Summer Fit™

Let's Get Ready for Seventh Grade!

Summer Fit Sixth to Seventh Grade

Author: Veronica Brand

Fitness and Nutrition: Lisa Roberts RN, BSN, PHN, James Cordova, Charles Miller, Steve Edwards, Missy Jones, Barbara Sherwood, John Bartlette, Malu Egido, Michael Ward

Healthy Family Lifestyle: Jay and Jen Jacobs & Marci and Courtney Crozier

Layout and Design: Scott Aucutt

Cover Design and Illustrations: Andy Carlson

Illustrations: Roxanne Ottley and Scott Aucutt

Series Created by George Starks

Summer Fit Dedication

Summer Fit is dedicated to Julia Hobbs and Carla Fisher who are the authors and unsung heroes of the original summer workbook series that helped establish the importance of summer learning. These women helped pioneer summer learning and dedicated their lives to teaching children and supporting parents. Carla and Julia made the world a better place by touching the lives of others using their love of education.

Summer Fit is also dedicated to Michael Starks whose presence is missed dearly, but who continues to teach us every day the importance of having courage in difficult times and treating others with respect, dignity, and a genuine concern for others.

Summer Fit Caution

If you have any questions regarding your child's ability to complete any of the suggested fitness activities consult your family doctor or child's pediatrician. Some of these exercises may require adult supervision. Children should stretch and warm up before exercises. Do not push children past their comfort level or ability. These physical fitness activities were created to be fun for parents and caregivers as well as the child, but not as a professional training or weight loss program. Exercise should stop immediately if you or your child experiences any of the following symptoms: pain, feeling dizzy or faint, nausea, or severe fatigue.

Summer Fit Copyright

Special thanks to the Terry Fox Foundation for use of Terry's photo and inspiring us all to contribute to making the world a better place for others each in our own way.

Printed in the USA
All Rights Reserved
ISBN: 978-0-9853526-0-8
www.SummerFitLearning.com

TABLE OF CONTENTS

Dear Parents,

Without opportunities to learn and practice essential skills over the summer months, most children fall behind academically. Research shows that summer learning loss varies, but that children can lose the equivalency of 2.5 months of math and 2 months of reading skills while away from school. In addition, children lose more than just academic knowledge during the summer. Research also shows that children are at greater risk of actually gaining more weight during summer vacation than during the school year:

All young people experience learning losses when they do not engage in educational activities during the summer. Research spanning 100 years shows that students typically score lower on standardized tests at the end of summer vacation than they do on the same tests at the beginning of the summer (White, 1906; Heyns, 1978; Entwisle & Alexander 1992; Cooper, 1996; Downey et al, 2004).

Research shows that children gain weight three times faster during the summer months – gaining as much weight during the summer as they do during the entire school year – even though the summertime is three times shorter. Von Hippel, P. T., Powell, B., Downey, D.B., & Rowland, N. (2007).

In the New York City school system, elementary and middle school students who placed in the top third of a fitness scale had better math and reading scores than students in the bottom third of the fitness scale. Those who were in the top 5% for fitness scored an average of 36 percentage points higher on state reading and math exams than did the least-fit 5%. New York City Department of Health. (2009)

Summer vacation is a great opportunity to use a variety of resources and programs to extend the academic learning experience and to reinforce life and social skills. It is an opportunity to give learning a different look and feel than what children are used to during the school year. Summer is a season that should be fun and carefree, but do not underestimate the opportunity and importance of helping children prepare for the upcoming school year. The key to a successful new school year is keeping your children active and learning this summer!

Sincerely,

Summer Fit Learning

FACT
You are your child's greatest teacher.

Purpose

The purpose of Summer Fit is to offer a comprehensive program for parents that promotes health and physical activity along side of academic and social skills. Summer Fit is designed to help create healthy and balanced family lifestyles.

Stay Smart

Summer Fit contains activities in reading, writing, math, language arts, science, geography and technology.

Program Components

Summer Fit activities and exercises are divided into 10 sections to correlate with the traditional 10 weeks of summer. Each section begins with a weekly overview and incentive calendar so parents and children can talk about the week ahead while reviewing the previous week. There are 10 pages of activities for each week. The child does 2 pages a day that should take 20-30 minutes a day to complete. Each day offers a simple routine to reinforce basic skills and includes a physical fitness exercise and healthy habit. Each week also reinforces a core value on a daily basis to build character and social skills. Activities start off easy and progressively get more difficult so by the end of the workbook children are mentally, physically and socially prepared for the grade ahead.

Stay Cool

Summer Fit uses core value activities, facts and role models to reinforce the importance of good character and social skills.

Stay Active

Summer Fit uses a daily fitness exercise and wellness tips to keep children moving and having fun.

Summer Fit includes a daily exercise program that children complete as part of their one-page of activities a day. These daily exercises and movement activities foster active lifestyles and get parents and children moving together.

Summer Fit uses daily value-based activities to reinforce good behavior.

Summer Fit promotes the body-brain connection and gives parents the tools to motivate children to use both.

Summer Fit includes an online component that gives children and parents additional summer learning and fitness resources at SummerFitLearning.com.

Summer Fit contains activities and exercises created by educators, parents and trainers committed to creating active learning environments that include movement and play as part of the learning experience.

Summer Fit uses role models from around the world to introduce and reinforce core values and the importance of good behavior.

Teaching the Whole Child

The Whole Child philosophy is based on the belief that every child should be healthy, engaged, supported and challenged in all aspects of their lives. Investing in the *overall* development of your child is critical to their personal health and well being. There is increased awareness that a balanced approach to nurturing and teaching our children will benefit all aspects of their lives; therefore creating well rounded students who are better equipped to successfully navigate the ups and downs of their education careers.

Supports Common Core Standards

The Common Core provides teachers and parents with a common understanding of what students are expected to learn. These standards will provide appropriate benchmarks for all students, regardless of where they live and be applied for students in grades K-12. Summer Fit is aligned to Common Core Standards.

Learn more at:
CoreStandards.org

Top 5 Parent Summer Tips

1 **Routine:** Set a time and a place for your child to complete their activities and exercises each day.

2 **Balance:** Use a combination of resources to reinforce classroom skills in fun ways. Integrate technology to help extend the learning experience.

3 **Motivate and Encourage:** Inspire your child to complete their daily activities and exercises. Get excited and show your support of their accomplishments!

4 **Play as a Family:** Slap "high 5," jump up and down and get silly! Show how fun it is to be active by doing it yourself! Health Experts recommend 60 minutes of play a day and kids love seeing parents playing and having fun!

5 **Eat Healthy (and together):** Kids are more likely to eat less healthy during the summer, than during the school year. Put food back on the table and eat together at least once a day.

Physical activity is critical to your health and well-being. Research shows that children with better health are in school more days, learn better, have higher self esteem and lower risk of developing chronic diseases.

Exercise Provides:

✔ Stronger muscles and bones

✔ Leaner body because exercise helps control body fat

✔ Increased blood flow to the brain and wellness at home

✔ Lower blood pressure and blood cholesterol levels

✔ Kids who are active are less likely to develop weight issues, display more self-confidence, perform better academically and enjoy a better overall quality of life!

Tips from a former *Biggest Loser*

Jen Jacobs
Former contestant of NBC's
The Biggest Loser

Jen Jacobs lost 114 pounds on Season 11 of NBC's *The Biggest Loser*.

Sedentary lifestyles, weight issues and unhealthy habits need to be addressed at home. It is more likely that your child will include healthy habits as part of their everyday life if they understand:

✔ Why staying active and eating healthy is important

✔ What are healthy habits and what are not

✔ How to be healthy, active and happy

Go to the Health and Wellness Index in the back of the book for more Family Health and Wellness Tips.

Warm Up!

It is always best to prepare your body for any physical activity by moving around and stretching.

Get Loose! Stretch!

Move your head from side to side, trying to touch each shoulder. Now move your head forward, touching your chin to your chest and then looking up and back as far as you can, trying to touch your back with the back of your head.

Touch your toes when standing, bend over at the waist and touch the end of your toes or the floor. Hold this for 10 seconds.

Get Moving

Walk or jog for 3-5 minutes to warm up before you exercise. Shake your arms and roll your shoulders when you are finished walking or jogging.

A healthy diet and daily exercise will maximize the likelihood of children growing up healthy and strong. Children are still growing and adding bone mass, so a balanced diet is very important to their overall health. Provide three nutritious meals a day that include fruits and vegetables. Try to limit fast food consumption, and find time to cook more at home where you know the source of your food and how your food is prepared. Provide your child with healthy, well-portioned snacks, and try to keep them from eating too much at a time.

SCORE! A HEALTHY EATING GOAL

As a rule of thumb, avoid foods and drinks that are high in sugars, fat, or caffeine. Try to provide fruits, vegetables, grains, lean meats, chicken, fish, and low-fat dairy products as part of a healthy meal when possible. Obesity and being overweight, even in children, can significantly increase the risk of heart disease, diabetes, and other chronic illnesses. Creating an active lifestyle this summer that includes healthy eating and exercise will help your child maintain a healthy weight and protect them from certain illnesses throughout the year.

Let's Eat Healthy!

5 Steps to Improve Eating Habits of Your Family

1) Make fresh fruits and veggies readily available.

2) Cook more at home, and sit down for dinner as a family.

3) Limit consumption of soda, desserts and sugary cereals.

4) Serve smaller portions.

5) Limit snacks to just one or two daily.

Technology in Middle School

Integrating more technology into your middle school students learning experience will allow your child to expand and use their knowledge exponentially. Technology is an important and natural next step in the learning process. It helps simulate real world experiences, allows them to interact with other learners and gives them the opportunity to access and work with information from around the world.

Encourage your child to use technology for more then social and entertainment purposes. Remind them that it is a learning tool as well. Technology gives them the opportunity to apply their mastery of basic skills and fundamentals in reading, writing, math and language arts in creative, fun and purposeful ways. It is a "next step" that is grounded in their ability to be an independent learner.

It is important to move forward with a balanced and mindful approach in order to avoid a sedentary lifestyle. Continue to put limits on screen time and encourage outside play and face-to-face friendships as part of a healthy and balanced household.

Bill Gates
Founder of Microsoft.

Extension Activities at
SummerFitLearning.com

KEYS TO TECH SUCCESS

1 Explore different technology resources and products with your child.

2 Utilize technology as a teaching tool to help extend and enhance their overall learning experience.

3 Develop learning activities that incorporate the utilization of technology. Show your child that technology is more then gaming and social networks.

4 Enforce responsible, ethical and legal use of technology.

Core Values in the Home

Understanding core values allows your child to have a clearer understanding of their own behavior in your home, in their classroom and in our communities. Core values are fundamental to society and are incorporated into our civil laws, but are taught first and foremost at home. Parents and guardians are the most important and influential people in a child's life. It is up to you to raise children who respect and accept themselves, and others around them.

Role Models

A role model is a person who serves as an example of a particular value or trait. Though it seems difficult to find positive role models, there are many people today, and throughout history who have exemplified in their own actions the values that we strive to have ourselves and teach our children.

Christa McAuliffe
A high school teacher who was chosen to be the first Teacher in Space.

Jackie Robinson
The first African American man to play Major League Baseball.

Wilma Rudolph
Olympic Athlete. The first American woman to win three gold medals in track and field.

Bullying

In recent years, bullying has become a leading topic of concern. It is a complex issue, and can be difficult for parents to know what to do when they hear that their child is being bullied or is bullying others. Bullying is always wrong. It is critical that you intervene appropriately when bullying occurs. Make sure your child understands what bullying means. Check in with your child often to make sure he/she knows you are interested and aware of what is going on in their social lives.

Learn more at StopBullying.gov

Books Build Better Brains!

Reading is considered the gateway to all learning, so it is critical as a parent or caregiver to assist and encourage children to read at all grade levels regardless of reading ability.

1. Create a daily reading routine. A reading routine provides the practice a child needs to reinforce and build reading and literacy skills.

2. Create a summer reading list. Choose a variety of books, including fairy tales, poems, fiction and non-fiction books.

3. Start a family summer reading club.

4. Discuss with your child a book that you are reading. Show your child how much you enjoy reading and ask them to discuss some of their favorite books

5. Combine summer movies with summer reading. Read the book before going to see this summer's blockbuster. If the book is not available, find a similar topic.

Read 30 minutes a day!

CYBER READERS: Books in a Digital World

With the increasing amount of digital content that is available, it is easy to access information and media on the go or at home. Currently, there are numerous studies researching how e-content is impacting how information is being retained and how it impacts classroom performance. It seems there are advantages for both e-content and traditional print, so it is important to cultivate a reading friendly environment that encourages and accepts both. More studies will likely show that there is material suited for learning in a digital format, as well as lessons that best remain in traditional textbooks.

Find these books at the library, bookstore or online. Summer is as much a time to read for enjoyment, as it is to maintain reading skills while you are away from school. We recommend you read for a minimum of 30 minutes a day during the summer - Happy Reading!

Something to Declare
By Alvarez, Julia

Tuck Everlasting
By Babbitt, Natalie

My Brother Sam Is Dead
By Collier, James and Christopher

With Every Drop of Blood
By Collier, James and Christopher

Out of Time
By Cooney, Caroline

Red Kayak
By Cummings, Priscilla

Mockingbird
By Erskine, Kathryn

Johnny Tremain
By Forbes, Esther

Games
By Gorman, Carol

House of Dies Drear
By Hamilton, Virginia

Hiroshima
By Hersey, John

Farewell to Manzanar
By Houston, Jeanne and James

Call of the Wild
By London, Jack

The Sea Wolf
By London, Jack

A Night to Remember
By Lord, Walter

Silent Storm
By Macy, Anne Sullivan

Dog Friday
By McKay, Hilary

The Glory Field
By Myers, Walter Dean

Sarah Bishop
By O'Dell, Scott

Lyddie
By Paterson, Katharine

Park's Quest
By Paterson, Katharine

Life As We Knew It
By Pfeffer, Susan Beth

Cast Two Shadows
By Rinaldi, Ann

Moon Dancer
By Rotkowski, Margaret

The Van Gogh Cafe
By Rylant, Cynthia

All-of-a-Kind Family
By Taylor, Sydney

The Bomb
By Taylor, Theodore

By Wartski, Maureen Crane
A Boat To Nowhere
By Taylor, Theodore

Dragonwings
By Yep, Laurence

When I Was Your Age: Original Stories About Growing Up
By Yep, Laurence

1.
```
      5319
      8374
      3268
    + 1258
    _____
```

2.
```
      0.48
      2.23
    + 1.99
    _____
```

3.
```
       876
     - 169
    _____
```

4. 2306 + 3217 + 9335 =

5. 2341 − 87 =

6. 785.32 − 45.8 =

7.
```
      57.29
    - 2.376
    _____
```

8.
```
       239
     x  72
    _____
```

9.
```
       408
     x 257
    _____
```

10. 519 x 67 =

11. 8.2 x 19 =

12. 41 x 8.3 =

14.
```
        87
     x 9.1
    _____
```

15.
```
       2.5
     x 7.3
    _____
```

16.
```
       927
    x 4.18
    _____
```

13. 641 x 2.76 + =

17. 8 | 696

18. 24 | 1704

19. 8 | 34

20. 1.5 | 55.5

21. 22 | 119 .02

22. 7.6 | 397.48

23. What is the Greatest Common Factor of 42 and 12?

24. What is the Least Common Multiple of 2, 3, and 5?

25. Circle the two equivalent fractions.
$$\frac{3}{12} \qquad \frac{1}{12} \qquad \frac{1}{3} \qquad \frac{1}{4}$$

26. Which fraction in each pair is larger?   a. $\dfrac{5}{6}$ $\dfrac{7}{12}$ b. $\dfrac{1}{6}$ $\dfrac{4}{15}$ c. $\dfrac{3}{4}$ $\dfrac{2}{3}$

27. Change the mixed number to a mixed fraction. $5 \dfrac{1}{3}$ _____

28. Add the fractions.

a. $\dfrac{2}{5} + \dfrac{1}{5} =$ b. $\dfrac{5}{8} + \dfrac{3}{4} =$ c. $7 \dfrac{1}{5} + 3 \dfrac{2}{3} =$

29. Subtract the fractions.

a. $\dfrac{4}{5} - \dfrac{1}{5} =$ b. $\dfrac{11}{15} - \dfrac{3}{5} =$ c. $8 \dfrac{4}{5} - 3 \dfrac{4}{15} =$

Multiply the fractions.

30. $\dfrac{2}{3} \times \dfrac{4}{5} =$ 31. $3 \dfrac{3}{2} \times 5 \dfrac{3}{5} =$

Divide the fractions.

32. $\dfrac{4}{3} \div \dfrac{2}{9} =$ 33. $6 \div \dfrac{6}{7} =$

Solve the proportion.

34. $\dfrac{6}{7} = \dfrac{n}{14} =$ 35. $\dfrac{5}{8} \div \dfrac{a}{24} =$

36. $\dfrac{67}{100}$ _____%   37. $40\% = \dfrac{2}{}$ 38. $0.43 = $ _____%

Match the following genres of literature with the phrase which best describes it.

1. ___ historical fiction	a. a story which may take place in the future
2. ___ science fiction	b. a story about a real person written by another person
3. ___ fantasy	c. a story which places fictional characters in a historical setting
4. ___ biography	d. a story with make believe creatures
5. ___ autobiography	e. an essay or story which is not made up
6. ___ myth	f. a story which may have a moral or teach a lesson
7. ___ mystery	g. a story about a person written by themself
8. ___ non-fiction	h. a story where a person may try to solve a crime

Match the following literary terms with their description.

1. ___ setting	a. the high point of a story
2. ___ sequence	b. the order of events in a story
3. ___ plot	c. time and place in which a story is set
4. ___ climax	d. exaggeration
5. ___ hyperbole	e. a brief summary of a story
6. ___ idiom	a. a direct comparison of two unlike things
7. ___ metaphor	b. a comparison of two unlike things using "like" or "as"
8. ___ simile	c. a phrase having a literal meaning and a figurative one
9. ___ personification	d. an expression not to be taken literally
10. ___ pun	e. attributing a non-human thing with human characteristics
11. ___ irony	a. repetition of vowel sounds in a phrase or sentence
12. ___ alliteration	b. saying one thing but meaning another
13. ___ assonance	c. words near each other beginning with the same letter
14. ___ rhyme	d. word whose name suggests the sound it makes
15. ___ onomatopoeia	e. words which end in the same sound
16. ___ moral	a. the viewpoint from which a story is told
17. ___ synonym	b. two words with opposite meanings
18. ___ antonym	c. the pattern of rhyme found in a poem
19. ___ perspective	d. lesson to be learned from a story
20. ___ rhyme scheme	e. two words with the same meaning

It was cold. There was no sign of grass, just white as far as the eye could see. The sky was a clear, sparkling blue. Even the blue looked cold. But, Erika didn't mind the cold. She was bundled up warmly. She even had hand warmers inside her plush mittens and some warmers in her boots. The only part of her really exposed to the cold was the horn that protruded from her forehead. It was blue, too, because that was its normal color, but she did feel the cold through the horn. Still, cold had always been part of Erica's life, and she didn't mind it.

1. This story is probably   a. a biography   b. a fantasy   c. non-fiction

2. What in the story tells you this? _____

_____

3. What season is Erika experiencing?   a. spring   b. fall   c. winter

4. Cite two phrases from the story which tell you what season it is. _____

_____

_____

_____

_____

_____

PARENT TIPS FOR WEEK 1

Skills of the Week

✔ Addition And Subtraction, Whole Numbers And Decimals
✔ Cell Parts, Plant And Animal Cells
✔ Comprehension
✔ Nouns, Noun/Verb Agreement
✔ Mesopotamia
✔ Characterization In Literature
✔ Ancient Egypt
✔ Pronouns
✔ Multiplication

Weekly Value Honesty

Essa Khan

Honesty means being fair, truthful, and trustworthy. Honesty means telling the truth no matter what. People who are honest do not lie, cheat, or steal.

Sometimes it is not easy to tell the truth, especially when you are scared and do not want to get in trouble or let others down. Try to remember that even when it is difficult telling the truth is always the best way to handle any situation and people will respect you more.

GET FIT TIME

Stretching is Very Important
Get into the habit of stretching every night before you go to bed, as well as before you exercise every day.

Play 60 Every Day!
Run, jump, dance and have fun outside every day for 60 minutes!

Health and Wellness

"Why are girls my age taller than boys?" Girls get a "jump start" on puberty and grow taller. Don't worry...boys will catch up in a couple years!

WEEK 1

HEALTHY MIND + HEALTHY BODY

Check the ☑ As You Complete Your Daily Task

	Day 1	Day 2	Day 3	Day 4	Day 5
MIND	☐	☐	☐	☐	☐
BODY	☐	☐	☐	☐	☐
DAILY READING	☐	☐	☐	☐	☐
	30 minutes	30 minutes	30 minutes	30 minutes	30 minutes

"I am honest"

_____
Print Name

Nuclear Envelope
Nucleolus
Nucleus
Smooth Endoplasmic Reticulum
Centriole
Golgi Body
Cytoplasm
Mitochondria
Rough Endoplasmic Reticulum
Plasma Membrane
Lysosome
Ribosome

DAY
1

All living things on earth are made up of cells.

A cell is surrounded by a thin wall called a membrane. Inside the membrane is a clear gel called cytoplasm. Cytoplasm contains proteins, amino acids, sugars, vitamins, ions, fatty acids and nucleotides. There are several parts to the cell. Mitochondrion produces the major portion of cell energy. The lysosome is a special digestive compartment. The Golgi Body is where proteins are put together to be sent to other parts of the cell. The smooth and rough endoplasmic reticulum are a system of membranes where proteins are synthesized. A ribosome is where protein chains are synthesized. Most ribosomes are attached to the outside of the endoplasmic reticulum, but some are free in the cytoplasm. The nucleus contains genetic material. This is where DNA is stored and replicated.

1. The nucleolus is inside the _____.

2. Two elements of the animal cell not mentioned in the paragraph are

_____ and _____ .

Adding four digit numbers

1.	6,238	2.	5,916	3.	2,730	4.	9,146	5.	8,095
	2,085		3,618		3,567		9,217		4,107
	3,419		2,430		9,184		8,350		3,268
	1,973		8,194		7,421		3,863		6,440
	+ 4,510		+ 2,105		+ 1,606		+ 2,584		+ 5,286

6. 2,306 + 4,165 + 7,839 =   7. 7,745 + 6,201 + 9,335 =

8. 5,026 + 7,139 + 7,835 =

DAILY EXERCISE
Jogging for Fitness 5
"Stretch Before You Play!"

Instruction
Jog 5 minutes in place or outside

Be Healthy!
Anytime you start a new exercise routine check with a parent!

DAY 1

Nouns

A noun names a person, place, or thing. Most nouns are easy to recognize – they are things you can point at, see, or touch. These are things like desk, dog, car. Other nouns are invisible. These are ideas like freedom, hatred, intelligence. They seem tricky at first, but are actually easy. Here is a strategy to help you identify them. Look at these words:

happy	liberty	stupid

Liberty is the only noun. How do you know? There is an easy test which tells you. Ask yourself, "Can I have it?" Can you have happy, No, but you can have happiness or joy. They're nouns. Can you have stupid? No, but stupidity, ignorance, intolerance – all these you can have. This test works because all of these idea nouns are things, and you can have things. Idea nouns are really thing nouns, they are just invisible things.

From the list below, circle the words which are nouns.

honesty	sad	honest	brave
charm	integrity	bravery	courage
funny	humor	kindness	mean
charity	fear	scared	hope
interesting	clever	angry	anger
talented	talent	childish	innocence
nervous	confidence	worried	manners

WEEK 1

© Summer Fit

Mesopotamia

Find these major cities and circle each one on map:

Assur

Babylon

Nineveh

Phoenicia

Sumer

Ur

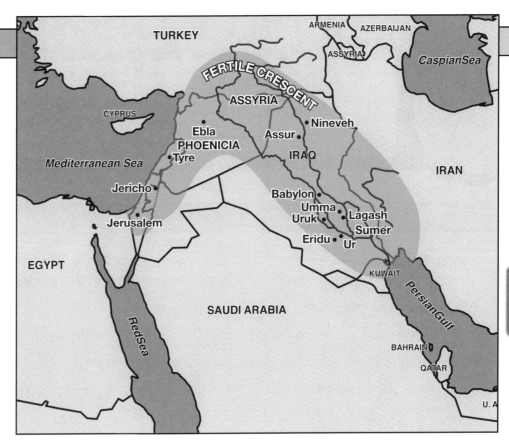

Many early civilizations grew around water sources. Water was important for growing crops as well as providing hydration for people and animals. One of the earliest civilizations began in the area known as the Fertile Crescent. This area is between two rivers, the Tigris and the Euphrates. In fact, the name Mesopotamia in Greek means "the land between two rivers."

Today, the Fertile Crescent includes the countries of Iraq, Syria, Lebanon, Cyprus, Jordan, Palestine, Kuwait, the Sinai Peninsula, and Northern Mesopotamia. It is a big place.

Adding four digit numbers

1.	2.	3.	4.	5.
0.48	9.00	14.14	23.62	46.09
0.17	17.87	9.82	10.62	3.99
+ 0.32	+ 3.65	+ 0.28	+ 4.75	+ 22.78

6. $52.94 + 16.07 =$

7. $0.821 + 0.976 + 1.088 =$

8. $37.62 + 0.976 =$

9. $0.09 + 5.027 + 23.784 =$

10. $324.9 + 28 + 14.006 =$

Strength

Go to www.summerfitlearning.com for more Activities!

DAILY EXERCISE
Inchworm
"Stretch Before You Play!"

Instruction
Do 10-15 times

Be Healthy!
Help set the table for dinner today!

Noun/Verb Agreement

DAY 2

When deciding if you are using the correct verb form, it helps to read the sentence aloud. **Choose the verb which agrees with the noun or nouns in the sentence. Circle your choice.**

1. Many people (agree , agrees) with my opinion.

2. Neither Bill nor Jose (want , wants) to watch the movie.

3. Both of the boys (like , likes) chocolate ice cream.

4. Moira and her friend (was , were) interested in learning to knit.

5. All of the songs on the play list (seem , seems) popular.

6. Everyone in the classroom (is , are) prepared today.

7. Ninety-two people (was , were) ready to jump in the pool.

8. Several of the books that were on sale (appeals, appeal) to me.

9. The big striped cat (don't , doesn't) like to sit in my lap.

10. George and Tatyana (don't , doesn't) come to this restaurant.

11. Either the boy or his sister (play , plays) in the band.

12. All the students (claps , clap) when the teacher declares a no homework day.

13. Anna Maria (was , were) dressed for a party.

14. The dogs in the neighborhood (bark , barks) at my cat.

15. The picture in the front hallway (hang , hangs) crookedly.

Subtraction Review

1. 876 - 234	2. 678 - 432	3. 237 - 156	4. 715 - 428	5. 6,254 - 193

6. 2,342 - 961 =   7. 9,228 - 1,417 =

8. 6,247 - 96 =

WEEK 1

Characteristics of Jo Marsh from Little Women

We usually get to know a person slowly, over time, but an author has to let you get to know a character very quickly. When we get to know someone we pay attention to what they look like, how they act, what they say. We also pay attention to what others say about them. These are some of the same methods reader use to learn about character traits, or qualities. In a story, look for clues to a character's personality and qualities by paying attention to several things:

The thoughts, feelings, actions and speech of the character
The thoughts, feelings, actions and speech of other characters
What the writer says directly about the character
The character's physical description

Read the following selection from Little Women, by Louisa May Alcott.

"Jo does use such slang words!" observed Amy, with a
reproving look at the long figure stretched on the rug.
Jo immediately sat up, put her hands in her pockets, and
began to whistle.
"Don't, Jo. It's so boyish!"
"That's why I do it."
"I detest rude, unladylike girls!"
"I hate affected, niminy-piminy chits!"
"Birds in their little nests agree," sang Beth, the
peacemaker, with such a funny face that both sharp voices
softened to a laugh, and the "pecking" ended for that time.
"Really, girls, you are both to be blamed," said Meg,
beginning to lecture in her elder-sisterly fashion. "You are old
enough to leave off boyish tricks, and to behave better,
Josephine. It didn't matter so much when you were a little
girl, but now you are so tall, and turn up your hair, you should
remember that you are a young lady."
"I'm not! And if turning up my hair makes me one, I'll
wear it in two tails till I'm twenty," cried Jo, pulling off
her net, and shaking down a chestnut mane. "I hate to think
I've got to grow up, and be Miss March, and wear long gowns,
and look as prim as a China Aster! It's bad enough to be a
girl, anyway, when I like boy's games and work and manners! I
can't get over my disappointment in not being a boy. And it's
worse than ever now, for I'm dying to go and fight with Papa.
And I can only stay home and knit, like a poky old woman!"

1. How does Jo feel about behaving like a lady? Cite 2 phrases from the story to support your claim.

_____

_____

_____

2. What does Jo do to act like a boy? _____

_____

Aerobic Go to www.summerfitlearning.com for more Activities!

DAILY EXERCISE
Jump the Line
"Stretch Before You Play!"

Instruction
Perform 10 times

Be Healthy!
Stretch every night before you go to bed.

Plant cells compared to animal cells

Plant and animal cells have many similarities. They both have Cytoplasm, Endoplasmic Reticulum, and Ribosomes. Both have Mitochondria, Golgi Apparatus, and a nucleus.

There are differences, too. Animal cells do not have a cell wall, chloroplasts, or plastids. Animal cells are generally round, with an irregular shape. Plant cells have a fixed rectangular shape. They both have vacuoles, but those in animal cells are much smaller than the one large vacuole of a plant cell. Centrioles are present in all animal cells, but only lower plant form cells. Animal cells have only a cell membrane, plant cells have a cell wall and a cell membrane. Cilia are present in animal cells, but rarely in plant cells.

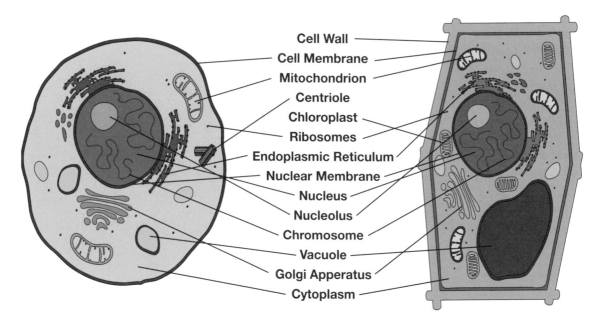

Cell Wall
Cell Membrane
Mitochondrion
Centriole
Chloroplast
Ribosomes
Endoplasmic Reticulum
Nuclear Membrane
Nucleus
Nucleolus
Chromosome
Vacuole
Golgi Apperatus
Cytoplasm

1. The flagellum is present in which cell? _____

2. The thicker cell wall is present in which cell? _____

3. Which cell has the larger vacuole? _____

4. Name two differences between the plant and the animal cell._____

_____

_____

Children were very important to the Ancient Egyptians. If a family could not have children, they tried magic, praying to various gods and goddesses, even placing letters at the tombs of dead relatives. They thought the relatives who were dead could possibly influence the gods. If nothing else worked, they might adopt a child.

Children were important because they carried on the life of the family. The boys would learn their father's trade. Girls would learn from their mothers how to run a house. Boys from wealthier families could also go to school. They learned religion, reading, writing and arithmetic.

Children were also supposed to take care of their parents as they aged. When the parents died, the sons would inherit the land. The daughters would inherit the household goods such as furniture and jewelry. If there were no sons, the daughter could also inherit the land.

1. What did sons contribute to the family?_____

2. What did girls learn to do? _____

3. What was one way people would try to be sure they could have a child? _____

_____

Subtract with decimals (Remember sometimes you need to add a zero for a place holder)

1.	2.	3.	4.	5.
7.26	23.87	67.18	263.1	201.81
- 1.14	- 1.6	- 9.236	- 5.29	- 160.78

6. $863.14 - 621.7 =$

7. $42.8 - 23.16 =$

Multiplication practice

1.	2.	3.	4.	5.
672	819	725	304	738
x 56	x 23	x 40	x 972	x 605

6. $467 \times 513 =$

7. $709 \times 76 =$

DAILY EXERCISE
Planks
"Stretch Before You Play!"

Instruction
Repeat 3 times for 30 seconds

Be Healthy!
Talk about your day with your family.

Pronouns

A pronoun is a word used instead of a noun. Using the correct pronoun is an important skill. Circle the correct pronoun in each set of parentheses.

1. I brought James, Charlie and (she, her) to school.

2. Henry, Tom and (I , me) did not believe what John, Bill and (she , her) said.

3. Jaime and (I, me) do not know whether Frank, Ben, or (he , him) will come.

4. (They , Them) and the girls are following us.

5. It is (I , me), not (he , him), who am to blame for the torn picture.

6. (We , Us) students have done our very best.

7. Sarai gave the book to Jose and (he , him) gave it to (they , them).

8. Dan and (he , him), as well as Maria and (I , me) met Grace and (he , him).

9. (They , them) asked (I , me) to go with (they , them).

10. Gabrielle can't go with (he , him) and (she , her).

11. (He , Him) and (I , me) are going out to dinner.

12. The students and (I , me) are having a good day.

13. (We , Us) and (they , them) are playing the final match.

14. My father sent Therese and (I , me) a card.

15. The principal was staring at (they , them) and (we , us).

DAY **4**

WEEK 1

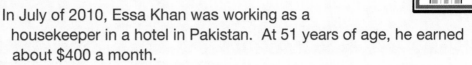

HONESTY - Essa Khan

In July of 2010, Essa Khan was working as a housekeeper in a hotel in Pakistan. At 51 years of age, he earned about $400 a month.

A Japanese worker had been staying in the hotel, and when he left, Khan found $50,000 in the room. He immediately contacted the hotel manager, who got in touch with the guest. Kahn said he never considered keeping the money. He said, "Times are hard for everyone, but that doesn't mean we should start stealing and taking things which do not belong to us."

The Governor of Punjab held a ceremony at the Governor's mansion to honor this act of honesty. The story has appeared in newspapers throughout the world. The governor, in praising Khan, said that his honesty had earned fame for Pakistan throughout the world.

An award for honest employees of the Serena Hotels has been named after Khan. He has also been rewarded for his honesty.

1. What is the capital of Pakistan?_____

2. Who do you know that demonstrates honesty? How do they do this?_____
_____
_____

3. Why might it have been difficult for Kahn to give back the money he found?_____
_____
_____
_____

4. What did the Serena Hotels name after Kahn?_____
_____
_____

Honesty – Memorize Your Value

"No legacy is so rich as honesty."

– William Shakespeare

Core Value Book List
Read More About Honesty

Nothing But the Truth
by Avi

Caleb's Choice
by G. Clifton Wisler

Moves Make the Man
by Bruce Brooks

The Shakespeare Stealer
by Gary L. Blackwood

Zach's Lie
by Roland Smith

.........TECH TIME!.........

It is fun to hear our words coming out of speakers. You can make this happen with a web 2.0 tool. Find a tool that will let you type a statement and then play it back to hear what you have typed. You could also find a tool that allows you to use a microphone with your computer to share a statement with your own voice and save it as an audio file. Do an Internet search to find a tool that will allow you to have fun with sound. Make a statement about a time you have been honest even if the easier route would be to lie or avoid the truth. Share this with a parent, have your parent rate your success in your workbook and then post it to our site. We all want to hear what you have to say!

www.SummerFitLearning.com

Bill Gates
Tech Guru and
Philanthropist
gatesfoundation.org

Play Time!
Choose a Game or Activity to Play for 60 minutes today!

YOU CHOOSE

_____

Write down which game or activity you played today!

Be Healthy!
Drink water instead of sugary soda drinks.

DAY 5

WEEK 1

1 2 3

PARENT TIPS FOR WEEK 2

Skills of the Week

- ✔ Multiplication and Division
- ✔ Greece
- ✔ Plot Summary
- ✔ Parenthesis
- ✔ Conduction
- ✔ Dashes
- ✔ Rome
- ✔ Convection
- ✔ Hyperbole
- ✔ Affixes and Roots

Weekly Value Compassion

Oprah Winfrey

Compassion is caring about the feelings and needs of others.

Sometimes we are so focused on our own feelings that we don't care how other people feel. If we consider other's feelings before our own the world can be a much kinder place. Take time to do something nice for another person and you will feel better about yourself.

Stretching is Very Important
Get into the habit of stretching every night before you go to bed, as well as before you exercise every day.

Play 60 Every Day!
Run, jump, dance and have fun outside every day for 60 minutes!

Health and Wellness

What are "growing pains?" No, they're not a disease. These pains are telling you that your body is growing up! Most of the time the pains are in the legs and hurt more at bedtime. Sometimes, they may even wake you up. The good news is that they go away around 13 years old. Doing the daily stretches in this book can help them feel better!

Check the ✓ As You Complete Your Daily Task

	Day 1	Day 2	Day 3	Day 4	Day 5
MIND	☐	☐	☐	☐	☐
BODY	☐	☐	☐	☐	☐
DAILY READING	☐ 30 minutes	☐ 30 minutes	☐ 30 minutes	☐ 30 minutes	☐ 30 minutes

"I am Compassionate"

_____
Print Name

Have you ever read the short explanation of a movie or TV show? That's a great example of how to write a plot summary. A plot summary can be a simple paragraph or a page or two, depending on the size of the piece and the amount of detail in the summary.

For example, for the movie *Night At The Museum*, you might read: A new night security guard at the Museum of Natural History realizes that an ancient curse causes the animals and exhibits on display to come to life and wreak havoc.

For the book *Where the Red Fern Grows*, you might read: A boy in the Ozarks wants desperately to buy two hound dogs, so that he can hunt. Despite family hardships and personal difficulties, Billy orders his dogs. He sneaks away from home to go into town to pick them up. Once he acquires the dogs, they all have a great series of adventures. He has to train the dogs, himself. His dad and grandpa give advice, but ultimately it is up to Billy. After many hunting trips, some close calls, and a tragic accident, Billy, his dad and grandpa take the dogs to a big championship hunt. Will they be able to compete against professionally trained, expensive dogs?

Choose a book you have read in the past year. Write a summary of at least 5 sentences. Be sure to cover the major plot points. Check your work for spelling and grammar correctness.

_____

_____

_____

_____

_____

_____

_____

_____

DAY 1

WEEK 2

Aerobic
Go to www.summerfitlearning.com for more Activities!

DAILY EXERCISE
Crooked Bunny
"Stretch Before You Play!"

Instruction
Perform 3 times in place or outside

Be Healthy!
Wash your hands before every meal.

DAY 1

Multiply 2 digit by 2 digit numbers, with 1 decimal.

Remember, when there is one decimal in the problem, there will be one decimal in your answer. Multiply as you normally would, then place the decimal to the left of the last number in your answer (thereby giving you one decimal in the answer).

1. 15
    x 2.3

2. 96
    x 6.1

3. 87
    x 4.5

4. 43
    x 1.7

5. 28
    x 3.5

6. 6.5
    x 7.1

7. 8.3
    x 5.6

8. 9.6
    x 4.7

9. 2.5
    x 12

10. 6.4
    x 7.5

11. 37 x 2.1 =

12. 64 x 7.5 =

Greece

Greek houses, in the 6th and 5th century BCE, were made up of two or three rooms, built around an open air courtyard. Larger homes might also have a kitchen, a room for bathing, and perhaps a woman's sitting area.

Greek women were only allowed to leave their homes for short periods of time. The courtyard was a perfect place for them to enjoy the open air, in the privacy of their own home. In fact, the whole family made good use of the courtyard.

The ancient Greeks loved stories, myths and fables. The family would gather in the courtyard to hear these stories, told by the mother or father.

Meals were usually eaten in the courtyard. Greek cooking equipment was small and light and could easily be set up there. The heat was kept out of the home and the courtyard was visually enjoyable for the dining experience.

1. What claim can you make about the climate of Greece based on this selection?

_____

2. What type of furniture might you find in an open air courtyard?

_____

WEEK 2

Conduction

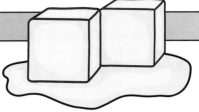

When two objects come into contact with each other, heat energy moves between them because the particles in one object collide with, or 'bing,' the particles in the other object. Transferred heat resulting from the collision of particles is called conduction. Conduction works best through solids, especially through materials such as metals. An example includes observing a raw egg fry as it hits a heated frying pan.

Try this activity: Put an ice cube in a Ziploc bag. Make a prediction about how long it will take you to melt the ice cube by using only your hands. When you are finished, reflect on this question: did the ice make your hands cold or did the heat from your hands cause the ice to melt. Cite information below to support your reflection.

_____

_____

_____

_____

_____

_____

Multiply 3 digits by 3 digits, with 2 decimals

Remember, wherever the two decimals are in the problem does not matter. You still need to put two decimal places in your answer. You always move from the right, even if there is a zero at the end. (In multiplication, you don't have to line up decimals.)

1.	508	2.	247	3.	247	4.	34.2	5.	6.42
	x 2.82		x 5.87		x 4.07		x 28.2		x 5 31

6. 632 x 1.23 =

7. 51.8 x 74.2 =

8. 3.29 x 167 =

DAILY EXERCISE
Ninja Crawl
"Stretch Before You Play!"

Instruction
Crawl for 5 minutes

Be Healthy!
Give your parents a hug.

DAY 2

WEEK 2   **5**

Correct Use of Dashes

- The dash is used to indicate a sudden or abrupt change in thought.
  Example: I will write the letter – but someone's at the door.

- The dash may be used to enclose material which could be in parenthesis.
  Example: Sometime next week – I forget when – I have an appointment.

- The dash is used before a word that sums up a preceding list of words.
  Example: English, mathematics, and science – these are important high school subjects.

Place dashes in the correct places in these sentence.

1. The boys need to pick up the trash but the bell just rang.

2. I have five dollars in my oh, no, I think I left my wallet at home.

3. I would ask or insist that you be quiet during the play.

4. Clothes, magazine, phone charger all I need for my little trip is packed.

5. This is very important are you listening to me?

6. I need three things to fix dinner flour fish and seasonings.

7. They wanted us Alice and me to meet them at the park.

8. I took Callie my calico cat to the vet.

9. Frank asked Bill to bring three things to the party music soda and chips.

10. Let's go to the park oh wait, we promised to meet Mary at the movie.

Do you have a place where you and your friends gather to meet? Maybe a favorite mall or park? The ancient Romans had a place to gather – the Forum. It was located in the valley between two of the seven hills where Rome was built.

The Forum was the main business center and shopping area for the Romans. They would do banking, trading and shopping. It was also a place for speeches. Government officials, religious leaders, or anyone who wanted to speak out was able to speak. In fact, good oration (public speaking) was considered a gift. The orator's purpose was to convince, to share ideas, but not to argue. People would stop their shopping or their visiting and listen to the speaker.

The Forum was also a place for religious ceremonies. There were temples to some of the gods that the people worshiped, so a shopper might stop and offer a gift to a god on their way home.

Festivals were also celebrated in the Forum. They might have to do with the seasons, a military conquest, or weddings.

Circle the things you would not find at the forum.

chariot	temple	sheep	car	benches
shops	mannequin	statues	food	
radio	aqueduct	mailbox	children	public speakers

Review Divide by 1 digit

1. 9 ⟌ 891   2. 6 ⟌ 822   3. 4 ⟌ 996   4. 6 ⟌ 547

5. 499 ÷ 9 =

6. 905 ÷ 6 =

Aerobic

DAILY EXERCISE
Burpies
"Stretch Before You Play!"

Instruction
Perform 5-7 times

Be Healthy!
Playing, running and jumping make you stronger.

Review commas, parentheses, dashes

Circle the number of each sentence that uses commas, parentheses and dashes correctly.

1. Several of my friends – Joanne, Marlene, Eve and Joan – are going to the party.

2. I am going to tell you a great story – but, the movie is ready to start.

3. Joe who is, my best friend, is meeting me at the mall.

4. I think the moose the cat and the cougar are very interesting animals.

5. Our class president (would you believe it) forgot to vote in the election.

6. Pennies, nickels, dimes, and quarters – these are the coins most often used.

7. She is going to Hawaii (a place) she always wanted to see.

8. Francis (who had brought his computer with him) googled the answer to the questions.

9. Most of the guests were eating (except for Ann who wasn't feeling well).

10. The price ($65) of the (shoes) seemed outrageous.

11. I just got a haircut – and it looks terrible!

12. Frank found pickles, onions, and tomato on his sandwich – which he loved.

13. The boys talked about cars movies and, music.

14. My friend – Sam – went with me to the movie today.

15. The teacher, Mrs. Brand, helped the students plan the car wash.

Divide 4 digits with decimal by 1 digit.

Remember that when the only decimal is in the dividend, the decimal in your answer needs to line up with the decimal in the dividend.

1. $9 \overline{\smash{\big)}\ 1.089}$ 2. $8 \overline{\smash{\big)}\ 200.8}$ 3. $7 \overline{\smash{\big)}\ 394.1}$

4. $332.4 \div 4 =$ 5. $31.38 \div 6 =$

Hyperbole (pronounced hi-per-bo-lee) is another word for exaggeration. We have talked about how hyperbole is an element of tall tales. People use hyperbole in everyday speech as well, and it is sometimes found in other genres of literature. Below are some commonly used examples of hyperbole. Write what each one means (without using exaggeration.)

1. I am so hungry I could eat a horse. _____

2. I have a million things to do. _____

3. I had a ton of homework. _____

4. If I can't buy that new dress, I will die. _____

5. He is as skinny as a toothpick. _____

6. This car goes faster than the speed of light. _____

7. That new car costs a bazillion dollars. _____

8. That joke is so old, the last time I heard it I was riding on a dinosaur. _____
_____

9. He's got tons of money. _____

10. You could have knocked me over with a feather. _____
_____

11. I've told you a million times. _____

12. He is older than the hills. _____

Convection

Heat energy transferred by the movement of a liquid or gas is called convection. When particles are heated, they move faster, expand, become less dense, and 'bang,' the particles rise. As the liquid or gas cools, the particles move slower, contract, become more dense, and 'bang,' the particles sink. This movement of heating, expanding, rising, cooling, contracting, and sinking is a continuous one. An example is to observe the amount of wind in the early morning compared to the afternoon. Wind is an example of a convection process in motion.

For this activity you need food coloring, distilled water, salt, a freezer tray for ice cubes, and two glass jars. Mix some of the distilled water with a few drops of food coloring. Freeze this into cubes. Fill two glass jars 3/4 full with distilled water. Add some salt to one of the jars and label it. Place a colored cube in each jar of water. Observe the movement of the colored water as it melts into the warmer water. Do not move the jars. Can you identify convection currents? Where is the colored water going? Is the colored cold water heavier or lighter than the warmer clear water?

Write three sentences telling your observations and conclusions.

_____
_____
_____
_____
_____

DAY
4

WEEK 2

DAILY EXERCISE
Dead Bug
"Stretch Before You Play!"

Instruction
Hold for 2 minutes

Be Healthy!
Always use sunscreen when you are playing outside!

Affixes and roots

Affixes are syllables or words attached to the beginnings (prefixes) or the ends (suffixes) of root words. A root word is the basic word, from which deeper meaning can be gained by adding prefixes and suffixes. Here are some common affixes and their meanings.

Anti – against or opposite   Pre - before

In – not   Pro – for

Ir – not   Sub - under

Mis – wrong   Super - above

Post – after   Trans – across

Use these meaning, and what you know of the meanings of the root words to define the following:

1. pro – British _____

2. inhuman _____

3. substandard _____

4. misspell _____

5. anti-inflammatory _____

6. superhuman _____

7. irregular _____

8. transatlantic _____

9. incorrect _____

10. postscript _____

DAY 4

WEEK 2

1 2

Compassion - Oprah Winfrey

Oprah Winfrey survived a childhood of abuse and neglect. She has become a well-known individual of influence and success. She uses her success and influence to reach out to others.

Oprah campaigned for a national database of convicted child abusers. She testified before a U.S. Senate Judiciary Committee on behalf of a National Child Protection Act. The "Oprah Bill," which established that database, became a law in 1993, and is available to law enforcement agencies around the country.

Oprah believes in using your life to help others. In 2000, Oprah's Angel Network began presenting a $100,000 "Use Your Life Award" to people who are using their own lives to improve the lives of others. She promotes other philanthropic ventures as well. One organization she has helped is the Oprah Winfrey Leadership Academy for Girls, near Johannesburg, South Africa. She initiated *Christmas Kindness South Africa*, which allowed 50,000 children from orphanages and rural schools in South Africa to receive food, clothing, and school supplies.

1. What is a definition of the word neglect? _____

_____

2. What is a definition of the word influence? _____

_____

3. In what country is Oprah's Leadership Academy for Girls? _____

4. After reading Oprah's story, how would you explain the value of compassion? Give an example of someone you know who demonstrates compassion.

_____

_____

_____

_____

Color a star for each time you show Compassion through your own actions this week.

 Write a 50-75 word essay describing one of your Compassion actions this week.

Compassion – Memorize Your Value

"We think too much and feel too little. More than machinery, we need humanity. More than cleverness, we need kindness and gentleness."

– Charlie Chaplin (1889-1977); Comic Actor, Filmmaker, Writer

Core Value Book List
Read More About Compassion

A Long Walk to Water
by Linda Sue Park

The Sin Eater
by Gary D Schmidt

Annie's Monster
by Barbara Corcoran

The Best Bad Thing
by Yoshiko Uchida

Madeline and the Great (Old) Escape Artist
by R. C. Jones

..........TECH TIME!..........

Slide show presentations are a way for you to take your knowledge and share it with other people. You can make a slide show of a vacation, of a special event in history, or a topic that you have studied. There are many tools online that will let you create a slide show and store it online. In at least 4 slides, share what you have learned about compassion and Oprah Winfrey. Show a friend or relative so they can learn about her compassion as well. Have someone rate your project.

www.SummerFitLearning.com

Bill Gates
Tech Guru and Philanthropist
gatesfoundation.org

Play Time!
Choose a Game or Activity to Play for 60 minutes today!

YOU CHOOSE

_____

Write down which game or activity you played today!

Be Healthy!
Take breaks from the sun by moving into the shade.

DAY 5

WEEK 2

1 2 3

PARENT TIPS FOR WEEK 3

Skills of the Week

- ✔ Division With Decimals
- ✔ Layers Of The Atmosphere
- ✔ Comprehension
- ✔ Persuasive Argument
- ✔ Greatest Common Factor
- ✔ Mali
- ✔ Figurative Language
- ✔ Multiple Word Meanings
- ✔ Fables
- ✔ Synonyms And Antonyms
- ✔ Least Common Multiple
- ✔ Geographic Theme Of Location
- ✔ Equivalent Fractions

Weekly Value Trustworthiness

Walter Cronkite

Trustworthiness is being worthy of trust. It means people can count on you.

You are honest and you keep your word. Sometimes it is easy to forget what we tell people because we try to do too much or we are constantly moving around. Try to slow down and follow through on what you say before moving onto something else.

Stretching is Very Important

Get into the habit of stretching every night before you go to bed, as well as before you exercise every day.

Play 60 Every Day!

Run, jump, dance and have fun outside every day for 60 minutes!

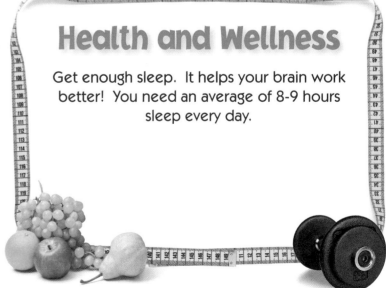

Health and Wellness

Get enough sleep. It helps your brain work better! You need an average of 8-9 hours sleep every day.

WEEK 3

Check the ✓ As You Complete Your Daily Task

	Day 1	Day 2	Day 3	Day 4	Day 5
MIND	☐	☐	☐	☐	☐
BODY	☐	☐	☐	☐	☐
DAILY READING	☐ 30 minutes	☐ 30 minutes	☐ 30 minutes	☐ 30 minutes	☐ 30 minutes

"I am trustworthy"

Print Name

Layers of the Atmosphere

Earth

10 miles

20 miles

20 miles

350 miles

39,600 miles

The Troposphere
life forms
weather
75% of atmosphere

The Stratosphere
ozone layer
24% of atmosphere

The Mesosphere
Cold
a few molecules
Shooting stars
burn up here

The Thermosphere
Fewer molecules
Large temperature
fluctuations

The Exosphere
Occasional
molecules
gradually escaping
into space

DAY 1

3

4

5

WEEK 3

Use the diagram to help you match each layer of the atmosphere with its description.

1. The layer that we live in, made out of the gases we breathe every day, is called the

_____

2. The layer which blends into the thermosphere, in which molecules may escape into space, is the

_____

3. The ozone layer, which makes up about 24% of the atmosphere is

_____

4. The layer with large temperature fluctuations and fewer molecules is

_____

5. This layer is cold, with few molecules. Shooting stars burn up here

_____

Divide numbers with decimal by 2 digits with decimal.

Now, you have to think. The decimal in the divisor means you need to move the decimal one place to the right and move the decimal in the dividend one place to the right. Then place the decimal in the answer immediately above the one in the dividend.

1. $2.6\overline{)738.4}$

2. $7.1\overline{)163.33}$

3. $63\overline{)114.03}$

4. $434.2 \div 5.2 =$

5. $348.08 \div 3.8 =$

Aerobic
Go to www.summerfitlearning.com for more Activities!

DAILY EXERCISE
Side Shuffles
"Stretch Before You Play!"

Instruction
10 Shuffles to the Right and Left. Repeat 2 x's

Be Healthy!
Exercise is good for health, but it also puts you in a good mood.

DAY 1

WEEK 3

Figurative Language

Figurative language is important to literature. Its usage provides depth, clarity, and interest to a selection. Some examples are idiom, metaphor, simile, hyperbole, and personification. Authors also use puns and irony. Figurative language can also be words put together in such a way as to catch the reader's interest because of the sound created, such as alliteration, assonance, rhyme or onomatopoeia. Here are some definitions and examples of commonly used figures of speech.

Idiom - words that have meaning different from their literal meaning – She was pulling his leg.

Metaphor – a direct comparison of two unlike things that have a specific thing in common – Life is a journey.

Simile – a direct comparison using the words "like" or "as" – Life is like a journey.

Hyperbole – exaggeration – He is a hundred feet tall.

Personification – giving human qualities to a nonhuman thing – The stars danced playfully in the sky.

Pun – a saying where one word or phrase has two meanings, a literal one and a funny one – Old owls never die; they just don't give a hoot.

Irony – A statement in which there is a discordance beyond the evident meaning - You study all week for a spelling test, then misspell your name.

Alliteration – repetition of the same beginning sound – The boy bounced the ball boisterously.

Assonance – repetition of a vowel sound – He rode on a proud round cloud.

Rhyme – having the same ending sound, at the end of lines of poetry or within a phrase – I had a fright in the bright night

Onomatopoeia – a word that imitates a sound associated with that word – Bam, bang, clank went the car.

Now it's your turn to have some fun. Write at three sentences using some of these types of figurative language.

1. _____

_____

2. _____

_____

3. _____

_____

Greatest Common Factor

When one number is divisible by a second, the second number is called a factor of the first. Two numbers may have some factors that are the same. These numbers are called common factors. The greatest of the common factors of two numbers is called their greatest common factor (GCF). An easy way to find the factors is to make a T chart. You begin with the smallest factor and the factor it needs to multiply to get the number. Then use the next factor, etc.

Example

36

1	36
2	18
3	12
4	9
6	6

Notice that 5 is not a factor of 36, so it is not on the chart. When the next number you could use is already on the right side, you have all the factors. Try using the T chart on the right to factor the number 48.

48

Now that you have the factors of both numbers, put a circle around the numbers that are in both charts (common.) Then decide which of the circled numbers is largest – that is the GCF. Remember that the GCF may be one of the numbers you are factoring.

On a separate sheet of paper, use T charts to find the GCF of these pairs of numbers:

1. 5 and 15 _____   2. 12 and 24 _____   3. 18 and 21 _____   4. 15 and 18 _____

In writing, argument does not involve anger. It involves using reason and logic to make a point. You are trying to persuade someone of your position, but you are not emotionally involved in the argument. During the summer, many people take a vacation. Parents don't go to work, children don't go to school. Sometimes people stay home but do a variety of activities available in their area. Other people decide to go somewhere else – either a favorite spot or a brand new place. Your task is to write a paragraph stating which you think is the better vacation (stay home or go somewhere) and why. You need at least three well-stated reasons. Use a separate sheet of paper if needed.

_____

_____

_____

_____

_____

_____

_____

_____

Strength
Go to www.summerfitlearning.com for more Activities!

DAILY EXERCISE
Reach and Rotate
"Stretch Before You Play!"

Instruction
5 times

Be Healthy!
Eat breakfast with your family.

DAY 2

4

5

WEEK 3

Mali

Around the year 1200, the kingdom of Ghana, in Africa, fell apart. The kingdom of Mali took over. The new king was a young man named Sundiata. He knew that trade was critical to Mali's success as a country, so he worked to restore trade alliances with Mali's neighbors. Mali grew in size under Sundiata's leadership. There were gold mines in the south and salt mines in the north. These both became very precious trade commodities.

Sundiata was a hero to his people. He was nicknamed the Lion King. Besides improving trade, he also built a strong military, to protect his country and the trade routes. He was a Muslim, but he believed in religious freedom. Unlike many kings of his time, when he conquered a new place, he did not make people convert to his religion, but allowed them to keep their own. He also allowed slaves to work for their freedom. He ruled for 25 years, and his people loved him.

1. Why would the nickname Lion King be an appropriate nickname for Sundiata? _____
_____
_____

2. Of the things Sundiata did to improve Mali, which do you think is most important? Why?
_____
_____

Multiple Meanings

Many words have more than one definition. It is a task of the reader to find the best meaning for the way the word is used in a sentence. **The nonsense sentences below confuse two meanings of the underlined words. Briefly tell what the two meanings are.**

1. The computer <u>mouse</u> ate the cheese. _____
_____

2. Hailey will take a <u>trip</u> next week on a banana peel. _____
_____

3. Spring is my favorite <u>season</u> and cinnamon is not. _____
_____

4. Everyone was <u>present</u> today, including the gift. _____
_____

5. In a <u>second,</u> he would win the medal between first and third. _____
_____

Use GCF to rewrite expression such as 36 + 8 = 4 (9+2). Find the GCF of the two numbers. Divide the two numbers by the GCF to find the factors that belong in the parenthesis.

1. 42 – 14 =

2. 36 – 18 =

3. 12 + 36 =

4. 15 + 18 =

5. 21 – 18 =

6. 44 – 12 =

7. 42 - 12 =

8. 21 + 18 =

9. 36 -24 =

10. 45 – 30 =

11. 21 + 42 =

12. 36 -27 =

Aesop's Fables

The legend is that a Greek man named Aesop was an ancient creator of many wonderful fables (a fable is a story which teaches a lesson or a moral). Tradition says that he was a slave who was able to earn his freedom because his master so enjoyed his stories. Many stories have been attributed to Aesop. There are also fables in many other cultures. One favorite fable attributed to Aesop is *The Lion and the Mouse*.

The lion was proud and strong, and king of the jungle. One day while he was sleeping, a tiny mouse ran over his face. The great lion awoke with a snarl. He caught the mouse with one mighty paw and raised the other to squash the creature who had annoyed him.

"Oh please, mighty lion!" squeaked the mouse, please do not kill me. Let me go, I beg you. If you do, one day I may be able to help in some way."

This greatly amused the lion. The thought that such a small and frightened creature as a mouse might be able to help the king of the jungle was so funny that he did not have the heart to kill the mouse. "Go away" he growled.

A few days later, a party of hunters came into the jungle. They decided to try to capture the lion. They climbed two trees, one on each side of the path, and held a net over the path. Later in the day the lion came loping along the path. At once the hunters dropped their net on the great beast. The lion roared and fought mightily, but he could not escape from the net.

The hunters went off to eat, leaving the lion trapped in the net, unable to move. The lion roared for help, but the only creature in the jungle that dared come near was the tiny mouse.

"Oh, it's you," groaned the lion. "There's nothing you can do to help me. You're too small."

"I may be small," said the mouse, "but I have sharp teeth and I owe you a good turn!"

Then the mouse began to nibble at the net. Before long he had made a hole big enough to allow the lion to crawl through and make his escape into the jungle.

MORAL: Sometimes the weak are able to help the strong.

1. Why did the lion let the mouse go free? _____

_____

2. How was the mouse able to help the lion? _____

_____

3. Why were the hunters not worried about leaving the lion? _____

_____

4. Give another example of the weak helping the strong. _____

_____

Aerobic Go to www.summerfitlearning.com for more Activities!

DAILY EXERCISE
Single Leg Pop-Hops
"Stretch Before You Play!"

Instruction
**Jump on each leg
10-15 times down
and back**

Be Healthy!
Make a healthy
sandwich for
lunch today
with whole
grain bread.

Synonyms

A synonym is a word that means the same or about the same thing as another word. Use of synonyms can help your writing become more interesting as it clarifies meaning and helps you to not be repetitive.

Read this myth about the White goddess of the moon, then find synonyms for the words listed below.

Artemis was the twin sister of the god of the sun, Apollo. She was ambitious, ruthless and hard-hearted. She was not gentle, like her mother Leto. She had a mind like a steel trap. When she wanted something, she went for it.

Artemis was resentful that Apollo had more of the world than she had. It wasn't fair! When Apollo came home the night after his first ride with the Horses of the Sun, Artemis was quite proud of him. But she said, "Look, brother," you've traveled all over – to the Hyperboreans and everywhere – all those beautiful places. You traveled in that fancy chariot with the swans and the dolphins. Now our father, Zeus, gives you the Horses of the Sun and nothing for me! It's not fair!" She went on to say that the next morning she would go with him to Mount Olympus. She would remind her father that she was his daughter, the Sun God's twin. If Apollo had the chariot of Helius to light up the day, she must have the silvery fire of Selene to light the sky at night. (Selene drove a silver chariot with two white horses over the night sky.)

Quite early the next morning the brother and sister rose up to Olympus. Zeus had not expected to see his lovely daughter; it had been a long time since she had visited. But when he saw her, this White Goddess, chaste and fair, he saw the logic of her request. What the brother could do in the day, the sister could do in the night. So he made the White Goddess the keeper of the silvery moon.

1. Find a synonym for the word pure.

2. Find a synonym for the word bitter.

3. Find a synonym for the word carriage.

4. Find a synonym for the word remorseless.

5. Find a synonym for the word anticipate.

Least Common Multiple

The first step in finding the LCM is to list 5 multiples of each number (knowing that the number itself is also a multiple.) So the next 5 multiples of 2 are 4, 6, 8, 10, 12. After you list the multiples of two numbers, you look for the smallest one that is the same in each list.

List the next 5 multiples of each number below.

1. 3, ___, ___, ___, ___, ___   2. 4, ___, ___, ___, ___, ___   3. 5, ___, ___, ___, ___, ___

4. 6, ___, ___, ___, ___, ___   5. 7, ___, ___, ___, ___, ___   6. 8, ___, ___, ___, ___, ___

7. 9, ___, ___, ___, ___, ___

Now, find the LCM of these sets of numbers.

8. 2 and 5 _____   9. 6 and 8 _____   10. 2, 3 and 5 _____   11. 3, 6 and 9 _____

Location

There are five themes in the study of geography: Location, place, movement, human environment interaction, and region (a good mnemonic device for remembering these is **Little Purple Men Hop Everywhere In Rome**).

Location can be exact or relative. An example of an exact location is your address. Map coordinates are another example of exact location. Relative location means where something is located in relation to something else. The Statue of Liberty is in a harbor by New York City.

The locations of ancient civilizations had a lot to do with what resources were available. People tended to settle near areas that had good land for farming, fairly level land for building homes, and rivers. Rivers were one of the most important resources people could find. The civilizations we have studied so far – Mesopotamia, Egypt, Greece, Rome, China, and Mali – were all located near major rivers.

Rivers served many purposes. Sometimes they were a barrier which prevented other groups of people from attacking and conquering, but people also did everyday sorts of things in rivers: they collected water for drinking and cooking, they used it for washing, they fished, they traveled to trade with other groups, and even took leisurely boat rides.

In India, civilization grew up near the Indus River Valley. We don't know as much about this society as some of the others we've studied, but in 1922, archaeologists uncovered the ancient cities of Harappa and Mohenjo-Daro. We know that the women wore lipstick, children had whistles and other toys, and artisans made beautiful pottery.

1. Give the absolute location of your home (your address) _____

2. Give a relative location of your home (what it is near) _____

3. List three reasons rivers were important to early civilizations _____

_____

_____

DAY 4

WEEK 3

1

DAILY EXERCISE
Grasshopper Crunch
"Stretch Before You Play!"

Instruction
Complete 10 on one side, 10 on the other

Be Healthy!
Take breaks from the sun by moving in the shade.

Antonyms

Antonyms are words that are opposites of another word. It's useful to recognize common antonyms. **In the exercise below, match the pairs of antonyms in each set**.

1. _____ abandon
2. _____ distinct
3. _____ delight
4. _____ loosen
5. _____ anxious

a. agony
b. tighten
c. keep
d. unconcerned
e. indistinguishable

6. _____ squander
7. _____ dilemma
8. _____ scanty
9. _____ partial
10. _____ plain

a. solution
b. complete
c. economize
d. ample
e. lavish

11. _____ failure
12. _____ accurate
13. _____ permit
14. _____ often
15. _____ fluid

a. mistaken
b. success
c. solid
d. forbid
e. rarely

Equivalent fractions

Fractions that name the same number are called equivalent fractions. A set of equivalent fractions might be $1/2 \approx 2/4 \approx 5/10$. Equivalent fractions are written by multiplying or dividing both the numerator and the denominator by the same number.

Examples:

$$\frac{1}{2} = \frac{1 \times 3}{2 \times 3} = \frac{3}{6}$$

$$\frac{10}{45} = \frac{10 \div 5}{45 \div 5} = \frac{2}{9}$$

1. $\dfrac{3}{9} = \dfrac{3 \div 3}{9 \div 3} = $

2. $\dfrac{1}{2} = \dfrac{}{14}$

3. $\dfrac{1}{5} = \dfrac{5}{}$

4. $\dfrac{8}{72} = \dfrac{}{9}$

Trustworthiness - Walter Cronkite

Do you trust what you see on TV or hear on the radio? A good dose of skepticism is often wise, Walter Cronkite was a newsman who was called the most trusted man in America.

Cronkite covered stories from World War II through the Vietnam conflict. He knew Presidents Truman, Eisenhower, Nixon, Kennedy, Johnson, and Reagan. He researched his information carefully, and was careful in his presentation of his stories. He said his job was to report the information, not to be a commentator or an analyst. Because he kept to the facts, and the facts were correct, the American public trusted him. If Walter Cronkite said something, it must be true.

Cronkite received many awards throughout his journalistic career, for his contributions to journalism. He was awarded the Presidential Medal of Freedom by President Jimmy Carter. From Princeton University, he was awarded the James Madison Award for Distinguished Public Service. His contributions to the broadcast business gave the American people someone they could trust.

DAY 5

1. Name 4 of the presidents Cronkite knew.

_____, _____,

_____, _____.

2. Define skepticism: _____

_____

3. Why did the American public trust Walter Cronkite? Give at least 2 reasons. _____

_____

_____

4. Which president awarded Cronkite the Presidential Medal of Freedom?_____

_____

_____

Color a star for each time you show Trustworthiness through your own actions this week.

 Write a 50-75 word essay describing one of your Trustworthiness actions this week.

Trustworthiness – Memorize Your Value

"Relationships of trust depend on our willingness to look not only to our own interests, but also the interests of others."

– Peter Farquharson

Core Value Book List
Read More About Trustworthiness

Wish You Well
by David Baldacci

The Cay
by Theodore Taylor

To Kill A Mockingbird
by Harper Lee

A Place Called Ugly
by Avi

The Trial of Anna Cottman
by Vivien Alcock

.........TECH TIME!..........

Telling stories can be a great way to share your experiences with others. Several web 2.0 tools allow you to do this. Search for one on the Internet. Create a storybook either: a) about a specific way that you have shown trustworthiness or b) a time when you saw trustworthiness in action. Make sure you have someone in your family see your story and rate it.

www.SummerFitLearning.com

Bill Gates
Tech Guru and
Philanthropist
gatesfoundation.org

1
2
3

DAY
5

WEEK 3

Play Time!
Choose a Game or Activity to Play for 60 minutes today!

YOU CHOOSE

_____

Write down which game or activity you played today!

Be Healthy!
Good sources of protein are meat, fish and eggs.

52 © Summer Fit

PARENT TIPS FOR WEEK 4

Skills of the Week

- ✔ Cross Products
- ✔ Olmec
- ✔ Spelling
- ✔ Comparing, Simplifying, Computation With Fractions
- ✔ Phrases Of The Moon
- ✔ Rhyme Scheme
- ✔ Sentence Fragments
- ✔ Aztec
- ✔ Similes
- ✔ Hyphens
- ✔ Constellations
- ✔ Metaphor

Weekly Value Self-Discipline

Jackie Robinson

Self-discipline means self-control. It is working hard and getting yourself to do what is important.

It is easy to lose interest in what you are doing, especially if it does not come fast and easy. Focus your attention on what you are trying to accomplish and try to block out other things until you reach your goal.

GET FIT TIME!

Stretching is Very Important
Get into the habit of stretching every night before you go to bed, as well as before you exercise every day.

Play 60 Every Day!
Run, jump, dance and have fun outside every day for 60 minutes!

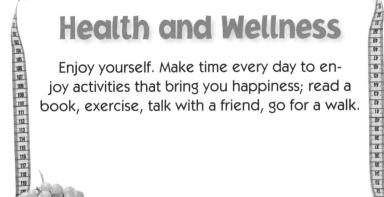

Health and Wellness

Enjoy yourself. Make time every day to enjoy activities that bring you happiness; read a book, exercise, talk with a friend, go for a walk.

WEEK 4

Check the ☑ As You Complete Your Daily Task

	Day 1	Day 2	Day 3	Day 4	Day 5
MIND	☐	☐	☐	☐	☐
BODY	☐	☐	☐	☐	☐
DAILY READING	☐ 30 minutes	☐ 30 minutes	☐ 30 minutes	☐ 30 minutes	☐ 30 minutes

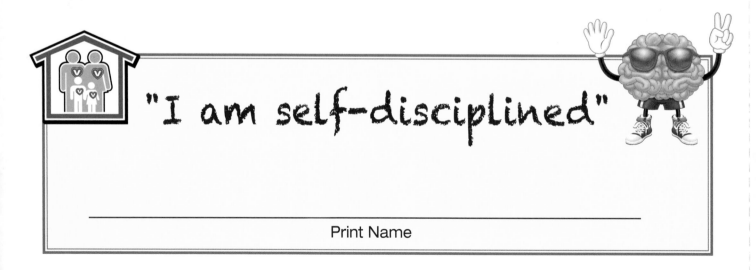

"I am self-disciplined"

_____
Print Name

Cross products

Cross products are a simple way to check if two fractions are equivalent.

Example: $\dfrac{2}{9}$ $\dfrac{4}{18}$ $2 \times 18 = 36$ $4 \times 9 = 36$ If the two crossed products equal the same thing, the fractions are equivalent.

Check the cross products to determine if the pairs of fractions are equivalent. Circle those that are.

1. $\dfrac{3}{9}$ $\dfrac{9}{15}$

2. $\dfrac{2}{5}$ $\dfrac{6}{10}$

3. $\dfrac{1}{5}$ $\dfrac{4}{16}$

4. $\dfrac{5}{5}$ $\dfrac{9}{9}$

5. $\dfrac{8}{12}$ $\dfrac{9}{13}$

6. $\dfrac{3}{8}$ $\dfrac{6}{16}$

7. $\dfrac{8}{12}$ $\dfrac{12}{18}$

DAY 1

Olmec

The first civilization we know of in Middle America (also called Mesoamerica) is the Olmec. These people built huge stone images of their rulers and their gods. Many were taller than a man, and weighed over 40 tons. Some of these were transported great distances, and to our knowledge they did not use wheels or animals. Makes you wonder how they managed it!

Look at the picture of the giant stone head. What does it tell you about the Olmec people? Did they think this god or ruler was kind or tyrannical? Was he intelligent or foolish? Was he handsome or ordinary?

If you were responsible for depicting the god of the Olmec people, how would you draw him? What facial features would you use? What designs or decorations would you incorporate?

Draw your version below.

WEEK 4

DAILY EXERCISE	Instruction
Ladders	**Run your course**
"Stretch Before You Play!"	**3 times**

Be Healthy!
Choose low-fat or non-fat foods whenever you can.

DAY 1

Spelling

Spelling is an important skill in communication. Below are several groups of words.
Circle the one in each group which is spelled correctly.

1. lenth   amoung   station   polece
2. lying   saylor   reapeats   picher
3. distanse   curtain   anser   carefull
4. plesure   propper   butcher   persanal
5. freinds   daughter   engin   somtimes
6. degrea   terible   dutey   surprise
7. companey   complaint   reletive   measur
8. passengers   twelfe   entranse   importanse
9. ninteen   hungrey   knowen   lining
10. remaned   nepheew   whisper   langwage
11. liberary   rhythm   ridiculus   legitemate
12. divine   knowlidge   assinement   budjet
13. condem   sciance   mathmatics   fulfill
14. permenent   asterick   kindergarten   analize
15. irelevent   admisable   attendance   canidate

Compare fractions

Write < or > to compare each set of fractions.

Example: $\dfrac{3}{5} > \dfrac{4}{7}$ $\dfrac{3}{5} = \dfrac{21}{35}$ $\dfrac{4}{7} = \dfrac{20}{35}$ Compare the new fractions $\dfrac{21}{35} > \dfrac{20}{35}$ so $\dfrac{3}{5} > \dfrac{4}{7}$

1. $\dfrac{5}{9}$ $\dfrac{4}{15}$	2. $\dfrac{4}{5}$ $\dfrac{7}{10}$	3. $\dfrac{3}{5}$ $\dfrac{3}{16}$	4. $\dfrac{7}{5}$ $\dfrac{3}{9}$	5. $\dfrac{5}{8}$ $\dfrac{3}{4}$	6. $\dfrac{1}{2}$ $\dfrac{3}{8}$

Rhyme Scheme

Remember that the rhyme scheme is the pattern formed by the rhyming words in a poem. Use letters to designate the lines that rhyme with each other. **For each of the poem segments below, write the rhyme scheme.**

Example: Fiddle-dee-dee by Eugene Field

There once was a bird that lived up in a tree,
And all he could whistle was "Fiddle-dee-dee" -
A very provoking, unmusical song
For one to be whistling the summer day long!
Yet always contented and busy was he
With that vocal recurrence of "Fiddle-dee-dee."   Rhyme Scheme: AABBCC

1.   An Astrologer's Song by Rudyard Kipling
        To the Heavens above us
        O look and behold
        The Planets that love us
        All harnessed in gold!
        What chariots, what horses
        Against us shall bide
        While the Stars in their courses
        Do fight on our side?

Rhyme Scheme : _____

2.   Children by Henry Wadsworth Longfellow
        Come to me, O ye children!
        For I hear you at your play,
        And the questions that perplexed me
        Have vanished quite away.

Rhyme Scheme : _____

3.   A Little Bird I Am by Louisa May Alcott
        A little bird I am,
        Shut from the fields of air,
        And in my cage I sit and sing
        To Him who placed me there:
        Well pleased a prisoner to be,
        Because, my God, it pleases Thee!
        Naught have I else to do;
        I sing the whole day long;
        And He whom most I love to please
        Doth listen to my song,
        He caught and bound my wandering wing,
        But still He bends to hear me sing.

Rhyme Scheme : _____

DAILY EXERCISE
Leg Lifts
"Stretch Before You Play!"

Instruction
Repeat 5 times

Be Healthy!
Yoga is a great way to stretch, and help you focus.

DAY 2

Sentence fragments

Many people get in a hurry when they are writing. Sometimes this causes people to write incomplete sentences. There are times when an author does this on purpose. To make a point, right? (That was an example.) However, very often it is not on purpose and it is confusing to the reader.

Mark each of the following sentences as **C** for complete or **I** for incomplete.

1. _____ Few rainy days in May.
2. _____ Luke always seems to be living in his own world.
3. _____ Even when it is full of music, food, and games.
4. _____ One very happy person in Silver City.
5. _____ Because it is quick and easy.
6. _____ She changes her plans if it is raining.
7. _____ The books on the table were overdue at the library.
8. _____ Sometimes it pays to look up.
9. _____ When I first saw this path.
10. _____ Toys of all kinds thrown everywhere.
11. _____ Mr. Jones gone to the market for groceries.
12. _____ Driving in the city in the early morning.
13. _____ When my cousin moved to New York, he had a hard time making new friends.
14. _____ Suzanne loved to go shopping with her mother and her aunts.

Phases of the Moon
Match the phase names with the description
New Moon
Waxing Crescent
Waxing Gibbous
Full Moon
Waning Gibbous
Waning Crescent

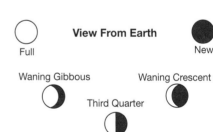

1. This moon occurs when the moon is on the opposite side of the earth; presents a full round disc. _____

2. The first of the moon phases (very little of the moon is showing). _____

3. Waxing means growing, and this moon is in the shape of a crescent. _____

4. A Gibbous moon is bulging out; this moon is still growing. _____

5. Waning is shrinking; this moon is again in the shape of a crescent. _____

6. This moon is shrinking and bulging at the same time. _____

WEEK 4

Aztec

When the Aztecs arrived in central Mexico, they found the best land already occupied by other groups. Normally when the Aztec came to a new place they would fight with the current occupants and take over the land. However this time, there was a legend involved. The legend said that when they spotted an eagle, perched on a cactus, holding a snake, they were to settle down. They were to live peacefully with their neighbors until they had gained strength. Finally, they were to build a glorious Aztec city, a city of their own.

They settled on the swampy land next to Lake Texcoco, where they began to build the most fantastic thing – floating gardens! This is an example of Human Environment Interaction. There wasn't the best land for farming in the swamps they initially inhabited. They built their own farmland by building rafts and anchoring them to the lakebed. They piled reeds and other vegetation on top of the rafts, and dirt on top of that. They used these gardens to grow chili peppers, squash, tomatoes, beans, and corn.

The Aztecs created more land by filling in the swamps and marshland. They built a glorious city in the middle of Lake Texcoco, named Tenochtitlan. The city had huge temples, open plazas, and a busy marketplace. There were "eating houses" and hairdressers.

The current capital of Mexico, Mexico City, is built on this same site. The lake is covered up except for a few small pockets of water and some underground waterways. The Aztec left a lasting reminder of their civilization.

1. Explain how the humans interacted with their environment in Tenochtitlan. _____

_____

2. What can you infer from the fact that the current capital of Mexico is on the same site as the

   Aztec capital of Tenochtitlan? _____

3. What did the Aztec do with their city or their gardens that was a surprise to you? _____

_____

Simile

A simile is a comparison between two unlike things that have something in common. It uses the words "like" or "as" to signify the comparison. In the description "shoots up taller like an india-rubber ball," the implication is that a rubber ball bounces very high, very suddenly and that sometimes the shadow becomes very tall, very suddenly.

What do each of these similes mean?

1. as alike as two peas in a pod _____
2. as big as a bus _____
3. as black as coal _____
4. as blind as a bat _____

In the following sentences, circle the two things being compared in each.

5. The sink was as clean as a whistle.
6. As Mark stood outside in the snow, he began to feel as cold as ice.
7. Claire was very tricky, causing her friends to think she was as clever as a fox.
8. After winning the science fair competition, Pierre was as proud as a peacock.

1

2

DAY 3

4

5

WEEK 4

Aerobic

Go to www.summerfitlearning.com for more Activities!

DAILY EXERCISE
Let's Roll
"Stretch Before You Play!"

Instruction
Ride for 20 Minutes

Be Healthy!
A calorie is a
unit of energy.

DAY
3

WEEK 4

Correct Usage of the Hyphen

Some compound words use a hyphen – some do not. Some examples are: eyewitness, eye shadow, eye-opener. You have to just know them or look them up in a dictionary. If you can't find it in the dictionary, assume they are two separate words.

Hyphenate a pair of adjectives when they come before a noun and act as a single idea. She is a friendly-looking woman. (If you could use "and" between the adjectives, do not hyphenate.)

When adverbs not ending in –ly are used as compound words in front of a noun, hyphenate. When they come after noun, do not hyphenate. He got some much-needed sleep. He got some sleep which was much needed.

Hyphenate numbers from twenty-one through ninety-nine, and all spelled out fractions.

Hyphens are also used to separate a word into syllables when the word has to be broken.

Circle the numbers of the sentences that are hyphenated correctly.

1. Marty needed a full-time job to pay for the books he needed for his classes.
2. Samantha had a sweet-sunny disposition.
3. The team needed six-teen points to win the game.
4. There were twenty-seven cans of peaches in the pantry.
5. I counted sixty-six cars on the train as it went by.
6. The restaurant boasted an award-winning hamburger.
7. We went to fif-teen houses trying to sell Girl Scout cookies.
8. They made a movie with a very low-budget.
9. The well-trained dog took first place in the championship contest.
10. The group used a specific decision-making process to arrive at a solution.

Simplify fractions

For most problems involving fractions, you will be asked to put the answer in its lowest term or simplify. To simplify a fraction, you divide the numerator and the denominator by the same number. You can divide both by the GCF.

1. $\dfrac{26}{39} \div \dfrac{13}{13}$ 2. $\dfrac{8}{24}$ 3. $\dfrac{12}{36}$ 4. $\dfrac{16}{40}$ 5. $\dfrac{7}{28}$

6. $\dfrac{14}{28}$ 7. $\dfrac{8}{40}$ 8. $\dfrac{24}{36}$ 9. $\dfrac{15}{24}$ 10. $\dfrac{9}{36}$

How constellations move

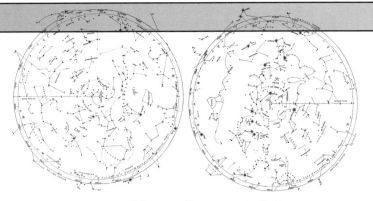

Have you noticed that constellations seem to move across the sky? This is because the earth rotates on its axis. The earth rotates from west to east. The stars maintain their position in the sky. We say a constellation has risen in the sky, but really the earth has rotated so that we can see particular constellations.

In addition, the earth moves around the sun once a year. The zodiac constellations are visible at different points in that orbit. For example, Orion is visible during the northern winter, but is on the opposite side of the sun during the summer, and therefore is not visible.

Try this experiment. Go out one night when the Moon is visible and try to find some stars that appear close to the Moon. You might want to draw a picture showing the Moon and the location of these stars. Try to go out the next night at the same time and compare your drawing to what you see. The stars you drew should be in about the same spot as the night before but the Moon will have moved. What happened? The stars are in the same spot because the Earth spun around once. The reason why the Moon isn't quite where you saw it the night before is because the Moon is orbiting the Earth.

1. Which moves, the earth or the constellations? _____

2. Orion is visible at what time of the year? _____

3. Why is the moon in a different place each night? _____

_____

Metaphor

Metaphors are comparisons similar to similes. The difference is that a metaphor does not use any clue words (whereas the simile uses "like" or "as").

Explain what is being compared in each sentence.

1. His grandfather is a pack rat. _____

_____

2. That man is a volcano ready to explode. _____

_____

3. Her eyes were fireworks. _____

_____

4. Joseph is a worm for how he treated his mother. _____

_____

5. Schools plant the seeds of wisdom. _____

_____

6. The test was a piece of cake. _____

_____

7. He showered her with gifts. _____

_____

DAILY EXERCISE
Knee lifts
"Stretch Before You Play!"

Instruction
**Repeat 5 times
with each leg**

Be Healthy!
Remember to say "thank you" to your friends and family.

1

2

DAY
4

Spelling

Find the word in the group which is not spelled correctly.

1. maintain   bachelor   canceled   comitted
2. safetey   relevant   restrain   department
3. vacation   beautiful   reletive   repair
4. objection   cabbage   wheather   aboard
5. personel   support   company   command
6. Tuesday   Wendsday   Thursday   Saturday
7. through   thought   throne   throughn
8. teacher   agread   thread   cheap
9. yesterday   village   question   arithmatic
10. breakfest   baking   surface   regular
11. December   November   Feburary   January
12. kitchen   remember   perfect   animel
13. address   weather   cieties   whether
14. uncle   guilty   grieff   judge
15. select   repair   trouble   caried

For some operations with fractions it helps to rewrite the fractions as mixed numbers or rewrite mixed numbers as fractions. To rewrite a mixed number, first multiply the denominator by the whole number. Next add the numerator to the product. Finally, write that sum above the denominator.

Example: $4\dfrac{3}{8}$	Step 1. 4 x 8 = 32	Step 2. 32 + 3 = 35	Step 3. $\dfrac{35}{8}$

1. $3\dfrac{2}{3}$ 2. $4\dfrac{3}{5}$ 3. $1\dfrac{5}{7}$ 4. $3\dfrac{5}{6}$ 5. $7\dfrac{3}{4}$

To change an improper fraction to a mixed number, reverse the steps.

Example: $\dfrac{35}{8}$	35 ÷ 8 = 4 r 3	The quotient becomes the whole number and the remainder becomes the numerator.	$\dfrac{43}{8}$

6. $\dfrac{5}{2}$ 7. $\dfrac{41}{7}$ 8. $\dfrac{32}{7}$ 9. $\dfrac{13}{9}$ 10. $\dfrac{25}{8}$

WEEK 4

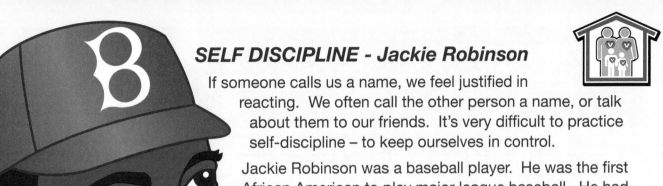

SELF DISCIPLINE - Jackie Robinson

If someone calls us a name, we feel justified in reacting. We often call the other person a name, or talk about them to our friends. It's very difficult to practice self-discipline – to keep ourselves in control.

Jackie Robinson was a baseball player. He was the first African American to play major league baseball. He had been playing in the Negro league, because in 1944, the baseball leagues were segregated. Branch Rickey, vice president of the Brooklyn Dodgers, wanted to change that and enlisted Robinson for that purpose. He made Robinson promise that he would not fight back when confronted with racism.

Players from other teams objected to playing against Robinson. Many fans jeered him. He and his family received threats. Some of his teammates threatened to sit out, but Manager Leo Durocher said he would trade them before he would trade Robinson. His faith in Robinson, coupled with Robinson's great athletic talent, and the self-discipline he employed to rise above the persecution, finally persuaded people to look beyond his color. He is considered by many to be one of baseball's greatest players.

1. What does it mean to say "the baseball leagues were segregated?" _____

_____

2. What was the position of Branch Rickey with the Dodgers baseball team? _____

_____

3. What promise did Rickey insist Robinson make? _____

_____

4. In addition to self-discipline, what qualities did Robinson employ to deal positively with the racism that he encountered? _____

_____

_____

Color a star for each time you show Self-Discipline through your own actions this week.

Write a 50-75 word essay describing one of your Self-Discipline actions this week.

Self-Discipline – Memorize Your Value

"In reading the lives of great men, I found that the first victory they won was over themselves...self discipline with all of them came first."

– Harry S. Truman

Core Value Book List
Read More About Self Discipline

Hatchet
by Gary Paulsen

Beyond the Divide
by Kathryn Lasky

The Dram Road
by Louise Lawrence

Touching Spirit Bear
by Ben Mikaelsen

Runaway
by Wendelin Van Draanen

.........TECH TIME!.........

Self-discipline is important in both how people control actions and emotions as well as how people stay focused on goals. Often teachers or parents will tell you that if you write things out it helps you to stay focused on your goals and therefore you are more self-disciplined. You can also do this online. Find a Web 2.0 tool that allows you to create a graphic organizer. There are many free sites that will let you sign up and create concept webs, mind maps and other various diagrams so that you can set your goals and see the steps that need to be taken. Try it! Pick a goal you need to meet and create an online diagram of the things that need to be done so you can accomplish it. Once you have it made, show a parent or friend.

www.SummerFitLearning.com

Bill Gates
Tech Guru and Philanthropist
gatesfoundation.org

Play Time!
Choose a Game or Activity to Play for 60 minutes today!

YOU CHOOSE

_____

Write down which game or activity you played today!

Be Healthy!
Instead of playing a video game play a board game.

DAY 5

WEEK 4

1 2 3

PARENT TIPS FOR WEEK 5

Skills of the Week

- ✔ Addition And Subtraction Of Fractions And Mixed Numbers
- ✔ Seasons
- ✔ Comprehension
- ✔ Intensive Pronouns
- ✔ Feudalism
- ✔ Spelling
- ✔ Water Cycle
- ✔ Historical Fiction
- ✔ Connecting Words
- ✔ Multiplication Of Simple Fractions And Mixed Numbers
- ✔ Metaphors
- ✔ Pronoun /Verb Agreement

Weekly Value Kindness

Oral Lee Brown

Kindness is caring about people, animals and the earth. It is looking for ways to help others.

Being nice to others catches on. When people are nice to each other they feel better about themselves and others. Small things make a big difference so when you smile, lend a helping hand and show concern for others– you are making the world a better place!

Stretching is Very Important
Get into the habit of stretching every night before you go to bed, as well as before you exercise every day.

Play 60 Every Day!
Run, jump, dance and have fun outside every day for 60 minutes!

Health and Wellness

Acne: those are the red bumps called pimples that a lot of kids and teenagers get on their skin. It is very common. Make sure to drink plenty of water and wash your face with a gentle face cleanser every day. No picking at them, it makes them worse!

WEEK 5

Check the ☑ As You Complete Your Daily Task

	Day 1	Day 2	Day 3	Day 4	Day 5
MIND	☐	☐	☐	☐	☐
BODY	☐	☐	☐	☐	☐
DAILY READING	☐	☐	☐	☐	☐
	30 minutes	30 minutes	30 minutes	30 minutes	30 minutes

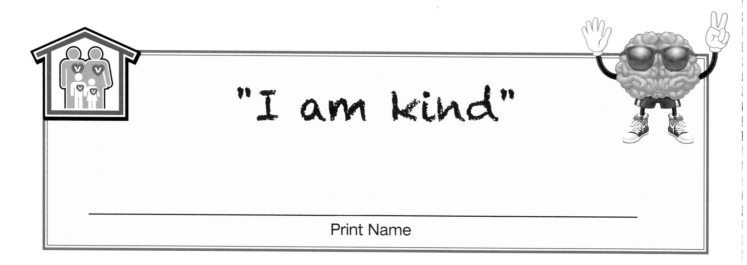

"I am kind"

_____

Print Name

Add and subtract fractions

1. $\dfrac{1}{3} + \dfrac{1}{3} =$

2. $\dfrac{3}{8} + \dfrac{2}{8} =$

3. $\dfrac{8}{9} + \dfrac{2}{9} =$

4. $\dfrac{4}{7} + \dfrac{5}{7} =$

5. $\dfrac{10}{27} - \dfrac{4}{27} =$

6. $\dfrac{9}{20} - \dfrac{3}{20} =$

7. $\dfrac{4}{5} - \dfrac{2}{5} =$

8. $\dfrac{9}{15} - \dfrac{4}{15} =$

9. $\dfrac{7}{19} + \dfrac{1}{19} + \dfrac{7}{19} =$

10. $\dfrac{11}{15} + \dfrac{2}{15} + \dfrac{8}{15} =$

Comprehension

The boys had been working all day. They were sweaty and dirty. Their hands had blisters from swinging the small ax and using the hammers, but they felt a great sense of accomplishment.

They were now the proud owners of a tree fort. They had spent days discussing the elements they wanted to include – two levels, a moat on one side of the tree, a tunnel leading from the base of the tree to a spot about 50 feet out. They had compromised a bit on the tunnel – it wasn't actually dug out of the ground. Instead, they had cleared the ground for the distance needed, then arranged branches to form the roof of the tunnel. They had to look quite a while to find enough curved branches to achieve this, but they did it.

The ladder was "borrowed" from Owen's garage. Tyler had supplied the planks for the floor by tearing apart an old, decrepit shed behind his home. Ahmed had requested the necessary nails from his dad, who had been reading the paper and only half heard what was said to him.

They had brought sandwiches for lunch, but now they were really hungry. It was getting dark and they knew they needed to go home, get dinner, and sleep, but they were reluctant to leave. So for a while, they just sat in the fort, listening to the noises of evening coming on, and enjoying their achievement.

1. What were the extra elements of the fort? _____
_____

2. Why were the boys reluctant to go home? _____
_____

3. Define the word decrepit _____
_____

4. What supplies did the boys need for their construction? _____
_____

5. Why would a group of kids want a tree fort? _____
_____

Aerobic

Go to www.summerfitlearning.com for more Activities!

DAILY EXERCISE
Jogging for Fitness 10
"Stretch Before You Play!"

Instruction
Jog 10 minutes in place or outside

Be Healthy!
Stretch before you exercise to help avoid injury.

DAY 1

Intensive pronouns

Intensive pronouns

Intensive pronouns are the words *myself, yourself, himself, herself, itself, ourselves, yourselves, themselves*. When they are used to emphasize the subject of the sentence, usually appearing right next to the subject, they are called intensive. (These same words are reflexive pronouns when they refer to the subject, but not emphasize it, as in *I gave myself a present*.)

Circle the intensive pronoun in each sentence.

1. The teacher told the student, "You yourself need to do all the work on this project."
2. I myself am tired of standing in line.
3. The hawk itself caught a rabbit.
4. The soldiers themselves marched in the parade.
5. The artist herself signed the painting.
6. We ourselves decided to put on a show.
7. My grandfather himself met John F. Kennedy.
8. We ourselves had nothing to do with the mess in the kitchen.
9. Mom told us, "You yourselves need to get your laundry put away."
10. We ourselves made all the food for the party.

The Reason for Seasons

We live in the Northern Hemisphere. It is summer when the North Pole is tilted toward the sun. At this time, the sun is high overhead and we receive strong sun rays. The sun shines for many hours each day. Its strong rays have a lot of time to heat Earth. In the far North, the sun shines for 24 hours a day. This gradually changes. Days get shorter and cooler, and the sun appears low in the sky at noon as the North Pole moves slowly away from the sun. Summer turns to fall, and then to winter. In winter, the North Pole is tilted away from the sun. We do not receive the strong rays and the sun is low in the sky. The sun shines for fewer hours each day. These weak rays do not have time to heat Earth. This explains the colder winters even though the sun is shining. Winter turns to spring and then back to summer as Earth completes one journey around the sun.

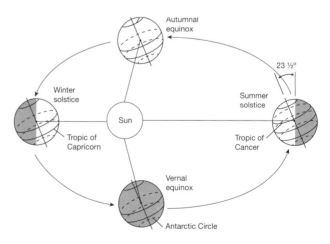

First remember to find the LCD and make equivalent fractions before adding or subtracting.

Example $\dfrac{1}{2} + \dfrac{1}{3} + \dfrac{1}{4} = \dfrac{6}{12} + \dfrac{4}{12} + \dfrac{3}{12} = \dfrac{13}{12} = 1\dfrac{1}{12}$

1. $\dfrac{8}{9} - \dfrac{5}{6} =$

2. $\dfrac{7}{8} + \dfrac{3}{5} =$

3. $\dfrac{7}{8} - \dfrac{2}{3} =$

4. $\dfrac{5}{9} + \dfrac{4}{27} =$

5. $\dfrac{9}{10} - \dfrac{2}{3} =$

6. $\dfrac{1}{9} + \dfrac{5}{6} =$

Feudalism

In Europe, you will find many rivers. During the middle ages, these rivers helped warring people enter European countries and try to conquer them. People began to group together, supporting one another, to repel the invaders. A system developed which was an agreement among the kings, lords, and knights. We call it the feudal system.

In the feudal system, the knights were vassals. A vassal is a person who serves someone else (in fact, the word vassal means servant). The knights would serve a noble or lord. They would be available when needed to protect the lord or his lands. In return, the knights would receive land of their own. A knight could be a vassal for more than one lord. This only worked as long as the lords he worked for didn't fight with each other!

The lords were vassals, too – they were vassals of the king. They had to support and protect the king.

There was another group of people at that time, but they were not really part of the feudal system, these were the peasants. They worked the land for the lords or the knights. There was the understanding that the lord or knight would protect them in case of attack. The peasants would grow the crops and tend the animals. They sometimes had a small plot of land for themselves.

1. Which group of people were not technically part of the feudal system?_____

_____

2. What was the agreement between the lords and the knights (what did each one get out of the system?) _____

_____

_____

3. What does the word vassal mean? _____

_____

_____

DAY 2

5

WEEK 5

DAILY EXERCISE
Chin-ups
"Stretch Before You Play!"

Instruction
Repeat 2 times

Be Healthy!
Stop eating when you are full.

DAY 2

WEEK 5

Spelling

There are words that sound the same but have different spellings. The correct spelling is important to the reader, because the spelling denotes the correct meaning. In the following sentences, circle the correct word to fit in sentence.

1. I could not see (threw , through) the curtain, so I missed the sunrise.

2. Javier did not want to (waste, waist) the delicious dinner, so he got a to-go box.

3. Many people are worried that global warming will cause (holes , wholes) in the ozone layer.

4. It was to (their , they're , there) advantage to get to the movie early.

5. Did you have to (weight , wait) long to buy your tickets?

6. There was a great (sail , sale) at the game store.

7. Did you decide (witch , which) costume you want to use for Halloween?

8. He looked outside to get an idea of what the (weather , whether) would be for the day.

9. Stefan was unhappy that he placed (forth , fourth) in the race.

10. Bonita and Allen said (their , they're, there) going to meet us at the mall.

11. Karl was so hungry that he ate the (hole , whole) pizza himself.

12. Please put the flower vase over (their , they're , there) on the coffee table.

13. Football players sometimes like to put on more (wait , weight) so they have more power.

14. Selena could not decide (weather , whether) or not to take French.

15. Hiekoti (threw , through) the football as hard as he could.

Water Cycle

The earth has a limited amount of water. So the water keeps recycling. We begin with the water in rivers, lakes, and oceans. The sun heats the water, turning it into vapor or steam. This goes into the air (a process called evaporation). When the water vapor in the air gets cold, condensation occurs, causing the vapor to form clouds. When the clouds have so much condensed water that they can't hold any more, we get precipitation (rain or snow). This falls to the earth and is collected back into the oceans, lakes and rivers. Where it falls to the ground, it will soak into the earth and become ground water. This is called the water cycle because it just keeps repeating.

Draw a diagram of the water cycle on a separate piece of paper. Be sure to include and correctly label evaporation, condensation, precipitation, and collection.

Historical fiction is a genre of literature which places a fictional story in a real time period of history in a realistic manner. Often this type of story helps the reader to understand the real historical events because they can identify with the characters in the story. You may have read <u>Number the Stars</u>, <u>The Shakespeare Stealer</u>, or <u>Al Capone Does My Shirts</u>. (If not, you may want to – they're very good books.)

Read the situations below. Decide if each one would be an example of historical fiction or not. If you think it is, mark it with a **Y**; if not, mark it with an **N**.

1. _____ Billy and his sister Veronica were headed into the mountains to look for berries. Berries were a nice, sweet treat after dinner, and when they were in season, the two brought home as many as they could. They had to be careful, however. When climbing around in the mountains, they might disturb some of the animals that made the mountains their home. That wasn't a problem if it was just some bluebirds, or small rodents. But if it were a mountain lion or a dinosaur, even a baby one, that could be very dangerous. They were glad they had found the dinosaurs stun guns in the market the last time they had flown to town, but weren't sure they really wanted to try them out.

2. _____ Francine and Amanda skipped along the dirt road, holding the large basket between them. They really enjoyed going to the market for their mother. They got to see all the new things that the merchants had gotten in on the latest ships. They sometimes got to visit with their friends. They were able to listen to the grown-ups gossip and talk politics (if they stayed quiet enough to not be noticed.) That was how they had heard about the Battle of Bunker Hill. They had listened to the grown-ups tell the stories, then rushed home to tell their parents.

3. _____ Kano loved his home along the Nile. It was such a big, beautiful river. He loved to watch the boats passing by, especially the Pharaoh's boats. They were so large and colorful. Once he even thought he saw the Pharaoh and the young prince.

4. _____ Nancy was very quiet leaving the house. If Mother heard her, she wouldn't be allowed to go. But it was all she had thought about for weeks. All the colorful banners, the interesting people, and all the unique animals! But most of all, she wanted to listen to the elucidators – the people who had come to share their knowledge of magic. She wanted to learn the spells to help her family's cow produce more milk, and make their garden grow more prolifically, and most of all, the spell to make her sister learn how to behave.

5. _____ Two nights to go. Two more nights and Paul's brother should be home. Paul wasn't sure why his brother had thought it so important to go to war. Paul didn't think it should be their fight. Yes, they lived in the South, and people said slavery was important to the economy. But Paul's family had never had slaves. They didn't believe in holding another human being in bondage. So Paul couldn't understand why Christopher had left to fight for the Confederate Army. But he didn't care anymore. Christopher would be home tomorrow and everything would be like it was before the war.

1

2

DAY
3

4

5

WEEK 5

Aerobic
Go to www.summerfitlearning.com for more Activities!

DAILY EXERCISE
Speed
"Stretch Before You Play!"

Instruction
Run 3 Blocks

Be Healthy!
Wash fruits and vegetables before eating them.

Connecting words in a narrative

Connecting words, also called transition words, are very important to the skill of writing. They serve a variety of purposes. They connect ideas, and also stress differences. They can indicate agreement, disagreement, results, and conclusions. They can also help keep the sequence of events clear. Circle the transition words in these sentences. Remember sometimes it is a phrase rather than just one word.

1. She wanted the shoes as well as the purse.
2. They wanted to sleep late on Saturday, however, the ball game was at 8:00.
3. Francois first went to the doctor; then he went to the pharmacist.
4. They were gone a long time, but when they returned, they were very happy.
5. Alice wanted a popsicle instead of an ice cream bar.
6. Anthony found the clue first, then he was able to find the hidden treasure.
7. They had to come home early because of the rain.
8. To summarize, there were eight members of the group present.
9. Caroline washed the dishes in addition to sweeping the floor.
10. Jim, together with Jennifer, decided to apply for positions as camp counselors.
11. They went to sleep right away, although none of the children thought they were tired.
12. Despite the storm warnings that had been broadcast, many were caught in the bad weather.
13. Tony learned to always have his phone with him, in case of emergency.
14. The family decided that, all things considered, it had been a good vacation.

Add/Subtract mixed numbers

Adding or subtracting the whole numbers is done like you normally do. Remember that to add or subtract the fraction part, the fractions need a common denominator.

Example

$$6\frac{1}{3} = 6\frac{5}{15}$$
$$+5\frac{2}{5} = 5\frac{6}{15}$$
$$\overline{11\frac{11}{15}}$$

1.
$$11\frac{2}{3}$$
$$-7\frac{3}{5}$$

2.
$$3\frac{1}{10}$$
$$+5\frac{3}{4}$$

Metaphor is a very effective tool in poetry. The device allows the poet to create an image through the metaphor that looks at something in a very unique way. Consider the poem Fog by Carl Sandburg.

> **FOG**
> The fog comes
> on little cat feet.
>
> It sits looking
> over harbor and city
>
> on silent haunches
> and then moves on.

You can imagine fog moving in the way a cat does. It is silent, as a cat often is. It creeps in and then moves on when it is ready.

Try to think of a metaphor for some ordinary things. In each case, explain how the original item and the metaphor are the same.

1. Paper _____

_____

2. Night _____

_____

3. Time _____

_____

4. A shadow _____

_____

5. A playground _____

_____

6. Your best friend _____

_____

7. Your room _____

_____

Strength

Go to www.summerfitlearning.com for more Activities!

DAILY EXERCISE
Heel Raises

"Stretch Before You Play!"

Instruction
Repeat 8 times

Be Healthy!
Say "please" when asking someone to do something for you.

1

DAY 4

WEEK 5

Pronouns in verb agreement

In a sentence, your subject and verb need to agree – a singular subject needs a singular verb. You would not say "They is happy," you would say "They are happy." You are probably familiar enough with most pronouns to be accurate, but indefinite pronouns cause a little confusion. These pronouns are singular: each, either, neither, one, anyone, everyone, someone, anybody, everybody, and somebody. These are plural: both, few, many, several. These can be singular or plural, depending on the noun to which they refer: all, any, most, none, some.

Circle the correct form of the verb for use in each of these sentences.

1. One of the children (is , are) sure that the books were turned in.
2. Many of them (is , are) worried about having too much homework over the weekend.
3. Somebody (has , have) left their locker open.
4. All of the musicians (says , say) that they are ready for the concert.
5. (Is , Are) there anyone ready to present their paper?
6. Anybody (is , are) welcome to participate in the history fair.
7. Each of the onlookers (remember , remembers) the situation differently.
8. Every one of Mary's friends (want , wants) her party to be a success.
9. Several of the animals (was , were) out of their cages.
10. Carol says they (play , plays) that song on the radio every day.
11. Some of the book (has , have) been read aloud to the children.
12. Some of the stories (has , have) been altered.
13. Neither person (is , was) willing to accept responsibility.
14. Both Marcella and Henry (believes , believe) Angela's story.

Multiply simple fractions Multiply the numerators; multiply the denominators; simplify.

Example $\dfrac{5}{6} \times \dfrac{2}{3} = \dfrac{10}{18} = \dfrac{5}{9}$

1. $\dfrac{5}{6} \times \dfrac{1}{5} = \underline{\quad} = \underline{\quad}$

2. $\dfrac{2}{5} \times \dfrac{3}{4} = \underline{\quad} = \underline{\quad}$

3. $\dfrac{5}{7} \times \dfrac{7}{9} = \underline{\quad} = \underline{\quad}$

4. $\dfrac{1}{5} \times \dfrac{1}{3} = \underline{\quad} = \underline{\quad}$

KINDNESS - Oral Lee Brown

Oral Lee Brown grew up in poverty. She struggled as a mother of three to make ends meet. She rose above her circumstances, owning a real estate office and a restaurant. She even created a popular peach cobbler dessert, which she marketed, but she believed in giving something back.

Through a chance encounter with a little girl in a grocery store in 1987, she became acquainted with Brookfield Elementary School in East Oakland California. She decided to "adopt" the class of 23 first graders. She told the children that if they stayed in school, she would pay for their college – and she began to put about ¼ of her salary into a savings account right then. She made regular visits to the school, helped tutor, met with parents, bought supplies, and tracked the children's progress.

19 of those children graduated college in 2003 and 2004. Three others went into trade schools. But Mrs. Brown's kindness did not end with those children. She has gone on to sponsor 5 more classes and more than 125 children. Helping others is the legacy of kindness given by Oral Lee Brown.

---

1. What is a synonym for poverty? _____

_____

2. What are three things that Oral Lee did that showed success: _____

_____

_____

_____

3. How much of her salary did Oral Lee set aside to help the children of Brookfield

Elementary School? _____

_____

4. How did the children demonstrate that they appreciated Oral Lee's sacrifice for them?

_____

_____

_____

Color a star for each time you show
Kindness through your own actions this week.

 Write a 50-75 word essay describing one of your Kindness actions this week.

Kindness – Memorize Your Value

"How lovely to think that no one need wait a moment. We can start now, start slowly, changing the world. How lovely that everyone, great and small, can make a contribution toward introducing justice straightaway. And you can always, always give something, even if it is only kindness!"

– Anne Frank

Core Value Book List
Read More About Kindness

Somebody Everybody Listens To
by Suzanne Supplee

Ruined
by Paula Morris

The Terrible Wave
by Marden Dahlstedt

Jane Addams
by Mary Kittredge

Their House
by Mary Towne

..........TECH TIME!..........

There are lots of web 2.0 tools that allow you to make your own small animation. Take a look at some fun sites that help you make an easy animated video. Find a tool you like online or through an online search. Create a brief animation about at least 3 ways to show kindness by giving back to others, just like Oral Lee Brown. Make sure to share it with someone, and enjoy the fun together!

www.SummerFitLearning.com

Bill Gates
Tech Guru and Philanthropist
gatesfoundation.org

Play Time!

Choose a Game or Activity to Play for 60 minutes today!

YOU CHOOSE

_____

Write down which game or activity you played today!

Be Healthy!
Eat all your meals at the kitchen table today.

DAY 5

WEEK 5

1 2 3

PARENT TIPS FOR WEEK 6

Skills of the Week

✔ Division Of Fractions And Mixed Numbers
✔ Renaissance
✔ Prepositional Phrases
✔ Gravity
✔ Compound Sentences
✔ Ratio
✔ Industrial Revolution
✔ Idioms
✔ Proportion
✔ Observatories
✔ Spelling
✔ Adjectives

Weekly Value Courage

Christine McAuliffe

Courage means doing the right thing even when it is difficult and you are afraid. It means to be brave.

It can be a lot easier to do the right thing when everybody else is doing it, but it can be a lot harder to do it on our own or when nobody is looking. Remember who you are and stand up for what you believe in when it is easy, and even more so when it is hard.

GET FIT TIME!

Stretching is Very Important
Get into the habit of stretching every night before you go to bed, as well as before you exercise every day.

Play 60 Every Day!

Run, jump, dance and have fun outside every day for 60 minutes!

Health and Wellness

Protect your great smile:)! Brush, floss and get your dental checkups.

WEEK 6

Check the ✓ As You Complete Your Daily Task

	Day 1	Day 2	Day 3	Day 4	Day 5
MIND	☐	☐	☐	☐	☐
BODY	☐	☐	☐	☐	☐
DAILY READING	☐ 30 minutes	☐ 30 minutes	☐ 30 minutes	☐ 30 minutes	☐ 30 minutes

"I am brave"

_____

Print Name

The Renaissance began partly as a result of the trade between the Far East and Mediterranean cities. The traders brought spices and gold from the East, but they also brought information about different cultures. Marco Polo, an Italian merchant, lived in the Orient for many years and wrote about his experiences. When he returned, he not only brought goods to trade, but ideas to share. This exchange of ideas and goods is part of the geographic theme of movement.

During the Renaissance, new ideas in many fields of thought abounded. Artists began to try new media, and new techniques. Philosophers looked at ancient history and philosophy, then took those ideas and infused them with renewed interest and new insights. Advances were made in medicine and science. New instruments, techniques, and theories led to growth in the area of exploration.

The Medici family was wealthy and powerful. They became patrons of the arts in Florence, Italy. A patron would basically hire an artist to work for only him. The artist would design and paint chapels and rooms, carve statues for decoration, and paint beautiful pictures for the patron.

One well-known scientist of the time was Galileo Galilei. He invented telescopes, a compass, and a thermometer. With the use of the telescopes, he was a ground breaking astronomer. He observed and noted four of Jupiter's moons.

Prince Henry of Portugal is also referred to as Prince Henry the Navigator. His contributions to the Renaissance included starting a school for oceanic navigation. He supported many explorers as they tried to find an ocean path around Africa.

What three things are mentioned as being brought back from the Far East by the traders?

1. _____

2. _____

3. _____

Divide fractions To divide by a fraction, multiply by the reciprocal of the divisor. Remember that the reciprocal is the fraction turned upside down. To divide a fraction by a whole number, change the whole number to an improper fraction. **Use a separate piece of paper to work the problems below.**

$$\text{Ex:} \quad \frac{5}{8} \div \frac{3}{8} = \frac{5}{8} \times \frac{8}{3} = \frac{40}{24} = \frac{5}{3} = 1\frac{2}{3}$$

$$\frac{2}{3} \div 4 = \frac{2}{3} \div \frac{4}{1} = \frac{2}{3} \times \frac{1}{4} = \frac{2}{12} = \frac{1}{6}$$

1. $\dfrac{3}{4} \div \dfrac{1}{2} =$

2. $\dfrac{2}{3} \div \dfrac{3}{4} =$

3. $5 \div \dfrac{5}{8} =$

DAY 1

WEEK 6

Aerobic Go to www.summerfitlearning.com for more Activities!

DAILY EXERCISE
Pass and Go
"Stretch Before You Play!"

Instruction
Get a Friend to Play
this Game With You!

Be Healthy!
Ask your
parents if
you can do
something for
them.

DAY 1

Prepositional phrases

Prepositions are words that show a relationship between other words. One way to look at it is the relationship between a fox and a log. The fox can go through the log, over it, around it, under it, near it, or in it, to list a few. There are some prepositions that don't work with the fox, such as during, after, except, about, and among. There are also some prepositions made up of more than one word, such as according to, in addition to, on account of and in spite of.

In the following sentences, circle the prepositional phrases.

1. The rabbit ran into the huge garden.

2. The little girl stood on the chair so she could see.

3. The book is always better than the movie according to some people.

4. The boys picked up trash in addition to raking the yard.

5. The dog lay between the flower garden and the little pond.

Rewrite these sentences, adding a prepositional phrase to each.

6. The cat ate her dinner. _____

_____

_____

7. Gabrielle is practicing her guitar. _____

_____

_____

8. Abram did his work. _____

_____

_____

9. Bill read the newspaper. _____

_____

_____

Divide mixed numbers To divide with a mixed number, change the mixed number to an improper fraction.

1. $\dfrac{3}{4} \div 6\dfrac{1}{2} =$

2. $9\dfrac{1}{2} \div \dfrac{6}{8} =$

3. $5\dfrac{1}{4} \div 2\dfrac{5}{8} =$

4. $5\dfrac{1}{4} \div 3\dfrac{3}{8} =$

5. $3\dfrac{1}{2} \div 2\dfrac{3}{5} =$

6. $7\dfrac{1}{2} \div 3\dfrac{3}{4} =$

DAY
2

Gravity

Gravity attracts all objects towards each other. Gravity has been around since the very beginning of the universe, and it works the same way everywhere in the universe, on all kinds of different objects, of all different sizes. The bigger an object is, and the closer you are to it, the stronger its gravitational pull is.

In the very beginning of the universe, gravity pulled atoms together to make stars and planets. Once the stars and planets had formed, gravity kept the planets in orbit around the stars, and moons orbiting around the planets. On each planet that is large enough, gravity keeps an atmosphere around the planet.

On Earth, gravity keeps the air around us (and everything else) from drifting off into space. Gravity also causes things to fall to the ground, causes the ocean's tides, and causes hot air to rise while colder air falls (which in turn causes wind). Gravity is everywhere!

1. _____ attracts all objects towards each other.

2. Gravity works everywhere in the _____.

3. In the beginning, gravity pulled atoms together to make the _____ and the planets.

4. Gravity keeps the planets in _____ around the stars, and _____ in

orbit around the planets.

5. Gravity keeps an _____ around planets that are large enough.

6. On _____, gravity keeps us from drifting off into space.

Strength
Go to www.summerfitlearning.com for more Activities!

Be Healthy!
Everybody gets bad breath, so remember to brush your teeth!

DAY 2

5

WEEK 6

Compound sentences

A compound sentence is one that has two or more simple sentences, usually joined by a connecting word. Sometimes an author uses sentences or varying lengths to make the writing interesting. The words used as connectors, or conjunctions, for compound sentences are: for, and, nor, but, or, yet, so. Except for very short sentences, a comma comes before the conjunction. **Use conjunctions to make each pair of short sentences one compound sentence.**

1. I do not like snakes. My friend, Alejandro, is very interested in them. _____

_____

_____

2. Carlos helped the younger children at recess. Carrie helped them after school. _____

_____

_____

3. My friend and I built a doghouse. The dog would not stay in it. _____

_____

_____

4. I tried to speak French. My friend tried to speak Chinese. _____

_____

_____

5. Kathleen forgot her lunch. She called her mother. _____

_____

_____

6. Robert threw his football across the room. Andrew caught it. _____

_____

Ratio

Mrs. B's class	Boys	Girls	Total
7th Grade	18	15	33
8th Grade	16	19	35
In Band	7	8	15
In Basketball	21	20	41
In Volleyball	15	17	32

A **ratio** is a comparison of two quantities. It can be written more than one way, but they are read the same way. If a ratio is written 2 : 3, you would read it, "Two to three". Another way to write a ratio is as a fraction, which may or may not be reduced to lowest terms.

If there are 18 boys in a class, and 19 girls, the ratio of boys to girls is 18 : 19.

Use the chart to write some ratios.

1) The ratio of boys to girls in band class is _____

2) The ratio of 7th graders to 8th graders is _____

3) The ratio of girls to boys in 8th grade is _____

4) The ratio of 8th graders to 7th graders is _____

5) The ratio of boys to girls in volleyball is _____

Challenge: What ratio could you simplify to have a final answer of 6 : 5? _____

Industrial Revolution

As people began to move from the country to the cities and towns, many people worked in their own homes, this was called Cottage Industry. Many women were part of the textile industry – spinning cotton into thread. A man named James Hargreaves invented a hand-powered spinning machine, that was a great improvement over the traditional spinning wheel. This allowed weavers to work faster, therefore increasing production. Factories were built beginning around the 1750s in England.

Factories were able to produce goods faster than the skilled craftsmen, and they could produce them for less money. People began to leave the cottage industries and work in the factories. Some of the advantages were that they didn't have to have their own equipment, they could leave their work at the end of the day, their pay was more secure (they didn't have to wait until a product was finished and hope the person who ordered it still wanted it).

There were disadvantages as well. The people in the factories worked long hours, in difficult conditions, and for little pay. Children often worked as long as adults in order to help their families have enough money to live.

An interesting note is that the early factories needed running water to power the machinery. So the manufacturers followed the example of the early civilizations, and settled near rivers.

1. Where did the early manufacturers have to build their factories? _____

_____

2. What were three disadvantages of working in the factories? _____

_____

_____

DAILY EXERCISE
Capture the Flag
"Stretch Before You Play!"

Instruction
Get Your Family and
Friends to Play

Be Healthy!
Ask your parents to buy 1% or skim milk instead of whole milk.

DAY
3

Idioms in Literature

Authors often include idioms in their work in order to make it more interesting. An idiom is a word or phrase that cannot be taken literally. Sometimes using an idiom explains a situation more clearly and easily than writing out an explanation.

Match the following idioms to their meanings.

1. ____ His bark is worse than his bite. A. Trick someone

2. ____ Pull the wool over his eyes. B. Mischief

3. ____ Every dog has his day. C. Everyone will have an opportunity.

4. ____ Monkey business D. He sounds meaner than he is.

5. ____ In a pickle E. Get it exactly right.

6. ____ When pigs fly F. In a difficult situation

7. ____ Hit the nail on the head G. Seem funny to someone

8. ____ The buck stops here. H. Will never happen

9. ____ A flash in the pan I. I take responsibility for this.

10. ____ Strike someone funny J. Something that looks great, but doesn't work out

Write an explanation for each of the following idioms.

11. The nick of time _____

12. Bite off more than you can chew _____

13. Hit the bull's eye _____

14. Fill someone's shoes _____

15. Curiosity killed the cat _____

16. Blow off steam _____

17. Clear as a bell _____

18. Eyes are bigger than your stomach _____

WEEK 6

An equation which states that two ratios are equal is called a proportion. There are two ways to write a proportion. This proportion is read, "40 is to 5 as 48 is to 6."

$$40 : 5 = 48 : 6 \qquad\qquad \frac{40}{5} = \frac{48}{6}$$

Write these situations as ratios. If they are equal, circle the ratio. They are equal if they form an equivalent fraction.

1. 75 correct out of 100
   150 correct out of 200

2. 15 out of 30 students
   25 out of 45 students

To solve a proportion, complete two equal ratios.

Example $\dfrac{30}{45} = \dfrac{6}{n}$ $\dfrac{30 \div 5}{45 \div 5} = \dfrac{6}{9}$ or 30 ÷ 6 = 5, so you must divide 45 by 5 to find n.

3. $\dfrac{3}{6} = \dfrac{n}{36}$

4. $\dfrac{56}{64} = \dfrac{7}{n}$

5. $\dfrac{8}{5} = \dfrac{24}{n}$

6. $\dfrac{27}{33} = \dfrac{n}{11}$

Observatories

An observatory is a place where very large and powerful telescopes are used to see into and study outer space. See if you can find the following words in the word search:

```
m   r   m   s   s   p   a   c   e   s
s   n   e   n   r   o   m   p   p   u
a   s   t   r   o   n   o   m   y   n
t   r   e   s   m   c   s   y   e   a
u   a   o   a   s   p   t   r   o   r
r   t   r   e   t   i   p   u   j   u
n   s   l   r   u   l   s   c   r   e
n   e   p   t   u   n   e   r   e   y
t   e   v   t   s   u   n   e   v   v
n   o   o   m   u   t   u   m   c   r
```

Astronomy
Jupiter
Mars
Mercury
Meteor

Moon
Neptune
Pluto
Telescope
Saturn

Space
Stars
Uranus
Venus

DAILY EXERCISE	Instruction	Be Healthy!
Lunges *"Stretch Before You Play!"*	**Repeat 5 times with each leg**	Drinking soda can add unhealthy fat to your body.

Common Spelling Mistakes

- Lose means to misplace something – Loose is the opposite of tight (Loose has room for 2 O's)
- Your means something belongs to you - You're, the apostrophe means a letter is missing (you are)
- Accept means to receive willingly – Except means to leave out
- It's, again the apostrophe shows something missing (It is) – Its means belonging to it
- Affect is a verb, meaning to act upon – Effect is a noun, the result of something
- Then means in the past- Than is a comparison (he is taller than she is)
- Weird breaks the rule of i before e – because it's weird
- A lot is NOT one word – it is two words
- Passed means to go by something or someone – Past means it has already happened.

DAY 4

Choose the correct words in the following paragraph.

Georgia was ready to (accept , except) her award. She was proud of the (affect , effect) her composition had on her classmates. She hoped (alot , a lot) of them would come to the presentation. It might be a little (wierd , weird) to be on stage in front of everyone, but she'd deal with it. It would be easier (than , then) doing a song and dance, for sure. She (passed , past) Abby on the way to the auditorium. She said hello and thought it would be really awkward to (loose , lose) her speech at this time. Then, she stepped on the stage to have her moment in the sun.

Adjectives

Adjectives are words that describe nouns or pronouns. They are often descriptive words, but can also be words that tell how many. Adjectives can also compare one noun or pronoun to another. These adjectives are positive (describing one thing), comparative (comparing two) or superlative (comparing three or more). Circle the adjective in each sentence.

1. My cute kitty is washing her face.
2. Max cooked a peppery sauce.
3. The windmill made a screechy sound.
4. Edna has the best race time of anyone.
5. I will be more careful than Marta.
6. Of the two of you, I hope the better person wins.
7. My cold is worse than Jerry's.
8. Black soot covered the chimney.
9. The cows went into the empty barn.
10. She danced in a shimmery dress.
11. There were nine boys in the class.
12. The guitar had a beautiful design.
13. The huge box waited to be opened.
14. Hank's chair was the most comfortable one in the house.
15. The blinding light gave him a headache.

WEEK 6

COURAGE - Christa McAuliffe

Courage can be defined as the ability to confront fear, pain, danger or uncertainty.

Christa McAuliffe was a teacher. Teaching is not a profession normally associated with courage. McAuliffe, however, was posthumously awarded the Congressional Space Medal of Honor. Pretty impressive for a teacher!

McAuliffe taught history, social studies, and civics in a junior high school. She developed and taught a course on "The American Woman." She also volunteered in her church, was a girl scout leader and raised funds for hospitals and the YMCA.

In 1984, along with 11,000 others, McAuliffe applied to NASA to be a "Teacher in Space." NASA's plan was to find a gifted teacher who could communicate to children from space. Although the space program had been in place since the 1960s, there were still dangers associated with space travel. McAuliffe knew this, but volunteered anyway. She faced the dangers and the uncertainties with a positive attitude, certain that she would be helping students. The space shuttle Challenger was launched on January 28, 1986, but exploded after the launch, killing all those aboard.

McAuliffe's example has led others to continue her quest. In 2004, Teachers in Space, a non-profit project sponsored by the Space Frontier Foundation began a project to again try to send teachers into space, to inspire and encourage young people's interest in space exploration.

1. Define posthumously: _____

2. Why is the Space Frontier Foundation trying to send teachers into space? _____

_____

_____

3. Find a word in the story that is a synonym for perspective. _____

4. Find a word in the story that is an antonym for safety. _____

5. What were some of the ordinary, non-courageous, things that McAuliffe did with her life?

_____

_____

_____

Color a star for each time you show Courage through your own actions this week.

 Write a 50-75 word essay describing one of your Courage actions this week.

Courage – Memorize Your Value

"Courage is about doing what you're afraid to do. There can be no courage unless you're scared."

– Eddie Rickenbacker

Core Value Book List
Read More About Courage

Alice the Brave
by Phyllis Reynolds Naylor

Red Cap
by G. Clifton Wisler

The Hero's Trail: A Guide for a Heroic Life
by T. A. Barron

When My Name Was Keoko
by Linda Sue Park

Steal Away
by Jennifer Armstrong

.........TECH TIME!..........

Have you ever made a word cloud? It is easy and fun to make one using online tools. You can take a set of words and create a collage to show what you think is important. You can make some words bigger than others. You can change the colors to make certain words stand out. You can do this for fun with friends or use it to creatively share the important pieces about something that you have learned. People have made word clouds with the Constitution, with a president's inaugural speech, with spelling words or with qualities they like in their friends. There are many web 2.0 sites that allow you to make free word clouds on the Internet. Do an Internet search to find a tool that will allow you to make a free word cloud. Using this tool, choose at least 10 words that stand out to you about Courage and brave actions of people like Christa McAuliffe. Create a word cloud to share what you have learned.

www.SummerFitLearning.com

Bill Gates
Tech Guru and Philanthropist
gatesfoundation.org

*Remember, web 2.0 tools are used to create and collaborate. So, share what you have done! Show your parents, guardian or friends and have them rate your project on this workbook page (provide a rating scale).

1
2
3
DAY
5

WEEK 6

Play Time!
Choose a Game or Activity to Play for 60 minutes today!

YOU CHOOSE

_____

Write down which game or activity you played today!

Be Healthy!
Try to eat 3 different vegetables today!

WEEK 7

Skills of the Week

- ✔ Percents And Decimals
- ✔ Milky Way Galaxy
- ✔ Pronouns And Antecedents
- ✔ Fractions And Decimals
- ✔ American Revolution
- ✔ Characterization
- ✔ Ratio And Scale
- ✔ Asteroids
- ✔ Myths
- ✔ Who And Whom
- ✔ Bar Graphs
- ✔ French Revolution

Weekly Value Respect

Harry S. Truman

Respect is honoring yourself and others. It is behaving in a way that makes life peaceful and orderly.

Sometimes we forget to appreciate that every person is unique and different. All of us want to be accepted and appreciated for who we are. Try to treat others the way that you want to be treated, even when it is difficult.

Stretching is Very Important
Get into the habit of stretching every night before you go to bed, as well as before you exercise every day.

Play 60 Every Day!
Run, jump, dance and have fun outside every day for 60 minutes!

Health and Wellness

Stay away from cigarettes! If you see other kids doing it, try to stay far from the smoke.

WEEK 7

HEALTHY MIND + HEALTHY BODY

Check the ✓ As You Complete Your Daily Task

	Day 1	Day 2	Day 3	Day 4	Day 5
MIND	☐	☐	☐	☐	☐
BODY	☐	☐	☐	☐	☐
DAILY READING	☐ 30 minutes	☐ 30 minutes	☐ 30 minutes	☐ 30 minutes	☐ 30 minutes

"I am respectful"

Print Name

Decimals can be written as a percent and any percent can be written as a decimal. The decimal 0.43 is read as 43 hundredths, meaning 43 out of 100, which can also be written 43%. 43% also means 43 out of 100, or 43 hundredths, which is 0.43

Change the following percents to decimals and decimals to percents.

1. 52% =

2. 63% =

3. 75% =

4. 17% =

5. 123% =

6. 0.43 =

7. 0.92 =

8. 0.75 =

9. 0.28 =

10. 1.54 =

DAY
1

2

3

4

5

Milky Way Galaxy

A galaxy is full of stars. Our sun is just one of at least 200 billion stars in the Milky Way galaxy. Our solar system is one of many solar systems, so is our galaxy. Our nearest major neighboring galaxy is called Andromeda. There are believed to be hundreds of billions of galaxies in the Universe.

The Milky Way is spiral shaped, as are other galaxies in the Universe, but some are elliptical and a few look like toothpicks or rings. How do we know what a galaxy looks like when the planet we live on is just a small part of the huge solar system that is one of many in the vast Milky Way galaxy? The Hubble Ultra Deep Field (HUDF) -- a very strong telescope -- can see beyond our galaxy and because it can, we have been able to see what other galaxies look like.

Decide if each statement is true or false.

1. _____ The Milky Way is the only galaxy.

2. _____ Our nearest neighbor galaxy is Andromeda.

3. _____ Our sun is one of at least 20 billion stars in the Milky Way Galaxy.

4. _____ The Milky Way is shaped like a ring.

5. _____ We know more about what is out in space because of the Hubble Telescope.

WEEK 7

DAILY EXERCISE
Mountain Climbers
"Stretch Before You Play!"

Instruction
Perform 3 x's for
60 seconds

Be Healthy!
Do not interrupt when someone is talking to you.

DAY 1

2

3

4

5

WEEK 7

Pronouns and antecedents

The antecedent is the noun to which a pronoun refers. In the sentence "Mary took her cat to the veterinarian for its checkup," <u>her</u> refers to Mary and <u>its</u> refers to the cat. For the first part of this exercise, circle the word or words to which each pronoun refers. (There may be more than one in a sentence.)

1. Bill and Fred went to their friend's house for dinner.

2. The teacher gave each girl back her paper.

3. The tree grew straight and tall in its pot.

When writing sentences using pronouns, the antecedent must agree with the pronoun in number and gender. This gets a bit confusing with indefinite pronouns, but there are a few rules to help understand this.

1. These indefinite pronouns are singular, and therefore must have a singular antecedent: one, everyone, someone, no one, anyone, everybody, nobody, anybody, somebody, each, either, neither. Most of these have "one" or "body" in the word, and those are singular.

2. These indefinite pronouns are plural and take plural antecedents: several, few, both, many.

3. These indefinite pronouns may be either singular or plural depending on how they are used in a sentence: all, most, any, none. If the sentence has a compound antecedent joined by or or nor, the pronoun agrees with the antecedent closer to it.

Circle the correct antecedent.

4. Each of the girls took (their , her) turn.

5. Neither Bob or Jack brought (their , his) shoes.

6. Most of the kids like (their , his or her) teacher.

7. Somebody should raise (their , his or her) hand.

8. Somebody in the girl's choir lost (their, her) notebook.

9. Either Yvonne or the boys found (their , his or her) ticket to the show.

10. Either the teachers or the principal volunteered (their , his or her) time.

Fractions to decimals.

Sometimes a fraction cannot be written with a denominator of 100. You can still write it as a percent by writing the fraction as a decimal. To do this, simply divide the numerator by the denominator.

Example $\dfrac{5}{8}$ = 5 ÷ 8 = 0.625	To write this as a percent, move the decimal 2 places to the right, giving you 62.5%. Don't go past 3 decimal places when dividing.

1. $\dfrac{7}{8}$ =

2. $\dfrac{50}{65}$ =

3. $\dfrac{26}{40}$ =

4. $\dfrac{8}{32}$ =

5. $\dfrac{9}{45}$ =

6. $\dfrac{17}{34}$ =

American Revolution

People from many countries came to settle in the Americas. In North America, colonies were founded all along the east coast. With the passage of time, Great Britain came to own or administer most of those colonies. For many years, the relationship between Great Britain and the colonies was a comfortable, positive one.

During the 1700s, European scientists and philosophers began to examine the world through reason rather than through religion. This period of time was called the Enlightenment. Some of the great thinkers were Locke, Voltaire, Montesquieu, and Newton. One of the ideas these men promoted was the notion of a social contract between government and the governed.

The American colonists began to feel that this social contract had been violated. They thought that the English government was taxing them unfairly, and not giving them a chance to have a say in the matter. They also felt that the government was using the colonies to supply resources to the mother country. However, from their perspective, the government was giving little or nothing back.

After a series of altercations between the colonists and the British soldiers, officials, and politicians, the colonists decided they should be their own country. They sent representatives to Philadelphia, who drafted a Declaration of Independence, which listed the reasons the colonies felt they deserved to be independent. The Revolutionary War was fought, the colonists won, and a new country was begun.

1. What idea did the Enlightenment thinkers promote which the colonists felt the British government had violated? _____

_____

2. What do we call the list of reasons drafted by the colonial representatives? _____

_____

DAILY EXERCISE
Push-ups (traditional or modified)
"Stretch Before You Play!"

Instruction
Repeat 10 times

Be Healthy!
Proteins build and replace tissues in your body.

Characters in a story

Characters are the people, animals, and imaginary creatures who take part in a story. The action generally centers around one or two main characters. The other characters in the story are the minor characters. They interact with the main character in order to move the story along.

Characters are revealed in a variety of ways. Often the author gives descriptions of the character. The interaction between the character and others in the story tells a great deal about the individual. Sometimes the author shares the character's thoughts and feelings as well.

Consider this excerpt from *20,000 Leagues Under the Sea* by Jules Verne. The book was published in 1870, when submarines were largely theoretical. Captain Nemo is the commander of a submarine, which he had himself designed and built.

"Ah, commander," I exclaimed with conviction, "your Nautilus is truly a marvelous boat!"

"Yes, professor," Captain Nemo replied with genuine excitement, "and I love it as if it were my own flesh and blood! Aboard a conventional ship, facing the ocean's perils, danger lurks everywhere; on the surface of the sea, your chief sensation is the constant feeling of an underlying chasm, as the Dutchman Jansen so aptly put it; but below the waves aboard the Nautilus, your heart never fails you! There are no structural deformities to worry about, because the double hull of this boat has the rigidity of iron; no rigging to be worn out by rolling and pitching on the waves; no sails for the wind to carry off; no boilers for steam to burst open; no fires to fear, because this submersible is made of sheet iron not wood; no coal to run out of, since electricity is its mechanical force; no collisions to fear, because it navigates the watery deep all by itself; no storms to brave, because just a few meters beneath the waves, it finds absolute tranquility! There, sir. There's the ideal ship! And if it's true that the engineer has more confidence in a craft than the builder, and the builder more than the captain himself, you can understand the utter abandon with which I place my trust in this Nautilus, since I'm its captain, builder, and engineer all in one!"

1. Nemo has been characterized as arrogant. Find evidence in the excerpt which supports this idea. _____

_____

2. Nemo is very proud of his ship. What are two of the things which he says make it ideal?

_____

_____

3. Why did Nemo say they did not have to worry about storms? _____

_____

Ratio used in scales

You could not draw a diagram of a house on a piece of paper because it is too large. Instead, we use scale, which is a type of ratio. Scale is also used on maps. Many people use scale drawings, such as architects, map makers and engineers. The ratio being used is usually in a legend or key. Use the following diagram and ratio to determine the actual size of the elements of this building. Use the measurement across as wide and top to bottom as long.

	1.5 in	0.5 in	1.25 in
1 in	Kitchen	Bath Room	Bedroom
1 in	Dining Room	Living Room	
	1.5 in	1.75 in	

Scale 1 in : 12 ft

1. Kitchen is actually _____ feet wide.

2. Kitchen is _____ feet long.

3. Living Room is _____ feet long.

4. Front of the building is _____ feet wide.

5. Side of building is _____ feet long.

Asteroid Fun Facts

- Asteroids are small bodies made of rock and metal that orbit the Sun.

- Asteroids are similar to comets but do not have a visible coma (fuzzy outline and tail) like comets do.

- Asteroids are also known as planetoids or minor planets.

- Asteroids vary greatly in size, some as small as ten meters in diameter while others stretch out over hundreds of kilometers.

- Objects under ten meters in diameter are generally regarded as meteoroids.

- The first asteroid was discovered in 1801 by Italian astronomer Giuseppe Piazzi.

- The asteroid belt lies roughly between the orbits of Mars and Jupiter in the Solar System.

- It is believed by many scientists and researchers that an asteroid impact was the cause behind the extinction of the dinosaurs around 65 million years ago.

Use at least five of these facts to write a paragraph about asteroids.

_____

_____

_____

_____

_____

DAY 3

WEEK 7

1
2
4
5

Aerobic
Go to www.summerfitlearning.com for more Activities!

DAILY EXERCISE
Moguls
"Stretch Before You Play!"

Instruction
Perform 3 x's for
30 seconds

Be Healthy!
Practice always makes you better.

Who and Whom

Two of the trickiest words in our language are who and whom. At least many people think so.

But here's a simple trick you can use to know when to use each pronoun. Make a question about the sentence. If the answer is he, the pronoun is who. If the answer is him, the pronoun is whom. For the sentence *(Who , Whom) wrote the letter?* You would respond **He** wrote the letter. Therefore the correct pronoun is Who. If the sentence is *The letter was written to (who , whom)?* the answer would be *The letter was written to **him***. The correct pronoun is whom.

Circle the correct pronoun for each of these sentences.

1. The children wondered (who , whom) their new teacher would be.

2. The package that came in the mail was addressed to (who , whom)?

3. We want to know on (who , whom) the trick was played.

4. Mrs. Jones consulted a lawyer (who , whom) she met in Indianapolis.

5. (Who , Whom) came to the door to get the pizza?

6. (Who , Whom) are you going to invite?

7. He doesn't know (who , whom) the president of the company is at this time.

8. You may give this award to (whoever , whomever) you please.

9. I can't remember (who , whom) told me that.

10. If I had known (who , whom) she was, I would have visited with her.

11. From (who , whom) have you gotten responses to your request?

12. The three girls (who , whom) were in the store were actually sisters.

13. No one could guess to (who , whom) the letter referred.

14. Do you know to (who , whom) I gave the key to the car?

350
300
250
200
150
100
50
0

■ 10:00 AM
■ 5:00 PM
■ 9:00 PM

Monday   Wednesday   Friday   Saturday

Number of shoppers in the clothing store

1. The store is the busiest at what time each day? _____

2. What is the busiest day and time for the store? _____

3. What reason might that be the busiest day and time? _____

_____

4. What day and time does the store have the least shoppers? _____

French Revolution

   Around the time America was fighting for independence, the people of France were becoming discontented. Their society was organized into three groups, called estates. The First Estate was made up of church leaders, the Second Estate was the nobles, and the Third Estate was everyone else (except the king – he didn't belong to any of these groups). The Third Estate included over 95% of the people.

   The First and Second Estates enjoyed a life of wealth and comfort. They collected money in the form of taxes and church offerings from the Third Estate, who were already living in poverty. When the Americans declared independence from Britain, some people in France decided to follow their lead and declare "independence" from the king and the upper classes.

   The French Revolution was very bloody and violent. By the time it was over, some of the original leaders had been put to death by those who had followed them. The royalty had been overthrown, but the French people felt that the rights due to them as French citizens had been acquired.

1. Which group of people made up the second estate? _____

_____

2. The poor, who were the majority of the people, were in which estate? _____

_____

3. Which estates enjoyed wealth and comfort? _____

_____

DAILY EXERCISE
Crunches
"Stretch Before You Play!"

Instruction
Repeat 5 times

Be Healthy!
Not everybody likes sports, and that's okay!

1

2

3

DAY 4

5

WEEK 7

Myth

A myth is usually a traditional story of events told as if they were history that serves to explore a group of people or explain a practice, belief, or natural phenomenon. Greeks and Romans both wrote myths to explain how they believed their societies began. They also used them to explore character traits in people. In the story of Daedalus and Icarus, Icarus was a typical child who thought his parent was being overprotective.

Most early civilizations created myths. Here is a Native American myth from the Lenape people.

WHEN SQUIRRELS WERE HUGE

Long ago, the squirrel was huge, and walked all over the place, in the valleys, in the woods, and the big forests, looking for smaller creatures to eat. He would eat all kinds of animals, even snakes.

Suddenly one evening he saw a two-legged creature running along. He ran after that two-legged creature, and finally he caught that person, and when he snatched him up he began to tear him to pieces. Finally he ate that person all up except for the person's hand which the giant squirrel was carrying in his hand.

While he was still busy chewing, all at once another person, an enormous person, was standing nearby. That person had a very white light shining and shimmering all around him, and when he said anything he roared like thunder and the earth shook and the trees fell down. He was the Creator.

The Creator said to the squirrel, "Now, truly you have done a very terrible deed. You have killed my child. Now, from this time on it is you who will be little and your children and your great grand-children will be eaten, and the shameful thing you did will always be seen (by a mark) under your forearm." Oh, the squirrel was scared, and he trembled with fear. He wanted to hide the man's hand, and he placed it under his upper arm. This story must be true because for a long time I have cut up and cooked many squirrels, and I have seen the hand under the squirrel's upper arm. We always cut that piece out before cooking the squirrel.

Answer each question **TRUE** or **FALSE**.

1. _____ Early people from many cultures told mythological stories.

2. _____ In the story, originally the squirrel was a very small animal.

3. _____ The person that the squirrel ate was the son of the Creator.

4. _____ The Creator is described as a weak, powerless person.

5. _____ The Creator wanted to reward the squirrel for his bravery.

6. _____ The squirrel wanted to hide the man's hand because it proved he had killed the man.

7. _____ The story suggests that there is a mark under a squirrel's arm which looks like a hand.

8. _____ This story is probably true.

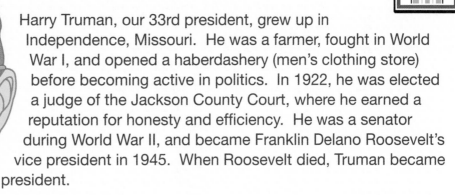

RESPECT – Harry S. Truman

Harry Truman, our 33rd president, grew up in Independence, Missouri. He was a farmer, fought in World War I, and opened a haberdashery (men's clothing store) before becoming active in politics. In 1922, he was elected a judge of the Jackson County Court, where he earned a reputation for honesty and efficiency. He was a senator during World War II, and became Franklin Delano Roosevelt's vice president in 1945. When Roosevelt died, Truman became president.

Truman had respect for the people of the USA. He worked hard to implement programs to help the poor and the elderly. In a 1946 letter to the National Urban League, President Truman wrote that the government has "an obligation to see that the civil rights of every citizen are fully and equally protected." He ended racial segregation in civil service and the armed forces in 1948. For the remainder of his presidency, he continued to fight against segregation.

1. What did Truman do with his life before becoming interested in politics?

_____

_____

2. What qualities did Truman demonstrate as a county judge?

_____

_____

3. What does implement mean?

_____

_____

4. Truman said that government has "an obligation to see that the civil rights of every citizen are fully and equally protected." How did Truman show that he believed this statement?

_____

_____

Color a star for each time you show Respect through your own actions this week.

 Write a 50-75 word essay describing one of your Respect actions this week.

Respect – Memorize Your Value

"We were taught to respect everyone, especially those who were older and wiser than we were from whom we could learn."

–BeNeca Ward

Core Value Book List
Read More About Respect

Apples and the Arrow
By Mary and Conrad Buff

A Day's Work
By Eve Bunting

Andy and the Lion
By James Daugherty

·········TECH TIME!·········

What does respect actually look like? Sometimes it is hard to visualize. President Truman did his best to show respect. Go online and fine a web 2.0 tool for creating a cover of a magazine or a book. Make a cover about Harry Truman, highlighting his qualities of respect. Get creative and then share what you have made!

www.SummerFitLearning.com

Bill Gates
Tech Guru and Philanthropist
gatesfoundation.org

1

2

3

4

DAY 5

W E E K 7

Play Time!
Choose a Game or Activity to Play for 60 minutes today!

YOU CHOOSE

_____

Write down which game or activity you played today!

Be Healthy!
Clean the kitchen without being asked.

Skills of the Week

- ✔ Integers, Computation With Integers
- ✔ Sonnets
- ✔ Observation
- ✔ Comprehension
- ✔ World War I
- ✔ Soliloquy
- ✔ Order Of Operations
- ✔ Ocean Water
- ✔ Appositives
- ✔ Regions Of United States

Weekly Value Responsibility

Jimmy Carter

Being responsible means others can depend on you. It is being accountable for what you do and for what you do not do.

A lot of times it is easier to look to someone else to step forward and do the work or to blame others when it does not get done. You are smart, capable and able so try to be the person who accepts challenges and does not blame others if it does not get done.

Stretching is Very Important

Get into the habit of stretching every night before you go to bed, as well as before you exercise every day.

Play 60 Every Day!

Run, jump, dance and have fun outside every day for 60 minutes!

Health and Wellness

Water makes your body work properly, so it is important to drink H2O throughout the day!

WEEK 8

HEALTHY MIND + HEALTHY BODY

Check the ✓ As You Complete Your Daily Task

	Day 1	Day 2	Day 3	Day 4	Day 5
MIND	☐	☐	☐	☐	☐
BODY	☐	☐	☐	☐	☐
DAILY READING	☐ 30 minutes	☐ 30 minutes	☐ 30 minutes	☐ 30 minutes	☐ 30 minutes

"I am responsible"

_____

Print Name

Integers Whole numbers and their opposites are called integers. Numbers less than zero are called negative numbers (an example is when you owe money). Numbers greater than zero are called positive numbers. Zero is neither positive nor negative. You can compare integers by looking at where they fall on a number line. The greater of two integers is always the one farthest to the right.

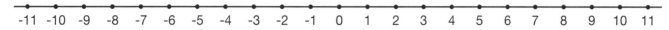

-11 -10 -9 -8 -7 -6 -5 -4 -3 -2 -1 0 1 2 3 4 5 6 7 8 9 10 11

Adding Integers The sum of two positive integers is a positive integer. The sum of two negative integers is a negative integer. To find the sum of a positive integer and a negative integer, you subtract the smaller absolute number from the larger one, then assign the sign of the larger one.

Example 3 + (-5) Think (5 – 3 = 2). 5 is larger than 3 and it's sign is negative, so the answer is -2. You can also use the number line. Begin at 3 and count 5 in the negative direction. You end up at -2.

1. 5 + 9 =

2. 13 + (-6) =

3. 14 + -3 =

4. 7 + (-10) =

5. -7 + (-2) =

6. -5 + 7 =

7. 4 + (-1) =

8. -2 + 0 =

DAY 1

2

3

4

5

WEEK 8

Regions of the US

Region is one of the themes of geography. A region is an area that has something in common. That something could be language, land formations, shared history or culture.

Different sources divide the United States into a different number of geographic regions. We are going to look at 7. There is a long region along the Atlantic and Gulf Coast, called the Coastal Plain. To the west of this and going from northern Georgia and Alabama to Maine is the Appalachian Mountain region. The largest region is call the Interior Lowlands, and reaches from eastern Ohio to Western Missouri and Illinois. The Great Plains is west of that, broken up by the Rocky Mountain region. Along the western coast of the U.S. is the Coastal Range. Between the Coastal Range and Rocky Mountains is the Basin and Ridge region. The division of these regions is based on the basic landforms found in each region.

1. In what region is your home located? _____

2. What landforms are located near your home? (Lakes, mountains, hills, flatland, oceans?)

_____

_____

3. What do you like best about the region in which you live? _____

_____

_____

Aerobic Go to www.summerfitlearning.com for more Activities!

DAILY EXERCISE
Racing Leap-Frog
"Stretch Before You Play!"

Instruction
Play with Friends!

Be Healthy!
Your body is growing and needs 8-9 hours of sleep every day!

DAY 1 | **Sonnet**

2 3 4 5

W E E K 8

A sonnet is a particular style of poetry. (The name comes from an Italian word "sonetto" which means little song.) Traditionally, it has 14 lines of iambic pentameter – huh!? That just means that every line has 10 syllables and every other syllable is stressed (soft – LOUD - soft – LOUD - soft – LOUD - soft – LOUD - soft – LOUD).

William Shakespeare, who lived in England in the late 1500s and early 1600s, is considered by many to be the greatest writer in the English language. He wrote about 38 plays, 154 sonnets, two long narrative poems, and several other poems. His sonnets followed a particular rhyme scheme: abab cdcd efef gg.

Sonnet 18 is perhaps the most well known of Shakespeare's sonnets.

Sonnet 18
Shall I compare thee to a summer's day?
Thou art more lovely and more temperate:
Rough winds do shake the darling buds of May,
And summer's lease hath all too short a date:
Sometime too hot the eye of heaven shines,
And often is his gold complexion dimm'd;
And every fair from fair sometime declines,
By chance or nature's changing course untrimm'd;
But thy eternal summer shall not fade
Nor lose possession of that fair thou owest;
Nor shall Death brag thou wander'st in his shade,
When in eternal lines to time thou growest:
　　So long as men can breathe or eyes can see,
　　So long lives this, and this gives life to thee.

The first line of this poem is very famous and often quoted. The next 11 lines, are the comparison of the person and summer. The last part of the poem tells how the subject is different from summer.

1. Line 2 says the subject is "more lovely and more temperate" than summer. What does temperate mean? _____

2. How does the poet say the summer is not temperate? _____
_____

3. Find the line that suggests that the subject will not seem to grow older. _____
_____

4. There is personification in line 11 – what word is it? _____

Subtract Integers

To subtract an integer, add it's opposite.

Examples: 3 – 9 = 3 + (-9) = -6   -9 – 4 = -9 + (-4) = -13   -6 – (-5) = -6 + 5 = -1

1. -9 – 12 =

2. 12 – 37 =

3. 42 – (-15) =

4. -6 – 2 =

5. 19-17 =

6. -19 – 17 =

7. -19 – (-17) =

8. 3 – (-7) =

9. -2 – 0 =

10. 0 – (-7) =

11. -13 – (-4) =

12. 12 – (-9) =

13. 1 – 0 =

14. 0 – 1 =

Observation Game

You will need a partner for this game. You also need 2 sets of 5 to 10 small ordinary objects, such as coins or Legos.   (2 dimes, 2 monopoly houses, etc.)

One person arranges the items from one set on a table. Set a timer for 30 seconds and the second person will study the arrangement on the table. At the end of 30 seconds, cover the objects. The second person now takes the second set of objects and tries to duplicate the arrangement. When finished, check the second arrangement against the first, awarding 1 point for each item the same. Be specific; not only are they in the same order, but for example was the coin heads up or tails, is it turned in the same direction? Use pen and paper to keep track of the score.

Now the second person arranges the objects and the first person tries to duplicate the arrangement. At the end of five rounds, tally the score for each player and crown the champion of observation!

PLAYER ONE :

PLAYER TWO:

Strength Go to www.summerfitlearning.com for more Activities!

DAILY EXERCISE
Chop n Squat
"Stretch Before You Play!"

Instruction
Repeat 10 times

Be Healthy!
Your brain works hard everyday, so put on a helmet!

Comprehension

Playing a musical instrument is a skill that takes time, effort, and a little talent. However, the rewards far outweigh the work that goes into it.

It is quite an accomplishment to learn even the basics of an instrument. You are mastering not only the skill involved in playing. You learn other technical aspects of your instrument: how it is made and put together, and perhaps even how to do simple repairs.

Very often a student learns the history of the instrument. Many instruments date back to pre-historic times. Then there are instruments which have been developed within the last century. A great many instruments are fashioned after previous instruments, but have been altered in some way.

Most instructors will also teach about composers. Some stick to just the more famous composers or time periods. Many prefer to focus on only modern composers. Some like to interject obscure, little known composers who often have composed something of which the teacher is especially fond.

Many people do not realize, however, the connection between music and math! Music in America is written with notes that measure largely in multiples of 2 (whole notes, half, quarter, sixteenths). A piece of music follows a pattern which is set up at the beginning of the piece – which note will get 1 beat in a measure and how many beats are in the measure. The math has to add up. In a measure which is supposed to have 4 beats, you could have a half note, a quarter note and 2 eighth notes. You could not have a half note, 2 quarter notes and an eighth note, because that would equal four and an eighth – too many beats for the measure.

Another way music is tied to math is in the scales we use. Most scales are based on 8 notes. We use the first seven letters of the alphabet to name the notes. Why don't we use the first eight? Because the last note in a scale is a higher version of the first note, and uses the same name.

Who would have thought music could help you with math? In addition, you learn some history, some culture, and a skill which can bring enjoyment to others as well as yourself.

1. Infer from the selection what the word obscure, in the fourth paragraph, means. _____
_____

2. What are two ways music is connected to math? _____
_____

3. What are the technical aspects you might learn with an instrument? _____
_____

4. The selection does not discuss practice, but to do well in anything we have to practice. How often do you think a person should practice a musical instrument. Explain your reasoning.
_____
_____

Multiply and divide integers

The product of two positive or two negative integers is always positive. The product of a positive integer and a negative integer is always negative. Remember that the product of any integer and zero is zero.

1. -4 x (-4) =

2. -8 x 3 =

3. 5 x (-6) =

4. -7 x (-8) =

5. -2 x 9 =

6. 5 x 7 =

7. 4 x (-8) =

8. -7 x (-9) =

The division rule is like the multiplication rule. The quotient of two positive or two negative integers is positive. The quotient of a positive and a negative integer is negative. Zero divided by any other integer is zero. An integer cannot be divided by zero.

9. 54 ÷ (-9) =

10. -63 ÷ 7 =

11. 72 ÷ 8 =

12. -36 ÷ (-6) =

13. -30 ÷ 5 =

14. 26 ÷ (-2) =

15. -27 ÷ (-3) =

16. -56 ÷ (-7) =

World War I

There are two wars that have been labeled as World Wars. They both began in Europe and involved some of the same countries. They are called World Wars because countries from around the world were involved.

World War I began when a Serbian man killed the Austrian heir. The Serbs felt they had been oppressed by the Austrians. The Austrians were allies with Germany. They declared war on Serbia. France and Great Britain declared war on Austria and Germany. Russia also declared war on Austria. Many European countries tried to stay neutral, but several joined one group or the other. America initially refused to take sides, but when Germans continued to attack ships in the Atlantic with Americans, America joined the Triple Entente (Great Britain, France and Russia). The other group was called the Triple Alliance; Italy joined this group.

1. Which countries were part of the Triple Alliance? _____

_____

_____

2. What event sparked the First World War? _____

_____

_____

DAILY EXERCISE
Bear Crawl
"Stretch Before You Play!"

Instruction
Crawl for 2
Minutes x 3

Be Healthy!
Eat a healthy snack like popcorn!

Soliloquy

One way to think of a soliloquy is that it's a speech you make to yourself. An author may have a character give a soliloquy in order for the reader to understand the character's thoughts and perspective. A more formal definition is a dramatic speech that represents reflections or unspoken thoughts by the character.

The following is a soliloquy by *Alice of Alice In Wonderland*. She has fallen down the rabbit hole after trying to follow the White Rabbit.

ALICE: *[Angrily]* Why, how impolite of him. I asked him a civil question, and he pretended not to hear me. That's not at all nice. *[Calling after him]* I say, Mr. White Rabbit, where are you going? Hmmm. He won't answer me. And I do so want to know what he is late for. I wonder if I might follow him. Why not? There's no rule that I mayn't go where I please. I--I will follow him. Wait for me, Mr. White Rabbit. I'm coming, too! *[Falling]* How curious. I never realized that rabbit holes were so dark . . . and so long . . . and so empty. I believe I have been falling for five minutes, and I still can't see the bottom! Hmph! After such a fall as this, I shall think nothing of tumbling downstairs. How brave they'll all think me at home. Why, I wouldn't say anything about it even if I fell off the top of the house! I wonder how many miles I've fallen by this time. I must be getting somewhere near the center of the earth. I wonder if I shall fall right through the earth! How funny that would be. Oh, I think I see the bottom. Yes, I'm sure I see the bottom. I shall hit the bottom, hit it very hard, and oh, how it will hurt!

1. What is the difference between a soliloquy and a dialogue? _____
_____

2. Why does Alice think a fall downstairs will seem like nothing? _____
_____

3. What does Alice use as her reason for following the rabbit?_____
_____

4. What did Alice say she had not realized before? _____
_____

5. Who does Alice seem concerned about during her fall? _____

6. Why would Alice think she would hit the bottom very hard? _____
_____
_____

1 2 DAY 3 4 5

WEEK 8

To evaluate mathematical expressions, remember the mnemonic device: **Please Excuse My Dear Aunt Sally**. Work anything in a parenthesis first, then exponents, multiplication and division next, and finally addition and subtraction. Within any of those groupings remember to work from left to right.

Example: $-3 \times 5 + 2 = -15 + 2 = -13$
$60 \div (5 + 5) = 60 \div 10 = 6$

1. $9 - 6.5 + (-4.1) =$

2. $-3.5 \times -1.4 \div 7 =$

3. $2 + [48 \div (14 + 10)] - 5 =$

4. $5 \times 9 - [-1.75 \times (-3.4)] =$

Ocean Water

For this activity you will need a clear bowl, a plastic bottle, table salt, and blue food coloring. Mix ¾ cup of water with 6 tablespoons of salt. Add blue food coloring to make the salty water a deep blue. Fill the bowl half full of water. View the bowl from the side as you pour the blue, salt water down the side of the bowl. Think about what happens when a fresh water river, such as the Mississippi River flows into a salty body of water such as the Gulf of Mexico.

5. Write a paragraph with at least 5 sentences to explain what you think happened in the activity.

_____

_____

_____

_____

_____

_____

_____

_____

_____

DAY
4

WEEK 8

DAILY EXERCISE
Side Step
"Stretch Before You Play!"

Instruction
Repeat 5 times in
each direction

Be Healthy!
Smile!

1
2
3

DAY 4

5

WEEK 8

Appositive

An appositive is a noun or a noun phrase that is placed next to another noun or noun phrase to help identify it. If I write, "A student raised his hand," you don't know who that is. If I write, "A student, Hank, raised his hand," then you know that Hank is the student.

Sometimes you need a comma to separate the appositive, sometimes you don't. If the information given by the appositive is essential, you don't use a comma. This would be the case is the sentence doesn't make sense without the appositive. An example is, "The musical group the Beatles wrote a many songs and were very popular in the 1960s." Without the name, the Beatles, the sentence is too vague to make sense.

If the information is not essential, the sentence makes sense without it. Then you set that phrase or noun apart with commas.

Insert an appositive phrase into the first five sentences.

1. I just finished watching my favorite movie, _____.

2. Juan's best friend, _____, went with him to the amusement park.

3. I forgot to feed my pet, a _____.

4. William Shakespeare, an _____ wrote many plays.

5. My school, _____, is a great school.

Decide whether the phrase is an appositive or a prepositional phrase. Mark the appositive sentences with an **A**; mark the prepositional phrases with a **P**.

6. _____ Carolyn played well in the 4th quarter of the match.

7. _____ Abraham Lincoln, the sixteenth president, wrote the Emancipation Proclamation.

8. _____ We'll meet at the park tomorrow.

9. _____ The movie last night, How The West Was Won, was an old one but a great story.

RESPONSIBILITY – Jimmy Carter

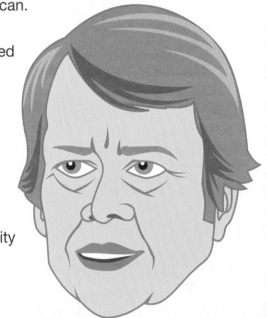

Once a person is no longer president, can they make a difference?

Jimmy Carter, 39th president of the United States, said, "We can choose to alleviate suffering. We can choose to work together for peace. We can make these changes – and we must." Even when we are not responsible for the suffering of others, we must be responsible for helping them whenever and however we can.

To help people follow through on this idea, Jimmy Carter founded the Carter Center. The Carter Center is dedicated to the protection of human rights, disease prevention, conflict resolution and the promotion of democracy.

In addition, Carter and his wife Rosalynn volunteer once a week for Habitat for Humanity. This group takes the responsibility of building and renovating homes for needy people in the United States and other countries. Carter and his wife don't just sit by – they hammer, and clean, and work with everyone else. Jimmy Carter has continued to take responsibility for those in our community who have difficulty helping themselves.

1. What is a habitat? _____

2. What are four things the Carter Center is dedicated to supporting?

    1) _____
    2) _____
    3) _____
    4) _____

3. If you were going to help build a home for a needy family, what factors would you look at to determine who deserved the home?

    _____

    _____

    _____

Color a star for each time you show
Responsibility through your own actions this week.

 Write a 50-75 word essay describing one of your Responsibility actions this week.

Responsibility Memorize
Your Value
"The price of greatness is
responsibility."

– Sir Winston Churchill

·········TECH TIME!·········

There are many aspects of being responsible. Online you can make fun and exciting brochures. Find a web 2.0 tool that will help you do this. Make a brochure that promotes responsibility and gives ideas of ways someone your age can be responsible.

www.SummerFitLearning.com

Bill Gates
Tech Guru and
Philanthropist
gatesfoundation.org

Core Value Book List
Read More About Responsibility

**Uncommon Champions:
Fifteen Athletes Who
Battled Back**
By Mary Kaminsky

**The Value of
Responsibility: The Story
of Ralph Bunche**
By Ann Donegan Johnson

Following Isabella
By Linda Talley and
Andrea Chase

1

2

3

4

DAY
5

WEEK 8

Play Time!
Choose a Game or Activity to Play for 60 minutes today!

YOU CHOOSE

_____

Write down which game or activity you played today!

Be Healthy!
Drink water
instead of soda.

Skills of the Week

- ✔ Unit Rate
- ✔ Scientific Method
- ✔ Alliteration
- ✔ Problem Solving
- ✔ Modern Europe
- ✔ Biography
- ✔ Statistics
- ✔ Scientific Classification
- ✔ Indirect Object
- ✔ Comprehension
- ✔ Transitive And Intransitive Verbs

Weekly Value Perseverance

Wilma Rudolph

Perseverance means not giving up or giving in when things are difficult. It means you try again when you fail.

Sometimes it is easy to forget that a lot of things in life require patience and hard work. Do not give up because it is hard to accomplish a task or to get something that we want. Focus on your goal and keep working hard. It is through this experience that you will accomplish what you want.

Stretching is Very Important

Get into the habit of stretching every night before you go to bed, as well as before you exercise every day.

Play 60 Every Day!

Run, jump, dance and have fun outside every day for 60 minutes!

Health and Wellness

You don't have to "diet" to be at a healthy weight. Eat different types of foods, including different vegetables and fruits, and stay away from the soda machine! Being involved in a sport or playing and getting physical activity everyday keeps you at a healthy weight, too!

WEEK 9

Check the ✓ As You Complete Your Daily Task

	Day 1	Day 2	Day 3	Day 4	Day 5
MIND					
BODY					
DAILY READING	30 minutes	30 minutes	30 minutes	30 minutes	30 minutes

"I have perseverance"

_____

Print Name

When a ratio compares quantities of different kinds, it is called a rate. The cost of each one of an item is known as the unit rate. The unit rate can be found by dividing the amount of money by the number of items. If a 6 pack of soda costs $4.20, then each soda costs $0.70. Find the unit rate for each of the following.

1. Susan earned $160 for selling 32 boxes of Christmas cards. _____

2. Prime Pizza brought in $656.27 for 73 pizzas. _____

3. The school play seated 1350 people in 30 rows. _____

4. Bill bought 8 tickets for $40. _____

5. Sam collected $325 for 50 books. _____

Scientific Method

Annie designed an experiment for her science class. Read the description and use your knowledge of scientific method to answer the questions.

Many people choose plant experiments for their first project, and so did Annie. She bought a special fertilizer which was advertised to help plants produce more, and larger flowers. She planted two plants of the same size in different containers with the same amount of potting soil. She put one plant in a sunny window and watered it daily with fertilized water. She put the other plant in a shed with no windows behind her house and watered it every other day with plain water.

1. What did Annie do wrong in her experiment? _____

_____

_____

_____

2. What would you do differently to test this product's claims? _____

_____

_____

_____

_____

DAY
1
2
3
4
5

WEEK 9

Aerobic

Go to www.summerfitlearning.com for more Activities!

DAILY EXERCISE
Towel Slide/Plate Push
"Stretch Before You Play!"

Instruction
Complete 5 times

Be Healthy! Brush your teeth in the morning, afternoon and before bed.

DAY 1

Alliteration

Alliteration is a device often used in poetry, but also in other literature, in which 2 or more words that are close to each other begin with the same sound. It helps provide a work with musical rhythms and adds interest and appeal. It lends flow and beauty as well as structure to a piece of writing. Poems with alliteration can be easier to memorize.

Alliteration is also used by advertisers to make slogans more memorable. It is also often used with children's stories to make them more fun to read out loud.

Here are some examples of alliteration in Edgar Allen Poe's poem The Raven.

Once upon a midnight dreary while I pondered <u>weak and weary</u>…

And the silken sad uncertain rustling of each purple curtain…

<u>Doubting, dreaming dreams</u> no mortal ever dared to dream before

---

Tongue Twisters are filled with Alliteration. Try saying a few of these tongue twisters three times in a row and quickly.

Peter Piper picked a peck of pickled peppers. A peck of pickled peppers Peter Piper picked. If Peter Piper picked a peck of pickled peppers. How many pickled peppers did Peter Piper pick?

Silly Sally swiftly shooed seven silly sheep. The seven silly sheep Silly Sally shooed shilly-shallied south. These sheep shouldn't sleep in a shack; Sheep should sleep in a shed.

Underline the words in each of the following sentences which demonstrate alliteration.

1. The calico cat caught several fat round mice.
2. The puppies ran round and round the playground.
3. Lovely yellow daffodils and ruby red roses filled the garden.
4. The orchestra performed the opus as beautifully as sweetly singing angels.
5. The sky was full of powder puff clouds.
6. The guitars and drums blended into a rich rhythm of rollicking tunes.
7. As they reached the top of the mountain, their eyes beheld the winter wonder below.
8. Clocks ticked and chimes rang as the boys waited wistfully for the lesson to end.
9. The friendly frog filled the air with his night calls.
10. It seemed that the library was filled with billions of books.

1. A 6 oz. can of beans cost $0.69. A 12 oz. can of the same brand costs $1.24. What is the best buy, four 6 oz. cans or two 12 oz. cans? What is the difference in cost?

_____

2. You are making a cake and you want to double the recipe. The original recipe calls for ¾ cup of sugar, 2 eggs, and 1 and 2/3 cup of flour. How much of each do you need for the cake you are making?

Sugar _____   Eggs _____   Flour _____

3. You want to buy 15 "To Go Mugs." How much will it cost if the price is 2 for $0.98? _____

4. You are looking at a diagram of a wall you want to cover with wallpaper. The scale is 1 in = 2 feet. How tall is the wall if the diagram shows 4 inches? How wide if the diagram shows 6 inches?

Height _____   Width _____

Modern Europe

There are 47 independent countries in Europe. Many people are familiar with the major countries in Europe, such as Great Britain and France, but not as familiar with some of the smaller countries (or those not in the news as much). Find and label these countries on the map.

Albania

Austria

Azerbaijan

Belarus

Bosnia & Herzegovina

Croatia

Czech Republic

Finland

Greece

Luxembourg

Monaco

Norway

Romania

Serbia

Turkey

WEEK 9

DAY 2

1 3 4 5

DAILY EXERCISE
Balance
"Stretch Before You Play!"

Instruction
Hold each for 15 seconds, then switch legs and repeat

Be Healthy!
Turn off the TV and play outside.

1

DAY 2

3

4

5

WEEK 9

Biography

The biography has been a genre of literature popular for hundreds of years. A biography is a story of someone's life, or a portion of that life, written by someone else. Sometimes a biography is written because the author admires the subject, sometimes because the author wants to point out the weaknesses or failings of a person.

An author researches the subject by reading other works about the person, perhaps the subject's diary or journal, and letters or essays written by the subject. The author tries to give the reader more than just basic facts. They try to include personal insights, reflections on the subject's personality, personal information regarding the subject.

Today, biographies are not just books. They may be television programs or movies, online sites, and magazine and newspaper articles.

Remember that biographies are supposed to be factual stories about a person's life. You can tell that a story is a biography if the subject is or was a real person, if the stories are realistic, and usually told in the third person.

Circle the titles or scenarios which would be biographies.

The Cat In the Hat

The Story of Thomas Edison's Childhood

George Washington's War Journal

George Washington's Journey to Mars

Peter Rabbit's Amazing Adventures

The Read Adventures of Rabbits

A story about how horses are trained

A story about a queen on the moon

Pizarro Conquering the Inca

Stories of the American Astronauts

Thomas Jefferson's Diary

The Presidents' Lives

The Diary of Anne Frank

The Wright Brothers and Their Airplane

A story about the current Queen of England

A story about a boy and his dinosaur

Write three sentences about whose biography your might like to read and why.

_____

_____

_____

_____

_____

_____

_____

Statistics is the area of math that takes a series of numbers and analyzes them using mean, median, mode, range. The mean is the average – you add the numbers together and divide by how many numbers are in the series. The median is the number that falls exactly in the middle if you put them in order from largest to smallest. If there is no middle number, you take the two in the middle and find the middle of those two. The range is the difference between the greatest and the least number. Mode is a number that appears more often than any other number in the series. (Sometimes there is no mode.) Give the mean, median, mode and range for each set of numbers.

	Mean	Median	Mode	Range
21, 19, 15, 11, 14	16	15	None	10
71, 23, 41, 63, 72				
29, 56, 43, 22, 61, 29				
125, 145, 189, 133				

Scientific Classification

Living things can be divided into 6 kingdoms: Plant, Animal, Protista, Fungi, Archaebacteria, and Eubacteria. Criteria for deciding which kingdom include cell type (complex or single), the ability to make food, and number of cells in the body. Plants, for example, are multicellular and consist of complex cells. They also make their own food. Plants are the second largest kingdom.

The animal kingdom is largest, with over 1 million species. All animals consist of many complex cells. They feed on other organisms.

Archaebacteria are single cell organisms. They are found in extreme environments such as boiling water and thermal vents, with no oxygen or highly acidic conditions. They are complex, as are Eubacteria. Most bacteria are in the Eubacteria kingdom. Most of these are helpful, like those that help produce yogurt and vitamins. Some, however, are not so helpful, such as the ones that cause disease. Some scientists group these two together as simply bacteria.

Mushrooms, mold, and mildew are part of the Fungi kingdom. These are multicellular and have complex cells. They were once thought to be plant cells, but they do not make their own food.

Protista seem to be a catch-all category. This kingdom is all things which are not plants, animals, bacteria, or fungi. Most are unicellular, but have complex cells.

1. Which kingdoms have organisms with single cells? _____

_____

_____

2. Which kingdom would claim as a member the lion? _____

_____

_____

DAILY EXERCISE
Jump Rope
"Stretch Before You Play!"

Instruction
Goal = 5 minutes
without stopping

Be Healthy!
Slow down
when you eat!

Indirect Object

If a direct object is the object of the action of the verb, what is an indirect object? The direct object answers the question "what?" The indirect object answers the question "to whom or for whom?" It is the noun or pronoun that is indirectly affected by the action of a verb.

In the sentence: **Bill played his grandmother a piece on his guitar.** Bill is the subject and played is the verb. He played what? A piece. He played for whom? His grandmother. Therefore, **piece** is the <u>direct</u> object and **grandmother** is the <u>indirect</u> object.

Note that if you use the word "for," as in **He played the guitar for his grandmother**, grandmother is now the object of the preposition for, but is still the indirect object of the sentence.

In the following sentences, circle the indirect object. If there is no indirect object, circle nothing.

1. The mother told the children a bedtime story.

2. Can you bring Julio a glass of water?

3. Claire played the piano beautifully and skillfully.

4. Helene baked the children of the neighborhood some cookies.

5. Dad bought the children each a new bike.

6. Emil gave his sister tickets to the new play.

7. Stewart gave us several options for activities after school.

8. The newspaper was well written.

9. Tell the teacher the reason you are late.

10. Show your dad the story you wrote.

11. Clint scored a goal for the team.

12. Omar sent his sister a postcard from Hawaii.

Mark Twain is probably best known for his books Tom Sawyer and Huck Finn, but he also wrote non-fiction. The following is an excerpt from *Roughing It*, based on events he experienced on a trip with his brother out west.

The next morning, bright and early, we took a hasty breakfast, and hurried to the starting-place. Then an inconvenience presented itself which we had not properly appreciated before, namely, that one cannot make a heavy traveling trunk stand for twenty-five pounds of baggage—because it weighs a good deal more. But that was all we could take—twenty-five pounds each. So we had to snatch our trunks open, and make a selection in a good deal of a hurry. We put our lawful twenty-five pounds apiece all in one valise, and shipped the trunks back to St. Louis again. It was a sad parting, for now we had no swallow-tail coats and white kid gloves to wear at Pawnee receptions in the Rocky Mountains, and no stove-pipe hats nor patent-leather boots, nor anything else necessary to make life calm and peaceful. ... I was armed to the teeth with a pitiful little Smith & Wesson's seven-shooter, which carried a ball like a homoeopathic pill, and it took the whole seven to make a dose for an adult. But I thought it was grand. It appeared to me to be a dangerous weapon. It only had one fault—you could not hit anything with it. One of our "conductors" practiced awhile on a cow with it, and as long as she stood still and behaved herself she was safe; but as soon as she went to moving about, and he got to shooting at other things, she came to grief. ... Mr. George Bemis was dismally formidable. George Bemis was our fellow-traveler.

We had never seen him before. He wore in his belt an old original "Allen" revolver, such as irreverent people called a "pepper-box." Simply drawing the trigger back, cocked and fired the pistol. As the trigger came back, the hammer would begin to rise and the barrel to turn over, and presently down would drop the hammer, and away would speed the ball. To aim along the turning barrel and hit the thing aimed at was a feat which was probably never done with an "Allen" in the world. But George's was a reliable weapon, nevertheless, because, as one of the stage-drivers afterward said, "If she didn't get what she went after, she would fetch something else." And so she did. She went after a deuce of spades nailed against a tree, once, and fetched a mule standing about thirty yards to the left of it. Bemis did not want the mule; but the owner came out with a double-barreled shotgun and persuaded him to buy it, anyhow. It was a cheerful weapon—the "Allen." Sometimes all its six barrels would go off at once, and then there was no safe place in all the region round about, but behind it.

1. What did Twain mean when he said "the owner came out with a double-barreled shotgun and persuaded him to buy it, anyhow." _____

_____

2. There is a bit of sarcasm in the first paragraph concerning the travelers' clothes. What did Twain infer when he said "we had no swallow-tail coats and white kid gloves to wear at Pawnee receptions in the Rocky Mountains, and no stove-pipe hats nor patent-leather boots." _____

_____

_____

Strength

Go to www.summerfitlearning.com for more Activities!

DAILY EXERCISE
Toe Taps
"Stretch Before You Play!"

Instruction
Repeat 10 times with each foot

Be Healthy!
Walk with your family before or after dinner.

Transitive and Intransitive Verbs

A transitive verb is an action verb that has an object to receive the action. (Remember you can answer the question "what" if there is an object.) Intransitive verbs are action verbs, but there is no object to receive the action. (You might be able to answer where, when, how, or why, but not what.) **In the following sentences, underline the verb and if there is an object, underline that, too. Write a T for the sentences that have a transitive verb, and an I for the sentences with an intransitive verb.**

1. _____ I knitted a blanket.
2. _____ Willow ate until she was stuffed.
3. _____ Candy rode her bicycle around the block several times.
4. _____ My mother baked several pies for Thanksgiving dinner.
5. _____ After the party, Brian moved the chairs back into the dining room.
6. _____ The book fell from my hand onto the floor.
7. _____ Leslie cried all night, and she couldn't seem to stop.
8. _____ I sold some books at the flea market.
9. _____ Ashley broke the window accidentally.
10. _____ The sun rose over the misty mountainside.
11. _____ The committee named a new chairperson during the meeting.
12. _____ The children slept peacefully.
13. _____ Natalia studies Russian in school.
14. _____ Bailey sits in the corner when she reads.

Problem solving

1. Jose is selling online music. His base pay is $5 a day, and he earns an extra $1 for every single song he sells. He wants to earn $100 this week. If he works Monday through Friday, and sells the same number of single songs each day, how many songs does he need to sell each day?

_____

2. If he sells 20 songs on Monday, what is the least he needs to sell the other four days?

_____

3. If he only sells 10 on Monday, what is the least he needs to sell the other four days?

_____

1 2 3 DAY 4 5 WEEK 9

PERSEVERANCE – Wilma Rudolph

Wilma Rudolph was not a healthy child. She had problems with her left leg and for several years had to wear a brace on it. Her family provided physical therapy for her, even though at one time she was told she may not even walk again. But Wilma and her family persevered.

By the time she was in high school, she began to play basketball. She later joined the track team and it was discovered that she was a talented runner. She participated in the 1956 and 1960 Olympics, winning 3 gold medals. Not bad for someone the doctors thought would never walk!

Wilma became a teacher and a coach. Her story was made into a television film and she was inducted into the U. S. Olympic Hall of Fame. She established the Wilma Rudolph Foundation to promote amateur athletics.

1. Who thought Wilma would possibly not walk after her leg problems? _____

_____

_____

2. What sports did Wilma participate in during high school? _____

_____

_____

3. What does the word amateur mean? _____

_____

_____

4. Number these events in the correct order from the story.

_____ Wilma was inducted into the U. S. Olympic Hall of Fame.

_____ Wilma won 3 Olympic gold medals.

_____ Wilma established a foundation to promote amateur athletics.

_____ Wilma was told she might not walk again.

_____ Wilma participated in basketball and track during high school.

_____ Wilma became a teacher and a coach.

Color a star for each time you show Perseverance through your own actions this week.

 Write a 50-75 word essay describing one of your Perseverance actions this week.

Perseverance – Memorize Your Value

"It always seems impossible until its done."

– Nelson Mandela

Core Value Book List
Read More About Perseverance

Fly, Eagle, Fly
By Desmond Tutu

I Knew You Could
By Wally Piper

Strawberry Girl
By Lois Lenski

·········TECH TIME!··········

Have you ever looked at a comic strip and learned something about someone else? This week you have learned about perseverance and the biography of Wilma Rudolph. How do you show perseverance in your life? Can you make a comic strip that shows your perseverance? Give it a try! Do an Internet search to find a tool that will allow you to make a free comic strip. Using this tool, create a three- frame comic strip showing how you have persevered at something in your life.

www.SummerFitLearning.com

Bill Gates
Tech Guru and
Philanthropist
gatesfoundation.org

Play Time!
Choose a Game or Activity to Play for 60 minutes today!

YOU CHOOSE

_____

Write down which game or activity you played today!

Be Healthy!
Acne, also known as pimples, is a normal part of growing up.

1
2
3
4

DAY 5

WEEK 9

PARENT TIPS FOR WEEK 10

Skills of the Week

✔ Autobiography
✔ Probability
✔ Modern Africa
✔ Percents Used In Different Ways
✔ Erosion
✔ Theme
✔ South America
✔ Central America
✔ Dependent Clauses
✔ Mood And Tone

Weekly Value Friendship

Hellen Keller and Anne Sulllivan

Friendship is what comes from being friends. It is caring and sharing and being there for each other in good times and bad.

It is fun to have friends that we play with, go to the movies and share our time, but it also is a responsibility. Our friends are people that we trust, protect, respect and stand up for even when it is not easy. We care about our friends and our friends care about us.

Stretching is Very Important
Get into the habit of stretching every night before you go to bed, as well as before you exercise every day.

Play 60 Every Day!

Run, jump, dance and have fun outside every day for 60 minutes!

Health and Wellness

If a friend tells you to do or try something that you feel uncomfortable with, don't do it! That's your body being smart! You are in control of your body and mind, not someone else.

WEEK 10

Check the ✓ As You Complete Your Daily Task

	Day 1	Day 2	Day 3	Day 4	Day 5
MIND	☐	☐	☐	☐	☐
BODY	☐	☐	☐	☐	☐
DAILY READING	☐ 30 minutes	☐ 30 minutes	☐ 30 minutes	☐ 30 minutes	☐ 30 minutes

"I am a friend"

Print Name

An autobiography is the story of a person's life or events in someone's life written by that person. Journals and diaries are considered autobiographical. Memoirs are also autobiographical. Jack London wrote a book called *The Road* with stories about his days as a hobo. Benjamin Franklin, Frederick Douglass, and Helen Keller all wrote about their own lives. Anne Frank wrote a diary which was published after her death. All of these stories are told by the individuals about themselves.

Autobiographies are usually written in the first person (I, me, we). The advantage over a biography is that you are privy to the subjects most intimate thoughts. The disadvantage is that people are sometimes less than frank about themselves, especially if there are things they are ashamed of or embarrassed about.

Read this short autobiography to find out about a girl named Veronica.

I loved belonging to a large family. I was the second child and the first daughter. Of the thirteen children, only two were boys: Curtis was the oldest and Paul was the fourth child. After me, as far as the girls, came Edie, Steffie, Jennie, Theresa, Cece, Liz, Sheila, Celeste, Miriam, and Tish.

People always express their sympathy for the boys, but I don't think they deserve any sympathy. Curtis was a great older brother, but he was very manipulative, as well. He was able to work the rest of us. I mean, on Halloween, he would get people to trade him one of something they had for two of something he had. But somehow, he ended up with the best stuff. We had more, but it wasn't as good. To this day, I dislike the game Monopoly, because you couldn't beat Curtis. Again, he would talk you into deals that seemed great, but in the end they benefitted him the most.

Paul probably had it a little tougher. By the time he got to high school, our father had left, and Curtis was entering the military. Paul had to deal with a bunch of teen-age sisters, and a mother, with no adult males in the picture. I like to think we helped him find and develop his feminine side, because he has matured into a thoughtful, loving husband.

Now, don't think we girls were always loving and sweet to each other. We had our spats, for sure. I'm a grown woman, now, but I still remember being so angry when one of the girls "borrowed" without my knowledge my favorite skirt, and when I got it back it had a terrible ink stain that would never come out. For the most part, though, we looked out for one another, helped one another, and we always loved one another.

1. Why did the oldest brother not deserve sympathy?_____

_____

2. How did Paul benefit from having so many sisters? _____

_____

3. What might be a disadvantage of being from a large family? _____

_____

4. What might be an advantage? _____

_____

DAILY EXERCISE
Jogging for Fitness 15
"Stretch Before You Play!"

Instruction
Jog 15 minutes in place or outside

Be Healthy!
Eat more whole grains like pasta, bread and rice.

DAY
1
2
3
4
5

WEEK 10

Probability

Probability is a measure of how likely an event is. For example, if you have a spinner with 6 numbers on 6 equal spaces, the likelihood of landing on any one number is 1 in 6. In other words, you have 1 out of 6 chances of landing on any number. If the numbers are 1 through 6, you have a 3 in 6 chance of landing on an odd number. This probability can be written as a fraction and can be simplified to 1/2 or 1 in 2 chance.

A glass jar contains 6 red, 5 green, 9 blue and 4 yellow marbles.

1. If a single marble is chosen at random from the jar, what is the probability of choosing a red marble? _____

2. What is the probability of choosing a green marble? _____

3. What is the probability of choosing a blue marble? _____

4. What is the probability of choosing a yellow marble? _____

Modern Africa

Africa is the second largest continent in the world. It is three times the size of the continental United States.

There are five huge river systems in Africa. The three biggest are the Nile, the Congo, and the Niger. The other two large river systems are the Orange and the Zambezi. Early civilizations developed along these rivers. One of the most well known is the civilization of Ancient Egypt. Rivers and lakes are still a major source of transportation and communication. They provide food in the form of fish. Fresh water is important for irrigation and for animals. Rivers also provide a very important source of power, hydro-generated electricity. Areas of dense population are centered along rivers and river basins.

Africa has rainforests, grasslands, and is home to the largest desert in the world, the Sahara. Africa does have a few mountain ranges, like the Atlas Mountains in the north. These are fairly large mountains, but they would seem small next to the Alps or the Himalayas. There are no huge mountain ranges in Africa.

1. Africa is the _____ largest continent in the world.

2. You could put the United States in Africa _____ times.

3. The three biggest river systems in Africa are the _____, the _____, and the _____.

4. Africa does not have any large _____.

There are many situations where it is appropriate to tip a person for the service they have given (in addition to the product you have purchased). People who wait tables in restaurants count on tips to supplement their base pay, so do hairdressers, newspaper carriers and cab drivers. Most people tip 10%, 15%, or 20%, depending on how good they thought the service was. An easy way to determine a tip is to begin with 10%, which is easy to figure. You simply take the amount being charged and move the decimal point one position to the left. So for a $45.23 bill at a restaurant, 10% would be $4.52. 20% is twice that amount, in this case $9.02. 15% would be 10% plus half of that. In our example, $4.52 plus $2.26, for a total of $6.78. **Figure the three percentages for each of the following amounts.**

1. $23.75   10% _____   15% _____   20% _____

2. $78.41   10% _____   15% _____   20% _____

3. $54.66   10% _____   15% _____   20% _____

Erosion

Erosion is the process that breaks things down. Rain and wind break down the earth and move the land. If an event occurs with strong rain or wind, you may see the effects of erosion very soon after. Most erosion, however, takes many years to effect a change.

As they age, mountains are worn down by weathering, mass wasting and erosion. Weathering takes place as rocks are broken down into smaller and smaller pieces due to the effects of weather. They do not move to another location, they just break down where they are. As water freezes and thaws, it breaks down rocks. Weathering can also be caused by chemical reactions.

Biotic weathering is caused by living organisms. A plant can grow through a split in a rock and make it worse. Animals digging is another form of biotic weathering.

The most common mass wasting is falling. Rocks, boulders, and dirt loosened by wind, rain, or freezing, simply fall downward.

Erosion takes place when materials move from one location to another. This happens when dust is blown down the side of the road or silt is washed down a river.

Unscramble the words by looking for them in the section above.

1. grehaeiwtn _____   4. coibti _____

2. osreoin _____   5. hicalemc _____

3. twiansg _____

Strength

Go to www.summerfitlearning.com for more Activities!

DAILY EXERCISE
Army Walk Push Up
"Stretch Before You Play!"

Instruction
Repeat 5-10 times

Be Healthy!
Learn a new joke today and tell it at dinner.

1

DAY 2

3

4

5

WEEK 10

Theme

Theme is the meaning or moral of a story. It is often a message about life or human nature that the author shares with the reader. It is different from the subject of a story – that is what a particular story is about, its characters, the important events. Theme is the meaning behind the story. Sometimes a theme is stated directly, as in some folktales and fables. Often, though, the author wants you to figure out the theme by paying attention to what is said and what happens in the story.

A typical theme might be that family is more important than anyone else, or honesty is an important trait to develop. **Lets look at the folktale "Stone Soup" to find the theme.**

A soldier was on his way home from the war. As he passed through a small village, close to nightfall, he realized he was very hungry. He stopped at a cottage and asked the woman there if she had any food to share with him. She was very wary of this stranger and so she yelled that she had no food and to go away!

The soldier moved away from the woman's house, but he didn't go away. He stood thinking for a minute, then he took from his pack a fairly large pot. He looked around and found an area near the road where he could build a fire. He filled his pot with some water from the nearby stream, and set it on the fire to heat. When he was sure the woman was looking out her window, he placed three very large stones in the pot.

The woman was very curious about this, so she shouted out the window and asked what he was doing? He replied that he was making stone soup. He said surely she had heard of stone soup before as it was a great delicacy in the homes of many rich people. She said she had not heard of it before, but was very curious.

He went on to say that of course, it would be better if he had a few vegetables: some corn, potatoes, perhaps a few carrots. She said that she had some of those and she would be glad to share if she could have some of the soup when he finished. And he told her that absolutely she could share, though it would be even better if they had a bit of meat in it. She excitedly said that she did have some meat they could put in. As he stirred all the ingredients in, he mentioned that a bit of salt and pepper would just about make it perfect, and wouldn't some biscuits and butter go nicely? The woman ran to the house to fetch the things he suggested.

Finally, the soup was ready, and the soldier and the woman had a fine feast. The soldier kindly let the woman keep the leftover soup, and she declared it was the best she had ever had.

1. What did the soldier trick the woman into doing? _____

2. What would you think is the theme of this story? _____

3. What did the soldier say to make the woman want to try the soup? _____

4. What is a delicacy? _____

Simple percent

Many teachers use simple percents to figure out your grades. They take an average of the scores you have earned and convert the number into a percent. Some teachers also weight grades. In other words, different categories are worth a different percent of your grade. They take the average of your tests, for instance, and count them as 35% of the final grade. Homework may be worth 20%, class work another 20% and quizzes the final 25%.
Use the chart below to help you figure out some possible grades.

	Tests x 35%	Quizzes x 25%	Homework x 20%	Class work x 20%	Total
Example	31.15	19.5	19	18.2	91.41
Francisco					
Emily					

Example: Test average 89, Quiz average 78, Homework average 95, Class work average 91
Francisco: Tests 76, Quizzes 79, Homework 95, Class work 90
Emily: Tests 92, Quizzes 89, Homework 71, Class work 85

South America

South America is the fourth largest continent and is located mostly in the Southern and Western Hemispheres. The Atlantic Ocean washes the Eastern Shore and the Pacific, the Western Shore. The second longest river in the world, the Amazon, runs through South America, as well as the Andes Mountains.

Spain and Portugal colonized most of South America, so Spanish and Portuguese are the most common languages spoken.

The world's largest tropical rain forest covers more than half of Brazil and runs through several other South American countries – The Amazon Rain Forest. Scientists think that about half of the world's species live in the rain forest. It is one of the last safe places for some animals, such as pink dolphins and jaguars. 40,000 plant species, 3,000 freshwater fish species and more than 370 reptile species exist in the Amazon.

Many people are concerned because of the deforestation that is taking place in the Amazon forest. People native to the forest are being displaced, as are many of the animal and plant species. Scientist fear that the deforestation will cause environmental problems because forests and rainforests absorb large quantities of CO_2 (carbon dioxide). CO_2 is harmful greenhouse gas mostly responsible for global warming and climate change. Many people fear that without rainforests a lot more of this gas will end up in the atmosphere causing global warming to be more severe.

1. Why are people concerned about the deforestation of the Amazon Rain Forest? _____

_____

_____

_____

Aerobic

Go to www.summerfitlearning.com for more Activities!

DAILY EXERCISE
Tree Sprints
"Stretch Before You Play!"

Instruction
Perform 3-5 sprints

Be Healthy!
Turn off the TV when you eat.

1
2
DAY 3
4
5

WEEK 10

Identifying a dependent clause

A dependent clause is a group of words that has both a subject and a verb, but cannot stand alone as a sentence. An example is: **Wherever she goes, trouble follows her.** Wherever she goes makes no sense without the rest of the sentence – it is incomplete. Another example is: **The only one of the seven dwarves who does not have a beard is Dopey.** Who does not have a beard is the dependent clause – because it is incomplete.
Underline the dependent clause in each of the sentences.

1. That is the ball that I was bouncing.
2. If at first you don't succeed, try something else.
3. Where is the package that I ordered?
4. Many people don't know who their state representative is.
5. I will fix some dinner when I get home.
6. Many planes fly over the city.
7. Even though he is angry, he is being polite.
8. Because I was late, I missed most of the movie.
9. Although I found the library book, I still owed a fine.
10. The crew had seen the whale, which was following the boat.
11. Since I have a large garden, it's helpful that I enjoy weeding.
12. Once Steven smashed the spider, Amy calmed down.
13. Even though it was dark, the children loved playing outside.
14. Grandma decided to put her garden behind the house where the land was level.

Simple Percent

Everyone likes to buy things on sale. Sale prices are usually calculated by using percent. If a shirt is usually $29.95, and the sale price is 20% off, the shirt is now $23.96 ($29.95 minus $5.99, which is 20%). Sometimes the item is already marked down a certain percent, and you have a coupon for another percentage off – then you really save!!

For each question, tell the amount saved and the final price

1. Original price $34.20, sale 15% off   _____ _____

2. Original price $42.50, sale 9% off   _____ _____

3. Original price $27.65, sale 25% off   _____ _____

4. Original price $36.75, sale 15% off, additional coupon 10%   _____ _____

Mood and Tone

Mood is the feeling the writer tries to create for the reader. The setting can affect the mood dramatically. A story that takes place during the London Olympics of 2012 will have a different mood from a story that takes place in the jungles of India.

Tone implies the writer's attitude toward the subject. A writer may use humor to write about a subject not thought to be serious, but a serious tone toward a subject thought to be important.

Highwaymen were robbers of the 17th and 18th centuries. They would stop the carriages of the upper classes. They were glamorized in song and story by the poor, who somehow felt avenged against the rich by the actions of the highwaymen. *The Highwayman* by Alfred Noyes tells one of these stories. Here are some excepts from that poem.

Verse One

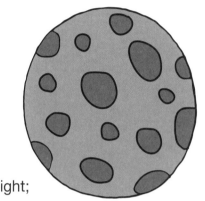

The wind was a torrent of darkness among the gusty trees.
The moon was a ghostly galleon tossed upon cloudy seas.
The road was a ribbon of moonlight over the purple moor,
And the highwayman came riding – Riding – riding –
The highwayman came riding, up to the old inn-door.

Verse Five

"One kiss, my bonny sweetheart, I'm after a prize tonight,
But I shall be back with the yellow gold before the morning light;
Yet, if they press me sharply, and harry me through the day,
Then look for me by moonlight, Watch for me by moonlight,
I'll come to thee by moonlight, though hell should bar the way."

Verse 8

They said no word to the landlord. They drank his ale instead.
But they gagged his daughter, and bound her, to the foot of her narrow bed.
Two of them knelt at her casement, with muskets at their side!
There was death at every window; And hell at one dark window;
For Bess could see, through her casement, the road that he would ride.

True or False

1. _____ The first stanza sets a pleasant relaxed mood for the poem.

2. _____ The words "riding – Riding – riding" give a sense of urgency to the poem, as

if the rider is hurrying to the inn.

3. _____ The second verse implies that the highwayman loves the woman.

4. _____ The words "death at every window" change the mood to one of danger.

5. _____ The tone suggests that the author really dislikes the highwayman's character.

Strength
Go to www.summerfitlearning.com for more Activities!

DAILY EXERCISE
Chin-ups
"Stretch Before You Play!"

Instruction
Repeat 2 times

Be Healthy! Smoking is one of the worst things you can do to your body.

Central America

There are 8 independent countries in Central America. Find and label these countries on the map.

1. Belize
2. Costa Rica
3. El Salvador
4. Guatemala

5. Honduras
6. Mexico
7. Nicaragua
8. Panama

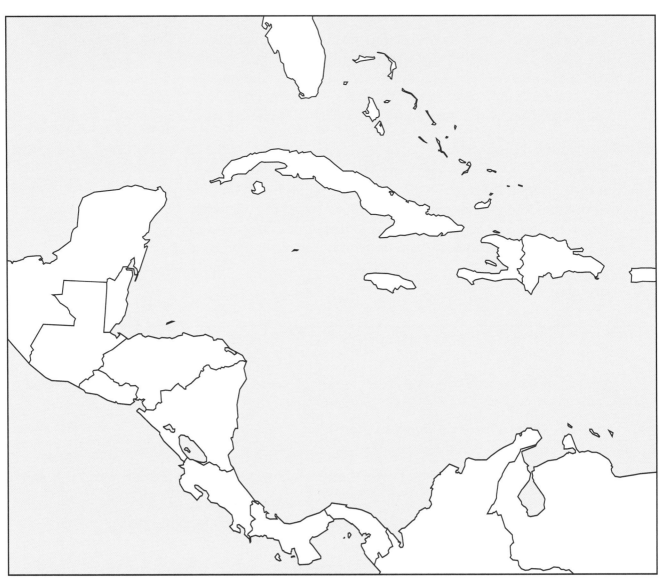

1 2 3 DAY 4 5 WEEK 10

FRIENDSHIP – Helen Keller and Anne Sullivan

Helen was less than two years old when an illness left her deaf and blind. Her family did not know how to help her, and as a result, she became an undisciplined and unruly child. Just prior to her 7th birthday, Anne Sullivan came to live with the Keller family, and changed Helen's life as well as her own.

Anne was only 20 years old and her own vision was severely impaired. She had lived a difficult childhood as a ward of the state of Massachusetts. She felt that obedience, patience, and love were the key to reaching Helen. In her biography, Helen wrote, "The most important day I remember in all my life is the one on which my teacher, Anne Mansfield Sullivan, came to me."

Anne stayed with Helen for most of the rest of their lives. She became more than a teacher – she was a mentor and a friend. Anne accompanied Helen when she traveled for pleasure and on lecture tours. When Anne married John Macy, she and her husband continued to live with Helen, until the Macys separated.

Anne and Helen lived and traveled together until Anne's death in 1926. When Helen died, her ashes were buried next to Anne.

1. Anne showed friendship for Anne by living with her and traveling with her. How do you show friendship to your friends? _____

_____

_____

2. What problem did Anne and Helen share? _____

_____

3. How can sharing a difficulty lead to friendship? _____

_____

_____

4. What qualities did Anne think would help her to reach Helen? _____

_____

_____

Color a star for each time you show Friendship through your own actions this week.

 Write a 50-75 word essay describing one of your Friendship actions this week.

Friendship – Memorize Your Value

"Wherever we are, it is our friends that make our world."

– Henry Drummond

Core Value Book List
Read More About Friendship

Charlotte's Web
By E.B. White

The Hundred Dresses
By Eleanor Estes-Louis Slobodkin

Because of Winn Dixie
By Kate DiCamillo

·········TECH TIME!·········

Friendships can take a long time to build. Friends go through many different experiences together. Look at the friendship between Helen Keller and Anne Sullivan. To give a visual idea of how their friendship developed through the years, you could use a timeline. Have you ever created a timeline on the Internet? There are many resources out there to help you do this. Find a tool online to create a time line of friendship between Anne and Helen.

www.SummerFitLearning.com

Bill Gates
Tech Guru and Philanthropist
gatesfoundation.org

Play Time!
Choose a Game or Activity to Play for 60 minutes today!

YOU CHOOSE

_____
Write down which game or activity you played today!

Be Healthy!
You may have a favorite food, but it's best to eat a variety.

1
2
3
4

DAY 5

WEEK 10

EXTRAS
Fitness Index
Family Health and Wellness Tips
Summer Journal • Book Report
Answer Key • Certificate of Completion

FITNESS INDEX

A healthy life is an active life. Kids need to be physically active for 60 minutes a day. Use the daily fitness activity to get moving. After 10 weeks of physical activity you have created a new and healthy lifestyle!

AEROBIC

Aerobic Exercise = Oxygen

The word "Aerobic" means "needing or giving oxygen." These *Summer Fit* exercises get the heart pumping and oxygen moving to help burn off sugars and calories!

STRENGTH

Strength Exercise = Muscle

Strength exercises help make muscles stronger. These *Summer Fit* exercises help build strong muscles to support doing fun activities around the house, school and outdoors!

SPORTS

Play Exercise = Sport Activity

Playing a different sport each week is an opportunity to use the *Summer Fit* oxygen and fitness exercises in a variety of ways. There are a lot of sports to choose from and remember that the most important thing about being *Summer Fit* is to have fun and play!

Warm Up Before Exercising

1 **Inchworm** – Put your hand on the ground in front of your feet. Walked out on the hands and then walk up on the feet. Do this 5 times.

2 **Knee Hug** – While you are slowly walking, pull your knee to your chest and hug. Do this 5 times on each leg.

3 **Toe Grab** – Toe Touch. Grab the toe behind your leg then touch the opposite toe with your opposite hand. Stand up and switch. Repeat 5 tines on each leg.

Warning:
Before starting any new exercise program you should consult your family physician. Even children can have medical conditions and at risk conditions that could limit the amount of physical activity they can do. So check with your doctor and then

Get Fit!

Aerobic Exercise = Oxygen

Aerobic exercises get you moving. When you move your heart pumps faster and more oxygen gets to your lungs. Movement helps burn off sugars and calories and gets you fit!

◆ **Jump the Line:** Use tape on a floor or chalk on cement to create a line. Jump front to back or side-to-side keeping feet together. **Goal = Jump 10 - 15 times back and forth**

◆ **Crooked Bunny:** Use 5 or more sticks, poles, or markers. Line them up leaving 2-3 feet space between each of them. Jump over each line traveling sideways over and back (right to left). **Goal = 3 - 5 times**

◆ **Burpies:** This is full body exercise is performed in four steps. Begin in a standing position. Drop into a squat position with your hands on the ground. Extend your feet back in one quick motion to assume so your body is straight. Return to the squat position in one quick motion. Return to standing position. **Goal = 5 - 7 times**

◆ **Side Shuffles:** Start with feet apart (parallel with one another). Jump up as high as you can and click together mid- air, landing apart in almost a partial squat, and continuing moving sideways in motion left and then right. **Goal = 10 shuffles to the right and 10 shuffles to the left**

◆ **Single Leg Pop-Hops:** Jump forward using only one leg in a continuous hopping motion and attempting to keep balance at the same time, jump back. **Goal = Jump on each leg 10 - 15 times**

◆ **Ladders:** Create 3 to 5 points of reference using different objects as markers to run and touch before returning back to starting position each time. Create different distances by moving your markers or reference points. **Goal = Run your course 3 times**

◆ **Let's Roll:** Put your lungs to work on your bike, skates or scooter. Don't forget to wear helmets and pads!

◆ **Speed:** Rest in between each block. See how fast you and your friends can run for one block. Time yourself and see if you can beat your original time. **Goal = Run 3 blocks**

◆ **Pass and Go:** This activity requires a second person. Ask a friend or someone from your family to play with you. The object of this activity is to pass the ball/bean bag back and forth counting by 2's get to a 100 as fast as you can. Have a stopwatch handy. Set a time you want to beat and go! Increase your goal by setting a lower time. **Goal = Beat your best time!**

◆ **Capture the Flag/ Get Your Family and Friends to Play:** Use scarves or old T-shirts for flags. Use a different color one for each team. Use chalk, cones, tape, or landmarks such as trees or sidewalks to divide your playing area into equal-sized territories for each team. Place one flag into each territory. It must be visible and once it is placed it cannot be moved. When the game begins, players cross into opposing teams' territories to grab their flags. When a player is in an opposing team's territory he/she can be captured by that team's players. If they tag him/her, he/she must run to the sideline and perform an exercise—for example, five jumping jacks or three push-ups. After they perform their exercise the player can go back to his/her own team's territory and resume play. The game ends when one team successfully captures the flag(s) from the other team or teams and returns to their own territory with the opposing team's flag.

◆ **Mountain Climbers:** Start in a pushup position on your hands and toes. Bring your right knee in towards your chest, resting the foot on the floor. Jump up and switch feet in the air, bringing your left foot in and your right foot back. You can also run the knees in and out rather than touching the toes to the floor. Continue alternating your feet as fast as you safely can for 30-60 seconds. **Goal = 3 times for 60 seconds each**

"Get Fit! Have Fun!"

- **Moguls:** Start in an extended plank/pushup position, jump so that your hands stay in place and your feet remain close together, but are moving as far to each side as they can. Jump left to right. **Goal = 3x's for 30 seconds**

- **Racing Leap-Frog:** In leapfrog there are two positions: the squatter and the leaper. Each player rotates these positions throughout the game. The squatter bends his knees and puts his hands firmly on the ground in front of him. His arms are placed between his knees and his head is tucked into his chest, mimicking a frog-like position. The leaper jumps over the squatter by placing her hands on his shoulders and pushing off the ground with her legs to leap over the squatter. Except for having her hands on the squatter's shoulders, the leaper should not touch the squatter while leaping over him. When playing leapfrog with two people, each person immediately rotates between being the leaper and squatter. Move in a forward motion placing hands either behind your head or out in front (to aid in creating distance) 10-15 total leaps could easily be used as a racing method.

- **Bear Crawl:** Find a large open space or a clear path. Start on your hands and feet and move forward just like a bear. Your knees should be slightly bent in order to keep your butt low and even with or slightly higher than your head. Your back should be relatively flat. Brace your abs and keep your head up or slightly neutral to see where you are going!
  Goal = Crawl for 2 - 3 minutes

- **Towel Slide/Plate Push:** Use this exercise for intervals using an object that can slide across the ground or floor. The exercise is simply to keep a firm grip on object and run it down to the other end of the room and back as quickly as possible…this can be done in many places including your backyard on the grass, in your driveway and a gymnasium. **Goal = Complete 5 times**

- **Jump Rope:** is the primary tool used in the game of skipping where you jump over a rope swung so that it passes under your feet and over your head. Here are some different jumps that you can do: **Goal = 3 - 5 minutes without stopping**
  Basic jump or easy jump: This is where both feet are slightly apart and jump at the same time over the rope. Beginners should master this technique first before moving onto more advanced techniques.
  Alternate foot jump (speed step): This style consists of using alternate feet to jump off the ground. This technique can be used to effectively double the number of skips per minute as compared to the above technique. This step is used for speed events.
  Criss-Cross: This method is similar to the basic jump with the only difference being that while jumping, the left hand goes to the right part of the body and vice versa for the right hand, with arms crossing in front of the body.
  Side Swing: This is a basic technique where the rope passes the side of the skipper's body, without jumping it. Usually the skipper performs a basic jump after a side swing, or a criss-cross.

- **Happy Feet:** Use your feet every chance you get today. Walk to a friend's house, to the store, around the park or wherever it's safe to walk. **Goal = Get your parents to walk with you after dinner**

- **Foot bag (need a hackey-sack)/ Play with friends!:** Gather players in a circle about 4-5 feet across. "Serve" the foot-bag to any player by tossing it gently in their direction waist high. Keep the foot bag in the air using any part of your body except your arms and hands. Pass the foot-bag back and forth around the circle for as many times as you can.

- **Tree Sprints/ Perform 3-5 sprints:** Find two trees that are 15-20 feet apart. Start with your left or right leg touching the base of the tree. On "go" sprint as fast as you can to the opposite tree, touch the tree trunk and sprint back to your start position. Continue sprints until you complete your goal or get tired.

- **Gassers:** Using a space about the width of a football or soccer field run/jog 1/4 of the distance lean down to touch the line or marker used then back to the start line. Immediately run/jog to the half-way point, touch the ground, and back to the start, run/jog 3/4 of the way and back then run/jog all the way and back. Goal = Start with one the first time you do this exercise and then work your way up to see how many you can do.

Summer Fit Tip

The more you workout and play with a partner the more they are likely to stick with it. Find a friend or someone in your family to exercise with everyday.

Jay and Jen Jacobs
Former Contestants of NBC's
The Biggest Loser

Strength Exercise = Muscle

Strength exercises make muscles stronger. When you build strong muscles you are able to lift more, run faster, and do fun activities around your house, school, and outdoors!

◆ **Inchworm:** This is a great way to develop strength, coordination, and flexibility. Kneel on the grass or other soft floor surface and stretch forward as far as you can while balancing yourself with your hands, palms down. Your hands and feet should be shoulder width apart. Raise your butt high and bend your head downward so you can see the heels of your feet. Slowly walk your hands until they are touching your feet. **Goal = 10 - 15 times**

◆ **Chair/bench Squats:** Try to keep your back up straight without leaning over too much, squat down and touch the chair with your butt (don't sit) and immediately come back up. **Goal = 5 to 10 times**

◆ **Ninja Crawl/ Crawl for 5 minutes:** Try to maintain a mostly flat back without straining. Keep your weight balanced equally on all four of your limbs. Don't sit too far back on your feet, and don't lean too far forward on your hands. Find a comfortable position that you can hold for a long time. Try to crawl with very little effort. Focus on your exhale, breath calm and slow. Try to crawl softly, quietly – move like a ninja. Try crawling on grass and sand– on flat and hilly surfaces. Crawl sideways, but keeping hands and feel on ground the entire time…aim for distance, longevity, and constant motion heading both right and left directions.

◆ **Dead Bug:** Sit upright and balance on your duff! All your limbs in the air (legs and arms) and balance as long as you can! **Goal = Hold for 2 minutes!**

◆ **One-legged Stand Ups:** Sit in the chair and come up on one leg 10 times (don't use the other leg!), then switch! **Goal = 10 times each leg**

◆ **Grasshopper Crunch:** Start by lying flat on your back, extend one leg and the opposite arm simultaneously, and crunch so that they come as close together as possible in meeting in the middle, then extend back out and return to starting position. **Goal = Complete 7 - 10 for each side**

◆ **Leg Lifts/ Repeat 5 times:** Start by laying flat on your back. Put your hands under your butt, right below your waist, palms down. This will keep your tailbone just off of ground. Raise your legs until they are just off of the ground. During the exercise, your feet must never touch the ground. Your goal is to you're your stomach tight and your legs as straight as you can during the exercise. Raise your legs as high as you can while keeping your knees straight. Lower your legs to their starting position. **Goal = 5 to 7 times**

◆ **Knee lifts:** Stand with your feet flat on the floor. Start by lifting your right knee up 5 times, always bring both feet together between each interval then change legs. When you feel more confident, bounce while you bring your knee up and alternate between legs. **Goal = 5 times each leg**

◆ **Chin-ups:** These are difficult because they use weaker arm and back muscles. From a hanging position, pull yourself up with your torso straight. Use your arms, without twisting your back. Try to raise yourself until your chest is at or near the bar. Hold for one or two seconds then lower yourself down slowly. **Goal = 3 to 5 times**

◆ **Heel Raises:** Heel raises strengthen the calf muscles. Stand with your feet a few inches apart, with your hands lightly resting on a counter or chair in front of you. Slowly raise your heels off the floor while keeping your knees straight. Hold for 5 seconds and then slowly lower your heels to the floor. Repeat. **Goal = Repeat 7 to 10 times**

- **Squats:** Start by placing your hands on your hips and stand with feet about shoulder width apart. Slowly move downward by bending your knees and keeping body straight by sticking out your butt. Squat as far down as you comfortably can, then slowly rise back up until you are standing straight. **Goal = 7 to 10 times**

- **Lunges:** Start by standing with your two feet shoulder length apart with your back straight and your arms by your sides. Simply lunge forward on one knee, count to two and then step back to your original position. After two counts lunge forward on your alternate foot. Always make sure that your front knee never goes beyond your toes. Make sure you keep your balance so you do not fall forward or to the side!
Goal = 5 times each leg

- **Push-ups (traditional or modified):** Practice getting your body into a straight position required for a pushup, by stiffening your body like a flat board. Get on the floor and rest on both forearms and toes, with your body stiff and straight off the floor. Keep your butt down without letting it droop towards the floor so it is straight with the rest of your body. When you are ready to start, take your forearms off the floor and place your hands where they were. Lower your body straight down until your chest almost touches the floor, and then push back up into your straight position. Keep your head up and look straight ahead. **Goal = 7 to 10 times**

To do a modified push up, get in your straight position and then rest on your knees. When you are ready to start, lower your body straight down while rocking forward on your knees to help take away some of your body weight. Push back up so you are in your original position. This is a great way to start learning push-ups and building your strength.

- **Crunches:** Start by sitting down on the floor, then bend your knees while moving your feet toward your butt. Keep your back and feet flat on the floor. Put your hands behind your head, or arms together in front of your body with your hands tucked under your chin. With your shoulders off the ground as the starting position, raise your head to your knees, using only core muscles. Then lower your body, keeping your shoulders slightly off the ground in the starting position. Try to keep your lower back on the floor and do not use your arms to pull yourself up. **Goal = 5 to 10 times**

- **Chop n Squat:** Start with legs wide, bring your feet together, then out wide again, reach down and touch the ground, and pop up. **Goal = 10 to 12 times**

- **Side Step:** Lung out to your right. Back leg straight, bend the right knee. Slid back and bend the left knee and straighten the right leg. Turn and face the opposite direction and repeat. **Goal = 5 times in each direction**

- **Balance:** Balance on one foot. Foot extended low in front of you. Foot extended low in back of you. Foot extended low to the side. **Goal = Hold for 15 seconds each leg, then switch and repeat 5 - 7 times**

- **Toe Taps:** Start by standing with your two feet shoulder length apart with your back straight and your arms by your sides. While jumping straight up, bring one toe forward to the front and tap while alternating to the opposite foot. Go back and forth between your left and right foot. Find a rhythm and be careful not to lose your balance! **Goal = Repeat 10 times with each foot**

- **Plank:** On the floor get on your stomach, get up on your elbows and have the elbows line up under you shoulders. Lift your body and legs off the floor and you are up on your toes. Hold this for 30 seconds to a minute. **Goal = increase each week with the goal of 2 to 4 minutes at the end**

Exercise Activities for Kids

Find What You Like

Everybody has different abilities and interests, so take the time to figure out what activities and exercises you like. Try them all: soccer, dance, karate, basketball, and skating are only a few. After you have played a lot of different ones, go back and focus on the ones you like! Create your own ways to be active and combine different activities and sports to put your own twist on things. Talk with your parents or caregiver for ideas and have them help you find and do the activities that you like to do. Playing and exercising is a great way to help you become fit, but remember that the most important thing about playing is that you are having fun!

List of Exercise Activities

Home–Outdoor:

Walking
Ride Bicycle
Swimming
Walk Dog
Golf with whiffle balls outside
Neighborhood walks/Exploring
(in a safe area)
Hula Hooping
Rollerskating/Rollerblading
Skateboarding
Jump rope
Climbing trees
Play in the back yard
Hopscotch
Stretching
Basketball
Yard work
Housecleaning

Home – Indoor:

Dancing
Exercise DVD
Yoga DVD
Home gym equipment
Stretch bands
Free weights
Stretching

With friends or family:

Red Rover
Chinese jump rope
Regular jump rope
Ring around the rosie
Tag/Freeze
Four score
Capture the flag
Dodgeball
Slip n Slide
Wallball
Tug of War
Stretching
Run through a sprinkler
Skipping
Family swim time
Bowling
Basketball
Hiking
Red light, Green light
Kick ball
Four Square
Tennis
Frisbee
Soccer
Jump Rope
Baseball

Turn off TV Go Outside - PLAY!
Public Service Announcement Brought to you by Summer Fit

Chill out on Screen Time

Screen time is the amount of time spent watching TV, DVDs or going to the movies, playing video games, texting on the phone and using the computer. The more time you spend looking at a screen the less time you are outside riding your bike, walking, swimming or playing soccer with your friends. Try to spend no more than a couple hours a day in front of a screen for activities other than homework and get outside and play!

Health and Wellness Index

Healthy Family Recipes and Snacks

YOGURT PARFAITS: 01

Prep time: 15 minutes
Cook time: 0
Yield: 4 servings
Good for: all ages, limited kitchen, cooking with kids

Ingredients:
2 cups fresh fruit, at least 2 different kinds (can also be thawed fresh fruit)
1 cup low-fat plain or soy yogurt
4 TBSP 100% fruit spread
1 cup granola or dry cereal

Marci Crozier
Former Contestant
of NBC's
The Biggest Loser

YOGURT PARFAITS: 02

Directions:
Wash and cut fruit into small pieces
In a bowl, mix the yogurt and fruit spread together
Layer each of the four parfaits as follows:
Fruit
Yogurt
Granola (repeat)
Enjoy!
Kids can use a plastic knife to cut soft fruit
Kids can combine and layer ingredients

Tips:
A healthier dessert than ice cream
A healthy part of a quick breakfast

It is important to teach children at a young age about the difference between a snack that is good for you versus a snack that is bad for you. It is equally important to teach your kids about moderation and how to eat until they are full, but not to overeat!

SMOOTHIES: 01

Prep time: 5 minutes
Cook time: 0
Yield: 2 servings
Good for: all ages,
limited kitchen, cooking with kids

Ingredients:
1 cup berries, fresh or frozen
4 ounces vanilla low fat yogurt
½ cup 100% apple juice
1 banana, cut into chunks
4 ice cubes

SMOOTHIES: 02

Directions:
Place apple juice, yogurt, berries, and banana in a blender. Cover and process until smooth

While the blender is running, drop ice cubes into the blender one at a time. Process until smooth

Variation:
Add ½ cup of silken tofu or ½ cup of peanut butter for extra protein.

Crunchy, Fruity Cobbler: 01

Prep time: 5 minutes
Cook time: 5 minutes
Yield: 4 servings (1 cup=1 serving)
Good for: all ages of children

Ingredients:
1 (15 ounce) can of sliced peaches, drained*
1 (15 ounce) can of pear halves, drained*
1/4 tsp. of almond or vanilla extract
1/4 tsp. of ground cinnamon
3/4 cup of low-fat granola with rai
*Canned fruit should be packed in

Crunchy, Fruity Cobbler: 02

Directions:
Combine the peaches, pears, extract and cinnamon in a microwave safe bowl. Stir well.
Sprinkle granola over the top.
Cover the bowl with a lid or plastic wrap, leaving a little opening for the steam to escape.
Microwave on high for 5 minutes.
Use potholders to remove the bowl from the microwave.
Let it cool a little, and then eat.

Health and Wellness Vocabulary

In order to teach your children the difference between healthy habits and unhealthy habits it is important to know and understand some of the basic terminology that you may hear in the media and from health experts.

Jay Jacobs
Former Contestant of NBC's *The Biggest Loser*

VOCABULARY

Calorie: A unit of measure of the amount of energy supplied by food.

Fat: It is one of the 3 nutrients (protein and carbohydrates are the other 2) that supplies calories to the body.

Protein: Is one of the building blocks of life. The body needs protein to repair and maintain itself. Every cell in the human body contains protein.

Carbohydrates: The main function is to provide energy for the body, especially the brain and nervous system.

Type 1 Diabetes: A disease characterized by high blood glucose (sugar) levels resulting in the destruction of the insulin-producing cells of the pancreas. This type of diabetes was previously called juvenile onset diabetes and insulin-dependent diabetes.

Type 2 Diabetes: A disease characterized by high blood glucose (sugar) levels due to the body's inability to use insulin normally, or to produce insulin. In the past this type of diabetes was called adult-onset diabetes and non-insulin dependent diabetes.

Sedentary lifestyle: A type of lifestyle with no or irregular physical activity. It pertains to a condition of inaction.

BMI: An index that correlates with total body fat content, and is an acceptable measure of body fatness in children and adults. It is calculated by dividing weight in kilograms by the square of height in meters. BMI is one of the leading indicators in determining obesity.

Obesity: Refers to a person's overall body weight and whether it's too high. Overweight is having extra body weight from muscle, bone, fat and/or water. Obesity is having a high amount of extra body fat.

Fiber: This is not an essential nutrient, but it performs several vital functions. A natural laxative, it keeps traffic moving through the intestinal tract and may lower the concentration of cholesterol in the blood.

Nutrient dense foods: Foods that contain relatively high amounts of nutrients compared to their caloric value.

Screen time: The amount of time a person participates in watching or playing something on a screen. The screen could be a television, computer, computer games, and a variety of electronics that interact with people utilizing a screen of various sizes. The American Academy of Pediatrics recommends no screen time before age 2 and no more that 1-2 hours of screen time for children over age 2.

Food label: Information listed inside a square box on prepared food packaging that shows the nutritional value of a product one consumes. It also gives the value shown as a percentage of the daily nutritional values that the Food and Drug Administration (FDA) recommend for a healthy diet.

Serving size: This term is used by the United States Department of Agriculture (USDA) to measure amounts of food. It is a tool for healthy eating.

Fat: is a source of energy. Fats perform many important functions in the body. There are healthy fats and unhealthy fats.

Monounsaturated and polyunsaturated oils: These contain some fatty acids that are HEALTHY. They do not increase the bad cholesterol in the body. Some of the foods in this category include fish, nuts and avocados.

Saturated fat: This "solid" fat increases bad cholesterol which can lead to it building up in the arteries and cause disease, more specifically, heart disease.

Trans fat: This fat is mostly found in processed foods and it contains unhealthy oils (partially hydrogenated). This type of fat has been shown to increase the bad cholesterol in the body and lower the good cholesterol.

Preadolescent: generally is defined as ages 9-11 years of age for girls and 10-12 years for boys.

Middle childhood: generally defines children between the ages of 5 to 10 years of age.

"School age": is another word for middle childhood.

"Tween": a relatively new term for a child between middle childhood and adolescence.

Health and Wellness: Child Nutrition

1. Preadolescent ("tweens") and school age children's growth continues at a steady, slow rate until the growth spurt they will experience in adolescence. Children of this age continue to have growth spurts that usually coincide with increased appetite. Parents should not be overly concerned about the variability and intake of their school-age children.
2. The importance of family mealtimes cannot be stressed enough. There is a positive relationship between families who eat together and the overall quality of a child's diet.
3. Continue to have your child's BMI-for-age percentile monitored to screen for over and underweight.
4. In this age group the choices a child makes about his or her food intake are becoming more and more influenced by their peers, the media, coaches, and teachers. These outside influences steadily increase as a child ages and becomes more independent.
5. School plays a key role in promoting healthy nutrition and physical activity, so try to participate in healthy, school-related activities with your child, such as walk to school days and volunteering in the school's garden club.
6. Limited physical activity, along with sedentary activities are major contributing factors to the sharp increase of childhood obesity.
7. Soft drink or soda consumption, which tends to increase as a child ages, is associated with increased empty caloric intake and an overall poorer diet. These soft drinks also are a major contributor to dental caries. Diet sodas have no nutrient value, though they are not high in calories.
8. Complications from overweight and obesity in childhood and adolescence are steadily rising. This is including type 2 diabetes (usually adult onset diabetes) and high cholesterol levels.
9. Those children in the age ranges of middle childhood and preadolescence are strongly encouraged to eat a VARIETY of foods and increase physical activity to 60 minutes every day. Parents should set a good example by being physically active themselves and joining their children in physical activity.
10. Parents with healthy eating behaviors and are physically active on a regular basis are excellent role models for their children.

Healthy Websites

www.myplate.gov

www.readyseteat.com

www.nourishinteractive.com

www.cdph.ca.gov/programs/wicworks

www.cdc.gov
(food safety practices, childhood diabetes and obesity)

www.who.int

www.championsforchange.net

www.nlm.nih.gov/medlineplus

Healthly Lifestyles Start at Home

Staying active and healthy is important because it will have a positive impact on every aspect of your life.

Marci and Courtney Crozier
Former Contestants of NBC's
The Biggest Loser

1   **Lead by example:** Your children will do what they see you do. Eat your fruits and vegetables, go for walks and read a book instead of watching television. Your child will see and naturally engage in these activities themselves.

2   **Limit Screen Time:** The American Academy of Pediatrics recommends no screen time before age 2 and no more that 1-2 hours of screen time for children over age 2. Instead of limiting screen time for just them, try regulating it as a household. Keep a log of technology time, note "Screen Free Zones" like the bedroom and try shutting off all technology at least 1 day a week.

3   **Talk at the Table:** Sitting down with the family for dinner gives everybody an opportunity to reconnect and share experiences with each other. Limit distractions by not taking phone calls during dinner and turning the television off.

4   **Drink More Water (and milk):** Soda and other packaged drinks are expensive and contain a lot of sugar and calories. Set an example by drinking water throughout the day and encourage your children to drink water or milk when they are thirsty. These are natural thirst quenchers that provide the mineral and nutrients young (and old) bodies really need.

5   **Portion Control:** There is nothing wrong with enjoying food, but try to eat less. Use smaller plates so food is not wasted and teach your children to tell the difference between being satisfied and overeating.

6   **Make Time For Family Play:** Instead of sitting down to watch TV together plan an activity as a family. Go for a walk or bike ride, work on the yard together, visit the neighbor as a family. It's a great way to reduce technology, but more importantly a great opportunity to enjoy time together as a family.

SUMMER JOURNAL

_____

_____

SUMMER JOURNAL

_____

_____

SUMMER JOURNAL

_____

_____

SUMMER JOURNAL

_____

_____

SUMMER JOURNAL

_____

_____

SUMMER JOURNAL

_____

_____

SUMMER JOURNAL

_____

_____

Summer Fit Book Report
Grade 6-7

Title: _____

Author: _____

Main Characters: _____

_____

_____

_____

Most interesting part of the story: _____

_____

_____

_____

Would you recommend this book to another student? Why or why not? _____

_____

_____

Did you like the way the story ended? Why or why not?: _____

_____

_____

Brief Summary: _____

_____

_____

_____

_____

_____

Math Pretest Answers

1. 18,219,   2. 4.7,   3. 707   4. 14,858
5. 2,254   6. 739.52   7. 54.914
8. 17,208   9. 104,856   10. 34,773
11. 155.8   12. 340.3   13. 1769.16
14. 791.7   15. 18,25   16. 3874.86
17. 87   18. 71   19. 4.25   20. 37
21. 5.41   22. 52.3   23. 6   24. 30
25. 3/12 and 1/4
26. a. 5/6   b. 4/15   c. 3/4
27. 16/3
28. a. 3/5   b. 1 3/8   c. 10 13/15
29. a. 3/5   b. 2/15   c. 5 8/15
30. 8/15   31. 12 3/5
32. 6   33. 7
34. n = 12   35. a = 15
36. 67%   37. ? = 5   38. 43%

Reading pretest answers

1. c   2. a   3. d   4. b
5. g   6. f   7. h   8. e
1. c   2. a   3. e   4. a   5. d
6. d   7. a   8. b   9. e   10. c
11. b   12. c   13. a   14. e   15. d
16. d   17. e   18. b   19. a   20. c
1. b   2. a horn in her forehead   3. c
4. cold, white (which is probably snow)

Exercise Answers

Week 1 Day 1

1. nucleus   2. Nuclear envelope, centriole,
1) 18, 225   2) 22,263   3) 24, 508   4) 33,160
5) 27,196   6) 14,310   7) 23,281   8) 20,000
Honesty, Charm, Integrity, Bravery, Courage,
Humor, Kindness, Charity, Fear, Hope, Anger,
Talent, Innocence, Confidence, Manners

Week 1 Day 2

Cities circled on the map – check a map
or a globe
1. 0.97   2. 30.52   3. 24.24   4. 38.99
5. 72.86
6. 69.01   7. 2.885   8. 38.596
9. 28.901   10. 366.906
1. agree   2. wants   3. like   4. were
5. seem   6. is   7. were   8. appeal
9. doesn't   10. don't   11. plays   12. clap
13. was   14. bark   15. hangs
1. 642   2. 246   3. 81   4. 287   5. 6,061
6. 1,381   7. 7,811   8. 6,151

Week 1 Day 3

1. Jo doesn't want to act like a lady.
Answers will vary – need two supporting
claims
2. She puts her hands in her pockets, and she
whistles.
1. animal   2. Plant   3. Plant
4. Any 2 differences

Week 1 Day 4

1. learned the father's trade   2. run a house
3. Answers will vary, but should reflect what
was in the section
1. 6.12   2. 22.27   3. 57.944   4. 257.81
5. 41.03   6. 241.44   7. 19.64
1. 37,632   2. 18,837   3. 29,000
4. 295,488   5. 446,490   6. 239,571
7. 53,884
1. her   2. I, she   3. I, he   4. They
5. I, he   6. We   7. he, them   8. he, I, him
9. They, me, them   10. him, her   11. He, I
12. I   13. We, they   14. me   15. them, us

Week 1 Day 5

1. Islamabad   2. Answers will vary
3. He could have found many uses for the
money for himself and his family.
4. An award for honesty

Week 2 Day 1

Summary paragraph of a book
1. 34.5   2. 585.6   3. 391.5   4. 73.1
5. 98 (98.0)   6. 461.5   7. 464.8   8. 451.2
9. 30   10. 480   11. 77.7   12. 480
1. Mild, pleasant climate   2. Answers will
vary – might include chairs, floor mats, tables

Week 2 Day 2

"heat energy moves between the two objects"
1. 1432.56   2. 1449.89   3. 1005.29
4. 964.44   5. 3409.02   6. 777.36
7. 3843.56   8. 549.43
1. trash – but   2. my – oh   3. ask – or
4. charger – all   5. important – are
6. dinner – flour   7. us – Alice and me – to
8. Callie – my calico cat – to
9. party – music   10. park – oh

Week 2 Day 3

Car, Mannequin, Radio, Mailbox
1. 99   2. 137   3. 249   4. 91.16 or 91 R 1
5. 55.44 or 55 R 4   6. 150.8
Sentences: 2-5-6-8-9-11-12-15: Should be
circled.
1. 0.121   2. 25.1   3. 56.3
4. 83.1   5. 5.23

Week 2 Day 4

1. I'm very hungry.   2. I have a lot of things
to do.   3. I had a lot of homework.
4. I'll be upset if I can't buy that dress.
5. He's very thin.   6. This car is very fast.
7. The car is very expensive.   8. That is a
very old joke.   9. He's very rich.   10 . I
was really surprised   11. I've told you many
times.   12. He's very old.
Answers will vary – should describe what was
observed during the activity
1. for the British   2. not human
3. below standard   4. spell wrong
5. not inflammatory   6. more than human
7. not regular   8. across the Atlantic
9. not correct   10. written after

Week 2 Day 5

1. Not taking proper care of someone or
something
2. To make a difference in someone's life, often
leading them in a particular direction
3. South Africa   4. Answers will vary

Week 3 Day 1

1. Troposphere   2. Exosphere
3. Stratosphere   4. Thermosphere
5. Mesosphere
1. 284   2. 23   3. 1.81   4. 83.5   5. 91.6
1-3. Answers will vary

Week 3 Day 2

1. 5   2. 12   3. 3   4. 3
Paragraph with three reasons
1. Answers will vary – may reflect that the
lion is considered kingly and Sundiata was
considered a good king.
2. Answers will vary.
1. tool to use with the computer, small rodent
2. Vacation, fall   3. Time of year, flavoring for
food   4. in attendance, a gift   5. amount of
time, coming after first   6. Place for money,
side of a river

Week 3 Day 3

1. 14(3-1)   2. 18(2-1)   3. 12(1+3)
4. 3(5+6)   5. 3(7-6)   6. 2(22-6)
7. 6(7-2)   8. 3(7+6)   9. 12(3-2)
10. 15(3-2)   11. 21(1+2)   12. 9(4-3)
1. Amused the lion to think the mouse could
help   2. Mouse chewed through the net
3. Hunters thought the lion could not escape
because he was unable to move
4. Answers will vary
Answers will vary

Week 3 Day 3 (continued)
1. clean, clear, neat (answers vary)
2. sharp, pungent, biting (answers vary)
3. car, coach, transport (answers vary)
4. ruthless, unmerciful, relentless (answers vary)
5. expect, foresee, await (answers vary)

Week 3 Day 4
1. 6, 9, 12, 15, 18   2. 8, 12, 16, 20, 24
3. 10, 15, 20, 25, 30   4. 12, 18, 24, 30, 36
5. 14, 21, 28, 35, 42   6. 16, 24, 32, 40, 48
7. 18, 27, 36, 45, 54   8. 10   9. 24
10. 30   11. 18
1. Answers will vary   2. Answers will vary
3. Any 3: protection, transportation, water for cooking and drinking, fishing, washing, enjoyment
1. c   2. e   3. a   4. b   5. d   6. c
7. a   8. d   9. b   10. e   11. b   12. a
13. d   14. e   15. c   1. 1/3   2. 7
3. 25   4. 1

Week 3 Day 5
1. Any four of the following: Truman, Eisenhower, Nixon, Kennedy, Johnson, Reagan
2. Not fully believing something or someone
3. Cronkite researched his information carefully, and was careful in how he presented his stories. His facts were correct.
4. President Jimmy Carter

Week 4 Day 1
Circle sets 1, 4, 6, and 7
Answers will vary
1. station   2. lying   3. curtain   4. butcher
5. daughter   6. surprise   7. complaint
8. passengers   9. lining   10. whisper
11. rhythm   12. divine   13. fulfill
14. kindergarten   15. attendance
1. >   2. <   3. <   4. >   5. <   6. >

Week 4 Day 2
1. ababcdcd   2. abcb   3. abcbdd
1. I   2. C   3. I   4. I   5. I   6. C
7. C   8. C   9. I   10. I   11. I   12. I
13. C   14. C
1. Full moon   2. New moon   3. Waxing crescent   4. Waxing Gibbous   5. Waning crescent   6. Waning Gibbous

Week 4 Day 3
1. They made farmland by building floating gardens.   2. It was a good site
3. Answers will vary
1. identical   2. very big   3. black   4. blind
5. sink and whistle   6. Mark and ice
7. Claire and the fox   8. Pierre and the peacock

1, 4, 5, 6, 9, 10
1. 2/3   2. 1/3   3. 1/3   4. 2/5   5. 1/4
6. 1/2   7. 1/5   8. 2/3   9. 5/8   10. 1/4

Week 4 Day 4
1. The earth   2. Northern winter
3. The moon is moving around the earth
1. His grandfather saves things just like a pack rat does.   2. The man has an explosive temper.   3. Eyes light things up.   4. He is low like a worm.   5. Schools are like farmers that plant something and something grows from it.   6. The test was easy, enjoyable.
7. He gave her many gifts, like the water from a shower.
1. comitted   2. safetey   3. reletive
4. wheather   5. personel   6. wendsday
7. throughn   8. agread   9. arithmatic
10. breakfest   11. Feburary   12. animel
13. cieties   14. grieff   15. caried
1. 11/3   2. 23/5   3. 12/7   4. 23/6
5. 31/4   6. 2 1/2   7. 5 6/7   8. 4 4/7
9. 1 4/9   10. 3 1/8

Week 4 Day 5
1. Baseball players of different races were not allowed to play in the same leagues
2. Vice President.   3. He would not fight back when confronted with racism   4. Answers will vary – could include positive self image, patience, respect

Week 5 Day 1
1. 2/3   2. 5/8   3. 10/9 = 11/9   4. 9/7 = 12/7   5. 6/27= 2/9   6. 6/20 = 3/10
7. 2/5   8. 5/15 = 1/3   9. 15/19
10. 21/15 = 16/15 = 12/5
1. tunnel and moat   2. wanted to enjoy their fort   3. falling apart   4. boards, nails, hammers   5. Answers will vary
1. yourself   2. myself   3. itself
4. themselves   5. herself   6. ourselves
7. himself   8. ourselves   9. yourselves
10. ourselves
Science – no answer needed

Week 5 Day 2
1. 1/18   2. 59/40 = 119/40   3. 5/24
4. 19/27   5. 7/30   6. 17/18
1. peasants   2. knights protected lords; lords gave knights land   3. servant
1. through   2. waste   3. holes   4. their
5. wait   6. sale   7. which   8. weather
9. fourth   10. they're   11. whole
12. there   13. weight   14. whether
15. threw
Water cycle diagrams will vary. Check online.

Week 5 Day 3
1. N   2. Y   3. Y   4. N   5. Y
1. as well as   2. however   3. first, then
4. but   5. instead of   6. first, then
7. because of   8. To summarize
9. in addition   10. together with
11. although   12. Despite   13. in case of
14. all things considered
1. 4 1/15   2. 8 34/40 = 8 17/20
3. 8 5/12   4. 814/10 = 9 2/5   5. 2 13/24

Week 5 Day 4
Answers will vary
1. is   2. are   3. has   4. say   5. is
6. is   7. remembers   8. wants   9. were
10. play   11. has   12. have   13. is
14 believe
1. 5/30 = 1/6   2. 6/20 = 3/10
3. 35/63 = 5/9   4. 1/15

Week 5 Day 5
1. Being poor   2. Owned a real estate office, owned a restaurant, created and marketed a popular dessert   3. 1/4 of her salary
4. The students did well enough in school to graduate from high school. They went on to college and trade schools.

Week 6 Day 1
Spices, gold, and information
1. 6/4 = 11/2   2. 8/9   3. 40/5 = 8
1. into the huge garden   2. on the chair
3. according to some people   4. in addition to raking the yard   5. between the flower garden and the little pond
6-9 Answers will vary

Week 6 Day 2
1. 6/52 = 3/26   2. 152/12 = 122/3
3. 168/84 = 2   4. 168/108 = 15/9
5. 35/26 = 19/26   6. 60/30 = 2
1. Gravity   2. universe   3. stars
4. orbit, moons   5. atmosphere   6. Earth
Answers will vary

Week 6 Day 3
1. 7 : 8   2. 33 : 35   3. 19 : 16   4. 35 : 33
5. 15 : 17   Challenge ratio of boys to girls in 7th grade
1. near rivers   2. Long hours, difficult conditions, little pay
1. D   2. A   4. C   4. B   5. F
6. H   7. E   8. I   9. J   10. G
11. At the last possible moment
12. Take on more than you can handle
13. Get it exactly right   14. Take someone's place   15. Being curious can lead to trouble
16. Relax   17. Very clear, easily understood
18. Took more than you can eat.

Week 6 Day 4
1. 75/100 = 150/200; should be circled
2. 15/30 = 25/45   3. 18   4. 8
5. 15   6. 9
Word Search:

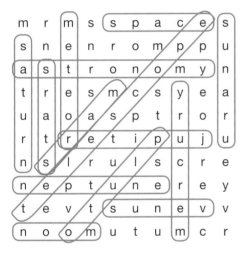

Accept, effect, a lot, weird, than, passed, lose
1. cute   2. peppery   3. screechy   4. best
5 more careful   6. better   7. worse
8. black   9. empty   10. shimmery
11. nine   12. beautiful   13. huge
14. most comfortable   15. blinding

Week 6 Day 5
1. After one has died   2. To inspire and encourage young people's interest in space exploration   3. Attitude
4. Danger   5. Answers could include taught school, volunteered in her church, was a girl scout leader.

Week 7 Day 1
1. 0.52   2. 0.63   3. 0.75   4. 0.17
5. 1.23   6. 43%   7. 92%   8. 75%
9. 28%   10. 154%   1. False   2. True
3. False   4. False   5. True
1. Bill and Fred   2. girl   3. tree   4. her
5. his   6. this   7. his or her   8. her   9. their   10. his or her

Week 7 Day 2
1. 87.5%   2. 76.9%   3. 65%   4. 25%
5. 20%   6. 50%
1. social contract   2. Declaration of Independence
1. You can understand the utter abandon with which I place my trust in this Nautilus, since I'm its captain, builder, and engineer all in one!
2. Any two: no structural deformities, no rigging to be worn out, no sails, no fires, won't run out of coal, no collisions, no storms
3. A few meters below the waves it is utterly tranquil.

Week 7 Day 3
1. 18 ft.   2. 12 ft.   3. 21 ft.   4. 27 ft.
5. 24 ft.
Answers will vary
1. who   2. whom   3. whom   4. whom
5. who   6. whom   7. who   8. whomever
9. who   10. who   11. whom   12. whom
13. whom   14. whom

Week 7 Day 4
1. 5:00 PM   2. Saturday 5:00 PM
3. answers vary: payday, people off work, weekend   4. Wednesday 9:00 PM
1. nobles   2. Third Estate   3. First and Second Estate
1. true   2. false   3. true   4. false
5. false   6. true   7. true   8. false

Week 7 Day 5
1. He was a farmer, fought in World War I, owned a men's clothing store   2. Honesty and efficiency   3. To begin something; to put into action   4. Worked to provide equality and quality of life for the poor, the elderly, and those discriminated against because of their race

Week 8 Day 1
1. 14   2. 7   3. 11   4. -3   5. -9
6. 2   7. 3   8. -2
Answers will vary
1. not extreme, mild   2. rough winds, too hot
3. Thy eternal summer shall not fade   4. Death

Week 8 Day 2
1. -21   2. -25   3. 57   4. -8   5. 2
6. -36   7. -2   8. 10   9. -2   10. 7
11. -9   12. 21   13. 1   14. -1
Science – no answer
1. little known   2. scale of notes, notes worth multiples of two, notes must add to the correct number of beats   3. how it is made and how to repair   4. Answers will vary

Week 8 Day 3
1. 16   2. -24   3. -30   4. 56   5. -18
6. 35   7. -32   8. 63   9. -6   10. -9
11. 9   12. 6   13. -6   14. -13   15. 9
16. 8
1. Italy, Germany, Austria   2. Serbian killed the Austrian heir
1. A soliloquy is one person talking; a dialogue is two people.   2. She has fallen a long way.   3. She wants to know what he's late for. Another answer is that there's no rule that says she can't follow him.   4. Rabbit holes are dark.   5. Herself   6. She is falling a long way, building up speed.

Week 8 Day 4
1. -1.6   2. 0.7   3. -1   4. 39.05
5. Answers will vary 1, 2, 3, Answers will vary
4. Author, poet, or playwright
5. Answers will vary   6. P   7. A   8. P   9. A

Week 8 Day 5
1. The place where a person or thing is most likely to be found; it's natural environment
2. Protection of human rights, disease prevention, conflict resolution, the promotion of democracy.   3. Answers will vary

Week 9 Day 1
1. $5 per box   2. $8.99 per pizza   3. 45 people per row   4. $5 per ticket   5. $6.50 per book
1. Annie had too many variables: both the water and the environment for the plants.
2. Students should indicate that the plants should both be placed in the same environment, and watered at the same time, the only difference being one watered with plain water and the other with the fertilizer.
1. calico cat   2. ran round and round
3. ruby red roses   4. sweetly singing
5. powder puff   6. rich rhythm of rollicking
7. winter wonder   8. waited wistfully
9. friendly frog filled   10. billions of books

Week 9 Day 2
1. two 12 oz. cans; $0.28 less
2. 1 1/2 c sugar, 4 eggs, 3 1/3 c flour
3. $7.35
4. Height 8 ft., Width 12 ft.
Check your map with a current map
The following should be circled: Pizarro
Conquering the Inca, The Story of Thomas
Edison's Childhood, Stories of the American
Astronauts, The Presidents' Lives, The Wright
Brothers and Their Airplane, A story about the
current Queen of England, Answers will vary

Week 9 Day 3
54, 63, None, 49 ;   40, 36, 29, 39 ;
148, 139, None, 64
1. Archaebacteria, Eubaceria, Protista
2. Animal
1. children   2. Julio   3. None   4. children
5. children   6. sister   7. us   8. None
9. teacher   10. dad   11. team   12. sister

Week 9 Day 4
1. The owner would shoot Bemis if he didn't
pay for the cow.   2. They would not need
those kinds of clothes in this setting anyway.
1. T, knitted blanket   2. I, ate   3. T, rode
bicycle   4. T, baked pies   5. T, moved chairs
6. I, fell   7. I, cried   8. T, sold books   9.
T, broke window   10. I, rose   11. T, named
chairperson   12. I, slept   13. T, studies
Russian   14. I, sits
1. 15 songs ($100 − 25 = $75, $75 ÷ 5 = $15)
2. 14 songs   3. 16 songs

Week 9 Day 5
1. Doctors   2. Basketball and track
3. Not a professional; one who does not get
paid for a particular act
4) 5, 3, 6, 1, 2, 4

Week 10 Day 1
1. He manipulated the others to get the best
of them.
2. He learned how to get along with women,
helped him become a good husband.   3 and 4.
Answers will vary
1. 6 in 24 or 1 in 4   2. 5 in 24   3. 9 in 24 or
3 in 8   4. 4 in 24 or 1 in 6
1. second   2. three   3. Nile, Congo, Niger
4. mountain ranges

Week 10 Day 2
1. $2.37, $3.55, $4.74   2. $7.84, $11.76,
$15.68   3. $5.46, $8.19, $10.92
1. weathering   2. erosion   3. wasting
4. biotic   5. chemical
1. give him all the ingredients for the soup
2. Answers will vary − could be It pays to
share, or people are stingy unless they think
they will get something.   3. It is a delicacy in
the homes of many rich people   4. a rare or
fancy food

Week 10 Day 3
Francisco: 26.6, 19.75, 19, 18, 83.35
Emily 32.2, 22.25, 14.2, 17, 85.65
1. people, animals, and plants will be
displaced; global warming issues
1. that I was bouncing   2. If at first you
don't succeed   3. that I ordered   4. who
their state representative is   5. when I get
home   6. over the city   7. Even though he
is angry   8. Because I was late
9. Although I found the library book
10. which was following the boat
11. Since I have a large garden
12. Once Steven smashed the spider
13. Even though it was dark
14. where the land was level
1. $5.13, $29.07   2. $3.82, $38.68
3. $6.91, $20.74   4. $8.63, $28.12

Week 10 Day 4
1. false   2. true   3. true   4. true   5. false
Check your map against a current map.

Week 10 Day 5
1. Answers will vary   2. Vision problems
3. Answers will vary. Could include that
sharing a difficulty helps people to understand
one another   4. Obedience, patience and love

Ferrets

3rd Edition

by Kim Schilling

for dummies®
A Wiley Brand

Ferrets For Dummies®, 3rd Edition

Published by: **John Wiley & Sons, Inc.,** 111 River Street, Hoboken, NJ 07030-5774, www.wiley.com

Copyright © 2021 by John Wiley & Sons, Inc., Hoboken, New Jersey

Published simultaneously in Canada

For general information on our other products and services, please contact our Customer Care Department within the U.S. at 877-762-2974, outside the U.S. at 317-572-3993, or fax 317-572-4002. For technical support, please visit https://hub.wiley.com/community/support/dummies.

Wiley publishes in a variety of print and electronic formats and by print-on-demand. Some material included with standard print versions of this book may not be included in e-books or in print-on-demand. If this book refers to media such as a CD or DVD that is not included in the version you purchased, you may download this material at http://booksupport.wiley.com. For more information about Wiley products, visit www.wiley.com.

Library of Congress Control Number: 2021930606

ISBN 978-1-119-72083-6 (pbk); ISBN 978-1-119-72084-3 (ebk); ISBN 978-1-119-72085-0 (ebk)

Manufactured in the United States of America

SKY10024585_012921

Table of Contents

Introduction

Numerous people have told me that a true love for animals may be genetically predisposed. Maybe this is true. Or maybe some animals just tug at our heartstrings a little harder than others. I believe both statements to apply to me. Although my love for animals may be termed "genetics" by the white-coated scientists in those sterile laboratories, I prefer to call what was passed on to me a blessing. I knew the moment my eyes locked onto a bouncing, chattering ferret that I'd been hooked by something mysteriously fascinating. Each one of my ferrets has provided me with much happiness and joy over the years. Even though all my ferrets, young and old, share in common the ability to make me break out in laughter with their habitual silliness, each one is a unique little fuzzball. And they continuously amaze me with their intelligence and social play.

Ferrets are fun and mischievous. They're cunning looters. They can steal and break your heart. They come in all sorts of colors and sizes. Ferrets can get into the littlest cracks and holes, both in your home and in your soul. They're bound to make you break out in uncontrollable laughter at least once a day. They steal any chance they can to dance and dook and chatter about. And when they're through amazing you with their antics, most ferrets love nothing more than to curl up somewhere warm with you and snooze the rest of the day away.

Sound like the perfect pet? Not necessarily. As a shelter director, my motto is "Not all animals make good pets for people, and not all people make good parents for pets." No two households, people, or lifestyles are the same. Although ferrets can bring you plenty of joy, they also can be quite challenging at times.

That's why I wrote this book about these amazing creatures. If you don't yet have a ferret, this book can help you decide whether a fuzzy is for you. And if you already have a ferret, this book can help you give him the best possible care. To boot, this book offers practical health and medical information. And everything from cover to cover is in cut-to-the-chase format — only what you need to know, in good ol' plain English.

About This Book

You have plenty to discover — and a lot of responsibility to take on — when you decide to adopt a ferret. Pet ownership isn't something to take lightly. You should always make a lifetime commitment when deciding to bring any pet into your home. This book helps you gain better insight into what's required so that you can make the right choices for your lifestyle.

This book doesn't require a read from cover to cover (of course, you can read it that way if you want to). Instead, this book is a reference guide. If you have a particular topic you want to research, you can turn right to the chapter that covers the topic.

Each chapter is divided into sections, and each section contains pieces of info about some part of ferret keeping — things like this:

>> Is a ferret the right pet for you?

>> How do I pick a healthy ferret?

>> What steps do I take to ferret-proof my home?

>> How do I set up my ferret's cage?

>> What medical conditions require a vet's care?

Foolish Assumptions

In writing *Ferrets For Dummies*, 3rd Edition, I made some assumptions about my readers:

>> You're one of the thousands and thousands of people out there who has a nagging child or spouse who whines daily about wanting to own a ferret. Or maybe you've had your emotions kidnapped by a ferret, and you want to make sure that a ferret is the pet for you before you adopt him.

>> Perhaps you're one of those lucky folks who already owns a ferret, and you want to know how to properly care for him.

>> You may be a volunteer or employee at a ferret shelter, humane society, veterinarian clinic, or pet shop. You've been given (or have volunteered for) the task of ferret-keeper, and you want to know about caring for these fantastic furballs.

>> You may be a "seasoned" ferret owner who's soon to discover that this book covers topics that you can't find in other ferret books, such as behavior challenges, alternative diet, and saying goodbye.

>> You may be one of the many who realize the growing need for — and importance of — enrichment in the lives of our ferrets and value the extensive information provided by this book on enrichment.

>> You may be a veterinarian who wants to know as much about the ferrets you treat — including basic history — as you do about the people who bring them in.

Whatever made you pick up this book, hold onto your hat, because you're in for the thrill of a lifetime!

Icons Used in This Book

To help you navigate this book full of great information, I include icons that point out helpful hints, fun facts, and things you'd be wise to keep in mind. In a nutshell, the icons do the following:

TIP

This icon provides tidbits of info that can make your life as a ferret mom or dad a little easier. Many of these tips were discovered by people, including myself, who learned some ferret-owning facts the hard way.

TECHNICAL STUFF

This icon points out interesting and sometimes technical ferret facts — some of which I stumbled upon while researching for this book. Not all this stuff makes for good dinner conversation, but you're never too old to learn. Consider this information interesting but nonessential.

WARNING

Don't glaze over the information accompanying this icon. Paying attention to what's here can save your ferret's life or prevent injury and illness — perhaps even major vet bills.

REMEMBER

The paragraph(s) accompanying this icon points out important stuff that you should store in an easily accessed part of your brain.

Beyond the Book

You can find a little more helpful ferrets-related information on `https://www.dummies.com`, where you can peruse this book's Cheat Sheet. To get this handy resource, go to the website and type *Ferrets For Dummies Cheat Sheet* in the Search box.

Where to Go from Here

If you're thinking about getting a ferret, or you want to know how to get a healthy one, start at the beginning with Parts 1 and 2. If you already have a ferret, you can delve into whatever chapter you want, hopping around as issues or problems arise, or as time permits.

Bottom line? Enjoy this book as it was meant to be enjoyed. Remember: People learn new things every day about ferrets. And the best teachers are our ferrets themselves. Don't be afraid to ask questions from the experts, such as your vet. Doing so is well worth the time, and it makes ferret parenting a much more pleasant experience. Besides, asking is the only way you can learn.

1

Is a Ferret Right for You?

Discover what a ferret is and isn't, from colors and patterns to wild and domestic classifications.

Uncover the secrets of ferrets in the past and present.

You'll get the lowdown on the legal aspects of owning ferrets.

Chapter **1**

What You Need to Know About Ferrets

To the undiscerning eye, she looks a little rat-like. But she acts and moves more like a cat. Sometimes, she fools you and becomes quite dog-like. She resembles some animals you see roaming your backyard or other curious critters featured on a nature television show. And at some point, you'll witness some people in a pet store pointing at a cage full of them, inquiring, "Good heavens, what in the world are those? Opossums?" I think not!

The lovable animal I refer to is the ferret, of course. She belongs to a colorful clan of creatures and often gets mistaken for different animals. In this chapter, I tell you all about the ferret's vast family, his close and distant relatives, and his interesting history. (And for you technical readers, I throw in all sorts of Latin lingo that may confuse even the professionals out there.)

The ferret's scientific name as of press time, preferred mostly by North-American scientists, is *Mustela putorius furo*. This name exists because of the beliefs concerning the function and nature of the ferret. For those of you who don't speak Ferret Latin, *Mustela* means "weasel" or "mouse killer." *Putorius* is derived from the Latin word *putoris,* meaning "stench," and *furo* is derived from the Latin word *furis,* meaning "thief." The word *ferret* itself is derived from the Latin word *furonem,* which also means "thief." Put all this together and you have one little "stinky mouse-killing thief." Although the historical ferret may have lived up to this dubious title, today's ferret is more often than not a cuddly little furball. For all practical purposes, I fondly refer to my ferrets as *Ferretus majorus pleasorus* in the comfort of my nonscientific home!

Some scientists who agree with me are now challenging the beliefs about ferrets — particularly some of the DNA evidence, as used in some paternity tests. The white coats doing most of the ancestral and DNA research are Europeans who prefer to call the ferret *Mustela furo.* Currently, several papers exist that support *Mustela furo.* The scientific name of our domestic ferret may very well change in the near future.

And before you actually run out and get your new family member, you must consider all the things your ferret will require of you — space, safety, and so on — so I cover these things here as well. After all, how can you promise to be a good mom or dad to your fuzzy if you don't even know what goes into good ferret parenting? Taking an honest look at the requirements can mean the difference between living happily with a new family member and taking on a major, unwelcome chore.

First Question: What Is a Ferret?

Although ferrets may look rodent-like with their long, pointed snouts and ticklish whiskers (see Figure 1-1), they're not rodents at all. Ferrets come from the order *Carnivora,* which simply means "meat or flesh eating." This order encompasses a huge group of animals, from Fifi the common lap dog to the mighty African lion. Within the order Carnivora, ferrets belong to the family *Mustelidae,* which they proudly share with such bold critters as the badger, wolverine, pine marten, and otters. Included in that family are both domesticated ferrets and ferret-like wild animals such as the weasel, European polecat, steppe polecat, black-footed ferret, and mink.

REMEMBER

The word *ferret* is appropriately derived from the Latin word *Furonem*, which means "thief." As a new ferret owner, you'll quickly realize just how thieving your new family member can be. As cute as this endearing trait may be at times, it has its downsides. It once took me over a day to find all the contents of my purse, which I foolishly left open in the presence of roving ferrets.

REMEMBER

Many ferret owners call their pets a variety of nicknames. Some of the names that I use throughout this book are fuzzy, carpet shark, snorkeler, furball, and fuzz-butt. I know that many more terms of endearment exist out there. Don't get confused!

Giving the Ferret a Physical: Examining Fuzzy Characteristics

Before you bring a new fuzzy home or in the early stages of your ferret parenthood, you need to become familiar with a ferret's physical inventory. When I say physical, I pretty much mean all the general stuff regarding a ferret's physical characteristics, from his paws and claws to his weight and remarkable (and not-so-remarkable) senses.

Take a look at Figure 1-2 if you really want to get down to the bones, literally, of examining a ferret's physical makeup! For information on ferret coats and colors, see Chapter 2.

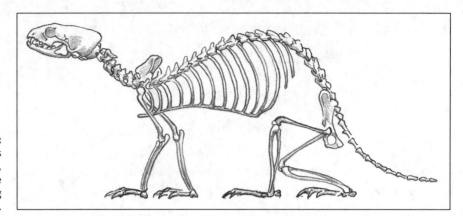

FIGURE 1-2:
A ferret's skeleton, displaying the ferret's long spine.

In the following sections, I introduce you to the physical characteristics of the ferret. My version of a ferret physical also covers other tidbits you should know, like color combos and life span, because knowing how to accessorize your fuzzy and how long you'll be caring for him is important.

Looking at the life span of a fuzzy

Since publishing the second edition of *Ferrets For Dummies* in 2007, I would have expected the six-to-eight-year life span of ferrets to have increased, yet I find it has stayed the same or even decreased slightly. Although I've still heard many stories of ferrets that have lived for up to nine or ten years, barring any unforeseen mishaps, my belief remains that a ferret's environment — his caging, disease, stress (including overcrowding), diet, and so on — plays a role in his short life span. As ferret owners discover more about the ferret and realize how important husbandry and the reduction of stress are, they might possibly see that increase in ferret life span within their own lifetime.

For now, though, you can only do your best to make your ferret's quality of life top-notch. At 1 year old, your fuzzy is considered full grown. At 3 to 4, he's considered middle-aged, and at 5 to 6 years of age, he's considered a geriatric, or an old fert! At this time, she may begin to slowly lose weight and start encountering debilitating illnesses. This is when things get tough and you're faced with difficult choices (see Chapter 17 for advice on saying goodbye to your fuzzy).

REMEMBER

As heartbreaking as it is, ferrets are prone to many diseases and may be genetically or medically flawed. Like most companion pets, whose life spans are short compared to humans, ferrets' lives are compacted into only six to eight oh-so-short years. The average human has 65 to 70 years to experience what a ferret experiences in under a decade. The ferret is an amazing trooper with a tremendous fight for life, and you can certainly do your part to help. See Chapters 15 and 16 for more on the conditions that can afflict your fuzzy and for tips on how to care for him.

In this corner, weighing in at . . .

A carpet shark's size makes him an ideal pet for both the apartment dweller and the homeowner. As is the case with some mammal species, unneutered male ferrets typically measure up to two times larger than females — called *sexual dimorphism.* There is a notable weight difference in the head and torso, where the male is wider and less dainty.

A typical altered female ferret weighs between a slim ¾ of a pound (0.3 kg) and a whopping 2½ pounds (1.1 kg) — and that's a big girl. Neutered males normally weigh 2 to 3½ pounds (0.9 to 1.6 kg), and unaltered males may weigh in at 4 to 6 pounds (1.8 to 2.7 kg) or more. In tape-measure terms, without the tail, female ferrets are between 13 and 14 inches (33 and 35.5 cm) long, and males generally measure between 15 and 16 inches (38 and 40.6 cm). A ferret's tail is 3 to 4 inches (7.6 to 10 cm) long. See Figure 1-3.

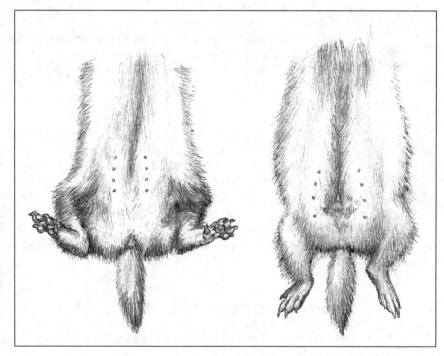

FIGURE 1-3:
Male ferrets are bulkier, with the location of the penis resembling belly buttons. Females are smaller and have vulval openings near the anus.

REMEMBER

Ferrets are kind of like humans in that they tend to bulk up in the winter. Sometimes ferrets gain 40 percent of their weight at this time of the year and then lose it in the spring (as do humans, right?). This isn't always the rule, though; some ferrets always seem skinny, and others are belly draggers all year round. Could it have something to do with health and/or exercise? Better check it out. (Parts 3 and 4 of this book cover various issues related to exercise and health.)

Getting to the point about claws and teeth

On each of a ferret's soft paws is a set of five non-retractable claws or nails designed for digging and grasping. Nature designed the nails to stay there for a ferret's benefit and survival, so you should never remove them. Frequent clipping, about every 7–10 days, is recommended (see Chapter 9 for more on grooming tips and Chapter 6 for more on ferret-proofing your home).

WARNING

Declawing your ferret is a big, fat no-no. For a ferret, declawing is a painful, mutilating surgery with way more risks than benefits. They need their claws for digging, grasping, walking, and playing. The base of the claw gives the ferret's foot added strength to support his weight. Removing the claws causes foot problems and/or pain when walking. If you think you'll be too lazy to clip your ferret's nails, you must recognize that a ferret isn't the pet for you.

Like all carnivores (see the first section in this chapter), ferrets have large canine teeth that can be rather intimidating. A ferret's teeth usually hang lower than his lip flap and are in full view. Although any animal with a mouth can and will bite under certain circumstances, I've found the biting ferret to be the exception rather than the rule. Most ferrets use their canine teeth to show off to their friends and to eat. When a ferret nips, she does it out of fear or play. An occasional warning nip may be a sign of the ferret's disapproval of one thing or another. (See Chapter 3 for more about the laws governing ferret bites.)

In this day and age, you would be hard pressed to find a veterinarian who would ethically lean on the side of declawing or defanging a ferret anyway. And many US and European governmental authorities have actually banned these mutilating practices on all animals.

REMEMBER

Make no doubt about it, the bite of a disgruntled ferret is painful and can draw blood. Take measures to make sure bites don't happen, and unless medically warranted for your ferret's health, don't alter his canine teeth; leave them right where they belong.

Making sense of senses

A ferret's senses vary in degree of acuteness (see Chapter 10 for more on ferret senses). Like human infants, a ferret's eyesight isn't that well-developed, and his ability to distinguish color is limited. A ferret can only see some reds and blues. Make no mistake about it, though: Even the most restricted ferret can and will find any object he wasn't intended to find (and his stubby little legs will help him steal the objects back to his hidey-hole). In a sense, all ferrets have sticky fingers: If they find it, it belongs to them. If they want it, it's theirs. You get the idea.

A ferret's sense of smell is far superior to a human's, and his little paw pads are more sensitive to the touch. Also, a fuzzy's sense of hearing is remarkable. If you open a bag of chips, for example, be assured that your ferret on the other side of your house will hear the bag opening and come a-begging. So, remember to whisper when discussing sensitive issues such as neutering or going on vacation.

Have I mentioned that ferrets have another sense? They seem to understand us humans. Scary!

Exercise and Time Considerations — Yours and Your Fuzzy's

When determining whether a ferret is the perfect pet for you, get introspective and look at your lifestyle. Ferrets are interactive and intelligent pets that need a lot of attention. If you want a pet that you can keep in a cage and look at every once in a while, you must accept that a ferret isn't for you. Fish are good when left in their tanks. Ferrets, on the other hand, are exploratory characters that aim to please their humans. Okay, they really aim to please themselves, but they tickle us pink in the process.

Ferrets need a lot of exercise and attention to be happy and healthy. Plan on allowing your ferret to spend no less than four hours a day playing in a safe, stimulating, enriched, ferret-proof environment. If you leave a fuzzy in a cage or unattended to too often, it actually leads to boredom and stress, which can in turn lead to serious health issues. Trust me, it will do you a world of good to get down on the floor with your ferret and let out your inner fuzzy. (For more information about enriching your ferret's life, check out Chapter 10.)

TIP

If you don't think you can provide your ferret with the proper amount of exercise and attention, and that's your only ferret hang-up, perhaps you should consider adopting two ferrets. Ferrets live to play and they play to live, so if you can't be an interactive human all the time, get your fuzzy a playmate. Besides, whereas one furball is intensely amusing, two (or more) are downright hysterical. In fact, I recommend getting two or three no matter what (see Chapter 4 for more on this advice).

If you let him, a healthy caged ferret will sleep 18 to 20 hours a day. Does this make these ferrets nocturnal or diurnal? Neither. I think they should get a category all to themselves. How about ferturnal? Most weasels are considered nocturnal, although they may change their sleeping patterns depending on habitat, competition, and food availability. Like their polecat relatives, healthy, free-roaming ferrets with little cage time should sleep only 15 to 18 hours a day. Strive to make your ferrets as active as possible.

Ferrets tend to be *crepuscular,* which means they usually pep up and come out at dusk and dawn, similar to deer. However, ferrets change their activity levels to meet their humans' schedules. For example, if you're a night owl and sleep all day, your ferrets will be night owls too. Just as weasels will adapt to best suit their survival needs, ferrets can be diurnal, nocturnal, or crepuscular. What sleeping patterns your ferret adopts is up to you! (For tips on your ferret's cage and bedding for sleep time, see Chapter 5.)

Taking a Whiff of the Odor Factor

All ferrets come equipped with a really "neat" scenting mechanism. Located just outside the ferret's anus on both sides are anal sacs filled with foul-smelling fluid. All carnivores have these sacs, including the beloved canine. A ferret's system is quite different from the human scenting mechanism, though, which is more often than not triggered by disagreeable food or the simple desire to offend. When excited, overstimulated, scared, or angry, your ferret will, without aim, discharge his secret weapon, called *poofing.* But the ferret's odor, although intentionally disturbing, rapidly dispels — just like yours! The following sections deal with a couple issues you face when playing the odor factor.

To descent or not to descent?

The majority of ferrets I've run across have been descented at a very early age — before they reach the pet trade. In other words, vets have removed their anal glands. Most ferrets are commercially raised in fuzzy farms where neutering and descenting occur before the ferrets can be shipped out. As a new owner, you have no real way to tell whether a ferret has been descented, however. The moment of truth comes at the moment of nasal impact.

Personally I don't recommend descenting ferrets. I find it an unnecessary and potentially harmful procedure. However, some ferret owners can't or don't want to tolerate the rare "poof" of odor expelled from the undescented ferret. Finding a vet who's performed this procedure before may be a challenge, but most experienced ferret vets may be willing to take on the challenge and should do just fine. Don't be surprised if you find that this surgery doesn't cut down on the odor as much as you thought it would. The anal glands are not the problem! Ferrets are musky critters with oil glands in their skin. And unneutered ferrets can be a wee bit smelly. Personally, I find the scent lovely!

AN EXPERT'S OPINION ON DESCENTING

"Despite information to the contrary, ferret farms continue to descent ferrets at a very young age to decrease their odor. Unfortunately, this has little effect on their natural odor and can lead to complications later in life, including difficulty with elimination, pain, and/or infection. As a ferret veterinarian, I only recommend this surgery if it is medically necessary to improve the health of the patient." According to Karen Purcell DVM, author of *Essentials of Ferrets: A Guide for Practitioners* (AAHA Press) and veterinarian in Roxboro, NC. Unless medically necessitated, I suggest that you leave your ferret be and pay more heed to his emotional state so you can control the odor. Some people actually like the smell. I myself love it. Those of you who have roommates will surely agree that ferret odor is more often the lesser of the two evils.

If you should happen upon a ferret with full scent capabilities in your search for a pet, take note, though: Descenting isn't necessary for living happily with a ferret. In fact, descenting is a North-American practice and is illegal in many European countries, who consider it unethical. The ferret's scent glands may be an important behavioral and social tool. Perhaps they use scent as a means of identifying one ferret from another or determining the health status of another ferret. Scent may also indicate where a ferret is in its breeding cycle.

Controlling your fuzzy's odor

The ferret's odor is unique and requires regular maintenance for odor control. You need to change his oil and rotate his tires every 3,000 miles, so to speak. Frequently changing his litter and bedding is the best way to control odor (see Chapter 9).

REMEMBER

Bathing your ferret often results in a stinkier fuzzy because his oil glands go into overdrive to replace the oils you washed down the drain. I only bathe my ferrets a couple times a year, and that seems plenty.

REMEMBER

There's always some odor involved with ferrets. Even the most well-cared-for ferret will have a slight musky smell. On average, the odor is no worse than a dog's smell; however, people's tolerances for smell are different. Obviously, if you let your ferret go for very long periods without a bath or if you become too lax with changing his litter box and bedding, his smell will become stronger. And keep in mind that poor diet and stress also contribute to the odor of your ferret.

Getting the Dish on Financial Matters

Ferrets are expensive pets. Whether you purchase your baby at a pet store, adopt her from a shelter, or have a neighbor leave her on your doorstep (see Chapter 4), you need to fork over not only emotion but also money. Investing in a ferret family member has many intangible rewards, but you must be willing to put out the cash when necessary to keep her safe and sound. The following list outlines the expenses you'll incur after adopting your fuzzy:

>> **Basic accessories:** This category includes such things as cages, toys, bedding, bowls, litter boxes, treats, and so on.

>> **Food:** Ferrets need high-quality ferret food, which is more costly than low-quality food. And the more ferrets you have, the more they'll eat. Are you willing to pay more for a high-quality food to keep your ferrets as healthy as possible? (See Chapter 8 for more on feeding your ferret.)

>> **Neutering or spaying:** Your new baby may or may not be altered, but unless you plan on breeding, which I caution you to think twice about, get him altered as soon as possible. Besides being the responsible thing to do, it'll cut down on the odor.

>> **Annual vet trips:** Besides regular checkups (see Chapter 12), your ferret should receive annual rabies and distemper vaccinations, as well as heart-worm preventives (vaccinations may be required by law; see Chapter 3).

As your ferret ages, the chances of him developing an illness or disease increases. Often, this means more frequent trips to the vet for special tests and/or medication. You owe it to any pet you have to provide quality medical care at all times.

TIP

The dollars can add up. Think about starting a pet fund, in which you put aside a few dollars each week in case an emergency comes up and you fall a little short financially. Also, pet insurance is becoming more and more popular among ferret owners. Do your research (starting with your veterinarian) to see whether insurance is an avenue to pursue. Either way, do yourself a favor and put aside some funds if you can.

Extreme Cage Makeover: Providing the Space They Need

You shouldn't bring a ferret to your home before you've completely and adequately set up his house for his arrival. Even though ferrets make great pets for both the house and apartment, you shouldn't compromise one luxury: His cage should be roomy, and you should make adequate room for it. (See Chapter 5 for more on creating a ferret cage.)

If your only available space is a wall that's supporting the world's largest beer-bottle collection, you should consider parting with the bottles or packing them up. Even if you could squeeze in both the ferret and the beer bottles, doing so wouldn't be a good idea. Your carpet shark could knock them over and break them, or your thief could manage to drag a bottle or two back to his secret hidey-hole!

Facing the Challenges of Ferret-Proofing Your Home

Ferrets are trouble magnets. From digging up the plants and carpeting, to stealing your stuff, to terrorizing the cats and dogs — if something can be messed with, a ferret will mess with it.

I compare this vigorous playtime madness to a human toddler on a double espresso. To combat the madness and protect your ferret, you need to ferret-proof your home — or at least the areas the little bugger has access to. It may be as simple as moving the houseplants, or it may be as involved as boarding up the cracks and crevices under your cabinets. Nature designed the ferret to search out your ferret-proofing failures. Therefore, ferret-proofing is a continuous activity as your curious fuzzy finds more and more flaws.

REMEMBER

If you even question whether something is unsafe, it's probably unsafe. Otherwise, you wouldn't give it a second thought. Expect the impossible, prepare for the worst, and hope for the best. What actually happens will probably be somewhere in between. For tips on how to make your home safe for your ferret, head to Chapter 6.

Ferrets and Kids

Ferrets can make good pets for single people living in apartments and for families in homes. I don't like to stereotype human children as a whole by saying this pet or that pet isn't good with kids. Usually, it's the other way around. Many kids aren't good around certain types of pets, although many are great. I was taking care of pets before I was even 10 years old, and I did so with great pleasure and responsibility. I didn't mind getting scratched or bitten, and I didn't mind the cage cleaning. I was an exception to most kids.

When it comes to smaller children such as toddlers, I worry as much about the ferret's safety as I do the child's. Ferrets are fast and move unpredictably, much like toddlers. The two in combination can result in disaster. Crushing injuries, such as a ferret being accidentally stepped on or squeezed, can lead to the ferret being injured, paralyzed, or even killed. A ferret in pain will often bite and injure whomever is in his path whether it is you or your toddler.

REMEMBER

Ferrets can be playfully nippy and squirmy, and they require a lot of attention and care. Most young children can and will activate the hyper switch in ferrets. And don't be fooled if your kid promises to be 100-percent responsible for his new ferret. You must evaluate your family members honestly before bringing a ferret home and expect that you'll be the main caretaker. See Chapter 7 for more on this topic.

Ferrets and Babies

In all my years of owning ferrets, exotics, and other pets, I have always addressed the topic of ferrets and babies rather head-on in an opinionated manner. It takes only a split-second for an interaction between a human baby and a ferret (or other pet) to go horribly wrong! A grasping baby can innocently squeeze a ferret, who may bite out of pain and or be seriously injured. I have read or heard about numerous seemingly unprovoked attacks in which small infants were injured by ferrets, some even during closely supervised encounters. It might be that babies smell funny, move funny, or even sound a bit funny, and although the majority of pet ferrets may be okay with meeting a human baby, why risk putting any ferret or baby in that position?

Ferrets and Other Household Pets

All animals have unique personalities, so to assume that one pet will get along with another is to be overly optimistic — an attitude that could lead to heartbreak. Multi-species interaction is a complex issue. I simply can't guarantee that your new fuzzy will get along with your other pets. And think about how your other pets might feel when they smell the little carnivore close by. Prey animals such as rabbits and guinea pigs might be fearful and stressed about the possibility of being your ferret's next meal. At the very least, house them in separate rooms. Ferrets are escape artists and have been known to kill small mammals, birds, and reptiles.

REMEMBER

Certain breeds of dogs are bred to hunt small animals, which the ferret is. And ferrets are bred as predators and may find birds, hamsters, and even small kittens as the perfect prey. Cats and ferrets often get along well, but you can't force a relationship that isn't there.

Having said all that, I don't see a reason why a ferret couldn't peacefully cohabitate in most homes if the owners use common sense. The key is to know your animals and their limits. Provide meticulous supervision at all times. When you introduce your pets, you may have to conclude that mixing the species just won't work in your home; be prepared to offer your ferret a safe place to adequately play away from all your other pets. (See Chapter 7 for more on introducing your ferret to other animals.)

Leaping over the Legal Hurdles

You should be aware of the legal aspects of owning a ferret. Before you consider the time, cost, adjustment, and olfactory aspects of ferret parenthood, do some digging to be sure that ferrets are legal where you live. What licenses may you need? What restrictions does your local government place on pet owners?

It's truly heartbreaking to lose a ferret to legal snags after investing so much time and love. Fortunately, I haven't experienced this pain firsthand, but I do shed tears when I read the emotional testimonies of people who've lost legal battles and ultimately their beloved fuzzies. For more information about the legal issues that govern owning a ferret, head to Chapter 3.

Chapter **2**

Understanding What Ferrets Are (And Aren't)

I t's important to discuss domestication when it comes to ferrets; the issue is at the center of a ferret's identity. Some people hold the mistaken belief that ferrets are wild animals, but that couldn't be further from the truth. Lumping them in with wild animals for regulatory purposes is, in my opinion, a crime (for more, see Chapter 3). In reality, ferrets are domesticated polecats, which means they're descendants of wild polecats that were domesticated by humans. This chapter will teach you about what it means to be domesticated and why ferrets are domesticated. It's really quite interesting.

You also discover in this chapter that ferrets are endearing critters that come in a multitude of colors and patterns, which I explain in detail. But ferret types don't end at colors. In your search for a ferret you may come across an angora or even a ferret-polecat hybrid, so this chapter prepares you a little for that unusual and exciting encounter. But you're not likely to encounter the ferret's rare and extremely endangered cousin, the black-footed ferret. So I'll introduce you to him here. You'll get to know about his plight and the heroic efforts of a group of people to reintroduce him back into the wild.

This chapter also burrows through the past and takes you into the present, taking note of historical ferret sightings — some of which are more like hallucinations. You find out why people prized the beloved ferret so much in the first place, and that common folk weren't the only ones who enjoyed the company of weasels. You also get a brief lesson on the art of ferreting, as well as a stern lecture on why your ferret should hunt only within the safety of your home.

Yes, Ferrets Are Domesticated

Domestication is a long process in which people selectively breed wild animals in captivity for human benefit. There are three main criteria for domestication:

» **Humans select the animals to be bred; the animals can't select mates themselves.**

In the case of unaltered pet ferrets, their breeding is under complete control of humans. People not only pair up the ferrets, but also can and sometimes do tell them when and when not to breed by using light cycles. They can take ferrets out of season by using vasectomized males or medications so that they can't reproduce. Humans can even have ferrets produce multiple litters per year or prevent them from having any litters in a year.

» **The animal experiences some type of genetic change that reflects the human selection and distinguishes it from its wild counterparts.**

Domestication has caused profound changes to ferret behavior:

- Domesticated ferrets by nature don't fear humans.

- They demonstrate prolonged litter behaviors toward other ferrets, which allows them to be housed with other ferrets.

- They demonstrate play behavior into late adulthood.

In addition to behavioral changes, the domesticated ferret features extreme changes to fur color when compared to wild polecats. Ferrets can be bred for a multitude of colors and patterns, and albinism occurs frequently.

>> **Humans derive some benefit from the domestication of the animal.**

People domesticated ferrets to be mousers because they wanted a polecat that could hunt mice and be predictably tame toward humans. By the end of the domestication process, that's exactly what they had. In the past and still today, people used ferrets in the sport of ferreting to hunt rabbits. Ferret domestication has also benefited humans in the areas of fur production, experimental science, and, of course, companionship.

Some domestication scientists would add a fourth bullet indicating tameness as a criterion, but not all domesticated animals are tame, which I can attest to as a keeper of wild animals. And some wild animals are tame, so tameness is relative.

WILL THE FERRET'S REAL DADDY PLEASE STAND UP?

A huge amount of mystery and controversy surrounds our little ferret friends' history — perhaps because all polecat groups are very closely related and can interbreed successfully (that is, they can produce viable hybrids). Nobody really knows how the ferret is related to the rest of the polecats, except that it *is* a domesticated polecat, and the European polecat *(Mustela putorius)* and the steppe polecat *(Mustela eversmanni)* may be involved. The most commonly accepted among several theories points toward the European polecat as having the most likely claim to ferret ancestry.

Although scientists have found little archeological evidence to support this idea, genetically speaking, today's ferret and the entire polecat group Subgenera Putorius (*Mustela eversmanni, Mustela putorius,* and *Mustela nigripes*) are practically twins. The most likely conclusion is that the domestic ferret is a polecat hybrid. But even a seemingly insignificant genetic discrepancy can mean the difference between a horse and a zebra or a dog and a coyote.

So, the studies move forward. However, it's quite possible that we may never know the real ancestry in our lifetime or in any other lifetime. For your purposes, all you truly need to know is that you're dealing with a unique little creature — more affectionate than ferocious, and so easy to fall in love with.

Getting to Know Fuzzies in the Past and Present

Domesticated ferrets have been around for about 2,500 years and have stolen the hearts of such people as Queen Elizabeth I and comedian Dick Smothers. They were avid sailors during the American Revolutionary war, and they've been skilled hunters from the time of domestication until now. It seems their talents abound. Since domesticating ferrets, people have found many uses for this wonderful animal, though it wasn't until several decades ago that the ferret actually started catching on as a lovable pet.

Ferrets throughout history

Tracking the ferret's timeline is both factually difficult and headache inducing. Many sources cite the people of Egypt as the original domesticators of ferrets, but we have no proof that this theory is true. Egyptian hieroglyphics portray images of weasel-like creatures, but several animals can fit the description — the mongoose being one of them. Prior to the domestication of the cat, the mongoose held the high esteem of snake catcher and keeper of the house in Egypt — and does so still today. Experts can logically conclude that these hieroglyphics don't show ferrets at all, but rather another animal native to the land. After all, you haven't seen reports of ferret mummies being discovered in Egypt, have you? And the Egyptians seemingly mummified everything! Additionally, the hieroglyphics date back almost 500 years prior to the domestication of the cat, which happened about 4,000 years ago.

The first known written reference to an animal likely to be the domesticated ferret popped up around 400 BC and was penned by the Greek satirical writer Aristophanes (448–385 BC). Later, in 350 BC, the Greek naturalist and philosopher Aristotle (384–322 BC) penned another reference. A ferret supposedly made an appearance in the Bible, but it turned out to be a mistake in translation. The word in question, translated correctly, means "small crawling things"; in modern day translations, it means "gecko."

Experts estimate that the ferret was introduced to North America a little more than 300 years ago. But only recently (in about the past 35 years) have most pet owners discovered the ferret's "fetching" personality.

Ferrets have always had a knack for meeting man's needs

Earlier civilizations must have found the ferret to be quite the efficient exterminator, because Caesar Augustus received a request around 60 BC to sail several ferrets to the Balearic Islands to control the rabbit population. And ferrets are no strangers to the seas; during the American Revolutionary War, several ferrets would roam the ships at sea to patrol for rodents. In fact, one ship was named after a ferret: In an 1823 newspaper article, a U.S. schooner, *The Ferret,* was reported to be chasing (capturing) pirates. People also used the small, flexible critters to navigate wire, cable, and tools through small openings and tunnels.

You can find many more documented reports on the use of ferrets to control pests and hunt small game. Supposedly, two of the greatest ferret keepers were German Emperor Frederick II (1194–1250) and Genghis Khan (1167–1227), ruler of the Mongol empire. The hunting of small game is called *ferreting* — a word still used today, both literally and figuratively (see the upcoming ferreting section for more on the topic).

Ferrets catching on

Ferrets have tunneled their way into the lives of many historical figures — from Caesar Augustus, who was asked for the working ferrets' services to rid an island of rabbits, to Queen Elizabeth I, who had a portrait done with one of her royal fuzzies. Ferrets have been frequent subjects of famous artists, such as Leonardo da Vinci. Other famous ferret humans include comedian Dick Smothers, American media personality and businesswoman Paris Hilton and actor Dave Foley. Ferrets have even weaseled into the theater, playing roles in such movies as *Kindergarten Cop, Garfield, Tale of Two Kitties, Starship Troopers, Star Trek: The Next Generation,* and *Beastmaster,* to mention just a few.

Ferrets have made brief appearances on some television shows. For instance, Dr. Wendy Winsted and her ferrets Melinda and McGuinn made a guest appearance on what was then called *Late Night with David Letterman.* They (the ferrets) performed the roll-over trick for a lap of milk and a bite of a stagehand's roast beef sandwich.

Ferrets also are a common source of punch lines and jokes. Take, for example, the television series *M*A*S*H.* Major Frank Burns was often referred to as "ferret face." I'm not sure where the insult lies, though. And David Letterman has frequently used the ferret in his Top Ten lists. I suppose I can see some humor in it. After all, I have some very weaselly friends. They know who they are!

Spotlighting the Sport of Ferreting

The sport of *ferreting* — hunting small game with ferrets — probably developed hand in hand with the domestication of the ferret. The ferret keeper, or *ferretmeister* (similar to a wisenheimer), would release a couple ferrets near rabbit burrows and send them in to find the game. Like today's pointers and other hunting dogs, working ferrets wore bells placed on their collars so their keepers could track them. A common misconception is that the ferret's job was to hunt. Far from the truth, it was simply supposed to chase the rabbit or other game out of its burrow. Often, the fleeing animal became entangled in nets that keepers used to prevent escape. The hunter then killed the prey with a club or gun or used dogs or hawks to catch the game. In modern days, the prey, often a rabbit, is humanely dispatched by cervical dislocation. Today, where ferreting is legal, such as the UK or Australia, ferret keepers often use GPS collars on their ferrets to keep track of them. That way, the ferrets are easily located and few are ever left behind.

Sometimes, a ferret would stay in the hole, eat its share of the catch, and then go to sleep! The aggravated keeper would have to send in another ferret tethered to a line to locate and awaken the stuffed, sleepy ferret. The keeper would then follow the line and dig out the ferrets and what was left of the carcass. Another option was to cover up all the exit holes except for one, set a mink trap, and hope the thieving ferret would be caught by morning. Nowadays, where ferreting is legal, a habitual offender is usually put up for adoption into a pet home rather than set out into the field again to be set up for failure.

Ferret keepers were sometimes poachers. The poachers would hide the ferret in his pants and take the fuzzy out at night to hunt. Poachers were possibly the first large-scale pet ferret owners. This makes sense if you consider that a poacher would typically spend more time bonding with and socializing his ferrets to reduce the risk of getting caught. As ferreting became more popular and the ferret gained respect, highly educated people took up the sport, and most people kept their ferrets in conditions far superior to what most people at that time experienced.

Many people in Australia and Europe still enjoy the sport of ferreting (see Figure 2-1); however, it's illegal in the United States and Canada.

I don't advise trying your hand at the sport of ferreting for many reasons:

>> It's illegal in the United States.

>> U.S. bunnies are nesters and not burrowers.

>> Your ferret can get lost, maybe even for good.

>> You may expose your ferret to a disease.

>> It's cold, dark, and scary in those rabbit burrows (to me, anyway).

>> Your ferret would prefer to be cuddled up with you in a safe, warm house.

>> Your ferret can drown in water-filled burrows.

>> Hey, what did a rabbit ever do to you?

FIGURE 2-1:
Here's a working
ferret teamed up
with a human
hunter.

FERRET LEGGING

You might know by now that ferrets love warm dark tunnels, so what could possibly go wrong by putting a ferret or two down your trousers? (Although this begs the question, "Why would you want to?") Ferret legging fanciers have been participating in what they've also called "put em down," for centuries, but this game of chance and endurance has only been gaining popularity since the 1970s. In this contest, this winner is whoever can withstand the consequences of, well, having ferrets in their pants. Only a brave or a stupid human would endure this. I'd be a downright ticked-off carpet shark if I were subjected to it. Some things to consider about ferret legging:

- Ferrets are fully fanged and fully clawed.

- Trousers are tied at the ankles and belts tightened to prevent ferrets from escaping.

- Underwear is not allowed to be worn so that ferrets can maneuver freely from one leg to the other.

- Human participants must be completely sober.

- Ferrets must not be sedated.

- Participants may only try to "dislodge" biting ferrets from outside of their trousers.

- Ouch!

(continued)

(continued)

The origins of ferret legging are somewhat disputed, but what isn't disputed is that Reg Mellor from Barnsley, England held the 1981 ferret legging world record with 5 hours 26 minutes until 2010 when Frank Bartlett broke Mellor's record with 5 hours and 30 minutes, raising 1,000 pounds for charity. This is amazing when you consider that 1972's ferret legging record was only 40 seconds, and it took a few years to break that record with just over a minute! The ladies' version of ferret legging, called "ferret busting" in which the ferret was put into a woman's shirt, was a complete bust and did not take off.

Although traditional ferreting is illegal in the United States, carpet sharks remain quite the charmers and are beloved snatchers of our small worldly possessions.

Picturing the Physical Appearance of the Domestic Ferret

Ferrets — those long, slender beauties — come in a variety of colors and patterns. Colors range from the easily recognized albino with her white fur and pink eyes, to the dark-eyed white (DEW) with her white coat and dark eyes, to the darker sables and all shades in between. As if colors weren't enough, ferrets also come in color patterns, which have to do with color concentrations or placement of white markings. Eye colors, mask shapes, and even nose colorings play roles in how your ferret may be classified. Color, however, should be the last factor in picking out your new ferret.

WARNING

What about naked, not-so-fuzzy ferrets, you ask? Hairless ferrets, unlike skinny pigs or hairless dogs/cats, are not bred to be that way. Hair loss in ferrets is almost always a condition related to adrenal disease and needs to be managed and treated by a veterinarian. It's also no reason to dump your ferret into a shelter, because it is manageable!

Ferret people are coming up with more and more definitions of coat colors and patterns all the time (maybe just to confuse the general public!), but many basic colors and patterns are defined for you. I present these in the sections that follow.

The spectrum of fuzzy colors

Every ferret has a color, and in that color is a pattern. Some colors and patterns change from season to season, and others will stay the same. Personally, when it comes to colors, I go by The American Ferret Association Standards. So, unless you bought a neon ferret, your fuzzy will most likely fall into one of the following categories that most ferret enthusiasts seem to agree on. (*Note:* These colors are show standards, so most ferrets won't match 100 percent.) Refer to the color photos in the middle of this book to see some of these ferret colors in their full glory!

REMEMBER

Groups of ferret experts argue over the names of shades of sables and silvers. You may find that one group calls one shade a fancy name and another group calls it something different. No matter how many color names the experts come up with, some ferrets will be lighter or darker than what their definitions specify. So, it seems the definitions may never end.

- » **Albino:** Resulting from a lack of pigment in the skin and eyes, albino ferrets range from a creamy white to a preferred snow-white color — both on the guardhairs and undercoat. All albinos have light- to medium-pink eyes, with ruby being preferred, and pink noses.

- » **Black:** The black ferret is absolutely stunning. His guardhairs are truly black in color. His undercoat is white or has a light golden cast, and his eyes are black or near black, with a nose to match. A speckled black nose also is acceptable.

- » **Black sable:** This ferret is such a dark brown that he actually appears black. He has a white or cream undercoat that barely shows through the dark guardhairs. His eyes should be dark brown to near black, with a nose to match. A heavily mottled (marbled), blackish brown nose is acceptable as well.

- » **Champagne:** This ferret is a light to medium tan or a diluted chocolate. His undercoat is white to creamy in color, and his eyes are light to dark burgundy. Like the chocolate, the champagne ferret's nose should be pink or beige, with or without the brown/beige "T" outline.

- » **Chocolate:** The chocolate ferret's coat is another shade variation of sable, but in a tasty shade of milk-chocolate brown. The ferret's undercoat has a golden cast to it or is white. His eyes are almost always brown but can be dark burgundy as well. The chocolate's nose is pink or beige, with or without the brown "T" outline; it can also be brick in color.

- » **Cinnamon:** The cinnamon's coat is a very beautiful shade of light reddish brown. His undercoat has a golden cast to it or is white. The ferret's eyes are light to dark burgundy. His nose may be pink, but a pinkish/beige nose with a brick colored "T" outline (or completely brick-colored nose) is preferred. However, many experts argue that true red cinnamons don't exist any longer.

- » **Dark-eyed white (DEW):** This category is one of my favorites. These beauties resemble albinos because of their white or creamy coats and pink noses. The exception is their eye color, which is a dark burgundy. The DEW pattern has 10 percent or less colored guardhairs in the form of a stripe, colored tail, spots, or a sprinkling throughout the coat.

The DEW ferret and DEW pattern are prone to deafness. *Waardensburg Syndrome* is a ferret condition that genetically links the white fur on the head to deafness (similar to the condition of deafness in many blue-eyed white cats). In addition to dark-eyed whites, pandas and shetlands/blazes (other ferret pattern types; see the following section) are often prone to deafness, though this isn't always the case. ***Note:*** Deaf ferrets make fine pets if you take extra care to properly train them and be careful not to startle them.

>> **Sable:** This ferret color is probably the most common. The guardhairs are a rich, deep brown, and they're evenly and densely dispersed. The undercoat on the neck, back, and belly is white or cream colored. The eyes are brown or close to black, and the nose is light or dappled brown. The nose may also have a brown "T" outline.

Guardhairs are the stiffer, longer, and more prominent pieces of fur that cover the shorter and softer undercoat. Guardhairs provide the ferret's coloration or camouflage and aid in waterproofing the fur. The undercoat also acts as insulation.

Did you know that ferrets, mainly white ferrets, can turn yellow to yellowish-orange? That stinky, naturally occurring oil (sebum) we've been talking about is yellow, and no amount of bathing will bring back your white ferret! In fact, bathing will only cause more production of oil and potentially more discoloration! Oil secretion is greater in the summer, causing your ferret to turn into more of a little grease monkey, but rest assured, he is also more comfortable, as the sebum allows air to circulate throughout his coat. Likewise, oil secretion diminishes in the winter so that the fur can return to the insulator it should be. Besides the oil, diet, aging, shedding, adrenal disease, and hormonal imbalances that occur during mating season contribute to the yellowish color.

Fuzzy color patterns

Ferret *patterns* are used to describe color concentrations and white markings on the ferret's body. With patterns, the main discriminating factors are the legs and tail, or *points*, and how the point color or mask shape (see below) relates to the rest of the body color. The following list presents the most commonly recognized ferret patterns. Flip to the color photos in the center of this book to see what some of these look like!

>> **Blaze:** These ferrets usually have smudges or rings of color around their eyes rather than masks. Small masks are acceptable, but full masks are not. A white blaze extends from the face up over the head and hopefully down the ferret's neck to the shoulders. All four of his feet have mitts or white tips; sometimes his knees are also white. Bibs, white or mottled bellies, and

roaning may also be present. He should have ruby or brown eyes, and his nose should be pink (with or without a lighter outline).

>> **Mitts:** Ferrets with mitts look like their paws have been dipped in white marshmallow fluff. They also have white bibs. A mitt's colors and patterns should be appropriate for his standards. The eyes should be a varying shade of burgundy, and the color standard should determine nose color. Knee patches and a tail tip may or may not be present.

>> **Panda:** Ferrets of any color that have white heads, necks, and throats. Some pandas have "rings" around their eyes, which is acceptable; all pandas should have four white mitts (or paws). Bibs and knee patches (yes, ferrets have knees) may be present, as well as a white tip on the tail. His eyes should be a shade of burgundy, and his nose should be pink (with or without a lighter outline).

>> **Roan:** This ferret almost has an even mixture of colored and white guardhairs. Typically, you want to see 50 to 60 percent colored and 40 to 50 percent white hairs. The color and pattern will determine the mask he needs to wear, along with his nose. For instance, a black roan mitt can have a hood or regular mask.

>> **Siamese or point:** These are ferrets of any color that have much darker points than body color. His mask is shaped like a thin letter V. Champagne versions of this ferret may have no mask (see the previous section for more on colors). The nose should be light in color, such as pink or beige, or have a "T" outline.

>> **Solid:** The solid ferret is slightly more concentrated in color than the standard ferret — ideally, 100 percent of the guardhairs will be colored. This means that you can't distinguish his points from the rest of his body, because the ferret's outer coat is solid in color. He should have a full T-bar mask and a nose color appropriate for his coat color (see the previous section).

>> **Standards:** This ferret pattern is perhaps the most common. The percentage of colored guardhairs should be approximately 90 to 100 compared to the white guardhairs present. The body appears lighter in color than the points (the legs and tail), which makes the points easily distinguishable from the rest of the body. Standards should have nose colors appropriate for their body colors standard and full or T-bar masks.

>> **Marked white:** This really neat pattern usually appears on a DEW with a smear of black somewhere on an otherwise all-white body.

REMEMBER

Hey! Where did my "silver" and "silver mitt" go? The silver, according to The American Ferret Association, is considered a "black roan." And you guessed it: The silver mitt is now the "black roan mitt."

Hanging up the question on ferret coat changes and colors

All this talk on colors and patterns may make your head spin, but don't get too hung up on it! Just like many animals, including some of our other pets, ferrets have fur cycles during which they shed out their old summer coats before their brand new winter coats come in. I emphasize "brand new" because this is not simply more fur lying in wait beneath the tired old spring coat just waiting to make its winter debut. It's a new coat all together. Each new coat on a sable may produce a darker sable with changing masks and graying hind legs, as he morphs throughout his life. A silver or roan will likely whiten up dramatically over time and become solid white. Don't get melodramatic over this normal progression. We all get a little light haired over time!

Also, don't be so surprised if your ferret gets turned around and sprouts a spring wardrobe in winter or fancies a winter coat in the spring. As far as experts are concerned, and they're still studying it a great deal, her shed cycle is greatly influenced by two hormones: prolactin and melatonin. The production of these hormones, which have been connected to hair growth, seem also to be linked to daylight length or photoperiod. So, how does that pertain to ferrets? Melatonin levels increase as days get shorter in most areas (darkness or dim light) and it decreases as the days get longer (brighter light). This melatonin production is needed for the normal development of your ferret's winter coat. Imagine if you will, the effects of keeping your ferret in a brightly lit room 24/7. Again, the theories continue, but the studies are strong.

Crazy ferret categories

Just when you thought colors and patterns might throw you for a loop, take into consideration that ferrets come in several different models, each with its own unique attributes. Not each "type" of ferret will be for everyone. While you're on this ferret fact-finding mission, I highly encourage you to take an honest look at your own present and foreseeable future lifestyle. Ask yourself what you can offer a ferret as a new member of your family, and what each type of ferret has to offer you, before making any decisions. The following gives you a look into the many options available to you.

>> **Farm/mill-bred:** Undoubtedly the majority of the ferrets sold as pets in the United States originate from what is known as ferret farms or mills, or mass producers of ferrets. Ferret kits are altered and descented prior to the age of 8 weeks, usually between 4 to 6 weeks just as their eyes are starting to open, before they're shipped out to distributors for sale. The presence of small tattoos in the ear may indicate which farm the ferret originated from, as well

as whether it is spayed or neutered (altered) and descented. Because mill ferrets are removed from mom prior to weaning, some may not learn proper ferret behavior such as bite inhibition or potty training. And early altering has negative health issues, such as an increase in adrenal gland disease. It is also thought that farmed ferrets are more prone to chronic and genetic diseases. These guys come in all colors and sizes, though the majority of farm bred ferrets in the U.S. tend to be smaller and more slender. Each ferret mill has its own reputation on the temperament of the animals they produce, ranging from lovey-dovey docile to gonna-gitcha! These ferrets are the ones most often found in shelters, because they are so abundant and probably the least of an original financial investment.

>> **Privately bred:** Generally speaking, ferrets that come from *reputable, responsible* private breeders tend to be healthier and possibly longer-lived than mill ferrets. Reputable breeders breed only the best ferrets — focusing on genetics, health, and temperament — in order to produce ferrets that are superior in musculature and health, both mental and physical. The focus placed on good genetics often leads to a decrease in disease, and late(r) altering decreases the rate of adrenal disease. These ferrets are uber high in energy and intelligence, do not tolerate physical discipline well, and require a great deal of out-of-cage time with mental and physical stimulation. With a privately bred kit you may not be able to choose among all those fancy colors, especially since some of the colors and patterns that occur are associated with genetic disorders or Waardenburg Syndrome. A good breeder will spend time with their kits — socializing, playing, feeding, and even helping to potty train them. They may be exposed to several types of foods and may be better adapted to a variable diet when they're placed in a new home than a mill ferret that was raised on kibble alone. A lot of hard work goes into a single privately bred litter. You'll find these beauties are a bit more expensive than mill ferrets, but they are a fantastic choice for someone who wishes to adopt a youngster and who has the patience to finish what momma ferret started.

Research your private ferrety well. Get ample references and be sure to visit the facility, if you're able, prior to putting a deposit down on your kit. Not all ferretries are equal. In fact, some are "backyard breeders" that keep their ferrets in horrible conditions. As such, their kits are often not properly socialized or ready for their new homes.

You may hear someone refer to their ferret as having a "whippet" or "bulldog" body type, and it's easy to see where they get these comparisons. Whippet body types have petite frames, narrow heads, longer snouts, and are quite fast and agile. In Europe, these ferrets might be comparable to the working/hunting type. On the other hand, the bulldog body type has a stockier, stronger build with a wider head and shorter snout. This ferret walks close to the ground, but will steal your sock just as efficiently as the whippet! In Europe, bulldogs would be comparable to the show and pet ferrets.

>> **Hybrids:** You will be hard-pressed to find a reasonable person who will place a hybrid into an inexperienced ferret home or a home with young children. A cross between a wild polecat and a domestic ferret, hybrids are incredibly intelligent, intense, and much more "wild" than their fully domestic counterparts. These critters require constant handling for socialization, and you can be fairly certain you are undoubtedly going to get bitten along the way. Although males tend to be bigger, females tend to be bossier, much like in the human race. Don't look for fancy colors here, because the polecat *du jour* (sable) is all you'll usually find in a hybrid. In terms of health and longevity, it's difficult to say whether the hybrid lives longer than your average domestic ferret, although it is reported that they are less prone to adrenal and heart disease. If you should find yourself with a hybrid in your home, be prepared to be challenged. Please provide an appropriate environment, as well as exciting and ever-changing enrichment for him. This will decrease boredom and possibly decrease the behavior issues.

>> **Angoras — full/half/semi:** The angora ferret is a sight to behold with its luxurious, beautiful coat and goofy, quirky personality. They can make wonderful additions to the right household and come in a variety of colors and coat lengths. The full angora is a genetic mutation so these ferrets have no undercoat, whereas half- and semi-angoras both have undercoats. Its coat can reach 5 to 6 inches in length and take up to a year to reach full coat length potential. Although the angora's coat will be shorter in summer than winter — normal shedding season applies — it will be distinctively longer than the coat of a standard ferret. Half-angora ferrets' coats get up to 3 inches in length, whereas semi-angora ferrets' coats grow to be up to 4 inches thick. You'd think grooming would be extensive for full angoras, but it's really not much different than that of a standard ferret, although you may want to consider a tasteful trim around the rearend to minimize dingleberries.

Besides lacking undercoats, most full angoras will also have nose cleft mutations. A nose cleft mutation is where visible clefts are present on either side of the full angora's nose. Oftentimes you may see tufts of hair coming out of the nostrils. Because the full angora is a genetic mutation, and also because full angora moms have difficulty producing milk after giving birth, it should be noted that full angora jills should not be bred unless a surrogate mom is ready and in place to take on those kits. Kits are highly fragile at birth and are easy to spot in litters with their oversized, blocky heads and tiny frames. Full angora kits mature 2 weeks behind their fuzzy counterparts until about 12 weeks of age, when they start to catch up in weight and size. Upper-respiratory infections may become problematic with full angoras due to the nose cleft mutation. With little protection to the airway and lungs, these guys don't stand a chance against inhaled sawdust, litter, or other irritants. Therefore, keepers of full angoras need to sweep and vacuum regularly. All Angoras are prone to some of the same problems as are standard ferrets such as lymphoma, adrenal disease, and insulinoma. However, like standard ferrets, all will undoubtedly steal your hearts!

When all is said and done, does it really matter the type of ferret you get? What is important is that it's the right fit for both of you. When choosing your first ferret, however, common sense should apply no matter what type you choose. Is it a healthy ferret? Is it comfortable being handled by you? Your ferret should be confident and full of curiosity as it explores you and its surroundings.

Not Just Another Color: The Black-Footed Ferret

The black-footed ferret, known as *Mustela nigripes,* is a small, carnivorous predator that lives in the wild and weighs between 1.5 and 2.5 pounds (0.7–1.1 kg) — approximately the same size as the mink and our domesticated fuzzy, or slightly larger than the weasel. In captivity, he may live as long as nine years, two to three times longer than expected in the wild. See Figure 2-2 to see what a black-footed ferret looks like. Compare it to Figure 1-1 in Chapter 1 to see how different the black-footed ferret looks from the domestic ferret. Refer also to the photo in the color insert.

FIGURE 2-2:
A black-footed ferret.

The black-footed ferret arrived in North America as an efficient predator, but it was in North America that he evolved into the specialized predator of prairie dogs. The black-footed ferret is known to be the only native North-American ferret and is the smallest of the polecats.

The black-footed ferret is considered by most to be one of the rarest mammals in the United States and perhaps the entire world. What has caused such a skilled hunter and cousin to our domestic ferret to earn such a title? It's no doubt that the plight of the black-footed ferret was caused both directly and indirectly by the human race. Sadly, his future remains uncertain.

This section describes the physical traits of the black-footed ferret and how our domestic ferret stands up in comparison. Here you also find an overview on how the black-footed ferret compares to our domestic ferret, where the black-footed ferret came from, where he's been, and where he's heading.

The one, true North American ferret!

The black-footed ferret adapted in North America long before the ferret was even domesticated. A close relative of the Siberian polecat, *Mustela eversmanii*, the ancestral black-footed ferret is thought to have come from northeast Asia, crossing at the point now known as the Bering Strait, between Russia and Alaska. The actual time period he scampered into North America remains uncertain. The estimates date as far back as 1 million years ago to as recent as 100,000 years ago.

Are black-footed ferrets really that different?

Black-footed ferrets and our domesticated fuzzies share many similar physical features, body size, and behaviors. Skeletally speaking, they're almost identical. Small differences appear in the skull. The domestic ferret has a shorter and more-rounded head and a slightly smaller nose. The domestic ferret's smaller ears give it an appearance of having a more pointed snout than the black-footed ferret. Both have strong front paws for digging and burrowing. The black-footed ferret has a more tubular tail unlike the tapered tail of the domestic ferret. It also has noticeably larger nocturnal eyes and broader ears needed for extra keen senses, along with a noticeably longer neck than the domestic ferret.

The black-footed ferret's nose is almost always solid black. He also always has the distinctive black feet, legs, and tip of tail. While our domestic ferrets can vary a great deal in color, shade, and pattern, only limited variations in shade of body color exist in the black-footed ferret. Always present is a white, cream, or buff full bib and a saddle of brown on his back. The saddle area is filled in with dark-tipped guard hairs that are lighter towards the roots of the hairs. Fur generally becomes lighter in shade towards and on the belly. All areas of brown can vary from light medium to dark depending on season and individual animal. Also very prominent on the black-footed ferret and almost all polecats is a white spot just above the top inner corner of each eye.

Habitat (or is that prairie dog?) destruction

The black-footed ferret's range was as vast as the prairie dog's. They thrived only where prairie dogs thrived, covering over 700 million acres. From southern Canada to northern Mexico, the prairie dog colonies were the life source for the black-footed ferret. Making up 90 percent of the black-footed ferret's diet, the prairie dog also furnished essential burrows, which were vital in providing shelter to the black-footed ferret. These burrows were safe havens that kept out the extreme weather and protected the black-footed ferret from predators. The burrows were also convenient places to whelp and rear offspring safely.

So with the essential presence of millions of prairie dogs inhabiting the territories, what could possibly push the black-footed ferret to the edge of extinction?

The most devastating human actions leading to the demise of the black-footed ferret weren't against the ferret at all but, rather, its food source — the prairie dog. Prairie dog colonies were viewed by local residents with extreme abomination for many reasons. Ranchers complained that the colonies competed with the local livestock for vital food. Agriculturists argued that they destroyed the land. Additionally, prairie dogs and other rodent species are highly susceptible to sylvatic plague, which was introduced by none other than the human animal, and this plague poses great health risks to humans and other animals.

Prairie dogs knew as well as people where the best living environment was. The locals didn't want their peaceful neighbors, and with the help of the U.S. government, that lead to rapid decimation of prairie dog populations.

The most reckless attack on the prairie dog came in the form of mass poisoning. Cans of cyanide gas were tossed into the burrows, or strychnine pellets were left disguised as treats. Contaminated carcasses were often eaten, which killed unaware diners, including black-footed ferrets, wolves, and eagles to name a few. Other animals inhabiting the burrows fell victim to these cruel assaults as well. The prairie dogs that survived the various strikes lost their habitat to land-clearing machines such as the bulldozer.

Experts estimate that up to 99 percent of the once-vast prairie dog range remains cleared of these peaceful critters, leaving only a few million acres with surviving colonies. In fact, legal poisoning and shooting of prairie dogs continues to this day.

With the black-footed ferret's food source practically decimated, its demise rapidly grew closer. In 1960, people realized that the black-footed ferret population might be in danger, but by then it was too late. By the mid-1960s, the first in-depth studies began to indicate how grim the future looked for the black-footed ferret. In 1967, the black-footed ferret became legally protected — only 116 years after being given its official scientific name in 1851 by John James Audubon and John Bachman. And in 1973, the black-footed ferret was one of the first animals to be placed on the current endangered species list.

The last wild black-footed ferret was initially thought to have been seen in 1974, but a small group was discovered in Wyoming in 1981 after a dog presented an unusual and unfortunately dead animal to its bewildered human. The newly discovered colony flourished and reached almost 130 animals. However, the population was destroyed by 1985. Turns out that most of the prairie dog population feeding this hopeful Wyoming ferret colony tested positive for the rodent-decimating sylvatic plague, known to humans as bubonic plague, killing both prairie dogs and ferrets.

Even more tragic was the fact that canine distemper, 100 percent fatal to black-footed ferrets, swept through the fragile group. This was as big a factor in wiping out the black-footed ferret as was plague. The race was then on to capture the remaining wild black-footed ferrets. There we were! Only eighteen ferrets were left in 1987. They stood on the brink of extinction again. Between 1985 and 1987, the very last 18 black-footed ferrets were rescued. The last-known wild ferret was taken alive in February 1987 in Wyoming — that is, before the reintroduction of the critters began taking place.

The Black-Footed Ferret Recovery Plan

The monumental goal of the Black-Footed Ferret Recovery Plan, developed and approved by the U.S. Fish and Wildlife Service in 1988 and revised in 2013, is to establish no less than ten geographically separate populations of wild, self-sustaining black-footed ferrets. This plan calls for the establishment of 1,500 breeding wild black-footed ferrets in order for the species to be stepped down from endangered to threatened, and 3,000 breeding adults in order to be removed from the endangered species list.

With the dedicated help of member organizations of The Black-Footed Ferret Recovery Implementation Team (BFFRIT), created in 1996, this goal is slowly being recognized. These organizations work with the U.S. Fish and Wildlife Service and act as advisory teams. According to their website, www.blackfootedferret. org: "Through a team effort, the agencies and partners involved on the Black-footed Ferret Recovery Implementation Team will promote strategic public awareness, understanding, and support, resulting in the successful recovery of the black-footed ferret and the conservation of the ecosystem upon which it depends."

Once thought to be extinct in 1980, more than 9,500 have been produced in captivity since 1987. Responsible for this are: Louisville Zoo, Toronto Zoo, The National Zoo-Smithsonian Conservation Biology Institute, The Phoenix Zoo, Cheyenne Mountain Zoo, and The National Black-Footed Ferret Conservation Center. More than 4,000 have been released into the wild since 1991. Approximately 700 exist today. The people responsible for the Recovery Program have gained a greater understanding of captive breeding and have successfully used artificial insemination (AI) to preserve precious genetic diversity. Maybe that number will double or even triple in another 25 years.

Captive breeding

Only since 1991 have attempts been made to reintroduce this species into the wild through captive-breeding efforts. In the beginning, these efforts were met with sobering obstacles. From the limited gene pool of only 18 captive black-footed ferrets, to the inability to successfully rehabilitate captive-reared juveniles into the wild, to the lack of habitat for release, the future looked grim for the black-footed ferret.

Today things are looking up because much has been learned about raising black-footed ferrets in captivity. Although black-footed ferrets retain some instincts, such as killing and eating prairie dogs, burrowing, and recognizing and avoiding predators, those instincts aren't as sharp as they would be had they been born in the wild. After all, they've been in captivity for 30 years!

For this reason, captive-born kits are now sent to survival boot camp for a month and a half to learn how to survive in the wild. Living in semi-natural, but protected, communities, the ferrets are allowed to sharpen their skills by interacting with live prairie dogs and living in real burrows. Preconditioning routines and procedures such as these have increased the survival rate of captive-born kits released into the wild threefold. Additionally, some sites have even been successful at transferring wild ferrets from one site to another, which is important for maintaining genetic distribution.

Progress being made

In the beginning years, only three states participated in releases: Wyoming, South Dakota, and Montana. Today things are quite different. In the U.S., there are now 30 different black-footed ferret reintroduction sites located in eight different states: Arizona, Kansas, New Mexico, Colorado, Utah, South Dakota, Wyoming, and Montana. Mexico and Canada also participate in the reintroduction project. The sites must be located where significant prairie dog towns still exist, so this means mainly federal, state, and tribal lands, although some private landowners have welcomed this endangered species as well.

Hurdles in recovery

Nothing worth doing is ever easy. Some things are in man's control, while other things aren't. Although significant progress has been made in The Black-Footed Ferret Recovery Plan, several challenges still remain. Unfortunately, all must be conquered in order to win the battle of the black-footed ferret.

>> **Political:** This is perhaps the biggest and longest-standing threat facing the black-footed ferret. It's not even against the ferret itself, but rather against its food source — the prairie dog. The biggest myth is that livestock suffer broken legs from stepping in prairie dog burrows. The fact is, cows aren't that stupid.

People also don't want their livestock competing for grassland. There are even state laws that mandate you eradicate prairie dogs from your land. The county will do it if you don't and then send you a bill later! Political pressure still exists to poison prairie dogs even on America's public lands. No prairie dogs. No food. No ferrets.

>> **Biological:** Black-footed ferrets are highly susceptible to both plague and also canine distemper. All states within range of black-footed ferrets have documented plague at some point in time. The Recovery Program is currently experimenting with a human plague vaccine to protect the black-footed ferret. Each ferret caught is given a series of two shots over a two week period. Although this vaccinates the ferrets, it doesn't help the prairie dogs. So, they use other tools, such as insecticide dust, to kill plague-transmitting fleas in prairie dog burrows. The Recovery Program is also experimenting with an oral vaccine to mass vaccinate prairie dogs.

>> **Economic:** This hurdle comes up almost everywhere help is needed. There simply isn't enough money to keep people in place to do what's needed. Finding more sites to put ferrets on also takes money, and raising money takes money. Without funding, the Recovery Program is doomed.

>> **Social:** Public awareness and education are missing components to the Recovery Program. How can anyone help a program they don't understand or even know about? Most people don't even know what a black-footed ferret even is. Says Travis Livieri of Prairie Wildlife Research, "Black-footed ferrets belong to every citizen, and it is our duty to restore this species." The people responsible for the Recovery Program need to do more public outreach. They need to view education as being as important as the recovery process itself.

Black-footed ferrets are one of the most recoverable species on the endangered species list. They're the "panda" of the prairie. The prairie dog is the keystone of the prairie. By preserving the prairie dog ecosystem, we're not only saving the black-footed ferret, we're also saving the swift fox, burrowing owl, ferruginous hawks, and mountain plover. They're all directly linked to prairie dogs. Bison and antelope also thrive in the prairie dog ecosystem. You can make a difference in saving these animals.

Although the government recognizes that the survival of the black-footed ferret depends directly on the survival of prairie dog colonies, some aspects of the government continue to support the mass killing of prairie dogs. It's possible that because the black-footed ferret is a specialized hunter and hasn't adapted to an alternate diet, people may soon lose these beautiful critters forever.

So, what can you do? First, you can learn about the prairie — what it is and its history. Did you know that you own a part of the prairie? It doesn't matter where you live! Find out which zoos have black-footed ferrets, and visit one of these magnificent creatures. Write to or call your local conservation office to find out how you can become directly involved in the fight to save your local prairies. And if you live in a state where prairie dogs reside, step forward and take action. Find out what you can do to help protect the prairie dog's future. And don't forget, you can go to www.blackfootedferret.org for more information on this phenomenal program!

Chapter **3**

Ferrets and the Law: Licensing and Other Issues

Some of you may be just beginning to develop a mild adoration of fuzzies; others have a fully developed love for the creatures that have melted the hearts of millions. The point is you care for the little critters, so it may surprise you to learn that ferrets actually are illegal in some cities and in some states as a whole. Places where ferrets aren't welcome or are downright illegal are called *ferret-free zones*. Likewise, *ferret-friendly zones* are places where ferrets are safe from the politicians and other ferret haters. The classification of your living area depends on how your local government categorizes the ferret.

This chapter explains how you can find out whether having a fuzzy is legal where you live. Obviously, you should obtain this information before you take a ferret into your heart and home. You may be surprised to find out that you may even need a license for your ferret, so I talk about that too. I also show you the rationale behind outlawing these critters, and I present the ramifications of being caught red-handed with a fugitive furball.

"A License? But He Can't Even Reach the Pedals!"

Some cities and states require that owners obtain licenses or permits for their ferrets. A license can be free (such as in my state of Illinois), or it can cost as much as $100 per year. In some places, fees are per ferret, so be sure you double-check the rules for your area by first calling your state's department of natural resources or fish and game department (whatever the state department is called). Next check with the county animal regulations, and finally your township. To get a license for your ferret, if even needed at all, you must follow the procedures provided by your governing entity.

Some permits are just useless pieces of paper, but not all permits come free of strings. For example, some require that you don't have children under a certain age in your household if you want to bring home a ferret, and some require proof of vaccinations and/or neutering/spaying.

Some states and cities don't regulate ferret ownership at all; however, that doesn't mean they look upon ferrets as welcome guests. Where ferret tolerance is low, confiscations or fines may be imposed routinely or randomly. Unfortunately, some cities are very confused; they say that permits are necessary to breed and/or sell ferrets but that it's illegal to own them. Huh? It can seem at times to be a conspiracy on the part of a few against the many ferret lovers. This is something we must deal with; all you can do is arm yourself with information, and jump through the necessary hoops.

Ferret-Free Zones and Why They Exist

Although the United States Department of Agriculture classifies ferrets as domesticated critters, some rogue state agencies still insist that domestic ferrets are wild animals. Others say that ferrets aren't wild animals but rather exotic animals. Still others believe that ferrets are domesticated but hold firmly to the idea that they're dangerous. Well, I'm here to tell you, without a doubt, the ferret is domesticated. But because many states regulate wild and exotic animals, and these states lump the poor ferret in where it just doesn't belong, ferrets end up getting regulated or discriminated against.

REMEMBER

For instance, California and Hawaii are the remaining U.S. states that continue to outlaw ferrets (many military bases all over the country also ban furballs). However, just because your state lists ferrets as legal doesn't mean your city does. Many major cities, such as New York, and some smaller cities remain in the dark ages as ferret-free zones. New Jersey requires an exotic animal permit for ferrets! The United States isn't the only nation with ferret issues. In 2002, New Zealand passed a law banning the sale, distribution, and breeding of ferrets. In Australia, ferrets are banned in Queensland and the Northern Territory. And South America has some pretty bizarre ferret laws as well! (Check out the section "Knowing the Law and the Consequences of Breaking It" to find out where to get this information.) While the lovable ferret continues to get wrapped up in bureaucracy, dedicated ferret freedom fighters continue to do their best to mow down misconceptions in the hopes of protecting and legalizing ferrets everywhere.

You may wonder how ferrets — these captivating bundles of energy and joy — can be such a source of controversy. It all lies in the myths and misconceptions department, as the following sections explain.

CALIFORNIANS UNITE!

One thing ferret people have in common is their devotion to their beloved pet ferrets, and Californians are no different. Ferrets have been illegal in their state since 1933 simply because some yahoo from the California Fish and Game Commission (FGC) accidentally included ferrets in a list of banned wild animals in their statute titled "The Importation and Transportation of Live Wild Animals." And since then, nothing — but nothing — has been able to sway them to fix this oversight. But all it really means is that Californians have to fight much harder for their rights and the rights of their fuzzies. Several organizations have sprouted up over the years to help change the regulations in California and one is especially worth noting due to their diligence in challenging the government to get ferret ownership legalized:

Ferrets Anonymous (www.legalizeferrets.org) is a nonprofit grass-roots organization made up of California ferret enthusiasts who are working to promote awareness of the domestic ferret in conjunction with their efforts toward ferret legalization. LegalizeFerrets. org publishes a weekly email newsletter, CLIFFNotes (California Legalization Initiative for Ferrets), every Sunday. Subscriptions are free. Just send an email to CLIFFNotes@legalizeferrets.org and request to be added to the mailing list.

What's it gonna be? Wild, domestic, or exotic?

Perhaps the biggest misconception about ferrets is that they're wild or non-domesticated animals — no different from the neighborhood skunks and raccoons. The truth is that ferrets are domesticated animals and have been for thousands of years. Ferrets depend on their humans for survival, so how can certain governments classify them as wildlife? The answer probably lies in how scientists named them way back when.

Depending on your school of belief, the ferret is either a species all to itself *(Mustela furo)* or a descendant of the wild European polecat *(Mustela putorius furo).* The ferret is "scientifically" known by the latter distinction, which is the legal glitch that many governments have used to classify fuzzies as wildlife. Many labels come with being classified as "wildlife" — people believe wildlife to be dangerous, unpredictable, and a disease risk. Most cities and states deem wildlife illegal to keep or require special permits in situations of ownership.

The scientific name of the fuzzy isn't the only thing standing in your way in many places:

>> Some people consider ferrets to be wild because they look so much like their cousins: the minks, weasels, and polecats. But just because you may look like a famous athlete doesn't make you part of his team, right?

>> One of the world's most endangered wildlife species, the black-footed ferret, happens to have "ferret" in its name, though it is wild and our ferret isn't.

Feral ferrets in my neighborhood?

Perhaps the most outrageous misconception about owning ferrets — or unfounded paranoia, actually — is the fear that pet ferrets will escape, unite in the wild, form large feral (wild) colonies, and develop their own organized crime rings. Okay, maybe I'm exaggerating a bit. But some governmental suits actually believe the part about the development of feral colonies. These politicians preach the idea that these colonies of roving feral ferrets will destroy native wildlife and livestock.

Here are some reasons why the feral-ferret scenario is very unlikely:

>> Ferrets are domestic animals (see the previous section), and they rely on humans for survival.

>> The majority of ferrets entering the pet trade are spayed or neutered.

>> Ferrets are indoor pets and escape is unlikely.

REMEMBER

Many species of domestic animals are capable of going feral, but for a colony to form, their environment has to be just perfect for them, and they have to have the necessary skills. In particular,

>> There must be several feral breeders around to make more animals.

>> There must be an open environmental niche.

North America has few open niches left for small predatory mammals such as the ferret. The niches are already filled with more competitive mustelids (a ferret's cousins), such as the American mink and the long-tailed weasel.

>> The animal must know how to escape from predators and find food.

These are just a few of the many reasons why the likelihood of ferrets taking over your environment is very small.

Should people fear rabies?

Zero reports have been made of a ferret transmitting rabies to a human, and only a handful of cases of ferrets carrying rabies have ever been documented. In fact, dogs and cats are at much greater risk of being exposed to rabies, thus putting you at greater risk. The following points should further solidify your argument to others (and to yourself) that rabies isn't a significant risk in ferrets:

>> Ferrets have little opportunity to come in contact with rabies-infected animals in the first place.

>> Infected ferrets are thought to carry dumb rabies and die quickly after becoming infected. (To compare dumb rabies with furious rabies, see Chapter 15.)

>> Research has concluded that out of the skunk, raccoon, and fox strains (in Europe) of rabies, to which the ferret is naturally susceptible, only the raccoon strain was shed in the saliva. The ferret was also remarkably immune to the European fox strain.

TIP

An approved rabies vaccine is available for ferrets to alleviate the fear of the disease being present. Part of being a responsible ferret owner is having your lovable fuzzball vaccinated on a yearly basis (see Chapter 12). Most cities and states recognize the rabies vaccine developed for the ferret as being protective against rabies, so for your sake and your ferret's, keep proof of her vaccinations on hand. A bite from your ferret without proof of rabies vaccination can cost her her life.

Knowing the Law and the Consequences of Breaking It

Ferret ownership isn't legal or tolerated everywhere. You need to check with an appropriate and knowledgeable agency before you bring home a fuzzy to get the exact details pertaining to ferret ownership where you live. Doing so can save your ferret's life. A good way to find out whether your ferret is welcome in your city or living area is to call your local Fish and Game Department, Department of Conservation, or Wildlife Department.

Another good source of information is your local humane society, because it's the society's business to know the local laws pertaining to all animals. But perhaps the best source of ferret law is your local ferret club or shelter, if your area has one. This is probably the safest source that will give you the most accurate information. After all, ferret people have the most invested in keeping their ferrets safe. Finally, check with your veterinarian. He has probably been treating ferrets and should know the general laws pertaining to them.

WARNING

Please, please *don't* rely solely on the advice or opinion of a pet-shop employee or breeder when it comes to ferret law. Even if these folks know your local laws, they may not be forthcoming in providing accurate information to potential buyers. This isn't true of all pet-shop employees or breeders, but why risk it? If you must ask one of these sources, be sure to get a second and third opinion.

So, say you get caught red-handed breaking your local ferret laws. So what?

First of all, the danger to your little fuzzy is great. Some ferret-free zones won't hesitate to remove your furry family member from her safe, secure home for good. If your ferret is lucky, she may get shipped to a shelter in a ferret-friendly zone where her life can begin anew. If she's unlucky, though, her life will abruptly end — all because of your carelessness and unfortunate misconceptions. Confiscation of your fuzzy is basically inevitable, but you may also get slapped with fines. Some fines are pretty hefty — like $2,000 per ferret offense.

2

Finding Your Ferret and Hanging Up the Welcome Hammock

Chapter **4**

On the Tail of a New Carpet Shark (Um, Ferret)

Most people who want a ferret as a new family member have an image of what the perfect ferret is. Friendly, sweet, loving, playful, adventurous — those are just a few of the characteristics ferret lovers dream about. But when it actually comes down to choosing a ferret for your home, friendly, sweet, and all the other adjectives get you only so far. You also need to think in terms of health, gender, and even age. And when you have all those characteristics figured out, you should consider whether you want to get more than one!

This chapter helps you choose the perfect ferret for your home and your family. I explain what the normal and ideal traits are and warn about some characteristics to avoid. Some sections talk about the differences in genders and ages. You may be surprised by what you discover in this chapter! When you have an idea of what type of ferret you're looking for, you can start to look in the right places to seek out your dream fuzzball. You have several options to consider, all with pros and cons, and I cover them later in the chapter.

Ferret Shopping 101

If you're new to ferret ownership (welcome to the club!), it's important to choose a healthy ferret with a pleasant personality to bring into your home. Only someone more experienced in ferret care should have the confidence to care for a ferret that needs special attention. The following list presents some tips to keep in mind when shopping for your new fuzzy friend:

>> Her fur should be soft, shiny, and full. She should have no patches of missing fur.

>> Her eyes should be clear and bright. No discharge should be coming from the eyes, ears, or nose.

>> Her underside should be clean and healthy looking. Look for signs of diarrhea or bloating, which can be evidence of parasites or illness.

>> The ideal ferret is inquisitive when you approach; she doesn't cower or run to a hiding place. She should be jumpy and playful.

REMEMBER

Don't view nipping in a young ferret as a warning sign. Nipping is normal for a youngster. However, you should avoid a ferret that bites aggressively out of fear. You should be able to recognize the difference. Problem ferrets hang on when they bite and draw blood.

>> Color should be your last deciding factor because many coat colors and patterns have a tendency to change and lighten over time.

"BUT I FELT SO SORRY FOR HER . . ."

I can't tell you how many people bring animals to shelters, ferrets included, because they didn't think long enough about their decisions to take on such a responsibility. I always ask people why they acquired their pets in the first place when they come to our shelter (I'm the curious type), and many say that they felt sorry for the animals. Getting a pet out of sympathy rarely leads to a win-win situation. Caring for an animal you know inside and out and have prepared for is difficult enough; taking on an animal that you know little about or that has underlying problems can lead to frustration, anger, and a sense of hopelessness.

Many wonderful breeder ferrets, pet-store ferrets, and shelter ferrets need good homes. Some of these ferrets require special attention; most do not. For information on finding your perfect ferret, see the section "Where to Find Your Ferret" later in this chapter.

Are You in the Market for a New or Used Ferret?

The decision you make about how old you want your ferret to be should be based on your experience and lifestyle. Some people automatically think that they should start off with baby ferrets; they have many reasons, some of which just don't make sense. The thought that you must begin with a baby so that she'll bond with you doesn't hold true in the ferret world. Most adult ferrets adapt well to change and will love you no matter how long you've had them. Other people like to use the "I want little Johnny and the ferret to grow up together" reasoning.

The fact is, both adult and baby ferrets make good pets. The following sections help you make your decision.

Starting off with a kit

Baby ferrets, or *kits*, are absolutely adorable and hard to resist. They're delightfully bouncy and mischievous, with a seemingly endless supply of energy. Adults have their fair share of spunk, but kits are just a tad bit more energetic than their adult counterparts.

TIP

If you have small children, I recommend that a kit not be your first choice. If you're alone or have only one or two other adults in your household, and you have a lot of extra attention to give, a kit may be just what you're looking for.

If you don't have small children, here are some things to know about kits before you purchase one:

>> Because kits are more active and playful, they can be more demanding of your time. They're also notoriously nippy while still in the learning and testing stage. Kits can and will bite!

REMEMBER

Biting isn't cute and shouldn't be encouraged through play. It can get out of hand and become a behavior issue if you don't deal with it immediately. To find out how to deal with biting, see Chapter 20.

>> You'll need to train and socialize a kit. You'll be the one who has to teach a kit what is and isn't acceptable.

>> You'll need to make sure that a kit has all her baby shots. Medically speaking, a baby fuzzy should already have received her first distemper shot by the time she goes home with you. She may need up to four shots, depending on how old she is and what medicine she's already received (see Chapter 12 for details).

Adopting an older ferret

Adult ferrets make wonderful pets. You don't have to purchase a ferret as a baby to get her to bond with you. An adult ferret will love you and display all the charisma and energy you could hope for. Unfortunately, thousands of wonderful adult ferrets wait patiently in shelters for homes simply because people believe that older ferrets are damaged in some way. Some people even dare to think that the adults aren't as cute as kits. I beg to differ! Almost all the ferrets I've owned have been hand-me-down adults. And each one, with its unique personality, melted my heart right away.

Families with smaller children, people looking for cuddlers, or even those of you who believe in rescuing before purchasing would make excellent homes for older ferrets. If this sounds like you, and you're thinking about adopting an older ferret, keep the following points in mind:

>> Because the life span of a ferret is relatively short (averaging 6 to 8 years), you may have less time to spend with an older or adult ferret. This isn't always the case, though. I've lost young ferrets to disease and had some of my older adoptees live years beyond the normal expectancy. The average life span is just something you may want to think about.

>> Generally speaking, older ferrets seem to be more relaxed with themselves and wiser to their surroundings, but they're still inquisitive and mischievous. Unless they fall ill, most adults are wildly amusing and playful. Some can get into just as much, if not more, trouble than their young counterparts! Adult ferrets just seem to have had the edge taken off.

>> Adult ferrets can be more set in their ways. Behavior difficulties, if they exist, can be more challenging to correct. Some adult ferrets have been neglected or abused, so they may need a little more understanding and patience. On the other hand, adults that have been treated well (and even some that have been neglected and abused) adapt well to new environments and have little or no difficulty bonding with their new humans.

REMEMBER

The majority of older ferrets have had at least one other caretaker. Most are already trained to use the litter box (see Chapter 19) and have been taught that nipping is unacceptable. However, adult ferrets that haven't been properly socialized may bite out of fear. If you decide that an older ferret is right for your home, take the time to play and socialize with the ferret(s) you consider for adoption. It won't take long to determine if any special needs exist, and then you must decide if you're capable of handling those needs.

Should You Pre-Order Blue or Pink Bedding (Get a Boy or Girl)?

A decision you have to make when looking to adopt a ferret is whether you want a male or female. This should be a minor role in your decision, because health and personality are the number one factors! Nature and nurture play roles in the physical and psychological make-up of each animal. Nature mostly defines the genetics of a species as a whole, defining its physiology and anatomy, as well as its sexual and social behavior. On the other hand, nurture, or environmental experiences influences such things as temperament, food preferences, and habits.

REMEMBER

Females are called either *jills* (unspayed) or *sprites* (spayed). Males are called either *hobs* (unneutered) or *gibs* (neutered).

Females typically are smaller and daintier than males. As boy ferrets mature, they tend to become more cuddly and couch-potato-ish. Females tend to remain more squirmish, as though they'd rather be anywhere else than in your loving grasp. I hate to hold fast to this stereotype, however, because I've had some females that were quite the opposite. Sometimes, all it takes to get a ferret — particularly a girl — to settle down is a bit of human intervention, such as rubbing her ear or another "grooming" gesture (see Chapter 9).

REMEMBER

Unless they're very sick or old, all ferrets are amusing bundles of energy with a propensity to please and make trouble, regardless of gender.

Pitting Altered versus Whole Furballs

Most ferrets that enter the pet trade come from mass ferret producers, so more than likely your ferret will already be neutered or spayed, negating a choice on your part. Sometimes the only way to know for sure is by a tattoo in the ear, though not all breeders tattoo their ferrets.

In the female ferret, spaying is a medical necessity. Unlike some mammals that go into heat for short periods of time, the female ferret stays in heat until she's bred. The unending heat cycle more often than not leads to a life-threatening condition called *aplastic anemia*. Spaying your ferret can save her life. In the male ferret, neutering is more of a behavioral necessity. It lessens aggression toward other male ferrets and urine marking on the ground (which also dramatically decreases the odor of boys).

Aplastic anemia is a condition caused by high levels of the hormone estrogen, which is produced when the ferret is in heat. A high level of estrogen suppresses the production of vital red and white blood cells in the bone marrow. As the disease advances, this suppression becomes irreversible. Secondary bacterial infections occur due to the lack of white blood cells to fight infection. The ferret's blood can't clot properly, so bleeding becomes a problem. Severe anemia sets in and an insidious death follows. Signs can be seen in ferrets that have been in heat for a month, and they can remain in heat for up to 6 months if unbred. How long it takes for aplastic anemia to kill a ferret depends on many variables.

If you plan to adopt a whole, or unaltered, ferret, you should have the altering procedure done by the time the fuzzy is 6 months old, unless you're planning to breed her. Commercial breeders alter their babies as young as 6 weeks old. Some people, however, suggest that males be altered as late as 12 months and females as late as 9 months so that they can reach full growth. Personally, I wait until 6 months for both the males and females.

Very few differences exist between altered male and altered female ferrets. In fact, every altered ferret I've ever met had his or her own unique personality that was unrelated to gender or age. All ferrets are amusing, hyper to various degrees, and easy to please, as long as you meet their needs. The following sections dig deeper into the behavior and characteristics of male and female ferrets and how they relate to sexual maturation.

Boys will be boys

You can identify your male as whole if his testicles begin to drop (appear) and his odor becomes stronger as the breeding season approaches. Like many animals, from the prairie dog to the moose, unneutered ferrets enter a period of breeding when all they can think about is passing on their superior genetic makeup. For ferrets, this breeding cycle may start in the spring and last six months, all the way until fall.

During the breeding season, males on the prowl can become aggressive toward other whole male ferrets, and sometimes towards their humans, too! During this period, a boy's weight also can fluctuate a great deal; he usually loses weight while staying preoccupied with the girls. Some males even become depressed or anxious if they fail to find the girls of their dreams for nights of unbridled romance.

For their own safety and the safety of cagemates, you should house unaltered males separately during mating season if you're not using them for breeding. But I suggest that you do them and yourself a favor and neuter.

Girls will be girls

Females, although less intent on finding the hobs of their dreams, enter a period of heat if left unaltered. You can easily tell whether your ferret is in heat because her vulva (genitals) swells a great deal from the increase in hormones.

REMEMBER

If you're faced with a female fuzzy in heat, your vet may choose to administer a hormone shot to bring her out of heat before spaying her. Or the vet may breed her to a vasectomized male to fake her out of heat before spaying her. Spaying your female while she's in heat is possible, but it's considered dangerous due to the risk of hemorrhaging.

WARNING

Swelling of the vulva can also be a sign of an incomplete or partial spay. Altering ferrets at a very young age can result in this rare surgical error. Unfortunately, a swollen vulva also is a common symptom of adrenal problems in a female ferret. Don't overlook a swollen vulva. If you have a ferret with this symptom, take a visit to an experienced ferret veterinarian; he'll yield the answers you need in order to proceed with the proper course of action.

"You Want *How* Many Ferrets?"

Perhaps you've already thought about what type of ferret you want, what gender you'd like, what kind of great cage you can make for your fuzzy, and so on; one question you may not have thought about, though, is how many ferrets to get, probably because you just assume that you'll get one. One ferret can be happy and content in a cage as long as she gets plenty of playtime out of the cage every day. However, if you have a busy schedule and your ferret won't get out of the cage as often as she should, you may want to consider getting two or three ferrets.

Quite a bit of controversy surrounds the social nature of our pet ferrets, which stems from the solitary nature of their cousin the wild polecat. One camp believes that ferrets, just like polecats, do not want or need the companionship of other ferrets, and thus forcing ferret companions on them may lead to unhappiness and stress. And we all know what stress does to the body! The opposite camp believes that ferrets are social animals and must have companions in order to thrive. So who is in the right? I personally believe the answer lies somewhere in the middle, but we, as caretakers, must read our ferrets with open minds when it comes to making the decision on whether to add another ferret, and to remember that each ferret is an individual.

TIP

Don't let the cost of food and supplies keep you from getting your single ferret a roommate. Cost of food and litter won't be that much more. If you're already caring for one ferret, housing two ferrets won't be that much different if that's the route you choose to go. In fact, having three is about the same! Now that I think of it, three can be a perfect ferret number (see the nearby sidebar for more). I used to think that one could never have too many ferrets. Experience has led me to change my mind. Groups of ferrets shouldn't exceed what a normal litter size would be — and the average litter size is five to eight kits. *The bigger the group, the more stress created.* If you'd like to adopt more than eight ferrets, you should consider breaking them up into groups.

Most, but certainly not all, altered ferrets will get along with other altered ferrets with little or no problem (see the previous section for more on altering your ferret). Sure, they'll go through their share of aggressive squabbles and fighting for hierarchy, but they'll eventually develop a bond. Even though ferrets have a deep-rooted solitary instinct, they'll come to view other ferrets as littermates and play and bop around accordingly (see Figure 4-1). As usual, there are exceptions to the rule, so you'll have to intervene when introductions and living situations go sour (see Chapter 7 for more on dealing with ferret introductions and living situations).

FIGURE 4-1:
Ferrets can make good companions for each other and usually play well together.

TECHNICAL STUFF

Ferrets aren't territorial to the extent that dogs are, but they are territorial critters by nature. In the wild, polecats are solitary and mark territories and chase off other polecats of the same gender. In a cage, ferrets have little microterritories and squabble over seemingly insignificant things. Although multiple ferrets usually share just about everything, from the water bottle to the litter box to the sock stolen right off your foot, they do make claims to certain things (such as a section on their beds).

Statistically speaking, it's easiest to introduce one gender to the opposite gender. (And all introductions should be made with altered ferrets, unless you want to have many more.) There tends to be more acceptance if you go this route. Introducing an altered boy to an altered boy also has a high success rate. Surprisingly, a female ferret generally has the most difficulty accepting another female ferret. Keep this in mind when considering adopting multiple ferrets. You can't make any predictions, however.

REMEMBER

Quarantining is the crucial process by which you isolate your new ferret until you know he's healthy and safe to introduce him to your existing ferret(s) without risk of passing illness. A period of two weeks is usually acceptable. This means you'll need a separate quarantine cage in which to temporarily house your new guy. Quarantine also can:

>> Establish a new ferret into his home without the stress of other nosy ferrets that might fight with him and stress him out even more.

>> Provide the new ferret safe, private time to bond with you!

>> Afford the newcomer an opportunity to slowly switch to the food you feed your current ferret(s).

IS THREE GOOD COMPANY?

I've heard many tales of a ferret becoming severely depressed when her long-term cagemate died. This is where adopting three ferrets ahead of time comes in handy. Having three means the loss of one ferret won't leave the other ferret completely alone, and you'll have time to bring another ferret into your life, if you choose, and the lives of the surviving ferrets at your own pace. But that's just my opinion, and some people think I'm nuts! Ferret lovers often wonder how they started with three ferrets and quickly end up with seven or more. That, my friends, is called *ferret math*. It's what ferret lovers blame for the mysterious additions and multiplications of ferrets. It just happens!

If you already have one ferret and are considering adding another, do so with some caution:

>> Introduce new furballs in neutral territories with neutral toys, just to be sure there are no bad feelings off the bat. See Chapter 7 on introductions.

>> An older ferret may not find the antics and energy of a kit or an adolescent as amusing as you do. On the other hand, a younger ferret may be just what the doctor ordered for the sometimes lazy and depressed carpet shark, assuming no serious illness is going on.

>> It's not unusual for the more dominant ferret to act a little bullyish and make the first tackle. They may screech at each other with humped backs and roll each other for a moment or two. Tails may get puffed like pipe cleaners or bottle brushes. One may take all the toys and stockpile them in a guarded corner or hidey-hole. These aren't unusual acts associated with introductions.

>> Watch for the warning signs of true aggression, like ongoing screeching and puffed tails. There should be little to no screeching, and tails should return to normal size within 10 minutes of the initial meeting. If one or both ferrets is doing more biting and screaming than playing after 5 or 10 minutes, call it a day and try again later.

WARNING

It's unusual to have one ferret kill another, but occasionally you'll come across an oddball that just simply hates other ferrets and makes an honest effort to injure the other. These guys should remain single. One ferret drawing blood or literally scaring the poop out of another ferret indicates a serious problem, and a mismatch has definitely occurred.

REMEMBER

A *solitary ferret* is a ferret that has reverted back to normal adult polecat behavior in terms of accepting other ferrets. In other words, she wants to live alone! Face it, ferrets are individuals, and a fair percentage just won't tolerate being with other ferrets. If you have such a fuzzy, you'll have to keep her separate from the others.

The bottom line is this: One ferret is amusing; two or more ferrets are a stitch. In and out of the cage, multiple ferrets wrestle and tumble together. They chatter and screech and fuss about. They steal each other's treasures and then collapse together in a cuddly pile until one decides to start the routine over again. If you're even questioning how many fuzzies to bring home, get at least two if they already get along!

Where to Find Your Ferret

You can adopt or purchase a ferret from many places and from many people. Where you go depends on your priorities, what you're looking for, and how far you're willing to go to get your ferret (to the ends of the earth, no doubt!). Pet shops and breeders are the places to go for kits, though shelters and private individuals may have them at times. Shelters and private individuals will have your adults, but pet shops and breeders may often have adults up for sale on occasion as well. To minimize the pains of introductions and quarantining, if you opt for bringing home more than one ferret, consider getting them from the same source. Almost all the sources I mention will offer multiples for sale or adoption. The following sections present the many different locales where little fuzzies are waiting for you as you read.

REMEMBER

No matter where they come from, most ferrets are very adaptable to new people and new environments. If you're generous with your time, patience, love, and ferret-friendly treats, you'll have a friend for life.

Perusing pet shops

Perhaps the most commonly thought of source for buying a ferret is the local pet shop. The goal of a pet shop is to sell to customers, not to make your life with a ferret harmonious, so you need to do your homework on the ferret and research your local pet shop before buying a new carpet shark. The following list presents some things to think about if you plan to get your ferret from a pet shop:

>> Pet shops are convenient, but your choice can be limited, because they usually only have a few commercially bred kits (baby ferrets) at any given time.

>> The majority of the kits come from mass producers (ferret farms). Occasionally, a pet shop will buy kits from a local breeder. You may even find an older fuzzy that wasn't bought as a kit or whose previous owner returned her.

REMEMBER

The majority of pet shop ferrets originate from mass producers or ferret farms where kits are removed prior to being weaned from mom. They may lack critical ferret socialization and behavior skills, which momma ferret teaches during the weaning period. You, as a new owner, may need to pick up where mom left off.

>> You may or may not get a health guarantee with your purchase of a ferret from a pet shop.

I suggest that you request a written health guarantee; if the pet shop refuses, look elsewhere for your ferret. Reputable pet shops usually sell healthy animals and therefore should be more than willing to offer written health guarantees.

>> Pet shops may be more expensive than many shelters. The expense may be well worth it if your ferret is in top health and has a great personality to match!

>> In good pet shops, workers play with the kits frequently to ensure proper socialization, and members of the staff have been trained extensively in the care of the animals they sell.

In less than desirable pet shops, staff members leave kits in their cages until potential buyers ask to see them. This practice can lead to poor socialization at a critical point in the ferrets' lives. In these pet shops, employees may be unknowledgeable in the care of specific animals, which causes them to recite misinformation to unknowing customers, and the shops won't offer solid after-sale support.

You need to find out whether the pet shop you're considering is one of the good ones; keep the following bits of advice in mind:

>> Don't purchase a ferret on your first visit. Make several visits to see how the staff truly cares for the animals.

>> Pet shops should be clean and tidy, as should the animal cages that house the potential pets. The animals should look and act healthy and have clean food and water.

>> Employees should be knowledgeable about the animals customers inquire about, or they should be willing to seek out the correct answers to questions. They should be sensitive to your concerns regarding ferrets without displaying the "sell sell sell" attitude.

I suggest that you see if the pet shop has printed educational materials about ferrets — for example, the pros and cons of having one, the guidelines to determining if a ferret is suitable for you, and information on general care. You can get and look over this information ahead of time to test the employees' level of knowledge about the pets they sell. However, a knowledgeable employee does not necessarily make for a knowledgeable pet shop, so look for warning signs that can lead to unhealthy ferrets, such as poor bedding, crowding, improper diet, or a supply of dirty water (or no water at all).

>> Try to find people who have purchased animals from your local shop and get their opinions. You also can check with the Better Business Bureau for prior complaints about the shop or call your local Humane Society to ask about the shop.

Picking out private breeders

A logical and common place to find a ferret for adoption is a private breeder — a private breeder can be an individual with a single breeding pair of ferrets or a fancy ferretry with up to a dozen breeding pairs. The biggest typically don't produce more than a dozen or so litters a year. Like pet shops, you can find good breeders and bad breeders. Locating a reputable breeder can be difficult because few private ferret breeders are out there. You can expect to pay two to three times more for a private-breeder ferret than a pet-store ferret.

TIP

A good source for finding ferret breeders is word of mouth in the ferret community, especially ferret clubs; other people may be able to point you toward respected breeders. Additionally, the Internet provides a wealth of information on ferret breeders and their ferretries. This latter option is a great starting place in your search for a private breeder, but remember: Buyer Beware. Do your research!

People breed ferrets for several reasons, and you must keep them in mind when trying to find a breeder. Some breed for money and profit; others breed because they love fuzzies; and for some, it's a combination of both. A good breeder will be very honest and up front with you about the responsibility of having a ferret as a pet.

REMEMBER

Although a good breeder should be pleasant and easy to talk with, you may end up feeling like you're the one being quizzed. This can be a very good thing. A breeder who's too eager to part with kits may be raising ferrets only for the profit and not for the well-being of the ferrets or the buyers.

Here are some more ways you can find out whether a breeder is reputable and a ferret lover:

» Try to get references from people who've bought kits from the breeder.

» If geographically feasible, travel to see the breeder's facility to get a sense of how the ferrets are kept.

» Ask the breeder about his motivation for breeding ferrets. A good breeder may say that he's breeding ferrets to improve the species.

» Ask the breeder about vaccination and vet schedules and any illnesses he has encountered with the ferret. Make sure, if you purchase a kit, that you get a written health guarantee from the breeder. An adoption (or purchase) contract should be available for you to see ahead of time.

» A good breeder will offer after-sales support. Ask if the breeder is willing to chat with you when you call with a question regarding your newly purchased baby.

» Ask about what happens if the ferret doesn't work out for you. Will the breeder take the ferret back? A responsible breeder will do this.

MY, WHAT BIG FERRETS YOU HAVE!

Private breeders often produce bigger ferrets than commercial ferret breeders or pet shops, usually because private breeders don't neuter/spay their babies early. Hormones play a role in growth . . . well, let me clarify this a bit. Early neutering causes males to be smaller due to lack of estrogen. However, this same lack of estrogen due to early neutering actually causes females to be *larger*. Most commercially bred ferret babies are altered at 6 weeks after birth.

Ferrets from private breeders usually are altered at the new owners' expense and discretion. A reputable breeder will discuss your options with you.

Note: A good breeder may have only one or two pairs of breeding ferrets, or he may have many more. Although you certainly don't want inbred ferrets, the amount of breeding pairs doesn't tell you if he does or doesn't practice good breeding.

REMEMBER

Purchasing a kit from a private breeder may have several benefits. *Reputable* breeders spend critical extra time socializing their kits and helping them to be good pet prospects. In addition, these kits may be exposed to various healthy food options during the weaning process so that new owners have less of a challenge moving their ferret between food items when they bring their new baby home.

Adopting from a ferret shelter

Perhaps the most overlooked location for adopting a wonderful pet ferret is a ferret shelter. At a shelter, you can find ferrets of all colors, patterns, and personalities. Some are youngsters that proved too energetic for their uneducated owners. Others are past their life expectancies and need gentle and loving homes for their final months. Some have been abused and/or neglected and require experienced, patient ferret homes. Others have been well cared for until their surrender. Many shelter fuzzies have special needs, such as daily medications or special feedings.

REMEMBER

If these things sound good to you, a shelter may be the perfect place for you to look. The number of ferrets that wind up in shelters is overwhelming. No matter what type of ferret you're looking for, a shelter is bound to have her. Adopting a ferret from a shelter is a great way to support the ferret cause. Want an extra perk? An adoption may mean a membership to the shelter's ferret club (if it has one). Membership could include newsletters, ferret shows, holiday parties, and fundraisers. So, along with adding a wonderful new family member, you get the chance to meet other furball fanatics and make a connection to a lifelong support group.

If you're considering getting your ferret from a shelter, heed the following information:

>> Shelters rely on ferret adoptions for financial assistance and to make room for incoming fuzzies. Many shelters have no less than 60 ferrets at any given time. Adoption fees at shelters usually are lower; they vary depending on the age and health of the ferret being adopted.

>> Most people work in the business of ferret rescuing and sheltering only because of their undying devotion to ferrets, so you don't have to worry about greedy or negative motives.

>> Expect shelter operators to conduct friendly yet thorough interviews with potential adopters. That's good and necessary in the shelter business. The job of the shelter folks is to put their ferrets into lifelong, loving homes. They want to find the best families for these homeless fuzzies.

>> Many shelters may have certain restrictions or requirements that breeders and pet shops may not have. For instance, almost all shelters require that the owners return the ferrets to the shelters if the relationships don't work out. Some have age restrictions on young children. Others want proof from landlords that ferrets are allowed. And still others require the entire family to be present for the adoption process. Every shelter has its own process.

>> Most ferret shelters have veterinarians who work closely with them to monitor the health of the ferrets in their care. Some shelters have blood work performed on older fuzzies just for peace of mind.

WARNING

I hate that I even have to mention this, but the ferret world, and even the animal world in general, is plagued with "pop-up" shelters. They spring up for various reasons, whether they're organized by people wanting free or cheap animals, so they tag themselves as shelters or they're organized by people who get in over their heads with their animals and label themselves as shelters in an attempt to collect money for vet care, food, and supplies. Additionally, a 501(C)3 or non-profit status means nothing about how the ferrets are cared for. Please research the shelter you intend to adopt from or even surrender your pet to. At the very least the shelter should be very open for a visit so that you can see firsthand how the ferrets are cared for.

>> Most ferret shelter staff members are highly knowledgeable in ferret husbandry and are eager to extend after-adoption support — when they aren't up to their elbows in work! After your adoption, you're bound to make friends with the shelter workers, which means a lifetime of support and continuing knowledge.

TIP

Are you starting to look for that perfect shelter ferret but don't know where to go? Start surfing the Web to research nearby ferret shelters. Here are a couple great places to start:

>> `www.ferret.org/links/shelters.html` (The American Ferret Association)

>> `www.ferretshelters.org`

Both sites keep up-to-date lists of ferret shelters around the world.

TIP

Still not sure if a ferret is the right pet for you? I have the perfect solution! Consider volunteering at a nearby ferret shelter, if even for just a day, to get some more insight into the character and habits of these amazing critters. Ferret operators and volunteers are usually quite upfront about the pros and cons of ferret ownership, as the last thing they want is for a ferret to be returned to the shelter. Their goal is to place ferrets into the right forever homes. They will certainly appreciate your help, as well!

Craigslist and other classified debacles

Craigslist and newspaper classified ads or the bulletin boards at veterinary clinics or pet shops can be wonderful sources for ferrets in need of homes. They can also be nightmarish emotional and financial set-ups for unknowing first time or newer ferret owners if they don't know exactly what they're getting in terms of ferret health and behavior. If you live in a larger city (one where owning a ferret is legal; see Chapter 3), it isn't uncommon to come across posted signs or ads for ferrets that need new homes. Sometimes, the sellers will be willing to part with cages and supplies as part of their fees.

Most often, the ferrets being sold through ads are older. The good news is that a previous owner can usually provide a wealth of background information on a particular ferret, if they are being upfront and honest, which you may not be able to get when adopting through other avenues. If you're hoping to adopt from a private individual who can provide as much background information as possible on your new ferret, adopting through an ad may be for you.

In these situations, you're most likely not going to get the niceties such as pre-purchase vet visits or health guarantees. The ferret(s) will come "as is," and "as is" frequently comes with the cage and all supplies. The adoption fee usually is worth that alone. The ferrets themselves should be outwardly healthy and have good temperaments.

Buyer beware: Like a pet shop, a private seller's ultimate goal may be getting rid of the ferret and getting cash in hand as soon as possible. Many sellers, though, are kind animal lovers who just want their fuzzies to go to more appropriate homes and want to recuperate some of their initial investments.

Rescuing the wayward weasel: Stray ferrets

Unfortunately, some people will find stray ferrets that are lost or have been abandoned by their previous caretakers. Always be cautious with a found ferret because you don't know what she's been through. She's likely scared and hungry and probably is very confused. She doesn't know if your intentions are good or bad, and she may bite out of fear or defense.

Ferrets are susceptible to rabies, so take this into consideration and take proper precautions if you find a stray ferret. The first thing you should do is protect yourself from being bitten and take the ferret to the vet for a complete checkup. Remember that the ferret doesn't need to have bite wounds for it to have been exposed to the rabies virus. Next, follow the proper quarantine procedures for a minimum of two weeks, housing the ferret in her own cage several rooms away from your other ferrets, feeding and cleaning her last, and wearing a different shirt over your clothes while handling that ferret.

Handle the ferret very cautiously, because if you're bitten, she'll need to be quarantined at the vet for a minimum of ten days, as required by most states for your own safety. Some states still require that the ferret be euthanized and be tested for rabies because her vaccination status is unknown.

If you find a lost ferret, you should make every attempt to find her home because someone may be grieving the loss of this little furball. Place an ad in your local paper and post notes on bulletin boards at pet shops, veterinary clinics, and other high-traffic areas. Many large newspapers allow you to place lost-and-found ads free of charge for up to one week. Be sure to leave out some specific identifying information in the ad so that the real owner can prove his or her ownership.

A found pet does not equate to "finders keepers!" Someone is most likely missing or even grieving their missing little guy. Nowadays, many lost-pet websites exist on the Internet, including several on social-media platforms such as Facebook. These may be great places to start looking for your found ferret's family. Beware of *flippers:* people who claim to be the owners only to turn around and sell the ferret once they've claimed it. Also, scammers looking for free pets may step up claiming to be the ferret's owner. For this reason, do not post identifying markings or behaviors. Quiz the owner and be sure to ask for proof of ownership before turning the ferret over.

Nowadays, microchipping domestic pets has become common procedure. A microchip can help you rescue a lost animal by tying the unique chip number to the owner. If you find a stray ferret, take the animal to your local veterinarian to have her scanned for a chip.

If the weeks go by and you don't find her home, you may decide that you want to keep her. Be sure to quarantine her before introducing her to your other fuzzies. She may be sick or have fleas. A trip to the vet with your newly found friend is a must. If you don't find her home and you can't keep her, don't abandon the little fuzzy. You can contact many excellent ferret shelters that would be more than happy to find your friend a proper home. You can also place an ad for the many ferret fanatics out there who may reply quickly to the chance to adopt a new pet.

Some people mistakenly identify minks and long-tailed weasels as ferrets. I've gone out on more than my fair share of stray ferret calls where I've come home with minks. Although these wild animals are awfully cute, minks can pack a powerful bite and shouldn't be approached. Be sure the critter you're "rescuing" is indeed a ferret!

Getting a Vet

Every ferret has different medical needs, and not all veterinarians are trained equally when it comes to the health and well-being of ferrets. Although ferrets are the third most popular carnivorous pet in America — topped only by dogs and cats — they're far less popular in the vet's office. Some vets just don't like ferrets; others get hung up on the common misconceptions people have about carpet sharks. Start off with recommendations from other ferret owners, or call your local ferret shelter to see who they use. If you're part of an online ferret group, start fishing for names of good vets that are in your area. It might even be worth a longer drive if it means getting to the right vet.

It's important to seek out a veterinarian who's comfortable and experienced with ferret medicine before you bring a new fuzzy into your home. You want to ensure that your ferret will have the best routine medical care available. More importantly, you won't jeopardize your pet's life while doing the panic shuffle if an emergency arises. You'll have done your research, and you'll know who to call.

To find out what to look for in a veterinarian and what questions to ask before you enlist his or her services, head to the chapters in Part 4.

Chapter **5**

Home Sweet Home: Preparing Your Ferret's Quarters

Before you bring your new ferret home, you should be completely prepared for his arrival. If you're all set for your new bundle of joy before he arrives, you'll spend less time "ferreting" for forgotten items and more time bonding with your baby.

This chapter presents the must-haves for your ferret to live comfortably and safely in your home, as well as the accessories that will enrich his quality of life. You find everything you need to know about ferret accommodations: from the house and furniture to the bathroom accessories and wardrobe. If you already have a ferret and all the necessary accommodations, please read this chapter anyway to make sure you haven't forgotten something. With so many things to think about, overlooking an item or two is easy.

Setting Up Fuzzy's Cage

Preparing the cage is where true fuzzball lovers often show their fanatical yet creative sides. Cages range from simple, single-level ranches to multilevel mansions with guesthouses. The cage you choose depends on your taste and what you can afford, both financially and spatially. The effort in choosing is worth it, though. After all, your ferret has to stay in his house when he's not out playing, so you should work on creating as stimulating an environment as possible. The following sections cover the necessary cage considerations, from size to location.

REMEMBER

Ferrets are carnivores. You should house ferrets only with other ferrets or by themselves. Although most pet ferrets don't recognize small animals as food, they may play small animals and birds to death. Many ferrets, though, have a strong predatory urge. I've known people who've lost rats, mice, sugar gliders, birds, and guinea pigs to pet ferrets. If you insist on interaction between your ferret and other animals, supervise them closely and cautiously.

Size matters: Picking the proper cage

The cage for one or two ferrets should be at least 3 feet wide x 2 feet deep x 2 feet high. This size is the absolute minimum. For households with more ferrets, I suggest going to multilevel cages. As with most pets, the bigger the cage, the better. Whatever size you choose, be sure your fuzzy's cage has enough space for a playroom, kitchen, bedroom, bathroom, and, of course, your baby. You wouldn't want to eat, sleep, and play in your toilet, and neither would your ferret.

Fuzzy blueprints: Making sure the design is right

Many, many types of pet cages are more than adequate for your ferret. Due to the complexity of the ferret's housing needs, though, ferret owners really should consider bringing in the custom ferret cage. This can be a cage special made by professionals or built with your own bare hands if you have the skills and talent. I recommend two things, however. First, make sure the doors are big enough so that you can put a larger litter box or even a nest box in the cage. And, if you do include larger doors, make sure you attach extra door latches to prevent gaps and escapes.

Construct a cage on your own, or with professionals, that fits all your ferret's needs. I present the keys to a good cage in the following list, and I go into greater detail in the sections that follow:

>> **Ample size:** The floor space should be roomy to allow for ample playing and comfortable snoozing.

>> **Good ventilation:** Poor ventilation combined with stinky, damp patches of urine and stool can lead to illness and disease.

REMEMBER

Avoid aquariums and similar enclosures for housing your ferret. These habitats lack proper ventilation and can cause serious illness. Besides being too small and cramped for an active carpet shark, they're made for fish, not ferrets!

>> **Small openings between wire and secure doors:** Ferrets are master escape artists. They'll try to stick their heads into or through any opening they can get their snouts into. They can and will push open doors with their heads.

WARNING

Severe injury or even strangulation can occur in an unsuitable cage. Make sure that your cage design features no large openings and that, if necessary, snap bolts reinforce the doors on the cage (*snap bolts* are the snaps at the end of a dog leash; see Figure 5-1).

>> **Sturdiness and easy access for cleaning:** Certain ferret cages come with pull-out trays to catch the litter and food crumbs that fall to the bottom. If you're lucky, you'll find or build a cage that has a built-in metal litter box that pulls out.

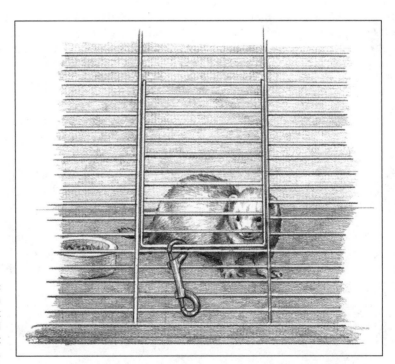

FIGURE 5-1:
Snap bolts can keep your ferret safely confined when you can't supervise him.

Materials

Perhaps the best types of ferret cages are made of sturdy galvanized wire. I prefer the black vinyl-coated wire because it's not only decorative but also easier on your ferret's feet. If the cage's floor is made of wire, be sure the little squares are no bigger than ¼ inch x ¼ inch. Ferrets have little feet, and spaced wire can be hard on their sensitive pads. And you certainly don't want anything wide enough for your ferret's feet to fall through.

TIP

A company I simply love is Kritter Koncepts, run by Barry and Kathy Fritz in Cambridge, WI. They make custom black vinyl-coated wire cages that are both attractive and affordable. You can reach Kritter Koncepts at 608-423-3124, or you can view their website at www.kritterkoncepts.net. If you're not up to waiting for a custom cage, I would suggest a bigger Ferret Nation or Critter Nation Cage.

In order to prevent injuries to ferret toes and feet, all wire cage floors absolutely must be covered. Otherwise, your ferret may end up with foot sores, broken toes, or worse! To keep your ferret's feet happy, consider the following options:

REMEMBER

>> You can cut a piece of carpeting and fit it into the bottom of the cage. If you use carpeting, you must take it out and wash it thoroughly or replace it as necessary. Dirty bedding usually accounts for most ferret odor, so your nose will tell you when the time has come!

You need to supervise ferrets with carpeted cages. They love to dig at the fibers, and some ferrets find the fibers simply delicious, which can be dangerous. Also, be aware that your ferret can snag its claws on carpet fibers and other fabrics, which may cause him to become trapped or injured. Keeping his nails trimmed will help (see Chapter 9), but it won't necessarily prevent this problem.

>> You can use a fitted piece of linoleum flooring or Plexiglas to cover the floor. I like the linoleum because it's flexible and the easiest surface to clean.

WARNING

Cages made of wood are impossible to completely sanitize, because the material is porous and easily absorbs urine. Your ferret may chew and ingest the wood, or damage to the teeth may occur. And certain treated woods can contain harmful chemicals. Three strikes, you're out! Likewise, certain metal surfaces may contain lead and zinc (which is just as toxic as lead; most cages no longer have lead, but the galvanizing process may still include zinc); when ingested, these materials can be harmful to your ferret. Do your cage research before you dish out the money to save yourself a pile of trouble in the end.

One story or multilevel?

Although a single-level cage will do the job, it just doesn't seem appropriate for the captive lifestyle of a ferret (see the chapters in Part 1 for basics on the ferret lifestyle and Part 5 for more on ferret psychology). Ferrets are active and inquisitive. And as ground dwellers, they love to burrow under piles of stuff. But they also enjoy racing up and down the ramps in a multilevel cage like the one in Figure 5-2. Multilevels also add more opportunity for you to attach cage accessories that are almost as important as the cage itself (see the later section "Acquiring Accessories and Other Stuff Fuzzy Needs").

FIGURE 5-2:
Most ferrets greatly appreciate multilevel cages.

Here are some factors to consider when creating/purchasing a multilevel cage:

>> The ramps in a multilevel should be made of wire (covered with a fabric ramp liner) because solid plastic ramps act more like slides than ladders.

>> Multilevel cages should have multiple doors for you to access the different levels.

>> You should consider adding an attachable litter box to the upper level.

>> At some point during the routine cleaning process, you'll have to reach into the far corners of all levels of the cage, so be sure you can access them.

>> You should provide snap bolts at the doorway gaps for extra security, especially if the doors are made of flexible wire.

TIP

Leave the single level cages for the hospital cages or for those ferrets that may be injured or too old to navigate ramps safely.

A home within a home: Finding a place inside for the cage

Placement of his cage is vital to the health and happiness of your ferret. If you can, place the cage where he can see you several times a day. It should be a quiet, comfortable place, conducive to snoozing when necessary, but it shouldn't be so far out of the way that the fuzzy's forgotten in your daily routine. Some ferret lovers actually dedicate entire rooms to ferrets and their cages. When I kept my ferrets in my home, my cages were connected by colorful tubes. I never knew which ferret would be sleeping in which cage! Sometimes, as many as eight were piled snuggly onto one hammock, although I had four to five hammocks throughout my maze of cages.

HEADING OFF CAGE RAGE

Cage stress, also known as *cage rage,* is often associated with a ferret's inability to escape to a safe place. You can identify a ferret suffering from cage stress by watching his behavior. Some signs may include the following:

- Constant pacing back and forth

- Gnawing on the cage bars (which can ultimately result in canine tooth fractures)

- Scratching incessantly at a corner of the cage

- Sores on his head and face from trying to push his way out of his confines

- Destruction in the cage, including the tipping of bowls and litter boxes, more so than "normal"

It's imperative that your fuzzy have somewhere dark and warm to hide and get away from all that's going on around him. You can use piles of fluffy bedding or a snooze sack, for example. Providing safety and security helps prevent cage stress. If you have a particularly nervous ferret (see Part 5 of this book for more on ferret psychology), you can cover part of his cage with a sheet or large towel.

Wooden parrot nest boxes can make great hidey-holes and sleeping spots for ferrets. In addition, a nest box can make for a fun climbing experience. Insert a few cuddly pieces of bedding into the box, and place the box into the cage or your ferret's play area. Watch for wood chewing. If you notice a lot of wear and tear, replace the box or scrap the idea altogether. Also, wood is porous and difficult to clean. Ferrets generally don't poop or pee where they sleep, but the young, sick, or disabled may be the exceptions to that rule. Check the nest boxes frequently for soiling and throw them out if they do become dirty. The urine will also eventually release ammonia, which is unhealthy for a ferret to breathe.

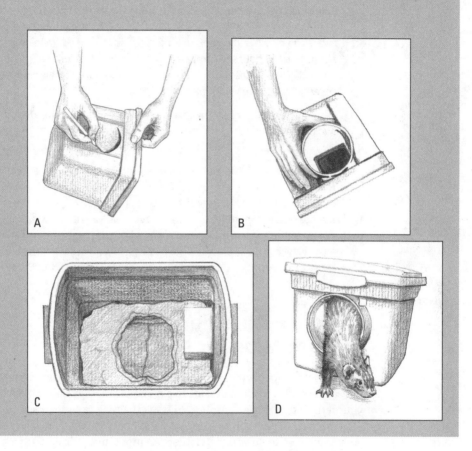

Here are some other pointers and reminders on indoor cage placement:

>> **Extreme blowing air can cause your ferret to get sick.** Drafts, or air movement itself, don't make people or animals sick. Cold air blowing continuously on the cage isn't good; however, cool air is fine. Also, hot air blowing continuously on the cage isn't good. Extremes are the problem, not the air movement itself.

Putting a cage near an outflow vent of an air conditioner or furnace is bad because of the dust and debris that may be blown out during the first few seconds. This can cause respiratory irritation or infection. It may also cause eye irritations.

>> **High humidity without good ventilation will cause distress.** Basements and small, poorly ventilated rooms often are damp and great breeding grounds for bacteria. If you must house your ferrets in a high-moisture area, use a dehumidifier.

>> **Too much light will interfere with sleep cycles.** It's important to have a cage site that can be darkened at night. Erratic photoperiods and long light cycles can be a health problem for ferrets, so they need to be able to have about 10 to 12 hours of complete darkness. (See Chapter 16 for info on adrenal gland disease.) Another option is some sort of light-eliminating covering over the cage for part of the day.

>> **Loud noise will stress your ferret and interfere with the sleep cycle.** Avoid placing the cage next to televisions or stereo speakers. The loud noise is very disturbing and if used at night can interfere with the normal sleep cycle.

>> **Place the cage on tile if at all possible, and pull the cage at least 6 inches from the wall.** A ferret's toilet habits can get sloppy, and you'll most definitely be cleaning both the floor and wall surrounding the cage routinely. You may want to consider putting up a large piece of acrylic glass to cover the wall closest to the cage. If you absolutely must put the cage on carpeting, invest in more acrylic glass or place a large piece of linoleum under the cage. Ferrets love to scoot up into the corners of their cages and poop out the sides!

A room with a view: Finding a place outside for the cage

As more and more people recognize the importance of natural lighting for ferrets, ferrets have been moving outside to experience Mother Nature first hand. Housing your ferret outside is a complicated issue that needs a great deal of consideration on your part, in addition to extreme diligence to health and safety. Not only does your cage have to be completely escape-proof and at least partially covered, but your ferrets also need heartworm, flea, and tick protection. And cage placement is one of the most critical aspects of keeping ferrets successfully outside.

I keep my ferrets outside, and they come in for personal playtime. They thrive outdoors, but I pay close attention to their needs, checking on them two or more times a day. I also have more than one ferret, so they can cuddle when it's cool out. Outdoor housing isn't for the lazy or the scatter-brained caretaker. Here are some tips on outdoor cage placement:

>> **Extreme cold and cold wind can kill.** Below-freezing weather exposure without a heated sleeping area, or exposure to freezing wind, can kill your ferret. Placement of the cage in the sun during the winter months is totally acceptable. You can cover one side of the cage for shade but place the nest box in the sun. Additionally, you need more than bedding to keep him warm. Nest boxes packed with straw will work. Avoid cloth, because it can get moist and freeze. Cloth also is a poor insulator. Move food, water, and litter boxes close to the nest box so that he'll come out to eat, drink, and go potty. Also, use a heated water bowl. You can purchase one online so your ferret won't snorkel during cold months. The best protection, though, is considering housing him indoors during the extreme winter months.

>> **More dangerous than the cold is the heat of the sun and high humidity.** Although ferrets enjoy the warmth that sunlight provides, direct sunlight with no relief can be deadly. Ferrets can get heatstroke or heat exhaustion if kept in hot places, even for just a short time. A temp of 80 degrees Fahrenheit or higher — especially with high humidity — is dangerous for your ferret. Be sure you shade a large part of the cage at all times so the fuzzy can escape the sun's hot rays. Place your cage under the comforting shade of trees if you have them. And be sure the nest box is always in the shade. Also, consider adding a litter box filled with water as a nice pool. Placement of cages on hot decks is ill-advised. Again, you should consider moving your ferret indoors when the weather becomes hot or extreme.

>> **Fenced yards are optimal.** Keeping your ferret's cage shaded in a fenced yard will keep predators such as foxes, coyotes, and dogs from getting to your ferret. It will also keep your curious neighbors out, thus keeping your ferret safe.

TIP

Some people think keeping ferrets outdoors is abusive. If done properly, it can be very healthy for your ferrets. With the exception of talking briefly about building an outdoor supervised play area for ferret enrichment (see Chapter 10), this edition of *Ferrets For Dummies* doesn't go into the specifics of constructing permanent outdoor enclosures, due to the complexity of the topic. However, I can recommend a phenomenal book that discusses this subject in great detail and length to anyone serious about outdoor housing. It's called *Ferret Husbandry, Medicine and Surgery, 2nd Edition*, by John H. Lewington (Saunders/Elsevier Limited). Even if you keep your ferret outside for only a few months a year, the book is well worth owning.

WARNING

Of course, there are some places that you should just flat out avoid putting your ferrets:

>> **Garages:** These are full of danger. Besides being devoid of healthy natural lighting, many garages can get overly hot in the summer and lack necessary ventilation. Most people keep chemicals that give off harmful fumes, such as

gasoline, in garages. And cars coming in and going out certainly add to the dangerous pollution.

» **Decks:** These heat up like a stove. Have you ever tried to walk barefoot across a hot wooden deck in the summer? It's like walking across hot coals or hot asphalt. A cage placed on a deck in the summer will roast in the hot sun, even if it's covered.

Making Your Ferret's Bed

Ferrets absolutely love to tunnel and nestle in their bedding, so knowing what and what not to use is important. Whether you cover the cage bottom is up to you (see the earlier section "Materials"), but be sure to fill bedroom areas with plenty of old T-shirts, sweatshirts, pillowcases, or towels. You want to provide good snoozing sites and hiding places for your ferret. One neat piece of bedding is simple to make: Simply snip off the legs of an old pair of pants or blue jeans. You can also buy custom ferret snooze sacks and fabric tunnels at any major pet supply store or online ferret supply store, but if you're handy with a sewing machine, you can easily make them. These accessories are attractive and cozy.

You should wash all bedding regularly to aid in reducing odors. Keep a clean, fresh supply of bedding on hand to use when you're washing the dirty stuff.

TIP

Some ferret owners have a blast decorating their ferrets' cages with custom-made hammocks, snuggle sacks, hanging cubes, and shelf and ramp liners purchased from individual crafters. One such crafter, Anna Senka, has become a favorite of mine with her Etsy shop SenkaCraftFactory, from which you can order both people and ferret stuff at reasonable costs. Products are high-quality, durable, and adorable! SenkaCraftFactory even allows you to customize your orders. Two paws up!

WARNING

Inspect your ferret's bedding routinely. Some carpet sharks find cloth an irresistible delicacy and chew holes in the fabric. These ferrets shouldn't have cloth. The danger comes from the ferret actually swallowing chunks of cloth. You'll find that certain ferrets need stronger types of fabric, such as denim, to prevent "cloth grazing." Small holes also pose a danger when your ferret is playing or digging around to get comfortable. He's apt to poke his head through a hole, and if he twists and turns just right, he may find himself trapped, and strangulation may occur. So toss the holey stuff. Finally, raggedy fibers and materials like terry cloth can catch on long claws, so toss the raggedy stuff and avoid fabrics like terry cloth.

Setting Your Ferret's Table

Picking out your ferret's food and water supplies doesn't have to be as tedious as picking out good china as a newlywed. However, not all food and water dishes will live up to your ferret's high standards, and he may put them through a battery of destruction tests before you can finally settle on the best feeding tools. Ferrets are extremely cunning little buggers. The average ferret can master even the most ferret-proof dish — meaning almost all dishes can be flung about the cage, tipped over, chewed up, pooped in, dug out, or slept in. You need to find the best possible dish and attempt to outsmart your ferret by adding a few clever accessories to keep the food and water clean and in their dishes. Remember, it's all in the presentation! The following sections show you the way.

WARNING

Did you know that "whisker fatigue" is an actual condition that your ferret can develop? Whiskers are complex little ticklers and are actually highly sensitive touch receptors that reach far beneath the skin of your ferret to connect with its nervous system. Overstimulation of the whiskers, perhaps from rubbing against the sides of a food dish that's too narrow or deep, may cause your ferret to act out. He may paw at the bowl to get the food out (more than usual). He may even start refusing food or water from the bowls. Make sure the bowls you choose are wide enough to prevent whisker fatigue. A stainless steel bowl made by Midwest Snap'y Fit is a great choice!

Serving your ferret's food with a sturdy dish

Pet dishes come in just about every size, shape, color, and texture. Their makers guarantee amazing things, such as non-tippable, indestructible, and easy to clean. And for the average pet, these claims are true. But a ferret sees a challenge in all that surrounds him, and a simple food dish is no exception. You need to choose the dish that best suits your ferret's needs. Remembering a few things may make your purchase easier and more successful. In the following sections, I prepare you for the food challenge that lies ahead and give you some bowl options.

REMEMBER

Stay away from food dish materials such as flimsy plastic and unglazed pottery or ceramic. Stick with stainless steel, thick plastic, or heavily glazed ceramic.

Fuzzy feeding challenges

Your ferret is bound to find the one weakness of the bowl you purchase for him. Bowls are gnawed on, tipped, and tossed. They're buried in bedding and even in litter boxes. Almost any bowl, attached or detached, is subject to becoming a sleeping area. Unless you buy an itty-bitty bowl or have a ferret the size of a housecat, you'll just have to be amused with this enchanting trait.

Less amusing is how many ferrets love to dig their food out of their bowls. This is another trait you must learn to live with. If your ferret cage has multiple levels (see the earlier section "Setting Up Fuzzy's Cage"), you can place the food dish anywhere on the top level or put it away from the corners on the lower levels (ferrets like to poop in corners). You should discard contaminated food immediately. Likewise, a poopy food dish is an unsanitary food dish; wash it right away.

Attachable bowls

You can fasten small metal C-clamps from a hardware store around the bowl, hanger, and side of the cage to prevent dish tragedy (see Figure 5-3). Although attachable bowls don't prevent digging, they do work to prevent tipping and catapulting. You can also drill a couple of holes in a sturdy plastic dish and fasten it to the sides of the cage with cable ties or even thin wire.

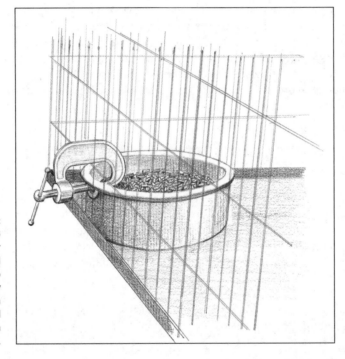

FIGURE 5-3: Use a C-clamp to secure your ferret's bowl, and you'll come to believe that they were made with the frenzied ferret owner in mind.

Another option is a wire dish hanger that simply hangs over the wire of the cage. If you choose this option, grab your pliers and bend the holder until it can't be lifted off the wire. Oftentimes, this type of holder falls prey to the "flip and tip" method of kill. With only the top fastened to the cage, the ferret can lift the bottom and fling the food out of the cage. A simple garbage tie or piece of wire can secure the bottom of the hanger to the cage, too.

Even attachable bowls have flaws. Not all are ferret-proof as far as becoming detached. The round stainless-steel bowls that fit snugly into an attached round wire hanger are great until the fit becomes just a tad loose. Being the predator he is, your ferret will sense the minute weakness of the dish. With a push and a shove of his back feet, a ferret lying on his back can easily flip the dish right out of its holder and into a soiled litter box. Quality ferret food certainly isn't cheap, so choose carefully the manner in which you present it to your ferret.

Weighted bowls

Unless your ferret is Hercules (and he may very well be), a heavily weighted dish or one made of a heavy material (such as thick ceramic) helps minimize the distance he can catapult the dish across his cage. If you can't fasten your ferret's bowl to the side of his cage, get the heaviest bowl possible — preferably one that's wider at the base to make it more difficult to tip over.

WARNING

Always place heavy ceramic bowls on the lowest level of the cage. On higher levels, these bowls can be quite dangerous if they're pushed off and tumble onto a fuzzy below.

Plastic bowls

If you're determined to buy a plastic food dish, make sure you purchase the heavy-duty type. The less porous the composition of the bowl, the more sanitary and easier to clean it is. Avoid lightweight plastic. It's easily damaged, and as a result of constant scratching and gnawing, small grooves and holes, which can be difficult to see, accumulate and harbor harmful bacteria.

To fully sanitize a plastic dish, you need to dip it into boiling water for about 5 minutes. You can also sanitize the bowl with a 30:1 water to bleach solution and let it soak for 20 minutes. Remember to wash it and rinse it well after soaking.

Hydrating your ferret

The water bottle is perhaps one of the greatest *and* least appreciated inventions made available to pet owners. You can easily clean it, it doesn't tip over, and it provides uncontaminated water throughout the day. The last point is very important, because providing a constant supply of clean, fresh water is essential to your ferret's well-being. *Note:* Water bottles work best when you fill them at least halfway, so keep this in mind when feeding and watering.

Bottle sizes vary, from those suitable for a mouse to those large enough for dogs and cats. A bottle that's too small yields little water and empties quickly. One that's too large, such as those designed for dogs, can be difficult for a ferret to operate because it requires a much harder push on the ball. Fortunately, bottle makers have taken some of the thought out of the process by making several specifically for ferrets. If you can't find a bottle at a pet supply shop, a guinea pig or rabbit water bottle is appropriate.

Picking out a bottle is just the first step. You also must attach the bottle to fuzzy's cage and train him to use it. Find out how in the sections that follow.

An older or weaker ferret, or even a ferret with bad or sensitive teeth, may find it very difficult to drink from a water bottle. He would prefer to become dehydrated rather than take an uncomfortable or painful drink, so be sure to read up on water bowls in the next section!

Attaching the bottle to the cage

Ferret water bottles are designed to mount on the outside of the cage (see Figure 5-4). Bottles hung on the inside of the cage are fair game; most ferrets will quickly seize and dismantle them. Also, outside mounting is convenient for you, because you have easy access to the bottle, which you should change daily.

FIGURE 5-4:
Water bottles should be secured from outside the cage.

As with anything your ferret sees, if his water bottle isn't firmly attached, you'll find it on the floor the next time you check his cage. And you'll have him staring pitifully out at you with his "What took you so long to get here?" look.

REMEMBER

A water bottle doesn't work too well if your fuzzy can't reach it. I've seen many people place their pets' water bottles way too high or way too low without even thinking about it. Position the bottle at a comfortable height so that your ferret doesn't have to strain himself by reaching too high or crouching too low to snatch a drink. Also, keep in mind the number of ferrets residing in the cage. If you have three or more in one cage, consider adding another bottle. For multilevel cages, providing water bottles on the top and bottom levels is a good idea.

Training fuzzy to use his water bottle

Most animals quickly discover that water flows from the tube when the stainless steel ball is gently pushed in. I have even witnessed my ingenious ferrets holding the ball in with a toenail to allow for more water to flow out.

Keeping the water bottle filled and the cage clean can be temporarily tedious, but it's well worth the effort in the end. Just through curiosity, most ferrets figure out the workings of the water bottle and do so without risking dangerous dehydration, illness, and possible death.

WARNING

A great many people are against using water bottles as the sole water source for their ferrets. This is for several valid reasons: Water bottles by design allow for only a small amount of water to flow through the tube at a given time. An impatient ferret may prefer to scamper off thirsty than to get his thirst quenched by a slow-flowing bottle. This state of being in chronic dehydration, as you can imagine, can wreak havoc on his little body, especially his kidneys. And if you have one of those determined little guys who insists on getting every little bit of H_2O out of that tube, dental damage may be the result of gnawing at the metal bottle stem for hours on end. I suggest you use a bowl in addition to a bottle.

Using a water dish

Water bottles are great, but because ferrets drink constantly throughout the day and night, it's a good idea to provide an additional, more easily accessed supply of water. The type of bowl you choose, as well as where you fasten the bowl, depends on your ferret. Heavy duty dishwasher-safe ceramic crock bowls work great to reduce tipping, but should never be used anywhere in a cage other than the ground level unless they're secured tightly in place to prevent them from becoming hazardous projectiles. Because most ferrets find rubber items a delicacy, avoid bowls with rubber bases, which are simply invitations to intestinal blockages. Your ferret will likely snorkel in her water bowl and fling it about the cage! Plastic or stainless steel attachable/lockable crocks are great alternatives since they can be securely fastened to the cage to minimize spillage. Regardless of the water bowl you choose, it should be located beneath the water bottle, if you have one, to help catch bottle drips and to keep ferret bedding dry.

Designing Your Ferret's Bathroom

Ferrets are naturally clean animals that can and should be trained to use a kitty litter box. Therefore, you need to equip your ferret's castle with a suitable bathroom. Believe it or not, you have some things to consider before running out and buying the first plastic cat box you see. The first thing is the size of the cage door through which you plan on shoving the litter box (this is where custom cages with built-in, pull-out litter pans can be convenient; see the earlier section "Setting Up Fuzzy's Cage"). In most instances, you won't have a problem, but be sure to double-check the size of your door. I've had many brilliant ideas foiled due to the width of the cage door! There are some very big housecats out there and some very big litter boxes.

You also need to consider the size of the cage and of your ferret family. Your ferret's cage should have at least one litter box, but large cages and cages with several ferrets should contain a minimum of two boxes. You'll find that corners are coveted spots for pooping, and a corner is the best place for a litter box. Keep that in mind when shopping for cages, as well.

Potty on! Choosing the right litter box for your ferret

The type of pooper(s) you have determines the most suitable litter box for you. His age and health status make a difference, too (see Part 4 for more on health issues). Ferrets like to fit their whole bodies — and then some — into their litter boxes. Here are some other things to think about:

>> Ferrets who aim high (those, for example, who scoot their butts up to the corners and aim for the peaks of the poop hills) need litter boxes with high sides. Ferrets that don't much care where they go (the ones, for example, who enter the box and squat down to do their business as soon as all four feet are in) are probably okay with a low-sided litter box.

>> As ferrets age, they may lose mobility in their hind legs, which can make getting into litter boxes more difficult. The same holds true for the sick or

injured guys. Invest in a low-sided box for a debilitated fuzzball, even if he has a temporary condition. The same goes for the super lazy ferrets. Gosh, did I just say that?!

>> Baby ferrets are full of energy, and they can and will get into almost anything. If your ferret is too small to get into a litter box, it may be too soon to be training him to use it.

>> If you have a super-duper big cage, a covered litter box may be feasible, but he may turn it into a bedroom, so keep watch! Perhaps you need a combination of both a low-sided box, which may do well on the bottom level (see Figure 5-5), and a high-sided box, which you can put on a top level if it fits, or vice versa. Also available are smaller triangular boxes that fit only in the corner of the cage. They sit low in the front and very high in the back. However, most ferrets prefer to use litter boxes that they can get all four feet in.

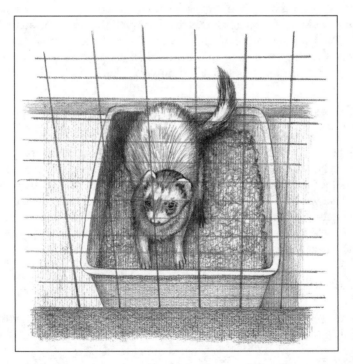

FIGURE 5-5: A ferret in a low-sided litter box at the bottom of the cage.

Finding the right litter box for your ferret may be a crapshoot at first. If you're a good observer, you can figure out what your ferret's litter-box needs are. On the other hand, I'm a good observer, and I have ferrets that make me move the boxes all around. I think they do it just to keep me on my toes!

Plastic litter boxes

Your ferret will most likely have a durable, plastic kitty litter box that comes from a pet shop or pet supply store. These are inexpensive and easy to replace when they become scratched up and worn out. Also, they come in many shapes and sizes to fit your ferret's cage and needs. You may also find a particular color that fits your choice of decorating.

TIP

Litter boxes rarely stay in one place in a ferret cage. They are pushed, pulled, flipped, and catapulted over to the levels below. However, making a couple of simple modifications to the litter box can improve your life with ferrets a great deal. One involves fastening the litter box to the sides of the cage using a couple of C-clamps. Another is to drill two holes on each of the sides you'll be fastening to the cage and then thread cable ties through the litter box and around the cage wire to secure it. Or — my favorite — insert steel U-bolts through holes in the litter box to fasten it to the cage.

What about those plastic boxes with rims around the top to help keep the litter in the box? Some people like this feature. I find the rim to be an ineffective weapon against talented litter pitchers, which most ferrets pride themselves in being. Additionally, most rims aren't fitted well enough to the litter boxes and become just another object tossed about the cage.

Slide-in metal litter boxes

Some ferret cages have built-in metal or Plexiglas slide-in/pull-out litter boxes. Just open the little door and pull out the box for easy cleaning. This type of box fits snugly into its own space, which eliminates the need to secure it. This may sound perfect, but it has its own problems. My ferrets drag their bedding into it, so I insert a short Plexiglas barrier to prevent this. Perhaps the worst thing about the metal-type pull out trays is that after a year or so — depending on the amount of urine it receives — the bottom of the metal pan slowly corrodes, which leads to holes.

Here are a few things you can do to prevent the corroding, or at least delay it:

» You can line the bottom and ½ inch of the sides with contact paper. The contact paper is okay, but it doesn't last very long and eventually peels or cracks when you clean it.

» You can cut a fitted piece of linoleum and place it on the bottom of the pan. This fix works fairly well, but you must remove the linoleum regularly for cleaning when urine leaks under it.

>> Another solution I've heard of is that you can spray the bottom of the metal pan with a safe coating, such as cooking spray, in between cleanings. You also can paint the bottom with a nontoxic paint or coating, such as Teflon.

TIP

Most metal pans are longer than a typical plastic litter box. However, I put a plastic litter box on my ferrets' favorite side of the metal box, and I fill the space that's left over with litter. So, my large metal box is divided into two, and the unprotected side gets little use — except for when I fail to clean the box as often as I should. This solution may seem to defeat the purpose of the built-in metal box, but the kitty litter box still fits in snugly, pulls out with the metal box, and isn't tossed about the cage.

Picking out the perfect litter

Don't think that the cheap, generic litter you can force your cat to use will do for your ferret. In most cases, cats are cleaner about their toilet habits. They go into the box, do their duty, politely cover it up, and exit quickly to be sure that no one saw who dropped the bomb. Ferrets are different. They dig and burrow in their litter. They toss it about as they roughhouse with each other or a favorite toy. Some drag their bedding into the litter box and go to sleep. A litter box is to most ferrets what a sandbox is to a creative child. Therefore, picking litter for your ferret requires more than simply picking up the cheapest litter in the kitty aisle of your grocery store.

The litter you choose for your fuzzball should be absorbent and as free of dust as possible. Also, get bigger pieces because litter gets stuck in the strangest of places and can cause illness. The following list presents the options for your litter-snorkeling fuzzy:

>> **Pelleted litters:** Many ferret fanciers consider pelleted litters the best litter for ferrets. It exists in many forms on the pet market and includes such products as: Yesterday's News (unscented preferred), Feline Pine, and Pine Pellet Stall Bedding. The latter two products have a pine odor, which may be offensive to some ferrets or even irritate some ferrets' respiratory tracts. Additionally, these two break down into sawdust when they get wet. Most are made from plant fibers or recycled newspaper. For the most part, pelleted litters rate high on the absorbency scale. Some of these litters are even considered digestible in case of accidental or intentional ingestion. Most varieties are fairly dust-free and free of perfumes, and they're difficult for a ferret to shove up his tiny nose. Although no litter is completely safe from the throws of ferret paws, pelleted litter is heavier and bigger, making it a little harder to toss overboard.

>> **Wood stove pellets:** This is by far one of my favorite ferret litters! Reasonably priced and made of compressed wood chips, wood stove pellets are also rapidly becoming a favorite litter among ferret owners. Wood stove pellets are inexpensive and do a great job of controlling odor. You can find this product at major home-improvement centers (near the fireplace stuff) and many other stores, but read the label carefully. Some are labeled "not for animal use" due to specific binding chemicals used. You will want "denatured wood litter pellets, kiln dried to remove harmful phenols."

>> **Silica-based litters (pearls, flakes, beads, or gel):** An expensive but attractive litter with a split personality. Some brands may cause silicosis, a non-cancerous, but sometimes fatal lung disease caused by prolonged exposure to silica dust. Others on the market claim to be "amorphous silica" or safe for the respiratory tract. And check out this fact: Because silica can expand to 20 times its original size when it meets moisture, it poses a huge risk of serious intestinal blockage should your ferret ingest it. Additionally, silica litter tends to be on the messier side. Just stay the heck away from it for the sake of your furbabies!

>> **Clay litter:** Clay litter, unfortunately, is very popular among both cat and ferret fanciers. It's cheap, abundant, fairly absorbent, and you can find it anywhere, even the grocery store. Most clay litters, however — even the ones that claim to be 99-percent dust-free — produce a ton of dust. Just because you can't see it when it settles after the initial pour doesn't mean the dust isn't there. Regular playing, digging, and walking on the litter upsets the dust, and remember, your ferret's center of gravity is much lower to the ground than other litter-using critters, so the risk of clay litter sticking to his or her naughty bits is much greater.

WARNING

Respiratory problems can develop over a period of time if your ferret inhales too much dust. Bits of clay litter (along with scoopable litter) easily find ways into a ferret's ears, eyes, nose, and mouth. Also, clay (and scoopable) litters can stick between a little ferret's toes, not to mention cling to his little butt when he scoots it across the litter after going. Additionally, because ferrets burrow through litter and sit in it, clay litter coats their hair and dries it out as well as attracting more dirt to the coat.

>> **Scoopable litter:** Scoopable litter is another popular choice. The absorbency of high-quality scoopable litter is excellent, making it convenient and easy to clean. It may have a pretty smell (before use, of course) or it may be odorless. Many, but not all, scoopable litters can be flushed right down the toilet along with the poop and urine. However, scoopable litter is incredibly dusty. The consistency is as fine as sand, making it easier to inhale and ingest. And, many, not all, scoopable litters turn into cement when they meet moisture. This is one I don't recommend for ferrets.

You must take extra caution with newly bathed or wet ferrets. Like dogs, ferrets go bonkers after baths. They roll around and wipe themselves across every surface available, including the litter box. Water + scoopable litter = cement. It dries quickly and can be very tedious to clean. Your ferret's eyes, ears, nose, mouth, toes, and behind can be subject to scoopable-litter impaction.

>> **Alfalfa-pelleted rabbit food:** Frequently confused for alfalfa-pelleted litter, rabbit food is cheap and can be found in bulk, but it does not make a good choice for litter in your ferret's litter box. Although it looks nice, some ferrets may be allergic to it or find the dust particles irritating. Be sure you know what you're buying!

>> **Corncob litter:** Although it's decorative to some degree, my experience with corncob litter says that you're just asking for trouble. First off, this litter is so light and airy that most of it is out of the litter box in no time. It isn't very absorbent, and it molds quickly; and mold can lead to respiratory disease. And many ferrets just can't resist nibbling on it a little, which can lead to a bowel impaction. Perhaps the only good thing I can say about corncob litter is that it isn't dusty.

>> **Newspaper:** You may find that a plain sheet of newspaper or shredded newspaper works well for your ferret's litter. Although it isn't pretty, newspaper is cheap and does the job. Litter/cage material is the only reason I subscribe to my local newspaper!

Puppy pee pads (disposable or reusable) in the corners of play areas or even in the litter boxes can also work well in place of litter. If you happen to have an ailing ferret, you'll be able to better examine his pee and poop on the pad. And if you also happen to have one boy and one girl, and you aren't sure who made the deposit, remember this: Due to the location of their genitals, girl ferrets pee and poop in the same spot, whereas boys pee in the front and poop in the back. As with all plastic, watch closely for chewing on the pee pads!

Acquiring Accessories and Other Stuff Fuzzy Needs

Ferrets are curious, active, and intelligent creatures. Picking out a suitable cage and throwing in the basic necessities isn't enough to make your fuzzy comfortable and happy. A ferret needs stimulation. You can add some extras to his cage, his playtime, and his life for his amusement and yours. Have a little fun and regularly rearrange his townhouse. Doing so also makes the cage look neater in your home. In the following sections, I introduce the accessories you can add to your ferret's cage and the accessories you can use to travel around with your fuzzy.

Fluffing up extra snoozing sites

No ferret's home is complete without at least one hanging hammock (see Figure 5-6). Hammocks come in all shapes and sizes. You can purchase one from a pet store or make one yourself. A hammock should be made from soft yet durable fabric and have hooks or clasps on all four corners to attach it to the top of the cage. Your fuzzy's hammock should be located near a shelf or ramp so he has safe, easy access to it.

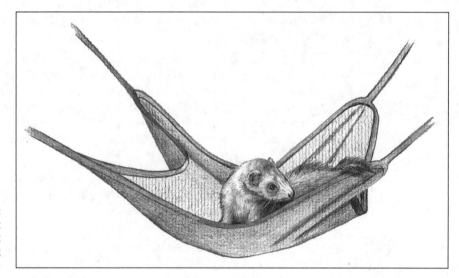

FIGURE 5-6:
A typical ferret hammock that can be hung inside the cage.

Some hammocks look more like hanging sleeping bags. Your ferret can choose to sleep right on top of it or snuggle between the two layers of fabric. I've had some ferrets who liked to squish inside a hammock with another pile of ferrets heaped on top of them. It reminds me of circus clowns crammed in a VW Bug (just when you think it can't possibly hold anymore . . .). Remember, a wonderful resource for awesome ferret cage bedding and people accessories is Anna Senka at her Etsy shop SenkaCraftFactory.

REMEMBER

You need to provide warm, dark places for your ferret to hide out and sleep in. Ferrets need to burrow and feel safe. You can utilize nest boxes for optimal stress control. A general rule is that the number of nest boxes should equal the number of ferrets plus one. If you don't give your fuzzy security, he'll likely suffer cage stress.

Because tunneling is a ferret's favorite extracurricular activity, you may want to hang some plastic tubes in your fuzzy's cage. Ferrets enjoy running through them and even curling up for a nap. The tubes are easy to clean and colorful, so they brighten up the cage area. You can find them in major pet supply stores or online ferret supply stores. They're made specifically for ferrets.

Ferret toys galore!

Ferrets are materialistic critters with an eye for valuables. Although you probably won't be able to prevent the thieving of some of your prized possessions, you can provide your ferret with his own valued toys. In addition to providing entertainment, toys help to satisfy your ferret's natural instinct to hoard food. But you need to know what toys are safe and what toys are bad ideas.

Good toys

Your ferret should be able to enjoy an assortment of toys both in the cage and out. Try to keep up with his level of intelligence and curiosity, and provide him with as much excitement as possible. Here are some toys you can use:

» Hard rubber balls (maybe even one with a bell safely inside)

» Cat toys that are made of hard plastic

» Plastic Easter eggs

» Ping pong balls

» Paper and plastic bags

» Cardboard boxes

» Small plush toys for dogs and cats (no detachable googly eyes)

» Human infant toys, such as plastic keys and rattles and terry-cloth-covered squeaky things

» Large ferret balls — the kind that have holes in them for entering and exiting

» Fun tunneling toys like PVC piping, clothes-dryer hoses, and ferret tubes

» Crinkly cat tunnels

» The best ferret toy ever: you!

You need to inspect toys routinely. Throw away any toys that have stuffing pulled out, and pay close attention to squeaky toys, because ferrets have been known to pull out the squeakers and ingest them. Do not use any toys that have small removable parts, such as googly eyes on plush toys, which might cause a blockage. Also, solid-colored PVC tunnels should be no more than 4 feet in length so that you can easily reach a ferret in distress should you quickly have to.

Toys to avoid

Exercise caution when purchasing playthings for your fuzzball. Most of the toys in the market are designed for dogs and cats. Ferrets love to chew and gnaw and destroy the stuff they covet so fiercely. However, their bodies don't process the junk in quite the same manner as dogs' and cats' bodies do. If your fuzzy eats something he shouldn't, you'll find occasional bits of foreign gunk, such as rubber or plastic, in his poop. More often, what doesn't choke him usually finds a nice place to settle in his stomach or intestine and causes just enough damage to warrant immediate medical attention — not to mention extreme panic for you. A best-case scenario: You can give a major dose of kitty or ferret hairball remedy (½ tablespoon) to help push it on through. A bad-case scenario: Fuzzy has to have surgery to remove the blockage. And the most awful scenario of all: Death that could've been prevented.

Here are some things you don't want to use as ferret toys:

>> Any toy made of latex or soft, flexible rubber/plastic, including unsupervised squeaky toys

>> Anything with small pieces that your ferret can chew off and swallow

>> Clear rolling balls (also known as rolling porta potties!) made for guinea pigs and chinchillas

>> Running wheels

>> Paper towel rolls or toilet paper rolls

>> Wall-mounted cat steps and ladders

>> Toys containing catnip (may contain essential oils to boost scent, which ferrets cannot metabolize!)

>> Objects small enough that your ferret can get his head stuck in them

>> Toys that show signs of ferret wear and tear

Your ferret will try to pilfer through your belongings and come up with a few toys you've obviously forgotten about, including socks, shoes, car keys, lipstick, and various other sundries. If you're a smoker, watch your cigarettes, too. Ferrets find them wonderfully fascinating, but they're not only toxic, but can also cause obstructions. You also should avoid bedding that contains foam rubber or stuffing.

Ferret owners should monitor their ferrets when it comes to playing with certain toys. For example, I don't include plastic bags in the "toys to avoid" list, mainly because ferrets love them! They make great enrichment toys. You do need to monitor their use, though. Don't leave the bags in the cage or unattended with your ferret. Bags and other potentially dangerous items can make great play items if you're diligent at watching and supervising the play. That's not to say, however, that all toys are safe even with proper monitoring. Some objects are flat out dangerous. Use common sense.

Leashes and harnesses for your ferret

Ferrets can learn to be walked on leashes, provided that they have comfortably fitting harnesses. Leashes and harnesses are especially important if you plan on taking your ferret outside for romps or when you have guests over who want to get to know your fuzzbutt. You can purchase many types of harnesses, but the long, slender body of the ferret makes him a difficult fit. You should choose a harness made specifically for ferrets — one that's H-shaped across the back and that fastens around the neck and belly (see Figure 5-7). Avoid cutesy vest-style harnesses, tempting as they may be, for several reasons: First, ferrets have a tendency to escape from these fashion statements. Second, because vest harnesses cover so much body surface, ferrets can overheat in them, especially outside in warmer weather. Third, these fabric harnesses can get wet, and a wet ferret is *no bueno*, particularly outside in the cold! Finally, cloth or mesh can easily get caught on things, causing it to tear or even cause strangulation.

Just like a puppy, your ferret will resist the sudden restraint on his freedom, so train him and get him used to it *before* venturing outside with him on a leash. He'll twist and turn and play tug of war as though he's truly claustrophobic and dying. He'll do the typical alligator roll and fake a horrible torture. Believe me — he'll get over it. As long as you can squeeze 2 fingers under the harness, you can be sure that it isn't too tight. Ferrets are master escape artists. Any looser and your ferret will be free in no time. Be patient and persistent with your teachings and reward him for good behavior. Unless you use the harness only when taking him to the vet, he'll eventually associate it with playtime. (For more tips on getting him used to the harness, see Chapter 19.)

Consider fastening a bell to your ferret's harness for your own sanity. After your little gal is used to the harness, she'll be exploring piles of leaves, tall grass, and bushes in no time. The sound of jingling will help you to keep track of her even if she's just at the end of the leash. Remember not to leave the harness on your ferret when you're not actively using it.

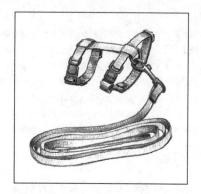

FIGURE 5-7:
Leashes and
harnesses keep
your ferret safe
outside and when
meeting people.

WARNING

Collars. See? I couldn't let it go! As a frequent Facebook reader, I have read post after post from devastated ferret owners who have either had their ferrets die or sustain severe traumas/injuries in freakish accidents caused by wearing collars. In the cases of injuries, some ferrets eventually recovered whereas other ferrets suffered permanent disabilities, such as blindness, neurological issues, deafness, and more. Again, don't do it!

Finding a good travel taxi

A travel taxi is probably one of the first accessories you'll want to purchase after you have your ferret's cage set up. After all, your baby needs to arrive home safely. Ferrets are neat, and it's fun to show them off, but a vehicle isn't a safe place to showcase your fuzzy. He can get stuck under the seat and under a pedal. He can obstruct your view by cruising on the dashboard. All this stuff can cause an accident, and an unrestrained fuzzy is too vulnerable to come out of a serious accident in one piece.

Consider the following when looking for an appropriate travel taxi:

» A simple, small, plastic cat carrier can comfortably accommodate a couple of ferrets for short trips to the vet or to grandmother's house. The carrier should contain a soft towel or other type of bedding for comfort and snoozing. Most carriers are designed for adequate ventilation, so that shouldn't be much of a worry.

» Avoid folding cardboard carriers that shelters or pet shops may send you home with. They lack proper ventilation for a ferret and can get hot quickly. It also doesn't take long for a ferret to figure his way out of one by scratching or chewing. Cardboard carriers can't be properly sanitized. You don't want to have ferret pee leak through the bottom of a cardboard carrier and onto your car seat.

» Carriers that open like suitcases are okay for short trips, but for longer trips, a carrier with a wire-grated, front-opening door (see Figure 5-8) is more appropriate. Larger carriers of the same type (made for small or medium-sized dogs) are appropriate for temporarily housing ferrets on trips, because one can hold a small litter box in addition to the ferrets and their bedding.

FIGURE 5-8: Pet carriers should be securely built with narrow bars to keep the ferret from escaping.

REMEMBER

As much as I hate to admit this, not everyone enjoys ferrets as much as I do. When traveling to the vet or other places, keep your ferret contained in case you run across one of these oddball people. My vet doesn't like it when I come waltzing in with a 10-foot snake draped around my neck. It scares the poodle owners! So I bring snakes to the vet in reptile carriers. Your pet carrier (minus the snake) is the safest place for your furball anyway. Strangers poking at him may be too much stimulation for your little guy, and he may nip out of fear or excitement. Unless you're in a comfortable and ferret-friendly environment, keep your fuzzy safe in his carrier.

Chapter **6**

Ferret-Proofing Your Home

At first, your home is a scary yet stimulating jungle to a tiny ferret, and she'll be chomping at the bit to find or cause trouble. And believe me, if she's able to find or cause trouble, she certainly will. Carpet sharks are notorious explorers and excavators. They like to push and pull and carry and toss every little household item they can. They can fit into the tiniest of tiny places and manage their way to the highest of spots. And they all put their leaping skills to the greatest challenge. Whoever came up with the phrase "Curiosity killed the cat" obviously hadn't been exposed to ferrets. Curiosity, although one of the ferret's most amusing qualities, can be her worst enemy.

Therefore, before your new fuzzy even walks into her new home, the environment should be ferret-proofed. In this chapter, you find out how to get your house ready for your new arrival. I also explain what habits you can change to keep your ferret safe and let you know how to cross off your next important priority: finding a good vet for your fuzzy.

Inspecting Your Home for Ferret Hazards

With the possible exception of a single closed-off room (a rubber-padded cell?) with no furniture, holes, or floor vents, most areas in a home can't be completely ferret-proofed. You have to be satisfied with doing your absolute best to minimize the possibilities of ferret tragedies. Like the parent of a toddler, you must keep your pet out of harm's way. However, unlike a human toddler, a ferret will rarely scream out for you when she hurts herself or gets wedged somewhere. Your fuzz-butt depends on you to remain vigilant at all times when she's out of her cage. (Learn about some great ferret-proofing hacks in Chapter 24)

The following list outlines some general guidelines for ferret-proofing your home:

» **Put up security gates to keep ferrets from danger zones.** Don't settle for easily climbed children's gates; those are just neat obstacles for a ferret to scale and master like a ladder. You may have to build something at least 3 feet high out of wood, Plexiglas, or another material that ferrets can't easily climb. Baby gates can be used if you creatively reinforce them so that they can't be climbed or squeezed through. Plexiglas and cardboard are your friends!

» **Be careful what you leave lying around your home.** Any object is fair game to a ferret. Some dangerous items include pen caps, rubber bands, cotton balls and cotton swabs, coins, latex/vinyl/rubbery things, sponges, jewelry, foam rubber, polyester stuffing, ear buds and ear plugs, dried foods, cigarettes, and bandages. Geez, the list could go on forever. Use common sense, and imagine you have a toddler cruising around just looking to push your buttons!

» **Don't store chemicals, such as cleaners or antifreeze, in accessible places.** Ferrets can knock the containers over, causing spills, and ingest poisonous chemicals. At the very least, they'll want to lick the containers just for a taste and may ingest chemical residue.

» **Put your medications out of reach.** You may be aware that prescription meds can be extremely dangerous and toxic to your ferret, but you may not know that many over-the-counter medications, such as Tylenol, can be as deadly as rat poison to your ferret.

» **Don't forget that ferrets can jump.** You should ferret-proof anything less than 30 inches off the ground or anything that your ferret can reach by climbing.

WARNING

Some people leave their ferrets out of their cages to go unsupervised all day. I believe only an extremely experienced ferret owner can pull this off without too many hitches. A person confident enough to leave a ferret unsupervised claims to know her ferret and the ferret's environment inside and out and knows the ways of ferret-proofing. But the debate over whether to cage your ferret is a heated one in the ferret community. It could be an entire chapter. Consider that ferrets have small heads and can fit through spaces two human fingers wide. Add that to their inherent curiosity, which did indeed kill at least the cat, and odds are, trouble will soon follow. And it is virtually impossible for any ferret owner, no matter how knowledgeable or diligent, to think of everything their ingenious ferrets can get into at any given time. You get the idea. I can't emphasize this enough. Think and prepare as though you have a toddler exploring your environment. Everything a toddler touches ends up in his mouth. A ferret isn't that different. The following sections lead you through ferret-proofing the different areas of your home and point out dangers that you may not have thought about. The bits of wisdom in these sections are made possible by all the close calls, injuries, and fatalities experienced by thousands of ferret lovers all over the country, including myself. Learn from our mistakes!

Laundry room

Utility/laundry rooms often are loaded with dangerous items, and they're practically impossible to ferret-proof, so you should keep these rooms off-limits altogether. Your ferret may decide to chew on the dryer vent hose and tunnel right out through to the scary outside. Even worse, your fuzzy could quickly crawl up into the clothes dryer to take a nap beneath all those soft clothes, especially when they're warm. You may not see her go in, and it will be too late when you do find her.

Kitchen

Block off your kitchen from curious ferrets if you can. You want to keep your fuzzy away from all those dangerous appliances in the kitchen. Here are a few of the ways your fuzzy can get hurt in the kitchen:

>> Refrigerators and other appliances have fans that can abruptly turn on and injure or kill your ferret.

>> Ingested fiberglass insulation can cause blockages or severe illness.

>> Stoves have pilot lights that can cause severe burns.

>> All appliances have electrical cords that can cause electrocution when chewed on.

>> Your ferret can get severely wedged inside a space in an appliance and suffocate before you get the chance to rescue her.

>> If you're like I am, you keep your bottom kitchen cabinets filled with cleaners that are poisonous if swallowed by your ferret. Child safety locks are a great invention!

I've known ferrets to climb into dishwashers, refrigerators, and freezers when no one's looking. You can imagine the worst-case scenarios! Ferrets are adventure seekers, and they'll try anything once. But sometimes once is all the chance they'll ever get.

Moldings, baseboards, and under cabinets

Get on your belly and make sure that all the moldings and baseboards in your home are intact and complete all around the rooms. You don't want any mystery spaces. Double-check with your hands beneath the cabinets to make sure that your ferret can't get up into the cabinets from under the ledges. Home builders often seem to skimp in this area.

Also check for holes that lead into walls or to the great outdoors. Any hole wider than one inch is a potential hidey-hole or danger zone. Board all these holes up. If a hole is less than one inch wide, decide whether your ferret can widen it with her teeth or claws. After all, drywall and similar materials are no match for a fuzzy's weapons.

Windows and doors

To prevent escapes and falls from high places, double-check the safety of your windows, doors, and screens. Make sure your screens are securely fastened and your doors are shut tight while your fuzzy is prowling. Also, you probably should-n't open any accessible window when your ferret is out and about. An exposed screen, likewise, isn't very hard to tear open or pull out with teeth or claws.

How big are the gaps between the bottoms of your doors and the floor? More than one inch? Better lower them to prevent your ferret from scooting under or getting stuck. Don't underestimate the average furball!

TIP

It won't take long for your ferret to realize that she has the strength and smarts to open some doors and windows. You can use snap bolts to keep her safely inside your home (see Chapter 5).

Floor vents and air returns

Your ferret may be able to pull off your floor vents and air returns if they aren't secure. I know my floor vent grates just lay loosely on top of the holes they cover (for decoration, I guess). After a ferret gets into a vent, she can tunnel through the house and get stuck somewhere or fall to a place where she can't get out. And here's something ferret owners (dog and cat owners, as well) often don't think about: Bells and identification tags on collars and even harnesses can get wedged/stuck in floor vents that are secured to the floor, especially when the ferret lies down on the vent. When he tries to get up, he is trapped and may struggle to get free, causing serious injury or strangulation.

Try to securely fasten any loose grates with small pieces of Velcro. It's effective, and you can hide the strips from view.

WARNING

Floor fans can be dangerous to your fuzzy. A moving fan blade can remove a toe, paw, or tail tip (or worse). If the blade protector on your fan (the cage covering the fan) is broken, your ferret may decide to explore and end up in deep trouble. Don't use fans near your free-roaming ferret.

Plants

Your ferret will try to taste all your plants, and some plants are poisonous when eaten. She'll also promptly remove every trace of dirt from the pot, because ferrets are excellent diggers. The problem is, some dirt contains harmful bacteria or chemicals from fertilizers or pesticides.

Heights

Look around you. Everything in your home is a potential stepstool, ladder, or launching pad, including your fuzzy's townhouse (see Chapter 5 for more on fuzzy cages). You may need to move or block certain items to prevent your ferret from getting too high up. Pay close attention to how accessible your stairwells, curtain rods, and countertops are. A significant fall almost always injures a ferret, and sometimes it can be fatal.

Electrical cords

Ooooh, electrical cords seem like yummy chew toys to the grazing ferret. In the eyes of pet owners, though, electrical cords are electrocution traps and fire start-ers. Try applying a safe, but distasteful substance on the cords, such as lemon juice or distilled white vinegar, to deter the ferret's gnawing urge. Another simple solution is to wrap electrical cords in aluminum foil. Most ferrets don't enjoy chewing on foil. However, the best solution is to keep all electrical cords completely out of your ferret's reach or to enclose them in special cable or cord moldings, available at home improvement stores.

WARNING

Bitter-tasting sprays are extremely popular products intended as chew and bite deterrents. In the past, these were highly recommended for use in training ferrets and ferret-proofing. This method has become highly controversial, however, because these sprays linger in the ferret's mouth and may cause foaming at the mouth and loss of appetite for several days. In addition to becoming extremely hungry, the poor ferret quickly becomes dehydrated. Also, at least one of the most well-known bitter spray products includes isopropanol, which is also the leading ingredient in rubbing alcohol. Isopropanol is twice as potent as the ethanol found in our favorite alcoholic beverages. Pretty darn scary for a tiny ferret that has no business hittin' the bottle in the first place!

Reclining chairs, rockers, and foldout couches

Many furniture items can be death traps. It's easy to plop down into a rocker or recliner and forget the danger of crushing your romping ferret in between the moving parts. I suggest that you don't use reclining chairs, rockers, or foldouts when your ferret is out playing or that you keep them out of your ferret's play-designated space. I, for instance, make everyone sit on the floor when my fuzzies are out and about!

Fireplaces

Nothing can match a walk on the wild side for your fuzzy, and fireplaces have it all: wood, dirt, and sometimes even rocks. If you want to keep your ferret and house soot-free, make your fireplace off-limits to snorkeling ferrets. You can invest in a heavy-duty fireplace grill that ferrets can't climb and that you can push flush against the fireplace. I went another route and installed glass doors on our fireplace.

Mattresses, couches, and chairs

Ferrets can easily crawl beneath most couches and chairs or the cushions on them, and they'll be tempted to do so. Mattresses are just as alluring. Those places make good hidey-holes, and the fabric beneath the furniture is awfully enticing. The danger is that you can squish your ferret between the cushions or under the chair if you unknowingly sit on her.

Many ferrets are tempted to dig and chew and tear at the underside fabric of furniture, often creating holes. Besides being detrimental to the furniture, chewing holes often allows furballs to find the stuffing that's revealed behind the protective fabric cloth. The same goes for mattresses. Ferrets love to chew on soft, foamy, rubbery things. If your ferret ingests the foam or other stuffing, intestinal blockage can occur.

Some ferret people prefer to use futons rather than traditional couches and chairs. Or, when the time comes to replace their furniture, ferret people choose to buy couches and chairs that are flush against the floor so their ferrets can't get under them. If these aren't viable options for you, you can turn your chairs and couches over and try to staple some heavy-duty cloth to the bottoms to keep your ferret out. Remember to staple close together so she can't get in between the staples.

Most ferret owners don't need to go to such extremes if they keep a close eye on their fuzzies during play time and inspect their furniture routinely for signs of destruction. And look before you sit!

Toilets, bathtubs, and buckets

Supervised recreational swimming can be fun for some fuzzies, but even the most athletic ferret risks drowning after a while. To prevent accidents, keep the lids down on toilets and keep bathroom doors closed when you have bathtubs full of water. Buckets of water or other liquids can also pose a drowning threat. Even if your ferret doesn't drown, she may become violently ill if she swims in a chemical of some sort.

Many bathmats and area rugs have rubber backings to prevent slippage. Unfortunately, these backings are delicious and sometimes deadly to fuzzies. Even the little rubber tips on door stops can block your ferret's intestinal tract when ingested. Watch for signs of interest in these items. You can easily pick up bathmats and rugs during playtime, and if necessary, you can remove the baseboard doorstops and replace them with stops that fasten to the tops of doors.

Cabinets

A ferret is quick to discover that she can easily pry open accessible cabinet doors. I don't recommend using most child latches as a solution. Most child latches are designed so that you have to slip your hand in and release the latches to open the cabinets. And if you can slip your hand in, the cabinet opens just enough for your ferret to come on in or get her head caught.

However, certain child latches are designed to work just fine. For example, one uses a magnet to release the latch on the inside of the cabinet door.

REMEMBER

Supervise your ferret when she's playing around cabinets, and be sure that they don't contain dangerous chemicals or small ingestible objects. Also, make sure that your low cabinets don't have holes that can lead to other awaiting dangers. For example, I have one cabinet that has a poorly fitted pipe coming through the bottom of it. I can see right down to the basement!

Trash cans

Garbage cans are simply irresistible to roving ferrets. Think of all the disgusting and dangerous items you throw away on a daily basis. Would you want a fuzzy kiss from a ferret that just had her nose in all that?

Keep all your garbage cans out of your fuzzy's reach when she's out. If she has access, she'll tip them over or find a way into them. Depending on what's in the trash, your ferret's curiosity could kill her or make her terribly ill. And who's to say you won't accidentally throw out your fuzzy with the trash if she climbs in and curls up for a snooze with a stinky banana peel? Fix your cans with sturdy lids and keep them completely out of your ferret's reach.

TIP

So, you can't put all your trash cans up high or fasten them tightly with sturdy lids. Tired of fishing trash out of hidey-holes? Exasperated at the thought of sweeping up half-dried coffee grounds for the third time this week? Try weighing down your garbage can. Place about five pounds of sand or smooth round pebbles in the bottom so your fuzzy can't tip the can!

Changing Some of Your Home Habits

Those of you with children may remember those selfish days when you could do anything your own way without needing to take others into consideration. Those of you without children may be there now! For every potential ferret owner: You can kiss your selfish days goodbye. Well, maybe the adjustment isn't as drastic as that, but you need to be prepared to adjust your habits and daily routine. Your furball is depending on you for survival.

The following list presents some actions you should make part of your daily fuzzy-owning routine:

» **Watch where you step, and don't carry stuff that blocks your vision.**
A ferret's favorite place to be and snooze is under things: carpets and rugs
(hence the nickname "carpet sharks"), clothing, pet beds, you name it. If it's on
the floor, step over it just in case!

Ferrets are quick and quiet. They can be underfoot in a flash. If yours are, you
may need to shuffle your feet when walking, a move known as the *Ferret
Shuffle*. Tread lightly, for a ferret is bound to be close at foot.

» **Check the clothes dryer and washer thoroughly before operating them.**
Also check carefully before you toss a load of clothes into the washer. Ferrets
aren't bulky and heavy like bricks. You'll hardly notice if your fuzzy has
burrowed into your dirty underwear (assuming you're not wearing them at
the time).

» **Don't plop lazily onto the couch or chair.** If your fuzzy isn't under the
furniture, she may be under the cushions. Also, the moving parts in a reclining
chair or sofa can injure or kill your ferret.

» **Don't leave small objects lying around.** Stealing is an endearing but
sometimes deadly ferret trait. If your fuzzy doesn't eat or chew a small object
up, she may hide it — and hide it well. You may not find your stolen objects
for a very long time. This is particularly annoying if the item your fuzzy steals is
valuable.

» **Don't open or close doors quickly.** You may startle or, worse, accidentally
injure your ferret. Garage doors, bathroom doors, and front doors are the
worst. And watch for heavy or self-closing doors! The same care should be
taken with cabinets, drawers, refrigerators, freezers, washers, dryers, and
dishwashers.

TIP

My friend, fellow ferret enthusiast Holly Ravenhill, has a great tip she shares with
people who inquire about additional ferret-proofing, because Heaven knows you
can't do enough! Holly says, "Train your family and friends! Any time you or anyone else enters or leaves the house, everyone yells *"ferret check!"* It's a great way
to remember to do a ferret head count and make sure no one escaped out the front
door." Great advice, Holly! Thanks for the tip!

Chapter 7

Introducing Fuzzy to His New Family

Bringing home a new ferret often means that you must face the delicate issue of introducing your new family member to your existing family members. It may not be as easy as you think. Take, for example, your domestic kitty that's used to being king or queen of the roost. An arrogant ruler, no doubt. Your cat will be dethroned, as will your spouse or any other member of the household, when your new ferret takes his spot by your side.

Knowing how to interact safely with your fuzzy on a one-to-one basis in his new surroundings is imperative, and this chapter tells you how. This chapter also offers insight into the social aspect of ferrets. These creatures aren't all they appear to be; they're even more wonderful than I can put on paper. That said, I discuss sticky subjects such as how to teach your kids to be safe and appropriate around fuzzbutts. Finally, I explain how to introduce your fuzzy to Fido and Fluffy, as well as to those neighbors who just have to stick their noses in your business.

WARNING

I believe you should quarantine any new ferret you bring into your home for at least two weeks until you know for sure he isn't sick. Although he may look healthy when you bring him home, he may be harboring parasites or a transmittable illness. Some serious ferret illnesses will flare their ugly heads only during stressful times, like a sudden change of environment. To quarantine, find a comfortable cage for your new ferret and house him at least two rooms away from your existing clan. Always feed and clean your new ferret last and remember to wash your hands thoroughly between handling ferrets. Wear another shirt over your clothing when handling your new ferret and leave it in the new ferret's room when you leave or go back and forth between ferret rooms. Most importantly, remind all members of the household to follow the same rules, or else the quarantine isn't a quarantine at all. When the quarantine period is over, the introductions can begin!

Ferrets as Social Animals

Ferret-owning humans swear up and down that ferrets are incredibly social critters. The fact is, polecats, ferrets included, are solitary animals with territorial tendencies. They don't act like dogs, which seek out other dogs, form packs, and travel around in groups. If you were to release three ferrets of the same gender in your backyard, they would more than likely go in three separate directions. In the wild, polecats defend their territories fervently against polecats of the same gender. (Naturally, if a member of the opposite sex enters a polecat's territory, she's more than welcome to stay awhile.)

The need to be solitary and territorial is, for the most part, kept under control by our beloved domestic ferrets under normal circumstances. But make no mistake about it: Although they play with and tolerate each other to the delight of all onlookers, ferrets maintain little unspoken territories, and at times they squabble with trespassers or thieves. However, there's a reason that thousands of ferret owners coo to themselves as they watch their babies pile in big sleepy heaps at the end of the day. Ferrets, after proper introductions, will more often than not view other ferrets as littermates and play about accordingly. They'll wrestle and dance as though they're the best of buddies, and in many cases, they can be the best of buddies. The simple fact is that ferrets establish a hierarchy amongst themselves and stake out microterritories in their tiny domains. In this way, are they really that different from us?

You and Your New Ferret: Making the Most of Your Friendship

Most ferrets enjoy the companionship of humans. It probably won't take long before your new fuzzy sees you as the perfect playmate — assuming you're willing to play nicely with him. To get to that stage, you have to make your ferret comfortable in your arms and in his surroundings. Sometimes, it takes a little bit of patience and extra understanding before you begin to feel that your ferret has bonded with you.

REMEMBER

Your body movements and tone of voice can influence his reactions to you. The age of your ferret and his history (some ferrets come with emotional baggage; see Chapter 20) also may determine how quickly he blends into your family.

Before you introduce your ferret to other family members, get to know him better and learn how to properly interact with him. The following sections show you how.

Hold me gently, please

In order to introduce your fuzzy to your family and to others, you need to become comfortable holding him — and he needs to be comfortable being held. Many healthy ferrets maintain the "I'd rather be anywhere than in your arms" position. In most cases, it has nothing to do with how you're actually holding the little guy (see Figure 7-1 for an example). There are always exceptions to the rule, though. I've run across many furballs who love to be held and cuddled. Usually, these guys are the older, more mature ferrets who have come to appreciate humans over the years.

To hold your ferret, support both his front and back legs in your arms (see Figure 7-1). Supporting his entire body is important. I can assure you that he'll try to move around quite a bit and probably try to crawl up your chest and onto your shoulder — maybe even onto your head! You can adjust his position, but remember not to squeeze his little body too tightly. You may find that sitting down and holding him on your lap works better for you. Use a treat such as salmon oil or pollock oil to entice him into staying put.

REMEMBER

If your ferret decides to nip you in protest of being held, don't reward the behavior by putting him down to play. You don't want to give in to his bad behavior, because he'll know what to do in the future when he wants down. Instead, if he nips, immediately tell him "No!" and place him in his cage. This way, your fuzzy will begin to associate biting with jail time (for more, see Chapter 19).

FIGURE 7-1:
Demonstrating
proper ways to
hold a ferret.

TIP

Scruffing, if done correctly, is a safe and painless way to hold a ferret when you need him to remain still for activities like trimming nails and cleaning ears. Simply grab the large, thick patch of skin behind his neck with your entire hand and lift him up. His hanging body should naturally remain still. You should support his bottom, especially if he's a heavy furball. However, note that the more support his bottom receives, the more he can move around. You should use scruffing mainly when more control is necessary for his safety or yours. Although scruffing is a scalding topic in the ferret community, with some saying it's abusive and others saying it's completely acceptable, remember, momma ferrets carry their kits around by the neck when moving them about. So do dogs and cats and other animals. No one calls DCFS on these furry moms. It's true that a small percentage of ferrets will actually become aggressive and reject you when you attempt to scruff them, however, so just don't scruff these few-and-far-between furballs. It's that simple.

Letting fuzzy set up shop in his home

I always advise people to allow their ferrets to get used to their new cages before they introduce them to the wonders of their new surroundings (Chapter 5 gives the lowdown on cages). This practice gives your ferret the chance to soak in all the new smells, both good and bad (people can give off funny scents!). Your ferret has a unique personality that you need to become familiar with. Only time will allow this to happen. Ease your ferret into your routine slowly; better yet, let him slowly ease *you* into *his* routine.

For starters, keep his cage in a convenient location — one that won't allow your 100-pound dog to rattle the cage every time she runs by. The following list presents some more cage tips:

» Don't allow the cage to become a resting shelf for your curious cat until your ferret has become comfortable with having that particular cat around (see the upcoming section "Fuzzy Meets Fluffy and Fido").

» Instruct children and other family members to keep their fingers out of the cage until your ferret has become comfortable with all the humans around (see the section "Preparing Your Child for the Ferret").

» If you like, you can partially cover the cage until you all get to know each other.

After a day or two of letting your ferret settle into his new home, take him to a different safe place, such as a bathroom. Sit down alone with some toys and let your ferret explore you at his own pace. Move slowly and quietly, talking softly as you encourage him to play. Watch his body language to see how comfortable he is with you. Some ferrets are more laid back and eager to accept the change in lifestyle. Others may maintain pipe-cleaner tails for hours until they become more relaxed. When you become comfortable with your ferret's temperament in his new environment, you can begin to give him more freedom. Let him roam first when the kids are at school and the other pets are confined to another area of the house and then move on from there.

The steps to successful bonding

Bonding with your ferret is an important part of establishing and maintaining a pet-loving, harmonious household. The rewards experienced as a result of properly bonding with your ferret will guarantee you a lifetime of love. The goal of bonding, after all, is to not only make life tolerable, but also to turn your ferret into a lap pet and you into a friend for life.

Establishing a bond isn't something that happens naturally or overnight. It takes effort, time, and trust from both parties, and it's an ongoing process. Here are some activities you can engage in to help cement your bond with your ferret:

>> **Playing:** Ferrets need frequent human interaction to remain happy, and you can provide this interaction and bond with your ferret by playing with him. Whether you get down on your belly and roll around with him or teach him new tricks, play is vital to your relationship. (See Chapter 10 for more information on play and enrichment.)

>> **Holding:** One of the best ways to bond with your ferret is to carry him around with you (see the earlier section "Hold me gently, please" for more on this topic). You can carry your ferret the old-fashioned way by cradling him in your arms and taking him with you from room to room, or you can just plant yourselves on the couch and watch television. Time carrying your ferret around should be limited, with frequent "down time" rests in between so that your ferret doesn't become too stressed and so he can take potty breaks.

>> **Grooming:** Grooming your ferret is a natural bonding tool. The activity mimics the way the ferret's mother and littermates would groom him in a familial environment. You should practice grooming rituals on a regular basis to enhance your bonding experience with your ferret; they'll help to soften even the most hardcore biter. (For more hygiene information, see Chapter 9.) The following are some grooming activities that promote bonding:

- **Face rubbing and cleaning:** Gently hold your ferret's head, and using your thumb or thumb and forefinger, stroke his face. I usually use both hands to hold a ferret's head, and I stroke his face with my thumbs from his nose back to his ears. For the cleaning part, you can take a warm, damp washcloth and gently stroke the face fur in the same direction the fur goes (with the grain).

- **Fur plucking:** Fur plucking is quite simple to do, but you must do it gently. Use your thumb and forefinger to gingerly tug on a tuft of fur on your ferret's head or neck. You also may tug on the fur located on his neck and belly; I've found these areas to be the most accepting, although you can pluck any part of your fuzzy's fur.

- **A warm, damp washcloth rubdown:** This is one of the most effective grooming/bonding methods, but it takes a little practice and getting used to for both parties. All you need is a small, damp (not wet), warm washcloth. Starting at your ferret's face and working your way back, rub him with the washcloth. Move in the same direction his fur flows. You may need to rinse and warm your washcloth periodically.

> Don't forget his belly, his bottom, and his genitals! Remember, what you want to do is mock his mother's behavior. A washcloth rubdown is not only a great way to bond with your ferret, but also a good way to help keep him clean — at least a little.

All these bonding rituals are easy and can be done just about anywhere and at any time — even while you're watching television. In addition to having a calming and soothing effect on the ferret, the grooming is good for your own blood pressure!

Fuzzy Meets Fluffy and Fido

If you love ferrets (or are thinking of getting one so you can fall in love), chances are you already have other pets in your home. You'll probably be able to introduce your ferret to your dogs and cats with no problems, provided that you take the necessary steps to minimize the natural tension between them. Not all ferrets have the same temperament; likewise, all cats and dogs have unique personalities that influence pet-to-pet relationships. In addition, some breeds of dogs (generally speaking) aren't as good with ferrets as others, and some are not meant to have relationships at all.

As a rule, ferrets get along better with cats. Ferrets and dogs together present unique conflicts that you should monitor closely. In the following sections, I explain how you can introduce your ferret to both cats and dogs, and I briefly cover other small animals in case you have your own miniature zoo at home! There is no proven formula, and caution should always be at the forefront of any interaction.

Heeeere kitty, kitty!

Ferrets and cats can make great companions, depending on their temperaments. I have three cats, and each one responds differently to my ferrets, and vice versa. Bella is usually neutral around my ferrets, often feeling too ancient and crabby to ferret around. Sometimes, though, she gets a wild hair up her heinie and waits patiently around the corner for a ferret to amble by so she can make a tackle. Crotchety old man Buzz has zero tolerance for any ferret behavior. He either stays up high or throws haphazard swats toward any fuzzy that's curious enough to cop a sniff. He then runs away and hides. Snipit, the youngest of the clan, is always up for a good wrestle. She tolerates ferret antics and enjoys getting down and dirty with all the furballs. They bite each other, take turns chasing, and play hide and seek. Snipit, however, usually wears down the ferrets. Eventually they'll run away and seek solitude in a hidey-hole after an hour or two.

You can do your part to try to make all your pet relationships like the one Snipit (or even Bella) and my ferrets have. To smooth the feline-ferret introductions in your house, follow these steps, one cat at a time:

1. **After your ferret gets comfortable in his new surroundings (see the previous sections), allow kitty to move freely about the outside of the ferret's cage while fuzzy is inside.**

   Let them sniff each other, and watch how they react. You may see no reaction at all.

2. **Take your ferret out of his cage and hold him securely while both he and kitty explore each other.**

   New smells are intriguing to ferrets. Both he and the cat may have puffed tails.

3. **If all seems calm so far, put your ferret down and watch cautiously as the two interact.**

   If conflict arises, end the meeting and try again later. It may take a few meetings before everyone is completely comfortable.

REMEMBER

Many people think that the ferret is the animal in the most danger during a cat-ferret encounter. My experience has been that most healthy adult ferrets can hold their own against cats and can even be more aggressive. Until you're sure that your ferret and cat can play nicely together, always supervise their games. Even after you become comfortable, supervision is a good idea.

WARNING

Adult ferrets have been known to kill kittens, so never leave an adult ferret and a kitten unsupervised. Better yet, let your kitten develop into an arrogant adolescent before subjecting her to ferret torture. It's only fair!

Nice puppy!

The relationship between a dog and ferret can be a little more complicated than the bond between a cat and ferret. Although cats come in different breeds, they all have pretty similar characteristics and are similar in size. Dogs, on the other hand, can be itty-bitty or massive in size and can be bred for certain personality traits and job functions. You must take your dog's size, bred-in job function, and personality into consideration when introducing your ferret to her.

REMEMBER

I've heard of many ferrets being killed by dogs, and the owners blame the dogs. The fault usually lies with the human who wasn't supervising the interaction or who didn't take into consideration the personality of the dog. It's your responsibility to keep your ferret safe and healthy; it's a dog's responsibility to be a dog.

Common dog/ferret characteristics

Although good dog–ferret relationships certainly do exist, I tend to mistrust most dogs around ferrets for several reasons:

>> Some breeds of dogs, like Terriers, Spaniels, and Hounds, are bred to hunt ferret-size game, and they may find a ferret awfully tempting. Supervise your ferret with these types of dogs with extreme caution.

>> Some dogs are very territorial. An otherwise laid-back, ferret-friendly pup may attack a ferret that ventures too close to her food, toys, or den. Keep your dog's stuff out of your ferret's territory, and watch for signs that your dog is getting possessive with other objects.

>> A nursing dog can get extremely aggressive toward other animals when she's protecting her litter.

>> Large or hyper dogs may inadvertently paw a ferret to death or injure the ferret's spine in an attempt to engage in play.

>> Some dogs don't like little animals or young animals and are very freaky around them. My favorite dog Ara was great with cats but was unpredictable around kittens.

>> Some dogs do well with ferrets until a fuzzy nips or chases them. A ferret is bound to nip and chase during play. If your dog can dish it out but can't take it, don't allow her to play with a fuzzy at all.

>> Some dogs just aren't good with other animals, including ferrets.

Of course, many exceptions exist, which is why you'll never know how an interaction will go until you try. Some nursing dogs allow ferrets to snuggle in with the rest of the litter. Some big dogs tiptoe gently around ferrets. Because every animal is an individual, you must decide how to allow your fuzzy to interact with your dog. Use common sense. If it feels or looks unsafe for your ferret, it probably is.

The Fuzzy-Fido introduction

Introducing a fuzzy and a dog should be almost the same as introducing a fuzzy and a cat. The main difference is that the process is slower. Just follow these steps:

1. **When your fuzzy is feeling settled in his new home (see the first section of this chapter), allow your dog to roam freely around and investigate your ferret's cage — with fuzzy in the cage and with you present.**

   Allow this type of interaction to take place for several days. Especially if you have a large dog, don't allow your dog alone with the cage. I have a friend who lost 7 ferrets to a large dog that tore apart the fuzzy cage in a matter of 15 unsupervised and devastating minutes.

2. **If the cage sniffing seems to be going well, take your ferret out and hold him securely; let your dog and ferret sniff each other.**

   You'll know things are going well if neither your dog nor your ferret is lunging at the other, or your ferret isn't cowering in the corner. If either is showing aggression, stop the introductions and try again the next day. Keep up the process until they become desensitized toward each other. This may take a month or more and may never work out at all.

3. **If the mutual smelling goes well, harness and leash your ferret and put him down on the ground with the dog in the room. Preferably another person should be in the room holding the dog on a leash, rather than allowing the dog to roam free.**

   Ideally, your dog's tail should be wagging and he should smell the ferret. Your ferret may or may not be interested in sniffing back. He may dance with excitement or just ignore your dog. Watch your dog for warning signs such as hackles up, baring teeth, or stiffened body. Every play interaction between your dog and ferret will be different from here on out and should be supervised due to the unpredictable nature of both animals.

REMEMBER

No matter how well a dog and ferret seem to get along, never leave them unsupervised. Be extra vigilant. Dogs can be funny critters, and I don't mean funny ha-ha. They're quick, and you may not be able to rescue your ferret if he needs help.

Ferrets and other small animals

Ferrets are predatory by nature. Allowing them to play with other small animals — such as rabbits, hamsters, birds, hedgehogs, guinea pigs, and lizards — is, in essence, messing with the laws of nature *and* the food chain. As I mention in Chapter 8, most kibble-raised ferrets won't even recognize smaller animals as food. However, the quick movements made by small pets may trigger the predatory reaction in your fuzzbutt. Even if a small pet stays perfectly still, your ferret's curiosity can take over, and, like a dog pawing during play, your ferret may kill the small animal accidentally.

Yes, of course exceptions to this trend exist, but I wouldn't want to risk the life of a small pet just to see if my ferret falls into the exception category. As a general guideline, keep your ferret separated from any animal his cousins may prey on in the wild. And remember not to house them in the same room!

Preparing Your Child for the Ferret

Some adults think young, innocent kids automatically know what to do and what not to do around animals. Not so. You need to teach your child about interacting safely with animals. Although some youngsters may have more common sense than their adult counterparts, an adult is still responsible for keeping both the child and the pet safe. In the following sections, I let you know what your kid needs to know before the introduction, and I take you through the process of making the introduction.

WARNING

Never allow any pet, ferret or otherwise, to interact unsupervised with a baby, toddler, or incapacitated person. Doing so is incredibly irresponsible. The human and the pet can get severely injured, particularly if the pet is a small animal such as a ferret or the person cannot properly fend for himself if needed.

Pause the cartoons: What your child should know beforehand

Children can activate the insanity button in even the calmest person or ferret. Fuzzies already are strung out on excess energy, and kids can easily manage to activate a ferret's overload switch. That's a given, and something you must deal with. Behavior aside, though, you must keep in mind that kids are smaller than adults. They're clumsier, and they have much higher pitched voices. These factors alone can make an already nervous ferret even more excited; when you combine the added hyperactivity a kid brings in, you can have double trouble.

Your job as a responsible adult and ferret-owning human is to teach your child what you know about ferrets in terms he or she will understand. When you're done explaining the following points to your kid, you can explain them again to any of his or her young friends who may also want to interact with your ferret:

>> Many kids get frightened easily around animals, particularly when they get nipped or scratched. Claws and teeth are sharp, and both can hurt. Explain to your child that ferrets are very active and playful and may not mean any harm.

>> Stress to your child the importance of not running around or roughhousing where ferrets are loose. Give age-appropriate reasons why so she'll understand.

>> Reinforce the importance of properly holding a ferret (refer to the section "Hold me gently, please"). Children have a tendency to squeeze things in order not to drop them. And they insist on holding things and then rapidly and without warning change their minds and let the objects or animals drop to the floor.

Insisting that your child always holds the ferret while sitting down is a good idea. That way, even if your fuzzbutt squirms away, he won't end up plopping to the floor.

TIP

For safety reasons, always supervise children when they're interacting with your ferret until you feel confident that they know how to properly play.

Fuzzy, meet Junior: Making the introduction

Kids can be quite unpredictable around and in their interactions with animals. The introductions you make are very important in educating your child about animal safety. It's important to go slowly and explain things as you go along.

The first step in the introduction phase is to go over the rules I mention in the previous section. When your child fully understands what you're saying, go over the following to help ease your ferret safely and comfortably into your child's life:

1. **Because most children automatically shy away from being bitten or scratched, make sure your child wears long pants and long sleeves to prevent your ferret from clawing.** This way, the child will find handling the ferret easier and safer.

2. **Start off slowly by having your child sit on the floor in the same room with the ferret.** Allow the ferret to approach your child on his own terms, but keep him from climbing on your child. This is a good time to practice patience.

3. **If the ferret seems relaxed around your child, and your child hasn't gone into hyper mode, pick up your ferret and demonstrate the proper way to hold him.** Point out his sharp claws and teeth and explain why it's important to properly hold the ferret.

4. **With your child still sitting on the ground, place the ferret in the child's lap and allow the ferret to get used to being with a new person.** Encourage your child to gently pet the ferret.

5. **If the meeting is going well and everyone is still calm, place the ferret into your child's arms, again showing her the proper way to hold the ferret.** Make sure you keep your hands just below the ferret in case your child

decides she no longer wants to hold him. If you feel comfortable with your child's comfort level, you can have her stand up and hold the ferret.

6. **If the you and your ferret both seem comfortable with how your child is handling the situation, demonstrate how to put the ferret back down.** At this time, you also can show your child how to properly pick up the ferret. Learning how to pick up your ferret and put him back down is just as important as learning how to hold him. Remind your child that she should never interact with the ferret without adult supervision.

With these simple guidelines, you should be able to determine how responsible your child will be with a ferret, and how your ferret will do with a child. Some kids and some ferrets take a little longer to get the hang of it. If this is the case with your loved ones, go slow! Never force a child or a pet to interact until both parties feel and act comfortable. Moving to the next step before your child and pet have mastered the prior step may lead to injuries.

Fuzzy Meets Fuzzy: Adding A New Ferret to Your Family

Introducing a new ferret to your other ferret pet(s) can be tricky business (and, remember, should only be done after the proper quarantine process). Like many other species of mammals, ferrets vie for top position. They do so through play wrestling and biting. Some ferrets are natural leaders; others are natural followers; and some would rather venture through life without ever encountering another ferret. You may not know which type you're bringing home until you see him spring into action.

Here are some bits of information to keep in mind when introducing your new ferret to his new family:

» Kits (very young ferrets) are perfect squeaky toys for older ferrets, although the kits rarely see it this way. Adult ferrets can be quite possessive of youngsters. They may try to drag them around and stuff them in hidey-holes while guarding aggressively against curious visitors.

» Newly introduced ferrets often display their frizzed tails for the first ten minutes or so. This behavior is normal. Pay particular attention when one ferret aggressively tackles another and performs an immediate alligator roll, because this behavior can signal trouble. A dominant ferret may take a lot longer to accept a new ferret and in some instances will act particularly aggressive.

Sometimes, a frightened ferret screams and hisses as the more aggressive ferret tries to engage in play. Ferrets play rough, but if one fuzzy seems overly bullied or frightened, separate him and try introducing again later.

>> Ferrets that have been isolated for a long period of time may feel particularly frightened at the sight of another fuzzy.

>> Although ferrets are capable of severely injuring — and even killing — another ferret, it rarely happens. Of course, you should always end the meeting if blood is drawn or if one poops or pees in fear, and you should always have a spare cage for the newcomer in case the introduction turns sour. Your quarantine cage is perfect for this.

REMEMBER

Some signs will almost immediately tell you that the new relationship probably won't work out: Drawing blood, one ferret literally having the poop scared out of him, and persistent screaming, to name a few. It may take only a few minutes for a newcomer to be welcomed, or it may take hours, days, or even months. Some ferrets just won't, under any circumstances, coexist. Most ferrets eventually learn to get along with other ferrets, though. If your ferrets only display bottle-brush tails and keep coming back for more sniffs, they should become best buds in no time.

That being said, you can do certain things to encourage a successful introduction and relationship between ferrets. I cover these actions in the sections that follow, as well as steps you can take to introduce multiple fuzzies.

Meeting on neutral ground

For your initial introduction, you should choose a ferret-proof room (see Chapter 6) that your established ferret hasn't yet explored. It should contain ferret toys, tubes and climbing furniture, as well as food and water. It should also contain secure nest boxes with small openings (see Chapter 5). Another neutral place can be in your yard, with all the ferrets harnessed and leashed.

When all parties are on site, place them together and watch cautiously to see how they react and interact. If the introduction is a rough one, place them in separate cages and try again later.

Messing with their sniffers

Ferrets have a tremendous sense of smell. They identify other ferrets and objects based on the unique scents they give off. The scent of a new ferret can be intimidating and provoke aggression or fear. So, you can take some actions to get their noses used to each other:

>> Because a lot of disagreements arise from one ferret not liking another's special smell, making them smell alike can help to curtail fuzzy tension. Your ferrets are probably due for baths anyway, so break out some safe tearless baby shampoo (use this type of shampoo only for this occasion) and give them baths (See Chapter 9 for more on cleaning). The boys will be busy feeling embarrassed at how girly they smell, and the girls will be busy walking with their heads held high. An established ferret will notice a newcomer, but everyone will smell pretty much the same at this point.

>> You can clean all toys and bedding in your main fuzzy cage before lumping them in together. Also, don't forget to clean the cage and change the litter boxes. These tasks give your new ferret ample opportunity to get his scent in the cage at the same time as the others.

>> You also can switch the cage bedding of the new ferret with the cage bedding of the established fuzzy, and vice versa. This way, they have no choice but to live with each other's stink. They'll either get used to each other or resent the other even more. Usually, they get used to each other. I use this tactic when introducing most animals to each other, from rabbits to foxes. Although it doesn't always work, it has a high success rate.

Forcing a relationship

Some ferret relationships require a little extra help to get going, to the point where it seems like you're forcing the relationship. Hey, no one said the intro would be easy! The following list presents a few more tips for helping your tough guys get through the initial bad times:

>> **Carry the buggers around together.** They may be so busy wondering where they're going that they'll forget their hatred for each other — even if just for a moment. Carry your ferrets everywhere you go in the house. Hold them on your lap together. Make them watch television with you — together! They'll resent you forever, but eventually they'll like each other.

>> **Stick the ferrets in a carrier together and take them to the vet for their shots and checkups.** Fear and anxiety have a bonding effect on both humans and animals. Your fuzzies can share the moment and hate you together.

>> **Allow them to share a tasty treat off the same spoon at the same time.** You also can allow them to enjoy a couple of irresistible licks of salmon oil or pollock oil from the same bottle.

>> **Bathe them together in the same tub at the same time.** They'll share a fear and anxiety similar to what they'll experience at the vet. Plus, the shared humiliation of the bath will lead to a bonding experience like no other.

> » **Let them duke it out!** It may be time to stop babying them. Let them spend a few (3) days screeching, chasing, bullying, and fighting, but no longer than that! Most of the time, ferrets work out their differences if you let them. Use your common sense, but keep in mind that it usually looks and sounds worse than it really is.

Easing your fuzzy into the business

Sometimes nothing you try seems to work, especially when you have one or two ferrets that just seem unwilling to let a newcomer into the group. As frustrating as it may be, you should do everything you can to help ease the new guy into the family. Because ferrets have a hierarchy amongst themselves, it's important to get to know everyone one by one, starting with the most submissive ferret. The theory is that by the time the ferret has met the most dominant ferrets, he'll already have been accepted by the more submissive ferrets and have become part of the family:

1. **Introduce your new ferret to a safe, neutral room with plenty of hiding spots (see the earlier section "Meeting on neutral ground").**

   The first thing he'll do is make his rounds to get to know the place and the new scents. After he knows the territory, he'll familiarize himself with the toys and other items in the room. He'll then dance about in play and silliness, just like any healthy ferret should do. Before long, he'll become bored with his surroundings and look to you for more to do.

2. **Introduce your most submissive and docile opposite-sex ferret into the room. (If your new ferret is a boy, introduce a girl.)**

   Now that your new ferret's attention is off the room, he can focus on the newly introduced ferret. If all goes well, you should see a fair amount of sniffing, some silly dancing, and some play about the room.

3. **Introduce your next most docile and submissive opposite-sex ferret into the room.**

   Repeat this process with all ferrets of this characterization.

4. **When you run out of opposite-sex ferrets to introduce, bring in the most docile same-sex ferret.**

   Repeat this process as well.

5. **What should remain are the unintroduced ferrets that are your typical aggressors.**

   The idea is that your new ferret will be assimilated into the group and become more easily accepted by the more aggressive ferrets with the blessing of the others.

REMEMBER

Although gender introductions can be unpredictable, boy ferret meeting girl ferret statistically has the best outcome. Boy ferret meeting boy ferret produces pretty good results, too. Girl ferret meeting girl ferret, on the other hand, can be more of a challenge.

If any of the previous steps fail at any point along the way, you should stop the introduction process and try again the next day. See the section "Messing with their sniffers" and bathe each of them right before starting the process again. Introduce salmon oil or pollock oil or another tasty treat when things start heating up and have them share a spoon. Take things you've learned in this chapter and incorporate them into this introduction process. Be creative. It may take several rounds of introductions or combinations of techniques. When all is said and done, there's no guarantee any introduction technique will work for your new ferret.

TIP

The art of butt sniffing is incredibly evolved, yet I wouldn't recommend you try this with your friends! Although we find it quite annoying and even embarrassing when dogs do it to us, butt sniffing actually serves an important role in telling the difference between individual family members, even identical twins. Our ferrets are no different. When ferrets are first introduced or reintroduced after a long time of being apart, it is thought that butt sniffing is not only fun, but it provides them a wealth of information of the other ferret such as gender and hormonal/reproductive status, diet, health status, temperament, and even whether he's met this ferret before. I might even venture to say that the more butt sniffing that occurs upon introduction, the less likely it is that serious squabbles will occur. Just a theory.

Heading Off Stranger Danger

Your new ferret may have several opportunities to encounter strangers when he enters your family and home. A meeting may take place at the vet's office or in the park during playtime (with you attached at the end of the leash, of course; see Chapter 5). It may be in your child's classroom during a show-and-tell or in your own home. You must realize that not everyone shares your fuzzy enthusiasm; some people will be taken aback at the quick display of curiosity shown by your ferret. Others may get annoyed at how bold your ferret can be as he tries to steal their possessions and mow through their hairdos. The good news is that you'll surely find people who are just like you and me. These people will be tickled pink at your ferret's charming personality.

Some ferrets are natural social butterflies; others quiver with nervousness when encountering new people or places. Use common sense; don't risk a stranger's health or your fuzzy's life if you already know that your ferret reacts badly to change or strangers. That said, here are some suggestions for dealing with strangers who come around your ferret:

>> When allowing a stranger to touch your ferret for the first time, keep your ferret's head under control. Offer the stranger your ferret's bottom and back to pet in order to minimize any chance of biting. Some people are nuts! Even a small nip might cause a well-known friend to report your pet for biting. We all know how that might end!

>> If you're entertaining guests at your home or if your kids have friends over, allow time for introductions; after the fuzzy curiosity has passed, it's best to keep your ferret caged. With so much else going on, supervising a roaming ferret becomes difficult. He can be mishandled or get injured with all the feet moving about.

>> If the stranger will become a frequent visitor to your ferret, give her a brief education on the common behavior of ferrets and on the proper way to handle them. I can't stress the education factor enough. That, along with common sense, has allowed me to safely show off my ferrets hundreds and hundreds of times with no tragedies or even close calls to report.

3

Basic Ferret Care and Feeding

Uncover the do's and don'ts of feeding your ferret the multiple diet options available.

Address all husbandry needs, from ferret bathing to cage cleaning and everything in between.

Know the safest way to travel with your ferret or ESA.

IN THIS CHAPTER

» **Hydrating your fuzzy**

» **Scanning the dietary requirements for ferrets**

» **Giving your ferret a traditional dry or wet diet**

» **Supplying an alternative (natural) diet**

» **Adding supplements and treats to your fuzzy's diet**

Chapter **8**

Filling Your Ferret's Belly

P roviding a suitable diet is essential for your ferret's good health, though feeding your fuzzy properly is easier said than done. The keys to a good diet are the proper amounts of

» Fat

» Meat-based protein

» Vitamins and minerals

So, what's the problem? Finding this perfect diet can be difficult and challenging for even an experienced fuzzy human.

That's why this chapter is extra-important. It covers the basic information you need to know about water — how much water to give and how often to give it — traditional diets, alternative diets, supplements, and treats. I also discuss the ferret's natural or evolutionary diet, a topic that in my opinion is important to know about in order to understand your ferret's nutritional needs. I even explain how to switch a ferret's diet if you find it necessary to do so; I hope I can convince some of you to do just that!

REMEMBER

Just as important is that your ferret's diet not contain, or have very minimal amounts of,

>> Fruits

>> Vegetables

>> Starches

>> Sugars

The wrong foods can lead to obesity, food-related illnesses, and a shortened life span. Surprisingly, to date no science-based diet/food studies in ferrets have been completed. So, just how big a part diet plays in terms of ferret diseases is still being discovered. Experts and owners alike know that it's big, however, and we may all be surprised at what will eventually be revealed.

Water, Water, Everywhere

No living thing can live without water, but not all water is equal when it comes to hydrating your ferret. Some ferret owners prefer to use bottled or distilled water. However, experts strongly argue that distilled water lacks many important nutrients that pets need, so you may want to avoid distilled water all together. Unless your tap water tests positive for high levels of harmful chemicals, tap water or even filtered water should be sufficient to hydrate your ferret. Make sure that your ferret's water bottle and bowl are full at all times!

Ferrets as Diners

I think I can safely say that no one has come up with the perfect solution when it comes to the question of what people should feed their domestic ferrets. There are so many factors that come into play, from owner preference to food availability to ferret health. I can't give you a single right answer. But I do know a lot about ferrets' dietary quirks and feeding needs. The following list presents some basics all ferret owners should know about their ferrets; the more you know about your ferret, the better you'll be able to choose the right diet for her:

>> Ferrets are *obligate carnivores,* meaning they meet virtually all of their nutritional needs by eating meat-based (animal-based) foods. They must eat meat!

>> Ferrets are *hypercarnivores,* meaning their anatomy, physiology, and behaviors are adapted to a strict carnivore lifestyle.

>> Ferrets *olfactory imprint* on their foods, which means their food-odor preferences are generally established by 6 months of age and finalized by 8 to 12 months. At this point, the older they get, the less likely they'll be able to recognize the smell of a new food as being yummy.

TIP

Knowing that your fuzzy olfactory imprints on his food, it makes sense to begin feeding him as many different varieties of foods as possible, as early as possible. Not only does this provide enrichment and stimulate his taste buds, but it also makes changing or introducing new foods less challenging!

>> Ferrets aren't built to digest fiber or plant matter. If you were to take a peek inside a ferret (not advised), you'd see that her large intestine is short and tubular and that the ferret lacks a cecum. The *cecum* is a blind pouch located at the junction where the small intestine ends and the large intestine begins; this is the place where fiber is bacterially digested (similar to the human appendix). Too much fiber in your ferret's belly leads to extra-squishy or mucousy poops.I mean, come on, even the mighty lion's cecum is better equipped to digest plant matter than ferrets'!

>> Ferrets may have a rapid GI transit time, depending on what food they consume. Food may pass in as little as 3 to 4 hours, which leaves little time to digest and absorb nutrients. In 6 hours, if fasted, the stomach usually is completely emptied. For this reason, feeding high-quality meat-based products and fat is even more important.

>> Ferrets can't digest milk as adults because of low levels of lactase.

>> Ferrets, because they're carnivores, have very simple gut flora (bacteria). Unlike in herbivores, fermentation isn't needed to extract the nutrients during the digestive process. Digestive additives such as *Lactobacillus,* found in yogurt, aren't important and won't help a ferret digest food.

>> The ferret's teeth are designed for tearing and cutting, not for chewing.

This list is just the beginning. This chapter is full of dietary information that should help you sort out the questions in your head!

Feeding the Traditional Commercial Diet

Traditional commercial diet formulas for ferrets have improved over the past decades as people have gained more knowledge and understanding of the ferret. But when it comes to dietary needs, your ferret is still no different from her polecat cousins: Her food should contain *taurine* (which helps keep her eyes and heart healthy) and be composed of less than 5 percent crude fiber, be between 20 and 40 percent crude fat and no less than 35 to 40 percent meat-based protein. Also important is the ratio of calcium to phosphorous, which should be 1:1, and although this value is not often listed on the label, most kibbles are usually adequate providers of these nutrients. When it comes to kibble and wet food, ferret owners have many options:

>> The pet industry has come out with several foods formulated just for ferrets. Many of these commercial ferret foods meet the protein/fat-level requirements, and some are considered among the better commercially available food choices for your ferret.

>> Some high-quality dry kitten foods have the necessary taurine, fat, and protein contents, but most don't. Before you make dry kitten food a staple of your ferret's diet, make sure the brand you choose has the nutritional content your ferret needs.

WARNING

>> Dog food isn't a source of proper nutrition for your ferret. It's usually too low in protein and too high in grains and veggies. It also doesn't contain the taurine additive that your ferret needs for healthy eyes and heart. Don't panic, however, if your furry snorkeler takes a dive into the dog's food bowl (when the dog isn't around, of course) and chows down on a piece or two of dog food. It won't harm him as long as it's a rare treat.

Don't expect a pet shop clerk to know what's best for your ferret. Many are fairly educated about the products they sell, but not necessarily the critters they sell. I've overheard one or two telling new ferret owners to feed canned dog food or only hamburger meat. I even heard one clerk tell a customer that ferrets are herbivores (plant eaters). Instead, read through the information in the following sections about what type of commercial diet to feed your ferret. In these sections, I discuss what wet and dry foods are and the pros and cons of feeding them to your ferret. I also talk about setting up a feeding schedule and what to do if you want to change from one diet to another. After you know the facts, you can get with your vet to go over your options.

Wet or dry food?

Some people like to stick with a dry food for their ferrets, and others prefer to feed their fuzzies moist food. Some people alternate between the diets, and some savvy ferret owners mix the dry and moist foods. I personally try to give my ferrets as much variety as possible. The following sections give you some things to think about when deciding what type of food is right for your furball.

DISSECTING PET FOOD LABELS

Pet food labels, even those from reputable manufacturers, can be and often are misleading. Unless the label says all the protein is from meat, you can be sure it isn't. The protein can come from other sources thrown into the recipe. The hair in a hairball is close to 100 percent protein. Fecal matter (trace amounts are allowed in by-products) also is made up of protein. Ick! So even if your ferret's food is 30 percent protein, how much of it actually comes from meat? Even if meat is listed as the top ingredient, that doesn't mean the meat is where all the protein comes from.

Most pet foods have meat or chicken by-products listed as a first ingredient. What the heck are meat and chicken by-products, anyway? Hold onto your lunch. By-products are leftover gunky animal bits that aren't fit for human consumption. They don't even qualify to be stuffed into a hot dog casing (that's really bad). By-products include such yummies as heads (chicken), skin, feet, blood, guts, beaks, tendons, stomach contents, discarded organs, and fecal matter (trace amounts). Once in a while, by-products may include bits of less-than-fresh meat. The protein from by-products may not be easily digested by your pet ferret. The key is the quality and wholesomeness of the by-products.

TIP

Ingredients are listed in order of highest percentage or concentration to lowest percentage or concentration. Remember to make sure there is no fruit and no sweeteners in the mix! The top five ingredients are key and should be: Meat, such as chicken, beef, or fish, and can be deboned or dehydrated (this should be listed first or second); meat protein isolate (should be listed first or second); chicken/beef/fish or another meat meal; meat by-products such as organ meats or eggs; and animal fats or oils.

Consumers don't even know why many additives are thrown into the pet food. Some say "to preserve freshness." Sure. Can you imagine? And did they remember to add all those essential vitamins, amino acids, and minerals that ferrets evolved eating? Some manufacturers may try their best to make up for it in some way, but how do we really know the job was accomplished? And ponder this: If a food was perfect, as each ad campaign suggests, why do the same manufacturers continuously release "new and improved" versions? This is evidence that the diet was NOT as complete as advertising suggested.

WARNING

Look at labels carefully and avoid foods with ingredients such as peas or pea protein, chick peas, sweet potatoes, or similar foods that have been closely linked to bladder stones. Many grain-free kibbles add these to their recipes, so beware!

Commercial dry (kibble)

Kibble is widely available, hygienically safe if you practice routine handwashing after handling, economical, and convenient, making it the most popular dietary choice among ferret owners. Many dry kibble options are available. They come in the form of kitten (least preferred) or ferret food. Some are at the top of my list, and others would go right into my garbage can. Some "nutritionally complete" ferret diets are available, but no matter what, if you're going this route, you need to choose only a high-quality ferret or kitten kibble for your furball.

If you want to feed your ferret kibble, keep this in mind: Ideally, the first five ingredients should be meat products, and the kibble should contain no corn, sweet potatoes, peas, or pea protein. The majority of kibble is poultry-based, but other meats are available as well. Avoid products that contain dried bits of fruits or vegetables, which ferrets can't digest.

REMEMBER

Ferrets can't chew kibble, so they swallow it in chunks; thus, it may not be digested properly, especially if the ferret has limited access to water. Ferrets must first hydrate kibble (guaranteed to less than 10 percent moisture) before proper digestion. And contrary to popular belief, dry kibble doesn't significantly help wear down the tartar buildup on a fuzzy's teeth. Hard kibble fed as a sole diet *does* cause tooth wear because it's very abrasive. Sprinkle a few drops of water or chicken broth over the hard food and microwave it briefly to help soften it up a little without making it the consistency of canned food. This minimizes damage to the teeth and improves digestibility.

This all sounds well and good, right? But dry kibble isn't all good for all ferrets. The following list outlines some cons of feeding your ferret kibble:

>> Kibble isn't mentally stimulating and is monotonous in taste. I know. I've tried it!

>> The heat and processing of the kibble may make some of the protein less digestible.

TECHNICAL STUFF

Kibble is an *extruded* diet. The ingredients are finely ground into a dough and then pushed or drawn through a "kibble-shaped" tube with heat and pressure. The dough is then cut and dried.

>> Starches/carbohydrates are used in the formation of kibble to hold the shape. Most kibbles have around 20 to 30 percent digestible carbohydrates, whereas a natural diet serves up about 7 percent carbs. Chew on that!

>> The higher than needed levels of carbs in kibble may contribute to diseases such as insulinoma (see Chapter 16), gastroenteritis, and bladder stones.

Commercial canned

Canned pet food is widely available, hygienically safe, economical, and convenient, and is therefore another popular choice among ferret owners. When looking for a canned food, you should stick with a high-quality feline or ferret food. The main ingredients should be meat products, and the food should contain no additional grains or sweeteners.

Canned ferret food has some benefits that you should consider when making the diet decision:

>> Canned foods are mentally stimulating.

>> Because many meat proteins are available, the tastes in canned foods are varied.

>> Canned foods are low in carbs and high in fat and protein.

Of course, canned foods have their cons, too:

>> High-quality canned feline or ferret food is easier on the teeth in terms of wear, but it may lead to faster tartar buildup.

>> Canned food lacks the nutrient density to be a ferret's sole food. Because it is about 70 percent water, ferrets need to eat a larger volume of canned food to get the same calories provided by dry food, which has only about a 1-percent moisture content. Ferrets' tummies are small, so they may not be able to get all their nutrient needs from canned food only.

REMEMBER

Depending on the brand, it's rare that a canned food would be a nutritionally better food than dry kibble. It's also slightly more expensive than kibble and can cause stinkier poops. Canned food shouldn't be the only food in the ferret's diet, but it would make an excellent addition to any main course, especially when served alongside kibble.

Setting a feeding schedule

Ferret owners influence how often their ferrets need to eat, because ferrets adapt their eating cycles to what and when they're being fed. For example, if you're feeding your ferret a kibble that's high in carbs, blood/sugar fluctuations can drive your ferret to eat more often — perhaps as often as every 4 to 5 hours. An even poorer diet could drive her to eat every 3 to 4 hours. However, if you're feeding a diet that's high in fat and meat-based protein, you'll leave your ferret satisfied for much longer — perhaps as long as 8 to 10 hours.

Some people think that leaving food out all the time leads to ferret obesity. They must be thinking of us humans! Normally, ferrets aren't gluttons and consume only the amount of fat needed to get the energy to terrorize their households in their normal capacity. This is called *eating to meet caloric need*, which is possible only when the ferret is eating a nutritionally complete food. If the ferret's diet is of nutritionally poor quality, your fuzzy will develop a nutritional deficit and will instinctively eat more to make up for it. This is called *eating to meet nutritional need*. If the poor diet also happens to be loaded with carbs (calorie dense), eating it can result in an obese ferret.

REMEMBER

If you think your ferret is getting chunky, take her to the vet to rule out an enlarged spleen or fluid in her abdominal cavity. Enlarged spleens are common causes of rapid weight gain.

Some ferrets get slightly wider with age, and some get wider in the winter. In general, obesity is rarely a serious problem in ferrets — especially if their diets are balanced.

Changing kibble diets

There are many reasons for needing or wanting to change your ferret's kibble diet. It can be a medical necessity. The food you're currently feeding may be discontinued. Or you may find something better out there for her. But it may be difficult to convince your ferret that she needs to change to the new type of food — especially if the fuzzy has been fed a different or improper diet before coming into your care. If this is the case, you need to switch the ferret over to the good stuff, despite any protest she may display. I've had some ferrets that would eat any type of cat, kitten, or ferret food, no matter what. These ferrets were likely fed a wide variety of foods at a young age. On the other hand, I've had some that refused all food until I could figure out exactly what they'd been eating before coming into my care. This is a case of extreme olfactory imprinting (see the earlier section "Ferrets as Diners"), and were used to only one type of food growing up.

The best way to switch your ferret's food is to mix her previous food with the new food of choice. Start off by adding just a small amount of the new food to the old. It's important not to switch completely to the new food immediately. Such a drastic change can lead to an upset tummy, diarrhea, and a generally crabby ferret. Gradually increase the amount of new food you include and decrease the amount of old food; do so over the course of 10 to 14 days. This process usually works well and gives your fuzzy's system a chance to get used to the change.

TIP

Don't sell that coffee bean grinder at the garage sale just yet! It's perfect for finely blending the old and new kibbles together to make a kibble "soup" that your ferret may find more palatable. Just take the mixture, add a little warm water and *voilà* — soup! If he still resists, try storing the new kibble in a ziplock bag with some of the old kibble until the smells of each kibble blend together. This can often make the switch easier.

If your ferret eats around the new food and devours the old, give her time and don't give up. The switch may take several days or even as long as several months, so patience and persistence are positive virtues. The health of your baby could depend on it.

If you own multiple ferrets and house them in the same cage, telling whether a ferret has taken to her new food can be difficult, because the ferrets eat from the same bowl. As the food level is quickly depleted, you may be unaware that your ferret is slowly starving, which can be extremely dangerous. Watch for any significant weight changes in all your fuzzies, particularly the newcomers. In fact, I recommend that you house a new ferret separately until you know for sure that she's eating what the rest of the gang is eating. This practice gives you the opportunity to monitor her food intake closely and prevent a possible slow starvation.

Serving Up an Alternative Diet

People have fed their ferrets man-made foods — mostly out of convenience or lack of anything else good to feed — since World War II. Recently, the ferret world has seen a growing movement to switch to more natural diets. A natural diet consists of feeding, among other things, meats, organs, and bones. Some people believe the only way to true pet health is to feed a diet that the animal evolved eating, and kibble certainly wasn't around 2,500 years ago, much less a century ago.

The following list presents what proponents of natural and evolutionary diets believe the benefits are:

» A natural or evolutionary diet ensures that your ferret is getting her essential nutrients. For example, those essential amino acids that the ferret can't produce herself are commonly found in the foods her wild relatives eat: rabbits, mice, rats, birds, frogs, lizards, and squirrels. Calcium is another example: Many man-made cat, kitten, or ferret foods lack quality bone meal, so ferrets are losing out on needed calcium.

» A healthy ferret on a varied and natural diet doesn't need to have food available at all times. The ferret's wild relatives eat only once or twice a day, sometimes even missing days when food is scarce.

>> Many people who feed their fuzzies a more natural diet believe that the variation of food consistency (bone, skin, meat, and so on) helps to flush out the intestinal tract, causing the ferret to be less prone to hairballs and other obstructions. The diet also helps to even out nutrient needs that are currently unknown.

>> The design of the ferret's jaw and teeth leaves her with limited chewing capability. Her teeth were designed for cutting meat and bone, but not all the time — at least not up to ten meals per day. Kibble can be as hard as or harder than bone, and its abrasiveness leads to wear on the teeth. A natural diet generally is easier on the teeth.

The following sections explain what I call a *natural diet* (raw or freeze-dried raw) and an evolutionary diet (small, whole prey). But first, you need to understand the polecat a little better. And you'll also learn about bones as part of the alternative diet. Finally, I explore the different ways you can feed the natural or evolutionary diet to your ferret.

REMEMBER

Most mainstream veterinarians are adamantly opposed to feeding raw meat diets, whether they're homemade or commercially prepared, and list many valid reasons why. Other vets and many holistic vets swear by the raw diet and give their valid reasons why as well. And each group refutes the other's reasons. Both sides sound right and reasonable. The only thing they agree on is that care and diligence are needed in handling raw food.

TIP

Although it's unknown exactly how the nutrient composition will be changed, it's possible to cook the diet to eliminate the risk of passing along any bacteria or parasites to your ferret. You can braise, steam, or microwave the food. This is also a good way to get your ferret switched over to the raw diet if this is what you choose to feed. Offer the food completely cooked or even slightly cooked to help get your ferret's system used to the change. Gradually mix in raw food with the cooked before switching completely to raw. See the section "Exploring the alternative way of feeding" for more advice on diet conversion.

Getting to know the wild polecat's diet

If I were to undertake the task of designing the perfect man-made ferret food, the first thing I would do is research. I would want to know what animal(s) was the ferret's closest relative and what it naturally thrived on in the wild.

Ferrets are descended from wild polecats, and experts know that both ferrets and polecats are obligate carnivores (see the section "Ferrets as Diners"). So, what do polecats prey on and eat in the wild? Mice, rats, rabbits, frogs, other amphibians, invertebrates, voles, small snakes, birds, eggs, and even some fish. Polecats often eat the entire carcass of smaller prey, from the organs to the bones, sometimes leaving the intestinal tract by the wayside. They also consume the fur of smaller prey and the downy part of birds as they eat the bodies. This natural diet is extremely low in carbohydrates. Most prey-animal carbohydrates originate from the animals' glycogen and blood sugar, with some possibly coming from the intestinal tracts of the animals. The diet also is high in meat-based protein and low in fiber. Additionally, this type of diet typically doesn't lead to dental disease. Admittedly, some polecats do get the disease, but the rate in polecats is much lower. The various textures of natural prey foods actually serve to massage the ferret's gums and help wipe the teeth clean.

Ferrets, if given the opportunity at a young age, would follow in their ancestors' dietary footsteps. Just for kicks, compare the evolutionary ingredients to the current list of ingredients found in your ferret's kibble. Nowhere in the polecat's diet would you find corn grits, corn meal, wheat, soy flour, rice, raisin puree, banana juice, cane molasses, corn sugar, dried potato products . . . well, you get the idea. Those are just some of the ingredients you may find in ferret kibble. What are food manufacturers thinking when they formulate our ferrets' food? They certainly aren't thinking of the evolutionary dietary needs of the ferret. (For more on an evolutionary diet, see the section that focuses on the topic later in this chapter.)

PMR (PREY-MODEL RAW), AKA FRANKENPREY

The concept of PMR is based on the belief that you can mimic your pet's evolutionary diet by combining whole, raw (emphasis on *raw*), natural foods. As such, this diet contains zero fruits, veggies, grains, or dairy. Although preparing and feeding PMR isn't for every furry owner, it has its pros and cons.

Proponents believe PMR

- Can lengthen life span

- Can prevent and even reverse illnesses/diseases in pets

- Improves the immune system

REMEMBER

One of the main reasons to switch to PMR is to provide your ferret with as much nutrition as possible, nutrition of a quality higher than that available in man-made diets, while still maintaining a diet that closely resembles a ferret's natural diet. The mere act of cooking can destroy, or at the very least alter, the fats, proteins,

(continued)

(continued)

vitamins, and minerals in the food. Although cooking may make some nutrients less available in some types of food, it may make nutrients *more* available in others.

- Improves pets' performance
- Improves coat and body odor
- Eliminates the need for dental cleanings
- Is more balanced than commercial kibbles

Many people "PMR" their pets on their own, using recipes they've gotten off the Internet or that they've concocted themselves. This isn't always safe. A homemade diet can be the best or the worst food you can feed your ferret! It's very difficult to get the right formula down; you could make your ferret sick by not having the right amount of this, that, or the other thing. Aim for a PMR formula ratio of 80% meat/10% secreting organs/ 10% bones (80/10/10) as a "loose" guide. Many seasoned PMR feeders adhere to a ratio of muscle meat (65 to 70 percent), edible bone (10 to 15 percent), heart (10 percent), liver (5 percent), and another secreting organ (5 percent). There are a few variations out there. Says veterinarian Susan Brown, "100 percent home-made diets — either raw, cooked, or a combination thereof — have been used successfully in some cases with individual animals. However, this requires real diligence to detail and having enough variety in the diet to cover all of the needs of the ferret, including trace vitamins and minerals. In addition, the owner has to prevent over-supplementation of various vitamins and minerals, because excessive amounts of some substances can be as great a health risk as not enough of these same substances. Currently there are quite a few quality diet choices for the small carnivore, and it is my recommendation that a ferret's diet should have a majority of its substance based on a commercial diet, whether it is a commercial raw, kibble, freeze-dried, or canned diet, or even better a combination of at least two of these forms."

Opponents of PMR believe

- The risk of transmitting bacteria and parasites to people and pets far outweighs the pros of feeding PMR. *E. coli* and salmonella are particularly of concern.

REMEMBER

First off, wash your hands and prep surfaces when you're finished with the preparation! It's that simple, no different than when you're cooking dinner for yourself or family at home. Second, a carnivore is built to digest and pass bacteria very quickly through its system. In carnivores, with their highly acidic stomachs and pH level of about 1.0, salmonella hasn't a chance of survival since it needs conditions of 4 to 8 pH in order to thrive. We know the transit time in our ferret can be as short as 3 to 4 hours. Because salmonella also requires at least 12 hours to reach incubation, it is digested and deposited harmlessly, albeit disgustingly, just outside the litterbox for you long before it can do any harm.

- The diet poses a particular risk to pet owners who formulate and mix the diets, especially for people who are young, elderly, or immuno-compromised.

- The diet is often nutritionally unsound and inconsistent.

- The use of whole bones can cause intestinal obstructions/perforations, dental fractures, and gastroenteritis.

If you like the idea of PMR, several commercially made raw and freeze-dried ferret diets are available, which I'll talk about later. They may be easier and more convenient to feed, as well as closer to the nutritional balance you're looking for. I also talk more about the controversy of feeding raw meat later in this chapter.

Keep the following things in mind when preparing and trying your hand at feeding 80/10/10 (5/5) PMR to your ferret:

- Some organs fall into the 80 percent "meat" category, such as: heart, lungs, gizzards, tongue, muscle and green tripe.

- Other meats can include: chicken, veal, duck, beef, fish, kangaroo, pheasant, turkey, venison, bison, buffalo, ostrich, emu, elk, pork, goat, rabbit and lamb. Do not feed harvested meat from carnivores such as: raccoons, fox, bear, coyote, wild pig/boar, and so on. And roadkill is a definite no-way!

- In the "secreting" organ category are: liver (vitamin A, folic acid, B vitamins, iron and copper), kidney (selenium, B vitamins, vitamin D), spleen (iron, tryptophan), pancreas (essential digestive enzymes), brain (DHA), thymus (hormones, which aid in immune function), and testicles (B vitamins, especially B12).

- Although 10 percent of the 80/10/10 ratio should be made up of secreting organs, 5 percent of that must be liver, thus the split to 5/5.

TIP

A liver is a liver is a liver, right? Wrong! Ruminant livers, or livers harvested from hooved cud-chewing animals such as cows, lamb, goats, and so on, are much higher in copper and should be fed at about 2 to 3 percent. Livers from animals such as turkeys and chickens have lower copper levels and should be fed at 5 percent. Although pork liver has no bioavailable copper, it too should be fed at 5 percent. And, no matter which source of liver you feed, adding more than 5 percent to the diet is not recommended due to the high content of vitamin A present.

- Bones may consist of whole prey, wings, feet, necks, frames/carcasses(chicken and ducks), tails and ribs. Remember never to feed dried out, brittle bones (baked, microwaved, and so on) that may be prone to splintering.

(continued)

(continued)

TIP

Getting the ratio down pat takes practice, and sometimes the proof is in the poo. A good hint that all is well with your furry carnivore is that he has *normal* poop, which will be small (less filler in a natural diet, so less to poop out). It will be firm, brown, and have little to no odor! Imagine that! Hard and white poop is an indication he's getting too much bone in his diet, so tone it down a bit! Loose poop is quite the opposite and may indicate too little bone in the diet or perhaps too much fat. You may have to experiment to see which one. As if loose wasn't bad enough, loose and stinky poop screams too much organ protein! But, you can do this! Patience.

The good, the bad, and the ugly on bones

Bones contain an incredible amount of good stuff, with calcium being the most obvious nutritional content. Bone marrow itself is made up of tissues rich in protein and fat. Bone and marrow contain high amounts of fatty acids, fats, iron, and other vitamins essential to the health of carnivores. Most of this good stuff comes from the ends of the bones, which are softer and easily bitten, chewed, and swallowed. The placement of the good stuff is beneficial, because the ends are the parts ferrets are most interested in. They usually leave the rest if they can find something else to eat.

Fact is, bones are wonderful sources of natural nutrition. If you think your ferret would benefit from the calcium and other nutrients in bones, you should try adding them to her diet.

Can feeding bones to your ferret cause harm? Certainly. So can feeding kibble! On extremely rare occasions, a bone splinter may cut the esophagus, causing internal bleeding. A fragment can even puncture the intestinal tract or stomach. But in my experience, these scenarios happen less frequently than a ferret choking on commercial food. Plus, the middle piece of a bone is the part that would most likely cause damage, and most ferrets eat off the ends of the bones only, leaving the middles for the garbage can.

If you're thinking of including bones in your ferret's diet, keep in mind the following:

>> Do not feed machine-cut bones, because they will likely have sharp edges that prove to be detrimental to your ferret.

>> Do not feed cooked bones of any kind. They may be hard and brittle, and they will be prone to splintering.

>> Avoid all weight-bearing bones, such as femurs or other long bones, because they are much denser than your ferret's teeth and may chip, crack, or wear the teeth down.

>> Large, soft bones can be smashed up into smaller pieces to reveal the highly nutritious and yummy marrow.

TIP

Getting your ferret to start munching on bones can prove challenging! Start with small, soft bones such as wing tips, drumettes, or ribs from small birds such as cornish game hens or quail. If you use drumettes, cut the "knuckle" off and toss it or smash it. Grab a cleaver and chop up the bone-in piece of meat into small pieces. Your meat-eater will hopefully be drawn to the deliciousness of the marrow and happily chow down on both the meat and marrow-covered bone.

>> Other acceptable bone choices are: rats/mice/guinea pigs (keep in mind that only adult rodents are nutritionally balanced, and these are actually considered whole-prey food items), frogs (all bones fed minimally due to extremely low-fat content), rabbit/Cornish game hen/quail/partridge/pheasant (all bones), chicken (wings, legs, feet and carcass), turkey (feet, neck, legs, wings, and ground carcass), and duck (wings, feet, neck, ribs and carcass).

>> Do not eliminate bones from your furry carnivore's diet due to your own worry. If you're still paranoid, smash the bones to bits and still allow your ferret to reap the benefits!

TIP

The Internet too often leads us to conflicting and or misleading information about our carpet sharks. There is, however, a fantastic source of reliable, up-to-date information, as well as ongoing support for ferret owners on the Internet: Holistic Ferret Forum has both a website (http://www.holisticferretforum.com/) and a Facebook group called Holistic Ferrets (https://www.facebook.com/groups/158560084258398/).

TIP

There are several great online sources to purchase ingredients for your ferret's PMR diet, which may prove easier or more convenient than your local grocery store or reptile feeder/supply house. Some tried-and-true companies you may like are:

>> https://primalpastures.com/collections/all-products (California)

>> https://www.primitivechoice.com/collections/raw-meat-items (Colorado)

>> http://www.rawfeedingmiami.com (Florida)

>> https://rebelraw.com/ (Georgia)

>> http://www.mypetcarnivore.com (Indiana)

- » https://www.rawdeliverymn.com/ (Minnesota)
- » https://pawfectlyrawne.com/ (New Hampshire)
- » http://hare-today.com (Pennsylvania)
- » http://www.texastripe.com/default.asp (Texas)
- » https://www.thogersenfamilyfarm.com/ (Washington)

E. COLI AND SALMONELLA

Both *E. coli* and salmonella are opportunistic little buggers that can live in the ferret's intestines without causing upset. Clinical signs range from mild gastroenteritis to more disconcerting signs such as tarry/bloody stools, anorexia, pale mucous membranes, severe dehydration, and even death. At minimum, treatment includes the appropriate antibiotics and fluid therapy. But the questions still left unanswered are how often are ferrets truly infected with debilitating *E. coli* or salmonella infections?

Let me first say people will always perceive some sort of risk when feeding food, especially raw. However, perceived risk is what you *think* the risk is *regardless* of what the *actual* risk is. Because of perceived risk, raw foods are under continuous scrutiny, which is rarely given to commercial foods.

Your immune system supplies the soldiers that guard the body against microbial intruders, such as the dreaded salmonella and *E. coli*. It's an adaptive system, so if you've never encountered an organism, you can get really sick and even die if suddenly exposed.

The same process is true when it comes to salmonella and *E. coli*. As strict carnivores, polecats come into contact with both organisms on a frequent basis. As a result, they have a natural immunity that helps protect them. This immunity could be genetic or acquired or a combination of both. However, some studies show that the immune system has to be "taught" to recognize the good from the bad. That's the basis of inoculations; you use a weakened, dead, or harmless variant to teach the immune system how to fight the living and dangerous invader.

There is no doubt that commercial raw foods are potentially contaminated with dozens of species of bacteria, any of which could result in disease or infection to the handler or consumer. This danger is not limited to raw meats, poultry, or eggs, but *all* raw foods, including raw vegetables and fruit. Salmonella and *E. coli* are the most commonly mentioned bacteria when discussing raw diets, but little empirical evidence exists to equate the perceived risk of infection to the actual risk. Arguments that the presence of salmonella in ferret feces proves it's a danger cannot be properly assessed without a baseline for comparison. A lot of emphasis is made of the risks of salmonella and *E. coli*, whatever they are, but little or no research has been done in ferrets that show —one way or another — that the presence of the bacteria constitutes an actual threat to the ferret or healthy individuals within their environment. And remember, the pH in our ferret's stomach is only around 1.0, and salmonella requires at least a 5 to 8 pH to survive and thrive, not to mention the GI transit time that quickly pushes out any bad bacteria.

The solution to feeding is a common sense approach to the problem. If you want to feed a kibble diet, then empty the dish of uneaten food each day, wash the dish in hot soapy water, and let it sit in the sun (or under a UV lamp) for an hour. Just because kibble is dry, it doesn't mean it can't be contaminated with salmonella and *E. coli*.

Likewise, if you want to feed a raw diet, keep in mind that you cannot predict if any food will be contaminated or not. If you're still uncomfortable feeding raw meat, it can be *briefly* seared with a propane torch (or on a hot barbeque) to kill surface bacteria without seriously harming interior nutrients. Or, it can be immersed in food-grade hydrogen peroxide to kill surface bacteria (many Internet stores carry the product). Perhaps the best way to kill as many bacteria as possible is to immerse the food in boiling water for about a minute only; again, to kill surface bacteria. Both searing and boiling will cook the contaminated surfaces, killing the bacteria, but allow the relatively sterile interiors to remain mostly uncooked, leaving important nutrients intact.

Choosing commercial raw or freeze-dried raw diets

Several pet food companies have developed commercially prepared raw or freeze-dried raw diets for ferrets or felines. These types of diets can be a great substitute for making the natural raw diet yourself. They're a little more expensive, but they're certainly more convenient and may be more nutritionally complete than homemade natural diets.

The pros of this type of natural diet include the following:

>> Some formulas are closer to the ferret's evolutionary diet, in terms of composition, than commercial canned food or kibble.

>> The diet is meat- and fat-based and is low on carbs.

>> Many of the nutrients are retained because this diet is unprocessed.

>> The diet may lessen the signs of and even prevent some GI diseases.

>> The diet is easy to feed, because the food usually comes in little medallions or freeze-dried chunks, which can be fed dry or reconstituted with water.

>> A wide variety of meat proteins are available; and the tastes are varied, making it more mentally stimulating.

>> Your ferret will have smaller and less frequent poops, because she'll digest more of the food.

>> You'll need to feed your ferret less frequently because of the natural nature of the diet.

TIP

The commercial raw or freeze-dried raw diet can be fed alone if it's a balanced recipe, but would also make an excellent addition to a kibble diet, or you can alternate this type of diet with kibble.

The diet, however, does have its cons, which include the following:

>> Composition can vary greatly from diet to diet.

>> The diet is hygienically questionable for you; you must use excellent hygiene practices if you apply the diet, just as you would when preparing a meal for yourself or your family.

>> You risk the transmission of parasites or bacteria to ferrets through the feeding of raw meat. However, I've already discussed multiple times up to this point how unlikely this is to happen.

>> It may or may not be nutritionally balanced.

This diet isn't recommended for use in homes with people who are immuno-compromised. You *can* cook this food by braising, microwaving, or steaming to make it safe. Chances are, you'll change the nutrient composition to some degree with cooking, but it isn't known to what degree.

The evolutionary diet: Feeding your pet small animals or insects

The *evolutionary diet* is simple. Essentially, you feed your ferret what she evolved eating. The polecat's diet is varied and includes, among other things, small mammals (rabbits, mature mice, weanling and older rats, and chicks), insects, amphibians, eggs, carrion invertebrates, and fish. The evolutionary diet is about offering freedom of choice and variety, and promoting the consumption of many different natural foods. Mimicking the evolutionary diet in captivity can be quite a challenge, though. Supporters of PMR and raw/freeze-dried raw diets claim to do it. But nothing can beat the real thing.

MEAT MATTERS

Many people argue that cooked meat (or eggs) is the ideal choice for diet. Others fight diligently to prove that raw is the best. Still others say, "If you must feed meat, feed it in the form of human baby food." And, of course, when discussing meat, there's always the issue of live or dead and the pros and cons of doing either. Well done or rare?

It's common knowledge that cooking meat kills off any harmful bacteria that may cause illness to the unfortunate diner. Some people suggest that you rinse raw meat in food-grade hydrogen peroxide to make it safe for pets. If you're comfortable with those answers, stick with them. However, I don't see little barbecue pits scattered throughout the forests, nor do I see dead coyotes, foxes, hawks, or other predators on the sides of the roads (unless they're car casualties). Carnivores eat raw meat. That's a fact of life.

If you're still unsure about raw meat, cut off the outside layer of the meat. The inside meat is generally sterile and safe. Make sure that the meat is fresh. I have fed live, fresh-killed, and thawed frozen meat to a number of animals over the years and have never had an incident of illness resulting from raw meat. Many Europeans continue to feed their ferrets mostly rabbit, and they're among the biggest, healthiest, and most muscular ferrets around.

Although clean raw meat (okay, cooked meat, too) is a wonderful food for ferrets, it can't be the sole food. Wild polecats eat the whole animal — bones, organs, and all. Domestic ferrets need all the good nutrients that come from the rest of the prey animal, not just the muscle meat. They also need some tooth resistance, such as tendons and fur, to help clean their teeth. The same goes for fish as a food source. It's good, but it shouldn't be the only food source.

Also, freezing may kill off some bacteria but doesn't generally kill off everything. And even if meat is cooked, post-cooking handling can seriously contaminate the food before it's even poured into your ferret's bowl. No feeding regime is without risk.

Because the ferret can consume an evolutionary diet, grow, survive, and successfully reproduce, the diet actually meets AAFCO (Association of American Feed Control Officials) requirements, the same as commercial kibble. (An important implication of the AAFCO requirements is that all modern diets attempt to match the evolutionary diet, making it the standard.) Although the evolutionary diet hasn't been studied in detail, its obvious success implies that it meets all the polecat's nutritional requirements, known or unknown. Tables 8-1 and 8-2 cover the nutritional content in many common types of vertebrate prey and invertebrate prey.

TABLE 8-1 ## Nutritional Composition of Vertebrate Prey

Mammal	Dry Matter (DM) %	Crude Protein (CP) %	Crude Fat (CF) %
Neonatal mouse	19.1	64.2	17.0
Juvenile mouse	18.2	44.2	30.1
Adult mouse	32.7	55.8	23.6
Neonatal rat	20.8	57.9	23.7
Juvenile rat	30.0	56.1	27.5
Adult rat	33.9	61.8	32.6
Neonatal rabbit	15.4	72.1	13.0
Adult rabbit*	26.2	65.2	15.8
Day-old chick	25.6	64.9	22.4
Green frog	22.5	71.2	10.2
Anolis lizard	29.4	67.4	N/A

*Dressed carcass

BOB CHURCH ON FREE CHOICE FEEDING

"The advantage of allowing the ferret free choice is that they will naturally select those foods that 'fill the nutritional gaps.' The hypothesis is that animals, if given free choice, will naturally select foods that meet their caloric and nutritional needs. Feeding this type of diet is simpler than it first appears. For example, I use two cafeteria trays, each with 8 small bowls, to feed my ferrets. One bowl may have crickets, another with large mealworms, another with chopped beef or pork, one with night crawlers, one with chopped up boiled egg, another with goldfish — you get the idea. About half of the bowls are filled with frozen mice. Once or twice a month, a SMALL amount of fresh finely minced fruit is offered. All feed animals were purchased after humane killing, or (in the case of the worms and insects) frozen to preserve nutrients and to eliminate escape. To lower the risk of binge eating of extremely favored items, they are given by hand. To reduce risk of food caching, the dishes are removed with all remaining food after about an hour. Leftover foods such as insects or frozen animals can be refrigerated and reused. With experience, it is an easy task to judge how much or little food is appropriate to offer. Every few days, all leftover or thawed food is dumped into a blender and turned into a 'prey shake' that can be frozen for future use as a food supplement, treat, or food base for sick ferrets. I have very little waste, no spoilage of cached foods, and no sick ferrets."

TABLE 8-2 ## Nutritional Composition of Invertebrate Prey

Insect	Dry Matter (DM) %	Crude Protein (CP) %	Crude Fat (CF) %
Crickets	30.8	20.5	6.8
Mealworms	38.1	18.7	13.4
Waxworms	41.5	14.1	24.9
Superworms	42.1	19.7	17.7
Earthworms	16.4	10.5	1.6
Cockroaches	38.7	20.9	11.0

Pros (and procedures) of the evolutionary diet

Pros of feeding your ferret the evolutionary diet (small whole prey) include the following:

>> It's the most nutritionally complete diet available.

>> The ferret retains all the nutrients.

>> The diet is mentally and behaviorally stimulating.

>> It may lessen the signs of and even prevent some GI diseases.

>> Produces smaller and less-frequent stools because of its high digestibility.

>> You don't need to feed your ferret as frequently.

This whole idea of feeding your ferret an evolutionary diet can be confusing in the beginning — especially when you're trying to figure out this business of prey. What is it, where do you get it, and what precautions do you take? Start small — give mice, feeder goldfish, chicks, mealworms, or crickets (for the daring) — and you may find that these food items work out just fine for your ferret. Or you may decide to upgrade to other items such as rats, small rabbits, small frogs, or small lizards. Whatever you decide or whatever your ferret likes, you can find prey animals at reptile supply stores or even most pet shops. Nowadays, you can even choose from hundreds of online sources to have your fresh, frozen prey and live insects shipped to your doorstep.

For people who want to feed a whole animal to a carnivore, the question is always, "Should a carnivore be fed a live or dead animal?" Mostly, this is a choice that addresses the owner's personal beliefs. However, it may be illegal to feed a live animal to another animal where you live.

My decision to feed pre-killed versus live rests on what type of carnivore I'm feeding and the experience of the predator. I feed my ferrets fresh-killed prey. Polecats, experienced ferrets included, are by nature efficient and quick predators that normally kill with a lightning-fast bite to the back of the neck. But most domesticated ferrets don't recognize small animals as food. Some are quick to kill; others play with the food until it happens to die. And some ferrets could care less and lazily watch a potential snack waltz on by. For a ferret eating a more natural diet, I see no reason to offer live food unless she's a quick predator. That's my opinion. I don't like to see the prey animal suffer anymore than it has to.

WARNING The majority of animal supply stores will give you a choice of purchasing most prey items live, frozen, or fresh-killed. It's a personal choice; go with whatever you're most comfortable with and what your skills and your ferret's skills are. However, I caution you to never feed a live rat to your ferret for the same reason I never feed live rats to my snakes: A rat can inflict serious wounds during a scuffle with even an excellent predator. Also, you should feed chicks, baby mice and baby rats sparingly. Although they're good for treats here and there, they are very low in calcium.

TIP Research the source of your prey foods! If the prey isn't healthy, it isn't healthy for your ferret. Does the supply store feed the prey quality foods? Are the animals free of parasites, bacteria, and nutritional diseases? How does the company dispatch (kill) the prey before shipping? How does it pack the prey for shipping? Does it offer guarantees? How long has it been in business? Don't ever feed a chemically euthanized animal to your ferret. She is likely to get very sick from the chemical(s) used to euthanize.

Cons of the evolutionary diet

The following list presents some cons of feeding the evolutionary diet (small whole prey):

» The practice is distasteful to some ferret owners.

» The diet can be expensive (although you can be economical and raise your own mice, rats or chicks for food).

» Some sources of animals aren't nutritional — they aren't free of parasites, bacterial infections, and nutritional disease. This is becoming less of a problem, however, because of active reptile-owning enthusiasts needing many of the same foods.

WARNING With so many feed-supply options available to you, you shouldn't offer your ferret an animal that's come from the wild. In fact, you may do way more harm than good. Many wild animals harbor parasites and bacteria that can be passed on to your ferret. Another thing to consider is poison/pesticides. Speaking from personal experience, I know of someone who lost a ferret when a wild mouse got into the cage. The ferret ate the mouse; unfortunately, the mouse had just eaten a load of poison that had been left out in the garage. Wild animals can pick up pesticides on the grass, bushes, trees, and even on driveways. Always get your prey from a reputable company or raise it yourself.

As distasteful as this diet may be for some ferret owners, it's important that you fully educate yourself on every diet that's available to your ferret. Diet is such an important part of your ferret's well-being. I'd be negligent to leave out this important choice.

AN AGGRESSIVE MYTH

Many people believe that feeding live animals (and some even believe raw meat) makes your ferret more aggressive. This simply isn't true. Domestic doesn't mean unnatural. It only means tame, made fit for domestic life, adapted or bred to live with and be of use to man. Humans are domestic. Does that mean we can't cater to our primal urges once in a while?

Take a good look at the average housecat. Some of these sweet, purring kitties can be killing machines, responsible for millions of wildlife deaths each year. While they can be quick killers, they more often than not kill slowly, often playing and toying with the victim before death. And yet, our housecats remain dear to our hearts, sharing our pillows at night and claiming us as their possessions in the morning by rubbing up against our legs. Why would a ferret be any different?

Many "reports" of aggression are usually easily explained with a bit of investigation. Many of the reports resulted from ratters or rabbiters who starved their ferrets to increase their hunter instincts. Many of these animals would have aggressively defended their meals, giving the illusion the meat made them aggressive. Also, meat was a favored food in those days of the milk and bread diet, making it something to defend. Ferrets were supposed to chase rabbits from the burrow, and when a rabbit was caught by a ferret, it was forcibly removed, increasing aggression.

All ferrets have a natural predatory instinct. It shows in the way they play with their toys as well as in how they interact with each other. Feeding your ferret what she would naturally eat in the wild won't unleash some fantasy wild beast inside. It only gives her an opportunity to experience and benefit from something more natural than what she's used to. In the end, she'll be the same lovable character, except maybe a little happier, healthier, and more energetic.

Exploring the alternative way of feeding

Perhaps the previous information in this section has sold you on a raw or evolutionary diet, but you're wondering how exactly to feed it to your ferret. After all, raw or live food may be a little messier than kibble. You'll certainly have to stay on top of the hygiene aspect of the feeding. And diligence will need to be at the top of your priority list. How you feed, though, depends on your ferret's manners and preferences and your setup.

REMEMBER

Some ferrets have nice manners and eat over their bowls; I don't know any of them, though. Many are hoarders who cache their food for snacks at a later date. And some may pick up their food and drop it a foot or two away from their bowls and eat it there. It's likely that most ferrets will behave differently each time they eat — especially if their diets consist of something they particularly like. Keep these thoughts in mind when developing a feeding routine for your ferret.

The following sections detail how you can convert your ferret to the natural diet and how you can cater your feedings to ferrets that roam free and ferrets that dwell in a cage.

TIP

The most important part of feeding your ferret a natural diet full of raw foods is hygiene. Your health (and your family's) is your top priority:

>> Wash your hands frequently, as well as your prep surfaces and any utensils you use.

>> Store the food according to manufacturer's instructions when applicable. Wash food bowls regularly and thoroughly.

>> Mop the floors where a ferret eats.

>> Wash ferret bedding and wipe down cage surfaces with a mild bleach solution more frequently (see Chapter 9 for more).

Converting your ferret to the natural world

Ferrets, like their polecat cousins, are olfactory hunters, meaning that they follow their noses to the dinner table. Whatever a ferret has consistently eaten during the first six months of her life, she'll see as the preferred food in the future — called *olfactory imprinting*.

Getting a ferret to betray her nose after chowing on kibble for so long can be challenging. However, it's well worth the effort if you're a true believer in the natural diet and want to broaden your ferret's culinary horizons. Of course, the conversion should occur when your fuzzy is as young as possible, but you *can* teach old ferrets new tricks. However, not all ferrets can be brought around — particularly the older kids. Make sure that you give it your all before giving up, though. Here are a couple steps you can take to start the process:

1. **If you haven't already been feeding canned food, start introducing high-quality canned ferret, cat, or kitten food to your ferret.** You can add the food in a separate bowl, but mixing it with dry food will usually force your ferret to taste it. Occasionally, you can switch to a high-quality canned dog food just for variety. The poopy smell gets worse with canned food, but the end result (oh crap, a pun) causes less-stinky poops.

2. **Invest in baby food.** Yep, you read that right. You can use meat baby food, from infant to toddler, as an enticement for your ferret to try a new food. The chicken variety works well. Rub some of it on the ferret's nose or front teeth if she won't readily accept it. She'll surely lick it off.

3. **Order grinds**. If you're extra nice to your local butcher, he may grind up a special blend to your specification, called *grinds*, made of meats, organs, and even bone if you so desire for you to take home to your finicky ferret. Grinds can also be very close to meeting a ferret's nutritional requirements and help to make the switch from kibble to a more natural diet. Grinds may also be purchased online from some specialty food stores.

Don't expect a change overnight. Persistence and experimentation are the keys to converting your ferret to a more natural diet. All ferrets are different. Some take several days to convert. Others take a week or so, or maybe even a month. After you get your ferret used to the idea of eating different food, though, you can step up your efforts and include more natural/evolutionary foods. Here are some tips to follow:

» **Put aside some freezer space for frozen mice.** Some people feed pre-killed chicks rather than mice. You usually can purchase pre-killed mice or chicks at a pet store — particularly one that sells reptiles. Store the animals in the freezer and thaw them as needed. After your ferret learns that a mouse or chick is food, the occasional frozen treat is okay. During winter, carnivores eat frozen meat all the time. When your ferret discovers that the mouse or chick is tasty, she'll be hooked.

» **Experiment with poultry.** You can chop up small pieces of chicken, turkey, or other poultry (bones and all) and allow your ferret to get a taste. You can use either cooked or raw poultry, depending on your comfort level, but remember the nutrients are not the same in cooked meat. If you don't want to make a special ferret meal, save a couple cut-up pieces after your next poultry dinner.

» **Become an organ donor.** Chicken, pork, and beef livers, as well as chicken and beef hearts, are great treats and are full of nutrition. Slice them up and offer the cuts to your fuzzy. Liver, by itself, is a great occasional meal.

>> **Be creative with hamburger.** Perhaps you've had those days when you mix anything you can find in the cupboards or freezer with hamburger. My mother called it "junk", but we ate it, and it actually tasted good most of the time. Cook up some beef and add ground bones or kibble. Form it in shapes like the kibble if you must. Just be creative.

>> **Use natural juices.** Many people forget how tasty the juices from cooked meats can be. I always use the juices as gravy over dry food. Natural juices can be a great introduction to a new taste, either in a separate bowl or over a small amount of kibble.

>> **Throw in some fishies.** Canned tuna in spring water is yummy to many ferrets. Try it. You also can try feeding other prepared fish, such as trout or salmon, cooked shellfish, shrimp, and crawdads. Feeder fish are yummy, too.

>> **Don't forget the bugs.** Even my dogs and cats eat bugs! Earthworms, crickets, cockroaches, and mealworms are tasty treats for your ferret. Your fuzzy, when she gets used to the idea, will eat only the squishy, juicy parts and leave the rest for you!

You may find that one of your ferrets loves liver, while another prefers hamburger. Remember, the natural diet is about freedom of choice! Conversion may take a little patience on your part. And don't forget that these natural foods spoil quickly. Don't let any linger around your ferret's cage or eating area for too long. If the food is still there in 12 hours, get rid of it! If you have to, try something different later.

A month or more of hamburger meat by itself or some other similarly bare diet is, by no means, a balanced diet. If your ferret is taking her sweet time fully converting to a balanced natural diet, she'll need to be supplemented with her familiar food even if it's kibble to ensure nutritional requirements are being met, if only minimally.

When your ferret finally switches to a raw food or evolutionary diet, she'll be likely to try just about anything, which is important because you don't want to stick to just one food item in this diet. She still needs a combination of soft and hard foods. Besides, some of the foods I mention in this chapter aren't complete diets. The combination of the foods is what makes them so good for your fuzzy. So don't rule out kibble for good. The biggest piece of bad news about natural diets? Your friends will often stare into your refrigerator in terror and decline dinner invitations!

Free-roaming ferrets

As a feeder of a raw, freeze-dried raw, or an evolutionary diet, it's up to you to reexamine and adjust your ferret's feeding habits and routines so that caching or other behaviors associated with free-roaming don't become hygiene problems in your home. Imagine the olfactory shock that will hit you three to four days after your beloved ferret has cached some raw meat or a mouse in a secret hidey-hole. And the biggest problem is that the hidey-hole remains top secret, and it's your job to sniff it out.

For beginners in the natural dieting world, I don't generally recommend feeding your ferret openly where she free roams, although many people do it with great success. The reason is simple: Some people aren't as hygiene-conscientious as they need to be when dealing with raw meat or prey animals. Although you may be fully aware of each and every hidey-hole your ferret has, meaning that you can retrieve uneaten foods at the end of the feeding (or day), you can't see the invisible trail left while the ferret was dragging the food there. Too many surfaces can become contaminated without you even knowing it.

TIP

I suggest you set up a "feeding playpen" — which is a small contained area that the ferret can't escape from — in a tiled room and feed your ferret in it. Let her have her fill for a couple hours or however long it takes. Some ferrets eat quickly. Some may take a while before showing interest in their meat or mice. That's the downside of putting a time limit on feeding. You want to give your ferret adequate time to eat her share, so get to know your ferret's eating habits.

The downside to the feeding playpen method is that you remove some of the enrichment aspects of the feeding. I like to encourage my ferrets to forage; I often hide their food, whether it's meat or mice or kibble, and they must sniff it out (for more on enrichment, see Chapter 10). If you get comfortable with your ferret's eating habits and your ability to handle raw meats and prey animals hygienically, you can begin to experiment with different feeding routines. You may find that feeding in an open area works better for you and your ferret. And you can even add an obvious-to-you hidey hole or two, such as an empty case of soda or a plastic pet igloo, where she can stash her catch of the day, making it easier to find leftovers. There's more than one way for this to work.

Caged ferrets

Yes, caged ferrets have to eat, too, and you have to be just as diligent when it comes to hygiene. A feeding playpen, which I describe in the previous section, works just as well for caged ferrets. Small rooms, such as bathrooms, work perfectly for feeding, also. Or you can simply feed the meat or prey animals in the upper level of your ferret's cage (see Chapter 5 for more on cage construction). Your ferret likely will pull the mice and meat down into her bedding. You simply shake out the bedding at the end of the feeding and put in fresh bedding. Some people just change the bedding on a daily basis. I find this to be an acceptable practice as long as you also wipe down and clean the cage on a regular basis to prevent an accumulation of harmful bacteria.

REMEMBER

Your ferret's cage is a haven for bacteria, no matter what you do. She'll poop in her litter box and possibly outside of it, and then walk in it and trudge through the cage and bedding. Bacteria multiply on her kibble, which she'll drop into her bedding. She licks her behind and then licks her water bottle or snorkels in her water bowl. Your ferret doesn't live a sanitary life, nor should she. In fact, like many other carnivores, she'll purposely stash her food in the most disgusting of places just to disguise the smell and hide it away from other predators. So don't be surprised to find food in the litterbox or under pee pads! The good news? Absence of immune-system-challenging microorganisms can actually be harmful to your ferret. Living in a sterile or super-clean environment may lead to immune problems later down the road. This is called the *hygiene hypothesis*. Google it!

Supplementing Your Fuzzy's Diet

A *supplement* is something you add to your ferret's diet to make up for what's lacking in her day to day feedings. If your healthy ferret is on a truly balanced and suitable diet, she doesn't really need supplements. Although supplements were a necessary part of a ferret's diet years ago, today most diets available to your ferret are better formulated, thus more balanced for a ferret. Often, giving supplements is more a matter of choice because a ferret enjoys the taste and sees them as treats.

The most common supplement is a fatty-acid oil supplement, which ferrets find pleasant. The right fatty-acid supplement can be just what the doctor ordered or it can be your worst nightmare. This section explains what you need to know about omega-3 and omega-6 fatty acids, which are the most commonly found fatty acids in pet-store supplements. Most supplements list the ingredients as I've listed them.

REMEMBER

Fatty acids, such as Omega 3 and Omega 6, which can be found in salmon oil, have to be incorporated into the cell membranes, so it may take several weeks for their effects to show. In fact, you may not see changes for two to three months. If possible, experts recommend that you split the daily dose, giving a half dose each in two 12-hour increments. Your ferret will still get a full daily dose, just not at once.

Omega-3 fatty acids

Omega-3 fatty acids, in general, have some great properties. They may slow the spread of cancer, reduce inflammation, lower blood pressure, and prevent ventricular arrhythmias. In addition to alpha-linoleic acid (ALA), the ingredients are as follows:

>> Eicosapentaenoic acid (EPA): Reduces inflammation in atopy, arthritis, autoimmune disease, seborrhea, and decreases cholesterol

>> Docosahhexoenoic acid (DHA): Reduces inflammation in atopy

Omega-6 fatty acids

Most quality pet foods contain adequate amounts of omega-6 fatty acids. Rich sources of this fatty acid include cold-water fish oils and the seeds of some plants such as sunflowers, borages, pumpkins, soybean, and flax. In addition to dihomo-gamma-linolenic acid (DGLA), the following list presents the ingredients in the supplement and the benefits (or detriments) they bring:

>> Linoleic acid (LA): Helps improve dry skin and a dull hair coat

>> Gamma linolenic acid (GLA): Reduces inflammation in atopy and autoimmune disease

>> Arachidonic acid (AA): Can *increase* inflammation

Savoring Treat Time!

Treats can be a vital part of your relationship with your ferret, as long as they're the right types and are given in moderation. Some fuzzies come to expect a favorite treat at a certain time of day or after performing a neat trick. They all beg for them no matter what. Of course, all ferrets deserve treats. But, before starting your ferret on treats, discuss doing so with your veterinarian. Some traditional treats can aggravate medical conditions such as insulinoma or chronic bowel disease. My goal is to get you away from traditional bad treats and onto healthy ones! Better safe than sorry. The following sections show you the way.

TIP

Next time you're shopping for your ferret's treats in the pet store, take a look at the ingredients. Do you see any meat in the lists? Many treats don't even contain meat, or if they do, the meat often is way down on the lists. What you find high on the list more often than not is sugar and even more sugar — maybe even more sugar and then some plant materials that aren't good for ferrets. Avoid these and stick to the meat-based treats.

Giving the good stuff

Here are some treats that you can offer your ferret in moderation (remember to feed these in very small pieces and very small amounts; even the good stuff can be harmful if overfed):

>> **Eggs:** Hard-boiled, poached, raw, or scrambled. Egg yolks (cooked or raw) are very nutritious. Eggs are perfect protein treats and are not only nutritious, but they serve many purposes. In addition to helping the ferret maintain a healthy and soft coat, the raw egg is an eggcellent hairball preventative. However, some people won't risk feeding raw eggs due to the possibility of germs or harmful bacteria. I've been over this business of harmful bacteria in food, yet still it's a personal choice.

TIP

When feeding raw eggs, stick to chicken or quail eggs, because duck eggs, in my opinion, are too large and often too rich for many ferrets. Feed the entire egg contents or yolk only, because egg whites can cause a biotin deficiency over time when fed alone. You should whisk the egg to blend the yolk and egg white, and serve one up per ferret once a week. Quail eggs, being so petite, may be given whole in the shell a couple times a week for perfect ferret enrichment!

>> **Meat:** Cooked or raw meats and organs are great treats. Special favorites are chicken livers and hearts. Beef and turkey pieces are good, also. If you have a dehydrator, you can make your own unseasoned turkey, salmon, beef, or chicken jerky to give as treats. Avoid processed meats such as lunchmeat, hot dogs or salami, because they're full of salt and additives.

TIP

A great treat for a half-dozen ferrets is to puncture a large fish-oil capsule (salmon oil without rosemary oil added is one of the very best fish oils!), pour the oil into a dish, cut up some raw chicken (no more than 1-square-inch pieces), and place the pieces in the oil. Heat the mix in the microwave until the chicken just starts to turn white. This may destroy some of the nutrients, but it makes a great occasional treat.Make sure the meat is not too hot before serving. You should feed no more than 1 teaspoon of salmon oil to a single ferret throughout the course of a week. More than that may cause runny poop.

>> **Insects:** Earthworms, crickets, cockroaches, and mealworms are tasty treats. Just about anything you'd feed reptiles or amphibians will make a great treat for a ferret.

>> **Small prey animals:** Mice, chicks, frogs, lizards, and rats all are healthy treats or main diet choices for your ferret (see the section "The evolutionary diet: Feeding your pet small animals/insects").

- » **Chicken baby food:** A single lick or two from a spoon or off your finger is a nice way to say "I love you" to your ferret, or "job well-done!" Most ferrets love the taste of the baby food. Remember, though, not to give too much as to spoil her regular meal.

- » **High-quality kibble:** Most ferrets view a piece of their regular kibble as a treat if you feed the kibble from your hand. If this works for your ferret, she not only gets a treat, but also isn't straying too far from her diet! This feeding method also is a good way to introduce a new food item.

TIP

I've found that ferrets see almost *any* type of cooking oil as a treat. Mine especially enjoy fish-oil treats, but they never turn down a bit of olive oil on the end of my finger. You can cut open a fish-oil capsule, which contains enough oil to "treat" a handful of ferrets. Like all supplements, you should do this infrequently. My rule is, *if your ferret wants a lot, she shouldn't get it very often.*

Avoiding the not-so-good stuff

There is such a thing as loving your ferret to death. Many dog and cat owners do so unknowingly with large amounts of treats and table scraps. Although some treats will be fine for your ferret if given in moderation, you should avoid some not-so-healthy treats altogether, no matter how much your ferret begs. When your ferret fills herself with junk, she decreases the amount of room she has for good food. The following list presents the not-so-good treats you should toss out of your ferret's diet:

- » **Alcohol and other high-sugar drinks/foods:** Too much sugar is a bad thing for a ferret. And a drunk ferret can quickly become a dead ferret. (Besides, you must be 21 to legally drink.)

- » **Coffee and tea products:** No caffeine, please. Like ferrets don't speed around enough.

- » **Dried fruits,** *including raisins:* Sorry guys and gals! These and other high-sugar fruit treats are on the banned list! Get them off your shelf!

- » **Fresh fruits:** These are super high in complex carbs and can't be digested by ferrets.

- » *Most* **commercial ferret treats:** Most are low in or absent of meat content but high in sugar. Check the labels carefully.

- » **High-calorie/high-sugar supplements:** The major ingredient of Nutri-Cal (and similar products), for instance, is molasses, which if given to an insulin-omic ferret when she isn't in the middle of a low-sugar incident can be unhealthy.

» **Cereals:** Treats must be low-salt and low-sugar (low-carb), and most cereals aren't. Two cereals frequently given to ferrets by their unknowing owners are Cheerios and Kix. Add these and all cereals to your ***banned*** list!

» **Veggies:** Vegetables may get lodged in the intestinal tract. Veggies also have little to no nutritional value for ferrets, and they come out the other end basically undigested if they make it that far.

» **Dairy products:** Many experts argue about lactose intolerance in ferrets. Some vets say it's prevalent, and others say it isn't. A single lick of milk or ice cream probably won't harm most healthy ferrets. In fact, owners frequently use heavy cream (the real stuff) as a high-fat supplement to add weight on and boost energy in a debilitated ferret. And cheese contains very little lactose, so very small amounts are probably safe, though still not recommended. Use your best judgment. If what you feed comes out the other end in smelly liquid form, your ferret probably is sensitive to lactose, but a little diarrhea from a small amount of dairy product won't harm her. And, by the way, goat milk contains almost as much lactose as cow milk, so don't even go there.

» **Seeds and nuts:** These things are indigestible and hard to pass, not to mention painful. They can cause blockages.

» **Peanut butter:** Although this is a high protein food, it's a plant-based protein, so it does your ferret no good. Additionally, even if it's not listed in the ingredient list, some peanut butter brands (some toothpastes, yogurts, and chewing gums, as well) contain the "all natural" low-calorie sweetener xylitol, which is toxic to pets.

» **Chocolate:** Contains theobromide, which, in high doses, can be fatal in some pets (such as dogs). No one knows for sure if chocolate is as dangerous to ferrets. Milk chocolate is generally much safer. The big problem isn't the trace amounts of theobromide in the milk chocolate; it's the tons of sugar. Don't panic if your fuzzy accidentally happens on a tiny piece of chocolate, but don't use chocolate as a treat.

» **Salty foods:** Save the beer nuts for the bar. A small taste here or there, though, won't kill a ferret.

» **Onions or garlic:** Don't share your dinner with your ferret if it's been seasoned or supplemented with either of these! Onions, although tasty, may cause a potentially fatal condition in ferrets called hemolytic anemia. And although garlic is guaranteed to keep the vampires away, it may also cause your ferret's kidneys to shut down, which is frequently fatal.

» **Fingers:** Just seeing if you're paying attention!

Chapter 9

Cleaning Time: Not All Ferret Fun and Games

Wouldn't you like to have a butler deliver your clean, happy ferret to you on the couch — and then get to work cleaning his cage and litter box — so you can just concentrate on the romping, playing, and cuddling parts? Okay, back to reality; most people don't have butlers, so they must face the routine chores of keeping ferrets. I'm talking about odor control, grooming, and general sanitation stuff here.

If you're anything like I am, you'll find it very satisfying to watch your gorgeous, clean, healthy ferret dash about with enthusiasm and then collapse in his unsoiled condo for a long nap. Besides giving you an opportunity to bond and discover possible health problems, cleaning and grooming are necessary for both your and your ferret's continued happiness and health.

In this chapter, I discuss the ins and outs of cleaning your fuzzy's cage, bedding, and dishes. I provide much-needed information on cleaning your fuzzy, too. Oh, cheer up. Into every life a little poop must fall!

Cleaning House for a Cozy Cage

When I say you need to regularly clean your fuzzy's house, I mean the entire house. What good is a sparkling cage if his bedding still has poop stuck in it or his toys are crusty from heaven knows what? Sometimes, people forget to do the whole overhaul. I admit it, I'm guilty at times. Just remember that you and your fuzzy will be happiest when the cleaning tornado hits the entire ferret condo. The following sections take you through the cleaning process for the cage, dishes, toys, bed, and toilet.

Doing your fuzzy's dishes

When I set out to clean my ferret's cage, I tackle dishes and water bottles first, because I think one of the most important aspects of good husbandry is providing clean, fresh food and water at all times. Because pooping and peeing are frequent activities with ferrets, you're likely to find an occasional mess in the food or water bowl or poop smeared on the side of one or the other or both. If you notice this, or an unusually dirty bowl, take the dish out immediately and clean it thoroughly. If you ignore it, the poop/dirt won't go away. Trust me, I've tried. Otherwise, regular cleanings with soap and warm water every couple days usually are sufficient. You should have extra food and water dishes, as well as extra water bottles on hand to swap with the dirty ones that you'll be cleaning.

Maintenance on the dishes and bottles is simple. Soap and water should be adequate when coupled with a gentle scrubbing (with a bottlebrush, for instance). You also can use a mixture of vinegar and water or baking soda and water. The key to good husbandry is to scrub thoroughly to remove any particle or algae buildup. And don't neglect the tube and stainless steel balls on the water bottle. Keeping these things free of mineral deposits helps eliminate any leakage and removes the risk of the metal ball getting stuck on gunk in the tube. Always remember to completely rinse before refilling.

TIP

A more effective cleaning solution is a mixture of warm water and a touch of bleach. At least once a week, clean all the dishes with the bleach and water solution (1:30). Unless you have bionic eyes, you can't see all the bacteria condos going up on your ferret's dishes. Come to terms with the fact that bacteria is there and wash frequently. Your ferret will thank you.

REMEMBER

Properly rinsing dishes is just as important as cleaning the dishes. Although a trace amount of soap won't kill your ferret, it tastes pretty bad and can cause diarrhea. In addition, the residue attracts more dirt and bacteria. Bleach, on the other hand, can cause your ferret to become very ill. Take care when washing the dishes, and be sure to rinse well. As a safeguard, I wash with soap and water after I use bleach. After all, can anyone be too careful when dealing with their precious furballs?

WARNING

Anything from a ferret cage may be contaminated with poop. Don't use the kitchen or kitchen sink when cleaning if at all possible because you can contaminate areas where you prepare food. Contamination can come with enteric bacteria like *E. coli* and salmonella from any pet-contaminated items that you clean in a kitchen. Instead, use a bathroom sink, bathtub, or laundry-room sink to do your cleaning. If the kitchen area is your only option, be sure to clean out the sink with a disinfectant and thoroughly clean any counter surfaces with disinfectant, such as Lysol or your bleach solution. And for God's sake, leave your dishwasher out of it! Just the thought of poo-water rinsing over my wine glasses after I've just finished a load of crappy ferret dishes and toys makes me gag.

Stripping his bed

Your ferret's bedding can get pretty raunchy after a while. Because ferrets spend so much time running in and out of the litter box, chances are good that traces of poop and urine will make their way to your fuzzy's towels or other bedding. Particles of litter and food crumbs get mixed in there as well. Your fuzzy spends a lot of time snuggling and sleeping in his bedding, so thoroughly washing his bedding at least once a week or more is important.

Doing ferret laundry is no different from doing human laundry. I use laundry soap and hot water. Sometimes, I add a half-cup of bleach to the load. If you like this suggestion, make sure that the finished laundry doesn't have a strong bleach odor; maybe even put it on the two-rinse cycle. If it still smells strongly of bleach, another regular wash with soap should fix the problem. If you're the type to opt for a more holistic approach, take a little white vinegar and add it to the "bleach compartment" in your washing machine. This can greatly reduce odors in washed bedding.

Before you toss in a load, though, consider the health of your washing machine. I always take ferret bedding outside and thoroughly shake it out before throwing it into the washer. That way, I discard most of the loose litter and debris before washing the bedding. Look for little poopies that may be stuck to the bedding and pick them off. You don't want to throw debris into your washing machine. Trust me, there's nothing like wearing a "clean" shirt with a poop stain on it! Worse yet is having someone point it out to you. I know this from experience!

Scrubbing (or scooping) the toilet

You should scoop litter boxes as often as you can, refilling them with litter as needed. Obviously, if you have many ferrets, it doesn't take long for the poop to start piling up. You'll notice the insides of the litter box getting pretty dirty after a short while, because most ferrets poop in the corners or at an edge. Some fuzzies hang their butts over the side, and the poop lands on the litter box edge.

Cleaning the litter box regularly helps reduce odor and the number of accidents that happen outside the box, because most ferrets hate to get their feet dirty — unless they're playing outside in the dirt and sand.

You'll soon find out that cleaning the litter box can be a nasty undertaking. Use common sense when cleaning the waste. I take out all litter boxes and empty them completely into the garbage at least once a week. Use a rag or dish sponge (not the one from your kitchen) to scrub the bottom and sides of the litter box. Usually, soap and water are sufficient. At least twice a month, I use bleach water to clean the box. Don't forget to clean the C-clamps that hold the litter box to the cage (see Chapter 5), because they can get quite nasty, too.

Tearing down the house

Cleaning the cage can be the most time-consuming and tedious chore. You should clean the cage at least once every couple weeks. I suggest that if the weather is nice, you drag the entire cage outside and hose that sucker down with high-pressure water. The rest of the time, you need to get on your hands and knees and reach into the cage to get it clean. (For more on a ferret's cage, head to Chapter 5.) Here are the steps I take:

1. **Pull out any catch pans in the cage so you can change the newspaper or catch litter.**

2. **Sweep up the displaced litter and food particles from the flooring.**

    A little hand-held vacuum is perfect for this task.

3. **Spray the flooring with a pet-friendly cleaner and wipe it thoroughly, remembering to leave no residue behind.**

    You can find ferret-friendly cleaners in most pet stores. You're finished with the easy part!

4. **This step is the hard part: getting any solidified poop off the corners of the wire shelves.**

    I use rubber gloves and pull off the waste. What doesn't come off with the initial tug I push off with a long, metal stick (such as a shish-ka-bob skewer).

You can also use a scouring pad, although the pad can be too abrasive and wear down any paint on the wire. A tool that works well is a nylon scrub pad — the kind you may use with a Teflon pan. It has a nylon mesh over a sponge. It doesn't ruin paint and it does a good job, after the cage has been wetted down, of getting crusty stuff off.

Toothbrushes aren't just for teeth anymore, so don't toss those old ones away! Discarded toothbrushes are absolutely perfect for cleaning those nasty, hard-to-reach spots in cages or for scrubbing crusty poops off of toys and such. Just don't confuse the cage-cleaning toothbrush for your real toothbrush down the road. On the other hand, if you get mad at your spouse . . . just sayin'.

5. **After you clear off most of the poop, use a wet rag and thoroughly clean all the areas of the cage.**

   If you have short arms like I do or a cage that's difficult to reach into, you may find that you can't reach one or two far corners that always seem to have a small bit of poop residue. That's when hosing can be most effective.

6. **Now you're ready to reassemble the cage.**

Getting the gunk off the toys

Don't neglect the fuzzy's toys when you're cleaning his house — a mistake often made by us humans. Assume they're dirty every time you strip the cage, even if they look clean. The toys get dragged about the ferret's litter box and buried in his dirty bedding. Check them daily, as well, for obvious signs of being pooped or peed on. The cleaning method you use depends on the type of toy in question. You can safely throw most cloth toys in the wash with the rest of his bedding.

As for plastic toys, I simply soak them in bleach water or plain, warm water until I can easily scrub off all the poopy grime. The important part is to always remember to thoroughly rinse the toys and leave no residue.

If you happen upon a toy buried beneath a pile of poop or in another messy situation, it's okay to just pitch it and buy your ferret a new toy. Some things are just too gross to clean. Plus, fuzzbutts deserve new toys as often as possible!

A wall full of turds!

Yep, you heard me correctly! Any seasoned ferret owner will attest to the fact that this magical occurrence happens when no one is looking, and it resembles a toddler's first attempt at splatter painting. I don't know how they manage, but your ferret can and will get poop stuck on the wall, especially if his cage butts up against it. (Yes that, folks, was a shameless pun.) What you do about this mess is up to you. If it's high enough on the wall, you might just hang a picture over it and call it a day. On the other hand, if you really want to remove the poop decor, as most of us do, the following might be of some help to you:

>> For easier clean-up, hold a warm, wet rag over the dried glob of poop for 5 to 10 painstaking, muscle-cramping minutes until it softens.

>> Use a spackle/putty knife or a flat plastic scraper to gently scrape the poop off the wall, being careful to not peel the paint or wallpaper off with it — much easier said than done!

>> Use the wet rag to wash away any remaining poo residue on the wall.

>> To remove existing stains on walls you can try: Nature's Miracle, bleach, Dawn dish soap, or even a Magic Eraser (be careful with the eraser because it may remove paint, as well!)

TIP

Cage-placement options are sometimes limited for ferret owners, and up against a wall may be all you have available. Consider these two anti-poop-on-the-wall hacks that will make your life so much easier and cleaner!

>> Fasten a large piece of Plexiglas on the wall behind the cage or slide the Plexiglas tightly between the cage and the wall to catch any splashes from the poop cannon. You will still need to clean the soiled Plexiglas surface as necessary. Plexiglas is relatively expensive, but it can be a one-time purchase if you're careful not to break it.

>> Hang butcher paper on the wall behind the cage. This is simple, economical, and easy to change-out after it gets dirty.

>> Hang a sheet on the wall behind the cage, or even drape it over the back of the cage. You can fasten the sheet to the top of the cage with clamps. Note that the sheet should be easy to remove and launder.

Scrub a Dub Fuzz: Navigating Bath Time

You have plenty to think about before bathing a smelly little ferret — such as choosing the right shampoo and knowing when and where to bathe him. Plus, not all ferrets like baths, so knowing what to do and what not to do can ease the anxiety both of you may be feeling. The following sections explain all the factors you must consider, and then I take you through the actual process of bathing your fuzzy.

One bath too many?

It's hard to believe that bathing a ferret may defeat the purpose — namely, making the fuzzy smell fresh — but it can be true. Bathing is important, but equally important is not washing your fuzzy too frequently. Bathing strips the skin and fur of their natural oils. The skin must work overtime to reproduce these oils in order to replace what you washed down the drain, making the smell worse initially. Excessive bathing also can lead to dry, flaky skin and coarse fur.

You'll probably notice initially that your ferret has a stronger smell than before the bath. Don't worry. The smell improves within a day or two.

REMEMBER

Unless your ferret gets into something really nasty, don't bathe him more than once a month if you have to bathe him at all. In all actuality, I suggest bathing him only a couple times a year. Look at it this way: It gives the scratches on your arms ample time to heal before you bathe the furball again!

Picking a shampoo

The shampoo you use on your ferret should be very gentle. Don't use strong shampoos or regular dish soaps; they can lead to dry, itchy skin and brittle fur. The majority of over-the-counter pet shampoos work well, as long as the shampoo is labeled safe for cats, kittens or ferrets. Your vet may carry some good shampoos that are great for sensitive skin. Dog shampoos often contain harsh chemicals that are safe for dogs but very harmful to ferrets. Although human shampoos aren't really advisable, a gentle tearless baby shampoo will work in a pinch. And, if your ferret is unfortunate enough to have fleas, be sure to read Chapter 14 before picking a shampoo and bathing him.

WHAT'S WITH MY FERRET'S TAIL ACNE?

Ferrets are prone to blackheads just like humans, although a ferret's usually show up on his tail. Often, hair loss and a reddish-brown, waxy film come with blackheads, which are caused by dirt and oil clogging their fuzzy pores. Although blackheads aren't too attractive, they're nothing to worry about. If you want to treat them, simply wash your fuzzy's tail every couple days (the tail only) with a shampoo that contains benzoyl peroxide or salicylic acid (which you can get from your vet). Gently scrub the tail with a washcloth and let the suds sit for a minute or two before rinsing.

Oatmeal — It's what's for baths

Perhaps the greatest discovery in ferret grooming is the soapless (colloidal) oatmeal bath! Not only will the oatmeal leave your ferret feeling refreshed, less itchy, and smelling good afterwards, but it also contains compounds that have anti-inflammatory and moisture-retaining properties. This means bath time without stripping oils and drying out skin!

Simply get some oats. Any will do as long as there are no added ingredients. Plain old fashioned or rolled oats are usually the easiest. Pour them into a sock or knee high/nylon. Tie off the sock to prevent the oats from falling out. Run a lukewarm (comfortable) bath and allow the water to run over the oats until the water is milky with oatmeal residue. You can also just swish the sock in the tub until the water is milky. This should take about five to ten minutes. To bathe the ferret, you can rub the wet oatmeal sock on him in the tub, use a wet wash cloth on him, or just let him swim around while you use your hands to gently massage his fur. Finish up with a quick rinse of fresh water before drying off your ferret.

WARNING

Dawn dish soap is wellknown for its use in treating wildlife that has been severely contaminated in oil spills. Although truly amazing commercials show waterfowl and other critters being gently bathed and freed of the deadly oil that entraps them and threatens their very lives, little do viewers know of the dangers that Dawn and other dish soaps present to our domestic pets. Dawn has been one of the most popular go-to solutions among pet owners for flea infestations, and while it may work, consider the fact that this detergent is designed to cut through grease and break apart/dissolve oils. How can this possibly be good to the health of our ferrets? It's not. Bathing your ferret in Dawn dish soap for any reason is highly discouraged for many reasons, including: 1) It strips the natural oils from the skin and fur, thus drying and damaging both, 2) The ferret's sensitive skin and airway may become irritated from the harsh chemicals in the dish soap, and 3) A variety of skin conditions, such as infections, burns, adverse reactions, and generalized irritation may occur simply from the much higher pH present in the dish soap. If you don't believe me, reach out to Dawn — you'll likely receive correspondence back from a brutally honest Dawn representative who will tell you in one form or another not to use it on your pet.

Choosing the crime scene

Where's the best place to bathe your ferret? The bathtub is an obvious choice. Many people look at bath time as a great opportunity for the water-loving fuzzy to play in the bathtub. This is okay, but limit the free swim to before the water gets all soapy and yucky. The downside to bathing in the tub is that it's tough on the human back and knees.

Many ferrets get so excited at the thought of bathing (yeah, right) that they poop in the water, so you may have to do some cleanup right away!

Sinks also are great places to clean a smelly snorkeler. The water flow from a sink faucet is a little gentler, and your back and knees will thank you. Avoid the kitchen sink for hygiene reasons; choose either a bathroom or laundry-room sink. Pull-out hoses/sprayers are good for easy rinsing.

Some people even let their fuzzies into the shower with them. Unless your ferret is comfortable with this method and manageable in the shower — or you shower with your clothes on — I urge you to take extra precaution. A naked human is an extra-vulnerable human!

Doing the deed

You need to do some preparatory work before you can begin the deed of bathing. First, you need some good supplies: an appropriate shampoo, plenty of clean, dry towels for both you and your ferret, and hip boots and goggles (for you). The water you prepare should be a temperature that's comfortable for a human child.

A ferret's body temperature is quite a bit higher than a human's (100–104°F). What feels warm to you may be a pinch too chilly for a ferret, causing fuzzy goose-bumps. Keep the water warm, but always test it before wetting your ferret; you don't want to scald the little bugger.

Fill the tub, sink, or basin with the water — just deep enough to submerge the ferret's body while allowing his feet to touch the bottom. This gives the anxious fuzzy a little extra security, because being unable to feel solid ground beneath your feet can be a terrifying experience.

Now you're ready to bathe. But what if your ferret isn't? The following sections give you some tips for bathing a water-shy ferret and take you through the normal bathing process.

Bathing a reluctant ferret

When it comes to bath time, not all ferrets enjoy water like their otter cousins. Some act like housecats when they get the slightest bit of water on their paws. Others, fortunately, take to it with Olympic-like style. Oftentimes, a ferret's first few encounters with water will determine his attitude. Whether your ferret's disdain for baths is due to his personality or to post-traumatic stress disorder, your job as a ferret human is to make the bathing process as pleasurable as possible.

If you can convince your fuzzy to look at bath time as a treat and reward, your battle may not be as big. Keep in mind that bathing the resistant ferret will not hurt him unless you're too forceful. You may need to lightly scruff him (see Chapter 7) and allow his feet to touch the bottom of the sink or tub to support his weight. Here are some more tips:

1. Allow him to play in the sink or tub for a moment without any water to get used to the crime scene.

2. Turn on the faucet just enough for a thin stream to come out, and allow your ferret to explore the water. Offer him a treat, such as a lick of meat baby food from a spoon, as a reward for being a good boy.

3. While he's still licking his chops, pick him up and put him under the warm stream of water. Offer him another lick of treat.

4. Slowly increase the flow of water until he's all wet.

5. Put your ferret down and offer him one more lick of treat. Continue onto the next section.

Water anxiety, of course, magically disappears *after* bath time. I frequently find myself spending time racing to keep my ferrets out of full coffee cups, toilets, and the dogs' water bowls. Bath anxiety may just be a control thing. Who knows for sure?

Wax on, wax off

I start a ferret's bath by lathering his back, because that's the easiest place to pour the shampoo. You can also pour the shampoo on your hands and rub your hands together before lathering him up. From there, I spread the shampoo evenly across all parts of his body, including the top of his head. Be careful not to get any soap in his eyes and ears. Some shampoos sting like heck, and your ferret will be sure to hold a grudge for next time. If you do get soap in your ferret's eyes, flush his face gently with water, using a cupped hand.

REMEMBER

A ferret with water-soaked fur is slightly heavier than a dry ferret, so take extra care to support his full weight during and after the bath. It can be tricky to lather up the rascal while he's trying to crawl up your arm. You almost need an extra set of hands — two to hold the ferret, one to pour the shampoo, and one to lather. Giving a bath is an art that's quickly mastered by the multi-ferreted human, though.

Keeping soap out of your ferret's mouth can be more challenging. Plenty of fuzz-ies seem to enjoy the taste of soap. Although this quirk may appear disgusting to some, I must defend the ferret by saying I also enjoyed the taste of soap when

I was a child. Unlike me, though, a ferret won't outgrow the taste. A little bit of soap won't hurt him, but keep him from sneaking in a lick anyway because there's nothing nutritious in soap and too much can make him ill.

After you have his body lathered up, you can get ready to rinse. Rinsing thoroughly is as important as lathering. Besides drying out his fur and making him itchy, soap residue left on the fur attracts dirt and gunk, and you'll soon have a dirty ferret again. For this reason, I suggest that you drain the water basin and use fresh, warm water to rinse. You can use a cup to pour the water over your ferret, or you can hold the ferret under the faucet — as long as the water pressure isn't too hard (see Figure 9-1). I enjoy using a hose that attaches to the faucet. Some sinks already have built-in hoses.

FIGURE 9-1: Lather your ferret's entire body before rinsing, being careful not to get soap in his eyes.

Don't drown the poor bugger while rinsing. In other words, don't pour water directly over his head. Use your hand to scoop water onto his head and to act as a washcloth. Remember to rinse the hard-to-reach areas, like the smelly armpits and throat. A well-rinsed furball is a squeaky-clean furball!

REMEMBER

Before you rinse, test the water temperature. Water that's too hot scalds, and water that's too cold causes your ferret to scramble for cover.

Drying out

If you think a dog makes a fuss after a bath, wait until you get a load of the ferret. Drying time is a major production, no doubt about it. For fuzzy, this is happy, hopping, dooking time — a time for puffed tails and sideways sashays. The ferret's main goal is to get as dry and as filthy as he possibly can in the shortest amount of time. This means he'll try to rub up against anything and everything he can, from the couch cushions to the dust bunnies behind the sofa — and that disgusting little spot you can't reach behind the toilet.

You want to prevent your fuzzbutt from undoing all your hard work, which means you must take it upon yourself to dry him or at least allow him to dry himself in a clean, safe place. First things first: Towel-dry him as best you can, making sure that you're gentle yet thorough in removing as much water as possible. Some people like to use warm towels to dry their ferrets. You can warm a towel in the clothes dryer or microwave, but make sure you don't let the towel get too hot.

REMEMBER

A great place for drying time is a bathtub filled with dry towels. You can also use a towel-filled bathroom (with drained tub and toilet lid down) or the play room filled with dry towels. Wherever you decide to let your ferret dry, though, keep in mind that he'll want to go to the bathroom soon after his bath. If he poops on your towel setup, he'll probably try to step in it, roll in it, and fall asleep in it. Drying time should be a supervised time. Besides, you wouldn't want to miss the drama for the world!

Some ferrets allow owners to use a hair dryer. (If you use a little round brush, you can give your fuzzy a little extra poof — just kidding.) For this method, use the warm, not hot, setting and keep the dryer moving so you don't aim warm air at the same part of the body for too long, which can cause burns (and split ends). Also, keep the dryer at least 12 inches from the body to prevent burns.

If after the drying antics your ferret is still damp, you need to put him in a place where he can finish drying off. The best spot is a warm place with no drafts. And unless his cage is clean, filled with clean towels, and temporarily has the litter box removed, that spot is out of the question.

Caring for Those Little Ears

A ferret's normal earwax is light or reddish brown. It should have very little, if any, odor to it. If it stinks, something is wrong. Some furballs need their ears cleaned more frequently than others. Some can go for long periods of time. Health, age, and season may determine how much wax your fuzzy produces, so be sure to consult with your vet and follow your nose to any possible problems. What your eyes may miss, your nose may discover. I, for one, use playtime as an opportunity to do a quick ear inspection.

REMEMBER

Ear cleaning should be done no more frequently than once every two to three weeks. Cleaning more frequently will cause more earwax production and more odor. In fact, earwax is protective and shouldn't be removed unless it's excessive or your ferret is about to enter a ferret show (see Chapter 10). Not cleaning the ears won't cause ear mites, deafness, or infections. In fact, ear disease in ferrets is pretty uncommon with the exception of mites, which are parasites transmitted directly from one ferret to another.

The only thing to clean when you clean a ferret's ears is the outer part — go nowhere near the ear canal (the hole). You're more likely to cause damage by poking around in the ear and shoving the normal wax into the ear canal. The following sections go through the preparation and the execution.

REMEMBER

Ear cleaning can be tough for a beginner, so I suggest you have your vet demonstrate the procedure once or twice until you feel comfortable with it. No matter how comfortable you become, though, your ferret will hate having his ears cleaned. If done too often or incorrectly, it may be painful and uncomfortable. Those cotton swabs may look tiny for your ears, but they seem like large wads of cotton to a ferret. The key to preventing injury due to panic is gentleness. If you don't think you can handle the ear-cleaning process, your vet should be more than happy to perform the procedure for a minimal fee.

Gathering supplies

To clean your ferret's ears, you definitely need some cotton swabs. Here are a couple other things you need to acquire before you begin:

>> **A good liquid ear cleanser:** You can purchase this product from most pet supply stores or from your vet. Make sure that the solution is safe for cats **and** kittens, because that means it will be safe for your fuzzy, too.

TIP

If you don't have a ferret-safe liquid ear cleaner, a little bit of water will do the trick. Again, over-the-counter cleansers should be labeled for kitten or ferret use. Never use rubbing alcohol, which can sting like crazy and dry out the ear. An occasional cleaning with hydrogen peroxide is acceptable, but keep in mind that this, too, may dry out the ear. Mineral oil, when used, increases the oily wax build-up, so avoid that, as well.

>> **A small dish:** Especially if you have a bunch of ears to clean, a small dish may be helpful. Pour a little ear-cleaning solution (or water) into the dish. You can dip the clean end of a cotton swab into the liquid instead of fumbling around to squirt some on the tip. Some people moisten the tips of several swabs before they begin. If you do, be sure you place them on a clean surface to prevent them from getting dirty.

TIP

If your cleaning solution is in a bottle with an easy-to-dispense "tip," I suggest you warm up the solution for the comfort of your ferret by placing the entire bottle in a glass of warm water for about 10 to 15 minutes. Swirl it around a bit to even out the temperature. Use your wrist to make sure the cleaner isn't too hot or too cold before squirting it in your ferret's ear.

Executing the ear clean

Find a quiet and comfortable place to clean your ferret's ears, and follow the steps in this list:

1. **Dip a clean cotton swab in the ear-cleaning solution (or squirt a little into the ear canal straight from the bottle)**

2. **Scruff or firmly hold your ferret (see Chapter 7).**

    Make sure that your ferret's bottom is supported when you're scruffing him, especially if he's a big guy. If he moves too much, you can lessen the bottom support a little until he settles down. You also can try getting a better hold of the scruff from the beginning.

3. **Using your scruffing hand, hold the tip of his ear between your fingers. With your other hand, use the moistened end of the swab to wipe the inside of your ferret's ear.**

    Some experienced ferret humans feel comfortable scruffing their ferrets with one hand and using the other to clean the ears. I prefer to have a helper hold my ferret. My arms eventually get sore from all the holding (especially in my multi-ferret household), and I like to have one hand free to hold my fuzzy's ear when I'm maneuvering the cotton swab in the other.

REMEMBER

Always use the moistened end of the cotton swab first. It loosens and scoops up a lot of the ear gunk. Starting off with the dry tip can be too abrasive on the ferret's sensitive ears. Moisture is needed to clean the ear.

4. **Using a circular motion, make contact with the inner walls and crevices of the ear to remove all the hidden gunk.**

WARNING

Only clean what you can see! Never push the cotton swab into your ferret's ear canal. You may damage his ear canal or pack the earwax deep into it, making it difficult to get out and hard for the ferret to hear.

A good guide is to make sure that you can see the tip of the swab.

5. **Repeat with your collection of moistened swabs until the tips come out with little or no ick on them.**

   Some ears require a repeat of the process with two or three freshly moistened swabs.

   Never reuse a dirty swab, and never dip a used swab into the cleaning solution. Doing so contaminates the rest of the cleanser.

6. **Using the dry end of a swab, repeat the circular wiping process to dry the ear.**

Your ferret will probably squirm during the cleaning process. If you hit a particularly sensitive or itchy area, he may even jerk a leg back and forth like a dog does when you find a perfect scratching spot. However, this isn't a feel-good reaction. Be gentler and pull out the swab in case you're in too deep. Remember, you can have a lick of salmon oil when you're finished as a treat for a job well done. Make sure that your ferret gets a taste, too!

Nailing Down the Manicure

The bottom line is this: Trimming his nails makes your ferret more comfortable. Fuzzies need their claws for many things, from walking and balance to climbing curtains and counter cruising. Overgrown nails can hurt the ferret, because long nails prevent his foot from resting flat on the ground. Trimming helps prevent the nails from splitting and getting caught on cage wires, carpeting, and bedding. Clipping your fuzzbutt's claws regularly also helps lessen the severity of human scratches and damage from digging.

You need to clip nails frequently because ferrets should never be declawed. A ferret's claws are non-retractable — like the claws on rabbits and dogs (cats have retractable claws) — so removing them would entail removing parts of his toes. Most veterinarians find this mutilating surgery too inhumane to perform, as do I, and it's becoming illegal to carry out in more and more municipalities.

The frequency of clipping varies from ferret to ferret, because nail-growth rates vary. Also, the amount and type of exercise you give your ferret factors in, because a lot of play may wear down his nails. On average, I find that I need to break out the nail trimmers every two to three weeks.

Now that you have the why and when down, you can get into the how. The following sections break down the clipping method you can use and how you can actually get the job done.

Choosing your clipping method

How you approach nail trimming depends on you and your ferret: You can use the scruff method, the distract method, or the sneak-attack method. The number of ferrets you have, your available time, the ferret's tolerance to nail clipping, and your ferret's distractibility are key factors in determining the method to use. The following list outlines these three methods:

TIP

>> **The scruff method** is probably the quickest way to trim nails. It steadies your ferret, gives you a better grip, and lessens the chance of over-cutting. It generally calms the ferret (and you), so it's great for beginners who are getting used to the art of clipping.

   If your scruffed ferret moves around a lot while you're clipping, allow him to lick a treat, such as meat baby food, while you scruff him. You can clip his nails quickly and easily this way; however, this method *does often* require two people if you're doing it carefully.

>> **The distract method** can take a little more time, but it's a nice way for you and your ferret to spend some quality time together. The method involves setting the fuzzy in your lap and placing a few drops of a treat like salmon oil, or another tasty substance, on his belly. While he busies himself licking it off, you can dive in and clip before he has a chance to object. This method doesn't work with all ferrets, but it can be worth a try.

>> **The sneak-attack method** is performed while your ferret is in a deep sleep. Depending on the quality of his sleep and your clipping talent, you may get all 20 nails clipped or just 1 or 2 before he wakes up.

REMEMBER

No matter what clipping method you choose, you should give a treat to your fuzzy during or after the manicure. You want him to look forward to his clippings!

After you decide how you want to approach nail trimming, take a good look at your ferret's nails so you know what you're dealing with. Most fuzzy nails are long, curving, and dagger-like. Some fuzzies develop thicker nails as they age. The nails on the back paws are much shorter because they wear down more quickly, meaning they can be more difficult to clip. But unlike many dogs, whose nails are solid black, a ferret's nails are white. The *quick*, or vein, is easy to see, so you know exactly how much nail tip you can clip. So you have that going for you!

Performing the clip

To perform the clip, I use fingernail clippers designed for human babies. Regular-size human clippers work well, too. Some people like to use cat- or dog-nail clippers, but I find them too awkward to handle when clipping such tiny nails. You also have a hard time seeing what you're doing because of the shape of the clipper. Whatever clippers *you* find most comfortable, make sure that the blades are sharp before you clip. Dull blades can cause the nail walls to crush, leaving the edges rough. Also, make sure that the lighting in the room is adequate.

To trim your ferret's nails, follow these steps (you can use any of the clipping methods for these steps):

1. **Take your thumb and first finger and hold the paw close to the toes, with your thumb on the bottom of the paw.**

2. **Use the pressure of your thumb to spread the toes.**

   Doing so makes going from claw to claw easier.

3. **Clip as much of the white nail tip off each toe as you can, leaving some white after the quick (the interior of a ferret's nail; see a cross-section of a ferret nail in Figure 9-2).**

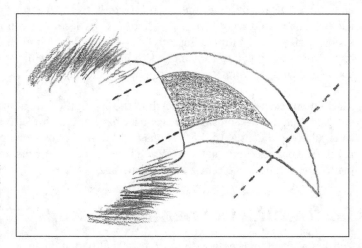

FIGURE 9-2: The quick contains blood vessels, so be sure not to cut a nail too short.

TIP

Cutting into the quick is painful and causes the ferret to bleed. Because accidents happen (perhaps you weren't paying attention or your fuzzbutt suddenly moved), have some styptic powder or cornstarch on hand to stop any bleeding that may occur. Apply directly to the tip of the bleeding nail. If those materials aren't available, try dipping the bleeding nail into a bar of white soap, beeswax, or flour. You also can try running cold water over it. I suggest postponing the rest of the manicure until after your ferret has forgiven your dreadful deed. If after 10 minutes the bleeding still hasn't stopped despite the above tactics, a trip to the vet may be warranted.

Even if the nail doesn't bleed, cutting too close to the quick can be painful, and your ferret will let you know. Take extra care with the back nails, because some have teeny-weeny nail tips. Look closely before clipping them. If the tips seem too short to clip, try filing them with a nail file, being careful not to scrape the fuzzy's sensitive paw pads.

REMEMBER

If you let your ferret's nails grow for a long time between cuttings, the quicks will grow longer and longer into the nails, allowing you to cut off less and less of the nails. This isn't a good thing. Cutting frequently causes the quicks to regress back toward the paws so that you can cut a good amount of the nails off, giving your fuzzy more freedom and less of a chance of snagging.

Chewing On Chomper Maintenance

As a routine part of your ferret's grooming process, you should check out his teeth and gums. Tartar will build up on your ferret's teeth, regardless of his diet. In addition, neglected teeth can go bad and/or chip, leading to abscesses that can seriously affect his health. Aging ferrets have more dental problems than younger ones, so it's up to you to sink your teeth into this chore while your ferret is still young and chipper. Your fuzzy's future health and happiness depend on it.

All children resist brushing their teeth in the beginning, and a fuzzy is no different. The good news is, most ferrets get used to having their teeth cleaned if you do so regularly and gently. In the sections that follow, I show you how to perform a regular dental checkup, and I go through the process of brushing your fuzzy's teeth. Soon enough, you'll be a brushing wizard!

Performing the dental checkup

The dental checkup is easy with most ferrets, although it can be quite a challenge with more difficult patients. Most of my carpet sharks sit in my lap with minimal fidgeting and allow me to lift their gums for a peek. Others need to be scruffed gently while I perform the dental inspection (see Chapter 7). I always like to have an extra pair of hands around so that I can concentrate on my findings. No matter how you handle the inspection, be gentle. Your ferret won't understand why you're poking around in his mouth, so take that into consideration.

You have two main things to look for when doing the dental checkup: the teeth and the gums.

REMEMBER

With the exception of small traces of tartar buildup, if you see something out of the ordinary in your furball's mouth, contact your vet right away to schedule a visit. Dental problems can be serious enough to cause death. Non-dental problems that are located in the mouth are almost always signs of an underlying illness. Regardless of whether you have a dental emergency, your vet should perform yearly dental exams on your fuzzy and remove any excess tartar or decaying teeth.

Teeth

First, you should take a peek at all his teeth. The grayish or greenish discoloration you may see is *tartar,* which forms from plaque. Buildup happens at the same time and at the same rate on all the teeth. However, the ferret's tongue acts as sort of a windshield wiper, helping clear away the gunk on the lingual side, or "tongue side," of the teeth. Because the self-cleaning is less efficient on the outer side, tartar builds up faster on the buccal side, or "cheek side," of the teeth. And buildup occurs even faster in areas where folds and crevices exist, such as on the carnassials or back teeth.

The stuff you see on the teeth isn't necessarily the problem, though; even small amounts of buildup can signal under-the-gum disease. Although tartar doesn't cause gingivitis — which is characterized by red, inflamed gums — it may exacerbate the problem by injuring tissue and increasing the progression of gingivitis. Various stages of periodontal disease can follow gingivitis and are marked by the actual recession of the gum line, as well as bone loss. At this point, the ferret's teeth lose their support, loosen, and fall out. Diseased teeth can be painful, can lead to serious infection, and can cause the ferret to stop eating.

Without tooth cleaning and regular vet checkups, buildup (and problems) can increase as your ferret ages. A small amount of buildup is expected and not necessarily a cause for concern; however, it can become your ferret's enemy if not kept in check.

Gums

The gums should be smooth, moist, and a medium-pink color. Red, inflamed gums are a sign of gum disease, and your ferret should be treated immediately by your vet. If they appear very light in color (whitish/grayish/bluish), your ferret may be seriously ill, so a visit to your vet is a must. If you notice isolated swelling over one or two teeth, you can suspect a tooth abscess. If you dare, stick your nose up to his mouth and take a whiff. Conditions such as gum problems and ulcers result in a case of bad breath.

Ulcers on the gums or on the inside of the lip flap are a common sign of the disease *insulinoma.* These ulcers usually are whitish in color, and sometimes they ooze. Your ferret may point out these ulcers or other dental problems by pawing at his mouth. Other signs include drooling and a crusty bib. Although insulinoma isn't necessarily a dental problem, it is something to keep an eye out for as long as you have your eye in his mouth. (For more information on insulinoma, see Chapter 16.)

If you notice your ferret has bad breath at any time — not just during a checkup — you should call your vet to schedule an appointment. In addition to being a sign of mouth ulcers and gum problems, bad breath may be an indication of liver or kidney problems.

Brushing his teeth

After you perform an exam and find that everything is okay, what can you do to prevent any future dental problems? Brush his teeth! You can make cleaning your ferret's teeth a regular part of your grooming routine. All you have to do is invest in a cat toothbrush (don't use your spouse's) or a human infant toothbrush. Heck, even a Q-Tip or gauze wrapped around your finger will work as long as the build-up isn't too bad. You could purchase a toothpaste designed for use on dogs or cats, although it seems that most ferrets find the taste disagreeable — even the meat-flavored ones. Instead, consider making your own healthier ferret toothpaste — just mix *human-grade* bone-meal powder (found in health food stores) with either a little water or salmon oil to the consistency of toothpaste. If you'd prefer, instead of bone-meal powder you can use ground-up cuttlefish bone (the chalky, almost pure calcium supplement used for birds) and mix that with water or oil.

Never use adult human toothpaste to brush your ferret's teeth. The fluoride in adult human toothpaste is thought to be poisonous to fuzzies, and ferrets don't know the meaning of "rinse and spit." Additionally, some toothpastes containe the deadly "all natural" sugar substitute xylitol, which can be very detrimental to your ferret's health.

To brush your ferret's teeth, follow these steps:

1. **Lift the lip and gently wipe his teeth with the toothbrush, Q-Tip, or gauze using up and down and back and forth movements.**

2. **Gently go over his gums with the toothbrush, Q-Tip, or gauze after you finish the teeth.**

   Pay particular attention to cleaning his gum line (where the teeth disappear into the gums).

Patience and gentleness are the keys to successfully brushing your ferret's teeth. After all, you're not sanding down old paint. Some ferrets tolerate having their teeth brushed after a while, but others may have to be scruffed. Use the method that's the least stressful on you and your ferret.

Breaking Out the Hairbrush

Some people choose to brush their fuzzies' fur as they would a dog's or cat's. Other people skip this grooming step; maybe they're lazy or just find it unnecessary. There's no disadvantage to brushing as long as you use a soft brush and you're gentle, but brushing does have three main advantages:

» Helps to keep your ferret's coat clean and free of debris

» Removes loose fur — an especially important thing because fuzzies are prone to hairballs, and hairballs can be fatal

» Improves bonding between you and your ferret

If you decide to brush your fuzzbutt, use a soft brush designed for kittens, rabbits, or other small mammals. These brushes generally are shorter bristled and just hard enough to remove loose fur without irritating sensitive skin. Stroke the brush in the same direction as the fur. Most furkids don't want to remain motionless for very long, so be aware that brushing can be a quick adventure. Some ferrets, however, enjoy this part of the grooming process and come to look forward to it.

Odor Control Tips 101 — A Summary

One of the biggest complaints many ferret owners have about their little war weasels is the "skunky" odor, but it doesn't have to be that way. Believe it or not, you have a lot of control over the odor that your ferret produces. Ferrets have two types of odors: one that the ferret himself emits and another that comes from the ferret's environment.

Let's get this out of the way. I love the sweet, musky smell of ferrets, especially an unaltered male (hob), and I daresay I'm not alone. It's music to my nose! Ferrets are born with anal scent glands, as well as musk glands that are scattered in the skin across the the body but more heavily concentrated around the face. Believe it or not, most of the odor comes from these musk glands or hormones (if unaltered ferrets are present) and not the anal sacs. So, what contributes to the odor, and what might you be able to do about it?

>> **Altering (spaying/neutering) your ferret:** Intact or unneutered/unspayed ferrets can be positively odiferous! And when males go into rut (breeding season) hormones abound! To attract the females, they use a special cologne called Urine with which they groom themselves in order to make themselves more desirable. If you're not planning on breeding your ferret, I highly suggest you alter or neuter/spay him or her. This will cut down on about 90 percent of the ferret's odor. Be sure to wait until the fuzzy is about 7 months old or later to alter, and even then it'll take about 30 days for the hormones to settle down. Most pet shops sell already-altered ferrets, so this is unlikely to be a concern of yours unless the spay/neuter was "missed" or "incomplete" when it was performed.

>> **Descenting your ferret:** There are many pros and cons to descenting your ferret, and reputable ferret veterinarians stand on both sides of the debate sharing valid points for and against the procedure (See Chapter 1 on Descenting). In many European countries, descenting is actually considered a mutilating procedure and is banned. Your ferret may "let one rip," but descenting has little to no impact on the overall scent of the ferret. Unlike the skunk, which has more developed anal glands than ferrets, and a spray that lingers for days and that travels far and wide (detectable by a human nose up to 3½ miles downwind!), a ferret's occasional "poof" is less potent and dissipates quickly. I say, if your ferret's anal glands are intact, keep them that way!

>> **Bathing your ferret:** I'm telling you now, resist the urge! Over-bathing your ferret is quite counterproductive and actually causes your ferret to smell worse! But how can this be? If you think about it, your ferret is covered in little glands, which produce musky oils. Bathing your ferret not only strips the skin and fur of these essential oils, but it leaves him feeling uncomfortably itchy, as well. This dryness causes the ferret's body to go into overdrive to replenish what was lost, thus producing extra stinky oils that get absorbed and stored by the dry, now-porous fur. The result is an extra stinky weasel.

>> **Cleaning those ears:** Dirty ears can stink, and ferret ears can produce lots of ear gunk. A little odor is to be expected, and you should properly clean her ears every two to three weeks to keep the odor under control. But if the odor is particularly offensive and the wax is super dark, almost black, your little guy might have earmites, which require a different intervention. (see Chapter 14 for information on earmites)

>> **Addressing bad breath:** Yep, it happens to the best of us, but bad breath in a ferret can be an indicator of many different things, so it's your job to stay on top of it. Brush your ferret's teeth and gums regularly with ferret-safe

toothpaste to prevent the build-up of smelly tartar. Build-up of tartar over time can lead to gum and tooth infections, which can be quite smelly, as well as indicative of serious conditions for your ferret. Some diseases, such as kidney disease, can be indicated by the presence of bad breath once other dental issues are ruled out. Never dismiss bad breath as "just one of those things."

Essential oils, perfumes, air fresheners (including plug-ins), other household deodorizers (and many other fragrances), and even many "green" products are toxic to ferrets (and cats), and should not be used on or around them. Ferrets (and cats) do not have the enzymes necessary to metabolize the phenol vapors, which build up to toxic levels in the liver over time. Tea tree oil, which is commonly marketed for and sold for ferret use, is especially toxic! There are many pet deodorizers on the market. Recognizing what's safe for your ferret might be a crapshoot. Remember, just because a product is branded for ferrets or described as safe on the Internet does not mean it's true! Having said that, address your ferret's odor directly with the methods discussed in this chapter. Do not attempt to mask it.

After you tackle his personal hygiene, you may notice there's still a bit of a stinky odor lingering in your humble abode. That's because you're not completely finished with the routine housekeeping and odor control. Let's talk about your carpet shark's environment:

» **Feeding your ferret a balanced diet:** Poop stinks. No way around it. However, the better the diet, the less offensive the smell. In fact, a really good diet should produce smaller, lower-odor poops. A poor quality diet produces crappy, smelly poops. Simply put, you get out exactly what you put in.

» **Constructing and cleaning the cage:** If you're reading this before you've gotten your first ferret, then perhaps I can talk you out of getting or constructing a cage made of wood. If you already invested in a wood cage, please consider re-investing in a new one. Odors from urine and ferret oils cannot be removed from wood after they've been absorbed. Uncoated wire gets rusty from water and urine, and it, too, will become porous and absorb the odors. Stick with plastic and coated wire materials for caging. At least monthly or more frequently, clean all inside cage surfaces with a very weak bleach/water solution or a weak white vinegar/water solution, making sure to remove all crusted-on poopies. Remove and replace disposable items such as cardboard box hidey spots even if they look clean. Trust me, they still smell! Don't neglect toys or other items in the cages, such as bowls and tubes. Clean them or switch them out for clean ones.

>> **Scooping the poop:** This is where many ferret owners fall down on the job and end up wondering why their weasels smell so bad. The truth is, it's not the ferret that smells, but rather the darn litter box that you've been neglecting for a week or more. Okay, maybe the ferret smells too, but it's only because she's had to drag herself in and out of a disgusting litter box. You *must* scoop at least the poop out of the litter box one to two times a day to keep the odor down. And once a week dump the entire litterbox out and clean it thoroughly before replacing the replenished box into the cage.

>> **Choosing your litter carefully** – There are so many litters on the market today. It can be downright confusing and frustrating to pet owners (see Chapter 5 for more on litter). Choosing the right litter can make a world of difference. The right litter cuts down on odor. It will be absorbent and be economical. The wrong litter may mold easily, be dusty, or contain phenols that are toxic to your ferret. The list goes on, so choose your ferret's litter wisely.

>> **Doing the laundry:** Your fuzzy's bedding looks clean, right? So why bother cleaning it? Wrong! Ferret oils and traces of urine, feces, food, bacteria, and God knows what are all over your fuzzy's bedding. Just because you can't see it doesn't mean it's not there, and it's for sure contributing to the odor you're smelling. Wash all bedding and fabric toys, or switch them all out with clean bedding and toys, at least weekly. And before you purchase any new bedding or toys for your ferret, ask yourself, will it fit in the washing machine or can it be washed? If the answer is no, resist the temptation.

REMEMBER

You want your ferret's bedding to be clean but free of odors. Avoid heavily scented detergents and fabric softeners. Look for a detergent that is free of fragrances, dyes, and chemical brighteners, such as Charlie's Soap. It may be more expensive, but well worth it to prevent allergic reactions or respiratory problems. If you find you must bleach your bedding, wash it again afterwards to remove the strong odor of the bleach, or put it through a second rinse cycle. And you can also add white vinegar to the bleach compartment in the washing machine for extra cleaning power.

WARNING

I'm sorry to say that air filters, although helpful to humans (and even ferrets) with some allergies, will not really help with odor control. This is a bummer, because I invested in about a dozen of them early on in my ferret career before I knew any better. And although this is more of a warning, I would be remiss if I failed to mention that ionizers or ozonators, once thought to be safe for pets, have now been put on the do–not–use list. This type of product intentionally emits ozone that oxidizes and destroys bacteria, fungus, mold, viruses, and mildew. It leaves high levels of ozone and pure oxygen in its place, which sounds like a good thing, right? Unfortunately not. One by-product, ozone, is actually thought to be hazardous to pets. And the odor-reducing properties? Ionizers may not be eliminating odor at all, but rather impairing the person's sense of smell instead.

Chapter **10**

Enrichment: Yours and Your Ferret's

Caring for your ferret means much more than providing her with fresh food and water. It's more than providing a roof over her head and cleaning up her poop, and it's even more than taking her for regular vet trips. Care goes way beyond that, which is where many pet owners fail in their responsibilities. Whether you own a dog, cat, bird, bunny, or ferret, your job is to keep your pet's life interesting and filled with enriching stimuli. In fact, her physical and psychological well-being depend on it!

Ferrets are as intelligent as small primates of the same body (and brain) size, which is proof that they need a lot of action-packed play and exploring time in a ferret-safe environment. Without a regular supply of stimulation, ferrets can become cage-crazy or depressed. Mentally, they can lose interest in their surroundings and their desire to explore or play. They may begin chewing on their cage bars and digging out their litter and food more frequently — basically, spending most of their time trying to find a way out of jail. Physically, they can become unfit and frequently will fall asleep on the hammock while watching reruns of old sitcoms. More importantly, the stress of having no enrichment can cause disease, such as ulcers, or make existing diseases worse.

This chapter is all about enrichment for both you and your ferret. I take the mystery out of the topic by further explaining what it is, why it's necessary, and what it does for ferrets. I try to give you enough information on ferret enrichment activities so that you can keep your ferret on her toes and even come up with your own enrichment ideas. I also guide you through some of the clubs, events, and resources available to you as a ferret owner. Take advantage of them. Here's to a happy and healthy life together!

Why Is Enrichment Necessary?

Like humans, ferrets possess an array of complex senses that need to be exercised on a daily basis. Imagine staring at the same wall for weeks on end. The sound of the same song playing over and over, which eventually becomes silent as you tune out the repetitiveness. Putting together the same puzzle so many times that you can do it in your sleep and you no longer enjoy the picture it creates. Your daily ration of macaroni and cheese squishing tastelessly in your mouth. You find some amusement in flinging it off your fork and watching it glob on the bare wall in front of you. The only smell filling your isolated room emanates from the toilet, which gets flushed every once in a while. Sound like torture? It is, and your ferret finds it excruciating as well. As a responsible ferret owner, your duty is to prevent your ferret from experiencing such depressing boredom. This presents quite a challenge to owners, because ferrets realize monotony in their surroundings rather quickly.

Humans tell our ferrets what and sometimes when to eat. We clean their cages and provide them with sleeping quarters. We introduce cagemates and take cagemates away. We medicate. We bathe. We groom. Humans are the ultimate ferret dictators, making most of their pets' life decisions for them. The basic goal of environmental enrichment is to get animals to interact with their environments, using their natural skills and behaviors, and to stimulate all their senses. You want to give your ferret something to think about, give her choices, and help her feel in control. Enrichment can also provide exercise, and it definitely relieves boredom.

What Does Enrichment Do for Ferrets?

What does enrichment do for ferrets? First of all, enrichment feels good! Enrichment can mean play! And what is play if not an activity that makes us feel good? This is a simple definition for an activity that utilizes a set of highly developed and often complicated skills. Dancing, chasing, dooking (a form of ferret talk), hopping aimlessly in many directions at once . . . all are fun, and all feel wonderful! If play makes your ferret feel good, what's wrong with that? Enriching your ferret's life is certainly better than risking cage stress and boredom that can make her feel bad and adopt a negative outlook. But enrichment does even more than make you and your ferret feel good, as I explain the following sections.

Relieves boredom and stress

Boredom can be a major cause of stress for fuzzies. Ferrets are physically and emotionally sensitive to their surroundings. They need stimulation and enrichment to keep from getting bored. And boy, do they get bored easily!

Facilitates bonding

Although their natural tendency is to live a solitary life, ferrets are frequently apt to enjoy the company of other ferrets — and sometimes even other types of pets. And experienced ferret owners can attest that their war weasels express great excitement when in their company. Through social enrichment, you can teach your ferret important social skills. Viewing each other much as they would littermates, ferrets brought together by adoption enjoy chasing each other and being chased. They rough and tumble and even steal from each other, testing their limits to the max. Sometimes, cats and dogs will partake in the ferret play as well, fostering supervised camaraderie and trust between species.

Enrichment is extremely important when it comes to bonding with humans, too! Enrichment activities are the only true ways for your ferret to get to know you and for you to get to know your ferret. Enrichment will increase comfort levels, establish limits, build trust, and strengthen bonds. Even a timid or aggressive ferret will build up more confidence and trust through enrichment activities.

TIP

Bonding enrichments also can help parents solve the problem of how to get their children interested in ferrets. Children often persuade their parents to get a ferret but soon get bored with it, and the ferret languishes in a cage for long periods of time. Bonding enrichments can help firmly connect a child to a ferret, which is great for all involved.

Keeps their senses alive and well

A ferret's every sense needs to be exercised routinely and equally to keep her sharp. Ferrets have an exceptional sense of smell; you'll frequently see your fuzzy with her nose to the ground as she sniffs out new and unusual things. Enrichment activities that call on this sense are great fun. Ferrets also benefit from games such as tag or pouncing, where they rely on their eyesight to hone in on victims. And what about touch, taste, and hearing? All very heightened senses that long to be tested. Keeping all this in mind, the possibilities for sensory enrichment are endless. (For more details on a ferret's senses, check out the section "Understanding Your Ferret's Senses.")

Helps to curb negative behaviors

Every ferret behavior is based on biological, medical, or psychological factors. A bored ferret can be a problematic ferret! So when you hear the term "cage crazy" or "cage rage," you can assume it means just that! A few symptoms of cage craziness include

>> Nipping or biting

>> Gnawing on cage bars

>> Fabric chewing

>> Pacing

This acting out is her way of letting you know that she's terribly unhappy. She's attempting to relieve some of the stress brought on by what's lacking in her life. This ferret needs some enrichment, stat!

Keeps the flab at bay

Lack of exercise or physical play contributes to chubbiness, whether you're talking about a human or a ferret. Physical enrichment activities burn calories and keep muscles toned and in shape. The ferret in its natural state is an extremely muscular critter, and you want to keep yours that way. Get your ferret out and exploring!

Encourages curiosity and creative problem solving

Enrichment is brain food! Enrichment not only increases the number of brain cells a ferret has, but also helps her brain recover from injury. Ferrets are both curious and adept problem-solvers. Providing enrichment will challenge your ferret by introducing new problems and encouraging the discovery of solutions.

Helps to keep bones, muscles, organs, and joints healthy

Physical enrichment improves joint and ligament performance, builds muscle, and increases strength. It also helps your ferret to build endurance when you're chasing her to retrieve your belongings! When humans exercise regularly, they preserve bone mass and increase bone density, because bones respond to mechanical stress by adding more bone tissue. It's likely your ferret gains benefits in this same way. Muscles and organs are exercised during physical enrichment and fed oxygen-rich blood, making them stronger and less prone to damage and infection. As they say, use them or lose them!

Improves heart health and overall circulation

Exercise and play gets a ferret's heart beating faster, thus facilitating rapid transportation of oxygen-rich blood and nutrients to all organs and areas of the body. As your ferret exercises, she engages in deep, rhythmic breathing, which assists her lungs in developing greater capacity and allows her to take in sufficient oxygen to nourish her cells. This is called *cardiovascular fitness*.

Enrichment play can also increase the size of her tiny blood vessels and improve the efficiency of the blood-delivery system. Physical play not only conditions the heart and lungs to work more efficiently during play, but also helps them work more efficiently during rest.

Makes humans smile and laugh

Ferrets are the ultimate in play therapy! It's hard not to find ferret antics worthy of giggles and smiles. All humans need to put aside time to laugh and have fun. Interacting with your ferret is a quick fix that rapidly dissipates anxiety, even if momentarily. It's a known fact that interacting with a pet in a positive way can reduce overall stress levels and lower blood pressure. And if that isn't a good enough reason to play with your ferret, how about the fact that she also giggles and smiles watching silly humans play along? You *and* your ferret will benefit from having fun!

Understanding Your Ferret's Senses

The pads on a ferret's paws are extremely sensitive. His face and nose are ticklish. His whiskers dance at the slightest sensation. His taste buds long to be awakened and stimulated with new tastes. Ferrets have an acute sense of hearing. They can hear a bag of treats being opened from across the house! That's right! Ferret senses are alive and well just like yours and mine. Understanding each sense will allow you to help your ferret live an enriching life. This section will teach you about the ferret's five senses. Every enrichment activity you implement will involve one or more of these senses. The more senses you stimulate, the better the enrichment.

Hearing

Ferrets have hearing that's at least comparable to a dog, meaning that it's excellent and highly developed. Reports indicate they can even hear frequencies as low as elephants can. Ferrets hear best in the range of 8 to 12 kilohertz (kHz). You can safely assume that your ferret can hear below and above the human ability.

Smelling

A foot of mud isn't enough to keep an innocent frog safe from a ferret, because the ferret's sense of smell is exceptionally strong. Her nose is so sensitive that she can likely sniff out water, which helps to explain how blind ferrets have little difficulty making their way to water bottles and bowls.

Unfortunately, a ferret's keen sense of smell can also be a disadvantage. The ferret's sense of smell causes her extreme *olfactory imprinting* — when a ferret "imprints" on food items by the age of 6 months old. This means that if she hasn't been exposed to the food by that age, she doesn't recognize it as food. When young, a ferret's smell cells that aren't exposed to specific types of odor wither away and die. Afterwards, because the ferret can't smell the food, she simply doesn't recognize it as something good to eat. (For more on this phenomenon, see the following section.)

Tasting

Experts and ferret owners don't know much about the ferret's sense of taste, but because it's closely tied to the sense of smell, they assume that ferrets also have a highly developed sense of taste. You'll certainly find that your ferret favors some tastes over others.

TIP

Because taste and smell are so closely tied together, you should expose a young ferret to as many food items as possible while she's young. That way, her smell cells will be more diversified and she'll be able to recognize more items as food when she grows into adulthood. This will allow you to provide a varied, free-choice diet and will give her a healthier life through adulthood (see Chapter 8).

Seeing

A common misconception is that the ferret's eyesight is exceptionally poor. Although the resolution (the ability to see fine detail) of a ferret's vision isn't as fine as a human's, and a ferret probably only sees limited colors — living in a world of grays, for instance — ferret vision isn't all that bad for a species that has adapted to see in the dark. Much of what's considered bad vision is probably an adaptation to living in cages, making ferrets appear more near-sighted than they actually are.

Touching

Ferrets have evolved to live in a dark, subterranean world. Consequently, they have a large number of specialized hairs sensitive to touch found around their mouths, on their necks, and even on their forearms! These special hairs "light" the way so they can move through dark areas with no light.

A ferret's foot pads also are very sensitive to touch; they have small hairs that probably help the ferret find her way in the dark. The hairs may reduce sound as well, helping her evade predators and sneak up on prey.

Recommended Enrichment Activities for You and Your Fuzzy

Many activities will allow you to have safe, enriching fun with your ferret — as long as you're fun-loving, creative, and well-prepared. In the following sections, I cover some of the enrichment possibilities for you. First, I give you pointers on setting up appropriate areas for your activities, and then I tell you about the activities themselves. The enrichment activities I present stimulate any of the ferret's five senses: smell, vision, touch, taste, and hearing.

TIP

A ferret's toy chest can quickly become full of all sorts of toys and miscellaneous objects. To keep it together, you can come up with a simple storage system that works for you. You can manage toys and enrichment items by storing them in size-appropriate bins or ferret-proof plastic containers. You can label the bins according to toy type, manner of enrichment (hearing, smelling, tasting, touching, or seeing), or even by weekly rotation. It also helps to keep one labeled bin aside to hold all items that need to be cleaned (for more on cleaning toys, see Chapter 9).

Organizing your ferret's play areas

A ferret's outdoor play area is essentially an enclosed, ferret-proofed place where she can run and play — a place that's safe from escape or predation from other animals. It should have all the following items for enrichment purposes:

>> Soil for digging

>> Water for splashing

>> Objects for climbing

>> Novel items for exploration

>> Tubes for running

>> Shade or protection from the heat

>> Dens for hiding and sleeping

Of paramount importance is ferret-proofing. Unless you're absolutely certain your ferret can't escape and that a predator can't get in, you shouldn't leave the ferret alone and unsupervised when outdoors.

REMEMBER

You must remember that ferrets are excellent diggers and can dig themselves out of most outdoor play areas. They're also excellent climbers, so you must confine any climbing opportunities to the middle of the play area with no chance for escape. (People like using wood climbing tools, because wood is difficult to climb.) Many people will line the bottoms of their outdoor play areas with wire and cover them with dirt to prevent digging escape. Other people choose to dig out the perimeter of the play areas and bury cement cinder blocks two to three feet deep in the ground. This option certainly stops the ferret from digging out, or at least gives you time to fill in the holes after they get that deep. You can always continue putting the cinder blocks above ground and then build a structure on them. The design of the play area is your choice, but it must be escape-proof and predation-proof.

A ferret's indoor play area is usually a room designated for the ferret. It may be just for the ferret, or it may be a common living area. It should be well ferret-proofed, and preferably tiled (see Chapter 6 on ferret-proofing). You can bring a little of the outdoors inside by providing a dirt dig box, a small pool of water, or a box of leaves, but the cleanup is obviously a little more involved.

Movement and physical-exercise activities

This section provides a couple specific enrichment activities that require physical exertion and movement. Other activities that fall under this category include play activities, leashed walks, wrestling, and anything that causes the ferret to work her muscles.

Dig it, baby

Ferrets love to dig, and you can honor that love by constructing a "dig box" for your ferret to play in. A dig box is simple to make, but it can be a messy endeavor depending on what you fill it with and what type of character your ferret is. On the other hand, it's so satisfying to watch your ferret letting loose and going all out in play. Just look at her smile behind that dirt mustache. If you're still worried about the mess, put a blanket or large towel beneath the dig box, and remember to put it on a tile floor! Here's what you need to do:

>> **Pick your container:** Cardboard boxes work, but they tip over easily and can only contain dry materials. They're okay if you're in a pinch, but they really limit you. Opt instead for a plastic tote, small kiddie pool, or Rubbermaid bin. The bin is great because you can cut the flexible lid in half (the short way) to contain much of the dig box contents while still allowing your ferret access to the inside for play. You'll also still have a great view of the antics going on in there. If necessary, attach a flexible hose, such as a dryer hose, to a hole in the side of the dig box so that your weasel can get up and into the box (and out, too!).

An even better idea is to use a clear bin so that you can see your ferret playing inside. You can cut a hole in the top of the lid for easy ferret access. Then you can cut a hole high on the side and insert a dryer hose into it so that your fuzzy can get in and out the fun way!

And who says you need a lid at all on your container. Mess is half the fun!

>> **Pick your contents:** This is where you get to go nuts too — nuts with imagination and fun. Just remember to be safe and to avoid adding any harmful items in your ferret's dig box. If you question yourself whether an item is safe or not, err on the side of caution and assume it isn't. Here are some common items used in dig boxes:

- Long grain white rice (*not* instant rice, which expands when moistened and may cause a blockage if ingested)

- Ping pong balls

- Play sand (as used in sandboxes) — wet or dry

- Shredded paper

- Plastic eggs

- Dry leaves

- Large dried beans (kidney, lima, etc)

- Pasta (shapes, not spaghetti)

- Potting soil or topsoil

- Peat moss

- Colored plastic balls (like those in a ball pit)

- Clean rags/towels

- Golf balls

- Crinkled up balls of newspaper

- Water (swim box)

- Dirty clothes

TIP

Here's your chance to show off your creative side. Toss some floating plastic balls into your ferret's swim box. Combine items from the list. Sink some toys and have him dive for the loot. And be sure to rotate items in your dig box to make sure your ferret doesn't become bored.

WARNING

Biodegradable packing peanuts — you know, the ones we've all tasted that mostly melt in your mouth — these can be dangerous to use in dig boxes, although many ferret owners do use them. Ferrets do seem to love these mysterious little things, but extreme caution should be exercised if you let your ferrets play with them. Some ferrets are attracted to the starch in the peanuts and will start eating them, which poses a blockage risk. Also, the real-deal Styrofoam packing peanuts should never be used in a dig box — they provide an even greater blockage risk because they don't dissolve at all.

>> **Throw in some treasures:** Hide some loot in the dig box for extra enrichment, and let her dig away to find it. Loot can be treasured toys or pieces of healthy treats, but if food is used, be sure to sanitize washable contents or dispose of contaminated content before the next dig box session. Here are some great additions to the dig box:

- Earthworms or other non-toxic edible insects (great in dig boxes containing sand, soil, or peat moss)

- A stinky shoe or sock

- Hard plastic cat toys with bells inside

- Empty pill bottle with large beans inside (childproof cap side on)

- A couple pieces of raw meat (*not* for use in soil or sand)

- Whole prey items, pre-killed (if you feed that way)

Ferret cheerleading

Invest in some cheap, plastic, multi-colored pom-poms, which you can find in most party supply stores. (Black and white would be the best contrast!) Now you're ready to try the following exercises:

>> Dance the poms above your ferret's head and watch her dance and jump up to catch them.

>> Race them along the floor to get your ferret to chase them or even ride them.

>> Wiggle the poms in your ferret's face and watch her go crazy!

TIP

This meets visual, hearing, and touching enrichments, assuming you complete all the exercises in this activity.

Social-development activities

This section presents some enrichment activities that relate to the social needs and development of your ferret. Other common types of social enrichments include face washing, grooming, petting, feeding by hand, and cuddling. (For more on grooming routines, head to Chapter 9.)

The washcloth rubdown

The washcloth rubdown is one of the most effective grooming/bonding methods, but it takes a little practice. All you need is a small, damp (not wet), warm washcloth. Starting at your ferret's face and working your way back across her body, rub your ferret with the washcloth. Move in the direction of her fur. You may need to rinse and warm your washcloth again during the activity to keep it fresh. Don't forget her belly, and particularly her bottom and genitals.

What you're doing is mocking her mom's behavior. This enrichment activity is not only a great way to bond with your ferret, but also a good way to keep her clean.

Sack 'o ferret

A great social enrichment activity is to get a bonding pouch or a sack and place your ferret inside. Carry her around while you do household chores or just sit with her and watch television or read a book. I usually have one hand in the pouch so that I can stay in contact with a ferret and play with her. Most ferret sacks and pouches have convenient straps so that you can hang them around your neck or over your shoulder.

Food-related activities

Enrichment activities that exploit the ferret's desire to eat can include giving tiny bits of "unusual" foods, such as tastes of human food; a tiny piece of pot roast; or even something unfamiliar such as a lick of brown gravy. Some examples of ferret-safe foods include meat-based baby food, cooked or whole whisked eggs, bits of raw meat, and nutritionally balanced kibble or canned food.

TIP

One useful food-related activity is the *stink trail.* Take a small piece of meat and "dab" it on the floor, making a trail to a hiding place. Be creative and make the trail zig-zag or go around the leg of a table. Watch your ferret follow the scent trail to the end!

Just the smell or experience of investigating food is enriching to a ferret, so even if your ferret doesn't eat the food, it isn't a failure of the enrichment. My friend Holly even invites her ferrets to sniff all the ferret-safe ingredients (no onions or garlic) whenever she's preparing dinner. Although they don't actually eat any of it, they get the benefit of experiencing the different scents.

Training exercises

This section presents some enrichment activities that encourage the training of your ferret to perform certain behaviors; others discourage your fuzzy from certain activities. Mostly, these activities are tricks (do's) and trainings (don'ts) that stimulate all your ferret's senses and help you out in the process!

Some fuzzies are cautious and anxious creatures; don't traumatize your ferret by insisting that she learn a certain training exercise if that trick obviously bothers her. Other ferrets will learn trick after trick. They may even teach you a few while still leaving room to invent new tricks of their own. Fuzzies are individual characters with unique personalities. All are extremely intelligent, but some have less interest in learning pet tricks. Having your ferret act like a ferret should be delightful enough.

Ferrets are instigators and live to cause mass mayhem. If you have multiple ferrets in your household, it only makes sense to isolate the furball trainee from the other ferrets before beginning any training session, but even so, use a room your chosen ferret is used to. Otherwise he'll spend the time exploring and you'll just be spinning your wheels out of frustration!

I beg your pardon?

The easiest trick to teach a ferret is to sit up and beg. The action comes naturally because ferrets often have to stand up high and peek for the things they want to pilfer. When your furball learns this trick, she may start running in front of you every chance she gets to beg for a treat, doggie-style. Teaching this trick requires that you have a favorite treat and a human hand — preferably attached to the rest of a human body:

1. **Sit on the floor with a treat in your hand or salmon oil on your finger.**

2. **Reach straight away from your body and let your ferret sniff the treat so she knows that it's there.**

   You can even give her a tiny taste.

3. **Slowly raise your hand until she has to raise herself to reach the treat.**

   Don't let her rest her front paws on your lap or grab your hand. If she does, gently nudge her away or move farther from her and start over. The idea is to get her to do the trick without cheating.

4. **While she reaches up to get it, use the command you want to stick with, such as "Up," "Beg," or "Sit up."**

   Choose a simple word or phrase and be consistent with it.

When your ferret begins to associate the verbal command with the treat, start using only the hand motion to prompt the action. *Note:* Deaf ferrets can't read lips, but they can read body language and beg for treats just as frequently.

Scooter, I think your human is calling

Many people have taught their ferrets to come a-runnin' when they call their names. Teaching this trick is almost the same as conditioning ferrets to respond to a squeaky toy or another noise with a treat in mind. However, many people proclaim that each of their ferrets knows her name separately from the others and that some even recognize the names of their cagemates.

You have a few ways to teach your fuzzy her name and have her respond to it. Repetition and reward play the biggest roles. Here's one method that works well:

1. **During playtime, grab a treat and then call your ferret's name.**

   If she doesn't even notice that a noise came out of your mouth, make visual contact with her and call her name again.

2. **Crouch down and let her know that you have something good to show her, all while calling her name.**

3. **If she appears interested and comes toward you, reward the action with a small taste of the treat.**

4. **Move farther away and call her name again, repeating the process several times; soon, she should figure out that her name really means a treat.**

TIP

Treats are great motivators and help while you train your ferret. However, an unfit fuzzy won't come running when you call her name because she'll be a slug from all the yummy treats. Use verbal praise and lavish petting as alternate rewards for desired behavior. Doing so will keep your ferret healthier, and she may enjoy the surprise of the reward. You can also call your ferret's name and squeak her favorite toy at the same time. This combination usually gets a furball's attention, and she'll come running to investigate. Keep calling her name and using the toy as added motivation. After she masters the trick, use the squeaky toy less and less until you cut it out completely.

You can make the trick tougher by hiding from your ferret and then calling her. Ferrets are extremely intelligent creatures. If your ferret knows a positive reward is at the end of the voice rainbow, she'll listen for her name and come bouncing eagerly to greet you.

Jumping through hoops

Having your ferret jump through hoops is a relatively easy trick to teach. All you need is a small plastic hoop (or something similar) that measures about 1 foot in diameter. Here's one teaching method that works:

1. **Hold the hoop upright on the floor between you and your fuzzy.**

2. **Show her a treat to entice her through the hoop; when she starts walking through to get the treat, say "Jump" and then reward her when she passes through.**

At this point, she has no clue what the heck you're talking about. She thinks you're nuts and just wants the treat. In time, though, she'll make the connection between the hoop, the command, and the treat.

3. **Gradually raise the hoop and try to entice her to jump through on command, using the treat during the early stages.**

TIP

You can get a ferret to jump through the hoop in several ways. Some ferrets will just jump through as you raise the hoop and say the command. Others will go under or around the hoop. If you have a difficult ferret, sit in a corner or narrow passageway to make it necessary for her to pass through the hoop. Always hold the treat up high so she has to look up and over the hoop rim to get to it. And don't forget to say "Jump" when the ferret passes through the hoop.

After your ferret masters walking through the hoop and learning the "Jump" command, you can try to place her on a slightly raised platform, like a pet carrier, and place the hoop in front of it off the ground. Raise the treat up high and say "Jump" as she hops through. This can help get your fuzzy airborne faster.

Several creative methods can teach this trick to your ferret. Tossing your ferret through the hoop and hollering "Jump," however, isn't a good way. Be gentle and creative, and pour on the praise for a job well done.

Roll over, Beethoven

A treat (such as a freeze-dried cat treat or piece of meat) can work wonders with teaching your ferret to roll over on command. Some fuzzies don't like to be placed on their backs and rolled over, so your ferret may give you a hard time at first. Not to worry; as usual, I know several ways to teach your fuzzy that have been successful in the past! Following is one method that works well:

1. **Hold a treat in your hand and allow your fuzzy to lick it.**

The treat will distract her while you gently roll her over.

2. **While still holding the treat, move it in a circular motion over your ferret's head while you roll her over.**

Many times at this point, a ferret's head will roll and her body will naturally follow as she tries to keep up with the treat.

3. **As she's rolling over — either on her own or with your gentle help — say "Over" or "Roll over."**

Be consistent with the term you use.

In the beginning, you may have to roll over a stubborn fuzzy 100 percent of the way. Eventually, you can taper off to a three-quarter push, to a half push, to a slight nudge. Your fuzzy should need only the motivation of a treat and the command by the time she has learned what you want her to do. When she associates rolling over with treats and affection, you may find her running in front of you and rolling over to get attention, be picked up, or get a treat. It's quite amusing.

TIP

Using the circular hand motion is great for teaching deaf carpet sharks that can't hear commands. They simply roll over as you give them the hand signal.

Diving for treasures

The diving for treasures trick is pretty cool and fun to watch, but to pull it off you need a ferret that's comfortable with water and likes to snorkel around otter-style. Here's how you teach your ferret to dive for treasure:

1. **Find a treat that sinks and is easy to spot underwater.**

   A small piece of raw meat is perfect for this trick.

2. **Get a large, empty litter box or something similar and fill it with water.**

3. **Place the treat in your open palm and rest your hand on the water's surface. Allow your ferret to grab the treat.**

4. **Repeat Step 3, but this time lower your hand just enough to soak the treat. Again, let your ferret grab it.**

5. **As your fuzzy gets used to this trick, lower your hand more and more until your ferret is (voluntarily) submerging her head in the water to get the treat.**

6. **When your fuzzy snorkeler becomes a pro at bobbing for goodies, toss the treat into the tub and watch her dive in.**

TIP

If she doesn't dive on in, bring the treat up from the deep and show it to her in the palm of your hand. As she sticks her head in to get it, drop the treat to the bottom again. She should go directly to it and snarf it up.

Sit, Ubu, sit! Good ferret!

Sitting is one of the easier tricks to teach your fuzzbutt, because gravity actually does most of the work. And if he already performs the "Up" movement with ease, which most ferrets are naturals at, this should come quickly after some practice. Here's how to do it:

1. **Hold a tasty treat about six inches above your ferret's head. He will naturally stand up tall to investigate the treat, then rest on his haunches in a sitting position as he moves closer to it.**

Holding the treat any higher than six inches above his head may cause him to jump for the treat.

2. **Say "Sit" as soon as your ferret settles into the haunched sitting position. While he's still in the sitting position, allow him to taste the treat, and repeat the command "Sit" calmly but assertively.**

   The repetition of the command and treat offering will eventually teach your ferret to associate his behavior of sitting with both the command and treat.

3. **Pet and praise your hard-working ferret after you give the treat.**

   Treats are nice, but this extra affection from you provides further positive reinforcement and aids in the learning process.

4. **Repeat this process no more than 10-15 times over a 20 minute time period.**

   Over-training your ferret may lead to your ferret's boredom or loss of interest in the process.

5. **You may or may not want to phase out treats as your ferret gets this down pat.**

   What are the odds you'll have a treat in your pocket every time you want to show your friends your ferret's new trick? There's a time and a place for treats. It just may not be all the time.

Using novel objects in activities

A *novel object* is one that the ferret is unfamiliar with. Ferrets love unfamiliar objects and always seem to favor them over anything else. New smells are the most important characteristic, but ferrets also enjoy new textures, shapes, graphic designs, tastes, and locations. As you read above, a simple, empty container is a great starting point. Make it a cardboard box and it's a win–win. The cardboard box itself can be novel for a day; turning it upside down makes it novel once again. Cut a hole in the side to make it novel after your ferret loses interest. Filling either container with dried leaves increases the novelty greatly. You get the idea. The following sections present a couple more enrichment activities that feature novel objects.

TIP

The nice thing about novel objects is that you don't have to spend a lot of money on them or get fancy with them. Ferrets don't care. Be creative with simple, safe household objects. The aforementioned dig boxes work well. A bin filled with crumpled newspaper (the hearing/touching senses) or an old boot (smelling) is a novel object that costs next to nothing.

Give your ferret something new and exciting to look at by creating a black and white checkerboard pattern for her cage or play area. You can use Plexiglas or wood for the wall. You can paint the checkerboard with non-toxic paint, or you can use tile or contact paper. It doesn't have to be fancy. Fasten or hang the board securely on the wall, low enough for the ferret to enjoy. You can even hang some toys from it. The idea is to give your ferret something sharply contrasting to look at (black and white works well).

Finding Your Own Enrichment at Ferret Clubs

Joining a ferret club is a great way to meet other ferret owners who share your love for ferrets. By staying in touch with ferret people, you can stay up to date with health issues and current events. You may even develop friendships that will last a lifetime! What could be better enrichment for you than that?

Ferret clubs exist all over the world, so you should be able to find one relatively close to home. Many clubs are associated with ferret shelters; others operate independently of shelters simply out of a love for ferrets. Many ferret clubs sponsor holiday parties with contests and games. Some even host ferret shows or fundraisers for ferret-related causes (see the following section for more on ferret shows).

Every dedicated ferret owner should consider joining a ferret club. For more information on joining a club in your area, check out `https://weaselwords.com/ferret-clubs//` which lists some clubs around the world.

Participating in Regional Shows, Club Shows, and Competitions

Life with a ferret doesn't have to end at home! A whole ferret culture is out there, waiting to be explored. Many people view ferret ownership as a livelihood like no other. Some owners live and breathe ferrets, scheduling their activities around playtime and feedings. But when, you may wonder, do these owners get out to play? I'm glad you asked!

People love to show off their fuzzies, whether the pets are bare-furred or dressed up in silly costumes. Ferret shows and fun matches are held all over, and some are downright serious business. You can find out about ferret shows by doing Internet searches or checking with the American Ferret Association, which keeps an up-to-date listing of the major shows in the United States. You can receive contact information for all shows and get complete show packets with details on entering your ferret in classes and fun matches. The following sections break down your show options and cover fun matches.

So, you want to show your fuzzy?

REMEMBER

The bottom line is this: Attending ferret shows, even as a spectator, is a great way to meet other fuzzy devotees and compare notes. You can swap stupid and silly stories, most of which are related to the bodily functions of ferrets. You can also learn about new medical treatments, get tips on overcoming behavioral problems, and find out the best ways to ferret-proof. Also, many vendors set up booths and sell ferret-related items at shows, ranging from food and ferret costumes to jewelry and other novelty items.

Of course, serious competition also exists. Rules, regulations, and standards vary from organization to organization. If you decide to show your ferret, know that she may be competing against generations of champions bred for show by private breeders.

Depending on the type of show and which organization is sponsoring it — such as The American Ferret Association (www.ferret.org) — you may have many entry classes to choose from (which I explain in the next section). And, depending on the show, points may be awarded to winners, just like with dog shows. To reach a certain level or tier in the show circuit, your ferret must obtain a certain number of points.

Naturally, looks aren't all that matter. Personality is a plus. Although points are awarded for clean ears, clean teeth, and a nice manicure, the most gorgeous, well-groomed ferret won't take home a ribbon if she bites the judge on the nose!

Preparing to bring home the blue ribbon

If you're set on showing your ferret, you need to consider several things. First up, what class will you enter?

>> **Specialty classes** are for ferrets to be judged on color standards (see Chapter 2 for a list of ferret colors). Some shows have extra specialty classes for shelter ferrets, geriatric ferrets, and handicapped ferrets.

>> **Championship classes** can be broken out by age, gender, and whether a ferret has been altered. Judges consider mainly body proportion, coat quality, and temperament. Champions may accrue points, making their babies more valuable in the future.

The most important part of showing your ferret is making sure she's up on her maintenance and manners, which includes the following (see Chapter 9 for grooming tips):

>> **Temperament:** Your ferret should be well-socialized and easily handled. A biting ferret or a ferret that's overly nervous around strangers should be left at home, because a bite will almost always mean disqualification (see Chapter 19).

>> **Nails:** You should trim your ferret's nails on a regular basis to keep the quick from growing too long with the nail. Preferably, you should clip your fuzzy's nails a couple days before the show so that they can smooth out, but don't clip them all the way down to the quick. Judges hate that. If you must clip them on the day of the show, make sure to use a nail file to round off the nails.

>> **Ears:** You can clean her ears the night before or the day of the show, but be sure not to discolor the fur in and around the ears. There should be no noticeable earwax.

>> **Teeth:** Dirty teeth will cost you points or a ribbon. Having gingivitis or red, inflamed gums also is a definite no-win situation! You should brush your ferret's teeth on a daily basis and take her to the vet for regular cleanings. A good brushing on the day of the show is warranted, but avoid scaling or scraping; you don't want to present a ferret with bleeding gums.

And have a toothbrush (or other tooth cleaning apparatus) on hand to get food out of her teeth at the last minute!

>> **Coat:** Unless the show is during shedding season or your ferret has adrenal gland disease, her coat should be soft and luxurious. Over-bathing may leave her skin dry and flaky. A poor diet also will leave her coat in bad condition. You can bathe your ferret the night before or the day of the show, using a ferret shampoo or baby shampoo, as long as you haven't bathed her too recently. A teeny, weeny dab of Vaseline between the toes is great for dry skin, as well.

After you have a class and your ferret is ready to present, you need to get ready for the show. You need to remember to bring many things along on the trip. The following list runs through your supplies:

>> Your show packet and confirmation

>> Proof of up-to-date vaccinations — canine distemper and rabies vaccinations, specifically

Many shows also require proof that your ferret has tested negative for ADV (Aleutian's Disease). (For more on vaccinations and diseases, check out the chapters in Part 4)

>> A large cage, carrier, and/or playpen for her to be able to move about

>> Extra food, water bowl, bottles of water, salmon oil

>> Camera

>> Small litter box and litter, scooper, paper towels, pee pads

>> Bedding and hammock

>> Plastic bags, wet wipes, two to three bath towels, sanitary wipes

>> Leash and harness

>> A grooming kit (including nail clippers, nail file, Q-tips, cotton balls, ear wash, toothbrush, hair brush, tissues, Vaseline, and coat-conditioner spray)

>> Extra money for shopping (the vendors are awesome!)

>> An extra suitcase to carry home all the goodies you purchase

>> Your ferret!

Fun matches

Fun matches are a great way to have fun with ferrets and their nutty humans. *Fun matches* are light-hearted competitions held during shows and can often be entered the day of a show. A little non-beauty related competition is good for the soul. Fun match contests have nothing to do with how beautiful and well-behaved your ferret is. They have everything to do with creativity, personality, and skill. Sometimes, it's just fuzzy luck that wins out.

Fun match contests often include the following:

>> **The yawning contest:** How many times can your ferret yawn in a set amount of time? The yawningest ferret wins.

The first ferret competition I ever entered was a yawning contest, and my Cookie took the prize. She yawned 7 times in 60 seconds. I was so proud! Back then, you could scruff your ferret, which helped the yawns come on.

Most contests now rely on natural yawns. I could win that contest, but none of my current ferrets could.

>> **Tube racing:** The first ferret out the other side of her tube wins.

Sometimes, you can use squeaky toys or stick your face through the exit hole to encourage your ferret through. I think my Nikki once curled up and went to sleep in a tube during a contest. We had to lift the tube and slide her out. Can't win 'em all!

>> **The great paper bag escape:** Each ferret is placed into a large paper bag. The top of the bag is neatly folded down. The first ferret to escape wins the contest.

>> **Silly pet tricks:** People come up with all sorts of silly ferret tricks, from rolling over to jumping through hoops. Ferrets perform their tricks in front of an audience and the audience favorite (judged by clapping) wins.

>> **The costume contest:** Ferrets are dressed up in unique and often adorable costumes, from chefs and doctors to geisha girls and ballerinas. Also judged by the audience's clapping.

Facebook and Other Internet Sources

The Internet is home to a wealth of ferret information. Some of the information is outstanding. Some is okay. Some isn't so great. Some is downright outlandish! Weeding through the good, the bad, and the ugly can be difficult, and I'm no expert when it comes to surfing the Web. It can be a scary place, so be careful and choosy about what you want to believe.

Well-recognized websites, Facebook groups, and Facebook pages are great places to start when it comes to gathering online information about ferrets. Patiently observe what goes on there so you can quickly learn who's been around the block and who the respected authorities are. The following are some great places to start:

>> **Facebook:** Almost everyone lives, breathes, and creeps on Facebook nowadays! If it's not a personal page, it's a business page, and even I have both! Here are some of my favorite ferret-related Facebook groups and pages that I believe all ferret owners, new and old alike, might benefit from. Listed in no particular order are:

- The Modern Ferret (https://www.facebook.com/themodernferret)

- Holistic Ferret Forum (https://www.facebook.com/groups/158560084258398/)

- American Ferret Association (`https://www.facebook.com/groups/americanferretassociation/`)

- Ferret-World (`https://www.facebook.com/FerretWorld/`)

- Ferret Community by Ferret-World.com (`https://www.facebook.com/groups/FerretCommunity/`)

- Ferret Care & Education (`https://www.facebook.com/groups/129363494438510/`)

- Ferret Lovers Community (`https://www.facebook.com/groups/ferretlove`)

- Greater Chicago Ferret Association (`https://www.facebook.com/groups/gcfaemail`) —Because they're my home base!

» **Websites:** There are many wonderful websites that exist out there for our ferret fanciers. Some of these have both Facebook presences and also websites. Here are a few in no particular order:

- Holistic Ferret Forum (`https://holisticferretforum.com/`)

- American Ferret Association (`https://www.ferret.org/`)

- Ferret-World (`https://www.ferret-world.com/`)

- Greater Chicago Ferret Association (`http://www.gcfa.com/`) —Because I love them!

Chapter **11**

Have Ferret, May Travel

S ome people think a vacation gives them time away from the kids and pets. Others wouldn't dare leave their loved ones behind — human or ferret. For me, lugging my many fuzzbutts to my dream destination just doesn't seem feasible or relaxing. It's difficult enough taking a spouse along for the trip! (Of course, you can always decide to leave your spouse behind and take off with your fuzzies.)

This chapter deals specifically with the sensitive subject of travel decisions. Do you travel with your ferret or leave him behind in someone else's care? You should take certain things into consideration when making this decision; much of it depends on where you're going and for how long. The decision you make is personal, of course; but whatever you choose, this chapter has you covered.

Fuzzy Is Going on Vacation!

If you decide that your fuzzy deserves a vacation too, or if you just can't bear to leave him behind, you need to do some pre-trip investigating and preparing. Depending on how you want to travel and where you're traveling to, taking your ferret may be a somewhat simple task, or it may be a major ordeal. No matter what, the health and safety of your ferret should be your utmost concern.

Traveling, even comfortably, is very stressful on your fuzzy. If your ferret accompanies you in your travels, the trip should be as relaxing as possible for both of you. This means giving your fuzzy ample playtime and attention as usual — if not more. It also means providing a comfortable cage to live in while away from home. Don't keep him in a tiny carrier. After all, if the trip won't be a vacation for your ferret, too, you should leave him behind where he can at least have familiar surroundings (see the later section "Leaving Your Furball in Good Hands"). Also, provide plenty of favorite toys to keep him amused and preoccupied when he isn't sleeping. As an extra bonus for keeping him busy, he won't be dooking, "Are we there yet? Are we there yet?"

Checking ahead

Before you leave on your trip, you need to make sure that your fuzzy is welcome at your destination — especially if you'll be staying in a hotel. Sneaking a ferret into a ferret-free hotel may mean an extra charge for you or an expulsion, leaving you nowhere to go. Be smart. Likewise, don't show up on your Aunt Mary's doorstep with ferret in hand without getting permission first. A call from your car a mile from her house isn't what I have in mind, either. Being considerate of other people helps ensure that your ferret will be treated well on his vacation.

If you'll be staying at a hotel that allows ferrets (and other pets, for that matter), you may be required to pay a little extra for your room or put down a refundable deposit to cover possible damage. Hey, there's a reason why it's becoming more and more difficult to find pet-friendly hotels! Most hotels are afraid of the mess that some pets leave behind. Keep your hotel pet-friendly by cleaning up after your ferret before you leave. (See the following section for tips on what you need to bring to ensure a clean and healthy trip.)

Many people forget (or don't know) that their beloved fuzzies aren't welcome in all cities and states. If your destination is a ferret-free zone (see Chapter 3 for info on these places), leave your fuzzy behind. If you'll be passing through a ferret-free zone on the way to your destination, consider what may happen if you get pulled over for a traffic violation, get in a car accident, or if your ferret suddenly requires medical treatment. Although the odds of being discovered on a simple journey through a ferret-free zone are remote, check the ferret laws of the towns you'll be passing through just to be sure. The penalty can vary from a simple warning to the confiscation of your beloved pet. It's up to you to chance it or drive a different route. No matter the situation, though, keep a health certificate and proof of rabies vaccination on hand.

Packing the necessities

Traveling with your ferret will be relatively easy, as long as you pack the necessary items to make his journey (and yours) comfortable. Whether you'll be going across the state line or heading to the other side of the country, you need the following basic items:

REMEMBER

>> Your ferret's first-aid kit (see Chapter 12 for a list of what should go in this kit)

Be sure to include an appropriate supply of medication that your ferret may need.

>> Proof of current rabies vaccination and a current health certificate issued by your veterinarian

>> A lasting supply of ferret food and a water bottle (see Chapter 8 for more on feeding your fuzzy)

>> A spacious pet carrier or travel cage to keep your ferret safe

TIP

The bigger the travel cage, the better — especially if you're going on a long trip. If you must travel with a small carrier, bring along a decent-sized cage for the duration of the vacation. Don't keep your ferret cooped up.

>> An appropriate harness and leash

>> A litter box and litter or puppy pads

>> Fluffy, snoozy bedding (don't forget to pack a change of bedding, too)

>> Cleaning supplies to clean up after your ferret; wet wipes, plastic bags, and so on (see Chapter 9)

>> Toys, toys, toys

>> An inescapable playpen

WARNING

Don't give your ferret any sedatives or tranquilizers of any sort while traveling. If you think your ferret must have a sedative, leave him at home or take one yourself and continue on with your travel plans!

On the Road or Flying High

We've come a long way since the horse and buggy! Getting to where you need to be has become much easier, whether you travel by plane, train, or automobile. Heck, you can even travel by ship, too! In this section, I talk about the most frequently used means of transportation — the scenic road trip and the zippy plane ride — so that you can make sure your ferret is comfortable and safe during his travels.

Road trip!

If you have the time (or if the thought of taking to the friendly skies makes you poof), you may decide to partake in a scenic road trip. Or perhaps the trip isn't long enough to warrant hopping on a plane. Although a road trip can be fun, you need to prepare for many things when driving with your ferret.

Road trip do's

When you decide to travel with your ferret (or children for that matter), you make a commitment to tend to his physical and emotional needs throughout the trip. This can be quite demanding. The following list presents some things you must do while on the road with your ferret:

>> Do keep your ferret in his carrier or cage to prevent accidents when you're driving. You don't want him running across your dashboard or hiding under your pedals!

>> Do make frequent rest stops and take the time to harness/leash your ferret for brisk walks. Also, resist the urge to let strangers handle your already stressed-out and excited fuzzy during stops. Stress is one of the conditions that can lead to unpredictable ferret behavior.

>> Do keep a copy of your ferret's rabies vaccination certificate and medical records in an easily accessible location.

>> Do offer your ferret water frequently during trips. A hanging water bottle or bowl in the carrier will continually drip or spill from the jostling.

>> Do keep your car cool and well-ventilated.

>> Do buckle in the carrier with the seat belt, if you can, for extra restraint.

>> Do remember to medicate your ferret, if necessary, at scheduled times.

TIP

If you're crazy enough to take a long, hot, summer road trip in a vehicle without air conditioning, bring along a cooler with several two-liter plastic bottles of frozen water. Keep one of the frozen bottles wrapped in a towel and in your pet's travel carrier to keep him cool.

"Hello and welcome!" says Heather, a beautiful champagne ferret owned by Mark and Debbie Fitzgerald.

Cats and ferrets together can make great friends. (See Chapter 7 for more on making introductions.) Xavier is a black roan mitt owned by Jared Deming.

SNF's Chili, owned by Suzanne Bergren, is waiting patiently for the third edition of Ferrets For Dummies to arrive.

Play enrichment such as this ball pit keeps a ferret's senses sharp and alive. (See Chapter 10 on enrichment.) Max is owned by Betsy Todd.

All ferrets need comfortable snooze spots; the more available to them, the better. (Read more in Chapter 5 about setting up house.) Molly is owned by Betsy Todd.

Many ferrets love to romp in the snow, but you should only allow such play under close supervision. Kali and Zeus are owned by Mark and Deb Fitzgerald.

Five-year-old ferret Sam is suffering from veterinarian-confirmed adrenal gland disease. The early stages of this disease more often than not cause fur loss or rat tail. (Chapter 16 tells you more about this awful disease.). Sam is well-loved by owners Mark and Deb Fitzgerald.

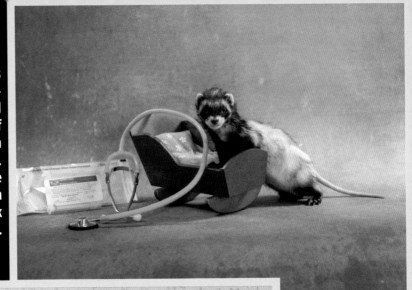

Kit-to-kit interaction is critical to the overall socialization and boundary development of the ferret. A ferret that grows up with boundaries is more like to be well-mannered in ferret-mannered way.

Every jill can be a princess with Mee Lai Kohana, owned by Mark and Deb Fitzgerald.

See Chapter 5 for the do's and don'ts of picking out safe ferret toys. Parker is owned by Mark and Deb Fitzgerald.

Don't let bad breath go on for long. It can be a sign of a very serious dental issue or even underlying disease. (See Chapter 9 for tips on dental care and hygiene.)

Love brings us together until...

Bad breath causes separation...

Posing a ferret is harder than it looks, but SH's Autumn Firelight, owned by Sally Heber, makes being a beautiful sable come naturally. And it does!

Ferrets can and will get their mitts on anything. This chocolate sable would surely drag this back to his hidey hole if allowed, showing you that size doesn't matter.

Know what goes into your ferret's mouth when he's out exploring, and never stop ferret-proofing. (See Chapter 6 for tips on ferret-proofing.)

Always supervise interactions between ferrets and other pets. (See Chapter 7 about making introductions.)

What is better than one ferret? A treasure chest full of ferrets! (See Chapter 4 about deciding on the right number of ferrets for your home.)

t's not easy being a sexy sable! Thunder is owned by Pat Stauffer.

Like most roans, this little girl's coat will lighten and possibly turn all white as she ages. (See Chapter 2 for more on colors and patterns.)

The right playpen set-up can offer a safe space for your ferret to explore his boundaries beyond his cage.

Ferrets are natural gardeners and will dig up all of your potted plants if you do not properly ferret-proof. Black roan mitt Xavier is owned by Jared Deming. (See Chapter 6 about ferret proofing.)

"Git along, Lil' Weasel. Git along."

"No s'mores for you!" Remember not to share sugary treats with your ferret. (See Chapter 8 for a list of good and bad ferret treats.) Ferrets owned by Mark an Debbie Fitzgerald.

Who's ready for goodies? Remember to stock up only on safe treats for your ferrets. (See Chapter 8 on treats.)

Ferrets are the adrenali junkies of the animal world. They need more supervision than your average pet. Xavier is owned by Jared Deming

WARNING

Ferrets are master escape artists. Take into consideration that your ferret may be able to get out of his cage or carrier in your vehicle. Also, a child or spouse may let him out without anyone knowing — a particularly scary situation if you drive with the windows down. And before slamming that car door shut, be sure your ferret is safe in his carrier where he belongs. In a car door versus ferret situation, the car door always wins.

Road trip don'ts

Driving with your ferret can be a challenge, and sometimes pets are the last thing on your mind. It's important to recognize the dangers associated with traveling with your ferret and be diligent in tending to his needs. You can prevent most accidents by using common sense or learning from others.

The following list presents some no no's for road trips with your fuzzy:

» Don't leave your ferret in the vehicle unattended when the temperature is extreme, and even when it's just sunny outside, the vehicle can quickly rise to an unsafe temperature inside.

» Don't leave him in the vehicle overnight while you snooze comfortably in a motel.

» Don't leave your ferret in his carrier with his harness or collar on. In fact, leave the collar at home or throw it away. (See Chapter 5 for the lowdown on collars.)

» Don't pack your ferret in the trunk. Besides being cruel, this treatment can kill him if the temperature is unstable or carbon monoxide leaks in.

» Don't fasten your caged ferret with the rest of your luggage on top of your vehicle. (You'd think common sense would prevail here . . .)

» Don't travel with a very sick, old, or pregnant ferret. The stress of traveling may jeopardize the already stressed fuzzy's health.

Taking to the friendly skies

Some extra requirements and considerations go along with traveling by air with your fuzzy. In addition to packing the necessary goods (see the earlier section "Packing the necessities"), you need to work on a couple pre-flight tasks:

» **Check with the airline to find out about any specific rules and regulations regarding traveling with pets.** Since 9/11, traveling with animals has become more restricted. Every airline is different. Most airlines no longer allow in-cabin pets, for instance. Although each airline has its own set of rules about flying with pets, you can be sure of the following typical requirements (be sure to follow all rules, including any that I may not cover here):

- You must make a prior reservation for your pet. Be sure to confirm the arrangement a couple days before takeoff. (**Note:** If you happen to find that rare airline that does allow in-cabin pet flying, you can almost bet it will issue an additional charge for in-cabin travel.)

- Your vet must issue a health certificate no more than ten days before takeoff. The certificate indicates that your ferret is current on vaccinations and is healthy and fit for travel. (Keep proof of his current rabies vaccination on hand, too.)

- You must provide an airline-approved carrier. If traveling in-cabin, your fuzzy's carrier must be small enough to fit beneath a seat. Also, your pet must remain in the carrier while on board. (Always call the airline to clarify what its definition of an "airline-approved" carrier is.)

REMEMBER

For health reasons, USDA regulations stipulate that airlines can't transport most animals via cargo during extreme hot or cold conditions. If you must transport your ferret through cargo, be sure to take the expected temperature into consideration.

» **Prepare your fuzzy's carrier for the airline regulations.** Most airlines have guidelines to make sure that your pet's carrier is properly labeled for identification. At minimum, you should do the following:

- Attach a label to the carrier that clearly lists your name, address, and phone number, along with the same information for an alternate contact from home.

- Attach another carrier label that states "LIVE ANIMALS," with an up arrow for any directionally challenged cargo handlers. Many airlines will supply these stickers if you ask for them.

- Include information about your final destination — such as city/state, hotel name, and phone number — in case you need to be contacted about your lost pet.

You also should make some food and water (bottle fastened above the food bowl) available to your ferret during flight, and his carrier should contain comfortable bedding — fuzzy snoozy stuff.

REMEMBER

Some airlines require that multiple pets travel in separate carriers. Three ferrets may require three carriers, which means more money for traveling.

Always book nonstop flights whenever possible when traveling with a fuzzy — especially if your ferret won't be traveling in-cabin with you. A change of planes is an added stress, and you run the risk of losing your furball in the shuffle between flights. Nonstop flights also are shorter, thus minimizing the length of an already wearisome situation. If your fuzzy must change planes, find out what precautions the airline will take to ensure a safe and timely transfer.

Going international

Unless you plan to travel abroad for a very long period of time, I suggest you leave fuzzy at home. I've heard of many international trips that went smoothly, but also of several that were nightmares for everyone involved. Traveling abroad with a ferret — whether you're moving permanently or vacationing — *can* go quite smoothly, though, if you follow the guidelines of the airline (see the preceding section) and destination country. With regard to the latter, be sure to research the following:

>> Does the destination country have a quarantine requirement?

>> Does your fuzzy's health certificate need to be translated into the appropriate language?

>> Does the destination country require that you obtain an import license?

>> Do you need to mail or fax the proper paperwork prior to you leaving the country? (Always keep copies on you.)

>> What's required to get through customs with your pet? (Usually, the proper documents get you right through.)

Most international flights have layovers before passengers continue on to their planned destinations. Almost all airlines allow passengers to visit their pets during layovers — if they've made prior arrangements. During this time, check on how your fuzzy is doing, and give him water, food, or any necessary medication.

Leaving Your Furball in Good Hands

You've decided to leave your fuzzy at home, in the care of capable handlers? Aaaaah, now this is a vacation! As much as I love fuzzies, I just have to get away from time to time, with no one to take care of but myself. Don't get me wrong, I always buckle with anxiety over finding the right person to watch my babies or the right place to take them to. And, of course, while I'm supposed to be relaxing on vacation, I'm wondering how all my kids are managing without me. Usually, when

I get home, I must face the reality that some other people can play Fuzzy Mom just as well as I do. It's quite an ego smasher.

The following sections outline your two best options for ferret care in your stead: sitters and boarding centers. Here you find out how to make sure that you leave your fuzzy in good hands so you can relax (or get your business done, as the case may be).

No matter who takes care of your ferret while you're gone, make sure that you educate him or her on ferret basics — especially those considerations unique to your fuzzy. For example, you should provide the following information:

>> The phone number where you can be reached and the name of the people you'll be staying with

>> An emergency phone number (or two) of someone close to home, such as a friend or relative

>> Your veterinarian's phone number and address, as well as the emergency clinic's phone number and address

>> A copy of your fuzzy's medical records in case he needs to go somewhere for an emergency

>> A copy of your ferret's rabies vaccination certificate or tag

>> An adequate supply of necessary medication, as well as exact instructions on how to medicate your ferret

Be sure to demonstrate the procedure (especially dosing) before you leave.

>> A written description of your ferret and his personality (attach photos next to each description if you have multiple ferrets to be extra helpful), including any necessary do's and don'ts

>> An adequate supply of food, along with precise written and demonstrated instructions on feeding (especially if you use a varied diet or you have a ferret that requires assisted feedings)

>> Detailed instructions on how to clean up after your ferret, supervise safe playtime, and watch for signs of illness or injury

>> A copy of *Ferrets For Dummies,* 3rd Edition!

When you leave your ferret in the hands of others, risk is involved. Nothing is foolproof. All you can really do is prepare your ferret's temporary caretaker as best you can. The more you educate, the better off everyone will be. More often than not, you'll arrive home to a happy, healthy ferret that's just darn glad to see you.

Let the interviews begin: Finding the perfect pet sitter

Many people scoff at the idea of paying strangers to come to their homes to visit with and care for their ferrets while they're away. But more and more people are choosing this option as reliable pet sitters gain experience and good reputations. Often, pet sitters come highly recommended by previous clients, veterinarians, friends, or neighbors. And pet sitters aren't just for vacationers anymore. Many people who work long hours choose pet sitters to assist in the routine care of their fuzzies.

If at all possible, pick a pet sitter who comes highly recommended by someone you trust. Request and carefully check the sitter's references. This person will have a key to your house and access to your belongings, not to mention the responsibility of the complete care of your fuzzy. Trustworthiness, reliability, and honesty are all musts.

Here are a few of the many questions you may consider asking a potential pet sitter:

>> How long have you been pet sitting?

>> Do you belong to an association?

>> Do you charge per day? Per ferret? Per visit?

>> Have you ever worked with ferrets? How long? How many clients?

>> What do you know about ferrets? Do you like them?

>> Who's your current veterinarian?

>> What's your procedure in case of an emergency?

>> Do you have a backup sitter in case of an emergency?

>> How often do you come to the house?

>> What do you do if the client runs out of food/supplies?

>> Do you medicate ferrets? Are you knowledgeable/experienced in medicating?

TIP

Depending on how much you're willing to spend, your pet sitter can make a daily visit or stop by several times throughout the day. The sitter may clean daily, every other day, or however often you request. The arrangements usually are based on a fee schedule. Discuss your options with the pet sitter before you leave, and get everything in writing.

You may choose a trusted neighbor or friend to be your pet sitter. With all the animals at my home/shelter, it takes several people to come in on a daily basis to help with upkeep when I go away. I feel like I'm leaving a 100-page manual behind, but I always feel better if I know the people who will be coming into my home. Keep in mind: A paid pet sitter usually does a good job because his or her reputation relies on it; a friend usually does a good job because a friendship depends on it. On the other hand, having friends watch your pets can be tricky and awkward if you're not happy with the job they did. Each situation is different. Go with the option that makes you feel most comfortable and works best for your ferret.

REMEMBER

Many pet sitters are more familiar with dogs, cats, and birds. It's up to you in some cases to educate the pet sitter on how to properly care for fuzzies. A good pet sitter should be willing to stop over once or twice before you leave to get acquainted with your fuzzbutt and his routine.

Away to camp: Boarding your ferret

If you can't find a reliable person to care for your fuzzy in your own home, you should board him while you're away. You have several boarding options:

>> Some veterinarians board pets for a fee, but busy vets = little ferret play time.

>> Some ferret shelters will watch your ferret temporarily for a fee if you promise to pick him up within a designated period of time.

>> A friend may agree to board a fuzzy houseguest temporarily.

>> Some professional boarding facilities house animals other than dogs and cats.

If you choose an unfamiliar person or place to watch your fuzzy, get references and check them out. Visit the home, shelter, clinic, or boarding facility to evaluate its overall condition. Don't leave your ferret there unless you're completely comfortable and have checked the cages for safety and security.

Make sure you provide emergency numbers, explicit instructions, and so on before you leave. Also, you may face a few more hurdles if you board your ferret while you're gone:

>> You may have to transport the ferret's condo to the home or facility.

>> You'll have to provide your ferret's food because his diet is likely to be unique.

>> You may be required to provide proof of current vaccinations or a health certificate.

TIP

If the person or boarding facility doesn't require proof of current vaccinations or a health certificate, I'd avoid that person or facility altogether. If the person or place doesn't ask you for proof of your pet's health, it probably doesn't ask other boarders for proof, either.

>> You may have to take the time to educate the caretaker on ferret-proofing and care so that he or she can go the extra mile while you're away. Many facilities aren't properly prepared to allow your ferret his daily freedom and exercise. Same goes for the homes of friends — unless you take the time to educate them.

WARNING

If you send your ferret to a boarding facility, shelter, or animal clinic, you run the risk of your fuzzy catching a disease or an illness from another animal. A friend's home isn't always safe, either — especially if the home contains other ferrets or animals. Make sure that your ferret is up to date on his shots (see Chapter 12).

Ferrets as Emotional Support Animals (ESAs)

It's no doubt that people adore their pets, ferret owners included. Besides offering enjoyment and enrichment in our lives, ferrets for *some* people can offer so much more as emotional support animals (ESAs). But only a small percentage of owners actually need ESAs, which function to assist an individual with a disability. Many individuals frequently confuse ESAs with service animals, and the ESA topic is a very heated one in the animal community. (See Figure 11-1.) Why, you ask? Because quite a few unscrupulous pet owners do damage to the reputation of ESAs by claiming their pets as ESAs simply to gain the few privileges or perks that come with having an ESA. It's unfair to those who truly need emotional assistance from their pet. And many online sources are popping up all over the place that will take your money in order to certify your pet as an ESA, and with a signed doctor's note, as well! This is a hoax in the making!

The Americans with Disabilities Act (ADA) specifically states, "A *service* animal means any *dog* that is individually trained to do work or perform tasks for the benefit of an individual with a disability, including a physical, sensory, psychiatric, intellectual, or other mental disability." Although the ADA limits service animals to dogs, it does state that entities "must make reasonable modifications in policies to allow individuals with disabilities to use miniature horses if they have been individually trained to do work or perform tasks for individuals with disabilities."

Comparison	Service	Therapy	Emotional Support
ADA covered: Rights to bring animal into public establishments	✓	✗	✗
Needs to tolerate a wide variety of experience	✓	✓	✗
May live with their disabled owners, even if "No Pets" policy in place	✓	✗	✓
May fly inside the airplane with their disabled owner	✓	✗	✓
Primary function is to provide emotional support, through companionship	✗	✗	✓
Specially trained to assist just one person	✓	✗	✗
Provide emotional support and comfort to many people	✗	✓	✗

FIGURE 11-1: Types of service animals.

So what about our beloved ferrets? They *can* be used as ESAs or "comfort animals," but because they aren't limited to working as ESAs and are in the pet category they are not covered by federal laws protecting the use of service animals. ESAs may be used as "therapy animals" as part of a medical treatment plan, but they do not have special training, like service animals do. Comfort animals or ESAs are often used for things such as companionship and therapeutic contact or to help in the relief of depression, loneliness, certain phobias, and anxiety. Overall, ESAs may improve their handlers' emotional, physical, social, or cognitive functioning.

Here are some other things you should know about ferrets or pets as ESAs:

>> **Public facilities:** ESAs aren't allowed in public facilities unless the facility is pet-friendly, such as a pet store. Service animals, however, are a different story. A no-pet policy cannot legally keep a service animal out. Additionally, bans against dog breeds such as pit bulls are prohibited around service animals.

>> **Employment:** We're all pretty clear that laws prohibit discrimination against people with disabilities, and that employers must provide "reasonable" accommodation. What you might not know is that allowing an ESA or service animal at work may, for many employers, be considered an accommodation. In this case, if the disability is not obvious, your employer may legally request

further documentation to establish the existence of the disability and to define the capacity in which the animal would help the employee do his or her job. ESAs and service animals may ultimately be excluded from the workplace for posing a direct threat or hardship to others in the workplace. However, it doesn't hurt to suggest a trial run with your ESA if your need to have one in the workplace is legitimate, and it's not just a case of your desire to be with your pet every waking hour.

>> **Housing:** The Fair Housing Act (FHA) also requires landlords or homeowners associations to provide reasonable accommodation to people with disabilities, and under the FHA, ESAs may qualify as reasonable accommodation. In this case, the animal is not considered a pet, and the accommodation may include waiving the pet deposit or waiving the no-pet rule. And, although landlords and homeowners associations may not ask about the existence, nature, or extent of the disability, your request for accommodation may lead to further demands for documentation specifying that

- You, the tenant, or a member of your family is a person with a disability

- The person with the disability needs the ESA for assistance

- The ESA actually assists the person with a disability

It's important to note the difference here between service animals and ESAs when talking about housing. Requesting documentation or certification would not be permitted where the ADA applies, such as in student housing, for example, when an animal that qualifies as a service animal is concerned. However, documentation may be requested for an ESA.

>> **Education:** This gets a little tricky. As you may have guessed by now, service animals are permitted. However, while ESAs rarely accompany students to school, situations should be reviewed on a case-by-case basis and will ultimately be at the school's discretion. Such cases are usually looked at by the student's 504 or IEP (Individual Education Plan) team.

>> **Ground transportation:** The laws are pretty clear when it comes to both public and private ground transportation in regards to service animals. No discrimination. Period. ESAs, however, do not share the same rights as service animals, and do not have to be allowed on ground transportation, no matter whether a no-pet sign exists.

>> **Air travel:** Even handlers with service animals may legally be subject to scrutiny by an airline seeking "evidence" that the accompanying animal is indeed a service animal. Although airline employees are limited in what they may legally ask about a service animal and its handler, you can bet an ESA and his person will be scrutinized even more thoroughly. Various types of personal documentation may be required to assist the airline in making its decision about whether to allow the ESA onboard. If you wish to travel by air with an ESA, absolutely call the airline ahead of time.

Unlike service animals, emotional support animals can be just about any animal, but there is certainly a huge difference between a service animal and an emotional support animal in terms of tasks and how they're viewed in the eyes of the law. Knowing the difference is key. Many pet owners are passionate about their pets, and ferret owners are no exception. It's certainly not unusual to desire to spend as much time with your ferret or other pet as you possibly can. Unfortunately it's also common for a lot of owners of *all* types of pets to attempt to pass off their pet as an ESA even when they don't need the use of an emotional support animal. This type of well-known deception has only led to more complicated scrutiny by the public and by businesses for those honestly and legitimately in need of an ESA.

4

Tackling Your Ferret's Health Issues and Treatments

Chapter **12**

Setting Up Your Ferret's Health Plan: Vets and First-Aid Kits

Health issues are inevitable for most creatures, and ferrets are no different. That's why you won't find many unemployed veterinarians! You can go through loads of trouble to safeguard your ferret, but something's bound to happen anyway. Some mishaps are preventable; others are not. Often, what has you running for the first-aid kit is an illness or an age-related problem. Here's the bottom line: If the situation is something you can learn from, soak up the lesson so you can prevent the episode from happening again.

All ferret owners need to arm themselves with certain information and tools for those "just-in-case" situations. That's what this chapter is all about. I discuss the process you should go through to select a qualified veterinarian for your fuzzy. Finding a good ferret vet at the very last, desperate moment can be difficult — if not life-threatening — so start right away. Even if you aren't facing an emergency, your ferret still needs routine checkups and vaccinations to ensure good health, so I cover these topics as well. I list the items that need to go into your very own fuzzy first-aid kit. Trust me, it's better to have an unopened bottle of Betadine solution sit for ages than to get caught in a situation where you desperately need it but don't have it. Finally, I show you how to prepare for emergency situations so you can care for your ferret in her most pressing time of need.

I get phone calls all the time from people asking me for advice about their sick ferrets. Remember: I'm not a vet, nor do I claim to be one. You shouldn't use this book in lieu of a visit to your vet. I purposely leave out dosage recommendations in this book because every ferret is different and every situation is different. You shouldn't diagnose your ferret, or give her prescription or over-the-counter meds, without a veterinarian consult. Also, providing first aid for your ferret doesn't mean you can forego a trip to the vet if the situation warrants it. Use your best judgment, and keep your ferret's health and happiness in mind at all times.

Selecting Your Ferret's Veterinarian

At some point, all responsible pet owners venture into a veterinarian's office. A vet handles your pet's routine care, answers questions about concerns you have, handles neuters/spays, and addresses any unforeseen emergencies. Your vet will become a part of your life, so knowing what to look for is important when searching for your ferret's doctor.

In your search for a vet, you'll encounter fancy, expensive veterinary facilities, modest, single-doctor practices, and many that fall in between. Don't judge a vet's abilities on looks alone. Rely on a vet's reputation, recommendations you receive, and your gut feelings.

In the following sections, I cover some questions you should ask potential vets and the importance of swinging by for a visit before entrusting your pet to a particular vet or clinic. And because your vet can and should be your ally in your ferret's care, I outline the ways you can develop a good working relationship with the doctor you choose.

Word of mouth is a wonderful way to find a good ferret vet. Talk to other ferret owners you know or who you can locate through your breeder or other acquaintances. Ask where they take their babies and what kind of care they receive. Call your local ferret shelter to see who people there recommend. With so many ferret-crazed people out there today, you're bound to find a good veterinarian! A few ferret enthusiasts have put together an extensive list of veterinarians across the world who treat ferrets. You can find the list at http://ferret.vet. (Note: to get to the search option, just click on the "view larger map" icon in the top-right corner of the page.)

Interviewing potential vets

In your search for a vet, don't be afraid to ask questions. Questions are your best tools. A good, professional veterinarian and staff will recognize your valid concerns and won't hesitate to answer your questions as completely as possible.

Begin by calling a clinic and asking whoever answers the phone if the doctor treats ferrets. Some don't and will refer you elsewhere. When you find a candidate that does treat fuzzies, do a little more investigation by asking the person on the phone if he has time to answer some questions. Better yet, leave a message for the vet to call you back. Make a list of the following questions and, of course, revise them depending on who you're talking to:

>> How long have you been practicing ferret medicine? How many ferrets do you encounter in a typical day or week?

>> Where did you learn to treat ferrets? (For a list of common veterinary tests and procedures for ferrets, see Table 12-1.)

>> Does your facility stock vaccinations for ferrets, such as one of the USDA-approved rabies vaccines?

>> Is your facility capable of properly housing ferrets that may need to be hospitalized? Can you handle overnight stays? Emergencies? After hours?

>> How do you feel about raw diet in ferrets? Or, if you prefer, what are your diet recommendations for ferrets?

>> What are your fees for routine care, such as checkups and vaccinations?

>> Do you accept CareCredit or arrange payment plans if necessary?

>> Do you perform routine surgeries (such as spaying and neutering) on ferrets? Do you have experience with the more difficult surgeries, such as splenecto-mies, adrenal surgery, or other tumor removals?

TIP

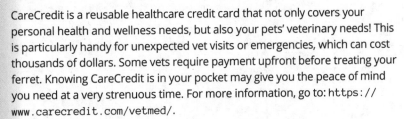

CareCredit is a reusable healthcare credit card that not only covers your personal health and wellness needs, but also your pets' veterinary needs! This is particularly handy for unexpected vet visits or emergencies, which can cost thousands of dollars. Some vets require payment upfront before treating your ferret. Knowing CareCredit is in your pocket may give you the peace of mind you need at a very strenuous time. For more information, go to: https://www.carecredit.com/vetmed/.

>> Can you handle and treat common diseases of the ferret?

>> Do you carry the Deslorelin (DES) implant for adrenal gland disease?

>> How do you stay up to date on the latest developments in ferret medicine and surgical techniques? What continuing education do you participate in?

Don't forget to be kind and courteous during the questioning, and always remember to thank the vet when you're through. The answers the vet and his staff give, and the general tone with which they give them, should give you a sense of whether this office is ferret-friendly. Do you feel comfortable with this doctor? If you don't, chances are your ferret won't either.

TABLE 12-1 **Ferret vet tests**

Test Name	Description	Time for Results
Basic exam	Palpation (feeling the body for lumps, enlarged organs [such as the spleen], or sensitivities), eye, ear, teeth, and weight check.	Instant
IDEXX diarrhea RealPCR panel	Detects bacteria, distemper, ECE, giardia, helicobacter, etc. Vets don't always do this so make sure to ask.	24–48 hours
Fecal Flotation	The first/default "poop test" vets do. Can detect parasites and fungal infections. (No bacteria.)	24–48 hours
IDEXX ferret GI profile	Tests for values similar to blood test, may be used for IBD diagnosis. Not too common.	24–48 hours
Urinalysis (pee test)	Can detect bladder stones, liver and kidney function, infections, etc.	24–48 hours
Dental probing	Evaluates dental health and identifies concerns.	1 hour
Dental X-rays	Identifies root resorption and fragments, abscesses, etc.	1 hour
Dental scaling	Requires anesthesia. Blood work is necessary first to make sure all organs are functioning correctly prior to anesthesia.	1 hour
Complete blood count panel	Can detect anemia, lymphoma, infection, among other things.	Instant; lab review may take 24–48 hours
Serum biochemistry profile	Evaluates organ function and dietary imbalances	Instant; lab review may take 24–48 hours
Blood glucose test	Evaluates blood sugar levels; helps diagnose insulinoma.	Instant
Antibody titer	Tests antibodies of a previous vaccine. There is no standard titer value for rabies.	24–48 hours
X-ray/radiograph	Won't show foam blockages or small tumors. Will show fluid build-up, heart disease, bladder stones, most blockages, larger tumors/masses, broken bones. Minor anesthesia may be needed; situation-specific.	Instant; lab review may take 24–48 hours
Ultrasound	For imaging soft tissue; can help diagnose heart disease, larger tumors, etc.	24–48 hours
Contrast X-ray	A contrast agent (barium, iodine, etc.) is swallowed and x-rayed (sometimes multiple times) to track digestion, highlight blockages, etc. Barium can be risky in certain situations.	3–4 hours
CT scan or MRI	For imaging soft tissue; more sensitive than ultrasound.	Varies — same day
Surgery	Blood word is necessary first to make sure all organs are functioning correctly and can recover.	Varies — same day

Test Name	Description	Time for Results
Adrenal Tennessee panel	Hormone levels are tested in the blood. Not always accurate and very pricey. Many people skip the test and diagnose/treat based on symptoms alone. Lupron shots treat adrenal and are given monthly. Preferred for ferrets who may be too ill to get the DES implant. The DES implant lasts 6-18 months, implanted in the shoulder. Melatonin implants last 4-8 months, implanted in the shoulder. Melatonin is less effective than DES but works well paired with DES.	24–48 hours
Biopsy	A sample of cells removed from tissue to test for cancer, IBD, etc., and help determine how to move forward. May be difficult for some internal locations. *Fine-needle aspirate* takes a small core sample to be analyzed under a microscope. A *Surgical biopsy* takes a section of normal and abnormal tissue and is sent for histology/analysis.	24–48 hours
Necropsy	Autopsy for animals; post-mortem exam to determine cause of death.	24–48 hours
Ear swab	Tests for ear mites, yeast, or bacteria.	Instant

Table courtesy Holly Ravenhill

Going for a visit

After you talk to a vet who seems qualified and meets your criteria, pay the doctor a visit. You want to see if this doctor is all he appeared to be on the phone or as described by other clients. First appearances usually are a good indication of how the vet runs his practice:

>> Are the office and treatment areas clean? Do they smell clean?

>> Were you greeted in a friendly manner by the staff?

>> Are the exam tables sanitized after each use?

>> Do technicians and vets wash their hands after handling animals?

If you already have your fuzzy, you can assume that she's probably due for a checkup. Now's a great time to see the potential vet in action with your furball:

>> Does the vet talk to your ferret in a calming way?

>> Does he handle your ferret with care and show genuine concern for both you and your pet?

It's very important that your new veterinarian listen to and acknowledge your concerns. You're the ferret's caregiver. If you've had her for some time, you know what's normal for your ferret. A vet who doesn't listen to you and learn from you may be too presumptuous to give your ferret the care that she needs — especially in emergency situations.

>> Does he explain what's being done in a concise and clear manner?

>> Does he answer your questions in an understandable fashion?

>> Does he seem rushed and preoccupied with other goings-on in the clinic, or is he focused on your pet?

Have you found a knowledgeable and caring vet who works in a clean, efficient, and friendly office? Congrats! If not, keep searching until you find a vet who meets all your requirements.

A good vet will have a network of other professionals he can rely on for support with difficult or unfamiliar cases. The willingness to reach out for help and to learn from others is a positive trait and one that should be looked for in a vet as well.

Developing a good working relationship

It's important that you maintain a comfortable and efficient working relationship with your vet built on trust and respect. Your veterinarian, like you, should have your pet's well-being at the top of his priority list. No one knows your pet like you do, and your vet will count on you to tell him when your ferret isn't quite herself. I can't tell you how many times I've brought in an animal that looked fine but that had a "look" about her that told me she wasn't quite right. In those cases, routine tests always revealed ailments. Your second sense is what can link you and your veterinarian in your quest to keep fuzzy healthy.

Here are some things you can do to develop a working relationship with your vet and make your interactions friendlier and more efficient:

>> **Keep accurate records.** Take the guesswork out of communicating with your vet. Write down how your ferret is acting when you think she's sick. Record what supportive care you've provided and how she's responded. List any medications and dosages you've administered and record any improvements or setbacks that you observe. And with all these observations, make sure you include times in hours and minutes.

>> **Know your animal.** If you can't bring your pet in to the office yourself, make sure you give the person who can your fuzzy's basic information. Vets get frustrated when people can't answer basic questions about the animals they bring in. Create a basic information card for your ferret that explains how you feed and house her, how you handle her, how she normally acts, what her issues are, and so on. Best-case scenario: Bring in your fuzzy yourself.

>> **Do what the vet tells you to do.** Give medications on time and at the correct dosages, and give them for as long as you're supposed to. Just as important, follow through with phone calls to the vet to give him progress reports.

>> **Ask questions.** Your vet's job is to not only treat your ferret, but also to answer your questions. Write down any questions you have before you get there and be ready to take notes when the vet is talking to you. Never feel foolish for asking questions!

>> **Stay educated, but don't be demanding.** You can do research on current health issues and be willing to learn what you can about your ferret's health. It's great to learn these things, but don't force what you learn on your vet, for multiple reasons:

- Your vet may already know the information.

- It shows a lack of trust and respect for your vet.

- Your vet will find it hard to work with a demanding know-it-all.

Instead, work as a team and offer up what you've learned. Seek your vet's professional opinion by asking how what you've learned can fit into your pet's diagnosis or treatment plan.

>> **Be honest.** Relationships are built on honesty and trust. Here are some specific situations when truth will keep your relationship with your vet strong:

- A vet doesn't want to hear "She was fine this morning" while looking at an animal that's obviously been in distress for days. Your vet depends on you to tell him everything that's going on. Your honesty may mean the difference between an accurate diagnosis and a misdiagnosis.

- Be upfront from the start about your financial situation. Don't make your vet guess what you can and can't afford to do for your pet. The cost of care is a sensitive area for both sides, so just be honest.

- Tell the truth about how you've followed through on treatment plans. If you didn't do what the vet told you to do, tell him so he doesn't assume that his plan doesn't work.

>> **Respect boundaries.** Never have another vet call yours to provide help without your vet's prior knowledge and permission. It not only catches your vet off guard, but also shows a lack of trust in and respect for him.

>> **Report problems you have at the vet's office.** If you should have a problem at a veterinary practice for any reason, report it to the proper staff member immediately. Voice your concerns respectfully and calmly, and be prepared to reach some sort of solution. Leaving the office angry or upset doesn't satisfy anyone or leave room for improvement. Vets want to clear up problems in their offices and prevent them from happening in the future.

>> **Leave your personal issues at home.** The vet's exam room or waiting room is no place to start arguing over whether your pet's treatment is worth X amount of dollars. Nor is it the place to announce to your spouse that you want a divorce. Come alone or agree ahead of time to table any heated topics you want to discuss.

The bottom line: Keeping the lines of communication open will help your vet give your ferret the best care he possibly can.

Putting Your Vet to Work with Vaccinations and Checkups

I'm one of those people who thinks that no matter where or when you get a new pet, you should make a visit to the vet within a day or two of her homecoming and continue with regular checkups from that point on. If you take your fuzzy in for a checkup every year (every six months for ferrets 3 years and older), your vet will be able to rule out any illnesses and vaccinate your ferret if she's due. I'm an advocate of regular vaccinations for pets. Vaccinations for ferrets keep your fuzzy safe from disease. Without them, ferrets are highly susceptible to canine distemper. They may also contract the rabies virus.

This section covers ferret checkups and vaccinations. You find out what your vet does for your kit (baby ferret) or for your grown-up fuzzy, and I let you know how to watch for warning signals that your fuzzy is having an allergic reaction to a vaccine or other medicine.

REMEMBER

I can't advise you one way or another when it comes to vaccinating your pet. The only person who can help you make vaccination decisions is your veterinarian. He should know how your fuzzy tolerated vaccinations in the past and how she'll likely tolerate them in the future. Discuss the pros and cons of vaccinating your ferret with your vet. Together, based on your fuzzy's history and future concerns, you can come up with a workable plan to keep your ferret safe.

Kits — The office visit

Baby ferrets (kits) receive some protective antibodies from their mothers, but these eventually start to wear away in stages as the kits age. Therefore, you must vaccinate your kit to counteract this gradual loss of protection. When you get your fuzzy, schedule an appointment to get her shots. Most farm-raised babies receive their first ferret-approved, modified live canine distemper shots at 4 to 6 weeks old. Private breeders usually give the first shots at 6 to 8 weeks.

WARNING

Confer with your vet and avoid using a distemper vaccine that has anything other than canine distemper vaccine in it — canine hepatitis, leptospirosis, parainfluenza, and so on, for instance. Ferrets shouldn't get vaccinated for these diseases. The USDA ferret-approved vaccines are strictly for canine distemper.

Distemper vaccine

Depending on your veterinarian, your ferret kit may be vaccinated for canine distemper — depending on its age at the time of the visit — according to different vaccine protocols (see Chapter 15 for more on canine distemper):

>> One vet may want to vaccinate for canine distemper at 8, 11, and 14 weeks of age.

>> Other vets prefer to vaccinate at 8, 12, and 16 weeks of age.

>> Ferrets over 16 weeks of age with unknown or no vaccination history only need two distemper shots, given three to four weeks apart. At this age, the ferrets receive the same protection as the kits that receive the full series of distemper vaccinations.

Rabies vaccine

The USDA ferret-approved rabies vaccine is a killed vaccine and is labeled for use after the age of 12 weeks. Some vets wait until the ferret is 14 to 18 weeks old, just in case the fuzzy's birthday got recorded incorrectly somewhere along the way. The rabies vaccine will prevent your ferret from contracting rabies if she becomes exposed. Additionally, the proof of rabies vaccination likely will keep her out of boiling water should she bite or scratch someone (see Chapter 3). Without this proof, she may be quarantined or possibly lose her life. For this reason, you can't skip the rabies booster for any reason.

WARNING

Although it's uncommon, some ferrets have allergic reactions to the distemper and or rabies vaccine (see the section, "Recognizing allergic reactions," later in this chapter, for the signs). The allergic reaction may happen only once or it may happen repeatedly, and the reaction may worsen with age. Some reactions can be life-threatening. In the past, experts recommended pretreating your ferret with an antihistamine such as Benadryl before either vaccine if your ferret had a history of allergic reactions. However, some vets, including Dr. Ruth Heller DVM, a ferret expert extraordinaire, feel Benadryl pretreatment may actually *cause* reactions in some ferrets, some possibly fatal. Pretreatment has also been implicated in leading to the onset of delayed vaccine reactions, which could possibly put you and your ferret in a huge life-threatening predicament if you've already left the vet and are home or headed for home. To avoid these problems, Dr. Heller advocates pretreating with an injection of the short-acting steroid dexamethasone. If your ferret has a history of severe, life-threatening allergic reactions to the distemper or rabies vaccine, and if she's strictly an indoor pet and has no contact with strange ferrets, you may want to consider skipping vaccines altogether. In fact, most ferret-knowledgeable vets will not even consider vaccinating a ferret that has reacted poorly to vaccinations in the past.

REMEMBER

The timing of the rabies shot can be an issue for you, your vet, and your ferret. Your ferret should receive the rabies and distemper shots at least two weeks apart to prevent any potential allergic reactions and also to identify which vaccine your ferret is having a reaction to, if there is any reaction at all. Keep that in mind when scheduling your ferret's vaccinations.

Overall kit checkup

In addition to the vaccines, your vet should set up an appointment to perform an overall checkup. The checkup should include testing your kit for internal parasites. To complete the tests, the vet requires a poop sample on your first visit. This sample also gives your vet an idea of how your ferret's digestive tract is performing.

An overall checkup should, at the very least, include these other elements as well:

» Weighing your fuzzy

» Listening to her heart and lungs

» Feeling her abdomen

» Checking her skin for external parasites and any abnormalities

» Checking her eyes, ears, and teeth

Adolescents and adults — the office visit

If you adopt an adult or teenage fuzzy whose vaccination history is unknown, you don't need to make four or five trips to the vet like you would with a kit, but you do need to make at least three. Your ferret should receive a canine distemper shot along with her initial physical exam (see the previous section for explanations of these processes).

You should bring your ferret back about three weeks later for a second distemper shot as well as a rabies shot (assuming she's older than 3 months) two weeks after that. Remember, you'll want to give the vaccinations at least two weeks apart.

TIP

If you adopt an adult ferret with a questionable background, vaccinate her just in case. Better safe than sorry!

Checkups for adult ferrets are a little more complicated. In addition to performing annual exams like a ferret kit would receive, your vet should do some extra palpating (touchy-feely stuff) to rule out enlarged organs (particularly the spleen) or suspicious lumps. Middle-aged ferrets, or those 3 years and older, are at an increased risk for disease and should have routine exams every six months. Disease can spread rapidly, so early detection and intervention are imperative. It's also recommended that your vet test blood glucose every six months, so speak to him about this. Other blood testing and X-rays for heart disease and so on can be done on a yearly basis.

TIP

Don't forget to bring a morsel of extra fresh poop, not dried up cement scraped off the wall, to your fuzzy's physical exam; you'll make your vet's day, and he'll be able to rule out parasites. And if you're noticing weirder than normal poops, request a bacteria test, as well.

REMEMBER

During your initial appointments with the vet, broach the topic of the dreaded heartworm disease. If you're a responsible dog owner, you should already know about it. Just like dogs and cats, ferrets are susceptible to heartworm, a mosquito-delivered disease. Even if you don't take your ferret outside, she isn't bulletproof, because mosquitoes can get into your house. For more information on heartworm — including recognizing its symptoms and treating it — head to Chapter 15.

Recognizing allergic reactions

Ferrets can have a reaction to the vaccinations given by veterinarians. This allergic reaction, called *anaphylaxis,* almost always occurs within 30 minutes of the vaccination injection, but it can occur up to 24 hours later. Anaphylaxis isn't very common; it can present itself as either a slight reaction or, at worst, a life-threatening condition.

The first 24 hours after the vaccination is the most crucial period; after that, your fuzzy should be in the clear. You need to remain vigilant during the initial period as you watch for signs of a bad reaction. Here are the signs of anaphylaxis:

>> Swelling around the eyes or nose

   A tiny lump where the needle went in isn't a reaction; a tiny lump is very common.

>> Vomiting

>> Diarrhea (may be bloody)

>> Lethargy (Usually, another sign should accompany the lethargy because a trip to the vet can be exhausting for your fuzzy.)

>> Pale mucous membranes (the tissue around the eyes or the gums)

>> Seizures (rare)

REMEMBER

A ferret that exhibits signs of anaphylaxis may not have a reaction to every single shot. Likewise, just because your ferret hasn't shown signs of anaphylaxis before doesn't mean that she never will. In fact, the odds of a vaccination reaction increase as the ferret ages.

TIP

I recommend that you wait around the clinic during the immediate waiting period (the first 30 minutes after the vaccine) just to be safe. It's important to immediately treat a fuzzy that's suffering from anaphylaxis, and also look for the Five Ps: Pinkness (lack of), panting, puking, peeing (uncontrollably) and pooping (uncontrollably). If you're already home when you notice the signs, pack right up and head back to the vet. On the way, keep your ferret warm (she may be experiencing the beginning signs of shock).

To treat anaphylaxis, your vet will most likely give your fuzzy an injection (yes, another one!) of an antihistamine and/or steroid. Some vets also administer fluids. (*Note:* Some vets like to pretreat a ferret with a history of vaccination allergy with one of these medicines just to be on the safe side.) This course of action treats the allergic reaction and heads off the shock, which can be deadlier to your ferret than the allergic reaction itself.

Titer testing

Vaccinations are a hot topic. People have long expressed concerns about overvaccinating their own children, and pets have recently fallen into that area of concern as well. After all, it only makes sense to avoid anything that causes adverse and possibly deadly reactions in ferrets, and vaccinations can be high on the list.

Scientists evaluate the immunity a vaccine produces by identifying their subjects' *titers*, that is, the number of antibodies in their blood. Although titer studies on ferrets are still evolving, it has been shown that the annual canine distemper vaccination provides an immunity that lasts far beyond a single year — studies show an immunity in excess of three years and possibly as long as a lifetime! Although the protective cut-off for ferrets has yet to be determined, one study showed that most vaccinated ferrets, developed titers at or above 64, compared to the proven protective level of 32 in dogs. That's twice the level than that of proven protection in dogs. Some of these ferrets' titers tested in the thousands. Those ferrets whose data extended over multiple years remained at equal titers despite having only received original vaccinations as kits. One might surmise these ferrets with such high titers are well protected from the disease for which they were originally vaccinated against in the first place.

Just how a vaccination stimulates immunity in a recipient can be an entire section itself, and is well worth the research. However, for our purposes, it's best only to know that you have some options out there. Titer tests can be done fairly inexpensively and only through your veterinarian — using an in-house titer test, which tests positively or negatively for titers, or a test sent to the specialized lab for this testing to be done (sent directly from your vet to New York State Diagnostic Laboratory at Cornell University). Regardless of which you choose, use the results of your ferret's titer test as a tool when discussing with your vet the pros and cons of vaccinating your ferret annually. As Dr. Ruth Heller, DVM states, "It is heartbreaking to give a medication for the sole purpose of protecting an animal, only to harm it instead. With a study showing that most ferrets develop good and longlasting antibodies in response to vaccinating, it becomes more possible to avoid such an occurrence."

Stocking Your Ferret First-Aid Kit

Perhaps you've already equipped your household with a first-aid kit for human use. A lot of what you put in your own first-aid kit also is useful for treating ferrets, but I recommend that you put together a first-aid kit strictly for your little fuzzy.

WARNING

Always consult your vet before including (and using) any over-the-counter products, medications, or supplements in your fuzzy first-aid kit. Using some common items to treat your ferret may actually aggravate certain illnesses or diseases. Also, you need to get the proper dosage amounts from your vet for treatments. It's easy to overdose a ferret on medication.

Every ferret first-aid kit should include the following items (*Note:* If you use something from the kit, be sure to replace it as soon as possible):

>> **Emergency phone numbers:**

- Your veterinarian's number

- The number to a 24-hour emergency clinic

- The number for the National Animal Poison Control Center

  To reach the National Animal Poison Control Center, you can call 888-426-4435. This service costs $75 per case — credit cards only.

- The number for the Pet Poison Helpline

  To reach the Pet Poison Helpline, call 855-764-7661. This service costs $59 per incident.

>> **Health records (include the following for each of your ferrets):**

- General health records with a corresponding identification photo of the ferret

- Current rabies certificates

- A list of prescription medications your ferret is currently taking

>> **Foodstuffs:**

- Jars of meat baby food — chicken or lamb (for the sick kid)

- Poopin Pumpkin (www.rockyscreaturecomforts.com)

- Light Karo syrup or Nutri-Cal (for a quick calorie boost or insulinoma crash)

- Unflavored Pedialyte or Gatorade (to rehydrate a dehydrated ferret)

- A can of prescription feline A/D, which you can get from your vet (easily digested food for the sickly)

- Oxbow Carnivore Care (an excellent, complete supplement)

- Canola or olive oil (may help to move bad stuff through)

- Royal Canin canned diet (for sick ferrets needing good nutrition)

- Salmon oil

- Feline hairball laxative or preventive (if your ferret hates salmon oil)

- Probiotic S. Boulardii and Prebiotic MOS (yeasts beneficial for carnivore digestion)

All ferret owners should know about Carnivore Care, which is available from Oxbow Pet Products. This highly palatable nutritional supplement is made with easily digestible protein that's suitable for carnivores such as ferrets. The supplement offers complete nutrition to ferrets with reduced appetites. For more information on this product, head to the website www.oxbowhay.com; you can call 800-249-0366 to order it (you can't order online). (See Chapter 8 for more on diet).

I've listed many different meat sources for your first-aid kit, but you don't have to stock them all. You can stock one or stock all. It's a personal preference. You may want to start off by including them all in case you get a sick ferret that turns out to be a picky eater. But if you decide to stick with one, Carnivore Care is my first choice.

>> **Cleaning solutions:**

- Betadine solution or Vetericyn for cats (for cleaning cuts)

- Nolvasan/chlorhexidine (for cleaning cuts)

  You can sometimes find this as an ear cleaner.

- Ear cleanser (for routine grooming)

- Eye wash/rinse (for flushing foreign bodies)

- Sterile saline solution (for flushing wounds)

>> **Bandages and wraps:**

- Gauze pads (for bleeding wounds)

- Gauze wrap

- Washcloths

- Vet wrap (self-sticking variety — you can find this in drug stores in the bandage section)

- Adhesive bandage tape (cloth tape works the best)

>> **Other health aids:**

- Styptic powder, beeswax, cornstarch, or block of white soap (for bleeding nails)

- Benadryl cream (*no* cortisone creams)

- Silver Sulfadiazine cream (SSD)

- Petroleum jelly (to help move a blockage and for lubricating a thermometer)

- Pepcid (for upset tummies)

I would be completely irresponsible if I didn't point out that I've removed a couple of items from the previous edition's first-aid kit, and for very good reasons! A great deal of time has elapsed since the 2nd Edition, and more research has shown that Pepto Bismol, when used over a long period of time, can cause neurological issues in your ferret. Therefore, it's no longer recommended by this author. Furthermore, and probably more important, is what's developed over time regarding the use of antibiotic ointments such as Bacitracin or Bacitracin-containing ointments such as Neosporin or Polymycin anywhere on your ferret. Bacitracin is toxic if ingested, and your ferret will surely lick it off if it's applied on any part of his body.

- EMT First Aid Gel (for wound healing)

- Sudocrem (for wound first aid)

- Preparation H (for prolapse — or make your own paste to apply by simply mixing granulated sugar and water together to a pasty consitency)

- Salmon or pollock oil (for mixing with medicine that tastes like you-know-what)

- Pediatric Liquid Benadryl (alcohol- and sugar-free for counteracting allergic reactions; see the section "Recognizing allergic reactions")

Tylenol (acetaminophen) is extremely toxic to ferrets even in very low doses. The liver metabolizes the medicine, and it will send your ferret into liver failure quickly, eventually killing your fuzzy. Many over-the-counter medicines contain acetaminophen. Therefore, even if it's in your first-aid kit, don't use any over-the-counter products without your vet's guidance and approval. You can prevent these types of fatal mistakes.

Poopin Pumpkin is a product developed by my fellow ferret enthusiast and good friend Barbara Clay. Over the many years as the shelter director of Rocky's Ferret Rescue & Shelter, she encountered ferrets with life-threatening furballs and other obstructions. No effective products existed for treatment, and risky invasive surgery was very expensive. Often the ferrets were so badly compromised that they couldn't even be considered as surgical candidates, and vets would recommend pumpkin as an alternate solution to try to purge the obstructions. Over a course of three years, Barbara developed Poopin Pumpkin, a concentrated dry product comprised of air-dried pumpkin powder and powdered whole eggs. Much to her delight, and after much testing, she had finally stumbled upon a highly effective recipe. That was in 2013. Now Poopin Pumpkin is a therapeutic supplement USDA approved for use in cats, dogs, and ferrets. It has been credited with saving the lives of ferrets in the U.S. and seven other countries! It's also used and recommended by vets, shelter operators, breeders, and personal owners!

For more information, visit Barbara's company website at https://www.rockyscreaturecomforts.com/.

Bene-Bac is one of the most widely recommended items when it comes to ferret first-aid kits, because it's designed to replace beneficial bacteria in the digestive tract after illness or diarrhea. What you may not know, however, is that it doesn't work for obligate carnivores, such as ferrets. The bacteria contained in Bene-Bac is made for omnivores and some herbivores. Using Bene-Bac won't hurt your ferret, but it won't help, either; it only helps you feel better!

>> **Miscellaneous items:**

- Heating pad (to help maintain a young or sick ferret's body temperature)

- Chemical or microwavable heating pack (portable heat for the young or sick ferret)

- Nail clippers and file

- Syringes (10 ml for feeding the sick ferret)

- Small blanket

- Flea comb

- Alpha Trak II (for testing blood glucose)

- Cotton balls and Q-Tips

- Eyedroppers

- Tweezers (to remove foreign bodies)

- Cotton balls and cotton swabs

- Ice pack (to reduce swelling or slow down bleeding)

- Rubber or latex gloves

- Scissors

- Pen light (to help you see wounds and foreign bodies)

- Pill crusher

- Rectal thermometer

  The normal temperature for a ferret is between 100 and 103 degrees Fahrenheit.

- Tongue depressors or popsicle sticks (for immobilizing injured limbs)

- Baby wipes (for general cleanup duties)

TIP

I also suggest that, whenever possible, you bring your first-aid kit to your ferret, as opposed to bringing your injured ferret to the first-aid kit. Make this easier by storing your first-aid supplies in a convenient and portable case. Fishing-tackle boxes and professional make-up boxes work great. You can also do a lot with Tupperware! Get one large bin and keep your supplies organized and labeled in smaller containers within that bin. Keep your first-aid case in a convenient and easy-to-reach location.

Ensuring Emergency Preparedness

Whether you've lived through them or have only heard about them, you know that real pet emergencies take place all the time. It seems like you hear more and more about disasters striking, leaving families and their pets with few options and nowhere to go. Disasters come in all shapes and sizes: floods, earthquakes, fires, hurricanes, tornadoes, and more.

Have you prepared your family and fuzzies to escape an emergency? Are you prepared to care for your pets during an emergency? Preparing for the collection and evacuation of your ferrets takes time, thought, and practice. Using the information in the following sections, you can take action and come up with a plan that best suits your situation.

The basic (quick) evacuation kit

The basic evacuation kit is for an emergency that allows for a small window of time to evacuate. Your only pet-related goal during a serious emergency is to get your ferret out quickly and safely. That's it. Anything else is just icing on the cake — and potentially dangerous icing at that.

The basic evacuation kit I suggest you put together is based on that one goal, making it quite simple. Here's what you need in this kit:

>> A flashlight (in case the lights go out)

>> A mesh pet carrier — (or fabric bag such as a thick pillowcase or something stronger to actually hold your ferrets in will work in a tight pinch)

>> A strong piece of rope (to tie the bag of ferrets shut; it should be about 2 feet)

>> A small fire extinguisher (to put out any small fires you encounter)

>> A police whistle, which you can purchase at an Army surplus store, or something equally loud and piercing (to call your ferrets)

The kit may seem too simple, but the purpose is to remain safe and get out fast. With this in mind, make sure you store the kit in a handy container and locate it in a convenient place.

REMEMBER

Most ferret owners have more than one ferret. Actually, many have an abundance of ferrets! For every four ferrets you have, you need to pack one fabric bag and one piece of rope. In a true get-out-fast-or-else emergency, one bag may do fine for up to six or seven ferrets, but the strength of the bag may decrease with each ferret you put inside.

Collecting and evacuating your fuzzy

The number-one rule in an emergency is to stay calm, because you know your ferret won't. When an emergency strikes, pick up your ferret and toss her in a sack or place her gently into the carrier — whatever the situation calls for. If you're using the sack method, tie it off securely with the rope. When your ferret is safe and secure, leave the house. You've done your job.

If you have more than one fuzzy, an emergency situation is no time to worry about who gets along with whom. Pick up your ferrets and toss them in the sack. After you tie it off securely with the rope, get the heck out of there.

WARNING

I'm in no way advocating that you should put your own life at risk to save the life of your pet. Trained professionals will come to the scene of an emergency to help you and your pet in times of crisis. Losing a pet is heartbreaking, but losing your life while trying to save a pet is catastrophic for many.

The deluxe (and orderly) evacuation kit

The basic evacuation kit is for a serious emergency that calls for quick action. The deluxe evacuation kit, on the other hand, is for an emergency that you know is coming, but that you have time to plan for. For example, a forest fire that's slowly making its way toward your home. Or a hurricane that's predicted to hit land in the next 24 hours. These are tragedies that you can prepare for with a little window of time. The deluxe kit is designed to be picked up and put in a car, taking up as little space as possible. Like the ferret first-aid kit and the basic evacuation kit (see earlier sections in this chapter), you should keep the deluxe kit in an area that's easily accessible and in a case that's ready to go.

In addition to the materials I mention for the basic kit, the deluxe kit should contain the following items; it may seem like a lot, but after you gather it up, you'll be done, and hopefully you'll never have to use the kit:

» **Foodstuffs:**

- Jars of chicken baby food
- At least a week's supply of your ferret's food, kept in a re-sealable container (swap out for fresh food regularly, if possible)
- Bottled water
- Pedialyte
- At least a week or two supply of any medication your ferret is taking

» **A basic first-aid kit:**

- Betadine/iodine solution
- Gauze pads/wrap
- Adhesive tape
- Antibiotic cream/ointment
- Salmon oil
- Heating pad or chemical heat packs
- Tweezers
- Cotton swabs
- Scissors
- Latex gloves
- Popsicle sticks
- Baby wipes
- Sanitizing gel
- Eyedropper
- A week's supply of medication (if necessary)

» **Restraint and identification:**

- Leash and harness with ID tag for each ferret
- Carrier or cage large enough for your ferret to move around in
- Copy of medical and up-to-date vaccination records

- Adoption/registration papers or other proof of ownership (including microchip number)

- Ferret identification card, which includes a recent photo, a written physical description (including tattoos and medical conditions), and a behavioral description

- An ID card with your name, address, phone number(s), and veterinarian's phone number

- Pre-planned emergency contact lists (veterinarians, family, and friends)

- Leather gloves (in case your ferret gets overly excited or scared and acts out in aggression)

» **Miscellaneous items:**

- Bedding (hammock, snooze sack)

- Hanging water bottle

- Non-tippable bowls

- Spoons

- Small garbage bags

- Dish soap

- Disposable litter tray

- Paper towels

Chapter **13**

Helping Your Hurt Ferret: First-Aid Basics

You must face the facts: Your little ferret friend is (or will be) a trouble magnet. No matter how much you love him or how much money you spend on preventive care, your ferret will eventually test your first-aid knowledge and your ability to work under severe emotional duress. Even if you keep your ferret confined to a cage all day and night (Caution: The ferret patrol and I will hunt you down and pummel you if you do!), you'll still have a misfortune here or there. And even the sweetest, most innocent ferret may have a mishap through no fault of his own.

This chapter covers the process of providing immediate first aid. I discuss how to identify and fix an easy problem and how to control a difficult one until your fuzzy can receive care from a medical professional. I explain how you can manage your ferret's pain during injury or illness situations. And I go through the steps you can take during your ferret's recovery to keep him comfortable and nourished. (The other chapters in Part 4 explain the serious diseases and illnesses you may come across and how you can treat them.)

Behaviors You Usually Don't Need to Worry About

You'll be happy to read that some funky ferret behaviors are normal. Like a grown man scratching his belly and dealing with indigestion after Thanksgiving dinner and then falling asleep during a football game, ferrets have a few peculiar behaviors that may startle you at first. Don't be alarmed. Many of the behaviors I list in the following sections often are harmless, and with the information here, you'll be prepared to deal with them and even predict their onset.

Shivering

Ferrets shiver for many reasons, but most of the reasons are simple and harmless. All ferrets shiver to raise their body temperature, which is necessary after sleeping more than half the day away! Shivering is a natural and effective temperature-raising method. Many also shiver when being scruffed. Remember to give a little bottom support to your shivering fuzzy in a scruffing situation (see Chapter 7). Frightened ferrets rarely shiver, but excited ferrets often do. If you suspect that your ferret's shivering is due to something other than these reasons, consult your veterinarian (for info on finding a qualified vet, refer to Chapter 12).

Itching and scratching

Ferrets are itchy critters, plain and simple. They'll sometimes awaken from a deep sleep just to feverishly scratch a sudden itch, and then they'll roll over and fall back to sleep. Or they'll stop in the middle of a mad dash across the room to scratch an itch. If you watch your ferret itch and scratch long enough, you'll begin to itch and scratch, too, because it makes most people paranoid about fleas. But scratching often is harmless and mainly annoying for the carpet shark.

REMEMBER If you do notice reddened areas, bumps, sores, or missing fur where your ferret is scratching, explore his environment, such as his bedding and what it was last washed in. Consider that skin tends to dry out a little during the colder months. And although uncommon, fuzzies can have allergies. Sometimes, too much scratching can lead to raw spots that you may need to treat topically. If this is the case, see your vet. If you've ruled out fleas and no fur is missing, you can probably chalk up the scratching to a typical ferret quirk.

Yawning

Yawning is such a common and interesting ferret quirk that ferret enthusiasts actually hold yawning contests (see Chapter 10)! Whether they're playing in your lap or backing into a litter box, yawns sneak out. They seemingly come out of nowhere. Could it have anything to do with how much sleep ferrets indulge in? And until recently I didn't know why furkids yawned while being scruffed — they do, and they do so considerably. According to Dr. Ruth Heller DVM, "The yawning and limpness [from scruffing] is related to the release of relaxation hormones. This is a physiological response so that babies go limp when Mom picks them up." So you see, scruffed ferrets are particularly vulnerable to yawning attacks. Although the effect of all the yawns seems nonexistent, people watching can be enticed into their own yawning attacks. I yawn as I write this!

Excessive sleeping

Sleeping excessively is common in ferrets, so don't take it as a sign that you're a complete bore. Sometimes, ferrets can sleep so hard that it appears they're in a coma or even dead. The fuzzies are warm and breathing, but they just won't wake up!

If you're a concerned mom or dad and insist on making sure that fuzzball is alive, you can try a few proven techniques. Start with the first and continue through the list:

1. Lift him up and call his name loudly.

2. Very gently rest your hand on his chest and wait for a breath.

3. Give his back or belly a few good rubs, but don't shake him violently.

4. Scratch him between the ears.

5. Scruff him gently (see Chapter 7) and wiggle him a bit if he still hasn't responded.

6. Put a dab of his favorite treat on his nose (see Chapter 8). The smell should get his little brain going; if not, he's probably sick.

7. Heavy sleeping may actually be a sign of an underlying condition such as insulinoma. As a *very* last resort, rub a tiny amount of Karo syrup on his gums; the sugar from this might just pull him out of his "crash."

Usually, this deep sleep (referred to as SND [Sleeping Not Dead]) is normal. When the ferret finally raises an eyelid to inspect the rude gate-crasher, you can rest assured that he's okay. You can play with the fuzzy a bit if you still feel the need to reassure yourself. It's taken almost a full minute to wake up one or two of my guys on some occasions, and it still scares the beans out of me. If an SND situation occurs frequently with the same ferret, a trip to the vet may be a wise idea. (Chapter 10 discusses enrichment, which may lessen the amount of sleep your fuzzy needs, along with the proper diet [see Chapter 8].)

WARNING

Sugar consumption is extremely dangerous for a ferret with *insulinoma* (See more in Chapter 16). Because of this, the use of Karo syrup with known or suspected insulinoma ferrets should be only in emergency situations. If it gets this far, a visit to the vet is probably a good idea.

WARNING

Although ferrets do sleep quite a bit, and some even enter the deep SND mode, be aware of sudden changes in your furkid's sleeping patterns. If he starts to sleep more often than usual, he may be giving you a sign of an underlying medical condition. Don't ignore sudden changes in behavior, because he may require immediate medical attention.

Sneezing, hiccuping, and coughing

With all the maladies fuzzies can get, you'd think sneezing, coughing, and hiccuping would be some more things to worry about. Not so. These conditions often are harmless and even useful for the fuzzy. Fuzzballs get around by sense of smell. If you watch closely, you'll see that your exploring ferret has his nose to the ground almost all the time. In the process, he's inhaling everything from dust bunnies to carpet fibers. He's bound to snort up bits and pieces of junk, and sneezing is the only way to clear his nose of it. When the sneezing attack is over, it's nose to the ground again.

Ferrets sometimes cough or hack as though they have something stuck in their throats. It's common and, more often than not, harmless. Coughing usually is a sign of a minor irritation to the throat or the reaction to a piece of kibble the fuzzy swallowed too quickly. If the coughing persists, though, contact your vet. Persistent coughing can also be a sign of several illnesses, including cardiomyopathy, so take note of how much coughing your fuzzy does and take him to see the vet. Better safe than sorry.

Hiccuping is a common and harmless fuzzy condition that results from the spasming of the ferret's diaphragm. In ferrets, hiccuping seems random and more of a bother to them than a condition to worry about. In humans, hiccuping often is a result of too much beer! Try giving your ferret a tiny lick of salmon oil to try to shorten the duration of the hiccuping.

Butt dragging

The skid marks your ferret leaves behind after he uses the bathroom are more than pretty decorations. They're ferret proclamations! Ferrets like to use butt dragging to tell other animals, including humans, where they've been and what their territorial boundaries are. Although the butt dragging may not actually leave a visual trail, you can bet your bottom dollar that he's left a scent behind. Not to worry; you may not notice the smell at all, but other ferrets and animals will smell it loud and clear.

If your fuzzy's butt dragging seems unusually lengthy or if he does it more and more frequently, you can have your vet check him for parasites or other conditions that may be causing discomfort, such as a serious prolapsed rectum. However, some ferrets actually get very minor prolapses after pooping, and they may butt-scoot until the prolapse corrects itself. This is quite normal.

TIP

Because most ferrets in the United States are descented, they don't leave much of a scent, but they still display the behavior. These ferrets are primarily trying to leave anal gland scent, not feces. Still, the scent trail is there. After all, a butt's a butt.

Drinking urine

No one knows for sure why some adorable little fuzzies engage in the obnoxious practice of urine drinking. Maybe they just want to gross us humans out. It may be a sexual behavior traced back to polecat relatives that groom themselves with their own urine in order to make themselves more desirable to females. Some ferret experts believe that drinking urine is just another way for a thirsty ferret to consume liquid. If you want to curtail the activity, make sure that enough water is always available. If you're really concerned about the amount of urine your furkid is lapping up, consult your veterinarian.

Honestly, although it seems disgusting to us, urine drinking is common for a ferret. It's a harmless act, unlike drinking too much beer, because urine is sterile, so ferrets aren't consuming a bunch of bacteria.

Pain Management and Care

Ferrets are quite the troopers! Their little bodies go through so much, and they put up a tremendous fight to live during even the most difficult of times. But ferrets, like so many other animals, are stoic creatures. They hide their pain in order to hide their "weaknesses," which would surely be death sentences in the wild. But if you know your ferret well (and make an effort to from the very first day you get him), you'll be able to tell that he's in pain, and there's no reason at all he needs to live that way.

Determining if your ferret is in pain

Couple the warning signs in the following list with your intimate knowledge of your fuzzy (or your fledgling knowledge) to tell if your ferret is in pain:

>> **Facial expression:** Squinting, muscles twitching on the top of his head, tooth grinding, dull eyes

>> **Appetite:** Reduced or absent appetite, dropping food from the mouth, difficulty swallowing or chewing, standing over food dish but not eating, selecting only soft foods

>> **Posture:** Tucked abdomen, lying on side with no ability to get up, inability to stretch out or curl up

>> **Activity:** Gait abnormalities (limping, holding limbs up, or dragging), restricted movement, trembling

>> **Grooming:** Failure to groom himself, poor coat appearance, excessive licking or scratching

>> **Self-awareness:** Protecting a body area, licking or chewing a body area

>> **Vocalization:** Crying or moaning periodically, vocalizing when defecating, urinating, or moving

>> **Attitude:** Unusual aggression, hiding more than usual, seeking comfort, bristling tail with depressed behavior, dull or uninterested attitude toward surroundings

>> **Response to being touched:** Protective, vocalizing, escaping, biting

REMEMBER

Some of the signs and behaviors in the previous list, while generally associated with pain, aren't solely indicators of pain. Some can be signs of other conditions. It all depends on your ferret. Pain can elicit extreme behaviors at opposite ends of the spectrum. Your ferret's pain may cause him to act unusually needy and seek comfort from you. Another ferret in pain may hide and isolate himself more than usual. No matter what, if changed behavior that can't be accounted for, or any of the listed signs are present, you can assume that something abnormal is going on. A call and visit to your vet are warranted.

Caring for a ferret in pain

You have many options to manage your ferret's pain, and fortunately the list is growing. Managing pain will keep your ferret comfortable and help him recover from surgery, illness, or injury. Pain management during and after surgery or for an injury or chronic illness should always be a part of routine supportive care. Speak to your vet about it to set up a pain management regimen.

You'll know the pain management regimen you and your vet have chosen is working when the signs of pain begin to alleviate and your ferret starts to act more like himself. If, however, the signs continue or worsen, you need to contact your vet immediately to discuss a change of plans.

The following list presents some of the most common pain medications currently used on ferrets by your veterinarian and or with your veterinarian's guidance only:

>> **Opioids:** Examples include buprenorphine, butorphanol, hydromorphone, and oxymorphone, and all are injections. These drugs are very effective for moderate to severe acute, post-surgical, or traumatic pain. They have a wide range of length of effectiveness, depending on which drug is used. Mild to profound sedation may accompany the treatment — the latter being a benefit if the pain is severe or a hindrance if you want to assess the level of pain. These drugs aren't good for chronic pain.

>> **NSAIDs (non-steroidal anti-inflammatory drugs):** Examples include meloxicam/metacam, carprofen, and ketoprofen. These medications have anti-inflammatory, pain-reducing, and fever-reducing properties. They can be effective for some types of acute and chronic pain. NSAIDs aren't recommended for ferrets that are pregnant, in shock, have stomach ulcers, or have kidney or liver disease. NSAIDs may also worsen gastritis.

Meloxicam/metacam should always be administered by injection and not orally due to the effects it has on the stomach and intestinal tract. It should be given only in very small amounts with Pepcid (an over-the-counter stomach acid-reducer that aids ferrets with gastrointestinal problems) over the course of only 2 to 3 days, and never be given in conjunction with prednisone.

>> **Local anesthetics:** Examples include lidocaine and bupivicaine. Vets use these drugs during surgery at the incision site to help block localized pain. Local anesthetics are short-term pain killers administered by injection only.

Tylenol (acetaminophen) is *extremely toxic* to your ferret, even in very low doses. It's metabolized by the liver and will send your ferret reeling into liver failure quickly before killing him. Additionally, ibuprofen, naproxen, and aspirin, once suggested for use, may also prove extremely toxic to your ferret. Never use an over-the-counter medication without discussing it with your veterinarian beforehand.

TIP

Many fuzzy owners and vets explore alternative pain management techniques, such as the following:

» Acupuncture, which can be very effective at managing certain types of pain

» Chiropractic care, which is limited to managing pain of the musculoskeletal system

» Herbal/homeopathic care, which may reduce some pain and anxiety. (**Note:** This option should be used only under the guidance of a veterinary professional who's familiar with the use of herbal/homeopathic medicine and its side effects.)

Use these options only under the direction and with the guidance of your trusted veterinarian (see Chapter 12).

Setting Up Fuzzy's Home Hospital Room

You can do non-medical things right at home to help alleviate anxiety and pain in your ferret. One of the most important parts of your ferret's treatment occurs during aftercare, which is where most of the problems begin and end. You can't become lax when your ferret needs special care that's critical to his health. Whether your ferret is injured, sick, recovering from surgery, or just plain elderly, you need to give special attention to the old and infirmed. Under the direction of your vet, you need to give medication exactly as prescribed, provide assisted feedings routinely, administer fluids when necessary, and so on.

And you have another critical step to take to get your ferret back to his old self: Make sure he has private space to which he can retreat:

» House him comfortably and in a quiet area.

» Be sure that no other ferrets, pets, or children can bother him.

» Keep his handling to a minimum, and keep it slow and easy.

Most post-surgical, critically ill, elderly, or injured ferrets have limited mobility or are prescribed restricted mobility by vets. The latter is for their safety while they heal and recover. Regardless of what your ferret's story is, he needs a hospital cage setup. Here's what you'll need:

>> **One cage approximately 2.5'-wide x 2'-deep x 2'-tall**

  The cage should have easy access to move in and out and have a big enough spot for a small litter box. It can have a small ramp leading to a low shelf, but a single story is preferable (see Chapter 5).

>> **One small litter box**

>> **Litter or shredded newspaper (for ferrets with incisions)**

>> **A water bottle and water bowl**

>> **Food dish (if he's eating on his own)**

>> **Plenty of fluffy bedding**

>> **His favorite toys**

REMEMBER

Your ferret needs to feel safe and comfortable, but you need to be able to check up on him often and provide him with the special one-on-one care he needs. The whole point of the hospital setup is to provide a safe recuperating spot for your ferret that's also convenient enough for you to do what you need to for your ferret. You also want to be able to get to your ferret quickly in case he's in distress. Therefore, forego putting any kind of nest box in the hospital cage. A nice pile of fluffy bedding is all that he needs for now.

TIP

To help with your fuzzy's need for security and sleep, cover the recovery cage with a towel or blanket. This will also help keep out drafts.

Feeding the Sick or Debilitated Ferret

Most ferret owners will, at some point, need to assist their ferrets when it comes to eating so that they continue to meet their nutritional and water-intake requirements (see Chapter 8). Your ferret may require supplemental feedings if he's sick or injured, old, has dental problems, or is recovering from surgery. No matter the reason, you need to follow through on assisted feeding four to six times a day if your fuzzy isn't eating on his own. The following sections give you a vet's guide to some recipes so you can create a meal that will help heal or sustain your ferret and the method for feeding your needy fuzzy safely and effectively.

The Assist Feed Recipe: Better than Mom's chicken soup

You need to make a special food mixture to feed your sick or debilitated ferret. The recipe I present in this section has been called many silly names that have nothing to do with ferrets. For our purposes, I'll simply call the recipe the *Assist Feed Recipe* and hope it catches on. It's relatively simple to make. The only requirements are that the concoction must be soft, easy to digest, full of energy-boosting calories, healthy, and yummy enough to make your ferret forget about resisting it.

You have several options when it comes to making the Assist Feed Recipe. Susan Brown, DVM, and co-author of *Essentials of Ferrets: A Guide for Practitioners* (American Animal Hospital Association), offers the following suggestions:

>> **Mix up Carnivore Care as directed:** Highly digestible protein sources make Carnivore Care an ideal choice when providing nutrition to ferrets that aren't eating or need supplemental feedings. It's made by Oxbow Company and can be purchased from your vet or directly from the company. You should have a small supply of this in your ferret first-aid kit (see Chapter 12). If you don't, before you pick up the Carnivore Care, you can substitute your ferret's favorite high-quality kibble and grind it up, mixing it with water.

>> **Mix Carnivore Care with Ensure or Resource 2.0 rather than water to increase calories and palatability:** You may need to add a smidge of water to thin the mixture a little.

>> **Mix the Carnivore Care as directed and mix in canned Science Diet A/D (no more than 50 percent of the total volume) to increase the fat and flavor.**

>> **Mix the Carnivore Care as directed and add some meat baby food (no more than 25 percent of the total volume) to put in more fat and flavor:** Baby food is the *least* complete thing you can feed your ferret for the long term. Beechnut is preferred.

>> **Mix the Carnivore Care as directed and add an all-meat canned cat food (no more than 25 percent of the total volume) for more fat and flavor.**

If your ferret is extra picky, you can also try a 50/50 mixture of kibble and Carnivore Care. The key is to find a flavor that's palatable to your ferret so that he wants to eat the food. As long as your main ingredient (good high-quality animal protein, low-carb kibble, or Carnivore Care) is adequate, you can experiment with other ingredients.

Mix the batch up until it's smooth and creamy. If you're a fuzzy chef extraordinaire, your ferret will lick your concoction right from the spoon or bowl with little hesitation. If you're a disaster in the kitchen, you may have to use a feeding syringe to get the stuff into his mouth. Expect a little ptooeying in this case. And see the next section for suggestions on how best — and how often — to get the food down.

TIP

Susan Brown would like me to give you the following advice: "Any of these supplements, even A/D alone or baby food alone, is fine for the short term (one week or less) or supplementing a ferret that is also still eating some on his own. However, if you are feeding the ferret all of the food he's getting and it's going to be long term, I would always opt for Carnivore Care alone or in some combination. If the ferret is very thin, you can use combo #2 or #3 to beef him up. You can reduce the amount of Resource/Ensure or A/D if the ferret gets overweight and go back to just Carnivore Care alone."

WARNING

Many published supplemental feeding recipes contain ingredients that aren't good for ferrets. Please *stay away* from the following items in particular:

>> Sugary items (such as honey, corn syrup, maple syrup, or Nutri-Cal)

>> Fruit (dried or otherwise, particularly raisins)

>> Grains

>> Vegetables

If you think about it, your ferret can only fit so much into his stomach. You can't waste that space on low-calorie, hard-to-digest, non-dense foods. Your fuzzy should be eating quality high-calorie food. Additionally, high-sugar foods, such as raisins, are tough on his pancreas and cause his blood-sugar levels to rise and fall rapidly. You don't want to add to your fuzzy's health problems!

The feeding method: Just as effective as the airplane into the mouth

The manner in which you feed your fuzzy his Assist Feed Recipe depends on his level of strength and willingness to eat:

>> **If your ferret is strong enough** and finds the Assist Feed Recipe appetizing, you can present it to him in a shallow bowl or allow him to lick it one spoonful at a time. He may even prefer to lick the recipe off your finger. No matter what, don't just place him in a cage with the bowl and walk away. Watch him and make sure that he's doing more eating than spreading it around his cage or other area. Also, if he has cagemates, be aware that they'll probably try to get to the food before he gets his share. That is why separating him in a hospital cage is so vital.

>> **If your ferret isn't strong enough** to feed himself, you'll have to feed him. If you do need to force feed, your first job is to take the word "force" out of your vocabulary. It's bad enough that the poor guy is sick. Don't make eating an unpleasant experience as well. (From here on out, I'll refer to this process as *assist feeding,* because that's really what you're doing.)

You can obtain a feeding syringe (it has no needle at the end) from your vet, or you can use an eyedropper (plastic, not glass) to assist feed your fuzzy. (*Note:* Eyedroppers can be a bit more time-consuming because they're smaller.) Suck up the formula into the syringe and squeeze a small amount into the corner of your ferret's mouth. He may crinkle up his nose and eyes with displeasure or surprise, but don't give up until you know he's had enough. Take the time to wipe his mouth and, if needed, your face, should the stuff go airborne during a violent ptooeying!

WARNING

Way too often, fuzzy humans are in a hurry to feed their sick babies. Forcing large amounts of food into a ferret's mouth can cause him to aspirate or choke. Feed him slowly and in small amounts. Let him set the pace. It may just take him awhile to get used to your cooking!

REMEMBER

Don't ever give up on a stubborn ferret that refuses to eat. Providing good nutrition and preventing dehydration are crucial to healing and/or prolonging the life of your ferret. You may end up with a ton of gunk on your body, but make sure that your sickie gets several cc's (3 to 4) of the good stuff four to six times a day. The feeding frequency can be less if he's eating a little on his own in between feedings.

Handling Actual Emergencies

Ferrets are tiny. They dehydrate quickly. They don't have very much blood, so they can't afford to lose much. Basically, fuzzies are stoic creatures, and unfortunately, they hide pain and illness too well. Sometimes, by the time you recognize a problem, it has become severe. The best prevention is to know your ferret's body language and behavior well. Your preparedness can save your furkid's life. And, unless the situation is as simple as a toenail cut too close to the quick, a visit to the vet as soon as possible is always a safe measure.

WARNING

If your ferret is in pain or scared, he may bite. Unless your ferret is new to your household, I can safely assume that your pet knows and trusts you. Your soft, reassuring voice may help comfort him and calm him down, but you should still exercise caution. (Head to Chapter 20 for tips on handling an aggressive ferret.)

TIP

Familiarize yourself with a nearby after-hours emergency hospital that's ferret-knowledgeable in case your ferret needs care when your veterinarian is unavailable.

In the following sections, I cover actual emergencies that you may encounter over the lifetime of your ferret. Some are common, such as dehydration and diarrhea, and others aren't so common, such as burns and electric shock. But these sections are designed to give you some basic information to prepare you for possible encounters with emergencies until you can get to the vet.

Shock

Shock is a common after-effect of traumatic injury or life-threatening illness, and it can cost your ferret his life. Shock is a serious medical emergency, and prevention and supportive therapy are essential. Check out the following list so you can recognize the big signs of shock:

» Rapid breathing

» Lethargy

» Shivering

» Faster than normal heartbeat

» Pale nose, skin, and ears

» Skin that's cool to the touch

» Grey to bluish gums

» Unresponsiveness or extreme anxiety

WARNING

Don't attempt to get a ferret in shock to eat or drink. Your fuzzy is having a hard time breathing, and his swallowing reflex just isn't there.

Get your ferret to the vet as soon as possible, trying to keep him warm on the way. Upon arrival, let your vet know what measures you've already taken and how your ferret has responded. Often, additional fluids are given subcutaneously by the vet to help speed the recovery. If your ferret is in shock due to blood loss, a blood transfusion from a healthy fuzzy can be lifesaving. It sounds extreme, but it has been done with great success.

Dehydration

Dehydration occurs because of abnormal fluid loss, which can happen if your ferret stops drinking or has severe or chronic diarrhea or vomiting. Except in cases where owners deny or restrict access to water or alter the water's taste, dehydration is almost always a sign of a serious underlying illness. Regardless of the cause, dehydration can be fatal if you don't address it immediately.

Some signs of dehydration include the following:

>> Dry, tacky gums

>> Low urine output

>> Weakened state

>> Difficulty opening his eyes all the way (constant squinting)

>> Loss of sparkle or glossiness in his eyes

TIP

Not sure if one of these symptoms means your fuzzy is dehydrated? How can you find out for sure? Try this technique: Pull up on the skin on the back of your ferret's neck or shoulders to make a "tent." Does the skin stay in this tented position for a second or more after you let go, or does it snap back to its original elasticity? Dehydration causes the skin to stay pinched up for a while and not flatten. The longer it takes his skin to flatten out, the more dehydrated your ferret is.

REMEMBER

Older ferrets or ferrets with adrenal gland disease lose a good amount of elasticity in their skin. In other words, their skin doesn't quickly snap back into place. Because of this, you may get a false result with the previous test, leading you to think your fuzzy is dehydrated. If your fuzzy is older or has adrenal gland disease, always look for the other signs of dehydration as well.

The immediate solution is to get fluids back into your ferret and get to your vet's office (or an emergency hospital) as soon as possible. By the time you determine your ferret is dehydrated, the situation has become an emergency and requires a trip to your vet. All supportive measures simply help stabilize your ferret until you can get him to professional help. To start, encourage your fuzzy to drink extra water or unflavored Pedialyte, and it gets the added benefit of consuming extra electrolytes with Pedialyte. Some people believe that warm chicken broth encourages drinking.

TIP

If your fuzzy refuses to drink at all, use a feeding syringe or an eyedropper to feed him the liquid. Hold your ferret in a normal standing position; don't tip him on his back. Be careful not to force too much liquid or squirt too quickly because he can choke.

Getting enough fluids into a dehydrated ferret is difficult. Often, a vet needs to administer extra fluids subcutaneously (under the skin) or intravenously (IV directly into the vein). Always take your ferret to the vet for treatment so you can find out what's making your ferret ill in the first place. Treating the underlying illness often prevents future bouts of dehydration.

Bleeding

Ferrets don't have very much blood in their bodies, so any wound that bleeds profusely requires immediate medical attention. The following sections show you how to begin treatment for common bleeding injuries; after you complete your initial treatment, all wounds or injuries should be looked at by a veterinarian as soon as possible, no matter the degree of the injury.

Bleeding from the ears, nose, mouth, rectum, or vaginal area is usually a sign of serious illness or injury. If you notice bleeding from one of these sources, visit your vet immediately or call a pet emergency hotline if your vet isn't available.

Treating injured nails

The most common source of ferret bleeding is a toenail that's cut too close to the quick (the pink, veined area of the nail). It's quite painful for your ferret; you'll hear him let out a series of small screeches to let you know that you screwed up. Here's how you can fix the mistake:

1. **Talk to him softly and hold him cautiously to inspect the damage (see Chapter 20 for tips on holding a potentially aggressive fuzzy).**

2. **Apply a small amount of styptic powder (or even cornstarch, beeswax, or white soap) with your finger to the tip of the bleeding nail.**

3. **Press hard for a moment and then release your finger.**

4. **If the nail is still bleeding, repeat Steps 2 and 3. Repeat several times if necessary.**

Styptic powder burns, and you may tick off your ferret, so be careful. Get the powder off your finger quickly because it will burn you, too.

A painless alternative to styptic powder is beeswax. Some people suggest pressing the nail into a bar of white soap (preferably a mild one). Other owners use cornstarch, baking soda, or flour to stop nail bleeding. These remedies may take longer to work, but you won't put your ferret in any more pain.

Seek veterinary care as soon as possible if your fuzzy suffers more than just a closely clipped nail; otherwise, the area may become infected. If the nail has been torn off, don't use powder to treat the injury. Rather, immediately apply pressure to the top of the toe, not on the toe tip, and seek veterinary attention right away. The blood will eventually clot on its own. Torn claws may need to be removed completely and require stitches, but that's a worst-case scenario.

Treating cuts

A laceration on your ferret can be serious. He may need a more extensive exam, stitches, and/or antibiotics to treat the injury, but that should come immediately after you provide initial care to your fuzzy's boo-boo. Remember, ferrets don't have a lot of blood to lose, so act fast! Follow these steps:

1. **Gently wash the laceration with cold water.**

2. **Apply gentle but firm pressure on the wound.**

Using something clean and dry is important — gauze or a clean washcloth, for instance.

3. **If possible, wrap the area with gauze and then use self-stick wrap to secure it to the wound.**

Wrapping may not be possible, however, depending on where the wound is.

Make sure that the wrap isn't too tight. Depending on the cause of the cut, your ferret may also be suffering from internal injuries that you can't see.

REMEMBER

4. **Head to the vet if the laceration is wide, deep, or appears red or irritated.**

A wound that won't stop bleeding needs immediate vet attention.

Vomiting

Vomiting can occur for several reasons, ranging from ingesting bad food, to an infection of the gastrointestinal (GI) tract, to an intestinal blockage. Keep a close eye on your vomiting ferret. Signs your ferret is about to vomit include excess saliva production, pawing at the mouth, and licking his lips. Sometimes, a small piece of ingested material will come up with vomit, and then the vomiting will stop. But if your fuzzy vomits repeatedly and shows the following symptoms, he possibly has an intestinal blockage:

>> Can't hold down his food

>> Shows no interest in food

>> Becomes depressed and lethargic

The only way to treat a blockage is to remove the object surgically. Not doing so may spell death for your ferret. Get to a vet as soon as possible!

People often swap the terms *vomit* and *regurgitate* back and forth, perhaps because the actions look the same to the undiscerning eye. In fact, they are two very different processes, and may have very different medical causes. Impress your vet by knowing the difference! *Vomiting* is an "active" involuntary process in which contents from the stomach and upper part of the intestines are forcefully ejected through the ferret's mouth. It may contain yellowish or greenish bile, phlegm, or partially digested food, and is usually accompanied by retching and abdominal muscle contractions. If you've ever had a cat or dog, this is the noise that has you leaping out of bed from a dead sleep to clumsily intervene. On the other hand, *regurgitation*, although equally gross, is typically a passive but involuntary process in which ingested goodies move backwards from the esophagus to the mouth or nose. It usually consists of undigested food, hair, mucus, and saliva. *Regurgitation* is not at all common in ferrets. In fact, it may even be a rare congenital or inherited condition. Some esophageal tract conditions can be the cause of *regurgitation*, as well as things such as foreign bodies, cancer, muscle disease, or poisoning.

Diarrhea (and other fecal issues)

Short bouts of infrequent diarrhea are quite common in ferrets. How can you tell if you're dealing with diarrhea? A ferret's normal stool is slightly soft but formed. Diarrhea is more liquid in form, and your ferret shows a higher frequency of pooping.

The cause of diarrhea can be very difficult to diagnose. The cause can be as simple as your ferret indulging in one too many treats (hey, we've all been there). Diarrhea can also be a sign of underlying diseases or illnesses or can result from changes in diet. An underlying condition may be easy to correct (influenza, for example) or difficult (eosinophilic gastroenteritis, for instance). But no matter what the cause, diarrhea can become life-threatening because your fuzzy is losing precious fluids and not absorbing all his food. You need to get treatment immediately and get to the bottom of the cause.

Diarrhea is cause for alarm if it becomes serious and frequent (lasts for more than a day). If your fuzzy's diarrhea persists, take him and a sample of some fresh liquidy poop to the vet immediately so she can rule out all the nasty things your fuzzy may have. The treatment may be as simple as daily doses of Pepcid and electrolyte-replacing fluids, but let your vet decide. A professional can learn a lot just from looking at a ferret's poop! Table 13-1 goes through the many properties a sick fuzzy's poop can have and lists the possible conditions associated with them. Be on the lookout!

To check for lower GI blood in your ferret's poop to be sure, take a poop sample and put it in a piece of gauze. Soak the gauze in warm water. If blood is in the stool, the water will turn red, and you'll see the color against the white gauze.

TABLE 13-1   **Poop and Possible Related Conditions**

Type of Poop	Possible Malady
Spaghetti-thin poop	Partial obstruction by a foreign body.
Green poop	A non-specific type of poop. The food possibly is moving too fast through the digestive tract, and the poop is green because the food isn't broken all the way down, It may not necessarily be cause for immediate concern. Anything that causes rapid passage or diarrhea can cause green poop — disease, food changes, stress, ECE (see Chapter 16), and so on.
Bloody poop	Fresh, bright-red blood usually comes from the lower intestine or rectum. Large amounts of blood may indicate a massive hemorrhage from the entire length of the GI tract.
Mucousy poop	One or two mucousy poops is nothing to concern yourself over. Simple things such as diet change or an acute stress reaction may cause this. However, the presence of consistent mucousy poops is something to talk to your vet about. Inflammatory bowel disease (IBD) or something equally sinister may be at play here and will need medical intervention.
Bubbly poop	Sometimes a bacterial overgrowth in the colon will cause a foul-smelling bubbly or foamy poop, which will require a visit to the vet. Make note, however, if your ferret has had a change in diet, is stressed, or is on a new medication, all of which may also cause bubbly poop.
Watery poop	This liquidy poop might not be cause for worry if it just happens once or twice, but anything more should be considered diarrhea and may lead to dehydration in your ferret. Caused when the food moves so quickly through the digestive tract that the colon doesn't have a chance to reabsorb the water in the food. Possible cases are stress and underlying illness.
Seedy poop	A non-specific type of poop. Malabsorption or maldigestion is taking place, meaning that digestion or absorption isn't happening the way it should. The seedy material is undigested fat and starch complexes. Seedy or "birdseed" poop can accompany any disease that seriously affects the small intestine. Low-quality ferret diets that are high in plant protein as opposed to animal protein may cause seedy poop, because the ferrets can't digest all the plant protein and starches. If you feed raw food that includes bone, you may see small pieces of bone matter in your ferret's poop. This often gives the poop a seedy looking appearance. This can be normal depending on what your ferret is fed.
Black, tarry poop	Results from gastric bleeding or gastric ulcers. The black color comes from the digestion of the blood, which occurs in the stomach. Significant bleeding in the stomach must be present in order for the ferret's poop to turn black. Another reason for black, tarry poop may be due to high iron and blood content in certain organs, such as liver and heart, fed to your ferret if you happen to feed a more natural diet.
White or chalky poop	Light colored or white poop may be the product of ferrets that are fed a natural diet high in bone material(s). If the poop is too white, your ferret may be getting too much calcium or bone.
Yellow or tan poop	Egg poo! Not only are the poops of ferrets fed raw eggs (yolks) squishy and poorly formed, they are frequently tan or yellow in color. This is the case even if you feed your ferrets other meats with the eggs.

In the case of treating severe diarrhea, your vet will request a complete history of your ferret in order to diagnose the cause. Be prepared to report the following:

>> The age of the ferret

>> How the ferret is living and with whom

>> The extent and duration of his symptoms

>> His current and past diet history

>> Other significant information you can readily give

Your vet may also want to perform blood tests, X-rays, or biopsies of the intestinal tract to help hone in on a proper diagnosis. Your vet will likely treat your ferret immediately for dehydration and may provide additional nutritional support before moving on to a treatment based on the diagnosis and the severity of the condition.

Seizures

A *seizure* occurs when the electrical impulses in the ferret's brain misfire. It can last from seconds to a few minutes and is a very scary thing to witness. Some seizures can occur very quietly and go unnoticed, but the majority involve the involuntary thrashing about of the limbs in combination with any of the following:

>> Loss of bladder/bowel control

>> Salivating

>> Vomiting

>> Involuntary vocalizations

REMEMBER

Seizures can be a sign of many different underlying conditions, from hypoglycemia (low blood sugar) to poisoning. They always merit a trip to the veterinarian's office immediately afterward, because you need to find the underlying cause and do everything you can to prevent future seizures.

I would only move a ferret if it's in a place that's dangerous. If he's already on the floor, leave him alone. In moving him, you may prolong the seizure or get yourself bitten. It's better to cover him with a light towel or washcloth to block out the light, which is a stimulus. Covering him to keep him dark may decrease the length of the seizure. Keep your fingers, pens, wallet, and any other objects away from your ferret's mouth when he's in the middle of the seizure and shoo away other ferrets and pets. If you have your wits about you, try to time the incident for future reference. (*Note:* Neither people nor ferrets have the ability to swallow their tongues during a seizure. That's a myth.)

WARNING

A ferret isn't in pain during a seizure, even if he's crying out. He's essentially unconscious and his body is going through involuntary muscle spasms. Don't try to hold your ferret down during a seizure. Restraining him can cause further injury — to him and to you. He may inadvertently and seriously bite you without even knowing what's going on around him. Because the jaws of a seizing animal/person clamp tightly shut, anything that gets in the way gets bitten severely. Also, restraining him is stimulating and may increase the length of the seizure.

In the end, you'll have a very wiped-out ferret. When your ferret's seizure ends, keep him calm, warm, and quiet. He'll be confused and shaken. You can offer him a little soft food, such as a high-protein canned food or meat baby food, to stabilize his blood sugar. If your ferret isn't feeling up to licking from a spoon or off a plate, offer the food from a feeding syringe. From start to finish, the ferret needs about 30 to 40 minutes to recover from the seizure, but get your ferret into the vet as soon as possible after the seizure ends. Seizures may cause irreversible brain damage, and the longer the seizure lasts, the more frequent the seizures become. Don't wait until morning to get to the vet. Find a 24-hour emergency vet even if the drive is farther and the cost is more. Your ferret depends on you!

Heatstroke

Ferrets are extremely susceptible to heatstroke — especially in temperatures above 80 degrees Fahrenheit. A heatstroke can quickly kill your ferret if you don't provide treatment immediately. Signs of heatstroke include

>> Heavy panting

>> Mucous coming from the nose or mouth

>> Extreme lethargy or limpness

>> Seizures

>> Loss of consciousness

Your main objective is to lower the ferret's body temperature slowly. A gradual decrease in body temperature is necessary to prevent shock. (A rapid decrease in body temperature can be as deadly as heatstroke itself.) First, get the ferret out of the sun and heat and give him water to drink. If you have an electrolyte-replacing drink, such as unflavored Pedialyte, use it if your ferret will drink it.

If your ferret is unconscious, don't try to get any liquid or food into his mouth, because he can choke. Just keep him cool and provide first aid until you can get him to the vet.

After you remove fuzzy from the heat and get some fluids in him, you can slowly lower his body temperature in many different ways:

>> Apply cool (not cold) water to body areas with less fur — the groin, lower stomach, and the feet, for example. You can place a wet washcloth on the key areas. The evaporation of the water on the skin cools the body and lowers his temperature.

>> Place your fuzzy directly in shallow, room-temperature water, keeping his head and the top half of his body above water. Don't submerge him in cold water because the shock of doing so can kill him.

>> Apply rubbing alcohol to his feet only, making sure not to miss his paw pads. You also can rub ice cubes on the ferret's feet.

>> Place the ferret in front of a fan. This method isn't as effective as the others, but it's better than nothing in an emergency situation.

No matter how you think your ferret is weathering the situation and responding to your treatment, get him to the vet as soon as possible. Often, the vet will give a ferret additional fluids to make up for those lost during the heatstroke. She may also recommend additional medications or other home support.

Take extra precautions in the warmer months to prevent heatstroke. Don't leave your ferret in a closed-up, hot car. Keep your ferret and his carrier out of direct sunlight, and be sure to give him extra water. If you take your ferret outside during the very warm months, bring along a bottle or two of frozen water. Wrap the bottles in towels and keep them in the carrier or cage.

Hypothermia

Hypothermia is a potentially fatal condition where the body's temperature drops below the level required for normal functioning of the internal organs. Some animals are more prone to hypothermia than others: Very young and very old ferrets, small ferrets with short hair, ferrets with no shelter in cold weather, wet ferrets, and ferrets undergoing surgical procedures. Signs of hypothermia include

>> Shivering (which often becomes violent)

>> Cool skin or skin cold to the touch

- » Slow, shallow breathing

- » Lethargy

- » Unresponsiveness

The hypothermic ferret needs immediate help from you to return his body temperature to normal. Depending on the duration and severity of the condition, tissue damage may already have occurred, so hypothermic ferrets should be warmed up very slowly. The following list presents some ways to accomplish this:

- » Run dry towels through the dryer to warm them up, and then wrap your ferret in the warm towels.

WARNING

A severely hypothermic ferret will be listless and unresponsive and therefore unable to move away from heat that you provide. Exercise extreme caution when you provide heat for a ferret so that you prevent burns. What feels warm to you may actually feel scorching to a ferret. Monitor the use of heat closely and keep watch over your ailing ferret to gauge his reactions.

- » If your ferret is wet, use a hair dryer on the low setting to dry him and warm him up.

- » Fill empty bottles, such as soda bottles, with warm water, wrap them in dish towels, and place them against your ferret's skin. The best placement is where your fuzzy has less fur, such as the armpit or the groin area. *Never* put an uncovered bottle against the ferret's skin; it may burn him.

- » Warm a heating pad on the low setting, place a towel over it, lay your ferret on top of it, and then cover him with a warm towel.

WARNING

Heating pads can be dangerous because they're the most common cause of overheating. Never leave your ferret unattended on a heating pad, and always keep checking the temperature of the pad and your ferret.

- » Grab some sealable plastic baggies or socks and fill them with uncooked rice or lentils. Warm them in the microwave for one to two minutes, wrap them in a towel, and place them on areas with little fur.

WARNING

When you come inside from extreme cold, it's hard to ignore how painful your fingers and toes are. Well, a severely hypothermic ferret may experience similar pain as his tissues warm up. As a result, he may bite or scratch at the areas and may even bite you in his time of discomfort. Be extra cautious when handling the fuzzy (see Chapter 20).

While your ferret is warming up, call your vet to discuss what else you should do. She may want to see your ferret for further examination. Additional veterinary care may include administering warm fluids intravenously and giving oxygen.

TIP

Lethargy and unresponsiveness also are common signs of hypoglycemia that goes along with insulinoma. It isn't uncommon for a hypoglycemic ferret to become hypothermic. If this situation happens with your fuzzy, take steps to warm him up, and if he's conscious and can swallow, give him a small amount of honey or sugar mixed with a little warm water. If he's unconscious, gently rub honey or sugar water on his gums. These actions may just save his life! Remember: This is a last-resort action!

Eye injuries

Ferrets can get very rough when playing with each other, and they can get into a lot of trouble on their own. Eye injuries aren't beyond the ferret injury realm. If your ferret receives a scratch to an eye, flush out the eye with cool water or a sterile saline solution. Any eye injury requires the attention of an experienced ferret vet, so waste no time getting there after flushing the eye.

REMEMBER

If you suspect that your fuzzy has foreign matter in his eye, such as litter or sand — which you can tell by a watery and squinty eye that lasts for more than an hour or so — don't apply pressure to the affected eye. Doing so can cause the particle to inflict further damage. Simply flush the eye and call your vet for instructions on how to proceed until you can get to the office.

Fractures or spinal injuries

Ferrets are extremely flexible and resilient, but occasionally bone injuries occur after a fall, after getting pounced on by a dog or child, or while getting folded up in a piece of furniture, for instance. If your ferret has a broken bone or an injured spine, he may be showing the following symptoms:

>> Limping

>> Showing resistance to moving

>> Dragging a leg or holding one up

>> Dragging his entire back end

Sometimes, it's hard to recognize a break without an actual X-ray, so a trip to the vet is necessary. The best course of action is to keep your ferret immobile and quiet while you seek immediate medical attention. Don't try to fix anything on your own. Place your ferret in a small carrier and keep him warm during the trip.

TIP

If you suspect his spine is injured, be extremely cautious. Spinal injuries can be devastating, if not fatal, so keep the ferret as still as possible in his small carrier. Wrap his body in a towel and get him to the vet immediately.

Poisoning

The world is a scary place for ferrets; even your home can be a source of harm. Most homes contain funky chemicals and cleaners, half of which humans don't remember storing. These chemicals and cleaners are poisonous to the little fuzzy. The most commonly encountered ferret poisons are rat poison and Tylenol. When your ferret finds and ingests these things, disaster ensues. Poisoning can also occur if you accidentally overdose your ferret on a prescribed medication.

Signs of poisoning include

>> Vomiting

>> Salivating

>> Pawing at the mouth

>> Diarrhea

>> Lethargy

>> Sudden weakness

>> Seizures

>> Unconsciousness

>> An overturned chemical bottle or chewed up cleaner container (okay, so not a symptom, but definitely a warning signal)

If you suspect that your ferret has ingested something poisonous or has taken too much medicine, take him and the suspected substance to your vet immediately. Try to figure out how much he ingested and how long ago so you can tell the vet. Treatment depends on the ingested substance. It can range from induced vomiting to medication. Only your vet will know the proper course of action.

Keep the following numbers close at hand and make sure that your vet has them for reference.

>> **National Animal Poison Control Center:** You can reach this nonprofit agency run by the ASPCA at 888-426-4435. The service costs $75 per case and accepts credit cards only.

>> **Pet Poison Hotline:** Another 24/7/365 service available throughout the United States, Canada, and the Caribbean. Initial consultation costs $59, and they can be reached at 855-767-7661.

Animal bites

People who own ferrets often have other animals in their homes. If you live in this type of home, you need to limit and monitor pet interactions closely to avoid bouts of aggression. If your ferret gets bitten by another household pet, wash his wound lightly with cold water and gently dab the area with hydrogen peroxide. If the wound is bleeding, apply pressure to slow the bleeding and get him to the vet immediately.

WARNING

Cat bites are particularly dangerous to both people and ferrets due to the amount of bacteria in cat saliva. Often, cat bites require special antibiotics. If your kitty bites your fuzzy, make an extra-quick trip to the vet.

If a neighbor's pet, a stray, or a wild animal bites your ferret, take him to the vet right away. If you know the animal that bit your fuzzy, find out if it's up to date on its rabies vaccination first. Although the incidence is extremely low and unlikely, your ferret can contract rabies from an infected animal. Prevention is the key. Watch your ferret closely for changes in behavior and report them to the vet. (For information on rabies vaccine and prevention, see Chapter 12.)

Electric shock

An electric shock can be severe enough to kill your little fuzzy. Electric shock is usually the result of a fuzzy chewing on electrical cords, which is why you need to keep cords in your home far out of your ferret's reach (see Chapter 6 for info on ferret-proofing your house). Be aware that chewed cords can also cause a fire. Check your home regularly for and replace any frayed or bitten electrical cords.

There's very little you can do for a ferret that's experienced electric shock except keep him warm and quiet until you can get him to the veterinarian. If he's lucky enough to survive, you can be almost certain he'll suffer damage to his teeth, gums, and mouth. You and your vet will then proceed with the proper treatment program for his injuries. Trust me, prevention is much easier on both of you!

Burns

Sometimes carpet sharks get into things they shouldn't (actually, more often than sometimes). It isn't their fault; it's in their nature. One serious side effect of this curiosity, burns, occurs because owners aren't paying close enough attention and allow the fuzzies to venture into unsafe territory. Burns can come from getting too close to fireplaces, cigarettes, ovens, and even pilot lights. Bathing your ferret in extremely hot water can also scald him. If your ferret suffers a burn, immediately apply cold water directly to the burned area. And if you can, apply an ice pack for no more than five minutes. After this initial treatment, get your ferret to the vet immediately.

Blockage protocol

Ferrets are notorious for eating things they have no business eating! This can lead them straight into serious trouble or have them knocking at death's door. If you see your ferret snarf down one of your favorite earbuds left on the side table, the following simple procedure may help you ward off tragedy. All you need is a can of pure pumpkin puree (*not* pie filling) and a jar of Vaseline or 100-percent petroleum jelly. *Note:* This method should only be used in emergencies:

1. **Feed your ferret 1 tablespoon of pumpkin puree immediately after the ingestion of the foreign body.**

   Remember, this is a high-carb food, so it should not be fed to your carnivorous ferret on a regular basis or in excess.

2. *One hour later,* **feed your ferret 1 teaspoon of Vaseline, which may be flavored with salmon oil to make it more palatable.**

3. **Repeat process for two to three hours. Within four hours, your ferret will hopefully present for you beautifully orange shaded poops, one of which should contain your once treasured, haphazardly ingested object.**

4. **When you see the object has passed, continue feeding 1 teaspoon of pumpkin to your naughty ferret for three to four days. This ensures that any remaining bits and pieces also make their way out the other end!**

It should also be noted that using the blockage protocol isn't 100 percent effective in all cases, and you should always be on the lookout for signs that your ferret isn't responding favorably. If your ferret begins to vomit or becomes severely lethargic or depressed, it's likely a sign that he has a total blockage, which needs immediate veterinarian intervention. If a vet-administered barium X-ray doesn't move the blockage along, the only way to save your ferret's life is through immediate surgery.

Chapter **14**

Ferreting Out Ferret Pests

Simply put, a *parasite* is an organism (or person) that feeds off another organism (or person) without giving anything back. You may even know one or two personally! Every living being is host to a parasite party or two — or maybe a hundred. Parasites come in all shapes and sizes. Some are internal, and some are external. Some are harmless and hardly noticeable; others can be quite damaging and difficult to miss.

This chapter deals specifically with external and internal pests that can bug the heck out of your fuzzy. I list these parasites and their warning signs and give you tips on keeping your fuzzy critter-free. I also shed some light on parasites, diseases, and germs that can affect both humans and their better halves, the carpet sharks.

Booting External Critters That Go Bite in the Night

They're ruthless and always hungry. Under a microscope, they look a bit like creepy prehistoric monsters. They're external parasites. Can anything be more annoying to the pet and pet owner than external parasites? Nothing that I know of.

These incredibly sturdy little ectoparasites need little to survive, and unfortunately, you and your ferret can be hosts to these ungrateful diners. In the sections that follow, I introduce many common external parasites that you must combat, and I give you the ammunition to kick them off your and your fuzzy's dinner table — namely, your skin.

Fleas

Fleas are the most common external parasites seen on ferrets. They spend most of their time building flea resorts in your rugs and couches and in any other cozy place they can find. One such cozy place is in your fuzzy's coat. Ferrets are just as prone to flea infestations as Fidos and Tabbys. But before you can safely rid your domain of these blood-sucking pests and prevent them from turning your frisky ferret into an illing itchy, you need to know what kind of army you're dealing with:

>> **Fleas are messy guests.** The act of feasting on your pet's warm blood triggers the female flea to lay thousands of eggs all over your home. Sometimes, you may observe a flea scurrying across its dinner table: your pet. More likely, you'll see only the end results of the flea's wild parties: the "flea dirt" left on the skin of your pet. This "dirt" is actually flea waste, which looks like tiny specks of reddish-black sand.

>> **Fleas are opportunistic little buggers.** Where there is wildlife, there are fleas. And plenty of them. Fleas can hitchhike right into your home on other pets, and although they can't live on humans, they can hitch a ride on your clothing or a picnic blanket, perhaps. And don't forget about the greatly appreciated, supervised trips your ferret takes to the wonderful outdoors. Through no fault of her own, your ferret may bring fleas into your house.

>> **Fleas love warm, humid places.** Fleas seek all warm-blooded victims. Although it may be warm and humid for only several months a year where you live, your battle against fleas is year round.

WARNING

Fleas can be more than a mere nuisance. A severe flea infestation can cause life-threatening anemia (a reduction in red blood cells, causing fatigue and weakness) in your ferret. Fleas also can carry parasites such as tapeworms and pass them along to your fuzzy. The bottom line: If your ferret has fleas, so do your other warm-blooded pets, and you need to get rid of them as soon as possible.

The following sections let you know how to check for these annoying critters and give you steps to take to free your home from their terrible reign.

Checking for fleas

Some indications of a flea infestation include small bites (tiny, red raised marks) or reddened areas or lesions on the skin due to plenty of scratching. Severe infestations may bring poor fur quality, thinning patches of fur, and fur discoloration. You may find yourself suffering some of the same scratching effects; don't be surprised if you have some bites around your feet and ankles if the infestation is severe (fleas can jump over 100 times their body length). Herein lies one of the biggest problems with fleas: Their tiny bites are painfully itchy. To a flea-allergic pet, the situation can be almost unbearable as she scratches out her skin and her underbelly becomes irritated.

To check your fuzzy for fleas, ruffle back her fur with your hands and examine her skin closely — particularly the belly. You should also inspect your ferret's bedding and change it often. You can shake out her towels or other bedding onto a white floor or a piece of paper and then distinguish the specks of kitty litter from the flea dirt.

Ridding your ferret and home of fleas

After you discover that fleas have invaded your home, you need to act to get rid of them as quickly as you can. The steps in the following sections give you the how-to. Before you treat your ferret for fleas, however, keep the following points in mind:

>> **If one of your pets has fleas, all your pets have fleas.** If you have several pets, you must treat them all, whether or not you see evidence of fleas on each one.

>> **What's safe for a dog may kill your ferret.** Controls such as sprays, dips, and flea collars aren't meant for fuzzies. Ferrets are hypersensitive to most of these products — particularly organophosphate pesticides. Even "ferret-safe" products can be harmful to a sick, geriatric, young (under 12 weeks old), or nursing ferret.

>> **You should consult with a veterinarian before applying any flea product on your ferret (or any pet, for that matter).** Your vet will make sure the product is safe and that your pet is healthy enough to withstand chemical treatment.

WARNING

With so many flea products on the market today, it's easy to get confused when it comes time to pick the best one for your ferret. Here's what you need to know while you're shopping. The following flea-treatment products are "toxic" to your ferret: Essential oils, Hartz, petroleum distillates, pyrethrins, flea collars, flea powders, permethrin, organophosphates, Biospot, flea dips, flea sprays, carbamates, and Defense. The good news is there are several good products currently available to use on your ferret including Advantage II for Small Cats, Advantage II for Ferrets (Over 1 lb), Advantage Multi, Frontline, and Revolution.

STEP 1: TREAT YOUR FERRET

To rid your ferret and home of fleas, begin simply by bathing your ferret with a safe, mild pet shampoo, such as oatmeal. Follow these steps:

1. **Gently bathe your ferret from head to toe — and remember the tail (tails have fleas, too).**

   Refer to Chapter 9 for detailed information on bathing your ferret. Here are some highlights: Don't forget your goggles, snorkel, and shoulder-length rubber gloves, and remember to prevent the shampoo from getting into the eyes, nose, mouth, and ears.

2. **Move the fuzzy to a warm, dry, flea-free place before you tackle her cage.**

   A travel carrier works well in times like these. After all, putting a squeaky-clean furball into a flea-infested cage doesn't make much sense.

WARNING

Not all shampoos are alike, and you'll want something ferret-safe and very mild. Oatmeal baths are preferred when possible. Avoid human shampoos, dog and cat shampoos, and dish soaps (which aren't even shampoos at all). I bring up dish soap because Dawn dish soap (see Chapter 9) is frequently recommended in the pet community for flea treatment. This chemical-dense product is harsh on your ferret's skin and fur, and may also be toxic. Not approved by this author!

TIP

Many ferret-safe commercial flea shampoos are available, but the chemicals contained in some of these products are concerning and may adversely affect your ferret's health. Additionally, flea-specific shampoos tend to dry out the ferret's skin and don't provide residual protection against fleas. Using a mild shampoo such as oatmeal removes flea dirt and soothes irritated skin. Although it won't kill existing fleas, it will wash many down the drain during the rinse cycle, and you'll be able to apply one of the ferret-safe topical spot-ons the very next day.

STEP 2: TREAT YOUR FERRET'S CAGE, BEDDING, AND OTHER STUFF

When your ferret is bathed, you're ready to tackle her cage and bedding. (*Note:* You have to do the same with your other pet stuff, too.) Follow these steps to treat these fuzzy fixtures:

1. **Remove all bedding from the cage and machine wash it in hot, soapy water.**

   If you prefer, you can place it in a sealed plastic bag and throw it away.

TIP

   Flea-treat all ferret bedding immediately before or after the ferret is bathed. Putting your newly bathed ferret into a cage with soiled, flea-infested bedding just annuls everything you've just done.

2. **Scrub the cage thoroughly with hot, soapy water and then dry.**

STEP 3: TREAT YOUR HOME

The third step — treating your entire home — is probably the most inconvenient and time-consuming of all the steps, and also it must be in complete conjunction with treating your ferret and its bedding. You may have killed the fleas on your ferret and the eggs on her bedding, but thousands of eggs may be getting ready to hatch all over your house, including in the baseboards, carpeting, and furniture.

You have several options for treating your home for fleas. The easiest way is to hire a professional exterminator. Other hands-on methods are foggers, sprays, and powders that you apply. As you decide what method to use, keep in mind that ferrets are remarkably sensitive to chemicals, so choose the safest and most natural method whenever possible. And always follow product directions when going it alone.

Before treating the environment with sprays or powders, it's imperative that you completely remove all your pets, including your ferret (and her cage/toys/bowls), from the premises until everything settles and dries. It isn't good for your ferret to be walking through wet sprays or having the powders settling on her body/stuff. Nor is it healthy for her to inhale the chemicals. Follow the directions on the bottles/can before returning your pet to your home.

REMEMBER

Because most commercial flea-killing products don't successfully kill all the eggs, larvae, and pupae, you may need to repeat this step 7 to 21 days after the first treatment, depending on which product you use. Make sure you seek out the advice of an expert.

STEP 4: STOP FLEAS FROM COMING BACK

You must make a regular effort to prevent reinfestation after you take the first few steps to treat for fleas. Here are some general suggestions:

>> Keep your pet's environment clean by vacuuming and scrubbing regularly.

>> Empty the vacuum bag after vacuuming each time, because fleas can survive in the bag and continue to lay eggs. The babies will hatch and leave the vacuum.

Worried about those pesky fleas hatching in your vacuum cleaner? Although flea collars aren't advised for use on your ferret — *ever* — you can cut one or two flea collars up and put the pieces in your vacuum cleaner bag or canister. Upon contact with the collar pieces, the fleas should soon die and not escape the vacuum.

>> Inspect and de-flea all incoming pets before they enter your home.

>> Treat your ferret regularly with one of the *monthly* ferret-safe spot-ons.

>> Treat all of your dogs and cats on a monthly basis with a safe flea preventative.

The following list presents products that you should use only in conjunction with your vet's blessing:

>> **Advantage II for Ferrets and also Advantage II for Small Cats (Bayer):** Both of these topical flea treatments are made with the ingredients imidaclo-prid and pyriproxyfen, and they kill fleas in all life stages. Not only do they begin working in 12 hours, but they also become waterproof after 24 hours of application.

The imidacloprid spreads evenly across your ferret's skin and coats the fleas through direct contact to provide full-body coverage. Imidacloprid attacks the flea's nervous system. Fleas die without having to ingest the imidacloprid by means of biting your poor ferret. Pyriproxyfen, however, is an insect growth regulator that attacks mostly young insects and insect eggs. Pyriproxyfen in effect mimics a natural hormone in insects and disrupts their growth.

>> **Advantage Multi for Cats (Bayer):** Made with the ingredients imidacloprid and moxidectin, Advantage Multi for Cats not only kills adult fleas and helps prevent future flea infestations, but it also aids in the prevention of heart-worms. It should be pointed out that Advantage Multi for Cats (0.4 mL size only) is the only drug that is FDA-approved to prevent heartworm in ferrets. At the time of this writing, there is no FDA-approved drug to treat heartworm disease in ferrets.

Applying a small amount of the liquid directly on the skin at the base of your ferret's skull provides up to 28 days of protection. The imidacloprid works the same way in this product as it does in other Advantage products. Moxidectin gets quickly absorbed through the skin into the subcutaneous fat and then moves into the bloodstream to prevent heartworm. Monthly applications are advised to protect against newly hatching fleas. Reapplication is recom-mended after bathing, but your ferret should receive no more than one application per week.

>> **Frontline Plus (Merial):** This product is made with the active ingredients fipronil, which paralyzes and kills adult fleas and ticks, and methoprene, which is an insect growth regulator. Methoprene also disrupts the normal levels of growth hormone, which makes the juvenile fleas stop growing, prevents the molting stage, and thus causes the death of the young flea. It's designed to be continually released onto the ferret's skin and fur for at least one full month after initial application.

Frontline Plus becomes waterproof two days after application; therefore, don't bathe your ferret during this period. If you must bathe your ferret before applying the product, wait at least five days after the bath before applying Frontline Plus.

It should be noted that Frontline (and its ingredients) were one of the first of the modern flea preventatives. As such, insects, such as fleas, become resistant over time. If you choose Frontline Plus as your go-to flea prevention and find that it's not helping, bathe your little guy thoroughly, wait a few days and apply a different topical product.

>> **Revolution Plus (Pfizer):** Made with the active ingredients selamectin and sarolaner, Revolution Plus is a topically applied product that prevents heartworm, kills adult fleas, prevents flea eggs from hatching, and treats and controls ear mite infestation. It also treats and controls sarcoptic mange and kills ticks. Selemectin is a member of the avermectin group of parasiticides, which to make a long complicated process understandable, paralyzes the internal or external parasites' nervous systems, causing death. Fleas are said to begin to die within 12 hours, and over 98 percent are typically dead within 24 hours of administration. Sarolaner is a member of the isoxazoline parasiticides. Both of these parasiticides kill fleas, mites, and lice, but by adding the sarolaner, this product has the benefit of tick killing power!

Revolution Plus has a very low adverse-reaction rate, and when compared to other products on the market, Revolution Plus has the broadest spectrum of prevention and treatment of parasites.

The wonderful thing about these products is that they kill the fleas before they lay eggs. If you stick with one of the appropriate monthly flea products with all your pets, chances are you won't often (if ever) need to go through the frenzied treatment process I describe in the previous sections.

TIP

Diatomaceous earth, or DE, has often been used to kill external parasites, such as fleas, in the captively kept animal world. So, how does it fit into ferret husbandry? DE, a powder which consists of silica and traces of other minerals, is only effective when it is dry. The jagged edges of each fine powdery particle, like shards of glass, can cause irritation to certain surfaces, and especially to the respiratory system of our sensitive ferret. Fleas and other insects that come into contact with DE dry up and die as the abrasive, clingy particles cause extensive damage to their exoskel-etons and suck the moisture from their bodies. Some flea larvae may be killed in the process, as well. However, DE does not affect flea eggs or flea pupae. The use of DE should be done with caution, and your ferret should not be allowed to play on carpet on which DE is sprinkled. Also, since DE has drying properties, it is advised not to use this directly on your pet, as it could cause dry fur and skin issues. Here are some helpful tips:

>> Purchase diatomaceous earth (you will want *food grade*, as opposed to filter grade, the latter which may be hazardous to your pet's health)

>> Wear gloves (protection from drying effects) and a mask (protection from respiratory irritation)

>> As a scoop and spreader, use a colander or pasta strainer with a handle, and tackle your flea infestation by sprinkling DE all over your home. Do not neglect baseboards, dog beds, carpets, rugs, hardwood floors, and upholstery.

>> Although inconvenient and somewhat messy, you should allow the DE to settle for at least three days, and remember not to let your ferret play where the DE is sprinkled.

>> This may kill your vacuum filter, or it may not, but after the allotted time is up, thoroughly vacuum up the DE and then empty your vacuum canister or bag.

Ticks

Ticks look like tiny brown crabs. When filled with blood, they resemble a raised mole on the skin. Ticks will appear without warning. They don't generally occur as an infestation, but rather as a single incident; perhaps you'll find up to several at a time if your ferret has been walking through infested brush areas. You should always check for ticks carefully after walks. The ticks may be flat, attached, but not yet filled with blood. Or they may be attached and already starting to fill up.

Here are a couple things to know about ticks:

>> Finding ticks can be difficult. You must feel beneath the fur for the tiny lumps. Ears are also great hiding spots for ticks.

>> Ticks can harbor some diseases, including Lyme disease, that can affect both humans and other animals. Some topical spot-on products, such as Revolution Plus and Frontline Plus, which are used to control fleas, are also effective in killing ticks.

Fortunately, although they're perhaps not for the squeamish, ticks are relatively easy to deal with. If you find one hitched to your fuzzy's skin, follow these steps:

1. **Using a pair of pointed — not squared off — tweezers or forceps (or even a *tick hook* — Google it!), grab the tick as close to the ferret's skin as possible.**

2. **Gently pull up, slowly and firmly, removing the tick, and making sure not to leave the tick's barbed mouth parts still attached to the fuzzy's skin.**

3. **After removal, what do you do with it? Drown the sucker in a small container with rubbing alcohol or soapy water. Easier yet, flush it down the toilet. Or, you can wrap it tightly in tape, making sure it can't escape, and throw it out. (I have no idea why you would do this if you have a toilet or even an outhouse.) But no matter what, avoid the temptation to crush the tick with your fingers! This is another way you might be able to get disease from it.**

4. **Clean the area of the bite with a wee bit of rubbing alcohol or antiseptic from your ferret's first-aid kit.**

WARNING

Don't burn the tick off of your ferret. Many people suggest this, but you run the risk of seriously burning your fuzzy. If the tick is embedded, I also don't advise digging the tick out of your ferret with a pair of tweezers; please consult with your vet!

Ear mites

Blood-sucking ear mites are common in ferrets. You can identify the issue by checking your fuzzy's ear canals for brownish-black gunk, which closely resembles coffee grounds. Ferrets with ear mites may show the following symptoms:

» Scratching feverishly at their ears

» Walking with a slight head tilt

» Shaking their heads due to the extreme discomfort

Their ears may also stink and be slightly discolored.

Treatment for ear mites is relatively easy (if you stick with it) and is necessary to prevent secondary infections that can be extremely painful and even result in deafness. Some vets may prescribe an ear ointment such as Tresaderm. Others may use injectible ivermectin. Ivermectin (the same as injectible ivermectin) mixed with propylene glycol or used by itself and applied directly into the ear canal also works. You can even use Revolution Plus (Zoetis), which is a flea-treatment and heartworm preventative, but which also requires a prescription from your vet. Another option is Advantage Multi for Cats.

Here are some other things you need to know about ear mite treatment:

>> Ear mites can pass between fuzzies and other household pets and vice versa, so it's important to treat all animals.

>> Wash all bedding frequently during treatments.

>> You can't eradicate ear mites with one application of medicine; you have to use a series of applications. A minimum of at least two treatments is going to be necessary depending on which medication you use, so it's crucial to be painstakingly thorough. Your veterinarian will be your best friend here.

Medications designed to kill the mites won't kill the eggs, which is why you have to repeat treatment. Mites hatch out after the first treatment. The second treatment kills the second batch of mites before they have a chance to lay eggs again and start the cycle over.

Sarcoptic mange (scabies)

As someone who's suffered from the dreadful pest known as sarcoptic mange (whose human form is known as scabies), I can testify that the condition is unbearably itchy and definitely no fun. This external bug is in the mite family and passes quite easily from animal to animal or from animal to human. Depending on your ferret's case, her symptoms may include itchy patches of hair loss on the belly, face, or legs or crusty skin with oozing, pimple-like sores. Sometimes, the scabies infestation attacks only the feet and toes, causing severe inflammation. Marked by scabby, swollen, red feet, foot rot often results in the claws falling out if left untreated. A vet can make a diagnosis with skin scrapings.

For treatment, you can choose really, really stinky vet-prescribed lime sulfur dips and shampoos, or you can go the simple route with oral or injectible ivermectin.

I am undoubtedly the laziest person I know, so I almost always opt for the path of least resistance as long as it's in the critter's best interests. So when it comes to flea, tick, mange, and ear mite treatment or prevention and heartworm prevention, I go for an all-around product. Such products may cost a little more upfront, but they save money in the long run. Products such as Revolution Plus or Advantage Multi for Cats are perfect for just that.

Battling the Internal Bugaboos That Threaten Your Fuzzy

It's bad enough that pests want to invade the outside of your little fuzzbutt, but some also want to take over your fuzzy's insides. Some internal parasites can be life-threatening and require immediate attention. You must stay vigilant for the warning signs and always take your little one to the vet if you suspect that something's wrong. In the following sections, I introduce some dangerous internal parasites and detail the warning signs that wave red flags so you can rush your fuzzy to the vet.

WARNING

Never, ever take on the role of doctor and medicate your ferret without your vet's guidance. Ferrets are tiny creatures and can overdose very easily. Some medications can be lethal in certain combinations. Also, you may cause more harm if you misdiagnose or fail to see other underlying health problems. Don't be hasty. Always get help from an experienced ferret vet who can diagnose and come up with the proper course of action (see Chapter 12 for more on finding one).

Heartworms

Heartworm disease is a parasitic worm (*Dirofilaria immitis*) infestation that attacks the heart. Where many mosquitoes buzz around, vets and ferret owners will see plenty of cases of heartworm. Ferrets are just as susceptible to this deadly disease as cats and dogs. In fact, many carnivores are. Even if your ferret doesn't go outside, mosquitoes can come inside.

Infected mosquitoes inject the larva into the ferret's bloodstream with a single piercing bite. The deadly parasite then develops and migrates to the fuzzy's heart, where the adult worms wreak cardiac havoc. It only takes a single worm to produce devastating results.

Signs

Signs of heartworm disease include the following:

>> Coughing or hacking

>> Lethargy

>> Fluid build-up in the chest and abdomen

>> Labored breathing

>> Pale lips, gums, and tongue

>> Hypothermia (low body temperature)

>> Heart murmur

>> Muffled heart sounds

>> Green color to the urine

Prevention

The best course of action against heartworm is prevention. Fortunately, you can acquire several effective options to prevent your ferret from getting heartworm:

>> **Advantage Multi for Cats (Bayer):** Made with the ingredients imidacloprid and moxidectin, Advantage Multi for Cats is said to not only kill adult fleas and help prevent future flea infestations, but also to aid in the prevention of heartworms. It should be pointed out that Advantage Multi for Cats (0.4 mL size only) is the only drug that is FDA-approved to prevent heartworm in ferrets. At the time of this writing, there is no FDA-approved drug to *treat* heartworm disease in ferrets.

Applying a small amount of the liquid directly on the skin at the base of your ferret's skull provides up to 28 days of protection. The imidacloprid works the same way in this product as it does in other Advantage products (See above flea section). Moxidectin gets quickly absorbed through the skin into the subcutaneous fat and then moves into the bloodstream to prevent heartworm. Reapplication is recommended after bathing, but your ferret should receive no more than one application per week.

>> **Revolution Plus (Pfizer):** Made with the active ingredients selamectin and sarolaner, Revolution Plus is a topically applied product that prevents heartworm, among many other things. Selemectin is a member of the avermectin group of parasiticides, which to make a long complicated process understandable, paralyzes internal or external parasites' nervous systems, causing death. Sarolaner is a member of the isoxazoline parasiticides.

>> **Heartgard (Boehringer Ingelheim Animal Health USA):** You can use Heartgard for cats or ¼ of the Heartgard for small dogs once a month. Be aware: Most fuzzies don't like the stuff!

TIP

Boehringer Ingelheim Animal Health USA, the maker of Heartgard, advises against splitting the pills or chewables. The company states that the effective ingredient (ivermectin) isn't evenly distributed throughout the pills or chewables, so you don't know for sure if your fuzzy is really getting an effective dose. Ferrets can handle large dosages of ivermectin. For example, a whole feline chewable Heartgard has less ivermectin in it than the dose a fuzzy would receive for treatment of ear mites. Because your ferret-knowledgeable vet will know all this information, and Heartgard is a veterinarian-prescribed medication, you should be given precise instructions from your vet on how to administer this preventative and at what dosage. If you're ever unsure, ask for clarification!

>> **Interceptor (Eli Lilly):** These tablets are small and easy to crush, and you can mix them into some baby food or salmon oil. Made with the active ingredient milbemycin oxime, Interceptor tablets need to be given once a month.

>> **Ivermectin (generic) (Merck):** Some vets prefer giving ferrets liquid ivermectin orally (or through injection) on a monthly basis. I don't suggest ever buying this product and treating your ferrets on your own and without the guidance of a veterinarian! This could prove very detrimental to your ferret.

Most vets prescribe the kitten dose of Revolution for a ferret when protecting her from fleas and ticks. This makes sense considering how little ferrets weigh. Some vet cardiologists, though, have suggested that this dose isn't strong enough to protect a ferret against heartworms; they say that the *cat* dose is the effective dose against heartworms. This may seem quite high, because cats can weigh so much more than ferrets, and you don't want to risk the life of your beloved pet! Therefore, always discuss this subject with your vet to make sure your ferret is kept healthy and adequately protected.

>> **Advantage Multi for Cats:** This is the only FDA-approved product for heartworm prevention (and flea treatment) in ferrets. The two main ingredients are imidacloprid (Advantage) and moxidectin. Like Revolution, it's a monthly topical applied directly to the skin on the neck or above the shoulders. In addition to heartworm prevention, Advantage Multi kills fleas, ear mites, and intestinal worms. The cat size (5 to 9 pounds) is the size approved for ferret use.

Before beginning a heartworm preventative, your ferret should test negative for heartworms, if possible. Fuzzies can be tested with the same in-clinic test that dogs get. Another detection method is a cardiac ultrasound, but it takes an experienced technician to visualize the heartworms in the ferret's heart.

Advantage Multi for Cats is the only FDA-approved drug currently available for heartworm prevention in ferrets. None of the other preventatives are approved for use in ferrets, but most have been tested in ferrets. Unapproved products are always used at the owner's risk. The manufacturers of these medications will not help out if there's a reaction or problem, such as not protecting the ferret against heartworms, because the use in ferrets is considered "off-label." They are used extensively by ferret owners, however.

Treatment

Infected ferrets usually die without treatment. Heartworm treatment, however, is relatively new in ferrets. Prednisone is often used during and after the treatment period. The safer option, with a high survival rate, is to treat more conservatively with ivermectin, doxycycline, furosemide, and prednisone. High doses of ivermectin slowly kills the adult heartworms. Furosemide treats the fluid retention; doxycycline kills the bacteria on the heartworms (Wolbachia), weakens the heartworms, and dramatically reduces the risk of adverse reactions to the heartworm treatment. Prednisone prevents dangerous blood clots from forming as the heartworms die. (Occasionally, diltiazem will also be used to treat the right-sided congestive heart failure that the heartworms can cause.)

Vets highly recommend cage rest during heartworm treatment. As you can see, prevention is much better and safer than treatment!

Extra care for your ferret

Along with extra rest, ferrets with heart disease should embark on a gentle exercise routine, with plenty of close supervision during playtime. Overstimulation may worsen the condition. Of course, common sense also dictates that frightening or startling these little heart breakers isn't a good idea. No barking dogs, firecrackers, or tuba playing, please. Ferrets with heart disease benefit from a low-sodium diet. Use only treats and Beechnut meat baby food with a low salt content.

Intestinal worms

Ferrets are susceptible to many intestinal worms, including roundworms, hookworms, tapeworms, flukes, and lungworms. Almost all intestinal infestations harbor the same symptoms:

» Dry, brittle fur

» Weight loss

» Diarrhea, mucousy or bloody poops, and/or worms in the poop (in rare, serious infestations)

» Abdominal bloating

» Weakness or lethargy

» Itchy heinie

- » Increased appetite with weight loss
- » Increased gas
- » Tender belly

Some intestinal worms are passed from one animal to another or to a human through an animal's infected poop. Some, like tapeworm, are passed through fleas or other intermediate hosts. Others can get into the system just by having their tiny larva burrow through the skin.

Although the symptoms generally are the same, treatment of intestinal parasites can vary depending on the organism you're dealing with. Some worms require oral medication in liquid or pill form. Others can fall to an injection (often ivermectin). Whatever the case, intestinal parasites left untreated can cause your ferret to have chronic intestinal problems and be prone to poor health. In rare instances, severe cases of intestinal worms can cause death.

REMEMBER

If you have more than one ferret and one of them has internal parasites, chances are you have more than one wormy fuzzy. Treat all your ferrets thoroughly, according to your vet's instructions. Don't forget to change their litter boxes and clean the cage to prevent reinfestation. If you also have dogs and cats, check them for parasites, too. Animals just love to get into poop!

Coccidia (coccidiosis)

Coccidia is a protozoan infection common in ferrets and other animals. The infection is picked up through the ingestion of infected poop and can be diagnosed by your vet if you provide a stool sample. However, a stool sample isn't always a fail-proof test. Your fuzzy may shed the oocysts (eggs) only periodically, which means you may test a poop on a day when no oocysts were shed. For the most accurate results, pick a poop that's bloody and mucousy.

Severe coccidia infestations can cause diarrhea, lethargy, dehydration, weight loss, loss of appetite, and, in severe cases, death. Kits (baby ferrets) are most susceptible to severe coccidia infestations and may have thin, brittle fur and a sparse coat. The kit's whiskers are stubby and broken off. In prolonged conditions, her heinie may appear red and swollen. Treatment often is successful if you catch the condition early enough. Many vets prescribe Albon (sulfadimethoxine) or Trimethprim and sulfamethoxazole (a generic antibiotic), or Marquis paste (Bayer) to treat coccidia.

Giardia

Giardia, a lovely protozoan, can get into you or your ferret via a water source (streams, lakes, ponds, and infected tap water, for example) or through the ingestion of infected poop. After gaining access to the intestinal tract, these buggers attack the inner lining of the intestine, causing an uncomfortable inflammation. Signs of giardia infestation include weight loss, bloating, diarrhea, and mucousy poops.

TECHNICAL STUFF

Giardia can be difficult to find under the microscope. You need a very fresh poop sample looked at immediately — like, while it's still steaming. Better yet, have your vet take a swab from the rectum. The very best course of action is to send a sample in a special solution to the lab for proper analysis and identification. Some people believe giardia is rare in ferrets, but others believe that it's very common and only shows its ugly warning signs when the fuzzy is stressed out. This is one parasite that's still being investigated.

The treatment suggested by a vet is oral medication — usually Flagyl (metronidazole). Some vets suggest Panacur (fenbendazole) as another option, although this medication isn't made specifically to combat giardia. For healthy fuzzies, some experts think that the symptoms may go away without treatment. I always suggest getting help. It may take up to a month to cure your furball, but your effort is well worth it.

TIP

Some medications — especially Flagyl — are so offensive to fuzzies that they projectile-ptooey them all over you. A treat such as salmon oil can come in handy. Mixing the medication with a yummy supplement can save you a laundry bill and reduce the rebellion on your ferret's part. Keep in mind, though, what you're medicating the fuzzy for in the first place; for example, ferrets with insulinoma shouldn't have sweet stuff.

Chapter **15**

Handling Viruses, Infections, and Other Conditions and Illnesses

N o matter how hard people try to stay healthy with good eating, exercise, and proper immunizations, millions of humans manage to get the worst viruses, respiratory infections, and flu every year. Your fuzzy is no different.

Experts have written entire books on the diseases and illnesses ferrets can contract. This isn't one of them. In this chapter, you simply get the basics on what you need to know about common ferret diseases and what you can do about them. This chapter deals with the most common diseases and conditions from the simple (flu) to the deadly (rabies) and from the serious (cardiomyopathy) to the not-so-serious (eye problems). As I make clear throughout this book, recognizing changes in your ferret's appearance and behavior early on can mean the difference between life and death. Even some of the presumably innocent conditions I describe in this chapter can take a turn for the worst or can be indicative of another more serious condition.

REMEMBER

A handful of signs seem to show up with almost all fuzzy ailments, which is just one more reason to leave the diagnosing and medicating to your experienced vet. Your ferret may be suffering from more than one malady. Also, you need to be aware that signs aren't set in stone. Your ferret may exhibit one sign or a combination of several. She may show none at all, especially in the beginning stages of an illness. The signs I list in this chapter are the most common ones for each illness and are here for reference purposes only. Don't wait until more signs appear before hauling your fuzzbutt to the vet.

Gastrointestinal (GI) Diseases

Gastrointestinal diseases refer to all those things that can go wrong with the stomach, intestines, or esophagus. The next few sections cover those GI ailments that can affect ferrets, and what you can do if you spot the symptoms involved.

Epizootic Catarrhal Enteritis (ECE)

Epizootic catarrhal enteritis (ECE), or "green slime disease," is a coronavirus that presents as an inflammation of the intestinal lining. In addition to the intestinal damage, as the disease progresses, the ferret's liver can be seriously affected, and the results can be deadly! Ferrets with ECE can't absorb food and water properly, causing life-threatening diarrhea. The disease is transmitted when a ferret comes in contact with the bodily fluids or feces of a sick ferret or via handlers of ill ferrets. For years, it was also called the "green mystery virus," but experts now know that a ferret-specific coronavirus causes ECE.

The fuzzies most at risk are older carpet sharks and very young ferrets. Ferrets that are already battling other illnesses, such as lymphosarcoma, adrenal disease, and/or insulinoma (see Chapter 16), also are at high risk. Healthy young and middle-aged furkids seem to get over ECE the fastest with the right support, almost as if the condition were the flu. In multi-ferret homes, you can expect most, if not all, of your fuzzies to get this disease within 48 to 72 hours after it enters the door. Baby ferrets bought from pet stores are frequent *asymptomatic carriers* of ECE, which means they can show no signs of having the condition. ECE also can enter your home on your clothes after you've handled a ferret with ECE.

The signs of this nasty disease can last anywhere from several days to several months. Many ferret kits are exposed to and infected by ECE through their mothers. It is believed that some of those ferrets, if not all, go on to become lifetime carriers. And although a ferret that has had ECE may always be a carrier, signs may subside and only again flare up during times of stress. Watch your ferret closely and get her to a vet the moment the signs become apparent. ECE is typically diagnosed by its characteristic timeline and clinical signs.

ECE is an extremely contagious disease that spreads from ferret to ferret very quickly. To safeguard your ferret, you need to clean, clean, clean. Follow these tips:

>> Don't let other people handle your ferret without taking precautions.

>> Wash thoroughly before and after you handle any ferrets.

>> Change clothing before handling your own little one after visiting with strange ferrets.

>> Make sure all new ferrets you get have been checked by the vet for parasites and given an overall clean bill of health before exposing them to others.

Some typical signs of ECE include the following:

>> Diarrhea that's initially bright green to yellow and full of mucous; it may be bubbly, foul-smelling, or slimy, and it may or may not be projectile diarrhea

>> Seedy poop, often yellowish in color (indicating undigested food)

REMEMBER

Not all that glows green is ECE! Green poop is not that uncommon in ferrets, and can be caused by stress or an upset tummy. Green simply indicates the food went through the ferret's system before the body could absorb the nutrients. On the other hand, if the poop is green but also watery or slimy, and if it persists, a trip to the vet is needed immediately to diagnose or rule out ECE.

>> Dehydration, often severe (see Chapter 13 on dehydration)

>> Lethargy and sleepiness

>> Extreme weight loss (up to 50 percent in severe cases)

>> Vomiting

>> Squinted, watery eyes (which is a sign of pain)

>> Oral and stomach ulcers

>> Coma

We have no cure for ECE as of press time. Also, no vaccine is currently available to protect against ECE, although experts are working diligently to develop one. And because ECE is viral, no medication can effectively combat it directly. However, some medications can be useful to manage some of the secondary effects of the disease, such as intestinal ulcers and intestinal pain. In addition, secondary bacterial infections may occur in an already weakened animal, and these too require treatment.

Some medications that have been successful (possibly in certain combinations) in treating secondary infections that occur along with ECE are:

>> Amoxicillin

>> Clavamox drops

>> Cefa drops

>> Baytril

Over-the-counter anti-cramping medications and tummy-coaters have been used in the past for treatment, but they aren't necessary and may cause more harm than good. Famotidine (Pepcid) or cimetidine may be used to prevent ulcers and excretion of excess stomach acid. Some veterinarians use an oral antiviral called "alpha interferon" with mixed results.

REMEMBER

Treatments vary by degree of illness and should be administered only under the guidance of your veterinarian. Not all medications work for every ferret. Your vet may find, through trial and error, the perfect medication to get your fuzzy through her ordeal. Every case needs to be evaluated on an individual basis. Please note that treatments of ferrets evolve over time as new medications are developed and new knowledge of diseases is gained. Your vet should be aware of current treatment protocols as they become available.

In healthier or younger ferrets, the disease should be treated like the flu unless signs become severe. The treatment, in addition to the secondary medications, is more complicated for other ferrets. An affected ferret will die of dehydration more quickly than she will starve to death, so keeping her hydrated is the most important part of supportive care. You must combat serious bouts of dehydration with subcutaneous fluids and/or electrolyte replacers, such as unflavored Pedialyte. Of course, you must pay attention to feeding your ailing fuzzy, too. The following bullets point out the care procedures:

>> Your vet should show you how to administer subcutaneous fluids. It takes 20 cc's or 4 teaspoons of fluids per pound of body weight three times a day to keep a healthy ferret alive. A dehydrated ferret needs more than that to stay alive. Your vet should determine how much subcutaneous fluids to administer and when to administer them. It's important to strictly use your vet as your guide, because it's actually possible to overhydrate or drown your ferret in fluids!

» Supplemental feedings with Assist Feed Recipe (see Chapter 13) three to four times a day has proven very helpful in supportive care. Assisted feeding is critical if your ferret isn't eating on her own. It also plays a role in reversing fatty liver disease, which is often the result of severe bouts of ECE. Additionally, assist feeding ensures that your ferret gets enough nutrition and helps keep her hydrated.

When your ferret is back on her paws again, be aware that her intestinal lining will be abnormal for some time, even after the signs seem to go away. She may suffer from periodic bouts of diarrhea and dehydration. Monitor your recovering fuzzy closely and for several months. Long-term damage to the lining of the intestinal tract may mean abnormal stools on and off for quite some time.

TIP

Oral fluids are equally important to a recovering ferret, so you can try to give water via spoon or syringe if your ferret isn't drinking from a bowl. The Assist Feed Recipe also will provide some oral fluids.

Ferret systemic coronaviral disease (FSCD)

This chronic, lethal disease of our beloved ferret is thought to be a mutation of the ECE virus. It was first seen in 2002, and has been reported thus far in Europe, the United States, Japan, the Netherlands, and South America. It is frequently compared to the dry form of feline infectious peritonitis (FIP) due to the presence of identical microscopic lesions seen in both ferrets with FSCD and cats with FIP. And although ferrets of any age can be infected with FSCD, it is more commonly seen in ferrets under a year old. Most likely this is due to immune suppression from stress-related factors such as weaning, altering, overcrowding, poor husbandry, vaccinating, descenting, and rehoming/shipping. Extensive signs of this disease include:

» Diarrhea (progressing from brownish-yellow to green-hemorrhagic)

» Weight loss and anorexia

» Inability to gain weight in growing ferrets

» Lethargy and hind limb weakness

» Vomiting, coughing, and sneezing

» Decreased drinking of water

» Teeth grinding

» Nasal discharge and rectal irritation

» Seizures (possibly prior to death)

» Intraabdominal masses and enlarged spleen

It is thought that this virus is transmitted from one ferret to another via the fecal-oral route, the same as with the FIP virus. Unfortunately, the disease is progressive and fatal. Ferrets typically die or are euthanized an average of two months after diagnosis with FSCD. Some veterinarians might suggest supportive care and heroic treatments. However, at this time and until a cure for this disease is found, such measures are merely prolonging a life of suffering for your ferret. It also prolongs heartache for you.

Covid-19 (SARS-CoV-2)

You may wonder what Covid-19 has to do with your ferret. Quite a few animal species are susceptible to, and have tested positive for, SARS-CoV-2, including ferrets that were infected experimentally in lab settings. Dogs, cats, mink, and even lions and tigers at a New York zoo have all had this disease. Most dogs, cats and big cats have had just mild upper-respiratory symptoms (sneezing, coughing, low grade fever, and lethargy), and have recovered in a few days.

Ferrets and humans are very similar where it comes to the receptor that is used for the virus to enter the cells. Sadly for ferret lovers, ferrets are now one of the main research animals in the race to learn more about Covid-19 and produce an effective vaccine against the potentially fatal virus. In studies, infected ferrets were able to spread the virus to other ferrets. Fortunately, the lab ferrets experienced only mild upper-respiratory symptoms with coughing and sneezing being the main problems. They all recovered in a few days. In a recent, real world study conducted by the Cummings School of Veterinary Medicine at Tufts University (North Grafton, MA), veterinary researchers monitored 29 ferrets in one household whose owners were sick with Covid-19. Despite the fact that the owners were still taking care of their numerous ferrets, the ferrets tested negative throughout the two-week study.

It should be noted, however, that according to the Centers for Disease Control and Prevention (CDC) transmission of SARS-CoV-2 is most frequently from person to person, but "it appears that it [SARS-CoV-2] can spread from people to animals in some situations, especially after close-contact with a person with Covid-19." And regarding transmission of SARS-CoV-2 from animals to people? The CDC says, "Currently, there is no evidence that animals play a *significant* role in the spread of SARS-CoV-2 to people. However, reports from infected mink farms in the Netherlands and Denmark suggest that in these environments there is the possibility for spread of SARS-CoV-2 from mink to people."

What should you do if you become sick with Covid-19? Out of abundance of caution, you should reduce your time with your ferrets and other pets, and especially no kissing, hugging, or close contact with your face. Ideally have another person take care of the pets until you recover from the disease and test negative. If you must care for your ferrets, wear a mask, wash your hands before handling your ferrets, and limit your time with them.

Intestinal and stomach blockages

The leading causes of death in ferrets under 2 years old are intestinal and stomach obstructions. Young ferrets mouth and taste everything from fingers to foam rubber. But older fuzzies aren't immune to this affliction. Blockages can occur when your overzealous carpet shark eats something that's too big to pass on through his system. Hairballs frequently cause clogs in ferrets (see the later "Hairballs" section). No matter the cause, if the ferret's body can't push the blockage out the other end, everything in her system backs up.

Blockages can occur anywhere in the digestive tract, from the throat to the stomach to the small intestine. Stomach blockages may move around, causing signs to appear and subside. A clog in the belly can last a long time and cause a slow wasting away. If it's a hairball, the mass slowly grows.

Here are some signs that your fuzzy may be blocked up:

>> Constipation

>> Tiny poop (looks like string cheese) or black, tarry poop

>> Bloating

>> Painful belly

>> Loss of appetite

>> Loss of weight

>> Vomiting

>> Mouth pawing

>> Severe dehydration

>> Teeth grinding

>> Face rubbing

>> Lethargy

>> Coma

>> Seizing (occurs after the blockage is complete and has been there 24 hrs or longer)

Attempting a diagnosis by feeling around the ferret's belly isn't fail-proof. Sometimes, large tumors cause similar signs and feel like an obstruction. Often, your vet will confirm your suspicions with an X-ray or ultrasound.

If you suspect that your fuzzy ate something she shouldn't have and it isn't life-threatening, you can start giving her Laxatone a couple times a day. Watch for foreign objects in anything that comes out the other end (*if* anything poops out).

TIP

Poop mixed with water makes identifying foreign bodies quite a bit easier. You can put some poop in a small sandwich bag, add a little water, and squish away!

WARNING

Keep in mind that it often takes more than Laxatone to fix a blockage problem. If you don't see the object coming out, get straight to the vet. Left untreated, a stopped-up fuzzy can die an agonizing death. Don't wait until the last minute to go to the veterinarian.

Exploratory surgery may be necessary to cure the ailment. After the blockage moves into the small intestine, surgery is imperative, or else a painful death can occur within a day or two. Vets recommend a soft diet for several days following the surgery (see Chapter 8 for tips on changing your ferret's diet).

WARNING

Because dehydration from failure to eat and drink is a serious problem, administering oral or subcutaneous fluids every few hours is imperative.

TIP

If you think pure canned pumpkin is just for Halloween, think again. This stuff is a great way to flush out your ferret's intestinal tract. If you think your ferret could have a blockage, offer her this tasty treat — as much as she wants. Most ferrets love it! Hopefully, it will flush out any foreign bodies. Word of caution: This doesn't work if the ferret's GI tract is completely blocked. If you think this is the case, contact your vet immediately.

Helicobacter Mustelae (H. mustelae) Infection

Helicobacter mustelae (H. mustelae) is a bacterium that resides in the stomachs of most ferrets. Although your ferret may harbor it after ingesting contaminated poop, she likely got it from mom, because it passes from mom to kit via exposure to the mom's poop. Unfortunately, this bacterium can be serious and cause disease.

Of course, H. mustelae may reside in your ferret's stomach for a lifetime without causing any disease. What makes the bug go from benign to gravely destructive isn't clear. What *is* clear is that serious bouts of H. mustelae infection may result in gastric problems, such as ulcers and *chronic atrophic gastritis.* Some ferret experts believe that this little bug can be serious enough to cause gastric ulcers — a theory that has mounting evidence to support it. In fact, almost all fuzzy ulcer patients are infected with H. mustelae. Most ferrets adversely affected by H. mustelae are over the age of 4.

REMEMBER

Atrophic gastritis is a chronic inflammation of the stomach lining, which leads to loss in function of many of the cells and the replacement of scar tissue. As a result, the stomach's ability to produce stomach acid is impaired, leading to severe digestive problems.

The presence of the infection causes an inflammation of the stomach lining. By attaching to the cells responsible for producing the protective mucosal lining of the stomach, the bacterium hinders the body's ability to produce mucous. This makes the stomach vulnerable to strong stomach acid, and the result can be burns or ulcers. H. mustelae infection also increases the pH of the stomach and impairs the stomach's ability to produce stomach acid; the latter is needed to digest food.

Here are the signs of an infection:

>> Vomiting

>> Loss of appetite

>> Loose stools

>> Excessive salivating

>> Dark, tarry stools

>> Lethargy

>> Teeth grinding

>> Painful belly

>> Enlarged mesenteric lymph nodes

>> Weight loss

It seems as though a ferret's own system can control this bacterial invasion under normal circumstances. Unless your fuzzy becomes extremely stressed out or is already weakened by disease or illness, the signs may not appear at all. The relationship between stress, disease, and illness, however, hasn't been proven to cause the bacterial rebellion. It's currently recommended that you treat only those ferrets that show signs of H. mustelae infection. After the signs appear, your ferret should be treated by a veterinarian immediately. Medication combinations that have been successful include Amoxicillin, Flagyl, and Pepcid for 4 to 6 weeks, or

Biaxin in combination with Amoxicillin for 2 to 3 weeks. These are just two of the current treatments out there. Other treatments are available, and there will undoubtedly be new and improved treatments in the future.

Eosinophilic Gastroenteritis

Eosinophilic gastroenteritis most commonly presents as a disease of the intestinal tract. However, it can involve other organs such as the liver, abdominal lymph nodes, pancreas, or skin. Eosinophils are a type of white blood cell that is released when some types of foreign invaders enter the body. These cells release a substance called *histamine* in their attempt to do battle, but unfortunately in large amounts histamine can instead start attacking the tissue around it. Histamines, by the way, are the same substances that cause your skin to swell after a bee sting. In the intestine they cause damage to intestinal lining. When the intestinal lining isn't functioning normally it can't absorb nutrients or water properly, resulting in diarrhea and weight loss. The foreign invaders that cause eosinophilic gastroenteritis are unknown at this time. Some veterinarians believe a food allergy is involved, but this hasn't been as yet substantiated. These vets may suggest a more natural diet may prevent eosinophilic gastroenteritis or help heal a ferret with the disease. Again, there is yet no scientific, only anecdotal findings.

The following list presents the common signs of eosinophilic gastroenteritis:

>> Severe diarrhea

>> Loss of appetite

>> Weight loss

>> Swollen ears and feet (in severe cases)

>> Skin ulcerations (in severe cases)

>> Abdominal pain (in severe cases)

Your vet can begin to make a diagnosis after reviewing the gastrointestinal signs I list in the previous section. Next comes a complete blood-cell count, which almost always shows a dramatic increase in eosinophils. The predominant signs coupled with the blood test should be almost conclusive. Definitive diagnosis, however, can be made by taking biopsies of the affected tissues — including intestinal or stomach tissue and the lymph nodes around the intestines. These areas often include large numbers of eosinophils in cases of eosinophilic gastroenteritis.

The prognosis should be good if you catch the disease early. With early diagnosis, medication and diet can work their magic and heal your fuzzy. Managing the signs and preventing future damage is your number-one priority. Unfortunately, too many ferrets are diagnosed with eosinophilic gastroenteritis when tissue damage is already profound. In these cases, prognosis is guarded to poor.

Because the exact cause of eosinophilic gastroenteritis remains unknown, we have no cure for the condition. Treatment is geared toward managing the current signs and preventing further damage to the tissues. A maintenance dose of a corticosteroid, such as prednisone, may be a lifelong necessity to prevent a relapse and further damage. *Corticosteroids* suppress inflammation and prevent large groups of eosinophils from forming; they also prevent them from breaking down as easily, thus blocking further tissue damage.

REMEMBER

A diet change is a must for ferrets with eosinophilic gastroenteritis, because it's suspected that food allergens may be culprits in this disease. If your ferret will eat mice or raw meat, a natural diet is the best choice in my book. (Chapter 8 has the full scoop on dietary options and changing your fuzzy's diet.) If not, you can start off by feeding your fuzzy turkey baby food in the beginning and graduate to Hills z/d diet, which you can get from your vet. Some vets even go so far as to say that the switch to a "hypoallergenic" diet can successfully wean a ferret off of corticosteroids. Some vets recommend a freeze-dried food, such as Stella & Chewy's Freeze-Dried products.

Megaesophagus

Megaesophagus is a relatively uncommon disease in ferrets. It's the result of the absence of or the decrease in the ability of the esophageal muscles (located in the throat and torso) to move food into the stomach. This breakdown in the muscles' ability can be a problem all its own, often with unknown causes, or it can be the result of an obstruction or damage to the nerves supplying the esophageal muscles.

The result of this loss of motility is that the esophagus swells as it fills with food and/or liquid. Some of the food may flow back up and out of the mouth, mimicking vomiting; some food may enter the ferret's stomach, making a sound much like water going down a drain. It isn't unusual to hear gurgling or notice that your ferret's breathing is impaired. *Aspiration pneumonia*, the result of inhaling food, also is a dangerous problem that these little ones face.

Your vet can make a diagnosis by using a barium swallow and X-ray, an endoscopy, a fluoroscopy, or clinical observation. There is no cure for this disease. The prognosis is guarded and depends a great deal on controlling the signs and meeting the nutritional needs of the ferret. You need to show a lot of care and dedication, because significant weight loss and dehydration are common with megaesophagus.

Your vet will use many different meds when dealing with megaesophagus, depending on which signs you're treating. You'll probably have to hand feed your ferret small, liquid meals three to five times a day for the remainder of your ferret's life. In the beginning, however, your ferret needs five to six meals a day to get her back on her feet. You want to start off with a soupy mixture and feed 10 to 15 CCs per feeding, using a syringe!

REMEMBER

Although a soupy mixture is needed, it can increase the danger of aspiration. You need to take great care during feeding. Keep your ferret's head in an elevated position and in line with its neck. Use a syringe to gently feed the soupy mix to the ferret. A little choking is common. If the choking continues or regurgitation occurs, allow your ferret to bring her head down to assist in bringing the food back up. Let her rest 20 to 30 minutes before trying to feed her again.

TIP

Some people suggest that you massage your ferret's throat and chest to stimulate swallowing. However, this practice can lead to regurgitation and aspiration. Holding your ferret in the upright position with her head at a 45-degree angle to the floor during feeding, and for 15 minutes or so after feeding, will help gravity take over and facilitate the flow of food into the stomach.

WARNING

Never use a water bowl for a ferret with megaesophagus, because her head position with the bowl can cause choking. You need to hang a water bottle high in her cage so that she has to stretch her neck up to reach for the water. This will minimize the risk of choking.

Dental Problems

Many things can go wrong with an animal's teeth. No toothy critter can hide from this fact — not even ferrets. Some fuzzy dental problems probably are genetic. Others can result from overuse and misuse of the chompers. Diet and physical health also may play a major role in the destruction of a ferret's teeth. Do your part and make sure your ferret gets a dental checkup during her routine exams at the vet's office. The following sections look at some problems that can occur in your fuzzy's mouth.

Faulty teeth

If you spend enough time with your fuzzy, you'll see her rough and tumble pretty hard with other fuzzies and her imaginary fuzzmates. She'll fall and crash into things. When she's cage crazy, she may gnaw frantically at the cage bars until someone rescues her. Plus, most ferrets are fed a hard kibble diet, too (see Chapter 8). Because of these things, fuzzy teeth endure a lot of wear and tear and abuse. For other fuzzies, teeth issues may be something they were born with. The following sections look at wear and tear and born problems.

REMEMBER

To help you get through the dental reading and your life as a fuzzy owner, here are a few terms that you need to be familiar with:

>> *Plaque* is a clear "biofilm" that's made up of cellular debris, oral secretions, plenty of bacteria, and some white blood cells. It adheres to the teeth rather quickly and stays there until it's removed.

>> *Tartar* and *dental calculus* are interchangeable words and result when minerals are added to the plaque, causing the plaque to harden. All tartar comes from plaque, but not all plaque mineralizes into tartar. Tartar is a hard material that starts to build up on the teeth at the gum line. It also adheres to the teeth and stays there until removal.

REMEMBER

You can help ensure your ferret's teeth get a clean bill of health at every vet visit by brushing his teeth regularly. And, by doing so, you'll also be giving your ferret an extra shot at living a long, healthy, happy life. Go slowly when first introducing your ferret to the practice of brushing his teeth. This is an unnatural situation for him, and patience will pay off in the end. Remember to brush his teeth at least twice a month, preferably weekly. (See Chapter 9 for more on brushing teeth)

>> In the presence of plaque or plaque and tartar, *gingivitis* can occur. This is an infection of the gums, or *gingiva*, caused by bacteria — usually those found in the plaque biofilm. Gingivitis is marked by red, inflamed gums.

>> *Periodontal disease* often is next to come and is marked by recession of the gum lines and actual bone loss. This is the stage where teeth lose their support, become loose, and fall out. Damage from periodontal disease is permanent, so you need to provide care to prevent the condition. (For more on this condition, see the following section.)

Wear and tear

Chipped, broken, and worn teeth aren't necessarily things to gnash *your* teeth over, unless you notice an obvious problem. But always let an experienced vet make that decision for you if you have any doubt. A vet can smooth out a chipped tooth if the surface is rough and irritating the inside of your ferret's lip. Breaks can be a little more serious. Exposed tooth pulp is painful and can lead to infections. Usually, a root canal or complete removal is warranted.

A chipped tooth may hide a more serious problem, such as a hidden crack leading into the pulp chamber of the tooth. The crack can result in a tooth infection that can spread to other teeth. Even worse, the infection can spread into the body and various vital organs such as the heart, kidneys, and liver. All chipped teeth should be checked by a vet; you can probably wait until her yearly physical, as long as you see no changes (such as discoloration, smell, or drainage). *Note:* All chipped teeth are at risk of future fractures and need to be watched.

Worn teeth are facts of life and will worsen as your ferret ages. Chewing hard kibble into manageable sizes for swallowing may be more difficult, so older fuzzies with worn teeth may need a softer diet (see Chapter 8 for more on switching a ferret's diet).

Growing issues

Your ferret may end up looking more like a Bulldog than a fuzzy weasel. Some poor furkids have teeth that protrude outward — usually, the canines are the culprits. Because these teeth prevent the lip flap from resting against the gums, the ferret's gums may become dry. And the inside of the lip gets irritated from the constant rubbing of the teeth. I've only had this situation happen to one ferret, and the offending teeth were the two lower canines. The problem was fixed by surgically clipping the teeth as far down as necessary and filling them with a safe, hardening substance (acrylic is commonly used).

If a ferret's tooth is severely deformed, completely removing it may be necessary. However, in small animals like ferrets, each tooth is an important part of the strength of the jawbone. Pulling teeth can compromise the jaw by removing a part of the load-bearing strength, along with the subsequent loss of bone that naturally occurs after the loss of a tooth. Therefore, this should be a last resort.

Some furkids actually grow extra baby teeth. Albino kids are notorious for this condition. Usually, all baby teeth are pushed right out when the adult teeth come in. Other times, they linger for several days before finally being squeezed out. If you notice a baby tooth that overstays its welcome, you probably should have your vet uproot it to prevent problems down the road. *Note:* Some adult ferrets have an extra incisor tooth (called a *supernumery tooth*); this condition is harmless.

Says ferret expert Bob Church: "About 5 percent (2 to 9 percent) of ferrets have an extra incisor tooth, and maybe 1 out of 100 of those have two extra teeth. A fewer number of ferrets don't grow all their teeth — usually a front premolar or the bottom tiny mandibular molar. On rare occasions, a ferret will have a tiny extra molar in the roof of her mouth. All these conditions are benign."

The dreaded dental disease

Gum disease, or *periodontal disease,* occurs with great frequency in ferrets — especially ones that are over 5 years old. Come to think of it, it happens in humans even more frequently. Humans are poor tooth brushers; and if we can't take care of our own teeth, we probably won't spend a lot of time on our pets' teeth.

The main cause of periodontal disease is the lack of a natural diet (see Chapter 8). Hair, bone, and other particles from a natural diet are extremely effective at massaging the gums and wiping away plaque and tartar. Other diseases, such as lymphoma, also can play a role in periodontal disease. Experts agree that you can greatly reduce the severity of the disease with daily tooth brushing and with more extensive cleanings performed by an experienced vet, as often as needed.

WARNING Unqualified people shouldn't scrape a ferret's teeth because they can cause scratches on the teeth that make tartar worse. Vets use ultrasound scalers to clear the teeth of the tartar and then polish them, making the scratches less of a problem.

The signs of periodontal disease include

>> Loose teeth

>> Discolored teeth

>> Stinky breath

>> Red, inflamed, or receding gums

>> Drooling

>> Mouth ulcers

>> Difficulty eating

>> Tartar and plaque build-up

>> Refusal to floss (okay, just kidding)

TIP At the very least, you should add dental checkups to your weekly or monthly grooming habits. In addition to checking for lumps, bumps, bruises, and other abnormalities, stick your head in your fuzzy's mouth and look for dental problems. For more on general care and grooming habits, head to Chapter 9.

WARNING Gum disease and ulcers of the mouth are serious problems by themselves. But did you know they can also be caused by renal disease, especially in ferrets five years and older? Renal disease can be diagnosed with blood tests and a urinalysis.

In addition to the lack of proper texture in a traditional diet, which provides gentle abrasiveness, eating fine particles of carbohydrates and changes in the oral pH contribute to periodontal disease. My answer to combating periodontal disease is to opt for the evolutionary or alternative diet, which offers various food items with varying degrees of texture. (See Chapter 8 for details about the diet.)

Heart Disease

Sadly, heart disease is a rather common problem in middle-aged and older ferrets. The most common type of heart disease seen in ferrets is dilated cardiomyopathy. We focus on these topics in the sections that follow, explaining the signs, diagnosis, and treatment phases of the diseases (and prevention when applicable). (Ferrets also can also suffer from hypertrophic cardiomyopathy and from heart valve disease.)

The ultimate means of establishing a diagnosis of heart disease is an ultrasound of the heart. An ultrasound is the only way to determine the actual cause of the heart problems:

>> If the heart walls are stretched and thin, a doctor can diagnose dilated cardiomyopathy.

>> If the heart walls are much thicker and bigger than normal, the doctor can diagnose hypertrophic cardiomyopathy.

>> If the heart valves are thicker than normal and not working well, the doctor can diagnose valvular heart disease.

>> If heartworms are seen in the heart, the doctor can diagnose heartworm disease.

Because the treatment for these four problems is different, a cardiac ultrasound is necessary to make the correct diagnosis and to select the correct treatment plan for your fuzzy with heart disease.

Dilated cardiomyopathy is most common in ferrets over the age of 3. It's a form of heart disease that causes damage to the heart muscle. Eventually, during the course of the disease, the heart stretches, enlarges, and weakens. Some of the heart muscle is replaced by scar tissue, making it impossible for the heart to contract normally. Inevitably, the blood flowing out of the heart decreases, and the heart becomes less efficient.

The exact cause of dilated cardiomyopathy is unknown at this time. Possible causes include viral infections and nutritional problems, such as deficiencies of taurine, l-carnitine, l-arginine, or perhaps even a deficiency of Coenzyme Q10 in the diet. The relationship of a taurine deficiency causing dilated cardiomyopathy has already been proven in cats. Unlike cats, however, ferrets don't improve when extra taurine is added to their diets.

How long your big-hearted fuzzy will live with dilated cardiomyopathy really depends on how fast her heart is deteriorating. If your ferret is diagnosed early, and you and your vet manage the signs properly, she may live for 2 or 3 more years.

Following are the signs of the dilated cardiomyopathy form of heart disease:

>> Labored breathing

>> Coughing

>> Pale or bluish gum coloring

>> Decreased or no appetite

>> Heart murmur

>> Lethargy

>> Frequent rests during play

>> Muffled heart sounds

>> Hypothermia (low body temperature)

>> Fluid build-up in the chest and abdominal areas

Ferrets with cardiomyopathy often have enlarged livers or spleens, as well. Frequently, a suffering fuzzy has a swollen belly. In this case, she probably has congestive heart failure, and the swollen belly results from a build-up of fluid in the abdomen. The ferret likely also has fluid accumulating in her chest and lungs.

Heart disease usually begins long before the diagnosis is made; however, a diagnosis also can be made before the onset of the signs. X-rays can be taken to look at the size and shape of the heart. Dilated cardiomyopathy heart disease causes the heart to be bigger and rounder than normal. An EKG can check for abnormal rhythms and conduction disturbances. And, of course, the best diagnosis method is an ultrasound, which I discuss earlier in this section.

Dilated cardiomyopathy generally is irreversible and has no cure. Treatment is designed to control the disease and slow down its progression. You can manage dilated cardiomyopathy with medication. The medications that vets commonly prescribe are

>> **An ACE inhibitor** — such as benazepril or enalapril

>> **A diuretic** — such as furosemide

>> **A muscle contraction strengthener** — such as pimobendan or digoxin

Only your vet and/or vet cardiologist can determine which medications and what dosages should work for your ferret.

Influenza (The "Flu")

Don't sneeze on your fuzzy, and don't let her sneeze on you, either! Your ferret is highly susceptible to human influenza A; you can pass it back and forth to each other if you're not careful. Influenza is the most common respiratory infection in ferrets. In healthy ferrets, recovery takes about five days. In weak or old ferrets, the sickness can be a little more serious, lasting several weeks.

Here are the signs that your ferret has influenza (ones we all, unfortunately, know so well):

>> Sneezing and coughing

>> Runny nose and eyes

>> Fever over 104° Fahrenheit

>> Lethargy

>> Wheezing

>> Diarrhea

>> Face rubbing

>> Loss of appetite

Unfortunately, the signs are so general and so common to other conditions that it can be difficult to identify the flu.

A little tender, loving care usually is all it takes to get your ferret through. However, antibiotics, fluids, and tummy-coaters may be necessary to combat severe bouts of the flu. Be sure to consult your vet. For severe sneezing, some vets may recommend an antihistamine. Be sure to wash your hands frequently after and in between handling your sicky. Your ferret won't think twice about sharing her miserable illness with you or other ferrets.

WARNING

Tylenol (acetaminophen) is extremely toxic to ferrets, even in very low doses. The liver metabolizes the medicine, which will send your ferret reeling into liver failure quickly before killing him. Many over-the-counter medicines contain acetaminophen. It's important that you don't use any over-the-counter products without your vet's guidance and approval. You can prevent many fatal mistakes.

If the signs persist for longer than a week, or your fuzzy shows signs of refusing to eat at all, you may not be dealing with the flu. Get to a vet immediately. A ferret with the flu is crabby and tired, but she isn't knocked completely on her butt. Also, look for abnormal discharge from her nose. A flu discharge is clear.

WARNING

Bacterial pneumonia can bubble up for several reasons — often due to a flu gone from bad to worse. In addition to having flu-like signs, pneumonia causes open-mouthed breathing or labored breathing along with severe, sometimes discolored, nasal goo. Bacterial pneumonia can kill your fuzzy quickly. The treatment depends on the type of bacteria producing the pneumonia. To make the diagnosis and prescribe the defense, your vet can perform a tracheal wash by introducing a small amount of saline into the trachea and then sucking it back up to perform a culture. This can be safely done under a general anesthetic and oxygen. Depending on the type of bacteria present, your vet may prescribe a dosage of amoxicillin, sulfadiazine and trimethoprim, enrofloxacin, or marbofloxacin.

TECHNICAL
STUFF

Ferrets, contrary to popular belief, don't catch the common cold, which is caused by a rhinovirus. However, ferrets can catch bacterial sinus infections, influenza A, and upper-respiratory infections, all of which can mimic cold-like signs.

Disseminated Idiopathic Myofasciitis

Disseminated idiopathic myofasciitis (DIM) is a disease that affects pet ferrets (*Mustela putorius furo*) between 5 months and 2 years of age, although the disease has been diagnosed in ferrets as old as 4 years. DIM is a severe inflammatory condition that affects primarily skeletal, smooth, and cardiac muscles, and surrounding connective tissues. First identified in 2003, DIM was considered by professionals for many years to be a hopeless, fatal disease. However, a fairly effective treatment protocol has been found to provide hope to DIM-affected ferrets, and today there are many long-term survivors.

Initial signs of DIM usually come on relatively quickly and commonly include:

>> A severe, persistent, fluctuating fever (often 104° to 108°F)

>> Severe lethargy and weakness

>> Dehydration

>> Enlarged lymph nodes or masses under the skin

>> Abnormal stools (green, dark, mucoid, and diarrhea)

>> Decreased appetite

Other signs that may occur with DIM include:

>> Sensitivity/pain when touched, especially in the rear

>> Increased heart and respiratory rates; many develop heart murmurs

>> Clear discharge from the nose and sometimes eyes

>> Labored breathing and coughing

>> Tooth grinding

>> Tiny orange dots on the skin

>> Pale gums

Although presumptive diagnosis of DIM can be made based on a ferret's clinical signs, a definitive diagnosis can best be made by obtaining surgical biopsies of skeletal muscle tissue. However, because some ferrets are too weak to undergo anesthesia and surgery, or because owners have financial constraints and cannot afford such biopsies, most ferrets are treated presumptively for DIM.

The prognosis for ferrets with DIM that are treated appropriately is relatively good; however, owners must realize that even a full recovery may take weeks to months. Furthermore, patience and consistency are critical to their ferret's recovery. Because many veterinarians and ferret owners have never heard of DIM, however, a DIM ferret make take time to be diagnosed appropriately. Some ferrets that have been sick for too long may not respond to current treatment protocol.

Urinary Tract Problems

Several urinary tract problems can pop up in carpet sharks. Many of the problems have similar signs, so a trip to the veterinarian is advisable upon the outset of signs — especially when you consider that urinary tract infections can become serious enough to cause kidney damage and even death. You need to have a correct diagnosis made and begin treatment as soon as possible.

Bladder or urinary tract infections

Bladder or urinary tract infections are caused most often by that irritating resident bacteria *E. coli* (found in poop, so keep that litter box clean). Staphylococcus is another bacterium that can be the evildoer. Although both males and females are susceptible to this type of infection, it seems more common in females in heat and females with adrenal disease (see Chapter 16).

Signs of a bladder or urinary tract infection include

>> Straining to urinate

>> Painful urination

>> Frequent piddles

>> Discolored or smelly urine

WARNING

If you notice any of these signs, take your critter to the vet immediately. Bladder infections can travel to the kidneys and cause major damage and death. By the time a full-blown kidney infection develops, your fuzzy may be so gravely ill that treatment can prove futile, so correct and early diagnosis is imperative.

Most experts agree that treatment with the proper antibiotics should continue for a minimum of two weeks; some opt for a three-week course of treatment. Stopping the medication too soon may cause the infection to flare up again. And the bug may be even stronger and more resistant to medications the next time around.

Prostate problems

Although male ferrets can get urinary tract infections — they may exhibit similar signs — your vet should first rule out a prostate problem, such as inflammation, cysts, tumors, or abscesses. Prostate woes may be diagnosed just by feeling for an enlargement. You may get to see a little pus ooze out of the fuzzy when his infected prostate is squeezed. Eeeeew! Because this male condition always is a result of adrenal disease (see Chapter 16), it may go away after you aggressively treat the adrenal condition.

Stones and blockages

Bladder or urinary tract stones (uroliths) are unfortunately becoming more and more common in our carpet sharks. Although not all of the causes of bladder stones are known, ferret experts have begun to zero in on several culprits. A poor diet high in ash or plant-based protein has been shown to play a major role in the formation of these painful stones. Other possible causes include bacterial or viral infections and even genetic links. Whatever the cause, a bladder stone is a painful condition and needs immediate veterinary attention.

The most common types of stones encountered are cystine (#1), followed by struvite, and calcium oxalate:

>> **Cystine stones:** Far different from struvite or calcium oxalate, cystine stones are the result of a genetic defect in the kidneys and were once an uncommon occurrence. Now, the breeding of ferrets with this defect has made the incidence rate rise dramatically. These stones are likely to be formed in acidic urine when the amino acid cystine, the least soluble amino acid, is not reabsorbed by the kidneys. As such, cystine stones are composed almost entirely of the amino acid cystine.

>> **Struvite stones:** High urinary pH, poor diet, and bacterial bladder infections are three contributing factors in the formation of these stones, which are composed of magnesium, ammonium, and phosphate. Struvite stones are less likely to form in an environment where the urine is acidic or below 6.4 pH. However, a plant-based diet and certain bacterial infections may cause the urine pH to skyrocket. In this environment, it may take less than one day for struvite stones to form. Therefore, ferrets should avoid plant-based foods, and bacterial bladder infections must be treated immediately with the proper antibiotics.

>> **Calcium oxalate stones:** Although calcium oxalate stones are very different from struvite stones, they are similar to struvite stones in that two main factors leading to the creation of oxalate stones are diet and urine pH. Formed from calcium and oxalate, it would make sense to stay away from any ferret foods (including treats and supplements) that are high in these ingredients (sweet potatoes, for example). Furthermore, oxalate is formed from the metabolism of plant-based protein and the metabolism of vitamin C, and calcium oxalate stones are more likely to develop in the presence of acidic urine pH.

WARNING

If the stones in your fuzzy's system get big enough or collect in the same area, blockages can occur. Your fuzzy will no longer leave piddle puddles at this point. Signs of a partial or full urinary blockage may include: Urinating small amounts frequently, leaking urine, straining when peeing, painful (vocalizing while) urinating, wet fur around the genitals, cloudy or bloody urine, foul-smelling urine, inability to urinate, rapid lethargy, and a depressed state. This situation is painful and deadly and requires immediate attention and treatment.

Because stones and blockages mimic infections, diagnosis can be difficult. Often, your vet can feel the large, urine-filled bladder or even the stones themselves. Use of X-rays has been successful in identifying stones in the bladder.

Treatment depends on the severity of the situation. It may be as simple as a change in diet (see Chapter 8), or it may require more drastic measures — such as surgery. A vet may also put your ferret on a regimen of antibiotics to help combat the problem.

Eye Problems

I believe that most every living thing with eyeballs is prone to cataracts and other afflictions of the eye. Naturally, ferrets fall into the group of susceptible animals. In fact, sight impairment is quite common in ferrets, and is *usually* nothing to be concerned about as long as you can recognize it and make provisions for your ferret. Ferrets, however, are very enduring, so it may take you a while to figure out your little ferret is sight-impaired. I had several fuzzies with cataracts, which are quite common. Some of these furballs were completely blind; others had partial vision. Sometimes eye problems in ferrets can be corrected surgically or medically. Don't worry if your ferret's eyes aren't fixable; a blind ferret or one with limited vision can find trouble as well as or better than a carpet shark with perfect vision. After all, they put much more effort into it!

What sort of things cause interference with sight in the ferret? To name just a few:

>> Retinal disease

>> Disease of the lens (cataracts or luxated [twisted] lens)

>> Disease of the optic nerve

>> Central nervous system problems that affect the vision center (stroke, seizures, head trauma)

>> Trauma to the eye globe causing rupture or puncture

>> Corneal disease (scarring from ulcers or trauma)

Ferrets don't see well to begin with. They see up close, but not very far away, making them near-sighted. Far superior are their senses of smell and hearing, which ferrets far more rely on when navigating about their day. A gradual loss of eyesight will cause most ferrets to slowly increase reliance on their other senses to "survive." It is not unusual for a blind ferret to memorize her surroundings (don't rearrange the furniture!) or even use a cagemate or two as "seeing eye ferrets."

Following are sure-fire signs of eye problems:

>> Your ferret seems more cautious about moving around.

>> She startles and backs off or snaps at you when you reach in to grab her.

>> She walks into things (especially if you rearrange the furniture!).

>> She repeatedly lifts her nose and smells the same thing.

>> She avoids open spaces and runs along walls or large objects.

>> Cataracts are visibly present in her eyes.

>> She places a call to your health-insurance carrier to see if laser surgery is covered.

TIP

Remember that your sight-impaired fuzzy still needs as much enrichment as all of your other furkids. Hone in on those senses she is "hyper" relying on, such as smell, touch, taste, and hearing. (Refer to Chapter 10 for enrichment ideas.)

TIP

If you're not sure if your ferret is blind, you can do the finger test. All my sighted ferrets rapidly chase, follow, or watch my finger as I move it from side to side. My blind guys just pop up their heads and listen to figure out what everyone else is doing. I love these guys. They're so cute!

REMEMBER

Blind ferrets adapt and function very well. However, you must take special precautions when dealing with a blind ferret. For example, you don't want to sneak up on her or startle her; instead, speak to her calmly and gently before interacting with her and especially before picking her up. You may need to take extra care when ferret-proofing your home to keep her away from falling dangers such as furniture or stairs. You can use scent mapping to help her learn her way around. You have many ways to improve your relationship with your visually impaired ferret!

Aleutian Disease Virus (ADV)

Aleutian disease (AD) is a contagious and potentially fatal ferret disease caused by a parvovirus. No vaccine is currently available. Named after the Aleutian mink, which is highly susceptible, ADV was first diagnosed on a mink ranch in the 1940s and then in ferrets in the 1960s. The biggest problem with this virus for the ferret isn't the virus itself, but the ferret's immune-system response.

When a virus enters the body, the body forms antibodies. These antibodies attach to the virus to help the immune system identify the virus as a foreign invader, thus triggering a defensive response to destroy it. In the case of ADV, a large complex of substances, not just the antibodies, bind with the viral particles and form an immune complex. These large complexes circulate throughout the body until they're deposited into the tissues of various organs; here, due to their size, the complexes cause inflammation. In small amounts, the complexes won't cause outward signs of disease; however, if the body deposits enough of these complexes into one area, the clinical disease may result.

Although transmission of ADV can occur through the air, typical transmission occurs through direct contact with the bodily fluids, such as blood, urine, saliva, and feces, of an infected ferret, or from contaminated cages, supplies, or humans. Practicing good husbandry and sanitation is the best way to prevent the spread of ADV. *Note:* The ADV can remain in a ferret-free home for up to two years.

Many ADV-positive ferrets never show clinical signs; and no one can predict if or when an ADV-positive ferret ever will. The signs of AD are variable and depend largely on the affected organs and secondary infections. The following list presents the possibilities; upon seeing a sign, head to your vet on the double:

>> Weight loss

>> Bloody (black, tarry) stools

>> Hind-end weakness

>> Lethargy

>> Anemia

>> Body twitching or seizures

>> Enlarged liver or spleen

>> Difficulty breathing

>> Anemia

>> Seizures

Science currently has no cure for AD and no way to predict how long a ferret that exhibits clinical AD-related signs will live. It depends on the severity of the damage to the organs. Unfortunately, most active cases of AD aren't diagnosed until the later stages of the disease, thus shortening the ferrets' lives.

Canine Distemper

Canine distemper is an unforgiving and miserable disease that's 99.9 percent fatal. In extremely rare instances, ferrets have survived, but all survivors have suffered neurological impairments. Because no treatment is available, prevention is critical. You can do your part to prevent the disease by vaccinating your fuzzy.

The canine distemper virus is extremely contagious and can be transmitted to your fuzzy via other infected animals. If you think your fuzzy is safe from canine distemper because she never leaves the house, you're dead wrong. You can carry this virus into your household on your shoes and clothing. The distemper virus also can live a long time outside of the victim's body. So be careful and do the right thing: Vaccinate your fuzzy. *Note:* Humans can't catch this disease from the poor victims.

The *incubation* period (the time it takes from the day of infection to the onset of signs) in your ferret may be as little as 7 days or as long as 21 days. When the signs appear, death usually occurs quickly, because the virus attacks many organs at once. On rare occasions, a fuzzy may suffer a longer, more miserable death. Because the prognosis is hopeless and the signs are unbearably miserable, if your vet makes a positive diagnosis, he should humanely euthanize your ferret as soon as possible. The extremely rare survivor will just suffer severe neurological damage and her quality of life will be poor.

Clinical signs of distemper include

>> Eye infection/discharge

>> Severe lethargy

>> Loss of appetite

>> Rash on chin, lips, and nose

>> Rash on belly and heinie

>> Hardened/thick paw pads

>> Diarrhea

>> Vomiting

>> Seizures

>> Coma

WARNING

Pet owners who decide against vaccinating for distemper run the risk of not only a single ferret becoming infected with distemper, but also the entire group. Think about this the next time you casually walk your unvaccinated ferret on a leash into a large chain pet store. A single ferret can come into contact with the virus — perhaps from a sick dog that visited the store, from the owner's shoe, or even during a vet checkup where an infected dog was in the office — and then become ill, going on to infect all the ferrets in the household before the owner realizes what's going on.

Diabetes Mellitus

Diabetes mellitus is quite the opposite of insulinoma (see Chapter 16). Instead of producing too much insulin, a hormone released by the pancreas, and which is also responsible for blood glucose regulation, ferrets with diabetes suffer from the inability to either produce insulin or to use insulin. When insulin isn't present in the ferret's body or when the body doesn't respond to insulin the way it was designed to, muscles and organs are unable to convert glucose into energy. The ferret's body has no choice but to steal from his own stashes of protein and fat in order to meet his daily energy needs until those reservoirs run out. This vicious cycle leads from gradual to major weight loss and eventually to a terminal condition requiring veterinary intervention.

High concentrations of blood glucose coupled with the ferret's inability to utilize accessible glucose as a source of fuel leaves the diabetic ferret with a multitude of possible symptoms. For example:

>> High blood sugar (hyperglycemia)

>> Increased urination

>> Increased or decreased appetite

>> Excessive thirst

>> Weight loss, often with overall body weakness

>> Lethargy

>> Depression

>> Fatty liver disease

Many experts believe that *diabetes mellitus* is not a spontaneously occurring disease. Instead, they think it is the result of a surgery on the pancreas to treat an insulinoma (see Chapter 16).

Quite simply put, the ultimate goal of treatment is to return the diabetic ferret's blood sugar to a normal or non-diabetic level. This may be achieved in a couple of ways, but it depends on the ferret's response to treatment. Injectable insulin, which is a pancreas-produced hormone that regulates the amount of glucose in the blood, is the treatment of choice. Additionally, your vet will likely advise you to deny excessive food to your ferret to prevent obesity, which can also be a problem with diabetic ferrets.

Although each case of *diabetes mellitus* is as unique as the affected ferret is herself, most cases can be managed without complications. With proper management, which may include a diet change along with the insulin, a diabetic ferret can live quite happily.

Enlarged Spleen (Splenomegaly)

The spleen (in ferrets and in other animals and humans) has several functions: For example,

» It serves as a blood purifier, filtering out bacteria and damaged cells.

» It provides the perfect environment for the cells of the immune system to learn how to counterattack an invasion of possible marauding organisms.

» It stores iron from old red blood cells, which is used to make new red blood cells. In ferrets and many other species, the spleen is an additional site for red and white blood-cell production.

» In some species, the spleen stores blood and releases it in times of need.

An enlarged spleen, or *splenomegaly*, is extremely prevalent in fuzzies, and no one really knows why. This problem often appears by itself, with no other underlying diseases. The ferret's spleen normally gets larger with age, but sometimes this growth is accelerated. One common thought is that the use of certain anesthetics rapidly causes this condition. The enlargement in this case is temporary only while the animal is under the effects of the anesthetic. Then the spleen goes back to normal. The spleen is very elastic, and may enlarge and go back to normal on its own as well when responding to the body's needs for more cells.

Diagnosing an enlarged spleen is relatively easy. Most experienced vets should be able to feel the enlarged organ by simply squishing around the ferret's abdomen. And an X-ray often confirms the size and condition of the organ. Care should be taken not to apply enough pressure to rupture a severely bulging spleen.

The shared expert opinion regarding treatment is to leave the spleen in if it isn't causing discomfort or other problems. In other words, "If it ain't broke, don't fix it." Fuzzies generally can live long, healthy lives with big spleens. Removing a spleen unnecessarily can put your baby in more jeopardy. On the other hand, if the oversized spleen is causing discomfort, lethargy, or loss of appetite, removal of the organ is necessary. Surgery to remove the spleen actually is straightforward, and the survival rate is extremely high — especially when no other illnesses are present.

REMEMBER

It might be a good idea to have your vet send out a sample of the spleen to a pathologist to determine the cause of the enlargement. Remember, illnesses or diseases caught early have a better chance of being treated more effectively.

Hairballs

Ferrets are prone to developing gastric hairballs, and hairballs can lead to intestinal blockages. Unlike cats, ferrets won't leave colorful wads of urped-up fur on your newly shampooed carpet. Ferrets are capable of throwing up, but usually the fur accumulates in the ferret's body until it becomes a large mass — a mass too big to go either up or down. Hairballs and other blockages (see the section "Intestinal and stomach blockages") can cause ferrets to become seriously ill — and they often cause death.

You should give your ferret a hairball preventative on a regular basis to help clean out her system. I give each of my ferrets a quarter-teaspoon of an easy-to-make homemade hairball preventative (one part salmon oil and one part pure petroleum jelly) weekly. Most ferrets like the taste of the stuff, although some need to get used to it. With more difficult types, you may need to insist that they take it — by placing it directly into their mouths with your fingertip or gently with a popsicle stick. You also can find commercial hairball remedies or preventives at many pet stores. Some ferret shelters and veterinarians also carry these products. Just remember that these may be sugar-dense for palatability and therefore may not be the best choice for your ferret over the long run, or for ferrets with health conditions that are exacerbated by sugar intake.

Rabies

Although ferrets are highly unlikely to contract rabies, the possibility does exist. Rabies, caused by a rhabdovirus, is passed through the saliva of an infected animal, most frequently through a bite that penetrates the skin. After entering the body, the deadly virus attaches to nerve bundles, reproduces, and migrates to the victim's brain. The virus then travels along nerve bundles until it reaches the salivary glands, where the animal can then pass it to another victim through a bite.

TECHNICAL STUFF

Many different strains of the rabies virus exist, including rodent, raccoon, fox, and skunk strains. Studies suggest that fuzzies are most susceptible to the raccoon strain, which they can pass on before death.

Rabies can manifest itself in one of two ways:

>> **Furious rabies:** With furious rabies, the infected animal exhibits intense aggression, biting, and foaming at the mouth.

>> **Dumb rabies:** With dumb rabies, the animal becomes lethargic and deathly ill, and wants little to do with people or other animals. Animals with dumb rabies don't attack and usually die quickly. Although ferret infection is extremely rare, studies indicate that ferrets will likely exhibit dumb rabies, with death occurring seven days (on average) after the ferret has been infected.

The following signs also suggest that your ferret may have rabies (although they can indicate a host of problems):

>> Disorientation

>> Loss of coordination

>> Muscle spasms

>> Difficulty breathing

>> Drooling

>> Nervousness

>> Hind-leg weakness

>> Passiveness

>> Hind-end paralysis

REMEMBER

Today, unlike many years ago, you have a choice on how much life "insurance" you're willing to buy for your lovable fuzzbutt, because you can give her a rabies vaccine. Some people want to weigh the pros and cons of vaccinating (the only viable con being a history of life-threatening allergic reactions), but the pros weigh heavily on the scale. Failure to vaccinate your ferret can lead to a miserable disease and death. To the true fuzzy human, the emotional cost of losing a ferret to a preventable disease is immeasurable. Proof of vaccination also may calm the fears of people who get bitten or scratched — and perhaps prevent confiscation of your pet (see Chapter 3).

Ulcers

By the time you're done reading about all that can go wrong with your fuzzy, you may be suffering from an ulcer yourself! Ulcers are one of the most common ferret diseases. An *ulcer* is an open sore, which can occur on the skin, eyes, or mucous membranes. For this section, I talk about ulcers of the gastrointestinal tract. The causes of ulcers are just about the same for fuzzies and humans:

>> **Stress, stress, and more stress:** The stress can come from illness, disease, grief (loss of a cagemate), low-quality food, injury, or even anxiety over the environment (overcrowding, abuse, small cage, poor husbandry, no exercise, and so on). (For more on helping your fuzzy grieve, check out Chapter 17.)

>> **Possible bacterial invasion:** The bacteria *H. mustelae's* presence may trigger a progressive inflammatory reaction in a ferret's stomach lining. The reaction weakens the lining and predisposes it to further damage. Ulcers, perhaps? No one knows for sure if bacteria can be directly linked to ulcers, but it sure can cause some serious damage to the tummy.

>> **Ulcer-causing substances:** These substances include alcohol, aspirin, and certain medications.

>> **Hairballs or other stomach foreign bodies:** Rubbing on the lining of the stomach in the same area over and over can cause severe irritation.

The signs of an ulcer include the following:

>> Lethargy

>> Tender belly

>> Face rubbing

>> Black, tarry stools

>> Teeth grinding

>> Loss of appetite

>> Vomiting (may be bloody)

>> Weight loss

- » Pale gums

- » Bad breath

- » Hunched posture (painful abdomen)

- » More aggression (pain)

If you notice any of these signs, take your ferret to the vet for an exam and diagnosis.

Having an ulcer diagnosed as soon as possible is important, because it's a very painful condition that may lead to death. Besides being unable to adequately digest their food, ulcer patients bleed internally from oozing blood vessels. For some reason, ulcer signs often are misdiagnosed as another intestinal or stomach problem. An effective diagnostic tool is a barium X-ray, which shows any signs of burned-out bellies or intestine.

Treatment of ulcers usually begins with antibiotic therapy, with medicines such as Amoxicillin and Biaxin to combat H. mustelae. Some veterinarians use Biaxin. To treat the ulcer itself, most vets use Carafate (which is most effective when given 10 minutes prior to feeding; consult your vet). Your vet may prescribe an OTC acid reliever such as Pepcid AC or Tagamet to relieve the burning and nausea that accompany ulcers. A bland diet is recommended during treatment (see Chapter 8 for tips on changing diet).

Because a ferret's body is always secreting stomach acid to help break down food, treatment can be long and tedious. It can and usually will take over a month for a ferret's ulcer to heal, and you should be prepared to treat the ulcer for a minimum of ten days after all signs have disappeared. Also, don't be surprised if your ferret gets another ulcer down the road. After she gets one, she'll be prone to getting more.

WARNING

If you allow your ferret's ulcer to progress without proper treatment, it may become so deep that it hits a major blood vessel and causes the suffering fuzzy to bleed to death internally. (The black, tarry stool associated with ulcers, for example, actually is digested blood and a sign of bleeding in the digestive tract.) If your ferret doesn't bleed to death, anemia may result from the constant rupturing of small blood vessels in the belly. Ulcers can also go all the way through the lining of the stomach and perforate, leading to the dumping of stomach contents into the abdomen and resulting in peritonitis and death.

Chapter **16**

Finding and Treating the Big C and Other Lumps

Unfortunately, whether you own one ferret or ten, you're likely to encounter ferret cancer during your time as a ferret owner. The three most prevalent cancer conditions are adrenal disease (which may or may not be cancerous), insulinoma, and lymphosarcoma. Symptoms and treatments vary, as well as prognoses.

As you'll see in this chapter, the Big C diagnosis is rarely an immediate death sentence. Many cases are treatable. Others are manageable, and your ferret may live a few more quality years after the diagnosis, with or without ongoing medical intervention. However, early detection and treatment are instrumental in adding quality months or even years to your fuzzy's life, so you need to watch for changes in your fuzzy's appearance, habits, and behavior. A good vet will trust your judgment that something isn't quite right with your fuzzbutt (see Chapter 12 for tips on finding a good vet). In this chapter, I discuss the three main types of ferret cancer. I also discuss chordomas and skin tumors.

Adrenal Gland Disease

Everyone has adrenal glands, including ferrets. These tiny organs are located very close to the kidneys. In a nutshell, *adrenal glands* are part of the endocrine system and produce extremely important hormones that help regulate electrolyte levels, increase musculature, and help the ferret in times of stress. Different areas of the adrenal glands are responsible for producing different hormones. For instance, small amounts of sex hormones, or "sex steroids," such as estrogen and progesterone, are produced by these glands. Adrenaline is also produced.

Adrenal gland disease is an extremely common syndrome in ferrets, and after many years of speculation, we now know several reasons why. The adrenal glands can start overproducing sex steroids that act the same way excessive amounts of the sex hormones testosterone and progesterone would act. Usually starting out as hyperplasia, the adrenal glands produce more gland tissue, which results in excessive hormone production. As the disease progresses, however, neoplasia (cancer) can develop. Fortunately for ferrets, *metastasis,* or spreading of the cancer beyond the adrenal gland(s) to other organs, doesn't happen often.

This disease can strike ferrets younger than 3 years old, but it much more commonly hits ferrets that are 3 years and older. Many reasons exist around the cause of adrenal disease:

>> Early neutering, which I define as neutering before puberty or prior to sexual development. Once removal of the ferret's sex organs (testicles or ovaries) occurs, there is no more regulation of the brain's sex hormone cycles. As a result, unchecked surges cause a stimulation of hormone production, such as estrogen, for example. The result is hyperplastic changes (an enlargement of a part or organ due to an abnormal increase in cell production) or neoplastic changes (abnormal growth of cells, causing either benign or malignant tumors) of the adrenal gland.

TECHNICAL STUFF

Many vets, and even ferret owners, seem stuck on their ferret's age when it comes to adrenal disease. They may not consider that a juvenile altered ferret could have adrenal disease, even if he displays one or two signs, simply because of his young age. It only takes the altering procedure to send the ferret's body into adrenal gland overproduction. Adrenal disease can hit ferrets as young as a few months old and certainly under 2 years old. I have seen it. Although it is uncommon, you should be aware of it. After you and your vet rule out other possible issues causing these signs, consider putting your ferret on a 3 month go-around with Lupron or a deslorelin implant to treat for adrenal gland disease. Better safe than sorry!

>> Adrenal gland disease is also caused by the unnatural light cycles that our "crepuscular" (active at dawn and dusk) ferrets experience while living in people's homes. These light cycles differ greatly from what the ferrets would experience naturally in the wild. After all, ideally ferrets should receive approximately 14 hours of total darkness each night. A prolonged photoperiod — that is, being subjected to longer periods of light — may decrease melatonin production and send hormonal messages to the ferret that it's breeding season.

>> Prolonged stress may also play a small role into the development of adrenal disease.

The signs of adrenal gland disease depend largely on which hormone(s) is being produced, the gender of the ferret, and the stage of the disease's development. Within these factors, the signs _may_ or _may not_ include the following:

REMEMBER

>> Hair loss on the tail/body

Hair loss on the tail and/or body is one of the most common signs of adrenal gland disease. However, it doesn't have to be present for adrenal gland disease to exist. Hair loss can come and go. A ferret may lose all her tail fur only to have it grow back thick and fluffy later on. Some may attribute this phenomenon to a seasonal coat change. It is, however, thought to be the early stage of adrenal gland disease — hyperplasia that temporarily resolves itself. As the disease progresses, hair loss usually starts on the tail and progresses up the body. The hair loss, if adrenal-gland related, is usually symmetrical. Sometimes, ferrets lose all but their socks and hats.

>> Excessive itchiness, with or without crusts, redness, or flaking

>> Swollen vulva in spayed females (see Figure 16-1)

>> Aggressive mating behavior (in neutered males)

>> Unusual aggressive behavior (in either gender) toward owners or cagemates

>> Difficulty urinating for males that develop enlarged prostates; partial or complete urinary obstructions

>> Anemia in both males and females

>> Some muscle thinning, weakness, or a potbellied appearance

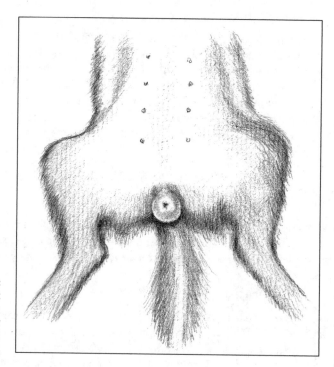

FIGURE 16-1:
Female ferret with swollen vulva caused by adrenal gland disease.

Making the diagnosis

Diagnosing adrenal gland disease can, at times, be pretty easy. In many cases, just looking at the ferret is enough. If she's experiencing serious hair loss alone or if the hair loss is coupled with any of the other common signs, she probably has adrenal gland disease. However, it's very important that you take your fuzzy to your vet as soon as you notice a symptom of the disease. The unfortunate thing is, a fuzzy can be suffering from adrenal gland disease and show no signs for a very long time. Your vet may get lucky and detect an enlarged adrenal gland during a routine physical examination, but this doesn't usually happen.

TIP

Because the adrenal glands are so tiny, an ultrasound of the abdomen may miss the early stages of adrenal gland disease. Running routine bloodwork and taking X-rays usually won't help in diagnosing adrenal gland disease, either. However, it's common for a ferret with adrenal gland disease to have another disease present, as well. Therefore, you should consider asking for additional bloodwork and X-rays anyway so that you and your vet can develop a treatment plan that's suitable for your pet's special needs.

After you discover some symptoms, you and your vet may opt to send a sample of your fuzzy's blood to the University of Tennessee, where experts can perform a test that's helpful in diagnosing adrenal gland disease. The experts can perform an adrenal-gland panel to evaluate the levels of sex steroids in your ferret's system. This is one way to zero in on a diagnosis — especially in cases where the diagnosis isn't so obvious.

Because the Tennessee panel isn't 100 percent accurate and can be expensive, most people decide to treat adrenal gland disease without the test. Many vets will also suggest surgically removing the affected adrenal gland(s) without going to extreme diagnostic measures if the major signs of the disease are already there.

Treating the disease

When it comes to treating adrenal gland disease, you have a few options to consider, which may be used independently or together. Many variables will come into play, such as the age and health of your ferret and your financial situation, but undoubtedly your vet will help you decide what's best for you and your ferret. One option, which is frequently recommended, is surgery. However, some medications have a positive effect in treating adrenal gland disease and/or managing its signs.

Surgery

Until implants (see "Medical treatment options," later in this chapter) became popular and more effective, adrenal gland surgery was a fairly common procedure. A ferret can live with one adrenal gland. Although we know that removing one gland shifts the burden of the gland function onto the remaining adrenal gland, and surgery is far less common due to effective implants, there may be a good reason for your ferret to undergo removal of her adrenal gland. For example, if the adrenal tumor is a rapidly growing one (carcinoma), or the vet is doing a surgery, such as an insulinoma surgery, and the tumor can be removed at the same time.

Your ferret may be a good surgical candidate if she's otherwise in good health otherwise and can withstand general anesthesia. Another option to adrenal gland removal is to *debulk*, or surgically remove, as much adrenal tissue as possible, followed by medical therapy. Post-operative prognosis is pretty good but depends on the tumors present and what else is going on inside the ferret's body. After the diseased gland(s) is removed, the signs gradually disappear. The ferret's fur usually grows back, although it can take many months. The fur also may be thinner and a different color.

Ferrets are prone to developing multi-organ diseases, so when your vet performs an abdominal exploratory surgery on your ferret, ask him to take a good look around inside your fuzzy. Your vet should check the condition of her adrenal glands, pancreas, stomach, intestines, liver, spleen, and kidneys, which only takes a couple extra minutes. Biopsies can be performed on anything suspicious, and your vet can remove anything obvious right then and there. Early detection of disease can prolong your fuzzy's life and make medical management more successful.

What if surgery isn't the right option for your ferret? Reasons may include the following:

>> Your fuzzy is at an advanced age.

>> Your fuzzy has other complicating diseases, such as advanced heart disease.

>> Maybe your own fears are preventing you from going the surgical route.

Well, if surgery isn't an option for you, fuzzies can live up to three years completely untreated. However, your ferret may experience behavioral changes, or other medical conditions may develop, such as prostate problems, as a result of untreated adrenal gland disease. Sometimes her fur will grow back at the next seasonal coat change. But affected ferrets usually lose more hair the next time around. And it may not grow back at all.

Medical treatment options

You do have good medical options to treat adrenal gland disease — some of which have been used with great results. The following list outlines some of these options and what they can do for your sick fuzzy: (*Note:* Not all adrenal ferrets are candidates for medical treatment. Speak with your vet about what's right for your furkid.)

>> Lupron depot (the long-acting lupron), also known as Lueprorlin in Europe, is a common adrenal medication that is safe for ferrets. The medication has very few, if any, known side effects and can be ordered directly from your vet. It acts by stopping the LH (Luteinizing Hormone) stimulation to the adrenal glands. In turn, the adrenal glands stop overproducing adrenal androgens and sex hormones. In carcinomas (cancer), Lupron may keep tumors from getting bigger, but Lupron does nothing directly to shrink tumors. Lupron can be an expensive treatment option, and it's necessary for the remainder of the ferret's life.

Lupron shots are a great option for ferrets that are older or more sensitive or for ferrets that may not be able to easily withstand even the light anesthesia that may come with the deslorelin implant.

Although you may not be able to prevent adrenal disease entirely, there are some ways you can help your ferret ward it off:

TIP

- Start deslorelin implants whether your ferret shows signs of adrenal disease or not. Suggested age to begin is approximately 6 months old.

- Speak to your vet about giving your ferret a melatonin implant.

- If possible, keep your ferret intact until she is between 6 and 8 months old. At minimum, let your ferret go through a full breeding season before neutering or spaying. Impossible to complete this one if your baby arrives already neutered or spayed.

- Keep them in the dark!! Ferrets need 14 hours of complete darkness, not dimness, a day. Turn off all the lights or cover her cage with a thick, dark blanket or a room-darkening curtain.

» Since the writing of the last edition of this book, Suprelorin implants finally made it to the U.S. This medication, also known as deslorelin acetate, works like Lupron, stopping the LH stimulation to the adrenal glands and turning off the overproduction of sex hormones and adrenal androgens. Within 14 days after the implant of deslorelin, most visible effects of adrenal disease decrease or completely disappear, and lost hair may return 4 to 6 weeks post-implant.

The implant, about the size of a grain of rice, is injected beneath the skin, which, in rare occasions, requires the ferret to be briefly anesthetized due to the size of the needle and the ferret's condition. Deslorelin does take 4 to 6 weeks to reach its maximum effect, but its ability to suppress adrenal-associated hormones can last anywhere from 8 to 20 months per implant.

It should also be noted that deslorelin may be used as a chemical contraceptive in unaltered male and female ferrets. It has been shown to be just as effective as surgical castration.

» Giving a ferret melatonin, orally or through implants (Ferretonin), is another popular medical approach to treating adrenal disease. Although implants are much more effective than oral administration, something is better than nothing. Oral melatonin needs to be given daily at the *same time* every day (7 to 8 hours after sunrise) in order for it to work — for many this equates to about 2:00 pm. Some ferret owners have used melatonin as a preventative. It works by lowering LH, sex hormone, and androgen levels. However, some are concerned that ferrets may develop immunity to melatonin after long-term use, rendering it relatively useless. Like Lupron and Suprelorin, it does nothing directly to stop the progression of the disease.

Melatonin implants can be used in conjunction with adrenal surgery or along with Lupron or deslorelin. In fact, your veterinarian may recommend it.

Prostate problems in the male ferret often are associated with adrenal gland disease. The overproduction of the testosterone-like sex steroid causes the prostate to enlarge. Some enlarged prostatic tissue can apply pressure on the urinary tract, leading to the ferret having difficulty urinating or creating urinary blockage. Ferrets can develop bacterial infections in the prostatic tissue leading to more serious disease. (Bacterial infections need to be treated with appropriate antibiotics.) Lupron or deslorelin, in high doses, inhibits the production of sex steroids, causing the prostate to shrink back to normal size.

Insulinoma

Insulinoma is one of the most diagnosed ferret cancers. A ferret with *insulinoma* has cancer of the insulin-secreting pancreatic cells, or *beta cells.* One of the pancreas's main roles is to release insulin as needed to regulate the ferret's blood sugar levels. It does its job by facilitating the movement of glucose out of the bloodstream and into the cells, which use it as a primary fuel source. In ferrets with insulinoma, tumors cause an overproduction of insulin. Too much glucose moves out of the bloodstream quickly, which causes rapid drops in blood sugar, or *hypoglycemia.* And without blood glucose, the ferret's brain and red blood cells are left with little to no fuel to maintain.

Insulinoma most often strikes ferrets after the age of 3. Sometimes, the disease goes unnoticed for a long time as the ferret's system fights to regulate its own blood sugar levels. During this time, the signs may not be overly apparent. When they do show up, some of the signs may include

>> Weakness and lethargy

>> Excessive sleep or difficulty waking up

>> Excessive salivation

>> Pawing at the mouth

>> Dazed and confused look

>> Loss of coordination

>> Rear leg weakness

>> Enlarged spleen

>> Tremors and/or seizures

>> Coma

REMEMBER

With insulinoma, the signs may come and go as the ferret's body works to counteract the swings in blood glucose by producing more glucose from the liver. Things that can trigger and aggravate the signs include exercise, stress, and diet. However, any of the signs warrants a trip to the vet.

Making the diagnosis

A vet usually obtains a diagnosis by drawing a *fasting* blood sugar level, in which the fuzzy goes three to four hours without food before the blood is drawn. Anything longer than three to four hours is too long for a ferret with insulinoma to go without food. Normal blood glucose levels are between 80 and 120. Having a fasting blood glucose level in the 70s is highly suspicious, but less than 70 is generally considered diagnostic for insulinoma. If you want to take the diagnostic process a step further, exploratory surgery will confirm the presence of insulinoma tumors.

Treating the disease

Your vet can help you determine the best course of action to treat insulinoma, based on your ferret's history and current condition. Surgery is frequently an option and may stop or slow the progression of insulinoma. Unfortunately, pancreatic tumors can be small and seedy nodules, located throughout the pancreas, making the treatment process surgically challenging. In some cases, the tumors are isolated nodules that can be more easily removed. And although surgery can stop or slow the progression of the disease, the condition is never completely curable. Tumors frequently return at a later date.

Your fuzzy may live for months to years after the diagnosis, with a lot of tender, loving care and a consistent management program, including medications and dietary changes (see Chapter 8). Some of the medications that vets have found to be successful in managing insulinoma are diazoxide (Proglycem) and corticosteroids (such as prednisolone or prednisone). Only your vet can determine what's best for your ferret.

WARNING

People often recommend that you add Brewer's yeast to the insulinoma patient's diet. I suggest that you *not* do this. The chromium in Brewer's yeast has been shown to actually lower blood sugar levels as opposed to stabilizing them, as once thought.

Every ferret owner should keep some Karo syrup or honey on hand, especially if you have a ferret with insulinoma. If your fuzzy *crashes* (shows extreme lethargy, weakness, or has seizures) due to low blood sugar, take a cotton swab and dab a little honey or Karo syrup on her gums. Do not use your finger or you risk being bitten by your disoriented ferret. The sugar helps to stabilize the ferret until you can get her to a vet, which you should do as quickly as possible. Follow up with some high-protein food like chicken baby food.

REMEMBER

Use this type of sugar boost in emergency situations only — to bring your ferret out of a hypoglycemic episode. Too much sugar can be dangerous for a fuzzy with insulinoma.

TIP

It's true that some ferrets may be genetically predisposed to cancers such as insulinoma. However, you still may be able to prevent it. Many ferret diets on the market are high in carbs/sugars and are linked to the onset of insulinoma in ferrets. The longer the ferret is on a high-carb diet, the more risk there is that she develops insulinoma as she ages. Consider a raw or freeze-dried raw low-carb diet for your ferret. Remember — the diet should have 75 percent or more animal-based protein.

Lymphosarcoma (Lymphoma)

Very common in beloved furballs is *lymphosarcoma* or *lymphoma,* a cancer of the lymphatic system (the organs and cells designed to fight disease). Many ferrets suffering from this type of cancer can have severely impaired immune systems, while other ferrets are *subclinical* — they have no overt signs of the disease at all. The cause of lymphosarcoma remains a bit of a mystery. Environmental and genetic influences are possible factors. Some experts are convinced that lympho-sarcoma is linked directly to a certain type of virus. The condition sometimes shows up in multiple cagemates, reinforcing the viral theory by implying some sort of viral transmission.

The two most common types of lymphosarcoma in ferrets are *juvenile lymphosar-coma* (lymphoblastic form), which hits furkids typically under the age of 14 months, and *adult lymphosarcoma* (lymphocytic form), which generally is diag-nosed in middle-aged and older ferrets. Because of the instances of subclinical ferrets, lymphosarcoma isn't always easy to recognize. Thankfully, many ferrets may show signs, including

>> Lethargy

>> Extreme weight loss

>> Diarrhea

>> Labored breathing

>> Loss of appetite

>> Enlarged spleen

>> Enlarged lymph nodes (locally or throughout the body)

Making the diagnosis

In juvenile lymphosarcoma, death can occur suddenly and with no signs, because the disease raids many organs at once. Vets often misdiagnose any warning signs that do exist in the youngsters as an upper-respiratory infection, pneumonia, or cardiomyopathy. This is due mainly to respiratory and circulatory distress resulting from large, fast-growing tumors that invade the chest cavity and squish the lungs.

Adult lymphosarcoma, on the other hand, is more often recognized by vets. Unlike with the juvenile version, classic lymphosarcoma frequently causes enlarged lymph nodes that a vet can easily feel under the jaw, the armpits and on the neck. The vet should confirm diagnosis with a biopsy of a lymph node, bone marrow, spleen, or chest fluid. Often, irregularities in the ferret's complete blood count or calcium raise a red flag, but that isn't always the case. It's always best to send out biopsy samples to a pathologist.

Treating the disease

Some fuzzy cancers, including lymphosarcoma/lymphoma, respond pretty well to chemotherapy. For many ferrets, chemotherapy provides a decent remission rate (with the exception of the intestinal form of lymphosarcoma), with life often prolonged 6 to 36 months from the start of treatment. However, this form of treatment can be very expensive, and not all cancer patients are good chemo candidates. You should talk to your vet about all your possible treatment options.

Some signs of lymphosarcoma can be alleviated temporarily with steroids, such as prednisone, but this treatment isn't a cure for the condition.

Chordomas

Chordomas are the most common musculoskeletal tumors found in the ferret. It's difficult to explain these icky tumors without first giving you a simple lesson on a complex matter of development. All developing embryos have certain tissues that develop to form their basic support systems, such as the spine (including the tail). Leftover embryonic tissue that doesn't develop into the skeletal structure rests in between the vertebrae. These remnants sometimes continue to grow, causing the formation of chordomas.

The mass often grows slowly at the tip of the ferret's tail, eventually giving the tail a club-like appearance. The tumor itself is made up of a bony center beneath a layer of cartilage and rough cells that resemble red, raw elephant skin. For the Herculean fuzzbutt, this tumor can be quite a weapon.

Chordomas are easily diagnosed and typically appear in fuzzies over 3 years old. The most common ferret chordoma is located on the tip of the tail. In some rare instances, a chordoma grows in between the vertebrae near the head, in a tumor called a *cervical chordoma.* This more serious tumor can cause compression of the spinal cord, at which point the ferret becomes physically impaired. Cervical chordomas also are more apt to spread and cause severe pain and neurological problems.

REMEMBER

Chordomas can present more than just cosmetic problems for your ferret. They frequently cause hair loss on and surrounding the tumor. Often, the mass becomes ulcerated and oozy. Because of its vulnerable location and the probability of trauma to the tail, vets generally recommend removal, which is a relatively simple procedure.

Itchy Growths: Skin Tumors

Skin tumors appear in all shapes and sizes on fuzzy friends. The good news is that the majority of these skin tumors are *benign,* or non-cancerous. However, all are capable of becoming *malignant,* or cancerous. Vets usually recommend the removal of the lump, bump, or ugly formation. Although the most common ferret skin tumors rarely develop into cancer, the possibility will always remain if you don't have a tumor removed.

Also, several types of skin tumors are itchy and easy to rub and irritate. Removing a tumor from your ferret eliminates the risk of her developing secondary infections from open sores. Be sure to send a tumor tissue sample to a lab for analysis, just for peace of mind. If your vet suspects cancer, removal of a nearby lymph node for biopsy also is a good idea to determine if the cancer has spread. You and your vet can determine a course of treatment from there. Remember: The earlier you act, the better chance you give your fuzzy!

Many types of skin tumors can afflict ferrets. The following sections touch on the most common skin tumors.

Mast cell tumors

Mast cells are directly related to the immune system. They produce histamines to combat foreign bodies in the ferret's system. For reasons unknown, these cells may migrate and form small tumors on the ferret's skin. The growths can appear anywhere on your fuzzy as a single tumor or multiple tumors.

Mast cell tumors often are round, slightly raised red lumps — button-like in appearance. Sometimes they're flat and scaly in appearance. Because of the ferret's constant production of histamines, this type of tumor is extremely itchy. You'll know something's up if you witness your poor ferret scratching feverishly at her skin (at the area of the tumor), causing excessive bleeding and oozing. Also, the site usually shows some hair loss and may be scabbed over from the constant irritation.

Although mast cell tumors often are malignant in other animals, they rarely become cancerous in ferrets. Nonetheless, because of the risk of infection and the obvious discomfort your fuzzy feels, you should be a nice human and have any mast cell tumors removed. Always have a biopsy done. You should also expect more, though, because they frequently pop up in other places.

Basal cell tumors

Basal cell tumors are slow-growing, wart-like nodules that feature little craters in the middle. They can pop up anywhere on your ferret. They're loose on the skin and move freely when you push on them.

Because of their raised presentation and mobility, basal cell tumors are easy to rub or scrape, which presents the possibility of infection. For these very same reasons, basal cell tumors are easy to remove, and you *should* have them removed. If removed properly by your vet, the tumors shouldn't recur in the same place.

Sebaceous cell tumors

Sebaceous cell tumors generally are tumors of the skin's oil glands or hair follicles. They're really funky in shape — sometimes branching out like cauliflower. They may appear as bluish-colored lumps just under the skin, although on the outside they can range in color from tan to brown to blue. Like the other common skin tumors, sebaceous cell tumors can appear anywhere on the fuzzy's body, and they're usually firm to the touch.

Removing sebaceous cell tumors is important because they often grow rapidly and can become cancerous. Besides, your ferret won't like sporting a vegetable-shaped mass for all the world to see.

TUMOR TALK

Allow me to try to unravel the mystery of tumors and the terms used to describe them. *Neoplasia* is the process in which cells grow in an abnormal and uncontrolled manner. The result is a *neoplasm,* also known as a *tumor,* which is made up of cells that serve no useful purpose to the body. Tumors may occur just about anywhere on the ferret's body — either externally on the skin or internally.

There are two types of tumors: *Benign* (non-cancerous) and *malignant* (cancerous). A benign tumor remains local, or at the site where it originally grows. Although it doesn't spread, or *metastasize,* to other parts of the body, it may grow big enough to become medically dangerous. Some tumors also have the potential to become malignant. A malignant tumor can metastasize through neoplastic cells being shed; these cells then travel to other areas of the body, such as the lungs, liver, brain, and lymph nodes. The rate of metastasis depends on the type of tumor and many other factors relating to the individual animal.

The suffix –oma doesn't designate a tumor as benign or malignant. For instance, lymphoma usually is malignant but may occur as a solitary tumor that doesn't spread; this is rare but possible (in people). An *adenoma* is a benign tumor — specifically a benign epithelial tumor having a glandular origin and structure. Adenocarcinoma is a malignant tumor originating in the glandular tissue. Carcinoma always means malignant; it's an invasive malignant tumor derived from epithelial tissue that tends to metastasize to other areas of the body. Approximately 80 percent of all malignant tumors are carcinomas (in humans).

You can't always tell whether a tumor is benign or malignant just by looking at it with the naked eye or by where it resides. A pathologist examines the tissues microscopically to determine the tumor type, which is why sending tissues off to a lab is so important.

Chapter **17**

Saying Goodbye When the Time Comes

Well, I suppose this topic had to come up eventually: death, the taboo and rarely-talked-about elephant in the room. Naturally, humans are never quite prepared for the death of a greatly cherished pet. The end always seems to come way too soon. And what's so unfortunate is that many humans don't know what they have until it's gone. Thankfully, many more humans cherish every breath their pets take, knowing all too well that each breath could be the last.

It's difficult to watch a beloved pet suffer. And for the true animal lovers, it never seems to matter how long the pets have been with them. I can still remember and feel the passing of every single fuzzy that has died since they first graced me with their presence. And with each death came the same questions, over and over and over again: Did I do something wrong? What more could I have done? Was this the right time to let go? Why this little girl? Why now?

This chapter deals with death head-on. In this chapter, I talk about knowing when to euthanize your pet. I discuss what you can learn from a post-mortem examination. I present some options for humanely and compassionately taking care of your deceased pet's body. Finally, I cover coping with the grieving process. I try to help you with your grief and your other fuzzies' grief so you can move on — but never forget.

Letting Go of Your Family Member

Sometimes, the only way people can truly show their love for their pets is to let them go. Pets count on humans day after day to make the right decisions for them, and the day will come when they must count on us to make that final, heartbreaking decision — to be selfless instead of selfish and end their suffering. In their eyes we'll see. In our hearts we'll know.

REMEMBER

It's time to let go when your ferret no longer enjoys life. His illnesses or injuries have been treated as well as they can be, yet he continues to suffer. Little hope exists, and your fuzzy's time from here on out will be filled with pain and misery. Stop. Look. Listen. Your ferret will tell you he's ready to go if you're willing to listen closely.

You can set up your ferret's final day with your vet, either in his office or privately at your home, depending on the vet. Humane euthanasia is painless to your little guy. It involves overdosing the ferret on an anesthetic, either by gas or by injection. Your baby will slowly fall to sleep. For the first time in a long time, he'll feel no pain; he'll be free from the suffering. In only a few short moments, he'll pass over the Rainbow Bridge — a term that comes from a poem with the same name, referring to an animal's passage from life to death — and be greeted by all the other pets that went before him. He'll once again be able to romp and play, and he'll watch you from afar until the day you can join him again.

And as hard as it may be for you, it will be comforting for your ferret if you're there with him. He'll want to hear your soothing voice and feel your touch while he leaves this world.

TIP

Many people ignore another important aspect to consider upon the death of a pet, be it from euthanasia or from a natural death. The other animals that the deceased pet had contact with — particularly any siblings or animals that were part of the fuzzy's social group — should be able to see and smell the deceased pet. It may seem "gross" to some people, but the remaining animals should be able to understand what happened so they can settle back into a normal life instead of always being concerned about where the deceased pet is. Other animals can have abrupt and dramatic behavioral changes when a beloved companion "disappears."

The other animals will have a far smoother transition if they have time to smell and see their dead cagemate. This may mean bringing the other social members to the vet's office, or at least a cagemate or two, or bringing the body home for a while and then returning it to the vet.

Learning from Fuzzy's Death with a Postmortem

It seems an impossible thought right after your ferret dies. No way will you allow a vet to operate on your newly deceased baby and examine him just out of curiosity. Well, you may want to think twice about your apprehensions. *Necropsies*, or *postmortems*, are performed shortly after the death of an animal and serve many important functions, which I outline in the following list.

A *necropsy* is simply a post-mortem examination of an animal. An *autopsy* is a post-mortem examination of a human, "auto" meaning "self" or "of the same species." *Postmortem* is Latin for "after death."

» **A postmortem may shed light on sudden, unexpected ferret deaths.** Not all animals give many warning signs before leaving this world. Some die quite unexpectedly and throw their humans into emotional tailspins. You may want some answers to the questions buzzing around in your head.

» **You and your other pets could have something to worry about.** The fear of something contagious enters everyone's head at one time or another. If your ferret's death is a surprise, you may want to know if you can expect more problems down the road or if you can prevent other surprises. And remember, animals can pass some icky cooties to humans, too.

» **A postmortem can provide invaluable information to the veterinary community about ferret disease and treatments.** Your fuzzy's death can assist other ferrets and their owners by providing precious data to veterinarians — data that can strengthen or weaken theories relating to ferret diseases and illnesses. The postmortem can also give clues as to what does and doesn't work in terms of treating ferrets. The more a vet sees and learns, the greater help the vet will be to ferrets in the future.

» **A postmortem may reveal internal genetic abnormalities, which sometimes are the result of poor breeding.** An examination can reveal diseases or illnesses that hadn't previously been identified in your ferret. As horrible as this may sound, if your ferret was a new purchase, you may be able to use the information from a postmortem to get your money back or to get a new ferret. At the very least, you may be able to help future fuzzies and owners from the fate you've witnessed.

>> **You can find out if husbandry played a role in the ferret's death.** Diet and environment play big parts in the health of a ferret. Experts aren't the only ones who can learn from their mistakes. I know I'd want to correct any deficiencies on my part and prevent future pet losses.

REMEMBER

For an accurate and complete postmortem, your ferret's body must be fresh. So what should you do if your pet passes at home and you want a vet to perform a postmortem? Place his body in a bag (double bagging is recommended) or container and put him in the fridge until the time comes. Don't freeze him or leave him at room temperature, because these environments can damage tissues and organs. Freezing, for instance, causes changes in tissues microscopically and makes it more difficult to do pathology or microscopic examinations. You can, however, freeze a body if you need to for just a gross postmortem or if you're looking for viral problems.

Your vet may or may not charge you for the postmortem. Most vets do charge a fee. It depends on their curiosity and desire to learn more about fuzzies. Some vets do the gross necropsy (dissecting and evaluating) for free and charge only for samples sent to pathologists or laboratories for testing.

If you choose to have a postmortem performed, your vet will, upon request, stitch up any incisions after the exam is completed. Your ferret won't look exactly like your little baby, but he won't look like Frankenfert, either. Keep in mind that the body is only the package that your fuzzy arrived in. He's no longer in there; he's opted for a superior package deal over the Rainbow Bridge.

REMEMBER

Having a necropsy performed is a difficult decision. I've always been told never to make a decision when I'm hungry, angry, lonely, or tired (HALT). You can probably throw grieving into that mix, too, but then it wouldn't spell a word. Chances are you aren't reading this material to figure out what to do at this very moment. You should think about postmortems now, before you're too emotional, and make a decision about what you'll do when your beloved ferret dies.

Selecting Fuzzy's Final Burrowing Place

What comes after the death of your ferret? Grieving, sadness, emptiness, anger, fear, loneliness. The list goes on and on. An important part of grieving, though, is putting some closure on the loss. A big part of getting closure is deciding what to do with your deceased pet. You have several options. It's no longer a choice between burying him in the backyard, tossing him out with the trash, or leaving him at the vet for convenience:

>> Some people have their pets cremated.

>> Some people have elaborate funerals at pet cemeteries complete with caskets and grave markers.

>> Some people have their pets freeze-dried or stuffed (taxidermied).

>> Some people opt for a simple or extravagant backyard funeral.

The following sections present some of these popular options.

Choosing cremation

Your vet will, upon request, properly store your deceased pet and arrange for a pet crematory to pick up the body for cremation. You also can take your pet directly to a pet crematorium with prior arrangement. Your cremation options are offered for different prices and vary from vet to vet and from crematorium to crematorium. If you choose this route, though, you usually have two main options:

>> A mass cremation without the return of your pet's ashes. The crematory disposes of all ashes according to the law.

>> A special cremation with the return of your pet's ashes. This includes a guarantee (complete with a certificate) that your deceased pet was cremated separately from other animals, assuring that all ashes are your pet's and only your pet's.

If you choose a special cremation, you need to think about your options for the returned ashes:

>> You can keep each pet separated in special containers. These containers can sit on special shelves or in other special places of honor.

>> You can have one big urn in which you keep all your pets together as a family.

>> You can bury the ashes or spread them in your pet's favorite *outdoor* place. I emphasize outdoor because your fuzzy's favorite hidey-hole in the play area probably isn't a good idea!

Your vet or the pet crematorium should be able to give you prices for these services and show you several urn styles. You can bypass your vet or the crematorium and even purchase urns online. Some urns are simple, and some are elaborate. The style you choose depends on your taste and your budget. You can add an engraved nameplate or simply have the pet's name etched in wood. Some people even add a little picture of the pets to the containers. This is a time for celebration of your pet's life.

WARNING

If you choose to receive only the ashes back without a special urn, be prepared for what you may get. Most of my pets' ashes were returned in small, white, plastic bottles or decorative tins. One time, though, some ashes came back in a clear plastic bag, which was both startling and disturbing to me.

TIP

Not all pet crematoriums are up to snuff. People, in some cases, get back way more than just their pets' ashes, or it may be apparent that not all the ashes could've possibly been returned. Be careful which crematorium you choose. Speak with your vet about the crematorium she uses. Call a referred crematorium and ask questions. If you're unhappy with the answers you get, you can take your pet to another place. The choice is yours. Some crematoriums even let you stay there while the service is performed.

TIP

A small portion of your pet's cremains (ashes) can also be made into a keepsake such as a beautiful piece of artwork or jewelry. A Google search should help you track down the perfect keepsake to fit your personality. My go-to company is called Spirit Pieces, which can be found online at www.spiritpieces.com. Their work is phenomenal!

Proceeding to a pet cemetery

No, a pet cemetery isn't anything like author Stephen King's portrayal. Thank heavens! In fact, pet cemeteries look a lot like human cemeteries, except much smaller. Many people love this resting option because they'll always have a special place to visit their beloved pets. Finding them, however, can be challenging, although some crematoriums have cemeteries on site. Pet cemeteries aren't all that popular, and many people don't even know they exist. Ask your vet to point you in the right direction, or contact a friend who has some experience with one. You can also perform an Internet search or check out the phone book under "pet cemetery."

The burial for your pet can be simple, such as you picking out a tiny site and delivering the body to the cemetery. Or it can be extravagant. You can have your ferret set up in a special coffin, and you can view the body in the funeral home before saying goodbye, just like at a human wake. Some places allow you to deliver the pet, in coffin, to the burial site and bury the pet yourself. Or you can follow a somber ground crew as they lead you to the burial site. You can purchase a head-stone so that your fuzzy's gravesite will always be marked with sentiment.

The pet cemetery burial option can be a costly endeavor. Pet cemeteries vary in policies and practices. I'm sure they also differ in prices and available packages.

Opting for a backyard burial

Backyard burials can be personal, private, and inexpensive, and they can mean everything to a grieving human. Many families with kids know exactly what I'm talking about. How many of you, as tearful children, made your family members gather around the toilet to bid farewell to the bravest, coolest goldfish that ever lived?

REMEMBER

Before you decide to bury your pet in the backyard, be sure to check city ordinances; backyard burials may actually be illegal in your area.

Headstones are optional for your backyard burial. For my old dog Ara, I custom-designed a headstone and had it etched in heavy granite by the stonecutter at the local cemetery. It took forever for the stone to arrive, but it was well worth the wait. Of course, after I spent $350, I started getting dozens of pet catalogs offering low-cost, simple pet headstones. But none could compete with my personal touch. (Read the sidebar "A personal story" for more about my sweet wolfdog, Ara.)

TIP

If your deceased pet was especially close to your child, you may want to encourage your child to celebrate the pet's life by personally making a headstone or grave marker. It's a wonderful way for the child to put a little closure on this huge matter of loss.

Note (actually a *Hubby Alert*): Just as a matter of clarification, my buried pets will be packed up and moved with me if I ever move from my house. They'll then be reburied in a beautiful place in my new yard. I've warned you, Hubby! You think I'm kidding? Here it is in writing!

Grieving for Your Lost Fuzzy

I'll tell you right off the bat: There's nothing worse than grieving a loss that no one seems to understand. People can sometimes make you feel worse about the death of your pet. Someone who has never had a pet may proclaim, "It's only an animal." Well, not exactly. Pets are family members that you grow extremely attached to. Your ferret has been a source of comfort and joy, as well as sadness and frustration. Many people view pets just as they view human children, but other people out there just don't understand.

I'm surrounded by people who just don't understand how I can cry over the loss of a ferret or any other small critter. A dog or a cat they'd understand — at least a little, so they say. And those who really have no clue rationalize, "It's not like they were humans." Those are the people to avoid. Those are the people who make me like animals more than people.

A PERSONAL STORY

One of the hardest decisions I've ever made was to put my 16½-year-old wolfdog, Ara, to sleep, but it was one I had to make. In the morning, he struggled to rise from his bed. He looked at me with sad, helpless eyes as I lifted his back end up for him. I saw that dignity still glowed dimly in his eyes, but the light was fading and I could tell he knew it. We romped slowly in the yard before our vet, Mike, arrived to put him to sleep. I questioned my decision as Ara walked up almost briskly to greet Mike. Maybe it wasn't time. I'd made this decision several times in the months before then and selfishly changed my mind just as Mike arrived. But Ara was almost 17 years old and was no longer happy. He fought to stay with us much longer than anyone had expected such a large dog to. We moved Ara's bed outside, and he quickly went to it. As he looked up at me, I could tell he trusted me to make the right decision. I held him closely while he left his broken-down body and passed over the Rainbow Bridge.

In my backyard, I have a beautiful group of large pine trees set in an imperfect row. Directly below their towering branches are many unmarked graves where dozens of critters rest. Directly north of these graves lies underground the most handsome, majestic, and loyal dog anyone's ever met. Ara Glen. His headstone reads, "Always Faithful, Always Loved." Ara is the keeper and protector of my critter graveyard. He watches over the little guys and guides them over the Rainbow Bridge. I visit his grave often when I need to talk, and I know he understands. This is why I planted him close to my heart.

After the death of your furry friend, surround yourself with people who do understand and don't think you're strange. I've seen people spend hundreds of dollars to remove tumors from mice, rats, and guinea pigs. It isn't the size or cost of the animal that matters; it's how much room he takes up in your heart.

So, you have my first bit of advice: Surround yourself with the right people. In the following sections, I give you more advice for dealing with your grief and for helping others through their grief.

Know you're not alone

You may feel crazy for feeling the way you do. Well, let me tell you, many of us out there feel crazy and silly right along with you. Don't let others kick you when you're down.

TIP

Many support groups are out there that deal directly with the loss of a pet. You can do a search on the Internet. If you can, visit the website www.rainbowsbridge. com. It's a neat site that has many wonderful tips and links to other pet-loss sites. It's also a virtual memorial site. If you visit this site or other sites like it, you'll find many hotlines and chat groups and even books dealing with grief issues, all available for you and your family members.

Face the feelings

A variety of different feelings will pop up at any given time after the death of your fuzzy. Feel them. Don't run from them. Remember that you're not alone. Your feelings are powerful, but they aren't unique. Among the emotions that will creep up for you to face are denial, anger, guilt, sadness, and emptiness.

Facing your feelings, however, doesn't mean beating yourself up about what you couldn't help. We all think we could've been better pet humans after our animals are gone, but hindsight is 20/20. Chances are, you were a wonderful parent. Feelings are temporary. Your memories will last forever, but the pain slowly fades after a while.

Give yourself time

Many people think that they should run right out and get new pets as soon as they lose the ones they loved so dearly. They think that doing so will fix the grief they're feeling. It won't. You know better than that. You can never replace a lost family member.

Give yourself time to grieve your loss. Pets aren't replaceable. You can certainly add to your family when you feel better, but taking on a new responsibility when you're grieving isn't fair to you, your family, or the new pet. Likewise, you shouldn't try to fix someone else's grief by giving a pet as a gift. Grief isn't something that can be fixed. It's something that you must work through over a period of time.

And when you're truly ready for a new pet, toss any feelings of guilt or betrayal out the window. Your deceased pet would've wanted you to move on and be happy with a new pet.

Help others deal with their loss

You may want to giggle inside when you see a child dragging an adult to the toilet for the ultimate farewell to Moby the goldfish. But you should recognize that the child is hurting. It's very possible that another person will feel the loss of your pet just as, or even more, deeply than you do. Respect other people's feelings by acknowledging them and providing as much support as you can. Each person is unique, and everyone has the right to grieve.

Don't forget that you have to help your other animals with their loss, too. Animals bond deeply with both humans and other animals. When my wolfdog, Ara, died, my hyper Doberman, Cassie, wanted to do nothing but sleep. She was lethargic and depressed. Several months later, I introduced two puppies to her, and she hated me for it. But they all play and get along today. However, she has never bonded to them the way she did with Ara. My point is, show all your grieving family members extra attention and love during the grieving period. (See the following section for much more advice on this topic.)

TECHNICAL
STUFF

Do pets really grieve? Many people, myself included, tend to project human emotions such as grief onto pets. The fact is, no one knows for sure if animals grieve, and the topic is a subjective one. Some will say the changes in behavior that an animal experiences after a death are due to the changes in environment — the safety and security of their "world" has been altered (a cagemate suddenly disappears or social structure is disrupted). Depending on the species and on the age of the animals and their health, it can affect them more or less dramatically. You need to understand the social behavior of a pet species to understand how the animals can respond to environmental changes.

Helping a Surviving Ferret Cope

Depression in animals isn't much different than depression in humans, except that animals don't have complex self-destructive thought patterns. The loss felt by a surviving ferret isn't to be underestimated, though. Surviving ferrets are affected very deeply. The signs are there. Lethargy and lack of appetite may be glaringly obvious, as well as their reclusiveness or clinginess. And it isn't unheard of for a lone ferret to die soon after his cagemate passes on. But you can do your part to help your surviving ferret get through these hard times. It isn't difficult. Ferrets are by nature solitary animals and usually do just fine on their own after a period of adjustment.

TIP

You need to give your sad fuzzy a lot of extra attention during his grieving stage. Spend more time developing and implementing enrichment plans to keep him busy and entertained (see Chapter 10). The worst thing you can do is isolate him. But be careful not to make too many abrupt changes in his life by suddenly carrying him around more often than usual and stressing him out. Over-babying him will only cause him to have more anxiety. Be aware of your own agitation and depression and keep him out of contact with that. He doesn't need to take on your stress as well. Realizing that life moves on will also help with your grief. If you get stuck in your grief, you won't be doing any favors to your ferret.

When dealing with a grieving ferret, many people ask, "Should I get another ferret? When will we know if it's the right time?" Many factors come into play when deciding whether to get a new ferret to keep your surviving ferret company. How old is your surviving ferret? If he's old and sickly, adding a newcomer is probably not a great idea. A surviving youngster may be a completely different story, because he may have many healthy years to share with another ferret. Take health and personality factors into consideration. What if your survivor doesn't get along with a new ferret? Are you ready to set up and maintain another cage and split playtimes? And the biggest question of all: Are *you* ready for a new ferret?

Many ferrets will benefit greatly from the company of a new ferret. But first and foremost, you need to make a commitment to your surviving ferret to truly meet his needs for consistent enrichment, which will keep him thriving. Enrichment is vital to a ferret, but even more so to a ferret that lives alone.

5

Ferret Psychology 101: Behavior and Training

Chapter **18**

Understanding What Fuzzy Is Trying to Tell You

Ferrets are extremely interactive critters. They use many different types of communication to get their points across — from body language to vocalizations to crazy behaviors. They can be notorious thieves and affectionate lap warmers at the same time. Watching them can be both amusing and baffling, but knowing what they're trying to say to you is important. It can mean the difference between a lick on the nose and a nip of the nostrils.

You'll surely encounter all sorts of captivating behavior, both good and bad, during your ferret rendezvous. My experience has been that the good encounters are far more plentiful than the bad. I spend more time laughing with my furballs, even when they're being devilish. In this chapter, I cover the main types of ferret communication so you can properly manage, care for, and play with your ferret. I discuss ferret vocalization, ferret dancing, fuzzy body language, and other unique behaviors. Hopefully, this chapter will help you recognize that you're not alone in thinking your ferret may be a little crazy . . . and will put to rest any fears you have that you're crazy for loving every minute of it.

Say What? Speaking Ferret-ese

For the most part, fuzzies are quiet. I mean, goodness, they sleep for hours on end! Occasionally, one of my furkids has a ferret dream and does a little whimpering in her sleep, but that's a rarity. During playtime, though, the vocabulary comes out. Ferrets use vocalization to send signals. Seasoned ferret humans (sprinkled with ferret poo) have personal terms for ferret vocalizations that they've come up with over the years. These terms are sort of like understood jokes between ferret and human. However, most fuzzy humans recognize a few terms universally. I cover these vocalizations in the sections that follow so you can speak the ferret language and understand what your ferret wants.

REMEMBER

Deaf ferrets aren't great at gauging their vocal communications around their humans or other ferrets. What comes out of your deafie might sound like a dying goose, or it may sound like any other ferret, except amplified ten times. Because a deaf ferret can't hear what's coming out of him, he may be very loud and vocal, which may also cause confusion and socializing issues with his playmates. I also know a husband that fits this description.

REMEMBER

People who don't understand ferret communication can become frightened or intimidated when encountering vocalizations for the first time. Recognizing the difference between a dook of happiness and a screech of anger is important. Not knowing may cause you to react improperly to the message being given. Humans often run into this difficulty with their human partners, too!

The dook

The most common ferret babble is known as *dooking* (also known as clucking or chuckling). It sounds like sort of a low-pitched, grumbling gibber. Ferret owners sometimes compare the sound of dooking to the noise clucking chickens make. Dookings are more often than not awesome sounds made out of sheer giddiness or excitement. The stimulation felt from wrestling with another ferret, rapid counter cruising, or even from exploring new smells, toys, and hidey-holes can cause carpet sharks to dook. Dooking often accompanies the happy weasel war dance! Nothing to worry about here; just enjoy!

I did say "more often than not" because you may have the misfortune of one day stepping on your ferret's tail and hearing him spew out the dook of pain! Unlike happy dooks, this is a machine gun rapid firing of dooks resulting from a sudden pain. It doesn't happen often, but you should know there's a big difference!

TECHNICAL STUFF

Mother jills (female ferrets) make a slightly different but similar noise to help their kits (baby ferrets) locate them when the babies are exploring their environment. Experts suggest that polecats also use a similar noise when first meeting each other, during dancing used to avoid conflict, and before and during ritual fighting.

The squeak

Let go! This game has gone too far! Commence with the squeaking! This jovial ferret babble, which is similar to dooking, is initiated during playful times that have crossed the ferret boundaries. Meant to be submissive noises, squeaking is one ferret's way of telling another ferret that he submits. Game over. Unfortunately, squeaking isn't always an effective measure against a stubborn opponent, and careful human intervention might be needed before the ferret play turns serious.

The giggles or hee-hees

My ferrets frequently get a case of the verbal "*hee hees*" while they're dooking. It's simply a delightfully serious attack of the ferret giggles, and yet it often causes concern for some ferret owners who believe their "laughing" ferret has a respiratory illness. I can totally understand that, because the hee-hees sound a bit like a panting dog or one that is hurriedly sniffing around. Calm down and laugh with your silly kids as they hop sideways in delight.

The screech or scream

The opposite of the dook is the certified sign of terror, the *screech* or *scream*. These noises are high-pitched reactions to extreme pain, fright, or anger. The screech/scream is a common defense mechanism and often is accompanied by or even replaced by rapid chattering. When you hear this warning cry, your job as a concerned parent is to jump to your fuzzy's defense. Her tail may be puffed and her back arched. She may have her mouth gaped open, and she may even be scooting backward. Go to her rescue immediately, but be sure to assess her body language before reaching down with your vulnerable hands.

WARNING

When rushing to help your fuzzy, do so with care. Most animals engrossed in pain, anger, or fright are capable of unpredictable behavior, and ferrets are no exception to this rule.

The squeal

The squealing ferret is often happy to see you, letting out tiny squeals of excitement as she asks for your attention and play engagement. But this confusing vocalization can also indicate that your ferret doesn't want to be held or even that she heard a startling noise. Let's muddy things up a bit more, as a squeal may often be a form of yawning, as she stretches awake from a nice nap.

The bark

Sometimes your ferret will surprise you and utter a noise that resembles a bark. Usually, the bark is one or two very loud chirps that come from a very excited or frightened furball. A friend of mine has a ferret that will bark if he tries to take away its treasured dried fish or jerky. Some humans bark if you prematurely remove their dinner plates, too.

WARNING

A ferret that's traumatized or excited enough to screech, hiss, or bark can take temporary leave of her senses and nail you good with her chompers — and it won't be her fault. Many situations can cause screeching, barking, hissing, or chattering — from a serious fight between two rival ferrets to having a tail caught in a door to coming face to face with a large, unfamiliar dog.

The honk

Ferret kits or adult kit-wanna-be's honk when they're nervous or lost. This honking noise helps "mom" locate and gather up her lost kit to make him safe and secure again. You're likely to hear this vocalization coming from young kits that have recently been separated from mom and placed into new homes. If this is the case, it's likely to stop as the kit gets more comfortable being away from mom and having your lovin'.

The hiss

The *hiss* is a warning noise in the ferret's vocabulary. I find a ferret's hissing noise quite amusing, even if she doesn't; it's sort of a cross between a "hee hee" and chattering. The noise can be in the form of long bursts of sound or short, hissy spats, depending on the situation. A hissing fuzzy can be a very annoyed, fearful, or angry fuzzy. However, ferrets often hiss at each other while engaging in play. No matter, take care when handling a hisser, especially when there's an arched back or bristled fur involved, as with a scream, because she can be so overly excited that you may be an unlucky recipient of her lashing out uncharacteristically.

TIP

zzzzzzz — Yes! Ferrets do snore. They may not sound like the freight train that comes from your bedroom every night, but some ferrets can even be heard snoring from quite a distance. This heavy breathing might even be accompanied by a twitch or two. Sweet dreams!

You Make Me Feel Like Dancin'! Interpreting Your Ferret's Jig

If you haven't figured it out by now, ferrets are animated critters with a complex array of behaviors. Often, a ferret's vocalizations (described in the previous section) are accompanied by particular movements and body language — such as opening the mouth, puffing the tail, arching the back, and so on — that resemble dances. Reading between the lines can be difficult, if not alarming, to people who don't know how to read ferret music. In the following sections, I help you interpret your ferret's dances and take action accordingly.

The dance of joy

I don't know of a ferret that hasn't mastered the dance of joy (see Figure 18-1). If you run across one, her ferret human is most certainly doing something terribly wrong. All healthy, happy ferrets partake in this frequent and brilliant performance. The dance of joy is an unadulterated sign of pure happiness and delight. (*Note:* These dancers are professional ferrets. Don't try these moves at home. Doing so may cause irreparable damage to your skeletal structure and harm your ego!)

To perform the dance, the ferret moves in all directions, sometimes at the same time. She may hop forward and sashay sideways, with a double twist back. Her mouth may be open and her back arched. No two dances are the same, yet all are amusing.

REMEMBER

The dance of joy is a great way to gauge whether your ferret is in shape. A very fit and energetic fuzzy will be the last one on the dance floor. Short bursts of dancing performed between short ferret naps are also common. If you find that your ferret is sleeping more than playing when she gains her daily freedom, try giving her more exercise (see Chapter 10). If her energy still seems low over time, take her to the vet for a checkup. You want to make sure that her lack of energy isn't more than just being flabby and out of shape.

FIGURE 18-1:
The ferret
dance of joy.

TECHNICAL
STUFF

It's probable that the dance of joy does a few things for the polecat:

>> The arched back, piloerection (frizzed-out tail), and sway make the animal look bigger than it is.

>> The side-to-side swings may confuse a potential predator or make the animal attack the tail rather than the head.

>> Several different species of weasels and polecats have used war dancing to confuse or distract potential prey, increasing the odds of getting a meal.

Ferrets do the dance as part of their "play fighting" behaviors. When doing the dance for a human or to play with another ferret (or just on their own), ferrets also open their mouths and sometimes dook.

The war dance

I like to call the war dance "dooking it out," even though dooks aren't associated with angry or fearful fuzzies (see the earlier section "The dook"). Sometimes, recognizing the war dance can be difficult because the dance of joy covers all the same basic body movements, including the notorious arched back. But an angry ferret often hisses or screeches as an additional warning. The war dance can be performed with or without a ferret partner. Your ferret may choose you as a partner or the family dog. Or she may pick out an inanimate object that happened to catch her off guard.

The war dance often features an arched back, which is the furball's way of appearing bigger than life. I call it basic trickery. The dance can be slow or fast, depending on the situation. Many angry ferrets back themselves into a corner, arched back and all, and screech or hiss with their mouths wide open. A very angry or frightened ferret also will let loose an A-bomb — a spray of musk — if they haven't already been descented. Although a frizzed-out tail often is appropriate attire for the war dance, it isn't always worn.

REMEMBER

If your ferret is in a bad situation, rescue the furkid quickly, but do so very cautiously. A bite that results from an upset ferret is rarely the fault of the ferret.

Decoding Your Ferret's Body Language

Ferrets do a lot more than dance when they're playing, inspecting, or exploring their environments. They always seem to be on mysterious quests, which sometimes feature about as much grace as a weasel in a lingerie drawer (not that I would know). Some ferrets appear to feel bored and frustrated at times. Some seem happy and silly. And others may just want to cool out in their hidey-holes. In the following sections, I cover some peculiar behaviors that ferrets exhibit alone and with each other. Hopefully you'll get the insight you've been looking for. Ferrets can be weird creatures!

The frizz look

A true sign of excitement, both good and bad, is the frizzed-out tail. I call it the "pipe cleaner tail," and others call it the "bottlebrush tail." The official term is *piloerection.* When humans get piloerection, we call it goosebumps. When ferrets get it, people call it frizzed or fuzzed. No matter what you call it, if you aren't reading the other signs that accompany the pipe cleaner tail, you may be in for a surprise. Remember, the frizzed tail is a sign of extreme emotion, good or bad. This ferret can be unpredictable.

The situation is similar to when dogs get hackles or when cats do that thing with the fur on their tails. Ferrets puff out the fur on their tails when they're frightened or angry (and are more prone to biting). However, the frizzy look can also be a sign of surprise or happy excitement. Each one of my furballs has a frizzed tail for several minutes after bath time. They're excited and overstimulated while they search for creative ways to dry off and undo all the cleaning.

The alligator roll and wrestlemania

Okay, so your ferret doesn't look like an alligator, but boy, can she flip and roll her partner in seconds flat! I've seen all my ferrets perform the alligator roll many times. The flip is just a form of playing or wrestling. The alpha fuzzy, or head cheese, is the master. She quickly grabs another fuzzy by the back of her neck and flips her upside down. Both carpet sharks then rapidly roll and wrestle about.

There are several variations of wrestling that almost always come into play when your ferrets are out of the cage. Many species of mammals participate in these mock battles to sharpen their survival skills and establish their rankings in the group.

REMEMBER

Ferrets can appear to be quite aggressive during normal play. The rough play, besides being fun, often is a way of establishing dominance. A ferret's skin is tough, and what appears to be ruthless biting may in fact just be a bothersome pinch to the recipient. (Ferrets use their paws for grabbing at other ferrets, for tackling, and for wrestling them to the ground, but their teeth are their main weapons.) One opponent may scream briefly in protest. Don't interfere unless you truly feel the game has turned into more than a game.

WARNING

The trouble comes when a fuzzy chooses a human hand or toe or a piece of clothing to perform an alligator roll on. Youngsters and overexcited ferrets in play mode do this a lot. Although it can be amusing and innocent at first, this behavior shouldn't be encouraged. If you choose to play along with the roll and wrestle with your ferret, use a toy to tackle and wrestle with rather than your hand. You don't want to encourage the fuzzy to bite your hand, and biting is almost always a part of this game.

The treasure hunt

Next time you get invited to a party in which the host sends you and the rest of the guests on a treasure hunt, grab your fuzzy to help in the search. Ferrets make excellent detectives. The job of the fuzzy is to explore every inch, every crack, and every scent of her environment, leaving nothing unexamined. A ferret's nose will be glued to the ground as she follows scent trails this way and that. She'll stop at nothing to get to know everything she can.

REMEMBER

Because of a ferret's determination and persistence to explore, proper ferret-proofing is essential to your ferret's safety (see Chapter 6). A ferret can find anything that you don't hide well enough. And when she finds it, she'll hide the stuff even better. This is called *cache behavior*. I've had ferrets present me with cherished items I thought I'd never see again. At first I wanted to show my excitement at the discoveries by rewarding the treasure hunters, but then I realized that they probably hid the treasures in the first place.

The chase is on

Most animals love to chase each other, but ferrets are the masters at the high-speed chase. The behavior may be the inner predator coming to the surface, or it may just illustrate the ferret's desire to have a good time. Regardless, you don't have to be a fuzzy to partake in chases. I've seen my cats and several furkids cruising around the house at the speed of fuzz. I've even done the ferret shuffle as quickly as I could to get away from a tailing carpet shark.

Overly excited or happy ferrets can appear to be quite nuts. They bounce off the walls, furniture, and body parts, often with their mouths gaping wide and teeth showing. This behavior is normal. Many people mistakenly believe this open-mouth gesture is aggression. Rather, it's an invitation to play, and it's all part of ferret fun and games.

WARNING

A ferret chase *can* be a dangerous behavior, though. Many dogs don't like to be chased by ferrets and will snap at them in retaliation. And kids who don't know how to properly perform the ferret shuffle shouldn't chase because they can easily step on fuzzies. The safest way for a person (adult or child) to play chase with a ferret is to be on all fours on the ground. The fuzzy almost always wins this way, and you reduce the risk of accidentally crushing her.

TECHNICAL STUFF

Did you know that ferrets and polecats aren't typically chase hunters? They hunt most of their food by uncovering it or by cornering it in tunnels. They move very rapidly if you startle them, however, as if to avoid becoming food for an owl!

Fuzzy stalking

Sometimes a ferret remains very still before pouncing on another ferret or toy. I call this behavior *fuzzy stalking* or *the ambush.* In this way, fuzzies are similar to cats, although ambushing isn't the preferred method of hunting by the ferret's wild relatives. A more serious variation of stalking is lunging. You may encounter the lunge when a ferret is becoming overprotective of a special toy or hidey-hole.

Tail wagging

Some ferrets wag their tails out of sheer excitement or stimulation. Some may even do it when they're upset. Tail wagging isn't as common in fuzzies as it is in cats, but it's hardly cause for alarm when it does happen. Youngsters seem more prone to this funny behavior. If your fuzzy is a tail wagger, you can say that you have a furkid with a tad more character than the rest of the furkids.

"Why Does My Ferret Do *That?*" Understanding Other Fuzzy Behaviors

Besides understanding vocalizations and body language, you need to know what other behaviors come with the ferret package. I get calls from people who proclaim excitedly that their ferrets hate the litter they've chosen. The ferrets toss or dump the litter constantly. They ask me what secret litter I use and what they can do to fix the problem.

Some ferret humans are relieved when I tell them that the problem probably isn't the litter. It's a natural ferret behavior to dig. Or it can be due to boredom and stress (see Chapter 10 for ideas on enrichment for your ferret). Some ferret humans want a quick fix and seem frustrated with my answers. I tell these people that ferrets are crazy, which is why people love them so much. In the sections that follow, I cover digging and the remaining fuzzy behaviors that you should recognize and understand.

Digging to China

A ferret's long claws weren't put there just for looks, you know. Any ferret owner will tell you that digging comes as naturally to a ferret as pooping. Normal targets of digging include cage corners, litter boxes, potted plants, and carpeting. If you think about it, though, the digging behavior makes sense:

>> Polecats, relatives of the ferret, are burrowing critters.

>> Polecats and ferrets hunt by sense of smell. When a wild polecat locates food with her sniffer, her claws dig in for the kill.

>> Ferrets inherently know that digging drives humans right up the wall!

REMEMBER

Another reason for digging that some people overlook is boredom or frustration. Although you can't take the urge to dig out of the ferret, you must recognize that ferrets need a lot of stimulation. Digging can, at times, be a way of saying, "Pay attention to me!" or "I'll get you for taking away my toy!" Or she may simply be attempting to get out of her cage. For tips on how to enrich your ferret's life and prevent stress and boredom, refer to Chapter 10.

TIP

Although you can't prevent a ferret from digging, you can do some things to prevent damage done by your excavator (for more on ferret-proofing, see Chapter 6):

>> Keep your plants up high or cover the soil with wire, large decorative rocks, or tin foil.

>> For carpeting, you can try to use plastic carpet runners or simply remove the carpeting where your fuzzy will be playing. Tile certainly is easier to clean, also.

Ferret fixations

Your ferret may become fixated on a certain object and treat it with extra-special care — even preventing others from getting near it. For some ferrets, "fixation" is the understatement of the year. When a ferret claims her love for an object, she often guards it tooth and nail.

My ferret Elmo discovered a toy from one of those fast-food kid's meals before I could even get it out of the plastic. It was a hard-plastic lion that he grabbed and ran off with to his hidey-hole. After he'd familiarized himself with it, he proudly brought the toy out to show off to his friends. But Elmo never allowed anyone to get too close to it. Like a mother protecting her vulnerable baby, this oversized carpet shark hissed warnings to the other ferrets to keep a safe distance.

WARNING

Ferrets will fixate on just about anything, regardless of whether or not it's safe. It's almost a natural reaction for us to quickly grab a harmful object from our ferret and pull it away, but avoid the urge to do this. A ferret acting possessive can pack a powerful bite, and you don't want your fingers to get in the way. Instead, distract the ferret using the sound of a squeaky toy or offer up a safe toy as an alternative. If you're brave and quick, you can distract by tickling his butt or belly until he releases the object. It is not advisable to scruff your ferret while he is being possessive with an object, as this may only make him latch on with more determination and make him agitated.

Elmo had many toys, but this one was never far from his sight. He carried it to the food bowl and dropped it in while he ate, and then he carefully buried it in his bedding when he was through. The toy even accompanied him to the litter box. Now that's true love!

The movers are here

What happens if your ferret becomes obsessed with something she just can't get her teeth around? Why, she simply tucks it under her belly and secures it there with her front paws. From there, the thief amuses any onlookers with her unique ability to scoot backward with the object in tow. Balls and small, hard objects often are subjected to this tuck-and-scoot method of moving.

And what if the object is too big to tuck and scoot? Well, her pointy honker isn't just for smelling and leaving nose prints on your eyeglasses. And her feet weren't made just for walking. Ferrets can not only drag around heavy objects, but also push them around (different from bossing us around). They use their noses and/or front feet to push items to the desired destinations. They'll try for hours to shove oversized items into obviously undersized locations. My fuzzies frequently try to drag me under the couch. I never have the heart to point out the flaw in their plan. I'm rather amused at watching them try to make it work no matter what.

A felon on your hands?

Ferrets would make excellent crooks if they weren't so darned blatant about their thieving ways. It's absolutely normal, even if sometimes annoying, for ferrets to steal objects and carry them off to their secret hidey-holes. Heck, the animal's name appropriately means "thief" (see Chapter 1). This thieving or hoarding is a *caching behavior*. It serves an important role in the survival of wild polecats: as a way for them to stock up on food for future shortfalls.

Almost anything the ferret can grab with her paws or carry in her mouth is fair game. From pieces of food to cigarette butts, you'll find the most unusual collections of goodies in the most unusual places. Purses, pockets, and backpacks are frequent targets for ferret raids. If you value any items your ferret may steal — such as car keys, shoes, and jewelry — I suggest that you keep these items up high or away from the ferret's play area altogether.

WARNING

Hoarding is one of the ferret's most endearing traits, but it can lead to trouble. Some stolen items are big, but others are dangerously small. Ferrets can ingest small items that can cause blockages. Remember this characteristic about your ferret when you ferret-proof your home (see Chapter 6). Plus, food that your fuzzy stashes can spoil or mold.

The zig-zag

Have you ever heard the saying a straight line for a ferret includes six zigs and seven zags? When zig-zagging, your ferret isn't trying to evade a pursuer, though that would be an excellent guess. Your ferret has inherited a unique hunting technique from her wild polecat relatives. Scanning the ground from side to side as she moves forward allows your ferret to cover more surface area and increases the odds of catching or unearthing a meal — or a dirty sock, in the case of your domesticated ferret.

BLAME THE FERRET!

In several plays written thousands of years ago, Aristophanes made fun of political opponents by calling them ferrets. He would imply that they stole public trust and funds in the same way ferrets stole bits of meat and shiny objects. The wording of these quotes may differ, and the animal mentioned by Aristophanes has been called a cat, marten, ferret, polecat, and house ferret. Thanks to Bob Church for providing these gems!

- In *The Acharnians* (425 BCE): "Happy he who shall be your possessor and embrace you so firmly at dawn, that you fart like a house ferret." **Note:** Reference to poofing.

- In *Wasps* (422 BCE): "But to-day men-at-arms are placed at every outlet to watch me, and two of them are lying in wait for me at this very door armed with spits, just as folks lie in wait for a house ferret that has stolen a piece of meat." **Note:** Reference to stealing meat.

- In *Peace* (421 BCE): "Let someone bring me the thrush and those two chaffinches; there were also some curds and four pieces of hare, unless the house ferret stole them last evening, for I know not what the infernal noise was that I heard in the house." **Note:** Reference to stealing meat.

- In *The Thesmophoriazusae* (411 BCE): "And how we give meats to our pimps at the feast of the Apaturia and then accuse the house ferret . . ." **Note:** Reference to giving meat (treasure) to others and blaming the ferret for stealing it.

- In *Plutus* (380 BCE): "Quick she drew back her hand, slipped down into the bed with her head beneath the coverlets and never moved again; only she let flee a fart in her fear which stank worse than a house ferret." **Note:** Reference to poofing.

Butt scooting

A skid mark here, a skid mark there: The unmistakable signs of the infamous ferret butt scoot! Ferrets and polecats may drag their butts across the yard or floor after going to the bathroom. This is your ferret's way of saying, "I was here!" Not all butt scoots leave visual evidence, but they all leave olfactory trails that tell other ferrets and animals that the area has been or is currently occupied by your fuzzy.

Coveting thy hidey-hole

Hidey–holes go hand in hand with ferrets, and the good spots are highly coveted if you have more than one fuzzy. In the wild, polecats use the burrows of other animals to nest in, but if none are readily available, they'll dig their own holes in tree root balls. They don't seem to stay in one spot for long; they'll pack up and move frequently. Domesticated ferrets also take advantage of hidey-holes when they find them. They'll hole up in them to sleep or rest and occasionally have to defend them from other ferrets. When your ferret can't find hidey-holes, she'll create them herself by digging or burrowing into mattresses, couches, or even your underwear drawer.

REMEMBER

Ferret behaviors are instinctual and serve purpose. Although you may find one or two of these behaviors highly annoying or inconvenient at times, ferrets should never be punished for doing what comes naturally. All you can do is ferret-proof as best you can on an ongoing basis!

Scoping out boundaries

Wild polecats spend a lot of time patrolling their territories in the wild, and a good amount of time is spent along the boundaries. Boundary patrols are conducted so that intruding polecats know the territory is currently occupied and they shouldn't enter. This reduces the amount of fights and decreases the chances of injury.

Domesticated ferrets inherited this territorial patrolling behavior. When first released from her cage or after a long nap, your ferret will first patrol the area before she starts to play. Along the walls, behind couches and curtains; she's simply retracing her territory and looking for intruders. Although you certainly hope she'll aim for the litter box, pooping along the edges, in corners, and even in doorways where intruders may enter is your ferret's way of putting up a fence, so to speak.

Chapter **19**

Putting Your Ferret through Basic Training: Easy as 1-2-3?

L ike a dog, a fuzzy doesn't come preprogrammed for use. You teach a dog how to sit, come, and heel; you must teach a fuzzy certain things, too — like how to mind his manners, use the litter box, and tolerate a harness and leash. These are basics of ferret life that every furkid should know. Some ferrets take to basic training quite quickly, but others need constant reminders of who's the boss. Teaching the basics of good manners means putting on your professor's hat and doing a little home-schooling with your new fuzzy. If your new ferret is an adult, chances are someone else has already home-schooled him, so you just need to keep him current on his skills.

As with any animal, including humans, patience and consistency are the keys to training success. You'll see what I mean when you bring your furball home. But just remember that the patience and effort are well worth it, because nothing can compare to the joy a socialized and greatly loved ferret will bring into your household. In this chapter, I cover the three basic training areas that require your effort, patience, and consistency: eliminating biting, bathroom training, and harness-and-leash socialization.

Just Say NO to Biting

Ferrets are similar to kittens and puppies in that they need to be trained not to bite. If you watch a human toddler closely, you'll be amazed at all the stuff that ends up in the kid's mouth. Chewing is how babies, human and animal, explore their environments and ease the pain of teething. Eventually the toothaches go away, but the nipping lingers on. Although the urge to nip lessens with age, an untrained adult ferret can be dangerously bold and aggressive with his chompers. Your job is to let your fuzzy know while he's young what is and isn't acceptable behavior. If you begin proper socialization and training when your ferret is young, you decrease the chances of him biting as an adult. (In this section, I talk about training baby ferrets, not adults that haven't been properly socialized. I cover getting help for the difficult adult carpet shark in Chapter 20.)

REMEMBER

Sometimes, training a youngster not to nip takes a lot of time and patience. The key to being successful is consistency. It can seem so cute at times to get the little guy all riled up and allow him to play-bite your hand. But you can't let your ferret bite during play and expect him to know that it isn't acceptable at other times and with other people. He won't understand that nipping is okay only when you're in the mood, so don't confuse him. Teach him one thing — not to bite — and stick to your guns. Believe me, if you have multiple fuzzies, the other ferrets will tell the kit just how far he can go with them. You should do the same!

It's important that you pay special attention to the do's and don'ts of nip-training your ferret. The following list presents some suggestions to help with training your fuzzy not to bite:

>> **Provide plenty of chew toys to help curb biting.**

TIP

Avoid toys with soft rubber, foam, vinyl, latex, or thin plastic, which will surely be chewed to bits and possibly ingested. Instead, use playthings made of fabric, maybe even a stuffed animal. These make great alternatives to your flesh as you're bite training, as well.

>> **Use a safe toy to wrestle with him rather than your hand.**

>> **Mist a safe, bitter bite deterrent on your hand when playing with him.**

After he gets a taste, he probably won't come back for seconds. This stuff is a nasty-tasting substance used to deter chewing in all kinds of pets.

TIP

You can prepare these easy-to-make bite deterrents at home. These may be safer than store-bought items and won't contain any harmful ingredients such as isopropyl alcohol:

- *Vinegar:* Combine two parts apple cider vinegar with one part distilled white vinegar in a spray bottle. Shake well before use.

- *Lemon juice:* Combine two parts lemon juice with one part distilled white vinegar in a spray bottle. Shake well before use.

» **Correct a nip immediately by scruffing the kit and very loudly saying "No" or "No bite."**

Scruffing is when you firmly grasp the loose skin on the back of the ferret's neck with your thumb and fingers and dangle the ferret. If he's really hefty, support his bottom slightly. Hissing (not screaming) loudly at the ferret after you say "No" is also very effective. Hissing is the tool a Mother Ferret or other ferrets would use to discipline kits. You can also lay (not tap) your finger gently across his nose after you scruff, say "No bite," and then hiss at him. Remember not to discipline in anger.You always want to remain calm, cool, and collected.

» **If you're holding the kit when he nips, don't reward him by giving him his freedom (in other words, don't put him down to roam free).**

Instead, place him in jail (confine him for no longer than 3 to 5 minutes, preferably in a carrier or somewhere other than his beloved home). His home should always be his comfort zone and not associated with punishment.

WARNING

» ***Don't ever*** **hit or bite your ferret in an attempt to discipline or train him, because aggression leads to aggression.**

Your fuzzy may also think that you're encouraging him to play harder. Hitting or biting him back is not only ridiculous, it is also an ineffective technique and frequently leads to bigger behavioral problems.

» ***Don't ever*** slather hot sauce on your hands or arms just to deter your ferret from biting or to give him a taste of his own medicine.

Hot sauce is, well, hot! Spicy hot! Not only does this not work, it falls under the abusive category in my opinion. Instead, try a little salmon oil to get him to associate your fingers or arm with pleasantness and licking instead of biting.

This Way to the Bathroom

If you read the other chapters of this book, you'll notice that I talk rather frequently about the ferret's bodily functions; that's because ferrets seem to poop about every 15 minutes or so while they're awake. Okay, not really. It just appears that way. And most ferret people spend more time telling animated stories and jokes about their fuzzies' notorious bathroom habits, and sharing pictures of poop art, than they do cleaning up after their kids. (Okay, I'll admit it, that's a little weird.)

Mother Fuzzy, if given the chance, will teach her kits to use the litter box. However, because many kits are delivered to new homes or halfway houses before mom gets the chance to teach them, the new human caretakers must do this dirty deed.

It's pretty simple to train a ferret that the litter box is his designated toilet. Although teaching them the purpose of the litter box is pretty easy, getting them to use it consistently is a crapshoot. Ferrets, unfortunately, don't have the greatest toilet habits. The following tips should help (for more on effective litter boxes and incorporating them into your ferret's kingdom, check out Chapter 5):

TIP

» **Keep your fuzzy's litter box in the corner of his cage.** A corner area is a magnet for a fuzzy butt. Ferrets prefer to back into a loading zone and unload.

» **Limit baby ferrets — or any ferret that's just learning to use a litter box — to smaller cages and play areas until the bathroom concept has sunk in.** Move your ferret to a larger cage only after he's potty trained, and add litter boxes to the higher levels if needed (see Chapter 5 for more on ferret cages).

As you expand your ferret's out-of-cage play area, increase the number of litter boxes you put in it. If a litter box is close by, your ferret will be more likely to use it. They are not like cats; they will not show great restraint and hold it until they reach the designated litterbox across the house. No! Any corner will do for your ferret. If you pay attention, your fuzzy will show you which corners are the best spots for litter boxes. Frequently pick him up and place him in a box until he goes. If he refuses, let him play for a few minutes and then repeat the process.

» **If your ferret is tiny (or ill), make sure his litter box has a low side or is small enough for him to climb in.** Don't forget, though. Ferrets are quirky and don't like any part of their bodies hanging outside of their toilets. Make sure the litter box has ample room for him to get into. Otherwise, he may poop elsewhere in protest.

» **When you wake your ferret for playtime, place him immediately in his litter box and wait until he does his duty.** When he does, you can let him come out. Don't be fooled by a faux poo; make sure he's really gone to the bathroom.

» **Until your fuzzy starts going consistently in his litter box, keep a little poo in the box as a reminder that the litter box is a toilet.**

» **If you catch your ferret straying from the plan (by backing into a corner, for instance), pick him up, firmly say "No," and then place him in the litter box until he goes.**

» _Always_ **praise your ferret for a job well done.** Use verbal schmoozing as well as petting.

If your otherwise litterbox-conscientious ferret starts missing the mark on a regular basis, it might be an underlying sign that something is amiss. Consider a trip to the vet to rule out GI or kidney issues, which may be causing him to go outside of the litter box.

Now that you have some tips in your potty-training arsenal for getting your fuzzy to use his box, you need to know the don'ts of bathroom training. The following list presents these don'ts:

>> **Never hit your fuzzy for having an accident.** Just be thankful he isn't a Great Dane!

>> **Never rub a ferret's nose in his waste when he has an accident.** This practice is abusive and serves no purpose. (It doesn't work with dogs, either.)

>> **Don't offer your fuzzy food rewards for going in his box.** You'll just teach him how to fake a poopy to get a treat.

I have some ferrets that back up to the edge of the litter box and then poop outside on the tile. This just proves that even when you do everything right, things can still go wrong. Go figure!

No healthy ferret wants to sleep in his or any other ferret's poop. However, you may find him dragging his bedding into his litter box and sleeping on top of it. You might want to consider placing some clean bedding into a clean litter box and adding it to your ferret's bedroom to see if that resolves the problem.

Harnessing Your Fuzzy for a Walk

Fuzzies are explorers by nature and can cover a lot of ground in only a few seconds. A fuzzy loves to wander around the backyard and explore outside, and it's nice for a ferret and his human to explore the outside world together. Unfortunately, without the proper restraint, it won't take your fuzzy long to get beyond your safe reach and into trouble. If you want to take your ferret outside to play, I advise you to always keep him leashed.

And nothing goes better with a ferret's leash than a harness for his long, slender body. I suggest that you choose an H-shaped harness designed specifically for ferrets (see Chapter 5). Personally, I don't like using collars. A tug on a collar can send the startled ferret into a frantic roll to get away from you. Also, a struggling fuzzy can often slip right out of a collar and scurry for freedom. I prefer harnesses because ferrets need less time to adjust to these new articles of clothing, and they're much more secure and safe.

As an extra precaution, you should consider fastening an identification tag to your fuzzy's harness in case he does escape. Some people even attach bells to the harness to keep track of the fuzzy's whereabouts.

The sections that follow show you how to familiarize your fuzzy with his harness and give you basic rules to follow when taking your fuzzy to the great outdoors to explore.

Getting fuzzy used to a harness

Before you take your ferret outside, get him accustomed to his harness and leash inside. Most ferrets struggle when you first put on the harness, but after awhile, most go about their business of exploring. Once in a while, though, I come across a rebellious carpet shark who takes more time to get used to the new constraint.

Start off slowly by following these simple steps:

1. **Get your ferret used to wearing his harness in the house while you supervise — but without a leash attached.**

   His harness should be just tight enough to prevent him from slipping out during a struggle.

2. **When he begins to forget about his new piece of clothing, add the leash and walk him around the house.**

3. **When he seems to accept his limited freedom, you can move to the outside world.**

I like to have my ferrets get all their struggling out inside the house, just in case. There's nothing like the panic that races through you as you're trying to catch a loose ferret outside.

Voilà. There's little more to this training than just harnessing your little guy. Some ferrets may need time to get used to having dead weight holding them back, but I've never seen a ferret revolt the way a puppy sometimes does. Ferrets don't heel or walk peacefully by your side like a pooch. The harness-and-leash method is merely a convenient way to tow you behind them as they go on their merry little ways.

A lot of people keep harnesses or tightly fitted collars on their ferrets all the time. Perhaps they leave the harnesses or collars on due to frustration or anxiety about having to put them back on later. I think this is a dangerous practice. Ferrets can and will get into everything and like to squeeze into small places. I advise you to never leave a collar or harness on your ferret while he's unsupervised, because it's very easy for him to get caught up on something and either get stuck or strangle himself, even in his own cage. If you have to battle to get the harness on, simply practice more often.

Following basic rules when you're out and about

The following list presents some basic rules for safety and sanity when you're outside with your fuzzy:

>> **Never tie your tethered ferret to something and leave him unsupervised.** Besides being an easy target for predators, your ferret will get bored and frustrated and do everything he can to escape, and he may just succeed.

>> **Never let your leashed ferret wander into shrubbery.** He can become entangled in the branches, and it will be difficult for you to rescue him. Worst-case scenario, he can get stuck and wiggle his way out of his harness.

>> **Never ignore the temperature.** You wouldn't walk your fuzzy across hot coals, so don't walk him on hot pavement. The fuzzy's paw-paws are very sensitive, you know. Likewise, those of us who've hopped frantically across a sandy beach know how brutally hot sand can get, and they don't make sandals for carpet sharks! Walking on snow is okay as long as your ferret isn't in it for too long.

REMEMBER

I strongly, strongly discourage the use of collars with ferrets for many safety reasons. If you're still not convinced after all you've read thus far and insist on using a collar on your ferret, consider the following while outdoors:

>> **Never use stretchy collars.** This type of collar is easy to pull off, especially if the ferret becomes entangled in foliage.

>> **Never use plastic collars or harnesses.** Your fuzzy will be tempted to chew on them and swallow the pieces. Even if the ferret wearing the collar doesn't chew it, a visiting playmate may.

Chapter **20**

Dealing with the Behaviorally Challenged Ferret

Some potential ferret owners, even after reading many books and magazines on ferrets, still aren't prepared for the endless behavioral possibilities they may face. You really can't know what all to expect until you've actually walked several miles with fuzzies attached to your shoes. It isn't just the new-comers who get all the surprises; many experienced fuzzy owners encounter unexpected problems after years of perfect fuzzdom. And consider this: It may be the ferret owner who's the problem and not the poor fuzzy.

This chapter is mostly about problem-solving and preparing you as much as pos-sible for the issues you may face. It deals with some of the reasons people give up their ferrets — in other words, it deals with the behaviorally challenged carpet sharks. I discuss the biters, the misunderstood ferrets of the world, and the aggressive beasts. You get the information needed to understand these fuzzies and reform them into acceptable members of the family.

Understanding Your Dracula in Fuzzy's Clothing

Once in a blue moon, a person will adopt a ferret that's just plain mean — in other words, she's a biter — and nothing much can be done about it. This is common in all pets, and ferrets are no exception. Most ferrets are loving and playful family members. Out of all the ferrets that have passed through my shelter or have remained as permanent residents, I've only encountered four severe biters. My experience has been that a lovable pooch is still far more dangerous than the typical fuzzy. But problem biters do exist, and you may adopt one someday.

The good news is that there's hope for the biting ferret. Most aggressive ferrets can be turned into gentle critters if their owners are willing to work on their relationships. If you're serious about being a fuzzy human, dumping a problem carpet shark at the nearest shelter should be your absolute last resort. This section is for the ferret lover who's willing to work to keep the ferret a part of the family.

Ferrets can bite for many reasons. Although you may not have all the colorful information about your fuzzy's personal history, you may be able to put the pieces together just by being a good observer. It may mean learning how to deactivate the bomb before it goes off, or it may mean taking time to convince your fuzzy that not all humans are evil. Usually, it's the latter (humans are the root of most biting evils).

REMEMBER

Not all ferret bites should be considered attacks. In fact, most aren't. Ferrets often have a good reason to bite; biting is sometimes the only way a ferret can communicate her needs or wishes. For example, a fuzzy can't reach up and smack you on the back of the head to say, "Tag, you're it." However, a nip on the ankle may be just as effective. Tag, by the way, is a favorite ferret game.

After you identify why your ferret is biting, you can address the situation appropriately. The following sections take a look at the most common reasons ferrets bite. (The later section "Socializing Your Biting Beast" explains what you can do to correct the problem, and Chapter 19 deals with training your ferret not to bite.)

REMEMBER

You must recognize the difference between playful biting and aggressive biting and try to correct both. An aggressive biter may bite you and hold on, or she may bite so hard that she draws blood. The pain caused by an aggressive biter is unmistakable. Playful bites include mouthing, light nips, and even "nip and runs." Although playful bites cause little to no discomfort, they may cause future problems.

I'm having growing pains

Baby ferrets are natural nippers. *All* kits can and will bite. They are, by nature, animals that face predation pressure. Young kits may react to startles by biting, simply as an instinctive reaction. Nothing is wrong with them; they just tend to react instinctively. And like all mammals, they explore the world with their mouths. And they have teething pains that can be severe at times, and gnawing on the closest available thing — your arm or a chew toy — helps to alleviate the pain. If your biting furball is a kit, I tend to think the situation really doesn't fall into the classification of "problem" — yet (see the following section).

Nobody told me not to bite

Many owners fail to nip-train their ferrets at an early age, when training is so crucial. The kit stage is the time when members of the ferret litter teach each other their biting limits. It is how a large male kit can play with a small female and not harm her. The rule ferrets learn is to never play harder than another ferret. An untrained fuzzy may be the owner's fault, the fault of a previous caretaker, or even the fault of a pet shop that failed to handle the cute babies on display. Perhaps the fuzzy you've adopted hasn't had limits set for her. Unfortunately, innocent kit nippers turn into bold biters if you don't stop the nipping early.

Often, people dump their nipping ferrets because they just don't know how to set limits and be the human bosses. The reason is due purely to frustration and lack of education. Chapter 19 covers how to nip-train a fuzzy. Educate yourself and don't give up on your little furball!

REMEMBER

Remember, ferrets learn from their playmates what is tolerable in terms of play biting. Their vocalizations are cues to let him know he's gone too far. A deaf ferret is at a serious disadvantage, then, because he cannot learn from those vocal cues. Training a deafie is sometimes more challenging because of this.

I'm in pain, darn it!

Your ferret has limited ability to say "Hey, my belly aches" or "I have these nasty bugs in my darn ears," so she may bite instead. Your biting furball may be suffering from a treatable condition, such as a severe ear mite infestation, or a more chronic disease, like adrenal disease. There are many, many medical conditions that can lead a ferret to bite.

Be a good human and be mindful of sudden changes in behavior. Many times she just isn't feeling well and needs your help. If the biting seems out of character, take your biter to the vet (warn the vet in advance about the aggression) for a complete physical. Rule out any illness or injury that may be causing your ferret to lash out in pain.

Resource guarding

In other words, "It's mine! Back off or I'll show you who's boss!" This possessive aggression is common in dogs, who can be aggressive when guarding food, a favorite sleeping spot, a coveted toy, or even his human. Some — okay, *many* — ferrets also share this often frustrating trait. Ferrets usually squabble only among themselves over resources, but if you get in the way, and the ferret sees you as a threat to his "treasure," you do run the risk of getting bitten. Training your ferret early in his life helps to curb this behavior, but it's no guarantee he won't display it later in life. After all, possession is nine-tenths of the law!

Provide plenty of toys, multiple food dishes, and hiding spots — way more than there are ferrets in your home. Practice taking away and returning toys to your ferret. Your ferret is less likely to get aggressive when he has grown comfortable with sharing.

I'm a manly or bully ferret

Unneutered male ferrets can (and probably will) be more aggressive than their altered counterparts. As with some teenage boys, it's the male ferret's hormonal duty to dominate whomever he can. Usually, an unneutered ferret chooses other male ferrets to bully. Female ferrets can also be targets of this type of male aggression. Sometimes, he'll bully the human who unknowingly tests his ferret manlihood. If you want to fix the aggression problem for this type of ferret, neuter that boy!

I'm facing a lot of change right now

Change, whether good or bad, is scary. Imagine this: Some giant picks you up, rips you out of your house, and plops you down in the middle of who knows where. Strangers are poking at you. Everything smells and looks funny. Some big, wet nose is sniffing at you and blowing snot on you. The new noises are enough to make your head explode. If you had a tail, it would be puffed out like a bottlebrush! You don't know whether to poop, run away, or bite. Heck, for all you know, you're in for the nightmare of your life.

A ferret in a strange situation may act scared and confused. Whether she's with a human she's loved and trusted for years or in the care of a brand new human, she doesn't know what to expect. When a ferret is under this much stress, she may bite. Give this ferret time to acclimate to big changes before rushing in and forcing her to bond with you. It may take hours, days, or weeks. But go slowly and let her explore new surroundings or new people.

Biting always worked before!

If your ferret was once under the care of another human (or perhaps you were the culprit), it's possible that she may have been trained to bite inadvertently. I don't mean "Caution: Guard Ferret on Premises!" I'm talking about a weenie human who gave the ferret her way every time she nipped. For instance, if the person picked up the fuzzy and she nipped, the person put her down and gave her freedom. Or perhaps when the ferret bit, the human thought that she must be hungry, so the person rewarded her with food. In other words, the ferret was training the human.

REMEMBER

Never positively reinforce a biting ferret. You shouldn't view biting as a cute way to tell you something.

I'm still fighting back

The main cause of a biting ferret is mistrust of humans. Humans can be pretty nasty animals. Some humans react violently or impulsively to stuff they don't understand; others are just jerks who thrive on being cruel. Unfortunately, animals are frequent victims of human abuse. In these cases, you can't blame a rescued fuzzy for remaining aggressive. Abused fuzzies learn several things during their abuse: 1) Attack or be attacked. 2) Hands equal hitting, feet equal kicking, and humans equal pain. 3) Every ferret for herself.

Working with an abused ferret takes extra time and patience. If you've ever been badly hurt by someone, physically or emotionally, you know how long it can take to trust again. Head to the following section to start the road to recovery with your scared fuzzy.

Some other reasons for my biting

Some ferrets react aggressively to particular noises, smells, or objects. My ferret Sybil (appropriately named), for example, came to my shelter with two other nutcases, Buster and Fidget. Sybil reacts aggressively when the dogs start barking, no matter where they are or why they're barking. How does she react? She runs up and bites me when they bark. Many ferrets react similarly to other stimuli, such as

>> New smells (especially on the hands or clothes)

>> The ruffling of newspapers

>> Vacuum cleaners

>> Brooms

>> Loud music

>> A squeaky toy

The list goes on. This is called *displaced aggression,* and there isn't always a reason why it happens. Some ferrets just get extra freaky around freaky people. This type of carpet shark may chase a timid person around the room and nip at his ankles. Most of these quirky ferrets are otherwise lovable and sweet, as most fuzzies are. The bottom line: If you're smart enough to identify the trigger, you should be smart enough not to trigger your fuzzy when she's out of her cage. (Oh, and by the way, most ferrets do have foot fetishes!)

Socializing Your Biting Beast

Not many fuzzies are just determined to be aggressive no matter what their owners do. A hopeless fuzzy case is a rarity. If you think you have an eccentric head case that you just can't handle, I suggest that you just haven't found the right approach or haven't been consistent with your technique. Your fuzzbutt may even be suffering from a combination of neuroses or a serious medical condition. Every ferret is a unique individual and responds differently to different methods of resocialization. Your job as your fuzzy's human is to find the best combination of love and gentle discipline.

In the following sections, you find out the best way to handle the biting ferret, as well as what to do if you should find yourself with a ferret hanging off your finger. With patience and consistency, using the tips here, you'll be able to turn your Dracula into a charmer in no time.

NORM AND HIS MAGIC TOUCH WITH AGGRESSIVE FERRETS

Norm Stilson of the Greater Chicago Ferret Association uses the same method to socialize all biting ferrets, and he has a tremendous success rate. He admits that his reconditioning process can take anywhere from a few weeks to a couple years. It depends largely on the severity of the ferret's mistrust of humans (in other words, how big of a jerk her previous human was) and how much time Norm has to work with the biter. Still, I've seen him in action, transforming the most hopeless biters into snuggly, happy fuzzbutts.

Norm uses the upper body grip, which I describe in the "Getting a grip" section, and spends a lot of time talking gently to the ferret. He uses his free hand to stroke the fur on top of the fuzzy's head and neck at the same time. He cuddles the fuzzy up against him (keeping control of the ferret's head) and even kisses the top of the fuzzy's head. Norm's version of the method, in my opinion, is the best.

Getting a grip

I find that the best way to handle an aggressive carpet shark is to firmly hold the upper part of her body from underneath, but with more control over her head — the *grip* method. You may have to distract her a little to seize her this way, but it allows you to hold her so she can't twist her head around to latch onto some vital part of your body. Simply follow these steps:

1. **Grasp your fuzzy by the scruff of the neck.**

2. **Take your free hand and hold her from underneath, just above her chest.**

3. **Wrap your fingers around the fuzzy's neck.**

   A paw may also go in between your fingers.

4. **When you're confident that you have the ferret safely but firmly in your grip, you can release the scruff.**

5. **Now you can use that free hand to smother her with gentle petting.**

This is a great handling method and doesn't require gloves (see the upcoming sidebar). And it usually works, too.

A GRIPPING QUESTION: GLOVES OR HANDS?

Some people think that thick gloves, made of leather, are great for working to tame the aggressive ferret. Gloves can help protect your hands from the serious ouchies an aggressive biter can inflict. Using gloves allows you to handle the fuzzy confidently and without fear if you're serious about taming her. If you're skittish around your aggressive ferret to begin with, this option may be the way to go. Another option is a fillet glove, which is thinner and has metal armor that prevents bites from getting through. You can find these gloves at sporting goods stores.

Although many people advocate using gloves to tame the biter, I believe that doing so may actually defeat the purpose. I think fuzzies find the feel of a gentle but firm human paw a little more soothing than the feel of a stiff, groping glove. Being held with a glove may feel a bit more like being manhandled, which may be why your furball is so ticked off in the first place. I've never used gloves. They're too bulky on my tiny hands, and I can't seem to hold a fuzzy comfortably. Also, I never want to give a ferret the impression that my skin is tough and can withstand such torture!

Getting unstuck

If a ferret bites you and doesn't want to let go (an uncommon behavior), you can use some techniques to get her off. Unless you're an experienced ferret handler, though, you'll probably be too busy panicking and overreacting to think about these techniques logically. Most people just try to fling the ferret from whichever body part she's latched onto.

With a little preparation and knowledge, you may be able to keep your wits about you in a latching situation and get unstuck. Some of the following tips may come in handy:

>> Place a tiny amount of safe, homemade bitter solution such as a solution of either white distilled vinegar and water or lemon juice and water into the corner of the ferret's mouth (use a cotton swab or small controlled spray). While she's *ptooey*ing out the taste, your finger will be *ptooey*ed out along with it. *Note:* You should always have some of this homemade bitter solution on hand, no pun intended. (See chapter 19 for instructions on how to make your own.)

WARNING

Don't ever spray any bitter solution directly into the ferret's face. Ever. Doing so is painful and cruel, and the fuzzy's next bite will be justified.

>> Hiss at the ferret to distract him into letting go.

>> Place your hand over his head and kiss him on the nose. Only for the brave and experienced owners!

>> Ask a helping hand to gently squeeze the carpet shark's jaws open and aid you in prying her off, one tooth at a time.

REMEMBER

A real fear biter can "jump bite," moving from your skin to the helper's skin. Be extra cautious. (See the earlier section "Understanding Your Dracula in Fuzzy's Clothing" for more on the reasons for biting.)

>> Have a helper thread a wooden chopstick behind the skin under attack. A gentle yet forceful twisting motion can loosen the bite grip just enough to allow for an escape without harming the ferret.

>> Drip some salmon oil over the tip of the ferret's nose. The ferret should automatically start licking the treat, releasing you in the process.

Although I often stress the importance of not rewarding biting with treats, giving a reward is justified during an extreme, prolonged bite. The object is to get unhooked without causing further trauma to you or the frightened ferret.

>> *As a very last resort,* find a cold body of water — such as water in a toilet, bathtub, or sink — and submerge her until her desire to breathe overtakes her desire to mangle you. You can also use cold running water from a faucet.

REMEMBER

The submerge method is a last-resort solution. Don't flush her down the toilet or drown her in the process. Bite wounds heal. Death is irreversible, and guilt haunts for a long time.

WARNING

Don't try to get your ferret to release by pulling her or jerking her away. In other words, don't try to send her for a flying lesson. Doing so only causes more damage, and you'll feel really stupid if you further injure yourself or your fuzzy when you have many better options.

The main thing to remember when being bitten is don't panic. Panicking usually makes the situation worse. If you know you're dealing with an aggressive ferret, you can opt not to handle her unless someone else is around to come to your rescue.

TIP

Some people avoid the use of scruffing altogether during bite training, because they don't want the ferret to associate scruffing with bad experiences or with getting in trouble. Rather, some prefer to save scruffing for activities that aid their ferrets, such as vet visits, administering meds, cleaning ears, and so on. However, this is a personal choice.

"I WILL PROBABLY BITE YOU EVEN HARDER IF YOU . . ."

If you opt for one of the following techniques to get your fuzzy to unlatch from a bite, you'll probably make the problem worse:

- Mist a bitter spray or another deterrent in your fuzzy's face
- Bite her back on the ear or head (some people actually do this)
- Flick her on the nose or head when she bites
- Hit her or throw her across the room
- Isolate her from the world for long periods of time
- Scruff her and shake her violently

Taming the critter

Depending on your ferret's personality and her past life experiences, she may or may not respond to certain methods of reconditioning. Some fuzzies learn quickly that humans can be trustworthy and can make great playmates. Others need quite a bit more time to come to this conclusion. This section presents some ideas that may or may not work for taming your biting ferret. Unfortunately, some may even make matters worse, but it may only be temporary. Don't give up on a tactic right away just because it doesn't work the first time. Winning over a biter takes patience and consistency. If, however, the biting gets more severe and more frequent after much patience and consistency, you probably should try a new tactic.

This list gives you some of the more obvious solutions you can try:

>> If your companion biter is an unaltered male, neuter him.

>> Rule out medical reasons for biting through a veterinary exam and get veterinary care for any illnesses or injuries.

>> If you know the biting trigger, such as barking dogs, don't subject your ferret to the trigger.

>> If your fuzzy is visually or hearing impaired (or very young), take extra care not to startle her when handling her.

>> Make sure that your ferret is well fed and given a proper well-balanced diet.

>> Dribble salmon oil on your skin to teach your biter that skin is for licking, not biting.

>> Spend more quality time with your ferret instead of keeping her cooped up in the cage for days on end.

And here are some more creative ideas; you can use these in combination with the previous solutions and with each other:

>> Put a safe, homemade bitter spray such as a white distilled vinegar or lemon juice solution on your hands so a bite doesn't taste as good.

>> Screech, growl, hiss, or loudly yell "Ouch!" or "No!" when the ferret bites (use simple words, not sentences). Some people do a quick, firm shake (no harder than another ferret would do) while verbally reprimanding the biter. Many ferrets see this as a sign that biting definitely isn't a good thing to do.

Some ferrets may bite harder if a verbal reprimand is accompanied by a scruff, especially if you include a firm shake. This is a definite individual thing.

Another method is to tell her, "I'm in charge, darn it!" and place her submissively on her back with a scruff. Hold her firmly in that position high up on her body to keep control of her head. After a few minutes, give her a timeout in her carrier.

» Sentence the ferret to short-term (no longer than 10 minute) jail time by placing her in a small carrier used only for biting. A fuzzy should always get a timeout immediately after biting.

REMEMBER

Timeouts are important for many forms of ferret discipline but should be used with care. Some people believe that an immediate timeout after biting is a reward to a ferret that wants to be left alone anyway. So, if you can, try to physically hold the fuzzy for several minutes after the bite occurs before you put her away for a timeout (see the section "Getting a grip"). However, if you're too angry to be rational or too busy cleaning up your wounds, you should put away the fuzzy immediately. If these timeouts don't seem to work, try the "I'm gonna hold you anyway" method to see if this form of dominance works better. And get your tetanus shot updated!

» If your fuzzy currently has no playmate, try introducing a fuzzy friend so that she'll have someone to rough and tumble with. She may be bored to frustration.

» Immediately substitute a toy for the human body part and allow the ferret to only bite that.

» Wrap the fuzzy securely in a towel and carry her around like a bundled baby. Talk to her and stroke the top of her head gently.

TIP

Don't use your ferret's cage as a timeout place. This can work one of two ways. It can make the ferret view her cage as a "bad place" where she doesn't want to go at any time, or the timeout can be viewed as a reward because the cage is where the ferret wanted to go in the first place. I think it is better to have a special, very small timeout cage — a cat-sized carrier would work fine.

REMEMBER

Aggression isn't a training or conditioning tool. In my opinion, aggression only leads to aggression, whether you're dealing with a human or a fuzzbutt. Chances are, what got you to this stage had something to do with a human who was being a jerk. So, throw away all the tough love and put on your compassionate hat. The biting ferret reacts positively only to a firm but consistently nonviolent approach. And don't forget to always reward your ferret for acceptable behavior. Ferrets are extremely intelligent and learn according to how you teach them. Heed what Bob Church, ferret guru and enthusiast, says: "A gentle hand grows a gentle ferret."

Bonding with the biting ferret

After all is said and done, I'm here to tell you that you simply cannot force a bond with your ferret any more than you can force a bond with the neighbor that just moved in next door. There are no guarantees. However, here are some tips you can follow to help foster a good relationship with your ferret and hopefully create that bond you desire:

>> **Patience and understanding:** Your ferret relies on you to teach him right from wrong, but he's not going to be perfect. Respond to him with patience and understanding, and he will respond to you positively, albeit in his own time.

>> **Never show fear:** Anxiety and fear causes physiological changes, such as changes in breathing rate and perspiration, as a result of the flight-or-fight response. We also give off chemicals called pheromones when we're scared or alarmed. It's very possible ferrets can smell these pheromones and sense when a person is scared. They may not attack us because of this, but I can certainly imagine them taking full advantage of us when we're in this state.

>> **Positive reinforcement:** In other words, don't be a jerk by responding negatively. Most creatures, including humans, respond best to positive reinforcement, and when negativity is thrown at them, it backfires. You want training to be a good experience. Always remember: Aggression leads to aggression.

>> **Redirection:** If your ferret is fixated on something, redirect him by using a stimulus, such as a clicker or even a clucking noise, to redirect him to you.

>> **Never hesitate:** If you're going to pick your ferret up, pick him up! Don't hesitate. Do so with confidence, and make your ferret feel safe and secure.

>> **Don't be a human-sized squeaky toy:** A high-pitched voice will surely activate your already-hyper little guy. And it's not funny to respond to his bites with squeals and giggles. This teaches him bad manners and sets both of you up for failure in the long run.

6

Breeding Ferrets: The Facts, Fallacies, and Plain Ol' Hard Work

Look honestly at the entire ferret breeding endeavor.

Understand ferret love from boudoir to cradle of kits.

Get a feel for the each of the ferret's developmental stages.

Chapter **21**

Should You Breed Your Ferret? Looking at the Big Picture

Being able to breed ferrets responsibly and successfully requires years of ferret ownership, a great deal of mentorship with a reputable ferret breeder, and even more research, among other things. Unless you meet the ownership requirement and can do the mentorship and research, I strongly urge you to have your ferret altered and leave breeding to the people who know exactly what they're doing and why they're doing it. Breeding ferrets is not like breeding dogs or cats. It's much more complex. It's much more expensive, and if you're looking for a profit, ferret breeding is not for you!

However, kits are simply adorable. What's more satisfying than raising a beautiful, healthy fuzzy? (Maybe giving a good home to an old fuzzy that was abandoned in a shelter.) Responsible private breeders offer an alternative for ferret people who want kits but don't want to go to pet shops. Responsible breeders are more interested in a kit's well-being than money, thus are more concerned about weeding out the less-than-desirable ferret homes. And private breeders get to spend oodles of time sharing their wealth of information with people who seek them out.

This chapter discusses breeder requirements that many beginner breeders haven't thought about. Before you begin breeding ferrets, find out whether you have what it takes. And, even if you decide that you do, ask yourself whether you should. Also, I discuss ferret shelters and why they exist, because every ferret in a shelter was once somebody's little baby.

What It Takes to Be a Responsible Breeder

REMEMBER

Breeding ferrets requires way more than just throwing two amorous fuzzies in a cage and hanging up the "Do Not Disturb" sign. Responsible breeders carefully choose their breeding pairs, and they breed for good temperament, good looks, and conformation. They're prepared for emergency medical situations and spend most of their free time caring for moms and kits (baby ferrets).

And responsible breeders don't just sell their kits to anyone. Money should be the last thing on a responsible breeder's mind. The honest truth is that unless you mass-produce hundreds of kits a year and sell them wholesale to pet shops, you probably won't make much money in the ferret breeding business. If you're lucky, you'll break even. If you're outstanding, you'll be in the red each year. A responsible breeder does the work because he or she simply loves the critter and wants to put the best ferrets in the best homes.

If you should stumble across a breeder who works alone, stay clear. Responsible breeders *network together*. They offer each other critical support and share husbandry knowledge. Striving for genetic diversity, responsible breeders share bloodlines. Additionally, they share records and pedigrees, which assist in calculating inbreeding variables and critter tracking. As a network, they have better access to foster moms and V-hobs. Responsible breeders know who's out there doing what, and they will quickly put the word out about irresponsible breeders. And because responsible breeders should take back any of their kits that are returned down the road, they even warn each other if they've gotten a kit back in bad shape from someone. Sharing of a "do not place" list prevents "breeder jumping" by which an irresponsible owner goes from one breeder to the next looking for another kit.

Alas, I can discuss much more that responsible breeders need to have and do, and I do so in the following sections.

Deep pockets

A ferret breeder must fork over money for the cost of caring for pregnant jills (unspayed females) and vulnerable kits (babies). In addition to normal care, breeders will always have unexpected expenses; have you thought about emergencies or unplanned situations? Responsible breeders must take the following costs into consideration:

>> Purchasing excellent breeding stock to get started. This may include extensive health testing of both parents to ensure their pedigree lives up to or exceeds the standards of breeding-quality ferrets — contributing only to the overall good of the species. It may also include import fees, licensing, airfare, overseas vetting, and many other costs.

>> Proper cages and setups for jills and kits (see Chapter 5 for more on ferret cages).

>> Routine vet care for moms and kits, including supplements and special diets required in order to maintain the health of mom and kits, both unborn and newly born. This also includes any medication needed.

>> First vaccination(s) and microchip for kits before they go to their new homes.

>> Veterinary wellness exams within 24 hours for kits leaving for their new homes.

>> "Fit to fly" health certificates or other health certificates needed for leaving home.

>> Optional "kit bags" filled with supplies, microchip and vaccination records, and miscellaneous other goodies to send along with the kits to their new homes.

>> Vet care for complications such as uterine infections and mastitis (infected and hardened mammary glands).

>> Emergency C-sections for jills in trouble. This is an extremely costly surgery in which you can lose both mom and the babies. It's not uncommon to lose the litter when a C-section comes into play. The reality is, breeders are sometimes faced with hard decisions. Some may choose to bear the loss of the litter and spay the jill to try to guarantee her life and to have her live out her existence as someone's beloved pet. Other breeders may choose to proceed with the C-section and pray the odds are in their favor. Although C-section technology for ferrets hasn't caught up with that of dogs and cats, I have heard of some ferret C-section success stories.

>> Having necropsies performed by a veterinarian on adult breeder ferrets or kits that have died unexpectedly or for no apparent reason. It helps to determine the cause of death. The necropsy may be costly, but it is a tool of the veterinarian world, and it teaches us all more about the animals we love. There cannot be advances made in our industry without necropsies.

>> Humane euthanizing of kits that have severe deformities or the cost of providing lifelong care for these babies.

>> Spaying bad moms (see the following section) or retirees — and providing lifelong care for them if you can't find good homes.

>> Providing lifelong care for any kits that you can't sell.

The emotional stake

Breeding isn't always smooth sailing, with happy births and successful adoptions; heartache is involved, and so are many decisions that you'd probably rather not have to face. Ferret moms, for example, may not be good moms at all. Kits can die from being cannibalized (eaten by mom) or neglected. It can be heartbreaking. Hand-rearing a newborn kit is next to impossible, so all you can do is watch.

TIP

Many breeders arrange to have two ferrets give birth within a few days of each other so that they can serve as foster moms if necessary. This plan doesn't always work, though — especially if the litters are large.

Before you decide to breed, ask yourself how you would feel about the following, because breeders face these situations at one time or another:

>> Enduring deaths from faded kit syndrome: These kits are seemingly normal until they start losing weight. Heartbreakingly, they just die for no apparent reason.

>> Moms having stillborn kits.

>> Moms cannibalizing or killing the kits: Usually caused by stress, such as too much human interference. Possibly the mom is too young or inexperienced or even that she's just a poor mom overall.

>> Losing kits because a mom refuses to nurse or is incapable of nursing.

>> Losing a mom during a difficult pregnancy, labor, or pregnancy-related illness.

>> Getting your hopes dashed when you find out it was a false pregnancy (which is common in ferrets).

>> Worrying about all the kits you help into the world and stressing over how they're doing in someone else's care.

>> Having kits with severe birth defects (malformations) euthanized. Some minor birthing accidents, such as a mom "overgrooming" a kit's tail or leg are considered defects but are usually cosmetic. On the other hand, some defects can be life-threatening, such as spine or heart defects or defective hips. If these problems are genetic, the entire line you've been creating will be lost. Such a thing has shut down breeders in the past.

>> Having fuzzies returned to you for one reason or another. Hopefully they're in good shape and won't require immediate veterinary care. Unfortunately, that's not always the case.

>> Losing contact with your kits. Let's face it. You can be extra careful when choosing that perfect home for your kits, but people can be jerks. They may break off contact with you or break the written contract you had. Depending on where you live, you may or may not legally be able to get your baby back even if you really want to try.

Time to care

Breeding ferrets, providing support during and after pregnancies for moms and kits, and finding perfect homes for your precious babies can be extremely time-consuming. You'll probably have to forgo your karate classes to do the following:

>> Search for (and research) a source of quality breeder ferrets, which are your initial financial and emotional investments.

>> Keep diligent records (financial and pedigree, as well as buyer/breeder contracts).

>> Talk to and learn from other responsible breeders.

REMEMBER

Responsible breeding *isn't* a competition; it's a shared interest.

>> Check your kits' weights regularly from birth to 5 weeks old to make sure that they're gaining weight, and take the necessary steps to correct problems upon discovery.

>> Chauffeur your ferrets to and from the vet.

>> Spend time socializing kits and begin training before they go to their new homes.

REMEMBER

Good breeders hang onto kits until they're at least 10 to 12 weeks old. Those who keep them a little longer suggest that doing so creates a stronger-minded and more self-aware kit, one that is independent and confident. On the other hand, it raises the overall costs incurred to keep these bottomless feeders an extra two weeks.

>> Spend an enormous amount of time on the phone talking to potential buyers and new ferret parents. Good breeders should be choosy about whom they sell their babies to, and they should provide ongoing before- and after-sales support.

>> Take care of kits that owners have brought back to you. A responsible breeder takes back kits that don't work out in their homes, which can be a burden over time.

RETIRING A BREEDING MYTH

Breeding animals isn't a way to teach a child about the miracle of life (and death, in many cases). If you feel your child is missing out in this area of knowledge, rent a video, buy some books, or tune in to the Discovery Channel or Animal Planet. These are great ways to spend quality time with kids and still teach them the value and beauty of life. Of course, also explain to your kids the devastating effects of overpopulation so that they'll understand why a video may be far more responsible than the real thing (see the final section of this chapter for more).

TIP

If you think you have what it takes to be a responsible fuzzy breeder, research the subject a little more. Call your local ferret shelter and put in a few hours of volunteer work each week. If you don't have time to do that now, you certainly won't have the time to breed ferrets responsibly.

Willingness to find out what you don't know

Responsible breeding means knowing a lot about ferret biology and genetics. For example, did you know that ferrets are similar to chinchillas in that breeding certain color variations may cause lethal genes? Additionally, new, exotic ferret colors being produced may be the result of mutant or recessive genes. No one knows for sure whether funky-colored ferrets will have more health problems down the road. How can you know whether you're creating one of these tragic situations?

In addition to biology and genetics, you need to know the rules governing the sale of ferrets. For example, when it comes to selling your kits, did you know that breeders who wholesale their ferrets (sell to pet shops, for example) are required to be USDA licensed? (Some breeders also have to be licensed by their state's Department of Agriculture; USDA is a separate federal licensing.)

REMEMBER

This places even more emphasis on the need to keep good records and maintain good husbandry practices. Inspectors can pop in at any reasonable time — unannounced — to inspect your facility, animals, and records. Also, ferret breeders may be required to have additional permits or licenses, depending on where they live.

WARNING

You need to remember that in some places it's still illegal to own ferrets. And in some states it's illegal to own unaltered ferrets after they've reached a certain age. Permits and licenses are almost always needed to breed, and on top of it you may need a permit for each ferret in the home.

ARE YOU *SURE* YOU WANT TO BREED FERRETS?

Again, anyone who is seriously considering breeding ferrets must do so out of *love* for the ferret and not for profit, because there just is no profit! Consider the following in all honesty if your brain is not convinced:

- **How long have you owned ferrets?** If it's not been at least 5 years, hang up your hat and keep enjoying your current ferrets.

- **Do you have a mentor?** As you have already read, no responsible breeder is an island. You must be part of a larger community for the good of the ferrets.

- **Are you a member of a local ferret club or ferret breeder club?** The more people you can reach out to and learn from, the better off you and your ferrets will be. Good reputable online clubs are also a great source of knowledge.

- **Who's going to buy your kits?** What does your local market look like? Can it support the number of kits you plan on producing? Are you planning on selling locally? Across the state? What about shipping? Lots of things to consider here!

- **Do you have an *experienced* ferret vet?** Remember: Not all vets see ferrets or are truly knowledgeable in ferret care. If you have one, is he willing to work with you in your breeding endeavor and give you access to necessary medications that cannot be acquired over-the-counter?

- **Can you perform basic injections?** As a breeder, and under the guidance of your veterinarian, you will undoubtedly be administering subcutaneous and intramuscular injections at home. You should know how to do this and how to administer life-saving fluids.

- **Do you have access to breeding software?** This will ensure accurate record-keeping and pedigree development, as well as calculating inbreeding variables.

- **Are you financially stable?** And actually, you should probably be a tad more than stable, because vet bills, high-quality foods and overall ferret supplies are extremely expensive. There are no cutting corners in responsible breeding!

- **Do you have the space?** Hobs have to be housed alone, and it's not unusual for jills not to get along, as well. And even if your jills can be housed together, they'll need separate maternity wards.

- **Do you have time?** Kits need *daily* handling from a very early age up until they go to their new homes. This helps to ensure proper socializing.

Avoiding a Need for More Shelters

If you love ferrets (and presumably you do if you want to breed them), you don't want to bolster the need for shelters. Most people have heard at one time or another the statistics on how many dogs and cats are killed each year in shelters. The senseless deaths of these once-loved pets number in the millions. As ferrets gain popularity as companion pets in households, the number of furballs that wind up in shelters also increases, as does the number of deaths of these homeless fuzzies.

Careless breeding by humans is the cause for overpopulation. The population of fuzzbutts at ferret shelters such as the Greater Chicago Ferret Association can fluctuate between 60 and 100 ferrets at a time. That's a lot of displaced furkids. Many are geriatric fuzzies that no longer fit into the perfect pet mold their humans have illogically created. These unfortunate souls get dumped for younger or different pets.

No ferret breeder can guarantee that every one of his or her kits will remain in permanent, loving homes. Too many people treat animals as property; they put little thought into getting pets and end up abusing them, neglecting them, selling them to the highest bidders, or giving them away to whoever shows up first. Some people even dump fuzzies into the wild to futilely fend for themselves, or they abandon them at shelters where their futures are unknown. This revolving-door syndrome gets passed on by example to children. It's morally and ethically wrong to treat any life with such disregard; this cycle needs to be stopped.

You can help stop this cycle by thinking long and hard about whether you should breed ferrets at all. If you can't meet the points listed previously in "What It Takes to Be a Responsible Breeder," you'll for sure be adding to the vicious cycle. But even responsible breeders can't guarantee they won't be a part of the cycle, because there are no guarantees on where the ferrets end up. Although it's true that overpopulation is a problem and breeding needs to be curtailed, the true problem lies with a human mentality that pets are disposable and the job of the shelter is to take in the unwanteds. The cycle stops with education and a change in mentality.

Chapter **22**

Unmasking the Details of Ferret Love

E ven if you've identified the perfect pair of furballs to breed (see Chapter 21), getting them to cooperate may be difficult. We humans tend to think that guys, no matter what species, have one thing on the brain and are always in the mood; the male ferret, or *hob,* however, has long bouts of "Not now, dear — I have a headache" syndrome.

Headaches aside, ferret courtship and mating often are primitively brutal and unromantic. After the deed is done and the male scoots off to put another notch in his chew toy, the female, or *jill,* needs some extra-special attention. Being the good human that you are, your job is to see that her needs are adequately met. This means more than just running out for a late-night pickle purchase; you must provide a whole lot of tender, loving care, supply a good place for her to hunker down, and fill her belly with extra-good stuff.

In addition to addressing the needs of a pregnant ferret, this chapter gives you an overview of the ferret's reproductive system and mating habits. We give a lot of emphasis to the do's and don'ts of breeding ferrets. This chapter also discusses the actual birth of the kits. Because the mortality rate in newborn ferret kits is high, I outline the basic things that can go wrong and explain what you may be able to do to help. This is a particularly important chapter to pay attention to if you're considering bringing more carpet sharks into the world. It's also great for people — especially shelter workers — who unexpectedly find themselves with pregnant ferrets on their hands.

REMEMBER

This chapter is by no means meant to be a step-by-step guide to breeding fuzzies. In fact, I hope to discourage you! The breeding process takes years to learn, and it's never mastered. It's an ongoing learning experience — a complex process. It is extremely time-consuming and God-awfully expensive. Although it may be rewarding, it will also undoubtedly break your heart time and time again. Consider the information here as background basics and an overview of typical things people encounter when breeding ferrets. If anything, this chapter is meant to further convince you to leave ferret breeding to experienced and responsible experts.

Fine-Tuning the Organs

Hormones and sexual maturity can cause wondrous changes in the appearance, behavior, and habits of our lovable ferrets. These changes occur over time as the body develops and peaks during the mating seasons, or *ruts,* when sexual maturity has been reached.

You need to know how ferrets develop and what changes you can expect to encounter in unaltered ferrets if you're considering breeding them. This brief section gives you an overview of the ferret's reproductive system and mating habits.

The boy (hob)

The male ferret's testicles begin to mature approximately six weeks after his birth. Full maturity takes close to six months, with some slowpokes waiting until eight or nine months to even start thinking about the ladies. You can tell when a hob is beginning that confusing time of puberty because his testicles begin to increase in size, mainly due to the increase in the male hormone testosterone. Also testicle size can change according to the photoperiod. Ferrets are tuned into the photoperiod to determine times of fertility. The testicle size is small and may appear "immature" in the non-breeding season (winter) and increase greatly in size in the breeding season — spring to fall. The increase in testosterone also causes the ferret to notice the girls a little more.

TIP

Boy ferrets that are ready to breed or that are in rut wear a discolored, yellowish undercoat, caused by an increase in oil production in the skin glands. Hobs also tend to lose weight and muscle mass during rut and often lose some of their beautiful fluffy tails. (This is known as *stud tail*.) Like teenage boys, they're at their smelliest during this time, and have only sex on their minds.

Mature males may tease the girls (only because they like them) and grab the backs of their necks to show them how much they care. Major welts and sometimes puncture wounds are often inflicted by new or inexperienced hobs upon jills within the first 24 hours of the courtship process, and these must be medically tended to by breeders. And as with an overactive male dog, behaviors such as pelvic thrusting and mounting and dragging various objects, people, and ferrets of either gender occur frequently. Hobs in rut are not picky, which is why good breeders house their hobs alone. They may also begin to stash ferret magazines under their snooze sacks and spend way too much time on the phone!

Nothing is safe from a hob in rut. Marking everything with a lovely mixture of sperm and urine, he ends up coating everything he has access to. Experienced breeders call this *snail trail* or *sliming*. Humans are not left out of the excitement! Hobs will run right over your feet and leave a snail trail, not only to mark their territories, but also to attract the jills-in-waiting. (Does this really work? Hmmm.) After breeding season, however, the male ferret returns to being just one of the stinky guys.

WARNING

If you haven't already figured it out, unaltered male ferrets are quite the smelly boys. They can be extremely aggressive toward other males and sometimes even their humans — especially when they're out to capture a female's heart. For this reason, unaltered boys don't usually make good pets when they're in breeding season.

The girl (jill)

Unaltered female ferrets become sexually mature at about 6 months of age under normal lighting conditions. The onset of *estrus* (the heat period) is closely associated with the increase in daylight during the normal seasonal change. Females that are exposed to shorter light days are late bloomers that reach sexual maturity as late as 12 months of age.

A female in estrus is easy to identify. Her pink vulva swells due to an increase in the female hormone estrogen. You may see a clear or slightly discolored discharge.

The female in heat may get crabby and sleep less (I refer to it as PMS, or Pre-Mustelid Syndrome). But unlike female humans, the ferret in estrus usually cuts back on her food intake. Some other stuff is going on inside her body, too.

The lining of her uterus begins to swell, and follicles containing eggs develop in the ovaries. Then she just sits back and waits for her dream ferret to come by and drag her off her fuzzy feet.

Making a love connection: Enter Neanderthal ferret

A female ferret should be bred about two weeks after the swelling of her vulva becomes noticeable (see the previous section). Typically, you should bring the female to the male's condo for the rendezvous. I recommend that you stay close to chaperone the first date to be sure the chemistry isn't overly explosive. Expect a lot of noise and commotion. The female may even adamantly reject the hob's advances. If he persists, she usually wins after a horrific fight ensues.

Many breeders recommend that you keep the breeding pair together for two to three days. Any longer than that and the male quickly gets on the female's nerves, causing arguments (and an occasional throwing of dishes). A lack of tolerance on the female's part often indicates that she has little buns in the oven.

REMEMBER

Breeding the female two days in a row may cause her to produce a bigger litter. If the ferret has fewer than two kits to nurse, she may come back into season while nursing and lose her milk. This occurrence is called *lactational estrus.* If this occurs, kits will need to be hand-reared or put with a surrogate mom.

REMEMBER

Romance and schmoozing are the last things on a male ferret's mind when he meets up with his dream girl. The male ferret practically tackles the female when he grabs her by the nape of the neck to mount her. He uses her to mop every corner of his condo, even though she may be screaming and biting in protest. When she goes into submission, he has his way with her, and it isn't uncommon for him to return for second or third helpings. No courtship is involved — unless you call clubbing her over the head and dragging her off by the fur to the nearest cave romantic. Some males are actually gentle, and their mates actually seem to enjoy themselves. But, for the most part, unaltered boys are no Don Juans.

The typical Mustelid love lasts an hour or so on average, with ten minutes being noted for some unimpressive fellows and an awesome three hours being noted for some marathon guys.

WARNING

The following list presents a couple things you should be aware of so you don't panic or cause injury:

>> Females often receive puncture wounds on the neck during the mating ritual, which usually requires some first aid. Blood is common, but violently shaking

the female and/or causing wounds serious enough for profuse bleeding isn't. Separate the pair immediately.

>> The typical mating ritual of ferrets — specifically the neck biting and prolonged intercourse — causes the release of hormones, which stimulates ovulation. Without the hormone, the female won't release her eggs and will remain in heat.

>> The male ferret's penis has a bony hook at the tip that causes it to become latched inside the female after he penetrates. And the male remains hooked until he decides that he's had enough — no sooner. Don't try to separate ferrets in the middle of the act. Besides ruining the mood, forcing a separation may injure one or both fuzzies.

Female carpet sharks are induced ovulators, which means that their eggs aren't released until mating actually takes place. Pressure on the cervix, caused by the act of mating, and neck biting stimulates the release of the eggs (ovulation) 30 to 40 hours after the deed is done. Sperm can survive in the female for 36 to 48 hours. As many as 18 (typically 5 to 13) eggs are fertilized. The vulva begins to dry and shrink after a week and returns to normal size in three to four weeks (longer if breeding took place long after estrus began).

REMEMBER

If the shrinkage doesn't begin after a week or so, your fuzzy hasn't established pregnancy, and you should set a new date with the male ferret.

What Happens If Your Unaltered Ferret Isn't Bred?

What if you decide not to breed your ferret after she goes into estrus? Not every ferret is bred every season for many reasons. But because female ferrets are induced ovulators, they remain in heat indefinitely until they're bred, and the result of a prolonged estrus can be deadly.

When a ferret is in estrus, her level of estrogen rises dramatically. This raised level of hormone, when in heat, suppresses the production of blood cells in the bone marrow. Prolonged suppression results in a condition called *aplastic anemia*. This condition is almost always fatal if left untreated because the ferret's red blood cells aren't replaced as needed and/or she'll succumb to bacterial infections from the lack of white blood cells. Some signs of aplastic anemia may include pale gums, hind-end weakness, patches of fur loss, and small areas of bleeding under the skin.

You have several ways to bring your female ferret out of estrus and harm's way:

>> Breed her to an unaltered male.

>> Breed her to a vasectomized male (known among breeders as a *V-Hob*). (The hormones are still going strong, but the road is blocked.)

>> Have a ferret-knowledgeable vet give her a proligestone hormone injection (the "jill jab") to fake her out of heat (see Chapter 12 for tips on finding a vet).

>> Have a ferret-knowledgeable vet inject a deslorelin implant, which lasts 8.5 to 20 months depending on the strength of the implant. A surge in hormones may cause her to appear to be in heat for up to two weeks after the implant, but that will subside. Note: Deslorelin will also stop a jill's current heat, but only if she's been in heat for less than three weeks. Deslorelin should not be implanted after that time due to bone marrow suppression that begins in four to five weeks after a heat cycle begins.

REMEMBER

A hormone injection and breeding to a vasectomized male are short-term solutions that cause a false pregnancy in your female. Some breeders believe a false pregnancy causes unnecessary emotional burden and stress on your jill. It's a personal choice. She'll eventually come back into heat and have the same problem. If you've decided that breeding your female isn't for you, you should proceed to the last suggestion.

>> Spay her! (See Chapter 12 for more information.)

Mothering the Mom-to-Be

About two weeks into your ferret's pregnancy, you should be able to gently palpate her belly and feel the small peanut-sized babies. However, she may not show the typical bulging signs of pregnancy until one month has passed. The kits should arrive in about 41 to 43 days (usually 42 days), barring any unforeseen circumstances. Until then, get ready to pamper and schmooze your fuzzy even more than you already do — for at least a couple of months. If you're a true ferret lover (and you'd better be if you plan on breeding ferrets), mothering isn't too difficult a job for you. Just triple your current efforts, because your jill will be in mommy mode and suffering from FMS or "ferret mood swing." Your care may very well be rewarded with a healthy litter of adorable kits. On the other hand, you must accept that complications are common no matter how well you care for her.

This section details what kind of care you should give to the mother fuzzy, from her feedings to her environment.

You should handle your pregnant ferret gently and very frequently to get her as comfortable with you as possible. This positive interaction between you and the mom is critical, especially if you need to physically intervene during or shortly after the birth. An unfamiliar hand poked into her nest may cause mom to reject and/or cannibalize her kits. For this reason, the person who handles momma ferret most often during pregnancy should be the only person to invade the nest if invasion becomes absolutely necessary. Also, jills can be aggressive when raising kits, so this is important to hopefully curb the aggression towards the main handler.

I suggest that you, as a serious ferret breeder, find another serious breeder (if you don't have another female to breed yourself) who will have a ferret giving birth around the same time as your little girl. Make prior arrangements to place your kits with the other nursing female if your mom proves to be an unfit mother (ferret moms aren't always good moms; see the later section "Some Problems You May Face After Birth"), because hand-rearing kits is next to impossible. (See the final two sections of this chapter for more on foster moms and hand-rearing.)

Most jills will only have a single litter of kits within a nine- to twelve-month period. However, the new mom may go back into heat just a few months after weaning her kits if she is exposed to extended lighting periods. A healthy ferret can have up to three successful litters per year, although most reputable breeders stick with one or two litters a year per ferret.

Strange craving? Keeping mom nourished

Pickles and ice cream aren't likely to be on the list of things your pregnant ferret will crave. However, a pregnant ferret does need some extra nutrition to maintain her strength, good health, and body condition before the kits arrive. Extra nutrition is necessary during the nursing period as well.

The following list presents some tips for keeping your pregnant ferret in good health and ready to deliver:

>> Experts recommend that a pregnant ferret's diet contain 35 to 40 percent meat-based protein and 15 to 20 percent fat. You should increase the number of daily feedings when the ferret begins to lactate, or produce milk. Most nursing moms are extra thin, so keep up on the extra nutrition.

>> Keep meat baby food or other healthy foods on hand for treats to feed during playtime and cuddling. Your ferret should also have her basic food (kibble, if you choose) available at all times, as well as plenty of fresh water (see Chapter 8 for more on normal ferret diets).

>> Many breeders supplement the pregnant and nursing ferret's basic diet with cooked meat and eggs. You can use a thicker Ferret Feeding Formula, or you can come up with your own creative recipes.

WARNING

Pregnant and nursing ferrets are prone to some ailments that can be life-threatening to both mom and the kits. It's important that you monitor your female's health and behavior closely. (For more information on mother fuzzy's ailments, see the sidebar "Conditions your female may encounter.")

Providing a maternity ward

You can keep pregnant fuzzies with other pregnant fuzzies, but you must separate them and give them a separate cage in a quiet private area or room at least 7 to 10 days before the kits are due. The private room should be a secure enclosure with extra bedding and a snuggly nest box. It should also be completely free of drafts, which is deadly for vulnerable kits. Providing a nest box is imperative, because it helps to keep the babies close together and warm. A baby that gets separated from the nest quickly chills and dies. The box also provides much-needed privacy for the new family. The following list runs through the many considerations you should make for your ferret's maternity ward, from the nest box to the environment of the entire room:

>> You need to create an enclosed nesting area to simulate the underground den area that a ferret would nest in the wild. You can use a wooden parrot nest box, which is better ventilated and controls moisture better than plastic. If you prefer plastic, head over to the section on building your own nest boxes in Chapter 5. The box should be clean and smooth to prevent injuries to the mom and kits. Openings to nest boxes should also be very smooth to protect mom when she enters and exits the box. Her belly and nipples will be vulnerable to abrasions.

>> Make sure the cage contains no openings greater than ¾"-x-¾" because newborns are about the size of the average pinky finger. If necessary, you can kit-proof the nursery by safely attaching cardboard, sheet metal, or acrylic glass "guards" inside the cage around the entire perimeter (they should extend 5 to 6 inches high).

>> Provide the appropriate bedding for the cage and box. Be careful about what type of bedding you choose. Avoid cloth or other materials that can snag little claws or unravel (stray fibers can strangle tiny heads and limbs). Many breeders use custom bedding that has no snagged threads. This is okay, too, but be aware that babies can be lost and suffocate in the "folds" of cloth. Keep a wary eye out! *Cross* shredded paper can work well, as can clean straw or hay.

"Mother knows best" is not just an old saying. Jills really do know what they want and need when it comes to their kits. If she's carrying them around all over the place, seems restless, or her babies are crying, try a different nest box or even different bedding. Perhaps she needs a different location.

>> Don't remove any extras that momma ferret adds. As her due date draws close, mom will begin to arrange her baby room just perfectly. She'll always pluck some fluffy wads of fur off her abdomen to line the nest with. The soft fur will be an extra comfort to the helpless kits. This also gives the kits access to the nipples later on and puts her skin closer to the kits for body heat.

>> Be quiet and limit your activity around the maternity ward as delivery approaches. No playing your bongos or allowing the dogs to romp around and shake the cage. Disturbances may cause mom to panic and eat her kits when they finally do arrive.

CONDITIONS YOUR FEMALE MAY ENCOUNTER

Unfortunately, your mother ferret may develop the following conditions, all of which require immediate veterinary attention:

- **Eclampsia:** Possibly related to diet and stress, this occurs late in pregnancy but before kits are born. Can kill both the mom and unborn kits. *Signs:* Loss of appetite, lethargy, dehydration, black/tarry poop, severe coat shedding. Exact cause is unknown.

- **Mastitis:** Bacterial infection in the mammary glands that occurs during the early stages of lactation. A common cause of mastitis is having rough edges on the nest box or too high an opening on the nest box. As mom drags herself in and out of the box, she continually irritates her swollen breast tissue, often receiving little abrasions or cuts that allow bacteria to enter. As kits get older, trauma caused to the mammary glands by their enthusiastic nursing may also contribute to inflammation and infection. *Signs:* Swelling, hardening, discoloration, and tenderness of mammary glands; anorexia; lethargy; inability to nurse kits (in severe cases).

Mastitis can be a lethal condition if not treated promptly by a veterinarian. You may notice the skin looking dark, almost black as teats and surrounding skin become necrotic or gangrenous — this is known in ferret breeding circles as the *Black Plague*. If this occurs, surgical excision to remove the dead tissue is often warranted, and teats may also be removed. It is urgent to move quickly on treatment, since

(continued)

(continued)

necrotic tissue spreads rapidly, putting the jill and all kits at great risk! Kits that are left behind will need to be hand-reared or tube fed, as they are no longer candidates to be foster kits, having been orally exposed to the bacteria that initially caused mom's mastitis in the first place. It is transmittable from one mom with mastitis to a healthy mom via the mouths of nursing kits! To aid in recovery, these moms are put on antibiotics and soaked in warm salty water, the latter being not-so-fun depending on your make and model of jill.

- **Nursing sickness:** Possibly related to diet and stress, this occurs shortly before or shortly after the kits are weaned. *Signs:* Loss of appetite, weakness, weight loss, lack of coordination, dehydration. Exact cause is unknown.

- **Vaginitis:** Results from general irritation to the vulva and secondary bacterial infection, often caused by bedding material such as hay, straw, and wood chips. *Signs:* Yellow discharge from the vaginal area.

- **Pyometra:** Bacterial infection of the uterus that occurs in unaltered, non-pregnant females. *Signs:* Pus discharge from vaginal area, distended abdomen from pus-filled uterus, lethargy, depressed appetite, increase in water consumption, fever.

Heading Off to the Delivery Room

This is an exciting time for you as you wait for the big day to arrive. You can be comforted by the fact that most ferrets give birth with little difficulty. Many experienced breeders will also administer a veterinarian–obtained injection of lutalyse to soften the jill's cervix before delivery. A few births will even require your vet's intervention. But most of the work will be done by your ferret. The following sections take you through a normal delivery and a difficult delivery to show you what to expect and what you need to be prepared to handle.

WARNING

No matter the delivery style, never assume (you or your vet) that the delivery is complete. Making sure that no kits are left behind is essential to the life of your ferret mom. Watch your ferret's behavior. If she seems distressed, make sure that you (if you're qualified) or your vet feels the jill's belly to rule out the possibility that another kit (dead or alive) is still inside her. Failing to check may lead to the death of your new mom and any unborn kits. If possible, wait to do any exams on her until she's at least fed her kits their first meal. A vet–obtained oxytocin injection administered under vet guidance by an experienced breeder will work to flush out the jill's reproductive system when all kits are accounted for.

The typical delivery

A normal kit delivery can happen quite quickly; two to three hours is typical for average-sized litters. In larger litters, the birthing process may take a little longer, with several kits arriving each hour. You and your vet should quietly observe mom for arising problems during this time, but don't disturb her unless absolutely necessary.

REMEMBER

Watch for kits still stuck in the placental sack. You'll have to help them out if mom fails to do so. She'll lick them clean and stimulate their breathing when they do get out. A kit stuck in the sack for too long will suffocate.

Allow mom to chew the umbilical cords in half instead of you cutting them. The crushing force of her chomp will keep the loose ends from bleeding. Also, make sure that mom eats all the placental material. As disgusting as this practice seems to humans, the placenta provides much-needed nourishment for the fatigued mom. It contains hormones that help the uterus to shrink and is also rich in iron (to promote milk production).

After this process, the new ferret mom usually curls up around her new kits, and they in turn immediately begin to suckle. Many ferret breeders agree that the first three days of the kits' lives are the most crucial. If the kits survive these difficult days, the chances of long-term survival are greatly heightened.

REMEMBER

Don't mess with that nest! Mom is a great housekeeper and will clean up after the birth, eating most of the afterbirth. You may remove any dead babies if necessary, but mom will usually eat them before you can get to them. Disturbing the nest during those first three days increases the likelihood of cannibalism or mom rejecting the babies.

The difficult delivery

Many kit deliveries are far from typical, unfortunately. Many things can go wrong with a delivery and lead to the death of a kit, the death of your ferret mom, and/or the need for an emergency cesarean section. The following list presents some common occurrences:

>> Kits born too quickly for mom may be a mass of entangled umbilical cords, resembling a small pile of spaghetti and pinky meatballs. Entangled kits can't nurse, and they get cold quickly and die. Also, limbs and lives may be lost due to the constriction of the drying cords and placentas around body parts.

>> Even though most kits die inside mom if they aren't delivered by the 44th day, some overdue kits can continue to grow, presenting problems if delivery ensues (by blocking the birth canal, for instance).

C-sections are not uncommon procedures. If you're a responsible breeder who loves what you do, C-sections are a no-brainer when it comes to the life of the jill (and kits) that's in dire distress and cannot birth on her own. If you're truly invested, financially and emotionally, in breeding, you'll already know that this lifesaving procedure and others that may precede or follow it can cost into the thousands of dollars. You will be prepared for the breeding investment *in its entirety*. If you aren't, don't breed. It's really that simple.

>> A kit in an unusual birthing position (such as its head tucked into its chest) almost always blocks the birth canal, where it can die and prevent the other kits from making their grand entrances. Unfortunately, those poor kits also die. And then mom cries, neglects the kits already delivered, and acts restless.

>> Kits with congenital defects often become stuck in the birth canal and die.

>> Small or overdue litters can produce dangerously large kits. Large kits can cause a holdup in the birth canal.

Depending on the cause of the difficult delivery, your vet may inject a labor-inducing drug or perform a cesarean section. It's a procedure that some ferret moms face. If the healthy mom is well cared for after the surgery, she almost always is physically capable of nursing and caring for her kits properly.

Some Problems You May Face after Birth

Hopefully all your kits will arrive safely and soundly. If so, you'll be happy as a clam and looking forward to helping raise the fuzzy family (or rehome them when they're old enough). What could possibly go wrong now? Many things, actually. You still have a long way to go before the babies are out of the woods.

Some ferrets just aren't cut out to be moms (or a human may make a mistake during a pregnancy to cause the ferret to become a bad parent; see the first section of this chapter for more). And even if you have the perfect mother fuzzy, situations may arise that prevent her from nursing her babies. In these situations, which I describe in the following sections, a foster mom is vital in helping keep the kits alive — unless the kits have already been cannibalized. And if your fuzzy mom dies during pregnancy or delivery, the role of the foster mom becomes even more vital. As sad as it seems, the possibility isn't that far-fetched.

A difficult mother

New moms that are nervous or uncomfortable often make poor ferret mothers. Some ferrets just weren't meant to be moms, so they reject or cannibalize their babies for no apparent reason. But reasons do exist, and they are valid to the fuzzies. The following list shows you how to avoid possible difficult situations:

>> **Fuzzy moms like their kits warm, so cold babies almost always are rejected.** If mom is away for a period of time (at a surgery, for instance), keeping the babies warm while she's away is essential. Or, if the kits wander away and get chilled, warm them up before returning them to the nest. (See the earlier section "Providing a maternity ward" for some tips.)

>> **Some moms require a meal before cozying up to their new babies.** If your ferret mom seems uninterested after delivering all those kits, offer her some warm canned food or her kibble moistened with warm water.

>> **Fluctuations in cage temperature, noise, and/or activity surrounding the nest can make a mom cannibalize or reject her youngsters.** Keep the area around the cage and nest calm. Now isn't the time to let the kids come in to see the new arrivals (see the earlier section "Providing a maternity ward" for more tips).

A mother incapable of nursing

REMEMBER

Some ferret moms simply don't produce enough milk, or any milk at all, for their kits to nurse on. One possible cause is mastitis (see the earlier sidebar "Conditions your female may encounter"). You (along with your vet) need to monitor the activity level and growth of all the kits at all times while they're nursing. Kits should gain weight daily, tripling by day 10 (see Chapter 23 for more). A kit that doesn't get enough nourishment slowly starves; he loses the desire to suckle, chills, and eventually dies. Weigh your babies daily, because a newborn ferret can live only three days without eating before he dies.

If the ferret mother is producing some milk, you can leave the kits with mom as long as you supplement the feedings with kitten-milk replacer. The best solution, however, is receiving the assistance of a foster mom (see the following section).

Calling on the foster mom

A breeder should try to have a foster ferret mom waiting in the wings in case an emergency arises with your momma — whether it's one of your own ferrets or a fellow ferret breeder's ferret. Most foster ferrets readily take new kits into their nests. Hopefully, your foster fuzzy is already nursing kits close in age to the ones being introduced. If she's a good milk producer, foster-nursing shouldn't be a problem for her, because ferrets can nurse more kits than they have available nipples.

HAND-REARING KITS AS A LAST RESORT

Hand-rearing a kit is an emotionally and physically exhausting endeavor that rarely pays off. The mortality rate, even with experienced ferret humans, is high. Kits need a mother's milk for at least ten days in the early stages of their lives. Successful hand-rearing is possible if you start with healthy kits that are 2 weeks old. In any case, you should give it your best shot if hand-rearing is your only option.

To hand-rear, give the kits kitten-milk replacer every two hours via a plastic eyedropper or bottle. Patience is one of the key components. Make sure you give the food in small amounts and very slowly to avoid aspiration pneumonia. Tube feeding is extremely difficult, even for the experienced, so take it slow. If you make it to week three, introduce the babies daily to a soft diet, such as canned cat or ferret food. The kits still need supplemental feedings until they reach 4 to 5 weeks old.

Whether you begin hand-rearing your kits at two weeks or three weeks, you should be weighing them daily to make sure they're gaining, not losing, weight. They're small creatures to begin with, and any weight loss should be looked at as significant enough to raise a red flag.

TIP

Most breeders will give a jill who failed at mothering, for whatever reason, a second chance to have success at it. However, it's time to retire her if she fails a second time. It doesn't make her any less of a ferret. It simply means she isn't meant for mothering. I get that!

TIP

The best way to introduce the "orphans" into the foster mom's nest is to first remove the foster mom. Allow the new kits to intermingle with the existing kits so that the new kits' scent becomes less distinct from the others' scent. If everyone smells the same, no one can complain!

In the rare instance that the foster mom rejects the kits (be sure to monitor them closely to watch for this), you need to find an immediate replacement. If you can't locate one, hand-rearing the kits is an option, but a very difficult one (see the sidebar "Hand-rearing kits as a last resort"). If the kits are less than 10 days old, they'll most likely die. The success rate increases with older kits.

Chapter **23**

From Birth to Bundle of Energy: Walking a Fuzzy's Timeline

I f you make it through the pregnancy and birthing ordeal — hey, it's stressful for all involved — you may be fortunate enough to watch a kit or two grow up. Healthy kits grow rapidly, both physically and emotionally. It won't be long before you're wiping away the tears in your eyes as you proclaim, "It seems like only yesterday Scooter was covered with newborn fuzz!"

This chapter takes you step by step through the developmental stages of carpet sharks. Some stages aren't too pleasant, but they'll be only temporary if you do your part as a good fuzzy human. From physical changes to behavioral changes, I tell you what to expect almost every step of the way and how to handle the changes to produce happy and healthy ferrets. However, keep this in mind: When it comes to fuzzbutts, nothing is set in stone!

Fuzzy Infancy: Birth to 3 Weeks

Kits (baby ferrets) are born into the world completely helpless and dependent on their mothers for survival. Their eyes and ears are sealed shut, rendering them blind and deaf. A small layer of fuzz covers their tiny bodies, which are smaller than a normal tube of lipstick (see Figure 23-1). Newborns typically weigh in at a whopping 6 to 12 grams. Most kits are born without any teeth, although baby incisors usually appear by day ten.

FIGURE 23-1:
These 3-week-old ferrets aren't much bigger than a tube of lipstick.

Healthy newborn kits have only two goals: getting food and keeping warm. Immediately after birth, they'll latch onto one of mom's nipples if allowed and remain there for a long period of time, gorging themselves on rich milk. Adequately fed newborns should gain between 2½–3 grams per day during their first week of life, doubling their birth weight by day five. Despite having just been squeezed through the birth canal and dropped into the cold world, newborn ferrets are active and mobile, although they have nowhere to go just yet. They explore their nest a tiny bit and start to develop the little muscles in their legs. They're able to recognize mom and siblings through smell. During the first few weeks, however, the young kits need to be stimulated by mama fuzzy to go to the bathroom.

During the second week of life, kits should gain about 4 grams per day. By 10 days old, they should've tripled their birth weight and should average about 30 grams. During the third week, the daily weight gain should be about 6 grams. And by 3 weeks old, your kits should be at least ten times heavier than when they were born.

At three weeks, the males and females are easier to tell apart (without cheating and turning them over). Females are daintier and have narrower heads. Boys are butterballs with their wide heads and stockier builds.

TECHNICAL STUFF

Even though fuzzies are born with their eyes closed, you can tell which ones are albinos because the color of their eyes shows through their thin skin. If you can't see dark color behind a fuzzy's semitransparent eyelids, you know you have a bouncing baby albino. (For more on fuzzy colors and what they entail, head to Chapter 2.)

Furball Toddlerhood: 3 to 6 Weeks

Kits that hit 3 weeks of age are working to rapidly develop their nest legs as they boldly explore their environment. Mom is still a part of their lives, keeping a close eye on kits that may wander too far away. Although the kits still rely on mom for the majority of their nourishment, natural weaning should begin at this age. The baby canine teeth and some baby premolars are beginning to erupt, and permanent incisor teeth are breaking through and pushing the baby incisors out. You can offer these kits a soft mush or canned food a few times a day (for more on diet, see Chapter 8).

REMEMBER

Weaning doesn't involve caging mom and plopping down a crock of odd-smelling mush in front of your confused kits. Weaning is a gradual process that should begin at the age of 3 weeks and be completed at around 6 weeks. Kits need time to adapt to the nutritional change. To wean effectively, first familiarize yourself with the diet information in Chapter 8. This is imperative, because you need to understand nutrition in ferrets. Starting out with canned food or a soft mush made with moistened kibble is only one way to start your babies. As kits get older, you should offer a variety of other foods, such as chicken and beef (either raw or cooked). A change of kibble and canned food is recommended. This is also the time to introduce small mice and insects if desired. The more variety offered, the better. The weaning process is messy as the kits delve face first into their food, but it's a relatively easy process. During these three weeks, the kits will naturally begin to rely less and less on mom and start to prefer the replacement diet you offer.

The fourth week is somewhat of a turning point in a kit's new life. His eyes and ears begin to show signs of opening up to the world. His soft, white fuzz should start taking on some color and pattern, giving you a glimpse into his future. More baby premolars also start to erupt around this time. Healthy kits should be eager to dive into the bowl of soft mush you provide and stuff themselves while still taking advantage of mom's milk supply. And although mom may still want to remind the kits to go to the bathroom, the kits should show signs of being the self-proficient poopers that their parents are!

By week five, a kit's eyes and ears have opened and he's ready to get into trouble! Kits at this age are extremely active and are starting to rough and tumble with their siblings. By week six, the kits should start eating more soft food and start relying less and less on mom for nutritional support. Some breeders introduce the dreaded first distemper vaccination at this age (see Chapter 12).

The Terrible Fuzzy Twos: 6 to 10 Weeks

Emotionally, at 6 to 7 weeks old, furball kits should be spending a lot of awake time playing mock-combat with their siblings. This play is important in developing hierarchy among the youngsters and preparing them for their futures as possible top furballs in their new homes!

At around seven weeks, ferrets should quit hanging on mom so much and start relying almost completely on the soft food you serve. Permanent canines are pushing through their sensitive gums, sometimes erupting just beside the baby canines. This is a pretty painful ordeal to the small fuzzbutt and can cause him to wallow in the throes of teething behavior (see Chapter 20). It isn't unusual to have kits with canine teeth side by side for several days until their baby canines finally fall out.

At 8 weeks old, kits should have four permanent canine teeth. They're now capable of eating the hard kibble that most other ferrets rely on. A kit should have a well-developed and varied diet by now, but if you haven't started this process yet, now is the time to introduce him to new tastes and smells. Babies are so impressionable!

Many private breeders begin to let their kits go to their new humans at around the age of 10 weeks (see Figure 23-2). Babies are usually using the litter box by now, and drinking from the water bottle comes easily. Some breeders, however, wait as long as 12 weeks before letting their babies go. The decision is up to the breeder and may be based on how comfortable he or she is with the person buying the ferret. Or it may just be based on personal policy. Whatever the case, there's really no disadvantage to waiting the extra four weeks for your youngster, other than possibly being a bit delayed in getting him on a varied diet.

FIGURE 23-2: These 8-week-old kits are just about ready for their new homes.

For those kits that received their first distemper shots at 6 weeks old, 9 weeks of age is the perfect time for the second attack on their heinies. For complete information on vaccination schedules, head to Chapter 12.

REMEMBER

Kits in the 6- to 10-week age range are extremely active in testing their humans to the limits. This age range is the critical training period, which many ferret humans fail to recognize. You need to handle your furkids frequently and gently. They need consistency and someone who's willing to teach them what is and isn't acceptable behavior. Because many kits arrive at pet shops at this age, they frequently don't receive the proper human guidance (for more on pet shops, see Chapter 4). Many of these toddlers become troubled teenagers for their unsuspecting humans. Therefore, as a responsible ferret breeder, you need to begin training as early as possible. (For information on ferret training, head to the chapters of Part 5.)

Adolescence Already? 10 to 15 Weeks

Your kits should have almost all their permanent teeth by 10 weeks of age. The little indentations on your fingers and arms are proof enough (see Chapters 19 and 20 for tips on biting training)! Kidding aside, if your kits received the proper fuzzy guidance during their terrible twos stage (see the previous section for advice and the chapters of Part 5 for tips), adolescence shouldn't be too bad.

By 3 months old (12 weeks), well-adjusted kits are discovering that humans can be fun companions. Although the activity level of kits this age still far surpasses the average human's energy levels (even with a double espresso), kits do begin to mellow a little bit (emphasis on a little bit). Ferret personalities become well-formed and defined during adolescence. Even though these kits are still highly influenced by the humans who interact with them, it's relatively easy to pick out the alpha males and females (top furballs) by watching them interact with their siblings and humans.

7

The Part of Tens

Ten great ferret-proofing hacks.

Ten delicious ferret recipes.

Chapter **24**

Ten Amazing and Creative Ferret-Proofing Hacks

s it at all possible that I can hound you anymore about ferret-proofing? I can go over it again and again, yet I will still hear stories of someone's fuzzy being injured or killed or escaping because of lack of ferret-proofing. Or worse yet, no ferret-proofing at all. Remember, ferret-proofing never ends. It's an ongoing saga, and if you have other humans in the household, it's a family affair. Take a look at these awesomely creative ferret-proofing hacks that may make your life a little easier. Or not. You be the judge.

Pool Noodles Be Gone!

Ferrets get into the smallest of places, and the spot in between your washer and dryer just calls out their names. Although you might be able to squeeze pool noodles into the crack, ferrets find the noodles easy to tear apart and delightfully delicious — but not so easy to pass. My friend Holly Ravenhill reminded me to instead take a blanket or large towel and roll it up tightly, and then shove it into the crack, fitting it snug enough so that the ferret cannot burrow beneath it or pull it out. *Voilà!* (See Figure 24-1.)

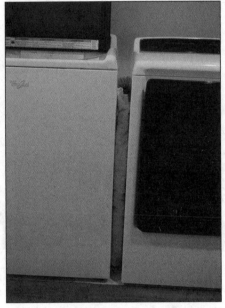

FIGURE 24-1:
Rolled up towel between a typical washer and dryer

Photo and hack idea courtesy of Holly Ravenhill

Up, Up, and Over — Not!

Ferrets are master climbers, master jumpers, and master escape-artists. In fact, I've never met a ferret that hasn't mastered the art of escaping from a ferret pen. I'm not sure who came up with this idea, but it's a brilliant solution to an age-old feisty ferret problem. This "climber stopper topper" is made of a simple piece of black flexible corrugated drain pipe that can be found at any larger hardware store. (See Figure 24-2.)

Although it looks simple to make, it takes a bit of talent to construct. You may lose a finger or two if you're not careful. If you have a neighbor who is great with power tools, particularly saws, you may want to trade him a six pack of Pepsi or beer in turn for his sawing services. Kevin Farlee, president of Washington Ferret Rescue & Shelter, offered the following advice when it came to constructing this altered pen:

>> Use a strong, sharp saw — a table saw or even a Japanese handsaw (see Figure 24-3).

FIGURE 24-2:
Simple PVC will prevent your ferret from escaping this pen

Photo and hack reference compliments of Washington Ferret Rescue & Shelter

FIGURE 24-3:
Japanese handsaws are sharp, but they do the trick!

Photo and hack idea courtesy of Kevin Farlee, president of Washington Ferret Rescue & Shelter

>> You'll be cutting lengthwise, so it's a good idea to draw a straight line down the tubing where you'll be cutting. This will keep you on track while sawing. (See Figure 24-4.)

>> Grab a friend who owes you a huge favor, because he'll be holding the front end of the tube while you cut away from him.

>> Don't cut off a finger or foot. Table saws and Japanese saws are *sharp*, and they don't discriminate between wood or fingers. If you're uncomfortable with working with saws, call someone who is savvy around power tools.

>> Just pop the tubing over the top of the pen, placing the edges of the pen into the newly sawed slat. Having two people do this can help the process move along a little faster.

You can use this modified playpen in your home, but what makes this so perfect is that it's portable. Perfect for ferret shows, playdates, travelling, or any event where your fuzzball will be away from home for a good length of time. *And*, ladies and gents, it works over baby gates, as well!

FIGURE 24-4:
Cut lengthwise
and draw a line
as a guide.

*Photo and hack idea courtesy of Kevin Farlee, President of
Washington Ferret Rescue & Shelter*

Cardboard Cut-Outs

Yep! The topic of climbing ferrets is a resonating one, and baby gates are frequently a go-to solution. Some are reasonably priced and others can break the bank. But most are no match for a ferret that will find its way around, under, over, or through the baby gate, leaving you begging for help from other ferret owners. Here's what you need to fix this irritating issue:

>> Purchase the baby gate that best fits the width of your doorway, making sure to choose one that the ferret cannot squeeze beneath or through the sides.

>> Measure the large climbable section(s) on the baby gate that you'll need to cover.

>> Measure and carefully cut thick pieces of cardboard to fit over each section.

>> Fasten the cardboard section(s) to the baby gate using cable/zip ties to hold the cardboard securely. (See Figure 24-5.)

Ferrets will always scratch at the cardboard, but if it's constructed well, the ferret shouldn't be able to conquer the wall to freedom. If you see wear and tear, however, be sure to replace the cardboard barrier.

FIGURE 24-5:
Contain just about any carpet shark with this hack!

Photo and hack submission courtesy of Claire Shannon

Yule Get Hung Up on Christmas

What ferret owner doesn't face the annual Christmas tree dilemma? Christmas trees: They're fresh. They're new. They smell good. And most of all, a Christmas tree is a mountain of branches that provides ample climbing opportunities for our mischievous furballs. Hang some ornaments from the tree and, well, most will end up in ferret hidey-holes throughout the house in no time. Although you could encircle the entire tree with a ferret-proof pen or get a smaller tree and put it on a table, why not do something a little crazy. Hang that sucker upside down from your ceiling. (See Figure 24-6.) That's right. I said it. Amaze your friends, and leave your family members rolling their eyes at holiday gatherings. They already think you love your ferrets more than you love them anyway. Suspending your tree is a labor of love, and it's a blast!

So, how does the average Joe hang a Christmas tree from the ceiling? I had to ask my husband, and what he came up with makes great sense. Safe, secure, and pretty darn easy!

1. **Lay the tree on its side and drill a hole into the very bottom of the Christmas tree trunk.**

2. **Carefully screw a 7/16" x 3 7/8" steel screw eye hook (see Figure 24-7) into the hole you just drilled in bottom of the tree.**

FIGURE 24-6:
Defying gravity is
not limited to
ferrets!

Photo and hack submission compliments of Karen Pedro

FIGURE 24-7:
Steel screw eye
hooks can be
found at most
hardware stores.

3. Locate a heavy beam in your ceiling and drill a hole into it.

4. Carefully screw a 7/16" x 3 7/8" steel screw eye hook into the hole you just drilled in the ceiling beam.

5. To save time and headache, fasten the hanging hardware to the eye hook in the ceiling before you hoist the tree. This can be a quick link or a heavy duty carabiner (regular or round).

6. Grab a friend or family member or two to help with the tree-hoisting project. At least one of you will need a ladder, and all of you will need muscles to lift the tree and maneuver it to attach.

Dual Purpose Door Blocker

Have you figured out by now that ferrets are diggers? We all know they'll dig to China if given the opportunity. And ferrets are as flexible as pasta noodles. Closed doors can provide some ferret-proofing challenges for fuzzy owners, from ferrets escaping beneath the narrow openings at the bottom to ruined carpeting from curious diggers. So, how do you combat this common problem?

One solution is to make the opening at the bottom of the door narrower to prevent the ferret from squeezing beneath it. But that alone won't protect your carpeting from the incessant digging. Purchase an inexpensive carpet runner or plastic carpet runner or even a scrap rug that can be measured and cut. Make sure whatever you get or cut fits widthwise beneath the opening of your door. Lengthwise it should be long enough so that your ferret cannot scratch it out and away from the doorway. (See Figure 24-8.)

FIGURE 24-8:
Runners beneath doors help to keep carpet sharks from tunneling beneath closed doorways

Photo and hack submission courtesy of Holly Ravenhill

REMEMBER

No landlord wants to find torn up carpeting in his rental unit. If you're a renter, this ferret-proofing hack may just mean the difference between losing or recouping your initial deposit when you move out.

TIP

The bottom of your door opening may be too wide for one runner to do the trick. No worries. Simply add another runner or more if you need to. This is less ideal with plastic runners that won't stick to each other, but you may be able to use Velcro in between the plastic layers to stick them together. And what about hardwood floors? Make sure you use rubber-backed carpet runners that grip to the floor.

Couch Cures

Everyone has that one ferret or five that will undoubtedly break into your couch, either from the bottom or from the top. It can be dangerous or even deadly for an exploring ferret. At the very least, it can be very annoying or costly for you, as his owner. Experienced ferret humans have worked hard over the years to match wits against their fuzzy counterparts to combat this problem. Take note of the following techniques.

To protect the underside of your couch:

>> Remove the legs from your couch and place the couch directly on the floor so that the ferrets cannot get beneath the couch at all.

>> If you can't remove the legs or don't want to, flip the couch over and cover the entire bottom of the couch with plywood (or a similar wood product), thick sheet or vinyl. Fasten the barrier to the underside with nails or staples. Don't forget to flip the couch back over.

To protect the cushions or topside of your couch:

>> If your couch sharks are burrowing in the couch cushions, throw up your hands in exasperation and call it quits.

>> Find a fitted couch cover/slip you can live with and fasten it over your current couch using nails or staples.

WARNING

This is one ferret-proofing hack you cannot be lazy about. Do a thorough check to make sure everything fits and you've fastened it all in such a way that your ferret cannot squeeze through any openings in the barriers. The barrier itself can become a hazard to your ferret if not done correctly.

TIP

Chairs and bed frames also provide similar hazards to your ferrets. Depending on the type of furniture you have, this hack may be adapted to work for chairs and bed frames, as well.

Fixing Floors and Revamping Ramps

Many ferret cages on the market today come equipped with wire floors and ramps, which seasoned ferret owners know can lead to broken toes or nails getting hung up in the wire, or even worse. Some owners use custom bedding to cover up the wire. I suggest you take it a step further and cover the ramps and floors before you add the bedding. You can use Peel-n-Stick vinyl tiles or Peel-n-Stick carpet squares for the floors. For the ramps, Peel-n-Stick carpet squares cut to size work well and prevent sliding. Both of these stick-on products are easily removed and replaced when necessary.

A Room with a View

Afraid your ferret might be getting into trouble behind your back? Undoubtedly he is. If you have a separate room for your ferrets, and many people do, you may want to see clearly into it. Keeping your ferret safe and out of harm's way is your duty as his human. An easy way to do this is by doing away with the modified baby gates and installing an easy-to-remove see-through Plexiglas guillotine-style door. (See Figure 24-9.) The following steps tell you how:

1. Use a router to cut straight "slide guides" into two 26" L x 1" W lengths of oak strips.

2. Screw the oak strips into the open doorway of the ferret room; slide guides exposed inwards.

3. Obtain your Plexiglas — ¼" thick x 24" tall — and slide it into the routed oak strip frame.

FIGURE 24-9:
This easy-to-remove guillotine door is perfect to spy on your ferrets.

Photo and hack submitted by Rose German, Founder of Ferret Fabulous Finds Auction House

4. Top the Plexiglas with a sliced rug core (the thick middle cardboard tube) to keep the jumpers from hurdling themselves over the top.

5. Duct tape the core to the Plexiglas, so that you can simply lift the "door" by lifting the core when you need to.

Wired for Trouble

There's more to successful ferret-proofing than possessing practical thinking. You need to be a creative, out-of-the-box thinker. At. All. Times. How many times have you been to an event and walked on or over those flat strips that cover exposed electrical cords so that you don't trip on them? Or maybe the event coordinators don't want you to squat down and gnaw on them. Who knows? I do know one thing; they're great for keeping your ferret from doing that, and they wouldn't even have to squat!

There are loads of different cord hiders, protectors, covers, and organizers available to choose from. Whatever you call them or whatever your needs are, something is out there for you. With a little effort and the right products, you can protect both the cords on the floors and the walls. This is a must for our little cord munchers.

Velcro to the Rescue

Whoever invented Velcro is one of my all-time heroes. Like its cousin duct tape, the uses for Velcro are eye-popping. In the ferret world, it can be a lifesaver. Consider all the drawers and cabinets that your ferret can and will open. All you need is a small piece of Velcro secured inside to help keep them closed. In my opinion, this is a better solution than the traditional baby locks that allow partial opening of the cabinets and drawers. Velcro virtually seals drawers shut until you open them with a little extra effort.

Chapter **25**

Ten Recipes that Make Your Ferret Go Mmmmmm

I believe that the key to good health for any animal is a well-balanced and varied diet. Whether you want to add some variety into your ferret's diet or need that perfect homemade "soup" for the sick or recovering ferret, I have the right recipe for you! This chapter provides some great recipes, compliments of several experienced and long-time fellow fuzzy lovers, for you to try with your ferret.

With a few exceptions, most of these recipes are easy to make. You may even get inspired to come up with one or two recipe ideas of your own.

TIP

My friend and fellow ferret guru Bob Church recommends feeding any new ferret recipe with some simple caveats:

>> He assumes that your vet has checked your ferret and has reviewed the recipe to determine if your fuzzy's health allows you to give him the food.

- Ferrets are olfactory imprinted, meaning they set their food preferences by the time they're 6 months old, so an older ferret may not want to try the foods right away (see Chapter 8 for more information on olfactory imprinting and converting your fuzzy to a new diet). If you put in some time and effort, though, you'll find that your fuzzy will accept most of these recipes. Younger ferrets and kits should accept them right away.

- Most of these recipes represent snacks or meals, not long-term diets. The recipes are designed to increase enrichment (see Chapter 10), offer variety, and increase dietary choice. Make sure you consult with your vet in order to ensure your ferret is getting a complete and balanced diet.

- Ferrets that eat a soft diet often will develop dental tartar. This also happens with hard, crunchy kibble, but the rate of deposit seems faster with the soft diet. Make sure you don't hurt your ferret while you're trying to help him! Tooth brushing and annual dental checkups are a must, regardless of the food your ferret eats.

REMEMBER

All of these recipes have been taste-tested and fuzzy-approved by the chefs' ferrets! And although most recipes include ingredient measurements, you can surely modify the foods for the specific needs of your ferret, and as advised by your vet. The measurements may require some trial and error on your part. It's likely that you'll never make two recipes the same, unless you write down exactly how much you choose to use of this, that, and the other thing.

Hobbit Delights

BY PLUMB STEPHANI OF MIDDLE EARTH FERRETRY

These healthy meat treats are a wonderful alternative to store-bought ferret treats, which are more often than not unsuitable for your ferret. Plumb says her ferrets are crazy about such yummies as freeze-dried hearts, gizzards, and livers. Duck, beef, and chicken, as well as quail eggs are coveted favorites. Preparation takes a while, but it's well worth it, and you can make a bunch at a time!

1 Gross out the local butcher and pique his morbid curiosity by buying up all of his spare parts . . . and by that I mean hearts, gizzards, livers, and so on.

2 Boil the organs until fully cooked — typically 45 minutes if you're using big whole pieces, and 25 minutes if the organs are cut into smaller chunks.

3 Drain the organs and let them cool off.

4 If they aren't already cut, cut them into smaller pieces. The bigger or thicker the pieces are, the longer they take to dry out.

5 Line a cookie sheet with parchment paper and spread the treats evenly across the cookie sheet.

6 Place the sheet into your freezer.

PLUMB'S TIP: The colder the freezer, the better the results. Frequently you will find that a deep freezer will work better than your fridge. And this whole process is no short-term endeavor either. To do it correctly, your treats need to stay in the freezer at least a week or longer, depending on how thick the chunks are. As the treats dry they will take on that ever-so-distinct white, freezer burned look and color that we all undeniably know. This is normal and a good thing for freeze-dried treats. When it's time to check for readiness, let a couple of pieces of various sizes thaw out. If they are squishy, they are not completely dried. If they're firm and crunchy, they're ready to store and serve up to your eagerly awaiting ferrets.

TIP

Another way of making freeze-dried treats is by using a food dehydrator. Just about any solid food item can go in there, but for ferrets things such as small chunks of organs, gizzards, and meats, including fowl, are used. It's quick and easy, but it's no match for the love and effort that go into Hobbit Delights.

Karen's Brew

BY KAREN PEDRO OF MAKE MY DAY FERRETS IN THE NETHERLANDS

This no raw-no kibble recipe is flexible in that it can be used as both a treat and also a meal. What separates one from the other is a mere addition or deletion of a good multi-vitamin for carnivores. Karen's Brew has been used for sick ferrets and as an alternative to feeding soaked or ground kibble or when raw is not advised.

½ gallon of water

4 chicken legs or whole chicken

2 fatty pork chops

2 eggs

3 ½ ounces of heart organ

1 ounce of liver

1 ounce of kidney

2 Tbsp ground egg shell

(Multi-vitamin powder for carnivores)

1 Boil water and add the chicken and pork chops. Let it simmer for 30-40 minutes until meat falls off the bone.

2 Take out the meat and the bone and pass the water through a colander and into another pot. Put it back on the stove and bring to a boil again. Then add the heart, liver and kidney. Cook without lid for 10 additional minutes.

3 Separate all the meat from the bones. Pour all the meat, organs and broth (no bones) into a food processor or blender and make a ground soup of it.

4 Put it back on the stove and bring it to boil while stirring.

5 Whip the eggs lightly. When the soup is boiling, take the concoction from the stove and add the whipped eggs. Keep on stirring until egg is solidified.

6 Let it cool, and at last add the ground egg shell.

7 Divide Karen's Brew into serving portions (perhaps use an ice cube tray) and warm before serving.

TIP

Karen explains the above recipe is great just as described above if you're only going to feed it as an occasional treat. However, if used more often or as a regular daily meal, it should be supplemented with multi-vitamins specifically developed and approved for use in carnivores. In the Netherlands, Karen uses the Dutch brand Puur, the carnivore supplement, made by Kiezebrink, a raw meat supplier. If this multi-vitamin contains calcium, you'll want to eliminate the egg shell from the preparation above. Note: If multi-vitamins are going to be added, only add them immediately before serving (right after heating).

Raw Soupy Recipe

BY HEATHER DOWNIE OF THE HOLISTIC FERRET FORUM

This raw–prepared meal was originally created to assist in helping ferrets switch over from kibble to raw and also as a convalescent meal for sick or hospice ferrets.

8 ounces *boneless* raw chicken (thigh meat preferred)

1 ounce raw chicken liver (or other raw liver)

1 ounce raw chicken hearts (equals 1-2 chicken hearts or 1 ounce of other raw heart)

½ to ¾ tsp *human grade* bone meal or crushed egg shell (air-dry egg shell and then crush with mortar and pestle or grind in a clean coffee grinder)

1 Weigh out the meat and organs (Helpful to chop the meat into small pieces first)

2 Add bone meal *or* eggshell

3 Put it all into a blender or food processor and blend, adding water until the consistency is that of a **thick** cream and no thinner.

HEATHER'S TIPS: Remember to use *human grade* bone meal powder. You absolutely don't want to know what's in the bone meal powder they manufacture and sell for pets! Also, if you have an emotional attachment to your blender, you'll want to absolutely avoid adding bones or tendons to this recipe, as they will kill your blender. Heather also states that while this recipe is fully balanced and can be used as a treat or a meal, it's not meant for long-term feeding, and tooth brushing may be a greater necessity.

Barb's Recipe for Hungover Ferrets

BY BARBARA CLAY, DIRECTOR OF ROCKY'S FERRET RESCUE & SHELTER AND DEVELOPER OF POOPIN PUMPKIN

No! Ferrets don't drink alcohol! But this one's named appropriately for its beneficial use with those obviously neglected ferrets that come in that look like they've been put through the wringer. It's a meal supplement intended only to be used about twice a week so that ferrets do not become dependent upon this tasty soup. Perfect also for ill and senior fuzzies!

½ cup of powdered *whole* eggs

1 heaping Tbsp Nupro Ferret supplement

1 jar of *Beechnut* Chicken-n-Gravy or Beef-n-Gravy

1 splash of hair of the dog (½ tsp salmon oil)

1 cup of warm water

1 Mix well and serve.

2 Save leftovers in an ice cube tray and freeze for later.

This recipe feeds 3-5 ferrets or one slightly hungry kid, although we don't advocate feeding this to your human child. Furthermore, her insistence on using Beechnut instead of a brand such as Gerber is due to the fact that Beechnut contains no cornstarch.

Ferret Bland Diet

BY KAREN PURCELL, DVM

There are so many variations of "duck soup" floating around the Internet today. It's difficult to tell one from the other or to know which are healthy and which aren't. Unlike in the beginning when duck soup was pretty straightforward, the recipes started getting fancier over the years. The Ferret Bland Diet is also a soup, but it gets ferret owners back to the simple basics.

1 can of vanilla Ensure

2 jars Beechnut turkey and broth baby food (meat only, no veggies)

1 cup of finely ground Totally Ferret or a mix of ferret kibble (NO cat food)

1 Finely grind the kibble in your blender and measure out one cup's worth.

2 Put the cup of ground kibble back into the blender.

3 Add the Ensure and baby food to the ground kibble.

4 Blend until smooth.

5 Add in any supplements and blend (only if recommended by your vet).

6 Pour into ice cube trays.

7 Melt 1 cube per ferret per meal.

REMEMBER

IT'S very important to remember that this no-frills transitional diet recipe is simply designed to get the poor ferret off of kibble, as it is too hard on them when they have gastritis.

TIP

Speaking of Duck Soup variations, I found a source of dry "Dook Soup" mixes created by Diane Wall of South Shore Ferret Care Rescue & Hospice, Inc. (southshoreferretcare.org) that I heard great things about. Each blend is made for a specific purpose, from adrenal and insulinoma to chicken allergy and hospice care. And of course there's the basic blend! Check them out!

Tui's Chewies

BY BOB CHURCH

Ferrets love to gnaw, and this treat will give your floor monkey something healthy and fun to gnaw on. Tui's Chewies aren't designed to be a replacement for commercially made chews, but rather an occasional alternative.

Water

Non-flavored gelatin

Chicken or beef, finely chopped

Beef or chicken bouillon

1 Dissolve the non-flavored gelatin in boiling water, per the instructions on the gelatin box.

You can make a super-saturated solution by adding enough water to where no more gelatin will dissolve; you'll still see some bits floating around.

2 Toss in the finely chopped chicken or beef.

3 Add some flavor with the chicken or beef bouillon.

4 Pour the mixture onto a cookie sheet (or cookie molds). Cut the mixture into rectangular shapes when it dries.

5 Place the shapes in a cool dehydrator until they're rubbery and hardened.

BOB'S TIP: You can also store the small, rectangular yummies uncovered in the freezer. Sometimes, the chewies will end up more like gummies; when that happens, you can just freeze them and serve them cold. Ferrets like them either way!

Family Dinner

BY CHARLIE O'KANE AT CAMP UDDER GUY

The below recipe was created specifically with poultry allergic furballs in mind, but can be fed to any of your ferrets to enjoy.

2 patties of *Dog* Stella and Chewy Red Meat Recipe

2 patties of *Dog* Stella and Chewy Lamb Recipe

1 patty of *Dog* Stella and Chewy Rabbit Recipe

½ jar of Beechnut beef baby food (no veggies)

2 *dashes* of salmon oil

1 *pinch* of powdered Taurine (if dog patties are used)

Add an egg yolk every 3 days

1 Warm up some water in a pan on the stove until it's simmering. Turn off and let sit.

2 Crumble the Stella and Chewy patties (or use a food processor) and put into a medium size bowl with a lid for future leftovers.

3 Add a pinch of powdered Taurine (if dog patties are used).

4 Add baby food, *dash* of salmon oil and egg yolk.

5 Add a bit of tap water.

6 Stir to mix it all up until you pretty much have a dry-ish ball.

7 Add a small amount of the hot water you've put aside.

8 Stir until it's a creamy consistency, adding more water if necessary to get there.

TIP

Charlie sets the ferret family dinner table with placemats and a family size bowl. If the crew isn't already there licking their lips and waiting on service, she gathers them for the feast to begin. Any leftovers after the family has had their share can be put back into the mixing container, placed in the fridge and added to at the next meal. Charlie also explains that ferret owners may substitute other flavors of Stella and Chewy in dog or cat versions if their ferret is not food sensitive. Sometimes they use Primal Foods for variety. And Charlie is proud to say that every ferret who has been at Camp Udder Guy takes to this soup immediately and will run and plead for dinner service each night.

Mickey's Meatloaf

BY BOB CHURCH

Okay, not everyone likes mother's meatloaf, but your ferret will love this one. You can cut Mickey's Meatloaf into small pieces that are wonderful for use in training or as special treats.

Ground chicken or turkey — uncooked

Chicken broth

One egg

Ground kibble

Whole kibble

Olive or fish oil

Spray oil

Ice cube tray

1 Mix all the ingredients (except the whole kibble and spray oil) like you're making a meatloaf (a mound of ground meat mixed with other ingredients).

2 Add just enough whole kibble to spread a piece per square inch.

3 Give the ice cube tray a light coating of spray oil and then fill the tray with the meatloaf.

4 Microwave the tray for a minute or two to harden the food, and then remove the miniature loaves from the tray areas.

You can store the pieces in plastic food containers in your freezer until needed.

BOB'S TIP: To serve, place a small meatloaf on a dish and microwave until you cook it throughout. Allow it to cool so you don't burn the mouth of your little floor monkey. Also, you can substitute ground beef or pork for the chicken or turkey if your ferret will accept it.

Clyde's Seaside Chunks

BY BOB CHURCH

The acceptance of this occasional meal is dependent on how olfactory imprinted your ferret has become, but if he's open to seafood, he'll gobble up the Seaside Chunks. You can cut up the food into tiny chunks to use as treats.

Crawdads, fish, small shrimp, and/or crab

Unsweetened gelatin

1 Make the gelatin according to the instructions, except that while you're mixing the gelatin, add small bits of seafood, just as you would fruit. (***Do not*** add fruit!)

2 Put the mix into small ice cube trays and store in the refrigerator until used.

Bluto's BARF

BY BOB CHURCH

BARF stands for Bones and Raw Food or Biologically Appropriate Raw Food. Although this treat may make you want to barf, your ferrets should love it as an occasional meal or offered as a special treat. Plus, you can be happy that Bluto's BARF is an excellent source of protein for your ferret.

½-inch frozen chicken chunks

Beef or chicken liver, partially frozen

Chicken hearts or gizzards, partially frozen

Chicken bones

Chicken broth

Frozen fat trimmings (about ⅕ by volume)

1 Mix the frozen meat ingredients (chicken chunks, liver, hearts or gizzards, and fat trimmings) in a bowl and cover the mixture with the broth.

2 Boil the chicken bones until the ends start to scratch under the pressure of your fingernail.

3 Cut the bones with poultry scissors into small chunks.

4 Add maybe a half-dozen pieces of bone to the bowl containing the meat and broth mixture.

5 Place that bowl in the microwave and heat until the broth is near the boiling point. Allow it to cool.

BOB'S TIP: This recipe seems to work better if you freeze the meat ingredients first and cut them with a cleaver into ½-inch chunks while still partially hard. You can serve this recipe as a soup, freeze it into small blocks for a treat, cook it into a paste, or add it as gravy to soften kibble.

Index

S

sable ferrets, 30

sacks, 194

salmon oil, 154

salmonella, 138–139, 142–143

salt, 158

sarcoptic mange (scabies), 280

SARS-CoV-2 (Covid-19), 292–293

schedule, feeding, 133–134

scratching, 246

screaming, 349

screeching, 349

scruffing, 110, 363

sebaceous cell tumors, 331

secreting organs, 138–139

seeds, 158

seizures, 263–264

senses

  enrichment for, 186

  overview, 12–13

  stimulating, 188–189

service animals, 217

sexual dimorphism, 11

sexual maturity, 392–394

  females, 393–394

  males, 392–393

shampoo

  choosing, 165

  for fleas, 274

shelters

  adopting from, 64–66

  breeding and, 390

shivering, 246

shock, 257

shopping for ferrets, 51–68

  adopting options, 61–68

Craigslist and other classified ads, 66–67

ferret shelter, 64–66

pet shops, 61–62

private breeders, 63–64

stray ferrets, 67–68

age, considering, 53–55

  adults, 54–55

  kits, 53–54

altered, 55–57

  females, 57

  males, 56–57

gender, 55

multiple ferrets, considering, 57–60

overview, 51–53

veterinarians, 68

shows, 200–204

Siamese ferrets, 31

sick ferrets. *See also* diseases and illnesses

  Assist Feed Recipe, 254–255

  feeding, 253–256

  methods for feeding, 255–256

single-level cages, 73–74

sitting trick, 198–199

size, cages, 70

skeleton, 10

skin tumors, 330–332

sleeping, excessive, 247–248

sleeping not dead (SND), 247–248

sliming, 393

small animals, 116, 156

smell, sense of, 13, 120–121, 188

snail trail, 393

snap bolts, 71

SND (sleeping not dead), 247–248

sneezing, 248

snoring, 351

soap, white, 259

social tendencies of ferrets, 108

social-development activities, 193–194

socializing biting ferrets, 374–380

solid ferrets, 31

solitary ferrets, 60

spaying, 57

specialty classes, 201

spinal injuries, 267

Spirit Pieces website, 338

spleens

  vet checkups, 233

  weight gain and, 134

splenomegaly (enlarged spleen), 314–315

sport of ferreting, 25–28

sprites. *See* females

squeaking, 349

squealing, 350

stalking, 355

standard ferrets, 31

Stilson, Norm, 374

stimulating senses, 188–189

stink trail, 194

stomach blockages, 293–294

stones, 308–309

stray ferrets, 67–68

stress, 185, 210

struvite stones, 308

stud tail, 393

styptic powder, 259

submerge method, 377

sugar, 157, 248

supernumery tooth, 300

superworms, 147

vaccinations *(continued)*
  kits, 230–232
    distemper vaccine, 231
    overall checkup, 232
    rabies vaccine, 231–232
  titer testing, 234–235
vaginitis, 400
vegetables, 158
Velcro, 422
ventilation, 71, 76
vertebrate prey, 146
veterinarians, 68,
    224–230
  developing good working
    relationship, 228–230
  interviewing, 224–227
  visiting, 227–228
vinegar, 362

vinyl-coated wire, 72
vocal communications,
    348–351
vomiting, 260–261

W
Waardensburg Syndrome, 30
wagging tail, 355
walls
  cage placement and, 76
  checkerboard, 200
  cleaning, 163–164
war dance, 352–353
washcloth rubdown,
    112–113, 193–194
water, 81–84, 128
waxworms, 147
weaning, 407

weight, 11
  enlarged spleens and, 134
  enrichment activities
    and, 186
white soap, 259
wild animals, 44–48
windows, 100
wood cages, 72
wrestling, 354

Y
yawning, 247
yawning contest, 203–204

Z
zig-zagging, 358
zinc, 72

About the Author

An Illinois native for all but the first two years of her adopted life, **Kim Schilling** resides in a south suburb of Chicago with her husband David of 28 years and teen-age sons, Sam and Josh. Josh joined the Schilling family after three years of grueling planning after which they all met at Christmastime 2009 in Ulan-Ude, the capital of Buryatia in Eastern Siberia, Russia. There they met their new son, six-year-old Sergei, and six months later, in 2010, in the blistering heat of June, they brought Sergei home. Joshua Michael, as shown on his new American birth certificate, has a gentle way with animals and loves them so. It has only strengthened Kim's theory that adopted souls tend to love the more fragile critters dearly. Perhaps they even like animals more than people, so she hints.

When Kim isn't writing or working as payroll manager for a large candy manufacturer, she's running the USDA-licensed non-profit organization she founded in the early 90s called Animals for Awareness. AFA is dedicated to the needs of displaced exotic animals. Its mission: Protection through education. You can learn more about Animals for Awareness by visiting: `https://www.facebook.com/AnimalsforAwareness`.

Dedication

To my awesomely quirky sons Sam and Josh for letting your individual personalities shine through, even though you each drive me up a wall at times, and for not batting an eye when I swear and throw things at the computer. Extra thanks to Josh for giving me permission to share part of his adoption story to the ferret world. To my hubby, David, who only gave me stink-eye occasionally when I yelled at him to turn his old-man music down because I was trying to write. Yet he offered up encouragement and pushed me to keep going. And finally, to my dearly departed bestie Dr. Mike Miller, DVM, just because he was who he was, and because his positive influence still continues to have a profound impact on me.

Author's Acknowledgments

Thanks to my writing shadow, Facebook poster, and greatest cheerleader, Holly Ravenhill, who confirmed and helped to identify key subject areas that needed updating. And a huge shout-out to my cozy *FFD3* Brainstorm Team for sharing many awesome ideas and answering my unending questions over the last year: Barbara Clay, director of Rocky's Ferret Rescue & Shelter and creator of Poopin Pumpkin; Plumb Stephanie of Middle Earth Ferretry and breeder of exquisite quality polecat hybrids, as well as half-, semi- and full-Angora ferrets; Karen Pedro of Make My Day Ferretry in the Netherlands; and Vondelle McLaughlin and Kevin Farlee of Washington Ferret Rescue & Shelter. Further thanks to Heather

Downie of the Holistic Ferret Forum for providing an awesome recipe and great insights into the world of ferret breeding. And thanks to Nancy Will and Marianne Tranborg Eriksen for joining in on the group discussions and adding two cents when desperately needed.

I cannot thank Katrina Ramsell, DVM, enough for getting accurate DIM information out into the ferret world. Big, big thanks to Jennifer LeBaron of Flair Photos and her awesome partners in crime, Debbie and Mark Fitzgerald, for the fantastic pictures for the color insert. And thanks to an old ferret friend, Bob Church, who continues to allow his timeless tidbits to be shared from edition to edition. A huge thank-you to Jerry Murray, DVM, for reading, constructively critiquing, and kindly suggesting edits for this edition. Karen Purcell, DVM, proved to be a cheerleader in her own way even if she didn't realize it, and I thank her for adding to the book with a quote and a recipe. Thank you, Tara Whitehawk, for sharing her Kibble Comparison Chart. Scarlett Gray-Saling, producer of the annual Ferret Buckeye Bash and proprietor of Scarlett's Happy Dookers Ferretry, provided so much insightful information on responsible breeding that I just can't express my appreciation. Thank you, Travis Livieri, for providing updated data on the black-footed ferret recovery project. Charlie O'Kane at Camp Udder Guy provided a unique and scrumptious ferret recipe. I appreciate both Rose German, founder of Ferret Fabulous Finds Auction House, and also Claire Shannon for contributing pictures and or ferret-proofing hacks. And a huge thanks to Ruth Heller, DVM, for priceless tidbits and overall support. Every one of you has been invaluable.

I would be remiss is I failed to mention other wonderful individuals and organizations that assisted along the journey in one way or another: Barbara Carlson, The American Ferret Association, Morgan Tangren, Dee Gage, National Black-Footed Ferret Conservation Center, Rebecca Wolfy Stout, Donna Weiss, Anna Senka, Sophia Le Blanc, Lynne Toole, Troy Lynn Eckart, Joan Vick, and Donna Spirito. Thank you so much to my editors, Christopher Morris and Kelsey Baird, for displaying great patience, understanding, and flexibility during my entire writing journey. I absolutely must give a huge shout-out to my lead AFA volunteer Christine Miller and AFA volunteers Kevin Courtney, Ricky Nogal, and Jack Malone for holding down the fort while I worked on the book. Finally, thank you to those on the Facebook groups Ferret Lovers Community and Ferret Care & Education, who responded to my various ferret-related questions. Heaven knows there have been so many hands in this recipe, being hooman I am bound to forget someone, and for that I'm deeply sorry.

Publisher's Acknowledgments

Acquisitions Editor: Kelsey Baird

Project Editor: Christopher Morris

Copy Editor: Christopher Morris

Technical Editor: Jerry Murray, DVM

Production Editor: Mohammed Zafar Ali

Cover Image: © Darri/Getty Images